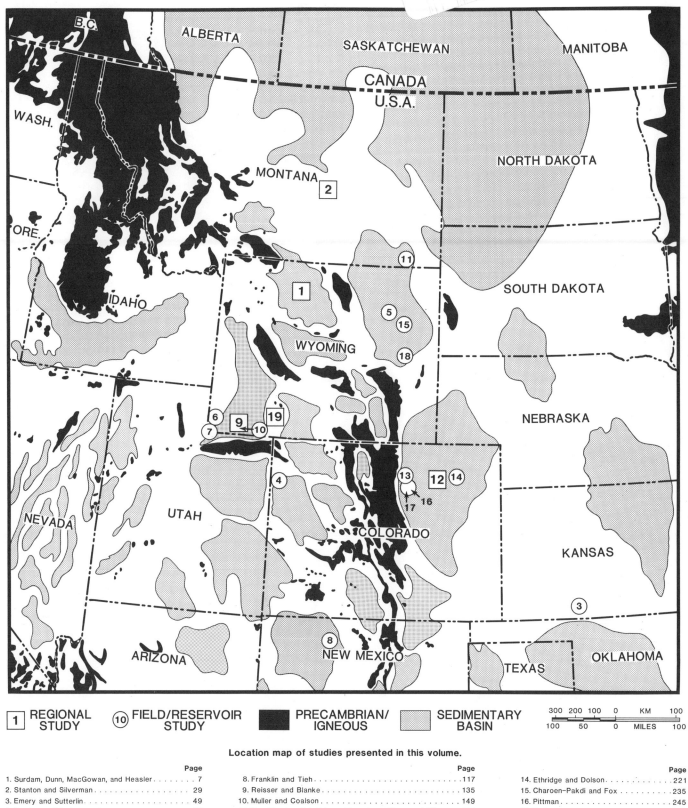

1 REGIONAL STUDY	**10** FIELD/RESERVOIR STUDY	PRECAMBRIAN/ IGNEOUS	SEDIMENTARY BASIN	300 200 100 0 KM 100	100 50 0 MILES 100

Location map of studies presented in this volume.

Petrogenesis and Petrophysics of Selected Sandstone Reservoirs of the Rocky Mountain Region

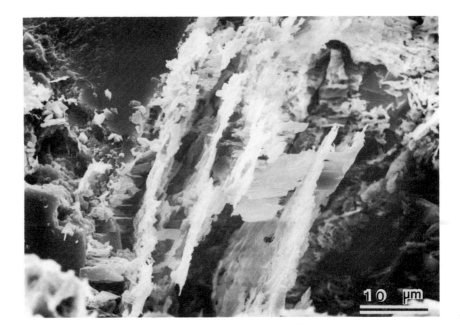

Editor-in-Chief:
    Edward B. Coalson

Associate Editors:
    Sanford S. Kaplan
    C. Wm. Keighin
    Chris A. Oglesby
    John W. Robinson

Published by:
    The Rocky Mountain Association of Geologists
    Denver, Colorado
    1989

President's Message

This is the second of a two volume series on the subject of petrophysical characteristics of Rocky Mountain oil and gas reservoirs. This volume deals with sandstones while the 1988 volume dealt with carbonate reservoirs.

The sandstone reservoir understood as a composite of its several aspects i.e., petrophysical, morphologic, and genetic framework is a necessary goal of the involved geologist. The knowledge and projection of these factors can guide right and rewarding decisions regarding the well, the pool, the field, and related prospects.

The authors and editors have made this guidebook a future reference for competitive pursuit of development and exploration of the subject Rocky Mountain reservoir sandstones. I join with the other geologist users of this volume in a sincere appreciation of the editors' and authors' efforts, the guiding RMAG plan and commitment, and the corporate contributors, which have combined to create this publication during a most difficult period of our profession.

Donald R. Hembre
President
Rocky Mountain Association of Geologists

Rocky Mountain Association of Geologists

Officers 1989

President . . . . Don Hembre
President–Elect . . . . Dennis Irwin
1st Vice–President . . . . Larry McPeek
2nd Vice–President . . . . Penny Frush
Secretary . . . . Fred Reid
Treasurer . . . . Robert Groth
Councilor . . . . John Osmond

Acknowledgments

As is any guidebook, this one is the result of the efforts and contributions of many people. It was conceived as the companion volume to "Occurrence and Petrophysical Properties of Carbonate Reservoirs in the Rocky Mountain Region", also published by the RMAG. People involved in starting this two-volume effort are acknowledged in the preface to the earlier book.

During the early stages of planning this book, valuable contributions of time and ideas were contributed by Barry Borak, Steve Fryberger, Steve Goolsby, Ron Jensen, Sandy Lindquist, David McKenzie, and Bob Weimer. Karl Arleth, Jim Castle, and Steve Fryberger also helped solicit papers, not an easy task in these parlous times for the oil industry.

Extremely helpful technical reviews of papers were provided by Bill Almon, Frank Ethridge, Tom Fouch, Steve Fryberger, Gus Gustasen, Wendy Harrison, Lee Krystinick, Sandy Lindquist, Dr. R.P. Lockwood, Randi Martinsen, Pete McCabe, Art Moore, Stan Paxton, Ed Pittman, Tom Ryer, Sharon Stonecipher, Steve Sturm, Rod Tillman, and Ted Walker. The authors and editors are thankful for the significant and careful criticisms of the manuscripts that these people made.

Ray Marvin shepherded the manuscripts through typesetting, layout, printing, and binding. As in past years, Ray's efforts were crucial in producing this book. Gary Hall assisted in pasting up papers.

Bass Enterprises Production Company (BEPCO) supported this book in key ways. BEPCO provided drafting (by Dan Poe) and secretarial support (by Kim Brady), as well as time for two editors (Coalson and Oglesby) to work on this book.

Funding for the color plates found at the end of this book was solicited by Robert Groth, Larry McPeek, David Moore, and Tom Sperr. Companies and individuals that generously donated the money necessary to pay for these expensive (but invaluable!) plates were:

Bass Enterprises Production Company

Chevron, U.S.A., Inc.

DeKalb Energy Company

Enron Oil and Gas Company

Exxon Company, U.S.A.

Marathon Oil Company

Mobil Oil Corporation

William Oline

Oryx Energy, Inc.

Shell Western E & P, Inc.

Terra Resources, Inc.

Total Minatome Corporation

RPI International supplied the basemap found on the front end-sheet, on which are shown the locations of the areas discussed in the papers. Petroleum Information provided digital field data summarized in the table found at the end of this book. We thank all of these people and organizations for the support they contributed to this book. We wish especially to acknowledge the efforts of the authors. Many of them had to deal with extraordinary complications, including layoffs, transfers, or actual loss of thin sections and other materials during corporate moves. The fact that they persevered in producing these articles despite the turmoil in the industry (and despite the demands of the editors) is much appreciated.

Abbreviations Used in References

AAPG = American Association of Petroleum Geologists
Abs. w/ Progs. = Abstracts with Programs
[abs.] = abstract
ACS = American Chemical Society
AGU = American Geophysical Union
Am. Min. = American Mineralogist
Ann. Field Conf. = Annual Field Conference
Ann. Mtg. = Annual Meeting
Ann. Tech. Conf. = Annual Technology Conference
Bull. = Bulletin
BGS = Billings Geological Society
Circ. = Circular
Clay Min. Soc. = Clay Mineral Society
Cont. Geol. = Contributions to Geology
CSM = Colorado School of Mines
DOE = Department of Energy
EOR = Enhanced Oil Recovery
Geochem. Jour. = Geochemical Journal
Geochim. Cosmochim. = Geochimica et Cosmochimica Acta
GSA = Geological Society of America
IAS = International Association of Sedimentology
IOSA = International Oil Scouts Association
Jour. = Journal of
Jour. Geoph. Res. = Journal of Geophysical Research
JPT = Journal of Petroleum Technology
JSP = Journal of Sedimentary Petrology
Mem. = Memoir
MGS = Montana Geological Society
Miner. Assoc. Am. = Mineralogical Association of America
Mtn. Geol. = The Mountain Geologist
MS = Master's
no. = number
OGJ = Oil and Gas Journal
PhD diss. = doctoral dissertation
Proc. = Proceedings of
Prof. Cont. = Professional Contribution
Prof. Paper = Professional Paper
Progs. w/ Abs. = Programs with Abstracts
Rpt. = Report
RMAG = Rocky Mountain Association of Geologists
RMS–SEPM = Rocky Mountain Section of Society of Economic Paleontologists and Mineralogists
Roy. Soc. Lon. = Royal Society of London
Sed. Geol. = Sedimentary Geology
SEG = Society of Exploration Geophysicists
SEPM = Society of Economic Paleontologists and Mineralogists
SPE = Society of Petroleum Engineers of American Institute of Mechanical Engineers
Spec. Pub. = Special Publication
SPEJ = Society of Petroleum Engineers Journal
Stud. in Geol. = Studies in Geology
Tech. Rpt. = Technical Report
U of CO = University of Colorado
U of KS = University of Kansas
U of WY = University of Wyoming
unpubl. = unpublished
USGS = United States Geological Survey
v. = volume
WGA = Wyoming Geological Association

TABLE OF CONTENTS

TABLE OF CONTENTS
(continued)

UPPER CRETACEOUS SANDSTONES

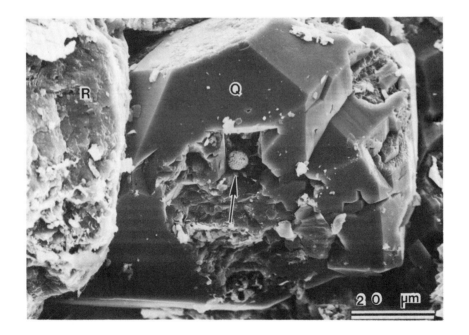

Well-developed quartz overgrowth (Q) partially enclosing a siliceous framework grain; isolated pyrite framboid (arrow) grew in a small, isolated pore in the fine-grained sandstone. Rock fragment (R) shows no more than microporosity. Turner Fm., sec 30 T46N R63W, Weston Co., WY. Depth 377 ft (115m). Photo donated by Bill Keighin.

Introduction: Editorial Philosophy and Summaries of Papers

SANFORD S. KAPLAN[1]
EDWARD B. COALSON[2]
C. Wm. KEIGHIN[3]
CHRIS A. OGLESBY[2]
JOHN W. ROBINSON[4]

[1]Independent Geologist, Denver, Colorado
[2]Bass Enterprises Production Company, Denver, Colorado
[3]U.S. Geological Survey, Denver, Colorado
[4]Colorado School of Mines, Golden, Colorado

CONTENT OF THIS BOOK

The major goal of this book was to document the petrophysics (i.e., the physical properties of greatest interest to petroleum geologists) and petrogenesis of important hydrocarbon–bearing sandstones of the Rocky Mountain states; these data are somewhat sparse and scattered in the literature. We also intended to publish data about the relationships between quality of hydrocarbon production and geology/petrography. Initially, there also were hopes of assembling a petrographic and petrophysical "atlas" of Rocky Mountain sandstone reservoirs.

We soon saw the impossibility of compiling a comprehensive atlas, due to the large amount of data required to characterize most Rocky Mountain sandstone reservoirs. However, while the content of this book is not global, we believe that the authors have documented some important and representative reservoirs and fields in the Rocky Mountains. We present petrographic, petrophysical, sedimentologic, and stratigraphic information that will be of use in exploration, exploitation, and scientific research in many basins and formations.

As for the goal of exploring controls on hydrocarbon production, it became evident upon receipt of the first few papers that the authors had taken basically different approaches. Almost all had investigated gross stratigraphic and structural controls, which of course are fundamentally important to petroleum geology. They also had described the diagenetic histories of their reservoirs, although in greatly varying degrees of detail and application to petrophysics. What differed were the applications of these data. Many authors emphasized the importance of facies architecture, structure, and diagenesis in determining patterns of fluid flow and productivity during primary, secondary, and/or tertiary production (Bowker and Jackson; Sercombe; Szpakiewicz et al.; Tillman). Some (James; Muller and Coalson; Pittman; Porter; Sercombe) explored problems in identification of pay from well logs and cores. Three papers (Higley and Schmoker; Keighin, Law, Pollastro; Surdam, Dunn, MacGowan, and Heasler) relate burial and thermal histories to the evolution of sandstone porosity. This diversity of applications of similar data reflects the

varied practical problems that geologists are trying to solve.

ORGANIZATION OF THE VOLUME

Many of these papers are essentially descriptive, as opposed to interpretive. Therefore, we follow guidebook precedent and present them in generally chronostratigraphic order. However, there is a common thread in most of the interpretations: the usefulness of diagenetic studies in prediction (or at least understanding) of trends in reservoir quality. This theme was addressed most globally in the first paper, by Surdam et al. Their results (discussed below) appear to constitute a benchmark against which to compare many of the other authors' observations of reservoir diagenesis.

The remaining papers describe "clean" sandstones of Paleozoic and Mesozoic age, or more–or–less shaley sandstones of Cretaceous age. Readers interested primarily in diagenesis would benefit from reading first the papers by Surdam et al.; Higley and Schmoker; and Keighin et al., because they describe regional diagenetic patterns in reservoirs that have undergone a wide range in burial depths. More–localized papers covering sandstones buried to shallow or intermediate depths are authored by Szpakiewicz, Schatzinger, Honarpour, Tham, and Tillman; Emery and Sutterlin; Pittman; Porter; Stanton and Silverman; Bowker and Jackson; Conner, Sullivan, and Tieh; Charoen–Pakdi and Fox; Franklin and Tieh; Weimer and Sonnenberg; and Ethridge and Dolson. James, Reisser and Blanke, Muller and Coalson, and Tillman write about deeply buried reservoirs. The reader interested in "testing" the observations of Surdam et al. (as we were) may find it helpful to read the papers in the listed order. The paper by Sercombe focuses on the effects of tectonic fracturing on reservoir quality, rather than on diagenesis.

The papers are followed by a section in which are found the color plates. Also, we include a subject index, a "first" for an RMAG publication.

HIGHPOINTS OF THE PAPERS

In the first paper in the book, "Conceptual Models for the Prediction of Porosity Evolution with an Example from the Bighorn Basin, Wyoming," Surdam et al. propose a general, conceptual model for diagenesis and evolution of porosity in reservoir sandstones, understood on the scale of sedimentary basins. They examine the complex changes in pore–fluid chemistry that control mineral reactions during progressive burial and provide case–sensitive "diagenetic pathways" that illustrate the influence of shallow, intermediate, and deep burial on porosity and permeability. Their short description of the Frontier Formation in the Big Horn Basin illustrates the application of the model to actual reservoirs. As with any model describing extremely complex natural phenomena, the reader is warned against applying the hypothesis slavishly, creating yet another "black box" that would be bound to fail at some point. For instance, as one reviewer (Harrison) pointed out, their discussion emphasizes so strongly the role that organic acids can play in intermediate burial that the reader (particularly those of us involved in petroleum extraction) might lose sight of the fact that these acids are not ubiquitous, and that diagenesis will proceed in the absence of organic contributions. However, their diagenetic pathways appear to be powerful tools for understanding and, possibly, forward modeling diagenesis in a wide variety of geologic settings and pore–fluid histories.

Clean, shallow sandstones of Pennsylvanian age are the subject of the next paper, by Stanton and Silverman, entitled "**Sedimentology, Diagenesis, and Reservoir Potential of the Pennsylvanian Tyler Formation, Central Montana**". The elusive Tyler sandstones are presented as valley–fill sequences in a low gradient, vertically aggrading, anastomosing fluvial system. The authors establish four diagenetic stages, including one that coincided with post–oil–migration uplift and erosion, and suggest that further work with sedimentologic and petrographic models may be useful in predicting reservoir occurrence. They postulate a surprising amount of solution porosity for such a shallow reservoir. They also provide exploration strategies that may reduce the stratigraphic risk in wildcatting.

In "**Petrologic Character of a Morrowan Sandstone Reservoir, Lexington Field, Clark County, Kansas**", Emery and Sutterlin give a detailed account of the physical characteristics of another relatively clean sandstone formation. These Morrow sandstones apparently were deposited as estuarine valley fill (our term) on a mesotidal coastline, and underwent a great deal of diagenesis. The authors consider both petrography and decline–curve analysis in determining a value for expected ultimate recovery (EUR). This is an example of application of petrophysical techniques to answer a common oil–field question, i.e., the effect that stratigraphy/petrology has on reserves. One question they do not answer is why the productive tidal channel sandstones pinch out in all directions away from the field and do not recur "on trend", a problem out of the domain of this careful field study but of interest to explorationists (Ray Marvin, pers. comm.).

Rangely Field has been the most prolific oil field in the Rocky Mountains (see tables at the back of this book). In "**The Weber Sandstone, Rangely Field, Colorado**", Bowker and Jackson divide the Weber Sandstone at Rangely into three major lithotypes and

characterize them by a variety of analytical methods. Eolian sandstones, which exhibit the best reservoir characteristics, show a surprisingly complex diagenetic history for such a shallow reservoir. For instance, the reservoir contains significant amounts of asphaltenes, a characteristic of Minnelusa reservoirs as well (see James, this volume). As might be expected of geologists concerned with an enhanced oil recovery project, they discuss the heterogeneities introduced into the reservoir by such features as crossbedding and small–scale stratigraphic changes.

In "**Diagenetic History and Reservoir Characteristics of a Deep Minnelusa Reservoir, Hawk Point Field, Powder River Basin, Wyoming**", James reports on a sandstone reservoir that has gone through a complex diagenetic history, including two stages of oil migration, and precipitation of asphaltene–like material. She postulates that early cementation by anhydrite preserved the original, relatively open grain fabric. After burial, anhydrite dissolution (prior to oil migration) apparently produced a reservoir with high porosity and large pore throats. The great efficiency of production from these, and perhaps other, Minnelusa sandstones appears to us to be a result of these diagenetic changes. So also may be the anomalously low cementation and saturation exponents James saw in this reservoir.

Also dealing with eolian sandstones, Tillman describes a reservoir composed of a complex combination of dune and dune–related facies in "**Sedimentary Facies and Reservoir Characteristics of the Nugget Sandstone (Jurassic): Painter Reservoir Field, Uinta County, Wyoming**". She reports that reservoir quality differs among these facies due to varying fabrics and diagenesis, and suggests that directional permeability trends are consistent with dune orientations. This is confirmed by field performance; the direction of maximum permeability is parallel to dune slipfaces. Her results are similar to those of Lindquist (1983, 1988), who described other, nearby Nugget reservoirs. Tillman also documents the effects that depositional and structural heterogeneities have on production and EOR efforts at Painter Reservoir.

In contrast, Sercombe discusses the relative non-importance of facies on reservoir quality of some Nugget reservoirs in "**Performance of Lower–Porosity Nugget Reservoirs, Anschutz Ranch East, Bessie Bottom, and North Pineview Fields, Utah and Wyoming**". He asserts that the primary control on gas productivity is tectonic fracturing, not deposition, in lower porosity Nugget reservoirs. In addition to adding a new facet to Nugget reservoir descriptions, his study also is an example of a methodical, integrated petrophysical project.

Variably shaley marine sandstones are described in detail by Franklin and Tieh in "**Petrography, Diagen-esis, and Reservoir Properties of the Dakota of the San Juan Basin, West Lindrith Field, Rio Arriba Co., New Mexico**". The authors discovered patterns in diagenesis that relate to original sandstone composition, texture, and depositional environment. Statistical methods are used to delineate three "diagenetic facies" (quartzose, calcitic, and shaley sandstones) which display profound differences in porosity, permeability, and immobile water saturation.

The paper also illustrates graphical methods of recognizing petro-physical "rock types" from log data in the absence of cores.

In **"Paleostructural Control of Dakota Hydrocarbon Accumulations on the Southern Moxa Arch, Southwest Wyoming and Northeast Utah"**, Reisser and Blanke describe the reservoir rocks and propose explanations for production anomalies in deeply buried Dakota reservoirs. They relate deposition, tectonics, diagenesis, and thermal history to reservoir quality. In their theory, emplacement of hydrocarbons in fluvial and deltaic Dakota sandstones halted diagenesis in, but not below, the gas columns, creating differential cementation. Paleocene and Eocene tectonics subsequently rotated the traps into their present configuration. The implications for exploration are spelled out.

The Dakota Sandstone also is the subject of Muller and Coalson's paper, **"Diagenetic and Petrophysical Variations of the Dakota Sandstone, Henry Field, Green River Basin, Wyoming"**. The authors conclude that the occurrence of authigenic clays, which are demonstrably more harmful to permeability than is quartz cement, is at least partly related to depositional environment. Channel sandstones make the best reservoirs and display remarkable amounts of solution porosity. It is found that diagenesis has created pore geometries that must be accounted for when interpreting log and DST data. Clay cementation is noted to occur below an intraformational unconformity within the Dakota; how this relates to Reisser and Blanke's thesis of differential diagenesis is not known.

Szpakiewicz, Schatzinger, Honarpour, Tham, and Tillman supply an intensive description of the production geology of a major oil field in **"Geological-Engineering Evaluation of Heterogeneity, Petrophysical Properties, and Productivity of Barrier Island/Valley Fill Lithotypes in Bell Creek Field, Muddy Formation, Powder River Basin, Montana"**. The authors utilize voluminous data synergistically to investigate predictability of fluid flow and residual oil saturations. Heterogeneities result from variations in depositional facies, diagenesis, and structure. Each of these factors affects primary, secondary, and tertiary recovery to different degrees. Some factors prove to be more predictable than others. As an interesting sidelight, the authors conclude that much dissolution in these rocks occurred very early, predating oil generation. Such early dissolution was not proposed for other reservoirs described in this volume.

Porosity and permeability are related to depositional environment, depth of burial, and thermal maturity in **"Influence of Depositional Environment and Diagenesis on Regional Porosity Trends in the Lower Cretaceous 'J' Sandstone, Denver Basin, Colorado"** by Higley and Schmoker. The authors present data from both the deeper Wattenberg Field and the shallower Kachina Field. Valley-fill channel sandstones are found to have the best reservoir quality throughout the basin. Thermal maturity is found to relate better to porosity than does depth. This regional paper sets the stage for the two papers following.

In **"Sequence Stratigraphic Analysis, Muddy (J) Sandstone Reservoir, Wattenberg Field, Denver Basin, Colorado"**, Weimer and Sonnenberg have updated earlier (1986) work on Wattenberg applying sequence-stratigraphy concepts to regional Muddy unconformities. The reservoir at Wattenberg, the marine Fort Collins Member, is interpreted as an extensive delta front sandstone. Post-depositional diagenesis of the reservoir by subaerial processes reduced both porosity and permeability. During this time, a regional lowstand surface of erosion developed, truncating the Wattenberg reservoir on all margins of the field. This truncation, in conjunction with early diagenesis, is put forth as the seal for this basin-centered synclinal field.

In **"Unconformities and Valley-Fill Sequences: Key to Understanding Reservoirs at Lonetree and Poncho Fields, D-J Basin, Colorado"**, Ethridge and Dolson discuss the deltaic, meander-belt, and marine depositional environments of the "J" Sandstone. They support Weimer and Sonnenberg's interpretation of a regional, sequence-bounding unconformity in the "J" Sandstone. They also focus on the petrology of the sequences, with emphasis on composition and diagenesis as they relate to the unconformity and to depositional environments. The authors conclude that most of the "J" porosity is secondary, resulting from diagenesis prior to hydrocarbon emplacement. Interestingly, the diagenetic history of both fluvial and marine bar reservoirs is similar, even though their depositional environments are not.

Charoen-Pakdi and Fox describe the reservoir properties of productive marine-shelf sandstones equivalent to the Frontier Formation. In **"Petrography and Petrophysics of the Upper Cretaceous Turner Sandy Member of the Carlile Shale of Todd Field, Powder River Basin, Wyoming"**, the authors propose an unusual diagenetic sequence in which there are two phases of oil migration and calcite dissolution. Whether or not multiple stages of oil emplacement and dissolution are the case, the existence of large amounts of solution porosity in these sandstones is significant.

The next two papers approach the same subject from different perspectives. Pittman examines the **"Nature of the Terry Sandstone Reservoir, Spindle Field, Colorado"** and concludes that these shaley sandstones contain mainly remnant intergranular porosity, resulting from deposition under high energy conditions on the crestal portion of offshore bars. His study focuses on wells in and immediately adjacent to Spindle Field. He illustrates a potentially very useful method (the so-called Winland equation) of using core porosity and permeability data to estimate effective pore-throat sizes, using it to delineate the trap; reservoir and nonreservoir facies have distinctly different distribution, size, and volume of pore apertures. The trap is presented as mainly stratigraphic.

While their conclusions are otherwise similar, Porter views Spindle Field differently from Pittman. In **"Structurally Influenced Stratigraphic and Diagenetic Trapping at Spindle Field, Colorado"**, she argues that both the Terry and the Hygiene reservoirs contain mainly secondary porosity, and that the trap is both stratigraphic and diagenetic. In these marine-shelf sandstones, reservoir properties are seen to result largely from diagenetic processes. In particular, she cites early occlusion of porosity by calcite cement, and subsequent dissolution of the calcite by fluids related to oil and gas generation, migrating along tensional fractures over basement fault blocks. Her data come from a wider area than do those of Pittman. This difference in conclusions illustrates the subjective nature of at least some geologic investigations (not necessarily a bad thing) and the effect that the scale of investigation can have on interpretations.

Conner, Sullivan, and Tieh deal with a very shaley reservoir in "**Depositional Environment and Mineralogy, Upper Cretaceous Teapot Sandstone, Well Draw Field, Powder River Basin, Wyoming**". Their work is mostly descriptive. However, they suggest the interesting possibility that the reservoir may have been drastically improved in its updip portions by waters moving downdip, leaching out unstable grains and cement. This is yet another reservoir in which dissolution is postulated as the source of effective porosity. The exact mechanism for this leaching event is not speculated on, suggesting room for further study (as do many of these papers).

In the last paper, "**Petrology and Reservoir Characteristics of the Almond Formation, Greater Green River Basin, Wyoming**", Keighin, Law, and Pollastro discuss the relationship of porosity and permeability to depth of burial, thermal maturity, diagenesis, and overpressuring. They infer that events associated with gas generation were central in improving porosity (or at least retarding porosity loss) during progressive burial. Again, dissolution of unstable minerals is seen as important in the development of reservoir characteristics.

CONCLUSIONS

Several observations follow from reading of these papers. First, the commonly stated supposition that sandstone reservoirs are petrographically simpler than are carbonate reservoirs is not true in these formations. In fact, mineralogy and diagenesis of these rocks are more complex than in many carbonate reservoirs. The major difference is that most of the diagenesis in these sandstones seems to have occurred later during burial history and affects a smaller percentage of framework grains, the bulk of diagenetic products being found in intergranular porosity. Consequently, the evolution of porosity in these sandstones is related more to thermal and pore–fluid histories than to conditions of deposition and very early burial as in many carbonate reservoirs.

Secondly, solution porosity in these Rocky Mountain sandstone reservoirs is very common. The implication of Schmidt and McDonald (1979) that sandstones are more affected by dissolution processes than we might expect seems to be true, at least for these formations. Of the 19 papers in this volume, 14 report the presence of significant amounts of dissolution porosity, formed both early and late in diagenesis. Several reservoirs apparently only produce because they contain solution pores. Thus, anticipation of dissolution processes is important, especially in the deeper exploration plays, because it provides a mechanism whereby reservoir–quality sandstone can be created at depth. Extensive dissolution porosity also seems to have dramatic effects on the resistivity

constants of log analysis, causing surprisingly low cementation and saturation exponents, with the potential for causing bypassed pay.

The bulk of the secondary porosity in these sandstones seems to have formed immediately before hydrocarbon emplacement, in accord with Schmidt and McDonald's (1979) contentions and with Surdam et al.'s model. Because all of the sandstones reported here are reservoirs for oil or gas, it is not possible to say how much dissolution would have occurred in the absence of organic acids and hydrocarbon generation.

Finally, it is apparent that studies of petrography, petrophysics, and petrogenesis have wide applicability to common oil–field problems. Even though the authors were not specifically requested to report on applications, petrographic information was used in these studies in discrimination of pay from non–pay, prediction and control of reservoir performance, and understanding of trends in reservoir quality. Many other potential (if not actual) petrophysical applications of petrographic data are reported elsewhere in the literature.

In fact, we believe that geologists have yet to fully realize the benefits of applying petrophysics and formation evaluation to everyday problems. Oddly, it was an engineer (Archie, 1950) who started serious discussion of the usefulness of determinations of porosity/rock types to formation evaluation, an observation that one might expect to emanate from a geologist. The methodologies of formation evaluation and petrophysics have been developed mainly by engineers and log analysts. However, as shown by the papers in this book, geologists studying cores can discover things about reservoir rocks that are central to successful formation evaluation, such as mineralogy, pore geometry, fluid characteristics, permeability, damageability, and heterogeneity. Conversely, it theoretically should be possible to extract useful information about these aspects of reservoir rocks from well logs, well performance, and pressure testing, even in the absence of core data.

Geologists, in our experience, generally do not exploit the methods and data of petrophysics. For example, easily available core data can be used to recognize differences in sandstone reservoir types (Coalson, Hartmann, and Thomas, 1985). Graphs of porosity versus permeability reveal consistent groupings for four common clastic lithologies (Fig. 1), a result of consistent differences in pore throat characteristics. Correlations such as these, although they are not much used, can assist both the explorationist and the exploitationist in maximizing discovery and development of hydrocarbon production (e.g., Sneider et al., 1981). However, the geologist who routinely uses even this simple plot is somewhat unusual.

On the other hand, it seems that geologists are displaying increasing interest in integration of traditional geological data (structure, stratigraphy, core descriptions, etc.) with data of reservoir engineering (log analysis, pressure–buildup analysis, well performance, etc.), an approach we might term "integrated formation analysis" (IFA). This interest reflects, we believe, a growing need for detailed reservoir analyses, primarily in field development.

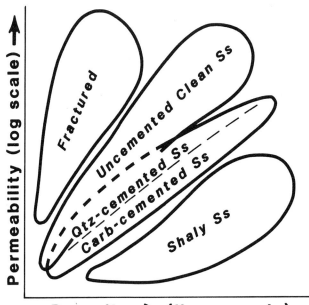

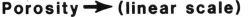

Fig. 1. Commonly seen patterns of porosity versus permeability in reservoir sandstones.

In order to test our observations, we took an informal, non-scientific poll of selected individuals in and associated with the oil industry (George Asquith, Pioneer Petroleum; W.H. Fertl, Atlas Wireline; Chuck Spencer, U.S. Geological Survey; Jack Thomas, Amoco Research; Norm Wardlaw, University of Calgary) regarding the present and future importance of rock studies and IFA to oil-field projects. (This hardly constitutes a rigorous database, but may be significant.) According to these gentlemen, perhaps 40–60% of all reservoir geology or engineering projects done in major companies today appear to involve IFA. (Presumably, in smaller companies the percentage is lower.) At least two logging companies (there may be more) offer extensive services in this area. Several state-sponsored agencies also are doing such integrated studies. At least some majors are conducting IFA studies using teams of geologists, engineers, and other specialists. In some companies (the most outstanding example probably being Canadian/American Hunter), IFA finds extensive application in exploration, particularly in the domestic play areas where there are large bases of subsurface data.

It appears that these kinds of analyses are becoming more sought after as domestic oil plays mature. As might be expected, IFA is applied primarily to exploitation projects, with significant successes being described in designing waterfloods, extending field pro-

duction, and identifying bypassed pay, especially in old producing wells slated for plugging. If field development geology is the future of petroleum geology, as Helwig (1987) and others contend, then the need for geologists to become more familiar with these methods is apparent.

It may be that too few geologists realize the usefulness of IFA–type studies in their daily exploration efforts. While excellent petrophysical research has been done by geologists, petrophysics just is not a routine part of exploration geological investigations. Papers documenting successful applications of petrophysics and formation evaluation to exploration for new oil, such as one by Schowalter and Hess (1982), are remarkably sparse. We believe that there may be many subtle fields left to be found that can only be discovered by methods of IFA. We believe that much opportunity exists to do subtle stratigraphic/diagenetic exploration, and to thereby find oil. Perhaps this should be the theme of a future guidebook.

CLOSING

It is our hope that the papers in this book will fuel interest in greater application of petrographic data to petroleum geology. While the role of such work in field development and exploitation is obvious, we believe that exploration efforts also would benefit. We therefore believe that petrographic and petrophysical analyses such as those reported in this volume will have an increasingly important role to play in petroleum geology. We suggest that geologists continue to build their familiarity with the disciplines of reservoir engineering, log analysis, and petrophysics and search for ways to apply these tools to exploration and exploitation.

REFERENCES

Archie, G.E., 1950, Introduction to petrophysics of reservoir rocks: AAPG Bull., v. 34, p. 943–961.

Coalson, E.B., D.J. Hartmann, and J.B. Thomas, 1985, Productive characteristics of common reservoir porosity types: South Texas Geol. Soc. Bull., v. 25, p. 35–51.

Helwig, J.A., 1987, Field development geology is the future of petroleum geology: AAPG Bull., v. 71, p. 1127.

Lindquist, S.J., 1983, Nugget Formation reservoir characteristics affecting production in the Overthrust Belt of southwestern Wyoming: JPT, p. 1355–1365.

Lindquist, S.J., 1988, Practical characterization of eolian reservoirs for development: Nugget Sandstone, Utah–Wyoming thrust belt: Sed. Geol., v. 56, p. 315–339.

Schmidt, V. and D.A. McDonald, 1979, The role of secondary porosity in the course of sandstone diagenesis, SEPM Spec. Pub. 26, p. 175–207.

Schowalter, T.T. and P.D. Hess, 1982, Interpretation of subsurface hydrocarbon shows: AAPG Bull., v. 66, p. 1302–1327.

Sneider, R.M. et al., 1981, Methods for detection and characterization of reservoir rock, Deep Basin Gas Area, Western Canada: SPE–AIME, 56th Ann. Fall Tech. Conf. and Exhib., Paper SPE 10072, 9 p.

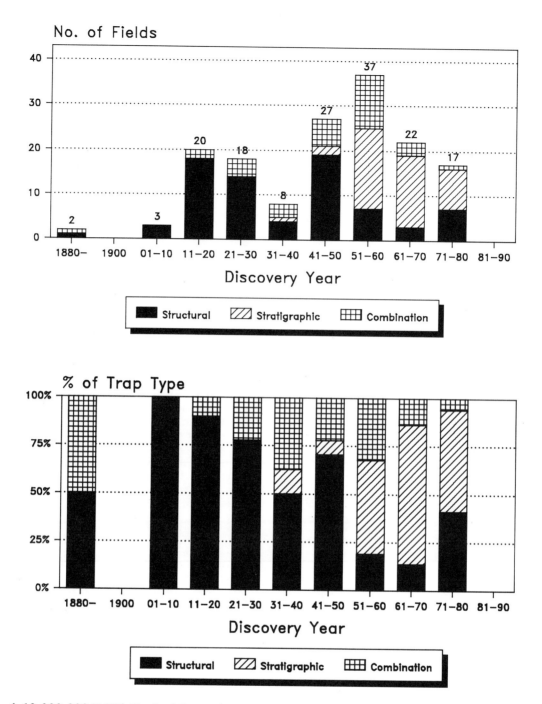

Large (>10,000,000 BOE) Rocky Mountain fields with sandstone reservoirs (n=155). Discoveries of different types of traps are plotted as the number of discoveried (upper graph) and as the percentage of total discoveries for that time period (lower graph). Trends in types of traps found illustrate the importance of surface–structure exploration in the 1920's, seismic exploration in the 1950's, and the higher resolution seismic of the 1970's, particularly in the Utah/Wyoming Overthrust Belt. The decline during the 1930's in success of exploration, then based almost entirely on prospecting for anticlines and fault traps, was interrupted by technological infusions of the 1940's, 1950's, and 1970's. Stratigraphic traps became exploration targets in the 1950's and continue to be successful. A greater percentage of stratigraphic traps now are being discovered as the "supply" of untapped structures identifiable with today's technology diminishes. Interestingly, no sandstone reservoir discovered since 1981 had produced 10,000,000 BOE as of August, 1988. However, Amos Draw, a Muddy Sandstone field in Campbell Co., Wyoming, was discovered in 1982, and comes close, having produced 8,509,000 BOE. Production data compliments of Petroleum Information. Compiled by John W. Robinson, 1989. See page 351ff for further information.

Conceptual Models for the Prediction of Porosity Evolution with an Example from the Frontier Sandstone, Bighorn Basin, Wyoming[1]

RONALD C. SURDAM[2]
THOMAS L. DUNN[3]
DONALD B. MacGOWAN[3]
HENRY P. HEASLER[2]

[1]Received February 14, 1989, Revised May 3, 1989
[2]Department of Geology and Geophysics, University of Wyoming, Laramie, Wyoming
[3]Enhanced Oil Recovery Institute, University of Wyoming, Laramie, Wyoming

The diagenetic modeling techniques presented in this paper result in a conceptual framework, whereby organic diagenesis can be integrated with inorganic diagenesis in a source–reservoir system during progressive burial. Predictions of porosity evolution in clastic reservoir intervals can result when this diagenetic information is combined with observations of the depositional fabric and near–surface and mechanical processes operative on the system.

The processes controlling progressive burial diagenesis are divided into three zones: 1) shallow burial, or from surface to depths equivalent to approximately 176°F (80°C); 2) intermediate burial, or approximately 176 to 284°F (80–140°C), and 3) deep burial, or 284 to 410°F (140–210°C). Each of these zones are categorized by a specific series of organic/inorganic interactions that control mineral stability, and porosity evolution through the respective time–temperature burial intervals.

The key to porosity prediction is to determine the spatial distribution of these organic/inorganic interactions during progressive burial. These interactions are kinetically controlled, and thus are best evaluated in time–temperature space. This can be done using a modified Tissot and Espitale (1975) kinetic maturation model. The application of this methodology is illustrated using a case history of the Frontier Formation from the Bighorn Basin of Wyoming and Montana.

INTRODUCTION

In this paper we demonstrate how to construct a conceptual model for the prediction of diagenesis in sandstone and shale sequences during progressive burial. The premise is that, in addition to depositional fabric and near–surface and mechanical processes, the interaction of organic and inorganic components control mineral reactions during diagenesis (Fig. 1). These physical and chemical processes provide a mechanistic explanation of why the diagenetic sequence shown in Table 1 is so common in sandstones that have undergone progressive and continuous burial diagenesis.

Exceptions can be found to this diagenetic sequence. However, they tend to be of local importance with respect to porosity evolution. An impor-

tant exception would occur if there were significant mixing of fluids, such as an influx of meteoric water, or hot deep brines. In the construction of this diagenetic model we therefore make the following assumptions:

1) There is no significant mixing of connate and meteoric waters below a depth equivalent to a temperature of about 176°F (80°C).

2) There is no subsequent mixing of connate waters with hot brines derived from significantly deeper portions of the basin.

Therefore, the rock–fluid system below depths equivalent to approximately 176°F (80°C) is closed. It should be noted that these assumptions do not negate fluid convection within the defined system, but they do restrict the fluid movement to within the system.

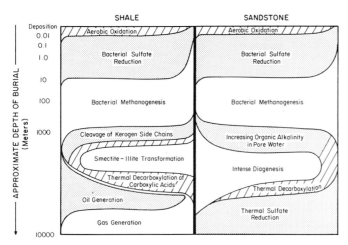

Figure 1. Typical diagenetic zones in shales and sandstones undergoing progressive burial. Depths are approximate. From Surdam et al., 1989c.

Table 1. Schematic of diagenetic mineral reactions and zones.

Shallow Burial (sediment/water interface ⇒ 80°C)

Compaction

Carbonate cementation
  Calcite
  Siderite
  Dolomite

Clay
  Infiltration
  Hydration/Reprecipitation
  Bioturbation

Silica cementation

Kaolinite precipitation

Intermediate Burial (80°C ⇒ 140°C)

Smectite ⇒ Illite	
Dissolution	Precipitation
Carbonate	Kaolinite
Feldspar (Plagioclase ⇒ K-feldspar)	Illite
Lithic fragments	Chlorite
Albitization	Ferroan carbonate
K-feldspar overgrowths	Quartz

Deep Burial (140°+C)

Dissolution	Precipitation
Ferroan carbonate	Pyrite
K-feldspar	Illite
Anhydrite	Quartz
Aluminosilicates	

SHALLOW BURIAL DIAGENESIS

Coupled with sandstone provenance and depositional fabric, the diagenetic processes characterizing shallow burial set the stage for most if not all subsequent diagenetic reactions (Berner, 1980), and therefore play an important role in porosity evolution (Surdam et al., 1989c). We here define "shallow" as the depth necessary to achieve 176°F (80°C), approximately from 5,000 to 10,000 ft (1.5–3 km), depending on the geothermal gradient. Significant shallow burial processes include: compaction or the formation of carbonates, clay cements, and of Fe-Mn oxide grain coatings; infiltration and alteration of clays and Fe-Mn oxides; and (of lesser importance) incipient

PROVENANCE CONTROLS ON POROSITY EVOLUTION

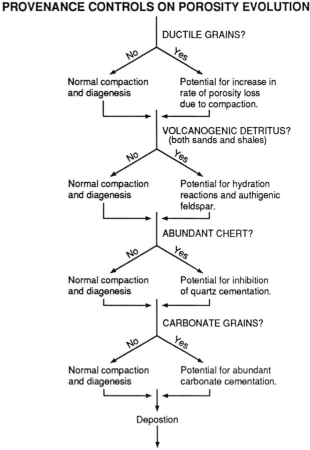

TO: NEAR-SURFACE PROCESSES AFFECTING POROSITY EVOLUTION

Figure 2. Controls of provenance on clastic diagenesis and porosity evolution. From Surdam et al., 1989b.

framework–grain dissolution, quartz precipitation, and grain replacement by carbonate. Some of these early diagenetic processes establish significant textural and mineralogical changes that can be recognized in deeply buried sediments, and which also are determinative to porosity enhancement or preservation at depth.

Early diagenetic processes can be very effective in accomplishing the following:

1) establishing fluid conduits for subsequent fluid convection,

2) preserving primary porosity by forming early grain coatings, (i.e., inhibiting later overgrowth formation),

3) preserving primary porosity by precipitation of early, non–pervasive cements that later can be removed (establishing high minus–cement porosities),

4) and irreversibly destroying porosity and permeability (i.e., completely occluding all effective fluid migration routes).

Sandstone provenance exerts a major control on diagenetic pathways taken by an arenite during burial (Fig. 2). Several near–surface chemical diagenetic processes also exert a strong control upon porosity evolution (Fig. 3). Mechanical processes which act upon porosity evolution include ductile grain deforma-

NEAR SURFACE PROCESSES AFFECTING POROSITY EVOLUTION

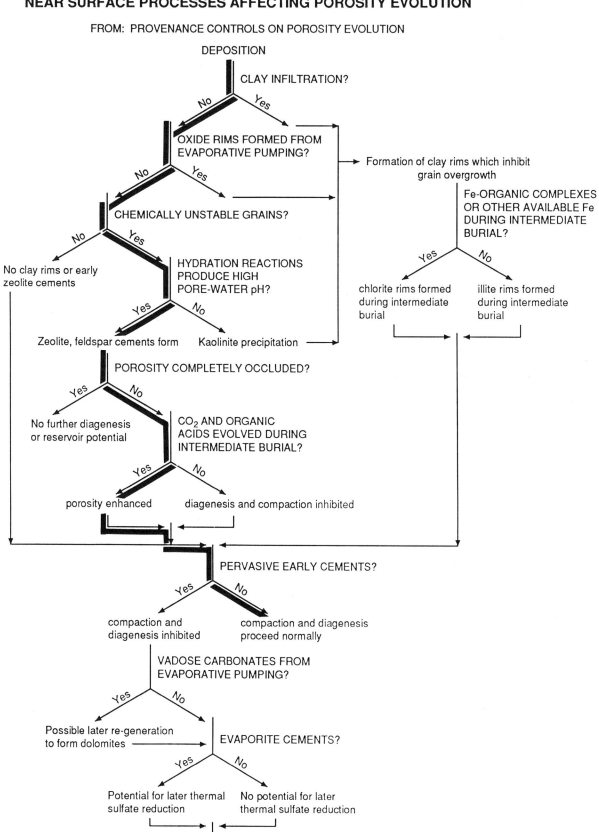

Figure 3. Diagenetic pathways for near–surface processes affecting porosity evolution. Heavy line shows diagenetic path taken by the Frontier Formation in the Bighorn Basin. Modified from Surdam et al., 1989b.

MECHANICAL PROCESSES AFFECTING POROSITY EVOLUTION

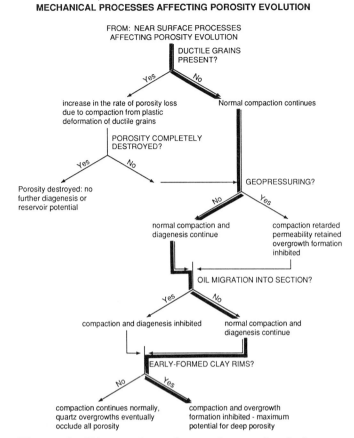

Figure 4. Diagenetic pathways for mechanical processes affecting porosity. Heavy line indicates diagenetic path of the Frontier Formation in Bighorn Basin. Modified from Surdam et al., 1989b.

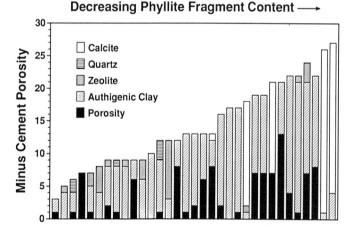

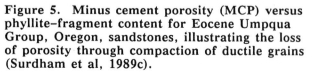

Figure 5. Minus cement porosity (MCP) versus phyllite-fragment content for Eocene Umpqua Group, Oregon, sandstones, illustrating the loss of porosity through compaction of ductile grains (Surdham et al, 1989c).

tion and grain packing changes (i.e., compaction) (McBride et al., 1989); geopressuring; and oil migration into the section. These processes (Fig. 4) may be operative from early through late burial.

Compactional Processes

The process most damaging to porosity and permeability during early burial is packing change and ductile grain deformation. Within the first few thousand feet of burial, porosity in a sandstone can be reduced by as much as 50% (Sclater and Christie, 1980). Excluding the effects of early cementation, the loss of porosity due to compaction in both sandstones and shales is maximized during early burial. The original composition of the sandstone plays a significant role in determining the magnitude of this effect, since detrital phyllosilicates and aggregate lithic grains containing them tend to behave plastically during compaction, contributing to the reduction of porosity. A good indicator of the extent of porosity loss due to compaction is the point–count–derived parameter, minus–cement porosity (MCP), which is the sum of the non-replacement, intergranular cements and remaining primary porosity. This value, when subtracted from the estimated original porosity, provides an approximation of the amount of porosity lost due to changes in grain packing and ductile grain deformation (Rosenfeld, 1949; Heald, 1956). Sandstones which contain large amounts of phyllitic–lithic fragments commonly show low MCP values due to the ductile behavior of the phyllitic grains. Surdam et al. (1989c) cite as an example the Eocene Umpqua Group sandstones of coastal Oregon which show increasing MCP values with decreasing phyllitic fragment content (Fig. 5). A further example is the contrasting reservoir quality of the Beluga and Sterling sandstones of the Cook Inlet Neogene which can be attributed to differences in provenance. Sandstones of the Beluga Formation, derived from a low–grade metasedimentary terrain, lost virtually all porosity in a few thousand feet of burial due to deformation of the ductile lithic grains. The sands of the Sterling Formation, derived from batholiths, contained abundant, but more mechanically stable, lithic fragments. Diagenesis of the phyllite–lithic arenites was inhibited by the permeability loss due to compaction and the shallow burial (Hayes et al., 1976).

Because of the control that grain size exerts on the variation of lithic grain content, various intervals within a depositional facies can be characterized by very different porosity vs. depth curves. An example is the Terry Sandstones (Upper Cretaceous offshore bars) as described by Pittman (1988 and this volume; see Fig. 6).

Carbonate Cementation

An effective way to regenerate original porosity at depth is by preserving it with early carbonate cementation before the rock has suffered significant mechanical deformation, and regenerate it by later dissolution. The major consequence of early cementation is to prevent or inhibit compactional effects and later fluid migration. If MCP is plotted versus depth for a sandstone characterized by early carbonate cementation, the observed MCP will be higher than the poros-

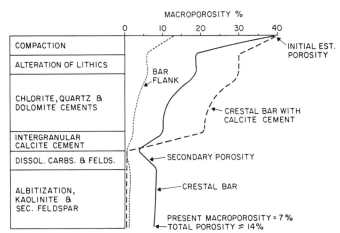

Figure 6. Evolution of the bar–flank and crestal–bar portions of the macroporosity of the Terry Sandstone during diagenesis. After Pittman, 1988. Reprinted and adapted with the permission of the Society of Economic Paleontologists and Mineralogists.

ity predicted by a typical compaction curve (cf. Surdam and others, 1989c). A large proportion of the original porosity can survive compactional effects. However, for this potential porosity to become effective, the cement must be removed. The wholesale removal of pore–filling carbonate cement from deeply buried sandstones has been postulated by several authors, most notably, Schmidt and McDonald (1979). However, the conclusion that porosity in deeply buried sandstones is the result solely of dissolution of pervasive intergranular cements is unlikely. The correspondence between the inhibition of progressive diagenesis and impermeable rock is observed so often that significant exceptions likely are rare. Also, the presence of some early carbonate cement is strongly tied to depositional environment and climate. Hence, to appeal to this process for globally observed deep porosity is unsatisfactory. More important to the preservation of primary porosity from the effects of compaction are the incomplete pore–filling or pore–lining cements that contribute to rock strength (Heald and Renton, 1966). For this reason it is important to understand the distribution of early cements; they can be of paramount importance during subsequent diagenesis.

Of the possible early cements in sandstones, carbonates appear to be the most volumetrically important (Berner, 1980; Gautier, 1985; Curtis and Coleman, 1986). In zones of abundant aerobic methane oxidation, large amounts of extremely carbon–isotopically light calcite will precipitate; however these conditions are rare (Gautier, 1985). In rocks exposed to vadose conditions for extended periods of time, significant carbonate cements can be precipitated by evaporative concentration because this process causes the pH to rise. Subaerial exposure on low–stand unconformities is an excellent setting for this process, and climate is a strong control.

Curtis and Coleman (1986) discuss in detail the processes controlling early carbonate cementation in

concretions associated with fine–grained sediments. They argue that isotopic evidence strongly supports the hypothesis that volumetrically important, early carbonate cements invariably are formed in either the zone of bacterially mediated sulfate reduction, or of microbial methanogenesis. Because we have defined our system to include both sandstones and shales, we feel justified in extrapolating from Curtis and Coleman's diagenetic model for fine–grained rocks to the source–reservoir system.

Curtis and Coleman explain the processes controlling the distribution and types of carbonate cements (e.g., calcite, dolomite, or siderite) formed during shallow burial in clastic sediments. They suggest that in sulfate–poor, bicarbonate–rich pore water systems characterized by the availability of Fe^{+2}, siderite should precipitate. In the absence of high concentrations of dissolved iron, the presence of Mg^{+2} or Ca^{+2} will favor the precipitation of dolomite or calcite, depending on the presence of SO_4^{-2} and the Mg^{+2}/Ca^{+2} ratio in the pore water.

Curtis (1978) and Berner (1981) described the diagenetic zones characterizing shallow burial from the surface downward as:

Zone 1) oxidation by molecular oxygen (Fig. 7), i.e., $CH_2O + O_2 \rightarrow H_2O + CO_2$. Usually this zone is a few centimeters thick, or the depth of burrowing.

Zone of Aerobic Bacterial Oxidation

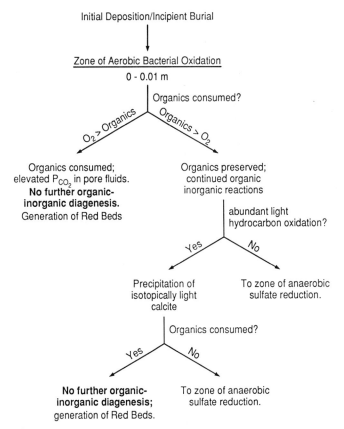

Figure 7. Reaction pathways for the zone of aerobic bacterial oxidation. From Surdam et al., 1989b.

Zone 2) bacterially mediated sulfate reduction, i.e., $2CH_2O + SO_4^{-2} \rightarrow HS^- + HCO_3^- + H_2O + CO_2$. Usually this zone is a few meters thick and limited by the availability of SO_4^{-2}.

Zone 3) bacterially mediated methanogenesis, i.e., $2CH_2O \rightarrow CH_4 + CO_2$. Usually this zone extends down to depths of approximately 1,000 meters (3,000 ft).

The introduction of CO_2 into the pore water as a result of oxidation, sulfate reduction, or methanogenesis does not result in the precipitation of carbonate minerals. As Curtis (1987) points out, the decrease in pH caused by CO_2 dissolution and H_2CO_3 dissociation will favor carbonate mineral dissolution. In a sandstone/shale sequence, significant carbonate precipitation requires a parallel reaction that consumes hydrogen ions or produces proton–consuming species. Reduction of Fe and Mn by oxidation of organic matter provides such parallel reactions (i.e., net hydroxyl production), for example:

$$CH_2O + 2Fe_2O_3 + 3H_2O \rightarrow$$
$$4Fe^{+2} + HCO_3^- + 7OH^-$$
(Curtis, 1987)

Thus, in an environment where either microbial sulfate reduction or methanogenesis is accompanied by Fe or Mn reduction, there is a high probability that a carbonate phase will precipitate.

As a sandstone–shale sequence passes into the zone of microbial sulfate reduction (Figs. 8 and 9), any available Fe and sulfate will be reduced and organic material will be oxidized. The mineral redox reaction is shown schematically as:

$$15CH_2O + 2Fe_2O_3 + 8SO_4^{-2} \rightarrow$$
$$4FeS_2 + 7H_2O + 15HCO_3^- + OH^-$$
(Curtis, 1987)

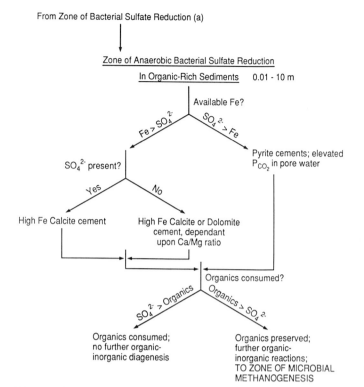

Figure 9. Reaction pathways for the zone of bacterial sulfate reduction in relatively organic–rich sediments with available sulfate. From Surdam et al., 1989b.

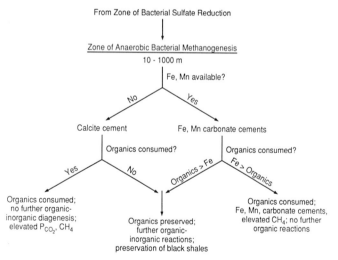

Figure 10. Reaction pathways for the zone of anaerobic bacterial methanogenesis. From Surdam et al., 1989b.

Pyrite precipitation is accompanied by a significant increase in bicarbonate concentration in the pore water. As a result, Fe–poor carbonates (calcite and dolomite) will form with highly insoluble Fe sulfides. With slightly greater burial, the sequence enters the zone of microbial methanogenesis (Fig. 10), where a combination of microbial methanogenesis and Fe re-

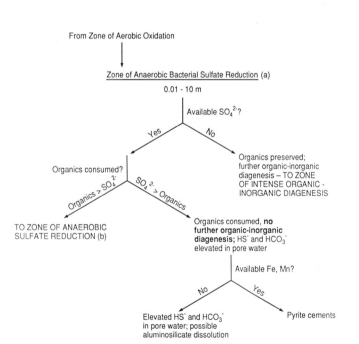

Figure 8. Reaction pathways for the zone of bacterial sulfate reduction in sediments with available sulfate, but which are relatively organic poor. From Surdam et al., 1989b.

duction is highly conducive to the precipitation of Fe–rich carbonate (Curtis, 1987). This process is approximated as follows:

$$7CH_2O + 2Fe_2O_3 \rightarrow$$
$$3CH_4 + 4FeCO_3 + H_2O$$

Thus, as a sediment passes through the zones of bacterially mediated sulfate reduction and microbial methanogenesis during shallow burial, there is ample opportunity to precipitate carbonate minerals depending upon the chemical pathway. The amount and type of carbonate precipitated will depend on the amounts and ratios of the key components: Fe, Mn, Ca^{+2}, Mg^{+2}, SO_4^{-2} and organic material.

The spatial distribution of early carbonate cements in the sandstone will depend not only on the availability and distribution of these key elements in the rock and pore fluid phases, but on burial rates and fluid flow mechanisms characterizing the system. Curtis and Coleman (1986), in constructing their model however, do not consider the dissolution of carbonate materials in the sands (e.g., shelly material) as a possible source of CO_2. This process must be considered, as it will have a profound effect upon the isotopic composition of any carbonate phase precipitated in these zones. Hence, one should not always expect a characteristic isotopic signature (e.g., positive C–isotopic signature from the zone of microbial methanogenesis) from carbonates precipitated in these zones.

Depositional environment has a strong influence on the potential for early carbonate formation, and on the sequence of microbial sulfate reduction and microbial methanogenesis (Curtis, 1987). This influence can be evaluated by interpreting the conditions characterizing early burial. This interaction will be a combination of the following conditions with the clastic inorganic and organic constituents:

1) sulfate-rich waters, e.g., typical marine or saline lacustrine waters

2) sulfate-poor waters, e.g., meteoric or fresh lacustrine waters

3) waters whose salinity is increased by evaporative concentration in the vadose zone

4) oxygenated conditions

5) anoxic conditions

As Curtis and Coleman (1986) point out, calcite precipitates from marine-influenced pore waters rich in dissolved sulfate. Dolomite is favored for similar waters depleted in sulfate. Siderite precipitates from meteorically derived pore waters (Figs. 7–10).

This model is predicated on continuous and progressive burial. If sediments were to experience significant uplift after passing through these zones, or if they were invaded by meteoric water, they would show a telogenetic overprint in the diagenetic sequence. For instance, light $\delta^{13}C$ isotopic signatures in carbonate cements (associated with pyrite) which are demonstrably post-compaction may be attributed to either uplift into the zone of microbial sulfate reduction, or the migration of sulfate-charged waters into the deeper pore water system.

Clay Minerals

Another very important early burial effect upon porosity is the addition of clay minerals into the sandstones at or near the sediment/water interface. Clay can fill pores, thereby damaging permeability; or it can be precursor for chlorite or illite rims which may help preserve porosity later. This addition can be accomplished by a variety of processes such as:

1) infiltration in fluvial sediments

2) bioturbation of marine and deltaic sediments

3) early hydration reactions in lithic–rich sediment, particularly those containing significant volcanogenic material

4) pedogenic processes commonly associated with unconformities

5) compaction of soft mud clasts

6) depositional regimes producing poorly sorted deposits (e.g., turbidity flows, episodic flow regime changes, etc.)

Pedogenic processes and bioturbation tend to result in significant degradation of porosity and permeability, and reduction in organic richness. The probable reason for this is that the processes of pedogenesis and bioturbation tend to fill pores with clay minerals, whereas infiltration and early hydration reactions generally tend to coat grains with clay and/or Fe–Mn oxides, thus inhibiting further compaction and diagenesis. Exceptions to these trends are: 1) quartzose sandstones which retain remnants of porosity and permeability due to the interference of the bioturbated clay, which inhibits quartz cementation, and 2) extensive infiltration of clays which completely fill intergranular pores (Moraes and De Ros, 1988).

For example, consider clay coats associated with eolian sandstones. Near–surface conditions typical of eolian settings, particularly in wet stationary dunes and arid alluvial fans, are characterized by periodic wetting and drying, in addition to evaporative concentration in a highly oxidizing environment. It is within this setting that the earliest diagenetic reactions occur, including incipient hydration and solution of unstable grains (e.g., mafic minerals and lithic grains) and the precipitation of clay and Fe–Mn oxide rims on framework grains (Walker et al., 1978; and Plate 1A). Dixon et al. (1989) have suggested that these early Fe–Mn oxide rims are the textural precursors to, and the reactants that form, chlorite rims in the Norphlet Formation of Alabama, a formation with greater than 20% porosity at 20,000 ft (6,200 m) depths. In contrast, chlorite rims in sandstones of the Tuscaloosa Formation of the Gulf Coast (which has similar porosity at similar depths) have been related to the availability of Fe from *in situ* dissolution of volcanogenic detritus (Thomson, 1979; Larese et al., 1984).

The distribution of the fine–grained volcanic detritus within fluvial channels could well be controlled by infiltration processes. Clay rims on framework grains have been shown to inhibit the development of quartz overgrowths by prohibiting nucleation (Heald, 1956; Cecil and Heald, 1971; Heald and Larese, 1974; Thomson, 1979; Larese et al., 1984; Dixon et al.

1989). Work by Matleck et al. (1989) indicates that the presence of infiltrated clays is related to the concentration of suspended load, fluctuating flow, lack of reworking, and the particle size of both the suspended sediment and the infiltrated sand. These authors note that many of these factors are strongly related to depositional environment. Infiltration of clays has been shown to be highly detrimental to reservoir sandstones if the volume of infiltrated clay is sufficient to occlude the intergranular pores (Moraes and De Ros, 1988). Therefore, it is essential to understand the processes characterizing the original depositional environment and the resulting reaction products if one expects to predict the distribution of porosity controlling factors, such as chlorite rims, in deeply buried sandstones.

Kaolinite

Second to carbonates, kaolinite is perhaps the most common alteration product formed during shallow burial. It is a typical product of weathering associated with high annual precipitation, low salinity waters, and relatively short contact time between first-formed weathering products and dilute waters (e.g., rainfall) (Barshad, 1966; Drever, 1988). Kaolinite is thermodynamically stable at low temperatures. However, increasing temperature and increasing ratio of cation to proton concentration decreases its stability in favor of other clays (Fig. 11). Kaolinite has been recognized as an early authigenic phase in reservoir sandstones (Fothergill, 1955; and many others since). It has been commonly recognized as forming from the alteration of feldspar and lithic fragments. Bjørlykke and Brendsdal (1986) and Aguado (1989) documented the abundant formation of kaolinite from detrital micas.

The link between kaolinite and dilute waters explains the tendency of kaolinite to be found in either non-marine deposits or those sandstones which are in hydrologic contact with meteoric waters. In the latter case, it forms as a telogenetic feature (i.e., as a result of uplift or meteoric water recharge) associated with unconformities, or sections which have remained in the shallow burial zone for long periods of time. Hence, the presence of significant amounts of kaolinite within a sandstone is broadly predictable in terms of depositional setting (non-marine vs. marine), composition (lithic and/or feldspar content indicated by provenance), and the possibility of later meteoric water recharge (continuity with updip and outcropping permeable beds or truncation by unconformities showing evidence of recharge). In addition to these associations, there is the potential for kaolinite or other aluminosilicate phases to form as the result of deeper dissolution of aluminosilicates and upward migration as an organo-aluminum complex (Surdam and others, 1984). Organo-aluminum complexes may be destabilized by mixing with lower ionic strength waters, or changes in temperature or pressure (Hatton and Hanor, 1984).

Chert

The presence of chert can reduce the amount of quartz cementation in a sandstone. Fine-grained chert does not typically form overgrowths of significant

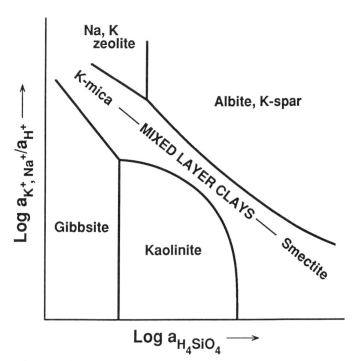

Figure 11. Activity space diagram for the H^+–Na^+–K^+–H_4SiO_4 system, schematically illustrating the stability relationships of authigenic feldspars, zeolites, and clays. After Drever, 1988. Reprinted and adapted with permission of Prentice Hall, Inc.

size (Heald and Renton, 1966). The quartz crystallites form minute terminations of varied crystallographic orientation which do not enlarge into a coherent overgrowth. The rate of overgrowth is reduced by two thirds when it has completed the formation of a euhedral termination (pers. comm., R.E. Larese, 1989). Essentially, the formation of the pyramid reduces the availability of dislocation or growth sites. Hence, if the chert does not substantially reduce rock strength, its presence in a quartz sandstone will normally result in a reduction of potential porosity loss by quartz cementation. Chert content follows grain size (Blatt et al., 1980); this effect will be most apparent in coarser clastics. Chert has had a significant impact on reservoir quality in many sandstones, most notably the Ivishak Formation of the North Slope, Alaska. Chert does not exert this positive effect in sandstones whose fluids have elevated silicon activities. In these cases, the extent of oversaturation produces extensive quartz growth regardless of the presence of chert, as suggested herein for the Cretaceous Frontier sandstones of Wyoming where abundant Si from dissolution of volcanic debris has negated the beneficial effects of detrital chert.

Volcanogenic Detritus

Another process that can be detrimental to porosity and permeability during early burial is the alteration of volcanogenic lithic and vitric material. Volcanogenic debris are highly reactive and particularly prone to hydration reactions. Hydration reactions result in three important effects: 1) an increase in pH,

2) an increase in Si activity, and 3) the formation of authigenic feldspars or hydrous phases such as clays or zeolites. These processes can be shown schematically as:

$$X\text{-silicate} + H_2O \rightarrow H\text{-silicate (``clay'')} + OH^- + X^+$$

where $X^+ = Na^+$, K^+, or $1/2\ Ca^{+2}$.

The first reaction product to form during incipient hydration typically is a clay mineral, but as the process proceeds, pH is increased to about 9, and a zeolite will form (Plate 1A). The precipitation of authigenic feldspar is favored over zeolites when Si activities are elevated and the activity of water is reduced, and, especially for potassium feldspars, when there are abundant nucleation sites (Kastner, 1971).

The products of these hydration reactions commonly completely occlude all effective porosity. Surdam and Boles (1979) have shown that this type of reaction in a volcanogenic sediment can reduce porosity by 10 to 20%. Galloway (1974, 1979) has discussed the early diagenesis of strongly volcanogenic sediments and illustrated their diagenesis with case histories from forearc basins of the Pacific Northwest.

The presence of volcanogenic lithic material can have a positive effect on porosity evolution. Larese et al. (1984) have shown that chlorite rims in the Tuscaloosa Formation can be attributed to the dissolution of volcanic lithic material.

In diagenesis of volcanogenic sandstones, clay and zeolite reaction products can be destabilized by organic acids and/or CO_2 evolved as the product of thermal maturation of sedimentary organic material (Crossey et al., 1984). Unless the early–formed reaction products have completely occluded porosity and permeability (as in many zeolite–rich sandstones), porosity enhancement can take place during later diagenesis. However, it is essential that organic–rich rocks be hydrologically connected to potential reservoir rocks with some remnant permeability, if porosity enhancement is to take place. The problem is that the organic–acid anions and CO_2 necessary for the dissolution or destabilization of clay or zeolite cements are generated by the diagenesis of source rocks (Fig. 1); source rocks are commonly are scarce in depositional settings characterized by a preponderance of volcanogenic material.

Quartz Cementation

Quartz cementation during early burial has the potential for both positive and negative influence on porosity evolution and reservoir quality: the loss of porosity by cementation may be offset by the increase in rock strength, which inhibits the loss of porosity by compaction. Early quartz cementation, although common in many sandstones, typically is not important volumetrically.

INTERMEDIATE BURIAL DIAGENESIS

With progressive burial, the sandstone–shale system enters the intermediate burial diagenesis zone, with temperatures of about 176 to 284°F (80–140°C) (Fig. 12, Table 1). In this zone, the most important porosity enhancing reactions take place: early–formed carbonate cements may be dissolved (or at the very least

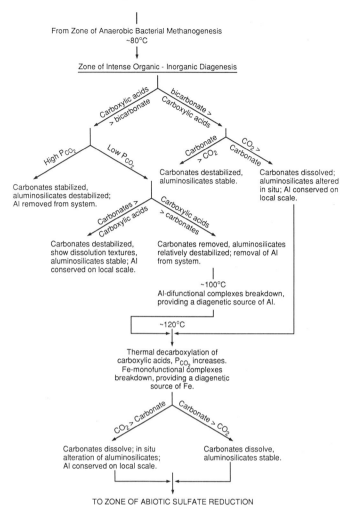

(modified from Surdam & others, 1984)

Figure 12. Reaction pathways for the zone of intermediate burial diagenesis (ca. 80 to 120°C, or 176 to 248°F). Modified from Surdam et al., 1984, and from Surdam et al., 1989b.

carbonate cements are inhibited from forming), and aluminosilicate framework grains may be dissolved. Therefore, porosity can be preserved or significantly enhanced.

Several porosity–destroying reactions also characterize this zone. For example, late ferroan carbonate cements are potential reaction products that typically occlude porosity (Boles, 1978). Also, there are a wide variety of reaction products such as kaolinite, illite, and chlorite that can form as a result of aluminosilicate dissolution. The imbalance between porosity–enhancing or preserving reactions and porosity–destroying reactions determines the net gain or loss of porosity.

In potential clastic reservoir facies, there typically is no demonstrable net gain in porosity due to aluminosilicate dissolution. In as much as Al is conserved in the source–reservoir system as a whole, some portions of the potential reservoir may be characterized by extensive aluminosilicate or carbonate dissolution, while other portions undergo the precipitation of dissolution products. The magnitude of porosity enhancement due to aluminosilicate grain dissolution depends on facies relationships, variations in original composition, formation of subsequent cements, availability of fluid conduits, fluid flux, and the proximity of organic–rich source rocks in hydrologic connection with the reservoir rock.

In contrast, carbonate–mineral dissolution and mass transfer apparently can occur on a scale larger than a specific reservoir and source rock system (Schultz et al., 1989). Thus, in order to predict the distribution and volume of enhanced and preserved porosity within a targeted clastic reservoir interval, it is essential to understand the processes controlling the determinative reactions.

The most important assumptions made in this paper with regard to diagenesis in the intermediate burial zone are that:

1) Total concentration of carboxylic acid anions can exceed 5,000 ppm. At these concentrations and at reservoir temperatures, they will buffer the alkalinity in the fluid phase in the early phases of intermediate burial (Lundegard and Land, 1989; MacGowan and Surdam, 1989b)

2) Difunctional carboxylic acid anions can be present at significant levels (as much as 1,000+ ppm) between 176 and 212°F (80–100°C)

3) With progressive burial and elevated temperatures (above 230°F, or 110°C) in this zone, the ratio of CO_2/carboxylic acid anions increases

4) The reservoir–source rock system is closed. That is, there is no mixing of the connate formation waters with meteoric water or deep basin brines from outside the system.

Support for these assumptions stems mainly from formation–water chemistry, kerogen composition and structure, and hydrous pyrolysis experiments (Carothers and Kharaka, 1978; 1980; Hatton and Hanor, 1984; Fisher, 1987; Surdam and MacGowan, 1987; MacGowan and Surdam, 1988a; 1989a and b).

Organic Acids and Mineral Stability

The carboxylic acid anions in interstitial waters associated with the intermediate burial zone have been attributed to a variety of origins. Among the most commonly quoted are generation by thermal maturation of kerogen, mineral oxidation of organic material, interaction of water and hydrocarbons (water washing), and bacterial action. A recent, comprehensive review of the origin, distribution and role of carboxylic acid anions in the diagenetic environment is presented by MacGowan and Surdam (1989a).

Carbonates

The stability of carbonate minerals during progressive burial commonly is evaluated simply in terms of pH and the aqueous species Ca^{+2}, H_2CO_3, HCO_3^-, CO_3^{-2}, and CO_2, from:

$$\Sigma CO_2 = H_2CO_3 + HCO_3^- + CO_3^{-2}$$

This results in a simplistic view where alkalinity is attributed solely to the aqueous carbonate species and the standard (and erroneous) explanation of carbonate stability in the zone of intermediate burial diagenesis being solely a function of partial pressure of CO_2 (Pco_2), and of Ca, Mg, and Fe concentration (Holland and Borcsik, 1965; Lundegard and Land, 1989).

In the zone of intermediate burial, temperatures range from 176 to 248°F (80–120°C) and the concentration of organic acid anions in formation water increases to the maximum concentration where the carbonate system is externally buffered by acetate (MacGowan and Surdam, 1989a). Under these conditions, these anions dominate alkalinity (Wiley et al., 1975; Carothers and Kharaka, 1978) and significantly affect carbonate stability (Surdam and Crossey, 1985a, b; Meshri, 1986). The pH of the waters will be buffered by carboxylic acid anions. The capacity of acetate to buffer pH is typically much greater than any aqueous carbonate species. Acetate commonly is the most abundant organic acid anion in formation waters; its maximum buffering capacity is at a pH of 5.4 (Martell and Smith, 1974; Carothers and Kharaka, 1978).

Lundegard and Land (1989) modeled the pH–buffer crossover points for calcite stabilization/destabilization in the system $Ca^{2+} - Na^+ - CaCO_3 - CH_3COOH - H_2O$ using computer simulations, and varying Pco_2. This is a first step in evaluating the buffer capacities of carboxylic acid anions and the aqueous carbonate species in carbonate reservoirs. However, as presently constructed, the model of Lundegard and Land has many problems and is of limited applicability to the understanding of organic–inorganic interactions and carbonate–mineral stability during diagenesis of clastic reservoirs in the zone of intermediate burial (Surdam et al., 1989c; MacGowan and Surdam 1989b).

At temperatures greater than 212°F (100°C), the carboxylic acids, particularly the difunctional species, begin to decarboxylate via:

$$HOOCCH_2COOH \rightarrow CH_3COOH + CO_2$$
$$CH_3COOH \rightarrow CH_4 + CO_2$$

resulting in increased Pco_2. At some point over the temperature interval of 248 to 320°F (120–160°C), the carboxylic acid anions will completely decarboxylate and the alkalinity again will be dominated by the carbonate system (internally buffered) (Surdam et al., 1984). Implicit in the decarboxylation process is the progressive elevation of formation water Pco_2. A trend of increasing CO_2 content of produced gases with depth in the Gulf Coast is described by Franks and Forester (1984) and can be explained by a process of: 1) generation of organic acid anions, 2) progressive decarboxylation of organic acid anions and concomitant increase in Pco_2 at temperatures greater than 248°F (120°C), and 3) loss, at temperatures somewhere between 248 and 320°F, of the buffering capacity of the carboxylic acid anion as concentration is diminished (Surdam et al., 1984; 1989c). As Pco_2 increases with a lack of an external buffer, the system will move toward lower pH and increasing carbonate solubility (carbonate–mineral dissolution or lack of precipitation). Individual cases may vary in detail depending in part on such variables as Fe^{+2} and Mg^{+2} concentration and sulfate reduction and hydrocarbon oxidation.

Although the products of aluminosilicate dissolution appear to be transported only relatively short distances (perhaps up to hundreds of meters), the products of carbonate mineral dissolution can be transported on the order of one km (Schultz et al., 1989). Ca^{+2} generated in the intermediate burial zone may be transported up section, and serve as a source of Ca for carbonate minerals forming in the zone of shallow burial. Schultz et al. (1989) working in the San Joaquin Basin suggest that the ultimate source of Ca in the carbonate cements is plagioclase dissolution.

Aluminosilicates

Surdam et al. (1984); Crossey, 1985; and Surdam and Crossey (1985a) have documented experimentally at 212°F (100°C) that the presence of difunctional carboxylic acid anions at concentrations found in formation waters (MacGowan and Surdam, 1988a and b) can increase the solubility of Al from aluminosilicate dissolution by over three orders of magnitude with respect to the inorganic solubility of gibbsite. The increase in Al solubility with respect to the inorganic solubility of kaolinite is even greater (MacGowan and Surdam, 1988a). Phenolic compounds such as hydroquinone and catechol have outstanding chelating characteristics and similarly increase the solubility of Al (Crossey, 1985; Surdam and Crossey, 1985b).

Destabilization or alteration of aluminosilicate framework grains is not sufficient to explain observed porosity–enhancement textures. For instance, the mineral must not only be destabilized, but Al and Si also must be transported from the site of dissolution as well, if net porosity enhancement is to occur. If they are not, the plagioclase will alter in situ to kaolinite or some other aluminous alteration phase.

In recent experiments conducted by MacGowan and Surdam (1988a) and MacGowan et al. (1988), andesine as well as whole–core material were placed in formation waters collected from Tertiary reservoirs in the southern San Joaquin Basin, California and from the Louisiana Gulf Coast. Samples were heated to 212°F (100°C) for two weeks. At the end of the experiment, there was 44+ ppm total analytical Al in the experimental solutions. Dissolution textures observed in the solid phase using scanning electron microscopy (SEM) were similar to those observed in the reservoir, demonstrating that significant amounts of Al and Si had been dissolved. Hansley (1987) demonstrated that garnet dissolution textures observed in the Jurassic Morrison Formation could be experimentally reproduced using organic acid anions as chelating species. These textures could not be duplicated using mineral acids. Thus, there is little doubt that aluminosilicate framework grains in the subsurface can be destabilized, and that Al and Si will be complexed and transported at concentrations in excess of the apparent inorganic solubility of common aluminous diagenetic minerals (e.g., kaolinite).

The stability of the organo–aluminum complex has been shown to be temperature (Surdam et al., 1984) and pH dependent (MacGowan and Surdam, 1988a). If the pH of the fluid carrying the complex is changed significantly (e.g., encounters carbonate–rich rocks, fluid degassing, changes temperature, or mixes with other subsurface waters), the complex may be destabilized, resulting in precipitation of minerals such as kaolinite. The stability of organo–metallic complexes also is dependent on salinity, bacterial activity and

P_{CO_2} and P_{CH_4} (Hatton and Hanor, 1984; Shock, 1988; MacGowan and Surdam 1989a).

It has further been demonstrated that these organo–aluminum complexes may be more hydrophobic than hydrophilic, and hence, once formed, partition into the oil phase (MacGowan et al., 1988). This would explain the low analytical Al values obtained for formation waters with high organic alkalinities produced from liquid hydrocarbon reservoirs actively undergoing intermediate burial diagenesis (MacGowan and Surdam, 1988a and 1989b); although the produced waters from these reservoirs typically contain less than five ppm Al, the produced liquid hydrocarbons commonly contain 100+ ppm Al. The same effect has been noted in hydrous pyrolysis experiments (MacGowan and Surdam, 1989b).

Crossey (1985) and Surdam and McGowan (1987) have shown that difunctional carboxylic acid anions typically have a lower thermal stability than monofunctional forms. As temperature increases, the difunctional acids decarboxylate to monofunctional forms and/or CO_2 and short chain alkanes. Thus, the difunctional forms should be more abundant in the 176 to 212°F (80–120°C) temperature interval than at higher temperatures. It has been demonstrated that difunctional carboxylic acid anions are much better chelaters of Al than are the monofunctional species (Surdam et al., 1984; Crossey, 1985; MacGowan and Surdam, 1988b). Thus, the sequential decarboxylation of difunctional species followed by monofunctional species determines the sequence of resultant mineral reaction products (Surdam et al., 1989c).

With respect to feldspars, it has been shown that calcic plagioclase is the most susceptible to dissolution by organic acids, followed in turn by albitic plagioclase and finally potassium feldspar (Surdam et al., 1984; Amrhein and Suarez, 1988). However, potassium feldspar is not immune to dissolution by organic acid anions, for in some cases potassium feldspar dissolution can be volumetrically significant (Land and Milliken, 1981; Yin and Surdam, 1985). Commonly, partially dissolved grains of calcic plagioclase are seen to be rimmed by authigenic potassium feldspar lacking dissolution textures (Dunn, 1979; Surdam et al., 1989c).

Organic acid anions complex a variety of components in addition to Al and Si (Huang and Keller, 1970). In treating wells, acetic acid commonly is used to complex Fe in order to keep it in solution. The data of Surdam and MacGowan (1987) and MacGowan et al. (1988) indicate that various metal–complexing organic anions compete in an intricate manner with each other in buffering pH and the complexing of various metals at reservoir conditions. It is apparent that no metal cation is complexed to the exclusion of any other metal cations by organometallic complexation in the reaction of formation fluids with core material (Surdam and MacGowan, 1987; MacGowan et al., 1988).

It is suggested that Fe–acetate complexes are stable at higher temperatures than are difunctional complexes such as Al–malonate. This speculation is based on the fact that monofunctional organic acid anions are stable at higher temperature than are difunctional species (Crossey, 1985). Hence, kaolinite, a possible product of Al–malonate destabilization, typically forms before and at lower temperatures than chlorite, a possible product of Fe–acetate destabilization. If calcic plagioclase is the dominant feldspar undergoing dissolution, then kaolinite commonly is the reaction product. The kaolinite–forming reaction primarily involves the recombination of Al from the organometallic complex with monosilicic acid. The formation of illite requires Al from the organometallic complex, monosilicic acid, and K^+. An ideal, observed source for the K^+ is the dissolution of potassium feldspar (Hower et al., 1976). In fact, the dissolution products of potassium feldspar contain all the essential components required to form illite. Thus, if potassium feldspar is dissolved, illite almost always will form somewhere in the diagenetic system (Surdam et al., 1989c).

In contrast, the formation of chlorite not only requires Al and H_4SiO_4, perhaps from aluminosilicate dissolution, but also a source of reduced Fe as well. Kaolinite or illite (depending on the activity of K^+) will form instead of chlorite in the absence of a reductant. If the system is reducing, the major competition for the Fe^{+2} will be pyrite, if there is a source of sulfur. Some potential reductants in sandstone/shale systems are H_2S, CH_4, and liquid hydrocarbons. All of these would be provided by thermal maturation of organic–rich portions of the system.

In summary, difunctional carboxylic acid anions provide an ideal mechanism to dissolve and transport significant quantities of relatively insoluble material in the subsurface during diagenesis, particularly over the 176 to 212°F (80–100°C) temperature range. These organic acid anions have been observed in formation waters at concentrations sufficient to increase the solubility of Al several orders of magnitude above the apparent inorganic solubility of kaolinite (MacGowan and Surdam, 1988). Therefore, carboxylic acid anions in formation waters will have a profound influence upon the stability of aluminosilicates and carbonates in the zone of intermediate burial diagenesis. At present, there is no other viable alternative for explaining the observed mass transfer of Al in the subsurface over this temperature interval.

It should be noted that the inhibition of authigenic mineral precipitation may characterize these "dissolution" episodes. This leaves petrographers with the unpleasant reality that fundamental events in the history of a sandstone may not leave recognizable and demonstrable textures behind.

Reduction of Fe and Mn Oxides

Assuming that organic material is expelled from shale into fluid conduits (Surdam et al., 1989c), several important reactions can take place in adjacent sandstones. For instance, any Fe^{+3} or Mn^{+4} will be reduced by H_2S. These reactions explain why many originally red (oxidized) reservoir sandstones are green or gray (reduced) in those portions that produce hydrocarbons (Dixon et al., 1989). It is fair to assume that those portions of the reservoir rock that remain red were not in significant fluid contact (e.g., no effective fluid conduit) with the organic–rich source rocks. There are outstanding examples of this

relationship in both the Norphlet Formation of Alabama and the Rotliegendes sandstones of the North Sea.

Ferroan Carbonate Minerals and Chlorite

The first carboxylic acid anions to decarboxylate with increased temperature are the difunctional species, followed at slightly higher temperatures by the monofunctional acid anions (Crossey, 1985; Surdam and MacGowan, 1987). Therefore, in the thermal window of 212 to 266°F, plus or minus 18 F° (100–120°C plus or minus 10 C°), the rock system is subjected to increasingly elevated P_{CO_2} (the product of decarboxlyated difunctional acid anions), but the alkalinity is still dominated by the monofunctional organic acid anions (i.e., acetate). Under these conditions, ferroan calcite or dolomite will be stabilized (Surdam and Crossey, 1985a and b). Isotopic temperatures calculated for these late ferroan carbonates are in the range of 230 to 260°F (110–130°C) (Boles, 1978). The appearance of ferruginous diagenetic minerals at this stage of burial may be explained by increased availability of iron due to the destabilization of iron-bearing organometallic complexes (e.g., iron acetate; Surdam et al., 1989c).

Shale Diagenesis

Sedimentary organic material in fine–grained rocks begins to undergo profound changes at approximately 176°F (80°C). These changes have a very significant effect on adjacent sandstones. O–bearing functional groups are cleaved from kerogen molecules with increased thermal exposure (Tissot and Welte, 1984; Surdam and Crossey, 1985a and b; Surdam et al., 1989b and c) (Figs. 13 and 14). These water-soluble, polar compounds most likely are transported out of the fine–grained rocks through microfractures, carried either by an incipient hydrocarbon phase or in an aqueous phase (MacGowan and Surdam, 1989). Significant quantities of organic acid anions are released to the aqueous phase in hydrous pyrolysis experiments (Kawamura et al., 1986; Kawamura and Kaplan, 1987; Surdam and MacGowan, 1987; Lundegard and Senftle, 1987; MacGowan and Surdam, 1989a and b). Also, the aqueous phase usually contains less than 1 ppm Al (S. Boese and R.C. Surdam, unpublished data). This apparently indicates that the carboxylic acid anions do not interact significantly with the mineral grains in the source rock; they must be sequestered from these reactive phases. The presence of high concentrations of carboxylic acid anions in the petroleum phase of hydrous pyrolysis experiments (Kawamura et al., 1986; Kawamura and Kaplan, 1987) and in some crude oils (MacGowan et al., 1988; MacGowan and Surdam, 1989b) has led to the speculation that they are carried from the source rock in an incipient oil phase, partitioning into the aqueous phase in the reservoir rock (Surdam et al., 1989c). Whatever the mechanism, the presence of high concentrations of carboxylic acid anions in some reservoir formation waters is *a priori* evidence that they are not consumed in reactions within the source rock.

Simultaneously in the fine–grained rocks, smectite is reacting to form illite. This reaction has the potential of releasing a variety of components, including Fe^{+2}, Si, and water (Eslinger and Pevear, 1988). This material may be transported into adjacent sandstones (Boles and Franks, 1979).

If sulfur is present, either as organic sulfur in kerogen or as sulfate in pore water, there is another set of reactions that can take place. These involve a series of linked hydrocarbon–oxidation and sulfate–reduction reactions that result in the production of H_2S, bicarbonate, and organic acid anions (Siebert, 1985; Machel, 1986).

As a sandstone–shale package enters the zone of intermediate burial diagenesis, carboxylic acid anions and other organic chelating species, H_2S, HCO_3^-, Fe^{+3}, Si, and water are released from fine–grained rocks into adjacent sandstones. In this strongly reducing environment, Fe^{+3} would be reduced immediately to Fe^{+2}. This is supported by recent thermodynamic calculations that show that diagenetic environments characterized by significant concentrations of carboxylic acid anions are bounded by oxygen fugacity values of −54.5 and −57 (Shock, 1988).

Alteration of Feldspar

Alteration of feldspar produces clays, zeolites, and other feldspars. Laumontite forms commonly in plagioclase–rich sandstones undergoing intermediate burial diagenesis. Accompanying or in place of laumontite is a more common phase, albite. Whether or not kaolinite forms rather than zeolites (with or without

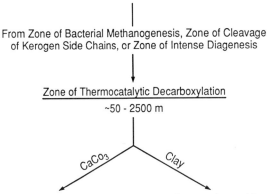

From Zone of Bacterial Methanogenesis, Zone of Cleavage of Kerogen Side Chains, or Zone of Intense Diagenesis

Zone of Thermocatalytic Decarboxylation
~50 - 2500 m

CaCO₃ / Clay

Carboxylic acids, n-alkanes, bicarbonate. Further organic-inorganic reactions in zone of intense diagenesis.

n-alkanes, elevated P_{CO_2}; further organic-inorganic reactions depend upon bacterial alteration of n-alkanes to more reactive species.

Figure 13. Reaction pathways for thermocatalytic cleavage of kerogen side chains in fine-grained rocks. From Surdam et al., 1989b.

SHALE DIAGENESIS
Thermocatalytic Cleavage of Carboxylic Acids from Kerogen

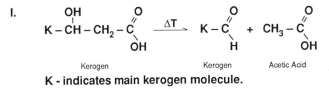

I.

Kerogen   Kerogen   Acetic Acid

K - indicates main kerogen molecule.

Figure 14. Reactions showing thermocatalytic cleavage of kerogen side chains.

albite) is determined by the cation–to–proton ratio and the availability of H_4SiO_4 (Fig. 11). Commonly in a replacement setting, dissolved feldspar is the source of these reactants. Hence, if the feldspar is potassic, a potassic phase is more likely to form, e.g., illite. Plagioclase more readily alters to kaolinite, albite, or laumontite.

Regional albitization of plagioclase in sandstone-shale systems in actively subsiding settings is common (Iijima and Utada, 1972; Land and Milliken, 1981; Boles, 1982; Gold, 1986; and Boles and Ramseyer, 1989). The zone of albitization occurs over the temperature range of 248 to 320°F (120–160°C) in Miocene and Oligocene sediments from the San Joaquin Basin of California (Boles and Ramseyer, 1989). By contrast, the zone of albitization in the Oligocene Frio formation of south Texas is much narrower; between 212 and 248°F (100–120°C). The zone of albitization in sandstones of the Texas Gulf Coast generally is from 212 to 266°F (100–130°C). Boles and Ramseyer (1989) suggest that the most important factors affecting the width of the albitization window are fluid composition (e.g., high Na/Ca ratios favor albitization), dissolution kinetics, variations in the thermal histories, and the structural state and composition of the precursor plagioclase (e.g., volcanic plagioclase would be susceptible to albitization at lower temperatures than would plutonic plagioclase; Pittman, 1989). This last factor may explain why some feldspars may be albitized while others are fresh (Boles and Ramseyer, 1989). "Stress–induced" albitization is common along highly stressed grain contacts and can occur at temperatures below 212°F (100°C) (Boles and Ramseyer, 1989).

DEEP BURIAL DIAGENESIS

Probably the process most devastating to porosity during deep burial (temperatures in excess of 284°F, or 190°C) is quartz cementation. Leder and Park (1986) suggested an empirical approach to predicting quartz cementation resulting from burial diagenesis. They plot porosity against depth for relatively clean sandstones from locations characterized by differing thermal regimes. Despite flaws in the model, these empirical curves are reasonable estimates of porosity-loss due to cementation and compaction for a sandstone undergoing progressive burial. However, there are well documented cases where significantly more porosity is present in sandstones than the Leder and Park model would suggest (e.g., Norphlet and Tuscaloosa formations) due to diagenetic processes not modeled by Leder and Park that inhibit quartz cementation. The problem is to evaluate the potential for the presence of these diagenetic factors. For the Norphlet Formation, Dixon et al. (1989) compiled a list of the most important diagenetic factors or processes responsible for the inhibition of quartz cementation with deep burial. These include chlorite rims, early migration of hydrocarbons, and geopressuring.

Abiotic Sulfate Reduction by Hydrocarbon Oxidation

As a sandstone–shale system exits the zone of intermediate burial and enters the zone of deep burial (at temperatures greater than 266°F, or 130°C), organic acid anions have been decarboxylated; the alkalinity of pore waters again are dominated by HCO_3^-. Siebert (1985) suggests that thermal (or abiotic) reduction of sulfate by hydrocarbons begins at approximately 284°F (140°C) and ends at 410°F (210°C). Siebert further suggests that the chemical evolution of many deeply buried and relatively exotic reservoir fluids can be explained by the reduction of sulfate by hydrocarbons and reaction of the resulting hydrogen sulfide with other minerals.

MacGowan and Surdam (1989) present a chemical divide model for diagenetic pathways possible in a clastic sequence over the temperature interval of 284 to 410°F (140–210°C), based on the observations of Siebert (1985) and Machel (1986) (Fig. 15). The pathways are defined by the chemical nature of the mineral materials and formation fluids present in a given clastic sequence. Hydrocarbons from the maturation of sedimentary organic matter, and sulfate from anhydrite dissolution, can undergo redox reactions to form calcite and hydrogen sulfide. These minerals become kinetically favorable at temperatures above about 284°F (140°C) (Siebert, 1985), but may form at temperatures as low as 212°F (100°C) (Machel, 1986). If there is more hydrocarbons than sulfate in the section and little available Fe, then the reaction series ends and the reservoir fluid is dominated by hydrocarbons with some hydrogen sulfide.

However, if sulfate is present in concentrations exceeding hydrocarbons, it can react with the previously formed hydrogen sulfide and CO_2 from the thermal degradation of kerogen decarboxylation of organic acid anions or the dissolution of carbonate minerals. The resultant formation fluid will be dominated by

hydrogen sulfide and elemental sulfur at higher temperatures. If Fe is available and sulfate is present in excess over hydrocarbons, the hydrogen sulfide and sulfur will react with Fe to form pyrite and protons. The protons generated from these reactions are then available to participate in mineral dissolution. If Fe is not readily available in the system, then hydrogen sulfide with subordinate carbon dioxide will dominate the reservoir fluid. Elevated concentrations of dissolved carbon dioxide can cause dissolution of feldspars. Chlorite and/or illite typically form as alteration products.

Acidic formation fluids generated by abiotic sulfate reduction can account for observed additional dissolution of feldspar, carbonate, and sulfate minerals, and formation of such products as late–forming illite, chlorite, and pyrite in clastics exposed to temperatures of 284 to 410°F (140–210°C) (Fig. 15). The porosity-enhancing and preserving potential of these reactions will be directly proportional to the availability and spatial distribution of hydrocarbons and sulfate.

DIAGENETIC PREDICTION

A series of important organic–inorganic reactions take place during progressive burial that are parallel to the inorganic reactions. The most important of these are shown as pathways in Figures 2 through 4, 7 through 10, and 15. The hypothesis presented in this paper has been that the organic reactions are serial, and that they exert significant control on the parallel inorganic reactions. Sandstone provenance and near-surface and mechanical processes also play an important role in the pathway of porosity evolution and clastic diagenesis (Figs. 2–4; Surdam et al., 1989b).

Our approach to prediction of diagenesis is to determine the spatial and temporal distribution of the organic reactions during progressive burial. This can be done using a modified Tissot and Espitale (1975) kinetic maturation model. This approach has been extensively discussed by Surdam et al. (1989c). Implicit in this methodology is the assumption that the reaction being modeled can be approximated by first-order reaction kinetics. At any time, the progress of the reaction of interest can be determined by calculating the transformation ratio (TR), which is the ratio of the reactants transformed into products, to the maximum amount of reactant available (Tissot and Welte, 1984). For practical purposes, the progress of the reaction of interest at a specific time can be determined from a plot of TR versus time. The inputs to a TR–time plot are 1) a time–temperature and burial history for the stratigraphic unit in which the reaction of interest is being evaluated, and 2) kinetic parameters (e.g., activation energy and frequency factor) for the reaction of interest.

Thermal Modeling Applied to Diagenetic Studies

Thermal modeling used in diagenetic studies is designed to give the best time–temperature history (TTH) for the reservoir and source rocks of interest. Errors in either the magnitude of temperatures or in timing of temperatures may result in serious misinterpretation of the maturation of source rocks (Tissot and Espitale, 1975) and the diagenesis of a reservoir

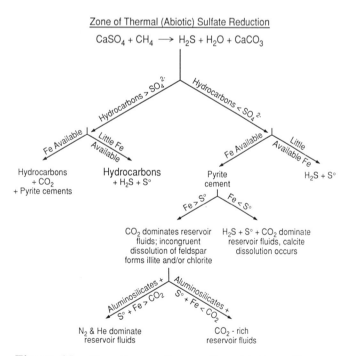

Figure 15. Reaction pathways for abiotic sulfate reduction by hydrocarbon oxidation. Adapted by MacGowan and Surdam (1989a) from Surdam et al., (1989b); based on Siebert (1985).

rock (Surdam et al., 1989c). Without a realistic thermal model, the prediction of hydrocarbon generation and porosity enhancement becomes a futile exercise.

Many factors should be considered when deriving a TTH for a diagenetic study. One very important constraint is the variation of terrestrial heat flow with time. For instance, regional tectonic events can produce severe perturbations in regional heat flow. The thermal effects of subduction, rifting, thrust faulting, igneous intrusion, or rapid uplift may be modeled either analytically or with numerical approximations. However, such approaches are very dependent on the quality of the geological data and the accuracy of models used to constrain them.

Heat flow also may vary areally. Depending on the contrast in thermal conductivities of rocks and the geometry of the layers, heat can be refracted. Heat may be transported by moving fluids, in which case the amount of heat flow variation will be a function of the mass flux of the fluid and the fluid flow path. Uneven heat sources, including intrusions or lateral changes in the radiogenic heat production in the upper crust, also may cause areal variations.

Chronostratigraphic data are important in constraining burial–history reconstructions and time–temperature histories. Because depth strongly affects temperature, a precise burial history is critical for construction of TTH's. Important aspects of burial history reconstruction include maximum burial depth, time of maximum burial, rates of burial, timing and magnitude of periods of uplift or nondeposition, and the lithology of all stratigraphic units.

Thermal models also require knowledge of the thermal properties of the rocks in the region of interest, such as thermal conductivity (for steady state models) and thermal diffusivity (for time–dependent models). All of these parameters vary with lithology.

Thermal conductivity is a measure of whether the rock is a relative insulator (e.g., shale) or conductor (e.g., quartzite) of heat. Thermal conductivity varies with porosity and thus with time. Representative thermal conductivity values can be assigned to rock units by estimation or measurement of porosities and bulk grain thermal conductivities. Thermal conductivity also is a function of lithology. For instance, it has been demonstrated that changes in the bulk mineralogy of sandstones due to progressive diagenesis can cause changes in thermal conductivity, and thus thermal history, of rock units (MacGowan and Surdam, 1988b).

Because the porosity of a rock unit changes due to compaction (grain packing changes and ductile grain deformation) during burial, this must be estimated in order to correctly predict changing thermal conductivities, and hence temperatures, through time. This is done by using exponential statistical fits of observed porosities versus depths (Athy, 1930; Dickinson, 1953; Magara, 1974). These curves should be refined iteratively. First, compaction modeling is used to calculate thermal and diagenetic models. Then predicted diagenetic excursions from the modeled porosity–depth profile must be used in calculation of thermal parameters. The diagenetic model must then be recalculated with these thermal parameters; such iterative refinements will produce a more accurate

model of the diagenetic system (MacGowan and Surdam, 1988b).

Data used to constrain TTH's can be categorized as either direct or indirect. Direct data constraints include drillhole bottom–hole temperatures (BHT's), measured heat flow values, measured thermal conductivities, and temperature measurements of bore holes. To be considered valid, a derived thermal model must reasonably match the observed present–day BHT's, other measured temperatures, and heat flow values. Indirect constraints on the TTH's include other models (such as the inferred tectonic evolution of a region) and maturation indicators such as production index (PI), vitrinite reflectance (Ro), thermal alteration index (TAI), time–temperature index (TTI), and clay–conversion temperatures.

The thermal models and some of the above parameters rely on varying assumptions. For example, a TAI of 3 correlates to an Ro of 0.6, which correlates to a production index of 0.2. Thus, the interpretation of the correctness of the TTH's can be difficult.

Kinetics of Diagenetic Reactions From Laboratory and Field Data

Once the time–temperature profile is determined, the next step is to measure the kinetic parameters for the reaction of interest. Hydrous pyrolysis is an experimental technique that has been used widely to study the kinetics of petroleum generation (Lewan et al., 1979; Winters et al., 1983; Hoering, 1984; Lewan, 1985). Hydrous pyrolysis experiments also have been employed in the study of the generation and decarboxylation of carboxylic acid anions (Kawamura, et al., 1986; MacGowan and Surdam, 1987; Surdam and MacGowan, 1987; Lundegard and Senftle, 1987; Kawamura and Kaplan, 1987); the best approximation of the natural system is to use whole source–rock aliquots and distilled water (Winters et al., 1983; Hoering, 1984; Burnham et al., 1987; Thyne et al., 1988; Surdam et al., 1989c).

The substitution of high temperature for time in very slow chemical reactions is common practice among classical kineticists (Levine, 1978), has been used extensively in inorganic geochemical and diagenetic models (Berner, 1980; Lasaga, 1981), and may be applicable to organic geochemical reactions (Price, 1983). Although Snowdon (1979) and Saxby (1982) point out that at extremely high temperatures, conditions within the experimental apparatus may not accurately reflect those in the geological environment, kinetic parameters derived from high temperature geochemical experiments have been employed successfully in modeling organic geochemical processes (e.g., Tissot and Espitale, 1975; Waples, 1980; Wood, 1988).

The generation, expulsion to the aqueous phase, and decarboxylation of carboxylic acid anions in hydrous pyrolysis and/or natural systems most likely reflect a series of reactions of varying reaction order, and not a single reaction of first–order (Price, 1983 and 1985; Drummond and Palmer, 1986). However, the data form fairly well behaved, straight lines in an Ahrrenius plot (Surdam et al., 1989c). Thus, we feel justified in approximating the reactions with first–order kinetic rate laws. These kinetics reflect not only the generation of the species from kerogen, but also their expulsion from the solid phase and their partitioning into the aqueous phase. For these reasons, these kinetic parameters are referred to as "pseudo–kinetics". Pseudo–kinetics have been measured for the generation of carboxylic acid anions (MacGowan and Surdam, unpublished. data), carboxylic acid decarboxylation (Kharaka et al., 1983; Palmer and Drummond, 1986; Boles et al., 1988; MacGowan and Surdam, unpubl. data), and the abiotic reduction of sulfate by hydrocarbon oxidation (Siebert, 1985).

The relative fraction of a diagenetic species is defined as the ratio of the amount of that species in solution to the total amount of that species that the source rock is capable of generating at any given temperature or time in the basin history (MacGowan and Surdam, 1987). The relative fractions of carboxylic acid anions, hydrogen sulfide, and bicarbonate from decarboxylation of carboxylic acid anions and abiotic sulfate reduction can be calculated by integrating pseudo–kinetic data and a TTH (Surdam et al., 1989c). By this method, we determined the relationship between changes in the diagenetically active aqueous species and the resultant mineral reactions (Table 2). These were used to construct diagenetic scenarios (Fig. 16).

The kinetics of other diagenetic reactions can be determined by observing various stages of reaction in the field and laboratory (Berner, 1980; 1981). Dutta (1986) used a modified Ahrrenius equation to determine the reaction kinetics for the smectite–illite reaction, based on the data of Perry (1969); Hower et al. (1976); and Freed (1982). Pytte and Reynolds (1989), using the data of Reynolds (1981) and Pytte (1982), determined the kinetics of this reaction and calculated it to be 6th–order (to approximate long term, low temperature conditions). Using the same technique, Surdam et al. (1989c) determined the kinetics of this reaction from field data for sodium smectite (Hagen, 1986) and for calcium smectite (Ramseyer and Boles, 1986), and from the experimental data of Whitney and Northrup (1988) (Table 3).

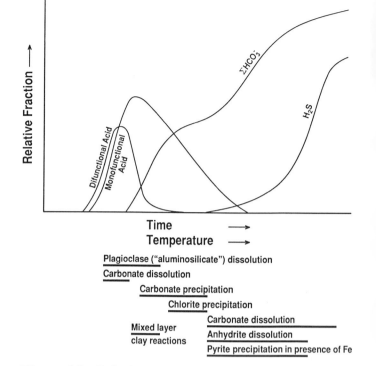

Figure 16. Relative concentrations of monofunctional and difunctional carboxylic acid anions as well as H_2S and HCO^{3-} through time for a Laramide–style basin.

CASE HISTORY: THE FRONTIER FORMATION, BIGHORN BASIN, WYOMING

The Frontier Formation (Upper Cretaceous) is of special interest because it provides good reservoirs in several basins across Wyoming. In the Bighorn Basin of Wyoming, the Frontier Formation includes sandstones and shales derived from the Laramide orogenic belt to the west and northwest (Goodell, 1962), as well as from local highs to the east and northeast (Van Houten, 1962). For discussions of the depositional environments and regional stratigraphy of the Frontier Formation in the Bighorn Basin, see Siemers (1975); Merewether et al. (1975); Goodell (1962); and Van Houten (1962).

Table 2. Diagenetic effects of changes in formation–water chemistry.

Cause	Effect
1) Monofunctional and difunctional carboxylic acid maximum	Aluminosilicate and carbonate mineral dissolution
2) Increased PCO_2 due to difunctional carboxylic acid anion decarboxylation; alkalinity dominated by monofunctional carboxylic acid anions	Carbonate mineral stabilization
3) Increased PCO_2 by monofunctional carboxylic acid anion decarboxylation	Late-stage carbonate precipitation; release of Fe from Fe-organic complexes allows precipitation of Fe-carbonates and conversion of early-formed kaolinite and smectite to chlorite
4) Loss of organic acid anion dominance in alkalinity; increased PCO_2	Carbonate mineral destabilization
5) Generation of H_2S due to thermal (abiotic) sulfate/hydrocarbon oxidation	Anhydrite dissolution, carbonate dissolution; pyrite precipitation in the presence of Fe

Table 3. Kinetics of the smectite–illite reaction.

Material	Activation Energy	Frequency Factor
Na-Smectite[1]	19.3±0.7 Kcal/mol	4.0×10^{10} my^{-1}
Na-Smectite[2]	20.3±0.9 Kcal/mol	1.64×10^{11} my^{-1}
Ca-Smectite[2]	25.7±3.5 Kcal/mol	5.19×10^{17} my^{-1}
Wyo. Bentonite[2]	18.5±1.5 Kcal/mol	1.99×10^{12} my^{-1}
Na-Smectite[3]	33 Kcal/mol	1.64×10^{21} my^{-1}

[1]Dutta, 1986
[2]Surdam and others, 1989c
[3]Pytte and Reynolds, 1989

General Petrography and Depositional Environments

The Frontier sandstones are lithic arenites (Goodell, 1962; Siemers, 1975). These sandstones have highly variable ratios of monocrystalline quartz to lithic fragments that generally decrease with increasing grain size (Blatt, et al., 1980). The lithics are chert and volcanic and sedimentary fragments. The adjacent shales contain fine-grained volcanic ash.

The degree of dissolution of feldspar and lithic fragments, and the amounts of feldspar and quartz cementation in Frontier sandstones were not explicitly addressed in prior investigations. We found that the amounts of these alteration products are highly variable and volumetrically significant. Both volcanic rock fragments in the sandstones and volcanic ash in the shales are partially or completely altered or dissolved. As discussed earlier, the presence of highly soluble volcanic debris results in elevated pH, and high cation and silicon activities. We suggest that this effect is responsible for the extensive feldspar and quartz overgrowths observed in the deeply buried Frontier sandstones (Plate 1B). This is in agreement with conclusions reached by Goodell (1962).

Siemers (1975) described the depositional environments of Frontier sandstones in outcrops on the western flank of the Bighorn Basin as marine bar and interbar in the lower portions of the formation, and prodelta, delta plain, delta margin, and nearshore marine in the upper part. All samples we have examined are from the upper third of the formation and are overwhelmingly from deltaic deposits.

These marine and deltaic rocks typically do not develop either clay infiltration or clay and/or Fe-Mn oxide coatings. Traces of siderite were observed in a few samples (Plate 1C), but it is not volumetrically significant. Early carbonate cements (forming prior to quartz overgrowth development, but after significant packing changes and ductile grain deformation) are present (Plate 1D) and typically associated with very fine-grained, laminated sandstones adjacent to organic-rich laminated mudstones. Hence, we can list the factors most important in porosity development:

1) The marine depositional systems operating in Frontier time were not conducive to the development of early clay and Fe-Mn oxide grain coatings. Therefore, the possibility of later clay coats inhibiting quartz cementation is greatly reduced. In addition, the depositional environments were not conducive to the formation of early carbonate cements.

2) The presence of volcanogenic material both in the sandstones and the adjacent shales provides material for early and late development of extensive quartz and feldspar overgrowths (Plate 1B).

3) Migration of hydrocarbons into the reservoir inhibited subsequent cementation. Hagen (1986) has shown that oil generation off-structure adjacent to the Elk Basin structure in the northern Bighorn Basin began approximately 60 Ma.

4) Basin-margin sediments and sediments in some central basin structures (e.g., Elk Basin Field) may have been exposed to the onset of intermediate burial diagenesis; however, progressive diagenesis and accompanying porosity loss did not occur because of subsequent uplift and cooling. This uplift may have resulted in telogenetic alteration, reducing reservoir quality (Plate 1E-F).

5) Deeper progressive burial along the basin axis caused the development of later feldspar and quartz overgrowths; precipitation of later carbonates postdating quartz overgrowths; formation of chlorite from the alteration of volcanogenic material; and subsequent minor late-carbonate dissolution (Plate 2A-D).

Diagenetic Models for the Frontier Formation

As a summary for this paper, we will construct a diagenetic model for the Frontier Sandstone as it passed through the intermediate and deep burial zones, using two burial histories, a general one for the basin center, and a more specific one for Elk Basin Field. The time-temperature profiles we used were constructed by Hagen (1986) and Hagen and Surdam (1989) (Fig. 17). The kinetic parameters for liquid hydrocarbon, acetate, and malonate generation, and for malonate decarboxylation are from unpublished hydrous pyrolysis data from Frontier source rocks. The smectite-illite transformation kinetics are from Surdam et al. (1989c) (Table 3). The thermal sulfate-reduction kinetics are from Siebert (1985). Acetate decarboxylation kinetics are from Palmer and Drummond (1986).

Our model of the diagenetic mineral distribution in the Frontier Formation (Fig. 18) is based on: 1) the distributions of organic acid anions, CO_2, smectite-illite transformation, and hydrocarbon generation; 2) the considerations listed in Table 2; and 3) our chemical-divide and pathway diagrams. During shallow burial, the marine sandstones in the Frontier were significantly modified by compaction, with only minor modification by chemical diagenesis (i.e., early carbonates and overgrowths). During intermediate burial, the most significant reactions modifying porosity

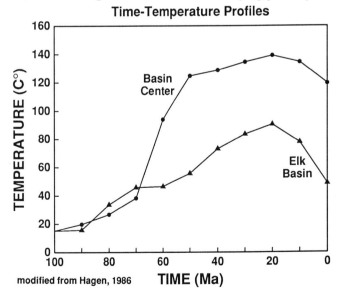

Time-Temperature Profiles

modified from Hagen, 1986

Figure 17. Time-temperature histories for the center of the Bighorn Basin and Elk Basin Field. After Hagen (1986) and Hagen and Surdam (1989).

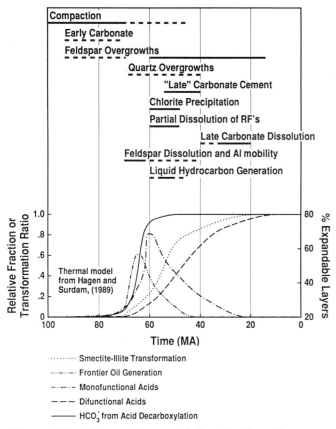

Figure 18. Diagenetic model for the Frontier Formation in the center of the Bighorn Basin. The model was constructed using the methodology of Surdam et al., (1989c).

included: 1) dissolution of feldspar (Plate 1C, Fig. 2), 2) dissolution of rock fragments (Plate 2 B–C), 3) precipitation of late carbonate (Plate 2A), and 4) precipitation of chlorite (Plate 2B–C). The first two reactions generated porosity, but the last two destroyed porosity. These four reactions define a narrow window of optimum porosity development (Fig. 18).

The zone of intense generation of liquid hydrocarbons occurred during a relatively short time (58 to 50 Ma). Fortunately, the zones of intense liquid hydrocarbon generation and optimum porosity development overlap; those sandstones that trapped hydrocarbons during this time are excellent exploration targets.

With continued burial, the Frontier sandstones left this narrow window. Reservoir quality decreased in sandstones not charged with hydrocarbons, due to porosity and permeability destruction by late carbonate, aluminosilicate, and silicate cements. Late carbonate dissolution is not a factor in the quality of liquid–hydrocarbon reservoirs because it occurred while liquid hydrocarbons were being thermally cracked to pyrobitumen and natural gas. In addition, the silicate cements that formed during deeper burial were not inhibited by chlorite rims, and destroyed reservoir quality. The Frontier Formation in the central portion of the Bighorn Basin has not been buried deeply

enough to initiate sulfate reduction by hydrocarbon oxidation.

Elk Basin Field

The Frontier sandstones at the Elk Basin oil field have had an optimum burial history for porosity preservation and enhancement (Surdam et al., 1989a). Hagen (1986) and Hagen and Surdam (1984) have shown that liquid hydrocarbon generation (i.e., TR between 0.2 and 0.4) in the deeper portions of the basin just west of the Elk Basin structure began approximately 60 Ma. The model for Elk Basin (Fig. 19) differs from the basin–center model (Fig. 18) because the Elk Basin anticline began to form between 55 and 52 Ma, reached maximum burial approximately 55 Ma, and was subsequently uplifted (Hagen, 1986; Surdam et al., 1989a). The diagenetic models are fairly similar until the time of the formation of the structure at Elk Basin. The zone of maximum porosity enhancement due to dissolution of feldspar, carbonates, and rock fragments during intermediate burial diagenesis took place from 65 to 52 Ma (Fig. 19). This coincided with the generation of liquid hydrocarbons in nearby source rocks. There was no formation of late carbonate or silicate cements; the window of optimum porosity enhancement was significantly expanded relative to that in the deep Bighorn Basin. The uplift and subsequent cooling of the Frontier Formation at Elk Basin also expanded the window of optimum porosity enhancement by reducing the effects of compaction, extending the interval of mineral dissolution, and inhibiting late silicate and carbonate cementation (Figs. 18 and 19; Plate 1C).

CONCLUSIONS

The diagenetic modeling techniques presented in this paper result in a conceptual framework in which organic diagenesis can be integrated with inorganic diagenesis in a source–reservoir system (Fig. 20). This approach allows the evaluation of porosity in a clastic reservoir at the time of hydrocarbon expulsion from the source rocks. When combined with subsidence profiles and time–temperature and sedimentological information, these modeling techniques allow the prediction of the temporal and spatial distribution of modified porosity in a clastic reservoir.

The integrated source– and reservoir–rock modeling techniques advocated in this paper have significant implications to the search for hydrocarbons. The largest uncertainty in most hydrocarbon prospects is the evaluation prior to drilling of the petrophysical properties of targeted sandstone interval. Where complex, diagenetically modified reservoirs, traps, and seals are the targets of exploration, the ability to make predictions of reservoir properties will be essential. The modeling techniques discussed in this paper allow the prediction of the spatial distribution of optimum porosity in the reservoir facies at the time of hydrocarbon migration. With the knowledge that results from the modeling techniques outlined in this paper, the largest remaining exploration uncertainty in both frontier and developed basins can be significantly reduced.

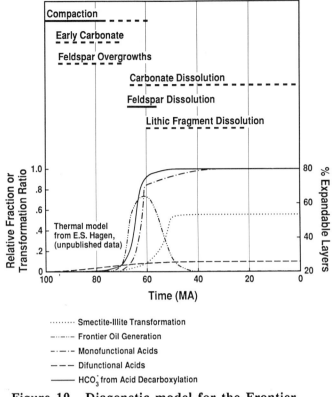

Figure 19. Diagenetic model for the Frontier Formation at Elk Basin Field. The model was constructed using the methodology of Surdam et al., (1989c).

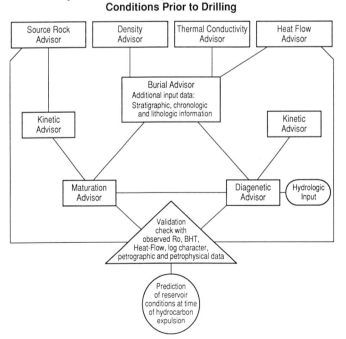

Figure 20. Integration of geological, geophysical, and geochemical processes necessary to produce holistic, predictive diagenetic model. From Surdam, et al. (1989c).

DEDICATION

This manuscript is dedicated to the memory of Hans P. Eugster. Hans demonstrated to us in the field how useful reaction pathway diagrams could be in unraveling chemical processes. The evaluation of diagenetic processes presented in this manuscript was significantly enhanced by our association with Hans.

ACKNOWLEDGEMENTS

We wish to thank the Department of Energy, grant DE-FGO2-87ER13805, for funding portions of this study. Amoco Production, Texaco, Mobil, Conoco, and BP Exploration companies also provided essential financial support for various aspects of the work presented in this manuscript. Their support is gratefully acknowledged. D.B. MacGowan and T.L. Dunn thank Dr. R.E. Ewing of the Enhanced Oil Recovery Institute of the University of Wyoming for financial support. We thank J.S. Bradley (Amoco Production) for thorough and thoughtful review of the manuscript. The manuscript was greatly improved with his help. We also thank the following University of Wyoming staff: S. Boese, M. Moraes, B. Aguado, L. Smith, P. Yin, B. Moncur, and G. Thyne, whose support was key to this research. Discussions with L.J. Crossey (Univ. of New Mexico), R. Siebert (Conoco), R. Vinopal (Texaco), P. Braithwaite and T. Tsui (Mobil), M. Beggs (BP Exploration), and L. De Ros and S. Anjos (Petrobras) also have been most helpful. The manuscript was also improved by the conscientious reviews of W. Almon, S. Paxton, and W. Harrison.

REFERENCES

Aguado, B., 1989, The B-3x-40 reservoir, Lake Maracaibo Basin, Western Venezuela: Diagenesis and reservoir heterogeneity, unpub. MS thesis, U. of WY, 293 p.

Amrhein, C., and D.L. Suarez, 1988, The use of a surface complexation model to describe the kinetics of ligand-promoted dissolution of anorthite: Geochim. Cosmochim. 52, p. 2785-2794.

Athy, L.F., 1930, Density, porosity, and compaction of sedimentary rocks, AAPG Bull., v. 14, p. 1-24.

Barshad, I., 1966, The effect of variation in precipitation on the nature of clay mineral formation in soils from acid and base igneous rocks: Proc. International Clay Conference, v. 1, p. 167-173.

Berner, R.A., 1980, Early Diagenesis: A Theoretical Approach: Princeton Univ. Press, NJ, 241 p.

Berner, R.A., 1981, A new geochemical classification of sedimentary environments: JSP, v. 51, p. 359-365.

Bjørlykke, K. and A. Brendsdal, 1986, Diagenesis of the Brent Sandstone in the Statfjord Field, North Sea, in D.L. Gautier, ed., Roles of Organic Matter in Sediment Diagenesis: SEPM Spec. Pub. No. 38, p. 157-167.

Blatt, H., G. Middleton, and R. Murray, 1980, Origin of Sedimentary Rocks: Prentice-Hall, NJ, 782 p.

Boles, J.R., 1978, Active ankerite cementation in the subsurface Eocene of Southwest Texas: Contrib. Miner. Petr., v. 68, p. 13-22.

Boles, J.R., 1982, Active albitization of plagioclase, Gulf Coast Tertiary: Am. Jour. Sci., v. 282, p. 165-180.

Boles, J. R. and S.G. Franks, 1979, Clay diagenesis in Wilcox sandstones of Southwest Texas; implications of smectite diagenesis on sandstone cementation: JSP, v. 49, p. 55-70.

Boles, J.R. and K.L. Ramseyer, 1987, Diagenetic carbonate in Miocene sandstone reservoir, San Joaquin Basin, Ca.: AAPG Bull., v. 71, p. 475-1487.

Boles, J.R. and K.L. Ramseyer, 1989, Albitization of plagioclase and vitrinite reflectance as paleothermal indicators, San Joaquin Basin, *in* S.A. Graham, ed., Studies of the Geology of the San Joaquin Basin, SEPM Pacific Section, Los Angeles, CA., p. 129-139.

Boles, J.S., D.A. Crerar, G. Grissom, and T.C. Key, 1988, Aqueous thermal decarboxylation of gallic acid, Geochim. Cosmochim. 52, p. 341-344.

Burnham, A.K., R.L. Braun, H.R. Gregg, and A.M. Samoun, 1987, Comparison of methods for measuring kerogen pyrolysis rates and fitting kinetic parameters: Energy and Fuels, v. 1, p. 452-458.

Carothers, W.W., and Y.K. Kharaka, 1978, Aliphatic acid anions in oil field waters-implications for origin of natural gas, AAPG Bull., v. 62, p. 2441-2453.

Carothers, W.W., and Y.K. Kharaka, 1980, Stable carbon isotopes in oil-field waters and the origin of CO_2: Geochim. Cosmochim. 44, p. 323-332.

Cecil, C.B. and M.T. Heald, 1971, Experimental investigation of the effects of grain coatings on quartz growth, JSP, v. 41, p. 582-584.

Crossey, L.J., 1985, The origin and role of water soluble organic compounds in clastic diagenetic systems, unpub. PhD diss., U. of WY, 135 p.

Crossey, L.J., B.R. Frost, R.C. and Surdam, 1984, The development of secondary porosity in laumontite-bearing sandstones, *in* D. McDonald and R. Surdam, eds., Clastic Diagenesis, AAPG Mem. 37, p. 127-149.

Curtis, C.D., 1978, Possible links between sandstone diagenesis and depth-related geochemical reactions occurring in enclosing mudstones: Geological Society of London Journal v. 135, pt. 1., p. 107-117.

Curtis, C.D., 1987, Inorganic geochemistry and petroleum exploration, *in* Advances in Petroleum Geochemistry: Academic Press, London, v. 2, p. 91-140.

Curtis, C.D., and M.L. Coleman, 1986, Controls on the precipitation of early diagenetic calcite, dolomite, and siderite concretions in complex depositional sequences, *in* D.L. Gautier, ed., Roles of Organic Matter in Sediment Diagenesis: SEPM Spec. Pub., no. 38, p. 23-34.

Dickinson, G., 1953, Geological aspects of abnormal reservoir pressures in Gulf Coast Louisiana: AAPG Bull., v. 37, p. 410-432.

Dixon, S.A., D.M. Summers, and R.C. Surdam, 1989, Diagenesis and preservation of porosity in the Norphlet Formation (Upper Jurassic), southern Alabama, AAPG Bull., v. 73, p. 707-728.

Drever, J.I., 1988, The Geochemistry of Natural Waters: 2nd ed., Prentice-Hall, NJ, 388 p.

Drummond, S.E. and D.A. Palmer, 1986, Thermal decarboxylation of acetate, Part II, Boundary conditions for the role of acetate in primary migration of natural gas and transportation of metals in hydrothermal systems: Geochim. Cosmochim. 50, p. 825-833.

Dunn, T.L., 1979, Mineral reactions in sandstones of the Lysite Mountain Area, central Wyoming: unpub. MS thesis, U. of WY, 81 p.

Dutta, N.C., 1986, Shale compaction, burial diagenesis and geopressures: a dynamic model, solution, and some results, *in* J. Burrus, ed., Thermal Modeling in Sedimentary Basins: Editions Technip, Paris, p. 149-172.

Eslinger, E., and D. Pevear, 1988, Clay minerals for petroleum geologists and Engineers: SEPM Short Course Notes, No. 22, 356 p.

Fisher, J.B., 1987, Distribution and occurrence of aliphatic acid anions in deep subsurface waters, Geochim. Cosmochim. 51, p. 2459-2468.

Fothergill, C.A., 1955, The cementation of oil reservoir sands and its origin: 4th World Petroleum Congress, Sec. 1/B, Paper 1, p. 301-314.

Franks, S.G. and R.W. Forester, 1984, Relationships among secondary porosity, pore-fluid chemistry and carbon dioxide, Texas Gulf Coast, *in* D.A. McDonald and R.C. Surdam, eds., Clastic Diagenesis, AAPG Mem. 37, p. 63-80.

Freed, R.L., 1982, Clay diagenesis and abnormally high fluid pressure: Proc. 52nd Ann. Mtg., SEG, Oct. 1982, Dallas.

Galloway, W.E., 1974, Deposition and diagenetic alteration of sandstone in northeast Pacific arc-related basins: implications for greywacke genesis: GSA Bull., v. 85, p. 379-390.

Galloway, W. E., 1979, Diagenetic control of reservoir quality in arc-derived sandstones: implications for petroleum exploration: *in* Aspects of Diagenesis, SEPM Spec. Pub., no. 26, p. 251-262.

Gautier, D.L., 1985, Interpretation of early diagenesis in ancient marine sediments, *in* Relationship of Organic Matter and Mineral Diagenesis, SEPM Short Course Notes, no. 17, p. 6-78.

Gold, P.B., 1986, Geochemistry and textures of authigenic albite from Miocene sandstones, Louisiana Gulf Coast: JSP, v. 57, p. 353-362.

Goodell, H.G., 1962, The stratigraphy and petrology of the Frontier formation of Wyoming, *in* R.L. Enyert and W.H. Curry, eds., Symposium on Early Cretaceous Rocks of Wyoming and Adjacent Areas: WGA 17th Ann. Field Conf. Guidebook, p. 173-210.

Hagen, E.S., 1986, Hydrocarbon maturation in Laramide-style basins: Constraints from the northern Big Horn Basin, Wyoming and Montana, unpub. PhD diss., U. of WY, 215 p.

Hagen, E.S., and R.C. Surdam, 1984, Maturation history and thermal evolution of Cretaceous source rocks of the Big Horn Basin, Wyoming and Montana, *in* J. Woodward, F.F. Meissner, and J.L. Clayton, eds., Hydrocarbon Source Rocks of the Greater Rocky Mountain Region: RMAG, Denver, p. 321-338.

Hagen, E.S., and R.C. Surdam, 1989, Thermal evolution of Laramide-style basins: constraints from the northern Bighorn Basin, Wy. and Mont., *in* N.D. Naeser and T.H. McCulloh, eds., Thermal History of Sedimentary Basins: Springer-Verlag, NY, p. 277-295.

Hansley, P.L., 1987, Petrologic and experimental evidence for the etching of garnets by organic acids in the Upper Jurassic Morrison Formation, northwestern New Mexico: JSP, v. 57, p. 666-681.

Hatton, R.S., and J.S. Hanor, 1984, Dissolved volatile fatty acids in subsurface, hydropressure brines: a review of published literature on occurrence, genesis and thermodynamic properties, Tech. Rpt. Geopress. Getherm. Act., Louisiana: Final Geological Rpt., 1 Nov-31 Oct 1982, DOE Rpt. #DOE/NV/10174-3, p. 384-454.

Hayes, J.B., J.C. Harms, and T. Wilson, Jr., 1976, Contrasts between braided and meandering stream deposits, Beluga and Sterling formations (Tertiary), Cook Inlet, Alaska, *in* Recent and Ancient Sedimentary Environments in Alaska: T.P. Miller, ed., Alaska Geol. Soc., Anchorage, Alaska, p. J1-J27.

Heald, M.T., 1956, Cementation in Simpson and St. Peter sandstones in parts of Oklahoma, Arkansas, and Missouri, Jour. Geol., v. 64, p. 16-30.

Heald, M.T. and R.E. Larese, 1973, The significance of the solution of feldspar in porosity development, JSP, v. 43, p. 458-460.

Heald, M.T. and R.E. Larese, 1974, Influence of coatings on quartz cementation, JSP, v. 44, p. 1269-1274.

Heald, M.T. and J.J. Renton, 1966, Experimental study of sandstone cementation, JSP, v. 36, p. 977-991.

Hoering, T.C., 1984, Thermal reactions of kerogen with added water, heavy water and pure organic substances, Organic Geochemistry, v. 5, p. 267-278.

Holland, H.D. and M. Borcsik, 1965, On the solution and deposition of calcite in hydrothermal systems, Symp. Probl. Postmagmatic Ore Deposits, Prague, v. 2, p. 364-374.

Hower, J., E.V. Eslinger, M.E. Hower, and E.A. Perry, 1976, Mechanism of burial metamorphism of argillaceous sediments, I. Mineral and chemical evidence, GSA Bull., v. 87, p. 725-737.

Huang, W.H. and W.D. Keller, 1970, Dissolution of rock-forming silicate minerals in organic acids: simulated first-stage weathering of fresh mineral surfaces, Am. Min., v. 55, p. 2076-2094.

Iijima, A. and M. Utada, 1972, A critical review of the occurrence of zeolites in sedimentary rocks, Jour. of Japanese Geology and Geography, v. 42, p. 61-63.

Kastner, M., 1971, Authigenic feldspars in carbonate rocks, Am. Min., v. 56, p. 1403-1442.

Kawaura, K. and I.R. Kaplan, 1987, Dicarboxylic acids generated by thermal alteration of kerogen and humic acids: Geochim. Cosmochim. 81, p. 3201-3207.

Kawaura, K., E. Tannenbaum, B.J. Huizinga, and I.R. Kaplan, 1986, Volatile organic acids generated from kerogen during laboratory heating, Geochem. Jour., v. 20, p. 51–59.

Kharaka, Y.K., W.W. Carothers, and R.J. Rosenbauer, 1983, Thermal decarboxylation of acetic acid; implications for the origin of natural gas, Geochim. Cosmochim. 47, p. 397–402.

Land, L.S. and K.L. Milliken, 1981, Feldspar diagenesis in the Frio Fm., Brazoria Co., Texas Gulf Coast, Geol., v. 9, p. 314–318.

Larese, R.E., E.D. Pittman, and M.T. Heald, 1984, Effects of diagenesis on porosity development, Tuscaloosa sandstone, Louisiana, [abs.], AAPG Bull., v. 68, p. 498.

Lasaga, A.C., 1981, Rate laws of geochemical reactions, *in* A.C. Lasaga and R.J. Kirkpatrick, eds., Kinetics of Geochemical Processes: Miner. Assoc. Am., Reviews in Mineralogy, vol. 8, p. 1–68.

Leder, F. and W.C. Park, 1986, Porosity reduction in sandstones by quartz overgrowth: AAPG Bull. v. 70, p. 1713–1728.

Levine, I.N., 1978, Physical Chemistry, McGraw-Hill, NY, 347 p.

Lewan, M.D., J.C. Winters, and J.H. McDonald, 1979, Generation of oil-like pyrolysates from organic-rich shales, Science, v. 203, p. 897–899.

Lewan, M.D., 1985, Evaluation of petroleum generation by hydrous pyrolysis experimentation: Phil. Trans. Roy. Soc. Lond., Series A, v. 315, p. 123–134.

Lundegard, P.D. and J.T. Senftle, 1987, Hydrous pyrolysis–a tool for the study of organic-acid synthesis, Appl. Geochim., v. 2, p. 605–612.

Lundegard, P.D. and L.S. Land, 1989, Carbonate equilibria and pH-buffering by organic acids–response to changes in PCO2, Chem. Geol., v. 74, p. 277–287.

MacGowan, D.B. and R.C. Surdam, 1987, The role of carboxylic acid anions in formation waters, sandstone diagenesis and petroleum reservoir modeling [abs.]: GSA Progs. w/ Abs., v. 19, p. 753.

MacGowan, D.B. and R.C. Surdam, 1988a, Difunctional carboxylic acid anions in oil field waters, Org. Geochem., v. 12, p. 245–259.

MacGowan, D.B. and R.C. Surdam, 1988b, The effects clastic diagenesis on thermal aspects of sedimentary basin models [abs.], GSA Progs. w/ Abs., v. 20, p. A258.

MacGowan, D.B. and R.C. Surdam, 1989a, The effect of organic/inorganic interactions on the progressive diagenesis of sandstones, in D. Melchoir, and R. Bassett, eds., Chemical Modeling in Aqueous Systems II: ACS Books, Washington D.C., in press.

MacGowan, D.B. and R.C. Surdam, 1989b, Carboxylic acid anions in sedimentary formation waters from the San Joaquin basin, California and the Louisiana Gulf Coast, Implications for diagenesis: Chem. Geol., submitted.

MacGowan, D.B., R.C. Surdam, and R.E. Ewing, 1988, The effect of carboxylic acid anions on the stability of framework grains in petroleum reservoirs: Proc. 4th Ann. EOR Symp., SPE, Paper SPE-17802, p. 621–630.

Machel, H.G., 1987, Some aspects of sulphate-hydrocarbon redox reactions, in J.D. Marshal, ed., Diagenesis of Sedimentary Sequences: GSA Spec. Pub. no. 36, p. 15–28.

Magara, K., 1974, Compaction, ion filtration, and osmosis in shale and their significance on primary migration: AAPG Bull., v. 58, p. 283–290.

Martall, A.E. and R.M. Smith, 1977, Critical Stability Constants, v. III: Other Organic Ligands, Plennum Press, NY, 495 p.

Matleck, K.S., D.W. Houseknecht, and K.R. Applin, 1989, Emplacement of clay into sand by infiltration, JSP, v. 59, p. 72–87.

McBride, E.F., J.C. Wilson, and T.N. Diggs, 1989, Compaction of Wilcox sandstones to 14,500 feet [abs.]: AAPG Bull., v. 73, p. 388.

Merewether, E.A., W.A. Cobban, and R.T. Ryder, 1975, Lower upper Cretaceous strata, Bighorn basin, Wyoming and Montana, in F.A. Exum and G.R. George, eds., Geology and Mineral Resources of the Bighorn Basin: WGA 27th Ann. Field Conf. Guidebook, p. 73–84.

Meshri, I.D., 1986, On the reactivity of carbonic and organic acids and the generation of secondary porosity, in Roles of Organic Matter in D.L. Gautier, ed., Sediment Diagenesis, SEPM Spec. Pub. no. 38, p. 123–128.

Moraes, M.A.S. and L.F. De Ros, 1988, Characterizacao e influenca das agilas de infitracao mecanica em reservatorios fluvias da bacia do Reconcavo, nor desto do Brazil, Boletin de Geociencias da Petrobras, (in Portuguese) v. 2, p. 13–26.

Palmer, D.A. and S.E. Drummond, 1986, Thermal decarboxylation of acetate, Part II, Boundary conditions for the role of acetate in primary migration of natural gas and transportation of metals in hydrothermal systems: Geochim. Cosmochim. 50, p. 825–833.

Perry, E.A. Jr., 1969, Burial diagenesis in Gulf Coast pelitic sediments, unpub. PhD diss., Case Western Reserve Univ.

Pittman, E.D., 1988, Diagenesis of the Terry Sandstone (Upper Cretaceous), Spindle Field, Colorado: JSP, v. 58, p. 785–800.

Price, L.C., 1983, Geologic time as a parameter in organic metamorphism and vitrinite reflectance as an absolute paleogeothermometer: JPG, v. 6, p. 5–38.

Price, L.C., 1985, Geologic time as a parameter in organic metamorphism and vitrinite reflectance as an absolute paleogeothermometer: Reply: JPG, v. 8, p. 233–240.

Pytte, A.M., 1982, The kinetics of the smectite-illite transformation in contact metamorphic shales, unpub. MA thesis, Dartmouth College, 78 p.

Pytte, A.M. and R.C. Reynolds, 1989, The thermal transformation of smectite to illite, in N.D. Naeser and T.H. McCulloh, eds., Thermal History of Sedimentary Basins, Springer-Verlag, NY, p. 133–140.

Ramseyer, K.L. and J.R. Boles, 1986, Mixed-layer illite/smectite minerals in Tertiary sandstones and shales, San Joaquin basin, Ca., Clay and Clay Minerals, v. 34, p. 115–124.

Reynolds, R.C., 1981, Mixed-layer illite-smectite in a contact metamorphic environment [abs.], 18th Am. Mtg. Clay Min. Soc. Proc., p. 5.

Rosenfeld, M.A., 1949, Some aspects of porosity and cementation, Producers Monthly, v. 13, p. 39–42.

Saxby, J., 1982, A reassessment of the range of kerogen maturities in which hydrocarbons are generated, JPG, v. 5, p. 117–128.

Schmidt, V. and D.A. McDonald, 1979, The role of secondary porosity in the course of sandstone diagenesis, in P.A. Scholle and P.R. Schluger, eds., Aspects of Diagenesis: SEPM Spec. Pub., no. 26, p. 175–207.

Schultz, J.L., J.R. Boles, and G.R. Tillman, 1989, Tracking calcium in the San Joaquin basin, Calif.: A strontium isotope study of carbonate cements at North Coles Levee, Geochim. Cosmochim., in press.

Sclater, J.G. and P.A. Christie, 1980, Continental stretching: an explanation of the post-mid-Cretaceous subsidence of the central North Sea basin, Jour. Geophys. Res., v. 85, p. 3711–3739.

Shock, E.L., 1988, Organic acid metastability in sedimentary basins, Geology, v. 16, p. 886–890.

Siebert, R.M., 1985, The origin of hydrogen sulfide, elemental sulfur, carbon dioxide and nitrogen in reservoirs: SEPM Gulf Coast Sec. Mtg., Abs. w/ Progs., v. 6, p. 30–31.

Siemers, C.T., 1975, Paleoenvironment analysis of the upper Cretaceous Frontier fm., northwestern Bighorn basin, Wyoming, in F.A. Exum and G.R. George, eds., Geology and Mineral Resources of the Bighorn Basin: WGA 27th Ann Field Conf. Guidebook, p. 85–100.

Snowdon, L.R., 1979, Errors in extrapolation of experimental kinetic parameters to organic geochemical systems: AAPG Bull., v. 63, p. 1128–1134.

Surdam, R.C., S.W. Boese, and Crossey, L.J., 1984, The chemistry of secondary porosity, in D.A. McDonald and R.C. Surdam, eds., Clastic Diagenesis: AAPG Mem. 37, p. 127–149.

Surdam, R.C. and J.R. Boles, 1979, Diagenesis of volcanic sandstones, in P.A. Scholle and P.R. Schluger, eds., Aspects of Diagenesis: SEPM Spec. Pub. No. 26, p. 227–242.

Surdam, R.C. and L.J. Crossey, 1985a, Organic-inorganic reactions during progressive burial: key to porosity/permeability enhancement and/or preservation, Phil. Trans. Roy. Soc. Lond., Series A, 315, p. 135–156.

Surdam, R.C. and L.J. Crossey, 1985b, Mechanisms of organic/inorganic interactions in sandstone/shale sequences, in Relationship of Organic Matter and Mineral Diagenesis, SEPM Short Course Notes, No. 7, p. 177–232.

Surdam, R.C., L.J. Crossey, E.S. Hagen, and H.P. Heasler, 1989a, Organic–inorganic interactions and sandstones diagenesis: AAPG Bull., v. 73, p. 1–23.

Surdam, R.C. and D.B. MacGowan, 1987, Oil field waters and sandstone diagenesis: Appl. Geochem., v. 2, p. 613–619.

Surdam, R.C., D.B. MacGowan, and T.L. Dunn, 1989b, Diagenetic pathways in sandstone/shale systems, Contrib. Geol., U. of WY Press, Laramie, WY, in press.

Surdam, R.C., T.L. Dunn, H.P. Heasler, and D.B. Mac-Gowan, 1989c, Porosity evolution in sandstone/shale systems, *in* I. Hutchinson and R. Hesse, eds., Burial Diagenesis Short Course Notes, Mineralogical Assoc. Canada, p. 61–134.

Tannenbaum, E., B.J. Huizinga, and I.R. Kaplan, 1986, Role of minerals in thermal alteration of organic matter–II: A material balance: AAPG Bull. v. 70, p. 805–812.

Thomson, A., 1979, Preservation of porosity in the deep Woodbine/Tuscaloosa trend, Louisiana, Gulf: Trans. GCAGS, v. 29, p. 396–403.

Thyne, G.D., D.B. MacGowan, and R.C. Surdam, 1988, Experimental determination of the production kinetics of petroleum and organic acids during thermal maturation of kerogen using laboratory hydrous pyrolysis [abs.]: GSA, Progs. w/ Abs., Rocky Mtn. Sec. Mtg., v. 19, p. 727.

Tissot, B.P. and J. Espitale, 1975, L'Evolution thermique de la matieré organique des sèdiménts: Applications d'une Simulation Mathematique, Rev. Inst. French Petrol. (in French), v. 39, p. 743–777.

Tissot, B.P. and D.H. Welte, 1984, Petroleum Formation and Occurrence, Sec. Ed., Springer-Verlag, NY., 699p.

Van Houten, F.B., 1962, Frontier formation, Bighorn basin, Wyoming, *in* R.L. Enyert and W.H. Curry III, eds., Symposium on Early Cretaceous Rocks of Wyoming and Adjacent Areas: WGA, 17th Ann. Field Conf. Guidebook, p. 173–210.

Walker, T.R., B. Waugh, and A.J. Crone, 1978, Diagenesis in first–cycle desert alluvium of Cenozoic age, southwestern United States, and northwestern Mexico: GSA Bull., v. 89, p. 19–32.

Waples, D., 1980, Time and temperature in petroleum exploration; application of Lopatin's method to petroleum exploration: AAPG Bull. v. 64, p. 916–926.

Whitney, G. and H.R. Northrop, 1988, Experimental investigation of the smectite to illite reaction: Dual mechanisms and oxygen isotope systematics: Am. Min., v. 73, p. 77–90.

Wiley, L.M., Y.K. Kharaka, T.S. Presser, J.B. Rapp, and I. Barnes, 1975, Short–chain aliphatic acid anions in oilfield waters and their contribution to the measured alkalinity: Geochim. Cosmochim. 39, p. 1707–1711.

Winters, J.C., J.A. Williams, and M.D. Lewan, 1983, A laboratory study of petroleum generation by hydrous pyrolysis, *in* M. Bjøroy, ed., Advances in Organic Geochemistry, 1981: J. Wiley and Sons, NY, p. 524–533.

Wood, D.A., 1988, Relationships between the thermal maturity indices calculated using Ahrrenius equation and Lopatin method: Implications for petroleum exploration: AAPG Bull., v. 72, p. 115–135.

Yin, P. and R.C. Surdam, 1985, Naturally enhanced porosity and permeability in the hydrocarbon reservoirs of the Gippsland basin, Australia: *in* R. Ewing, ed., Proc. 1st WY EOR Symp., EOR Institute, U. of WY, p. 79–109.

Microporosity formed by dissolution/leaching of a feldspar grain. Sample form Almond Fm., sec 2, T19N R99W, Sweetwater Co., WY. Depth 4,487 ft (1,368 m). Photo donated by Bill Keighin.

Sedimentology, Diagenesis, and Reservoir Potential of the Pennsylvanian Tyler Formation, Central Montana[1]

PETER T. STANTON[2]

MATTHEW R. SILVERMAN[3]

[1]Received September 17, 1988; Revised April 5, 1989
[2]Consulting Geologist, Denver, Colorado
[3]Gustavson Associates, Boulder, Colorado

Sandstone reservoirs of the Pennsylvanian Tyler Formation were deposited in the narrow Central Montana Trough that connected the Williston Basin with the western continental margin. The Lower Tyler Member is comprised of discontinuous sandstones within a sequence of dark gray shales. The Bear Gulch Member is a lithographic limestone. The Upper Tyler Member consists of a basal sandstone overlain by interbedded red shales and carbonates.

The Lower and Upper Tyler members are valley–fill sequences deposited by low gradient, vertically aggrading, anastomosing fluvial systems. Channel–fill sandstones are straight to sinuous, one–half mi (0.8 km) wide, and 25 to 35 ft (8–11 m) thick. Multistoried channels are common. Tyler sandstones are typically well–sorted, well–rounded, very fine– to medium– grained quartzarenites and sublitharenites. Sedimentary structures are predominantly uni–di– rectional planar–tabular crossbeds. Interchannel sediments, including natural levee, crevasse splay, and lacustrine deposits, make up the bulk of the formation. They consist of gray shales which contain thin, upward–coarsening sandstone cycles and rare coals.

Four diagenetic stages have been identified. Stage I, early burial diagenesis, typically con– sists of pyrite and siderite authigenesis in a reducing substrate. Opal, chlorite, hematite, and/or dolomite formed locally by vadose diagenesis. Stage II, related to erosion of the overly– ing Alaska Bench Formation, consists of anhydrite, chlorite, dolomite, and quartz precipitation. Stage III, deep burial diagenesis, resulted from thermal maturation of organic material and includes cementation by kaolinite and ferroan dolomite. Stage IV, due to regional uplift and fresh water flushing from the west, is marked by dedolomitization and subsequent precipitation of pyrite and calcite.

Potential reservoirs are exclusively channel sandstones in which reservoir quality is con– trolled by the extent of cementation. Both sedimentologic and petrographic models can be used to predict reservoir occurrence.

INTRODUCTION

The Tyler Formation (Pennsylvanian) in Central Montana has been a primary target for petroleum ex– plorationists since the 1940's. Success has been spo– radic; excellent oil fields have been discovered, but at a relatively low success ratio. Geologists are faced with notoriously unpredictable occurrences of reser– voir–quality sandstone.

The study area includes townships 9–13N and ranges 24–33E (Fig. 1). It encompasses virtually all current oil production from the Tyler Formation in Montana. In the subsurface, the top of the Tyler Formation ranges in depth to over 6,000 ft (1,829 m). The unit is deepest to the south and east. It crops out approximately 15 mi (24 km) west of the study area.

The purpose of this investigation was to apply modern concepts of sedimentology and clastic petrog– raphy to the problem of locating Tyler reservoir sand– stones. The study was completed in three phases: subsurface correlation and mapping using well logs, interpretation of sedimentology based on examination of cores and core chips (Table 1), and petrographic analysis of 25 thin sections from potential reservoir sandstones. Petrographic analysis was restricted to lithologies with reservoir potential. Clean sandstones from both producing and non–producing wells were examined; shaly sandstones and other low reservoir–

REGIONAL DATA: Tyler Formation, Central Montana
Producing Interval: Lower and Upper Tyler members
Geographic Location: Musselshell and Rosebud Counties, Montana
Present Tectonic Setting: Central Montana Uplift
Depositional Setting: Big Snowy Trough
Age of Reservoir: Early Pennsylvanian (Morrowan)
Lithology of Reservoir: Well sorted, fine- to medium-grained quartzarenite
Depositional Environment: Anastomosing fluvial system within an alluvial valley–fill sequence
Diagenesis: 1) siderite, pyrite, rare opal; 2) anhydrite, chlorite, quartz overgrowths; 3) kaolinite, ferroan dolomite, minor dissolution; and 4) dolomite dissolution, calcite, pyrite, ferroan calcite

Porosity Types: Intergranular with minor dissolution
Porosity: Field averages from 8 to 19%
Permeability: Field averages from 8 to 1,000 md
Nature of Traps: Stratigraphic, structural, combined, paleostructural/stratigraphic, and diagenetic.
Entrapping Facies: Channel abandonment and interchannel levee, splay, and lacustrine deposits
Source Rocks: Heath Formation (Mississippian) limestones and shales
Timing of Hydrocarbon Migration: Laramide (?)

REPRESENTATIVE FIELD: Breed Creek Field
Discovery Date: 1976
Reservoir Depth: 4,800 ft (1,463 m)
Reservoir Thickness: 25 ft (8 m)
IP (average): 74 BOPD
Areal Extent: 520 acres (210 ha)
Original Reservoir Pressure: 1,945 psi
Cumulative Production (6/88): 1,100,000 BO
Estimated Oil in Place: 5,000,000 BO
Approximate Ultimate Recovery: 1,750,000 BO
Oil Gravity: 32° API
Water Saturation: Logs 25–35%; core 4–33%
Porosity in Pay: Maximum 27%, average 17%
Permeability in Pay: Maximum 185 md, average 13 md
Reservoir Temperature: 120°F (43°C)

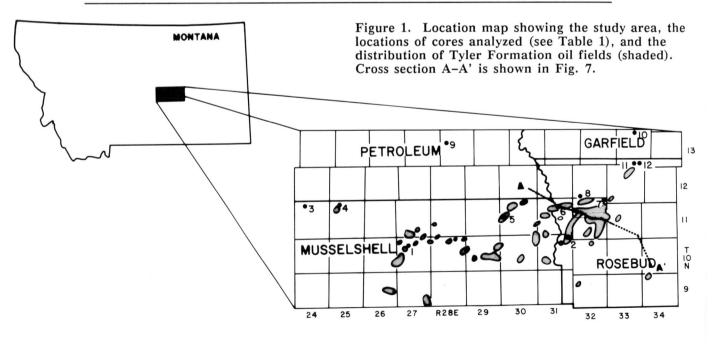

Figure 1. Location map showing the study area, the locations of cores analyzed (see Table 1), and the distribution of Tyler Formation oil fields (shaded). Cross section A–A' is shown in Fig. 7.

Table 1. Tyler Formation cores utilized (Complete descriptions are included in Stanton, 1986).

Well Name	Location	Interval (ft)
Dome Petroleum 8–9 Bigwall	9–10N–27E	3,711–3,761
Polumbus 1–6 Kincheloe	1–10N–31E	4,737–4,789
Marnell Res. 1 Marnell Hydra Federal	5–11N–24E	1,078–1,094 1,174–1,183
Petro–Lewis 15–5 Mang	5–11N–25E	2,529–2,560
Petro–Lewis 9–18 Shellhammer	18–11N–30E	3,925–3,967
McAlester A–4 Montana Federal	10–11N–31E	5,238–5,299 5,331–5,341
Champlin 2 Coffee	1–11N–32E	5,770–5,858
Huckabay 2–32 Kincheloe	32–12N–32E	5,345–5,387
Champlin 1 Alvin C	12–13N–28E	3,647–3,709
ARCO 1–3 BNRR–Coastal	3–13N–33E	4,250–4,356
Milestone 44–33 BN	33–13N–33E	4,895–4,952
GPE 71 Ranch	34–33N–13E	4,817–4,836
GPE 3 BNI	35–13N–33E	4,833–4,862

potential lithologies were not. Petrographic techniques included thin section petrography and scanning electron microscopy (SEM).

PREVIOUS INVESTIGATIONS

Investigations of the Tyler Formation stratigraphy in Central Montana include: Freeman (1922), Mundt (1956a, b), Norton (1956), Willis (1959), Krantzler (1966), Maughan and Roberts (1967), Harris (1972), Fanshawe (1978), Maughan (1984), and Nobel (1984). Early authors believed the Tyler was Chesterian in age, while later studies propose that it is Morrowan to Atokan. Alternatively, Scott (1935), Gardner (1959), Horner (1985), and Williams (1981) place the lower portion of the Tyler section in the Chesterian Heath Formation (part of the Big Snowy Group), and the upper portion with the Morrowan to Atokan Amsden Group.

A compilation of field summaries edited by Tonnsen (1985) contains the most up–to–date information on the Tyler's petroleum potential. Earlier field studies include Chuman (1956), Foster (1956), Varland (1956), Staggs (1959), Carlson (1967), Poole and Starkweather (1969), and McDade and Starkweather (1969). Cooper (1956), Todd (1959), and Fanshawe (1978) relate reservoir distribution to paleotectonics.

Relatively few authors have analyzed the sedimentology of the Tyler Formation. Mundt (1956a, b) interpreted Tyler sandstones as fluvial channel deposits. Willis (1959) proposed that the sandstones were offshore marine bars; subsequent authors generally follow Mundt's interpretation. Maughan (1984) suggested that Tyler sandstones in Central Montana are marine shoreline deposits. Nobel (1984) described measured sections and shallow cores northwest of the study area and proposed deposition in a tidal flat/tidal channel complex. Carbonate sedimentology has been addressed in an analysis of the Bear Gulch Limestone Member (Williams, 1981).

REGIONAL TECTONIC SETTING

The Tyler Formation in the study area was deposited in a narrow east–west trending basin called the Central Montana Trough or Big Snowy Trough (Fig. 2). The Central Montana Trough connected the Williston Basin with the western continental margin via the Snowcrest Trough in southwest Montana (Maughan, 1984). It was flanked to the north by the Alberta Shelf and to the south by the Wyoming Shelf. The trough was considered a structural sag by Mundt (1956a) and Fanshawe (1978). Maughan (1984) suggested that it was a rift or aulocogen bounded to the south by the Musselshell lineament. Post-Tyler erosion has destroyed any evidence of a northern fault margin (Harris, 1972; Maughan, 1984).

Two stages of post–Tyler tectonism were described by Fanshawe (1978). He identified an episode of uplift with some associated folding and faulting at the

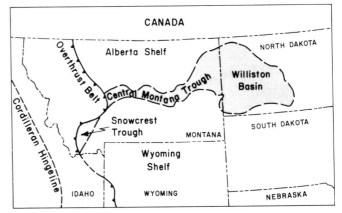

Figure 2. Principle paleogeographic elements during Tyler deposition. Boundaries of Central Montana Trough and Williston Basin (shaded) are delineated by subcrop limits of the Lower Tyler and Bear Gulch (adapted from Maughan, 1984).

end of Alaska Bench (Amsden) deposition. This corresponds to an erosional period which lasted until Jurassic time. Later tectonism resulted in structural reversal, forming the Central Montana Uplift with associated anticlinal and domal features. This readjustment occurred during either Laramide or Eocene time.

NOMENCLATURE AND AGE

Stratigraphic nomenclature of the Upper Mississippian and Lower Pennsylvanian formations in Central Montana has been a subject of much controversy. Two schools of thought have developed since the 1920's. One school defines the Tyler Formation as a heterogeneous sequence of varicolored shales and white and red sandstones, distinct from the underlying black shales and limestones of the Heath Formation of the Big Snowy Group (Freeman, 1922; Mundt, 1956a and b; Norton, 1956; Foster, 1956; Willis, 1959; Krantzler, 1966; Maughan and Roberts, 1967; Harris, 1972; Fanshawe, 1978; Maughan, 1984; and Nobel, 1984). The opposing school does not recognize any Tyler Formation, but includes the lower, typically dark colored strata as a member of the Heath Formation and the upper, typically red, strata as the lowest member in the Amsden Group (Scott, 1935; Gardner, 1959; Williams, 1981; and Horner, 1984). The argument is based on the ranges of fauna collected from the Bear Gulch Limestone, which locally divides the lower and upper Tyler units.

A further complication to the nomenclature is the location of the Mississippian–Pennsylvanian boundary, which has significance as a worldwide depositional hiatus. Maughan (1984) and most other authors who recognize the Tyler Formation place the boundary at the Heath–Tyler contact. Williams (1981) and other authors who do not recognize the Tyler Formation place the boundary at the Heath–Amsden contact (top of the Bear Gulch Limestone). Resolution of the problem is not within the scope of this study. The stratigraphy utilized for the study (Fig. 3) recognizes the Tyler Formation as a lithologically distinct, mappable unit comprised of three members, for which Maughan (1984) employed the names Stonehouse Canyon, Bear Gulch, and Cameron Creek. Geologists in the petroleum industry, however, generally use the terminology recognized by Harris (1972), in which the Stonehouse Canyon and Cameron Creek members are termed the Lower Tyler and Upper Tyler members, respectively.

REGIONAL STRATIGRAPHY

The Lower Tyler Member forms a narrow, east-west trending band across the center of the study area. It ranges in thickness up to 320 ft (98 m) and thins rapidly to zero to the north and south (Fig. 4). The unit consists of dark gray to black, carbonaceous shale with several discontinuous, buff to light gray sandstone bodies. These sandstones have been informally designated "C", "B", and Stensvad sandstones, in ascending order. The basal sandstone commonly rests on the Heath Formation and contains pebbles derived from that unit. The gross and net thicknesses of sandstones typically are greatest where the Lower Tyler Member is thickest.

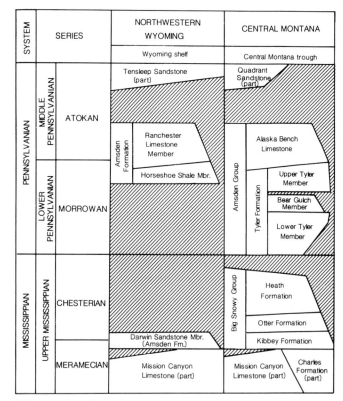

Figure 3. Stratigraphic nomenclature of the Central Montana Trough and adjacent Wyoming Shelf (adapted from Maughan, 1984; and Harris, 1972).

The Bear Gulch Member conformably overlies the Lower Tyler Member. Where the Lower Tyler is absent, the Bear Gulch Member rests directly on the Heath Formation. Its occurrence is limited to the northern half of the study area, where thickness ranges from 140 ft (43 m) at the northwest corner to a zero edge at its southern and eastern limits. The Bear Gulch thickness is controlled by an unconformity on its upper surface, where it is overlain by the Upper Tyler Member (Foster, 1956; Harris, 1972; and Williams, 1981). The Bear Gulch consists of medium to dark gray, extremely dense lithographic limestone thinly interbedded with calcareous black shale and marl.

The Upper Tyler Member unconformably overlies the Bear Gulch Member or, where the latter is absent, the Lower Tyler Member. The interval is thickest (Fig. 5) coincident with the area where the Lower Tyler Member is thickest. In the study area, the Upper Tyler ranges in thickness from over 200 ft (61 m) to less than 50 ft (15 m) in the north and south. A basal sandstone, commonly termed the "A" Sandstone, typically occurs at the Upper Tyler/Bear Gulch contact. The "A" Sandstone characteristically is light gray to red, grading upward into dark gray to red shales with thinly interbedded limestones and dolomites (Harris, 1972; Maughan, 1984; and Nobel, 1984). The Upper Tyler Member grades upward into the base of the Alaska Bench Formation.

SUBSURFACE MAPPING

The Tyler Formation has been penetrated in over 1,500 wells, most of which were drilled in the last 30 years. Petrophysical logs are available for almost every well. The traditional log suite (Fig. 6) includes resistivity–SP and sonic–gamma ray logs. Many wells are evaluated without density or neutron porosity logs, largely because sonic logs are thought to indicate more accurate porosity values in the presence of sandstones containing such dense minerals as pyrite, siderite, and hematite.

A log cross section (Fig. 7) illustrates the general criteria used for correlation throughout the study area. In addition, Tonnsen (1985) presented type logs and field summaries for numerous Tyler fields. The basic field data for one representative Tyler field (Silverman, 1985) are included in the Reservoir Summary.

Structural mapping on a variety of geologic markers is valuable, but the most widely used regional datums are the tops of the Upper Tyler and of the Lower Tyler (Fig. 8). The top of the Upper Tyler can be picked consistently on both well logs and seismic data.

Major structural features flanking the study area include the Big Snowy Uplift (west), Bull Mountains Basin (south), Porcupine Dome (east), and Cat Creek Anticline (north). The southwest–plunging Sumatra Anticline is the most prominent fold within the Tyler trend. Other closures include Big Wall Dome, Ivanhoe Dome, and Melstone Anticline, all of which produce oil from the Tyler. Major east–west, high angle reverse faults traverse the study area and include the Sumatra Fault on the north and the Willow Creek Fault to the south.

Stratigraphic mapping indicates that the thickest Upper Tyler Sandstone bodies accumulated along the margins of the thickest Upper Tyler trend (Fig. 5). Sandstone thickness principally represents the "A" Sandstone, a fluvial channel deposit within an alluvial valley–fill sequence (Fig. 7). "A" sandstones occur in isolated pods along the valley's axis and southern margin, and range up to 50 ft (15 m) in thickness.

The Lower Tyler Member (Fig. 4) has a very limited areal distribution. As with the Upper Tyler Member, the Lower Tyler represents filling of an alluvial valley (Fig. 7). The valley was 7 to 15 mi (11–24 km) wide, and over 300 ft (91 m) deep, with relatively steep margins. Lower Tyler sandstones are concentrated along the basin axis (Fig. 2). Net sandstone thickness, which ranges up to 100 ft (30 m), is an accumulated total for multiple, separate sandstone bodies. Lower Tyler channels typically followed the basin axis (longitudinal rivers, as defined by Miall, 1981). Multistoried channels are common, accounting for the thickest net sandstone values.

SEDIMENTARY FACIES AND ENVIRONMENTS OF DEPOSITION

Analyses of 12 conventional cores, in conjunction with regional subsurface mapping produced for this study and previously published works, suggest that sandstones of the Tyler Formation were deposited in a series of fluvial channels. Evidence for this conclusion follows those points originally outlined by Mundt (1956a), and includes sandstone–body geometry and subcrop pattern, grain–size distribution, sequence of sedimentary features, and channel–base lag deposits.

Inclusions of wood, leaves, and carbonaceous material, as well as the vertical association with rooted horizons and rare coals, contribute to the fluvial interpretation.

Fluvial Channel Facies

Channel deposits as delineated in the subsurface are straight to sinuous and average one–half mi (0.8 km) in width, with an average thickness from 25 to 35 ft (8–11 m). This results in a width/depth ratio between 50 and 100, which suggests a mobile channel belt (Friend, 1983; Miall, 1985). This ratio probably is a maximum, however, because subsurface correlations tend to include sandy–levee and crevasse–splay deposits in the channel width, while excluding fine–grained abandonment fill from the channel depth. In addition, detailed cross sections at Ivanhoe, Keg Coulee, South Little Wall Creek, Melstone, Stensvad, Sumatra, and Winnett Junction fields (Tonnsen, 1985) indicate that these channel deposits are comprised of several closely spaced channels. Each channel may be only a few hundred feet in width.

Tyler channel sandstones are very well sorted, medium to fine grained, contain a thin basal lag deposit, and fine upward slightly to very fine–grained sandstone at the top. Two conglomeratic sandstone units (seen in the GPE No. 3 BNI and Champlin No. 2 Coffee wells) apparently derived much of their coarse bed load from intrabasinal overbank deposits.

Sedimentary features in channel sandstones are dominated by unidirectional planar–tabular cross beds, dipping from 10 to 25°, in sets 4 to 12 in. (10 to 30 cm) in thickness. Crossbeds likely were deposited as foresets of migrating linguoid or transverse bars. Crossbeds commonly are separated by 0.4 to 2 in. (1 to 5 cm) beds of ripple– and climbing–ripple–laminated sandstone which contain rounded, flattened shale pebbles and flasers. These ripple laminae probably were deposited in front of prograding sand waves as current and counter–current ripples due to formation of separation eddies (Jopling, 1965; Collinson, 1970). Ripples also may have formed over or between migrating bars during falling water stages. This interpretation of the channel bedforms precludes the need for tidal currents as employed by Nobel (1984).

Convoluted beds and fluid–escape structures occur rarely in the channel sequence, and suggest slumping of oversteepened bedforms between flood episodes, or contortion of sediment due to shear stress of flow. No evidence of exposure of bar tops was observed in any core.

Reduced flow regime or partial abandonment in channel deposits is indicated by ripple–, climbing ripple– and wispy–laminated, very fine– to fine–grained sandstones at the top of many channel deposits. Abundant angular shale pebbles in discrete horizons in cores from the Polumbus No. 1–6 Kincheloe (Fig. 6; Table 2, Unit 3) and Arco No. 1–3 BNRR Coastal wells probably were derived from caving of bank margins in channels and/or splay channels during partial abandonment (Putnam, 1983). Total abandonment is suggested by slumped and microfaulted sandy shale horizons in the Champlin No. 2 Coffee and Polumbus No. 1–6 Kincheloe (Fig. 6; Table 2, Unit 4) wells, and a greening–upward shale and coal interval in the

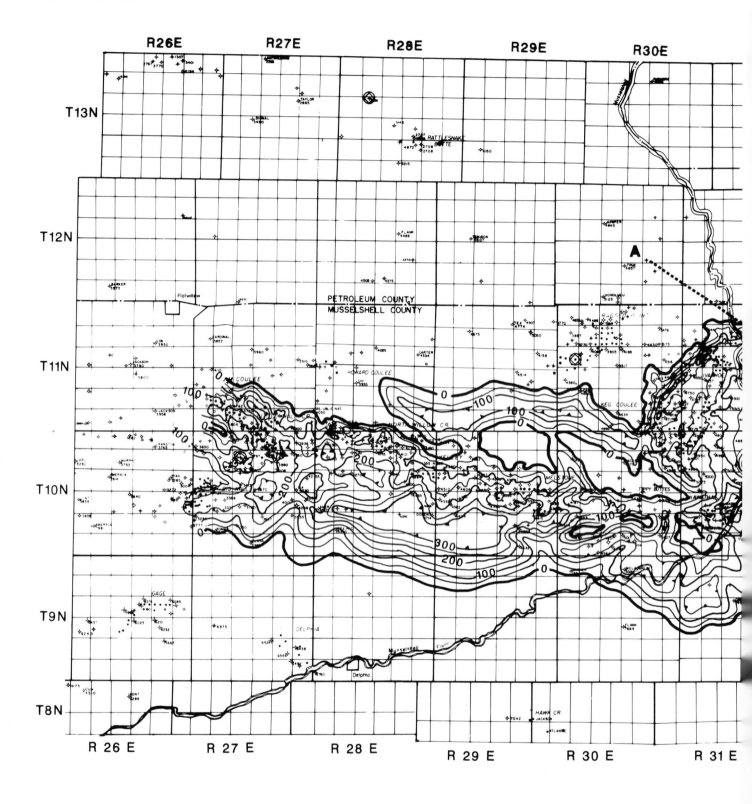

◎   CORES ANALYZED FOR STUDY

Figure 4. Isopach map of the Lower Tyler Member, contour interval = 100 ft (30 m). Data from over ⟶

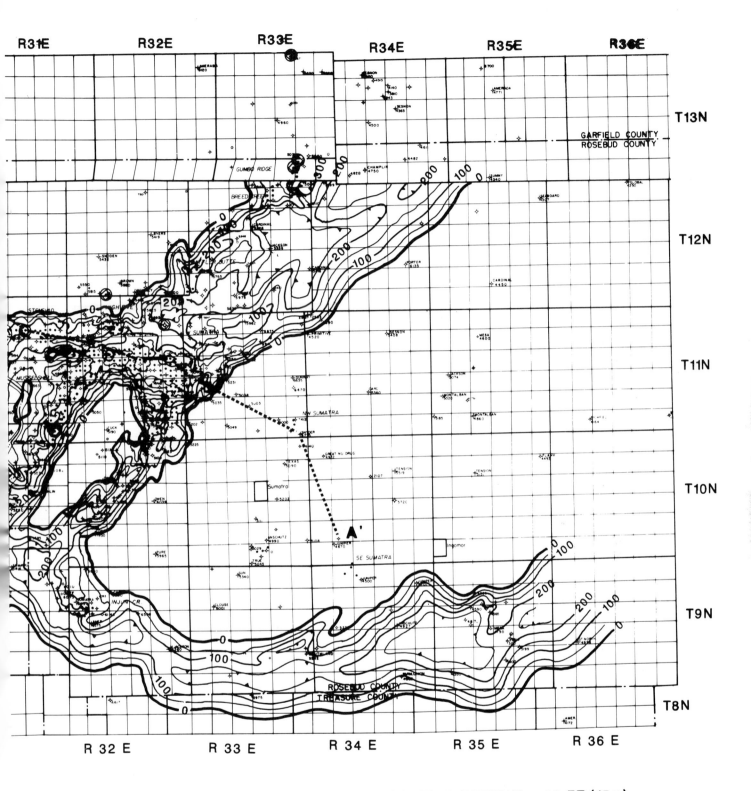

CONTOUR INTERVAL : 50 FT (15m)

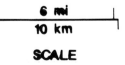

SCALE

1,300 wells are utilized (adapted from Freedom, 1982).

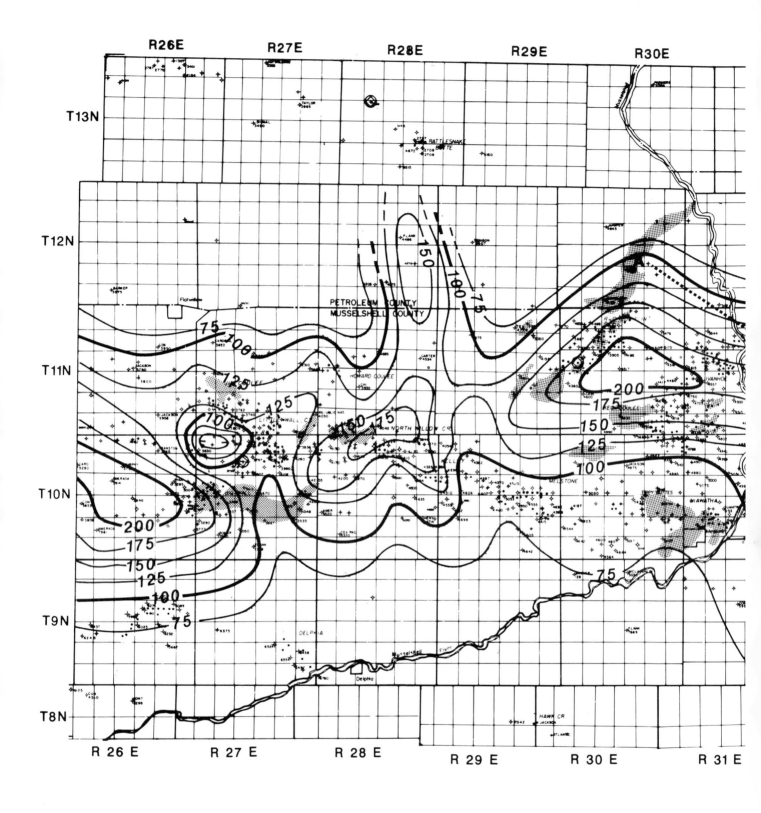

◇   CORES ANALYZED FOR STUDY

▨   TOTAL UPPER TYLER SANDSTONE THICKNESS > 20 FT (6 m)

Figure 5. Isopach map of Upper Tyler Member, contour interval = 50 ft (15 m). Limited well data ⟶

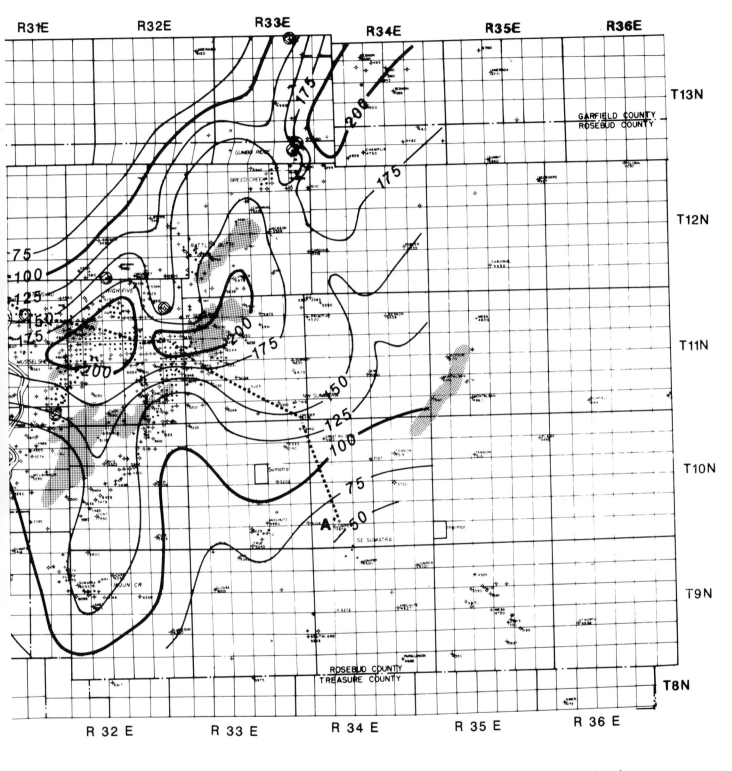

CONTOUR INTERVAL : 25 FT (8m)

6 mi
10 km

SCALE

utilized (adapted from Stanton, 1986; and Freedom, 1982).

Figure 6. Typical logs with core description, Polumbus 1-6 Kincheloe, Sumatra Field, SE NW Sec 1 T10N R31E.

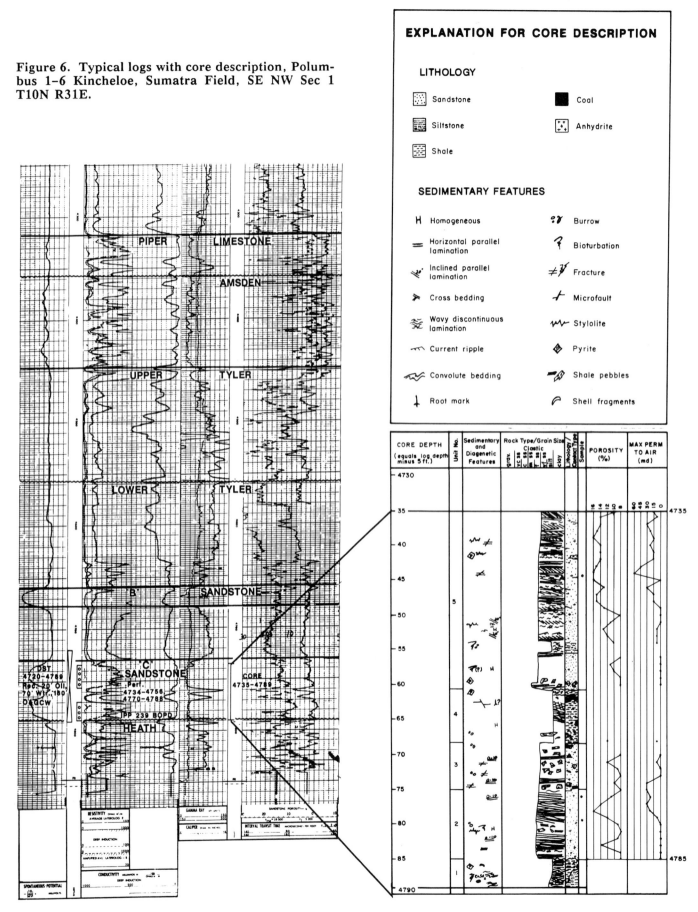

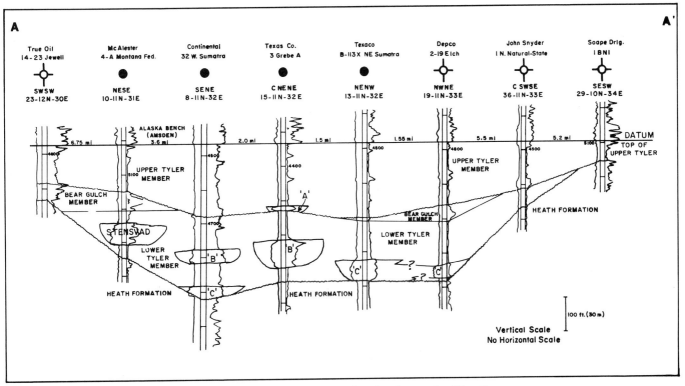

Figure 7. Stratigraphic log cross section A-A'. Location is shown in Fig. 1.

Table 2. Typical core description, Polumbus No. 1-6 Kincheloe. A graphical representation is included in Figure 6.

Unit 1: 4,789.0-4,785.5 ft; Heath Formation

Medium gray to tan siltstone which becomes shaley upward, grading into pyritic, organic-rich, highly fissile black shale. Shale contains pyritized microfossils. Burrowing is rare.

Unit 2: 4,785.5-4,775.0 ft; Fluvial Channel Facies (active channel-fill)

Tan, lightly oil-stained, anhydrite-cemented, very well sorted, well rounded, medium- to fine-grained sandstone. Shale intraclasts and rare fossil fragments occur from 4,781 to 4,783 ft. Shale intraclasts range up to 2.4 in. (6.0 cm) in length. The unit is characterized by low-angle laminations and unconformably overlies Unit 1. Locally, bedding planes contain carbonaceous material as flattened pebbles and stylolites.

Unit 3: 4,775.0-4,768.3 ft; Fluvial Channel Facies (partial abandonment-fill)

Light gray, anhydrite-cemented, well sorted, fine grained sandstone. The unit contains numerous angular mudstone intraclasts and several anhydrite nodules. Intraclasts range up to 4.0 in. (10.0 cm) in length. The base of the unit is gradational from Unit 2.

Unit 4: 4,768.3-4,761.0 ft; Fluvial Channel Facies (grades from abandonment-fill to interchannel to possible marine)

Dark gray, homogeneous mudstone which becomes laminated and micro-faulted upward, then grades into coaly, black shale and black to dark gray mudstone. This upper mudstone contains a scour surface which is overlain by pyritized fossil fragments. Fossil fragments include crinoid and bryozoan debris.

Unit 5: 4,761.0-4,735.0 ft; Fluvial Channel Facies (active channel-fill)

Light tan, lightly oil-stained, very well sorted, fine- to very fine-grained sandstone. The unit is comprised of alternating beds of clean, cross-bedded sandstone, interbedded with thin beds of sandstone which contain carbonaceous material, flasers, and shale pebbles. A one foot (0.3 m) thick bed of dark gray, bioturbated, sandy shale occurs at 4,755 ft. The unit is lightly cemented by dolomite and anhydrite. The base of the unit unconformably overlies Unit 4, and contains shale pebbles derived from that unit.

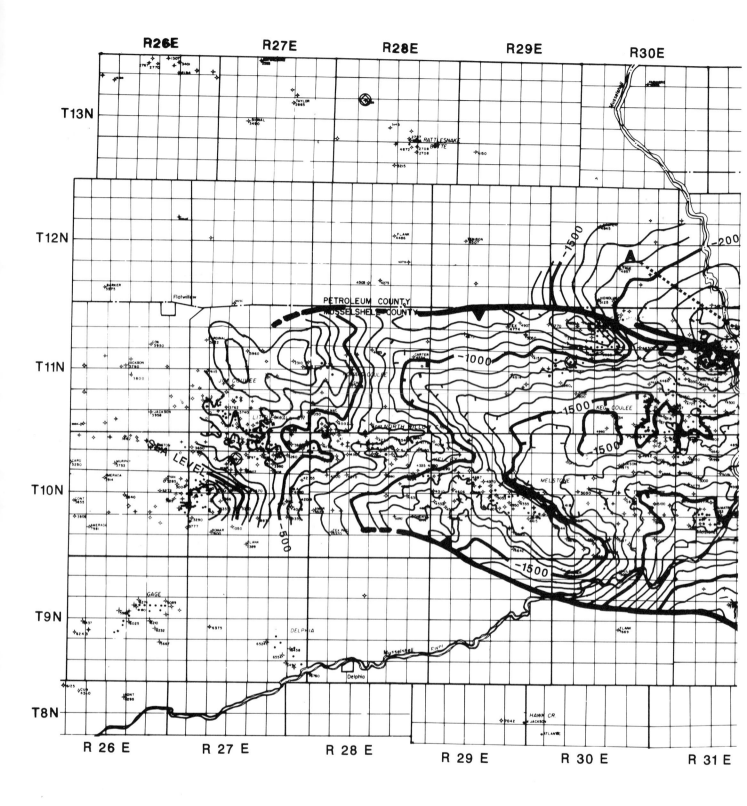

◇   CORES ANALYZED FOR STUDY

Figure 8. Structure map, top of Lower Tyler, contour interval = 100 ft (30 m). Data from over 1,300 →

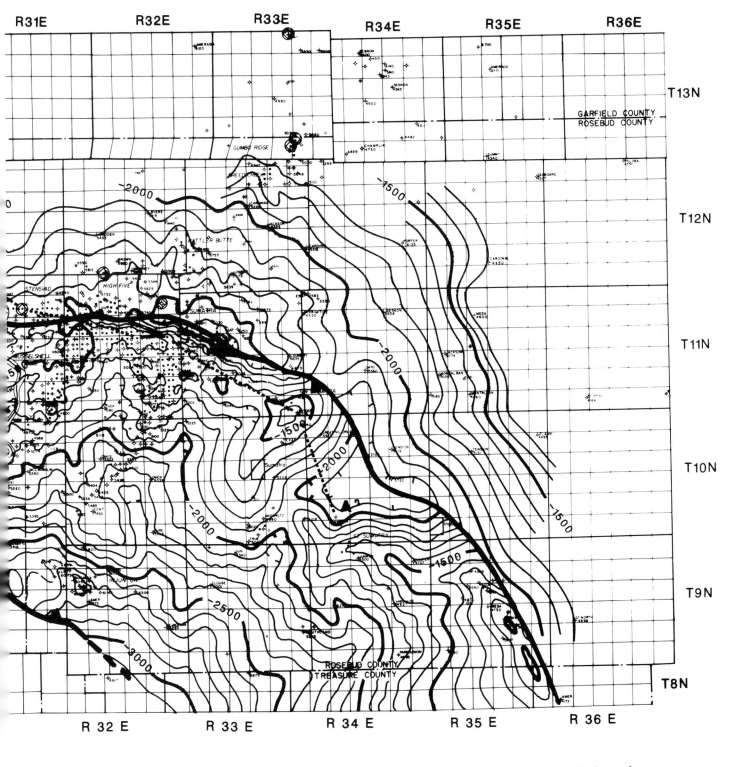

CONTOUR INTERVAL : 100 FT (30m)

6 mi
10 km

SCALE

wells are utilized (adapted from Freedom, 1982).

Huckabay No. 2–32 Kincheloe well. Part or all of a bioturbated, interbedded sandstone–shale sequence in the Dome No. 8–9 Bigwall core also may be an abandonment sequence overlying a thin channel sandstone.

Levee, Splay, and Lacustrine Facies

Deposits from interchannel regions are characterized by light to dark gray, very carbonaceous, very fine- to fine-grained sandstone with wavy interbeds to flasers of medium to dark gray shale. A thin coal bed occurs in the Champlin No. 1 Alvin C well, although rooting was not observed. Siderite nodules and pyrite are common diagenetic features in Tyler interchannel sediments.

Sandstone–shale sequences typically are organized into upward–coarsening cycles which grade from laminated shale to ripple- and climbing-ripple-laminated, very fine–grained sandstone. In several instances, the cycle coarsens further into cross-bedded, fine- to medium-grained sandstone.

Cycles range in thickness from several inches up to five ft (1.5 m), and are sharply overlain by the laminated shale of the next cycle. Shales contain carbonaceous material and woody debris on bedding planes, and display rare sand–filled burrows. Rarely, bioturbation has homogenized sandstone–shale cycles.

Upward–coarsening sandstone–shale cycles are interpreted as crevasse–splay deposits. The laminated nature of shale beds, the absence of rooting, and the range from rare burrows to pervasive bioturbation suggests that crevasse splays were deposited in lakes or bays. Very rare bidirectional ripple laminations in the Champlin No. 1 Alvin C well may have formed by the interaction of flood- and wind–influenced currents. The thin coal horizon in that well lacks a pronounced root zone, and may represent rafted organic material. The buff-colored, intraclast lime wacke–packstone in that core probably is a fresh–water lacustrine limestone deposit.

Dark gray to black, calcareous, sparsely fossiliferous shales occur in several cores. They typically are featureless, with only rare burrows and sparse ostracods(?). Willis (1959), Williams (1981), and Maughan (1984) noted the presence of fresh- to brackish–water ostracods in the Tyler Formation. These Tyler Formation shales probably represent low energy deposits of muddy, fresh–water lakes, brackish bays, or estuaries. A thin, dark gray shale in the core from the Polumbus No. 1–6 Kincheloe (Fig. 6; Table 2, Unit 4) contains a normal marine fauna, including bryozoan and crinoid fragments. This bed is the only horizon examined which clearly represents marine sedimentation.

Bear Gulch Limestone

The transition from the Lower Tyler shales to the Bear Gulch Limestone is not present in any core. Williams (1981) determined that the contact between these units is conformable. She described a Bear Gulch fauna comprised of planktonic and nektonic organisms, with a very limited epifauna, and proposed deposition beneath a highly turbid water column with lower than normal marine salinity.

Uppermost Upper Tyler Beds

The Upper Tyler Member above the "A" Sandstone was not well sampled in the cores available for this study. Analysis of rotary cuttings, field observations, and descriptions of this interval in the literature indicate that it is comprised of red to gray shales with thin interbeds of limestone and sandstone. The limestones typically are one to three ft (0.3 to 1.0 m) in thickness, and range in composition from mudstones to ooid bioclast grainstones. Maughan (1984) noted the presence of brachiopods, pelecypods, gastropods, and millerellids within these beds. Sandstones are white to red, and irregular to lenticular bedded (Willis, 1959). A thin sandstone at the top of the Petro-Lewis No. 9–18 Shellhammer core probably is an example. The development of dolomite/hematite nodules in this sandstone suggests subaerial exposure. Although little detailed sedimentology has been done, most authors believe this sequence represents a transgressive shoreline deposit, and is gradational upward to the shallow marine Alaska Bench Formation (Mundt, 1956a; Willis, 1959; Harris, 1972; Maughan, 1984; and Nobel, 1984).

Fluvial Model

Sedimentary environments interpreted from the Tyler Formation in the study area indicate the presence of narrow fluvial channels in an extensive floodplain/lake complex. Channels show little evidence of lateral migration; instead, abandonment sequences described in several cores suggest that channel avulsion was a common process. In light of these characteristics, a low gradient fluvial system is proposed. Sandstone geometry suggests an anastomosing channel morphology with well-developed levees constraining channels (Fig. 9).

Descriptions in the literature of modern anastomosing river systems are not common. Smith (1983) re-

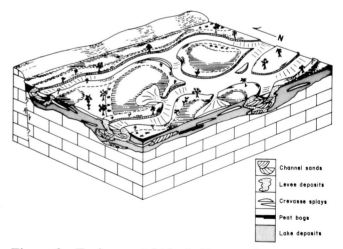

Figure 9. Facies model block diagram for an anastomosing fluvial system (from Stanton, 1986, as modified from Smith and Smith, 1980; Smith, 1983; and Miall, 1985). The brick pattern represents Mississippian Big Snowy Group sediments into which an alluvial valley has been incised. Channel location is controlled by topography on the Mississippian unconformity.

viewed anastomosing reaches of the Columbia and Saskatchewan rivers in Canada. He described narrow, stable channels flanked by an interchannel complex of lakes, marshes, and peat bogs. Channel bedforms are dominated by sand waves with planar–tabular crossbed sets. Fining–upward sequences within the crossbeds are interpreted as flood–cycle deposits. Channel deposits are 15 to 45 ft (5–14 m) thick and up to 900 ft (274 m) wide.

Smith (1986) studied anastomosing river deposits of the Magdalena River in northwestern Colombia. Here, channel deposits are larger, with an average thickness of 90 ft (27 m) and width of 1,800 ft (549 m). The vertical grain–size trend is uniform. Fining–upward cycles are absent. The interchannel region is dominated by a complex of lakes, marshes, and bogs, but very little peat has accumulated in the subsurface deposits.

Tyler channel deposits are similar to Smith's (1986) example in their uniform vertical grain–size trend and the paucity of coal. Although fining–upward cycles are not evident in cores, flood cycles in channels may go unrecognized because of the uniform sediment size available. In the interchannel regions, cyclic crevasse splay deposits probably represent flood events.

Smith (1986) discussed factors controlling organic accumulations in the floodplain complex of anastomosing river systems. Thin coals in the Tyler Formation have been described by Mundt (1956a), Willis (1959), Harris (1972), Maughan (1984), and Nobel (1984). Several poorly developed coal beds occur in the cores described for this study. Smith (1986) attributed the lack of significant organic accumulations in the Magdalena River system to high rates of subsidence and sedimentation. A similar mechanism probably suppressed organic accumulation in the Tyler Formation. It is possible, however, that coals are better developed in portions of the Central Montana Trough that were isolated from channel processes. These regions are not thoroughly explored because reservoir potential is minimal.

The width–to–depth ratio for Tyler channel deposits is greater than twice the value calculated for Smith's (1983, 1986) anastomosing channels. The inclusion of splay and levee deposits and multiple channels in the width measurement, coupled with the exclusion of fine–grained abandonment fill from thickness/depth estimates tends to maximize the ratio for Tyler channels. Given the limitations of establishing channel geometries in the subsurface, the relative importance of the width–to–depth ratio to the proposed model is not known.

Basin–Wide Implications of Sedimentology

Given the presence of an anastomosing fluvial system, several conclusions can be drawn regarding depositional conditions in the Central Montana Trough during Tyler time. First, the channel morphology necessitates a low gradient, with rapid continuous vertical aggradation (Smith and Smith, 1980; Smith, 1983). Aggradation can be caused by basin subsidence, rising sea level, or both. Because the basin has been described as a graben or aulocogen (Maughan, 1984), subsidence seems the more likely

mechanism. Eustatic sea level changes also should be considered, however, because of well documented Carboniferous glaciation (Crowell and Frakes, 1972). Second, sediment influx must have kept pace with subsidence in order to maintain an alluvial plain. When sediment influx lagged, lacustrine, estuarine, or marine waters would have inundated the basin (Smith, 1983). Such a scenario probably accounts for deposition of the Bear Gulch Limestone Member. Third, a humid climate is surmised to account for the well–developed wetlands with rare coals. This conclusion is consistent with the paleogeographic reconstruction of Scotese et al. (1979) which places the Central Montana Trough as a northwest–southeast trending tropical basin north of the Carboniferous equator.

SANDSTONE PETROGRAPHY

Twenty–five sandstone samples selected from eight conventional cores were subjected to petrographic and SEM analyses. Samples of both producing and non-producing intervals in the fluvial channel facies were chosen to determine the effects of modal constituents, depositional textures, and diagenetic alterations on potential reservoir lithologies. Shaley sandstones were not deemed potential reservoirs and, consequently, were not sampled.

Detrital Constituents

The samples analyzed are quartzarenites and sublitharenites (Fig. 10); the principle detrital component is monocrystalline quartz, characterized by undulose extinction, vacuoles, and very rare abraded quartz overgrowths. Polycrystalline quartz is a minor constituent. Feldspar grains are extremely rare, accounting for one percent or less of framework grains. Lithic rock fragments typically comprise less than six percent of the framework grains. They include clasts of mudstone, chert, and phosphate (bone fragments?).

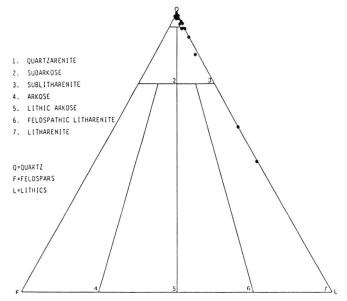

1. QUARTZARENITE
2. SUBARKOSE
3. SUBLITHARENITE
4. ARKOSE
5. LITHIC ARKOSE
6. FELOSPATHIC LITHARENITE
7. LITHARENITE

Q=QUARTZ
F=FELDSPARS
L=LITHICS

Figure 10. Ternary QFL diagram showing modal composition of Tyler Formation sandstones. Analysis is based on 250 points per sample (from Stanton, 1986). Classification scheme from Folk (1974).

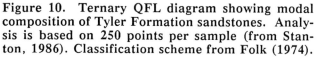

Three samples from the GPE No. 3 BNI well (4,847.1 ft/1,476.4 m, 4,858.0 ft/1,479.7 m, and 4,859.3 ft/1,480.1 m) contain 14 to 53% lithic grains. These samples, derived from conglomeratic channel sands, contain large intraclasts, including mudstone, siltstone, hematitic rock fragments, and phosphate fragments, as well as pieces of carbonized wood.

Detrital heavy minerals occur in trace amounts and include tourmaline and zircon, with very rare sphene, apatite, epidote, rutile, and orthopyroxene. Detrital intergranular matrix includes clay (0 to 13.2%) and carbonaceous material (0 to 4.4%) which typically occur together in flasers and thin laminations, suggesting deposition under slack water conditions.

Textural Features

Tyler sand grains are moderately to very well sorted, rounded to well rounded, and very fine to medium grained (Plate 1A). The largest clasts typically are coarse-grained. Rarely, sandstones are poorly sorted, subrounded to rounded, conglomeratic, and medium to coarse grained.

Compaction of samples has been slight, as indicated by grain-to-grain relationships and abundance of intergranular constituents. Grain contacts are predominantly tangential, with subordinate amounts of long contacts and a few floating grains. Intergranular constituents, including porosity, dead oil, detrital matrix, and cements form a combined modal abundance of 20.8 to 51.6%. The high end of this range indicates extensive grain replacement and/or displacive cementation. Quartz overgrowth cementation, however, commonly has reduced compaction and preserved primary intergranular porosity.

Visual porosity in thin sections ranges from zero to 14.4%, with mean pore diameters of 0.05 to 0.25 mm, and maximum diameters of 0.25 to 2.50 mm. Log porosity is much higher in many wells; values as high as 28% have been recorded. The discrepancy suggests that more-porous sandstones occur in the Tyler Formation than were penetrated in the available cores. Log porosities also include non-effective microporosity in clays, matrix, and partially dissolved grains.

Interparticle pores are the dominant type; their size is approximated by the mean pore diameter. Dissolution pores, typically accounting for less than 10% of the total porosity, are larger and determine the maximum pore diameter. Micropores, including pores smaller than 0.005 mm, occur in all samples in trace amounts, within detrital and authigenic clays and within some partially dissolved grains.

Provenance

Tyler sands likely were derived from a reworked sedimentary source terrane. Evidence to support this interpretation includes the high degree of compositional and textural maturity, rare abraded quartz overgrowths, and a generally stable heavy mineral suite. Non-quartzose detrital grains were derived principally from reworking of underlying Heath strata, or from intraformational shales and siltstones. Feldspathic components in the original sediment were a minor constituent, even after accounting for intrastratal dissolution.

Diagenetic Alterations

Cementation

Tyler sandstones have been cemented by a series of authigenic minerals. Carbonate cements, including calcite (Plate 1B), ferroan calcite, dolomite, and ferroan dolomite (Plate 1B, C) are abundant, typically forming pore-filling crystal mosaics and/or poikilotopic crystals. Siderite occurs in seven samples (principally from the GPE No. 71 Ranch and No. 3 BNI wells) where its morphologies include aggregates of tiny rhombohedra (Plate 1D), spherules (Plate 1E), and nodules.

Gypsum and/or anhydrite occur in most samples and display the same habit, associations, and diagenesis. They form large poikilotopic crystals (Plate 1C), and rarely, polycrystalline pore-filling mosaics. They are discussed as one cement phase, termed anhydrite for convenience, throughout the remainder of the text.

Silicate cements include widespread syntaxial quartz overgrowths (Plate 1D and F), locally abundant pore-filling and grain-replacing chalcedony (Plate 2A), and megaquartz (Plate 2B). Other silicate cements are kaolinite, chlorite, and mixed-layer illite/smectite clays. Kaolinite occurs as pore-filling aggregates of tiny hexagonal crystals which typically are confined to dissolution pores (Plate 2C, D). In two samples (Polumbus No. 1-6 Kincheloe, 4,775.9 ft/1,454.7 m and Marnell Resources No. 1 Marnell Hydra Federal, 1,182.5 ft/360.2 m) kaolinite is common to abundant as a widely distributed pore-filling cement. Chlorite occurs in four samples in identifiable quantities (Petro-Lewis No. 9-18 Shellhammer, 3,953.5 ft/1,204.2 m; Huckaby No. 2-32 Kincheloe, 5,366.5 ft/1,634.6 m; and GPE No. 3 BNI, 4,836.0 ft/1,473.0 m and 4,847.1 ft/1,476.4 m). It forms characteristic grain-perpendicular rims of platy crystals arranged in a "honeycomb" or "cardhouse" morphology (Plates 1F, 2B and E) and has crystallized in voids formed by partial dissolution of mudstone fragments. Elsewhere, traces of clay were identified tentatively as mixed-layer illite/smectite and chlorite, typically associated with dissolution pores and authigenic kaolinite in those pores.

Pyrite occurs in trace to common abundances in most samples as tiny pore-filling crystals, and rarely as spheroids. Hematite is rare to common in two samples (Petro-Lewis No. 9-18 Shellhammer, 3,920.0 ft/1,194.0 m; and GPE No. 3 BNI, 4,859.3 ft/1,480.1 m). Hematite forms pore-filling or grain-coating crystals and, locally, has heavily stained or replaced grains.

Dissolution

Evidence of minor dissolution of detrital components occurs in every sample. Dissolution was limited by the compositional maturity of the sediments; unstable grains presumably have been removed from the system during first-cycle sedimentation and diagenesis. Dissolution pores are associated primarily with relict debris of feldspars. Many of these pores later were filled by authigenic kaolinite and traces of mixed-layer illite/smectite. Shale intraclasts also have undergone some intrastratal dissolution, as well as replacement by (or subsequent reprecipitation of) chloritic clay.

Dissolution of cements has occurred locally and contributed to reservoir potential. Cements that exhibit dissolution textures include anhydrite (GPE No. 3 BNI, 4,836.0 ft/1,473.0 m, Plate 2D and E), ferroan dolomite (Marnell Resources No. 1 Marnell Hydra Federal, 1,182.5 ft/360.2 m, Plate 2C and F) and calcite (Petro–Lewis No. 15–5 Mang, 2,550.5 ft/776.9 m, Plate 1B).

Diagenetic Sequence And Geochemical Implications

The sequence of mineral authigenesis can be subdivided into four stages (Fig. 11) with several variations in Stages I and II. Stages I, II, and III represent successively deeper stages of burial diagenesis, while Stage IV resulted from uplift and flushing by fresh water from the western flank of the basin (Fig. 12).

Stage I, characterized by pyrite and siderite cementation, represents early diagenesis. Bacterial reduction of sulfate and fermentation of organic matter led to reducing, slightly alkaline chemistry with a high activity of bicarbonate. Initial pore fluids derived from the fluvial system probably were fresh. Locally, samples also are cemented by alternating cycles of siderite and pyrite (Plate 1E), siderite and silica (Plate 2A), and silica and chlorite. These occurrences suggest fluctuating water chemistries, possibly due to vadose processes. One sample (Petro–Lewis No. 9–18 Shellhammer, 3,920.2 ft/1,194.1 m) contains a nodule of hematite and dolomite, and may indicate fluctuations in groundwater chemistry.

Stage II diagenesis is characterized by anhydrite and quartz–overgrowth cementation with local precipitation of chlorite and/or dolomite. Cement stratigraphy in anhydrite nodules indicates that anhydrite cementation began first, followed by chlorite and quartz. Eventually, all three cements precipitated simultaneously. The abundance of anhydrite indicates a shift in pore–fluid chemistry to oxidizing, saline wa-

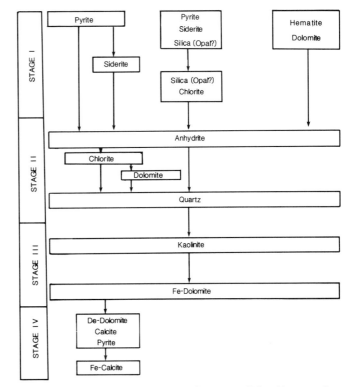

Figure 11. Flow chart showing possible diagenetic sequences affecting Tyler sandstones.

ters. This event probably corresponds to either deposition or erosion of the overlying Alaska Bench Formation.

Stage III diagenesis includes cementation by kaolinite followed by ferroan dolomite, and locally followed by infiltration of oil. This stage is attributed to thermal maturation of adjacent source rocks with the resultant production of organic acids and bicarbonate. Where oil was emplaced, subsequent

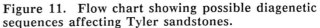

STAGE	CEMENTS	Eh − 0 +	pH 7	TDS 200‰	P_{CO_2} $10^{-3.5}$	CATIONS	ANIONS
I Early Burial Diagenesis	Pyrite Siderite					Fe^{+2}	S^{-2} HCO_3^-
II Sub-unconformity Diagenesis	Anhydrite Chlorite Quartz					Ca^{+2} H^+ Fe^{+2} Mg^{+2}	SO_4^{-2} $H_3SiO_4^-$
III Deep Burial/ Thermal Maturation	Kaolinite Fe-Dolomite					H^+ $Al(OH)_2^+$ Fe^{+2} Mg^{+2}	$H_3SiO_4^-$ HCO_3^- $C_xH_y(CO_2)_z^-$
IV Uplift and Basin Flushing	De-Dolomite Calcite Pyrite					Fe^{+2} Ca^{+2} Mg^{+2}	S^{-2} HCO_3^-

Figure 12. Diagenetic stages affecting Tyler sandstones, with proposed geochemical conditions.

diagenetic alterations typically were inhibited. Dissolution or replacement of anhydrite occurred, at least in part, during Stage III.

Stage IV diagenesis occurs in samples from two wells (Petro–Lewis No. 15–5 Mang and Marnell Resources No. 1 Marnell Hydra Federal) along the western margin of the study area, where the Tyler Formation is quite shallow, less than 2,000 ft (610 m). The stage is characterized by dissolution of ferroan dolomite and precipitation of pyrite, calcite, and ferroan calcite (Plate 2C and E). These alterations are attributed to regional uplift and infiltration of fresh waters from the outcrop belt. Oil which coats Stage IV cements (Petro–Lewis No. 15–5 Mang, 2,550.5 ft/776.9 m, Plate 1B) indicates a secondary oil migration event into some late formed hydrocarbon traps.

RESERVOIR POTENTIAL

Reservoirs in the Tyler Formation are fluvial channel sandstones typically less than one–half mi (0.8 km) wide, with an average thickness of 35 ft (11 m), but ranging to greater than 100 ft (30 m). Most fields are comprised of a complex of narrow channel sandstones which are each a few hundred feet wide, clustered in close lateral and vertical proximity. Channel complexes range from linear to sinuous and have proven difficult to follow in the subsurface.

Facies relationships indicate that Tyler sandstones were deposited as active channel fill in a low gradient, anastomosing fluvial system. The system developed within two large alluvial valleys scoured into the Heath Formation, and later into the Bear Gulch and Lower Tyler members. The combined effects of local topography and basin subsidence controlled stream distribution. Consequently, channel sandstones typically occur in the thickest portions of the Lower and Upper Tyler members.

Effective mesoporosity as determined by point count analyses ranges from zero to 14.4%, but appears to be much higher in logs of many wells. Mesopores have a mean pore diameter of 0.05 to 0.25 mm, and are commonly well interconnected. Moderate to good permeabilities commonly occur wherever mesoporosity is greater than 10%.

The textural and mineralogical maturity of Tyler sandstones has had a positive effect on reservoir quality. Sandstones typically are very well sorted, well rounded, medium–grained quartzarenites. Quartzose framework grains helped minimize compaction and maintained primary porosity. The few non–quartz detrital constituents include shale fragments, feldspar grains, and detrital matrix. Shale pebbles and detrital matrix commonly are concentrated along laminations and flasers, locally reducing porosity and permeability. Dissolution of feldspars and shale fragments contributes a minor amount of porosity to most reservoirs.

Cementation was the primary control on reservoir quality. Pore–filling anhydrite, dolomite, ferroan dolomite, and calcite form non–porous patches. In most samples, these patches are small (a few millimeters in diameter) and surrounded by porous sandstone. In these instances, extraction of fluids is not severely inhibited. Locally, excessive crystal growth has resulted in reservoir destruction.

Silica, siderite, kaolinite, and chlorite cements are less detrimental to reservoir quality. Silica, typically occurring as syntaxial quartz overgrowths, acts to enlarge the effective grain diameters. This has two effects: permeability is reduced due to narrowing of pore throats, and overall compaction is reduced by broadening of grain contacts. Thus, minor quartz overgrowths help to preserve reservoir potential, whereas extensive overgrowth development has severely reduced permeability to fluids. In samples from the GPE No. 3 BNI and No. 71 Ranch wells, pervasive precipitation of silica (originally as opal?) and siderite has severely reduced porosity.

Authigenic clays include kaolinite and chlorite. Kaolinite is present in small amounts in nearly every sample. It typically occurs in grain–dissolution pores and, in that habit, has little effect on reservoir quality. Locally, kaolinite is abundant and has eliminated reservoir potential. Chlorite occurs in several samples as a grain–rimming clay. In these rare instances, it presents the problems of reduced permeability, increased water saturation, and potential formation damage during acid treatments. Based on the samples analyzed, however, chlorite is not widely distributed. Mixed-layer illite/smectite clays were identified in trace amounts in several samples, but are not considered a potential problem.

OIL PRODUCTION

Production was first established from Tyler sandstone reservoirs in 1937 at Big Wall Field, an anticlinal trap in T10N, R26–27E. Approximately 80,000,000 BO have been produced from about 25 Tyler fields (Petroleum Information, 1988). They range in size from unnamed, noncommercial, one-well pools to Sumatra Field (T11N, R31–33E). Sumatra has estimated ultimate reserves of 45,000,000 BO from combination structural–stratigraphic traps in "A", Stensvad, "B", and "C" sandstones. Recoverable reserves from all known Tyler fields combined exceeds 110,000,000 BO. Associated gas is produced in each field, but represents an economically minor product. Several fields have experienced successful secondary and tertiary recovery projects.

Average field size is 3,500,000 BO; eliminating Sumatra reduces this figure to 2,000,000 BO. Over 20% of the fields will produce more than 5,000,000 BO. Almost 50% will yield over 1,000,000 BO. Production–decline curves of many fields reveal rapid declines from initial rates of 100–300 BOPD/well and well lives exceeding 10 years (Fig. 13).

Lower Tyler producing wells have an average ultimate recovery of approximately 150,000 BO. Several wells have produced over 500,000 BO, often due to stacked pays. Average pay thickness and recovery factor are 25–30 ft (8–9 m) and 200 BO/acre-ft, respectively. In 16 Upper and Lower Tyler reservoirs (data from Tonnsen, 1985), porosities and permeabilities Lower Tyler reservoirs cluster in the 12–19% and 50–300 md ranges (Fig. 14). Wide variation in values for Upper Tyler reservoirs may reflect significantly higher clay content in the uppermost sandstones versus the prolific basal Upper Tyler "A" Sandstone.

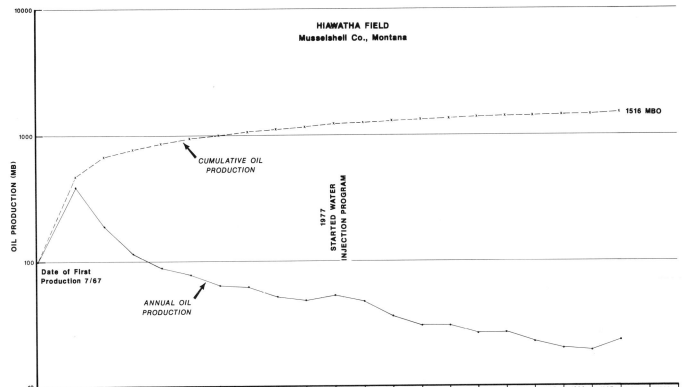

Figure 13. Annual and cumulative oil production curves, Hiawatha Field, Musselshell County, MT.

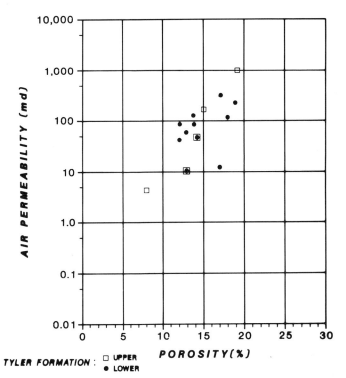

Figure 14. Graph of average reservoir porosity vs. permeability for 16 Tyler Formation fields. Data from Tonnsen (1985).

EXPLORATION CONCEPTS

To maximize the success of Tyler exploration, a program of integrated high resolution seismic stratigraphy and detailed sedimentologic analyses is recommended. Seismic surveys oriented perpendicular to thick isopach trends have been shown to locate channel complexes and reduce certain elements of stratigraphic risk. Oriented cores should be cut in exploratory wells through the entire interval of interest, regardless of reservoir sandstone presence; the interchannel regions contain important lithologic and paleocurrent information. For example, in wells that miss the channel sandstones, paleocurrent directions obtained from levee and crevasse–splay deposits can be used to determine the direction back to the channel. Sandstone/shale ratios and thicknesses of crevasse splays also may indicate relative distance to the channel. Crevasse splays are fan–shaped, and thin both parallel and perpendicular to the channel trend with increased distance from the splay channel. Thus it may require directional information from several wells, or from several splays in a vertical sequence, to pinpoint the direction to the channel.

Paleocurrent data have been used to determine the reservoir trend for drilling successful step–out wells within the channel. Core is preferred to dipmeter logs in order to maximize facies information if the channel is missed. Also, because channel avulsion was a common process, fine–grained abandonment fill locally occurs in channels. Differentiation of overbank from channel abandonment deposits is critical because the former is beyond the confines of the channel while the latter is within it. Locating potential reservoir sandstones from these two environments requires two very different exploration solutions.

Petrographic analyses suggest that diagenesis was controlled by several basin–wide events. With further work to delineate the timing and distribution of cementation stages, the diagenetic model can be used to identify favorable areas for exploration. Three promising avenues of investigation are apparent initially. First, the relationship between anhydrite cementation and the Alaska Bench/Piper unconformity should be investigated. If Stage II diagenesis is due to this unconformity, then patterns of groundwater transportation and paleostructure may distinguish regions of promising reservoir potential from tightly cemented areas. Second, the timing of Stage III diagenesis and primary oil migration should be established and related to paleostructure. If migration into sandstones occurred prior to structural inversion, then the possibility exists for diagenetic trapping mechanisms. Finally, secondary oil migration is indicated by oil staining of Stage IV cements. Stage IV diagenesis has been related to regional uplift with fresh water flushing the formation from the west. Subsequent dissolution of dolomite and calcite has created potential reservoirs.

ACKNOWLEDGMENTS

Generous support of this project by the following companies is gratefully acknowledged: Champlin Petroleum (now Union Pacific Resources), AGAT-GeoChem Consultants, and TOTAL Minatome (and its predecessors, Texas Gas Exploration and CSX Oil and Gas). This paper would not have been possible without the assistance of Theodore R. Walker and Penny Frush. Steve Sturm provided many excellent suggestions in his technical review.

REFERENCES

Carlson, K.P., 1967, South Keg Coulee Field, Musselshell County, Montana: Mtn. Geol., v. 4, p. 91-94.

Chuman, D., 1956, Melstone Oil Field: *in* Judith Mountains – Central Montana: 7th Ann. Field Conf. Guidebook, BGS, p. 110-112.

Collinson, J.D., 1970, Bedforms of the Tana River, Norway: Geogr. Annaler, v. 52A, p. 31-55.

Cooper, G.G., 1956, The Tyler Formation and basement faulting: BGS Guidebook No. 7, p. 82-85.

Crowell, J.C. and L.A. Frakes, 1972, Late Paleozoic glaciation: V, Karroo Basin, South Africa: GSA Bull., v. 83, p. 2887-2912.

Fanshawe, J.R., 1978, Central Montana tectonics and the Tyler Formation, *in* The Economic Geology of the Williston Basin, Montana, North Dakota, South Dakota, Saskatchewan, Manitoba: 24th Ann. Conf., Williston Basin Symp., MGS, p. 239-248.

Foster, D.I., 1956, N.W. Sumatra field (Montana): *in* Judith Mountains – Central Montana: 7th Ann. Field Conf. Guidebook, BGS, p. 116-123.

Freedom Resources, 1982, Central Montana Tyler Study, unpubl. proprietary report.

Freeman, O.W., 1922, Oil in the Quadrant Formation of east-central Montana: Engineering and Mining Jour., v. 113, p. 825-827.

Friend, P.F., 1983, Towards the field classification of alluvial architecture or sequence: Spec. Pub. IAS, v. 6, p. 345-354.

Gardner, L.S., 1959, Revision of Big Snowy Group in central Montana: AAPG Bull., v. 43, p. 329-349.

Harris, W.L., 1972, Upper Mississippian and Pennsylvanian sediments of central Montana: unpub. PhD thesis, Univ. of MT, Missoula, Montana, 252 p.

Horner, J.R., 1985, Stratigraphic position of the Bear Gulch Limestone (lower Carboniferous) of central Montana: International Congress on Carboniferous Stratigraphy and Geology, v. 9, n. 5, p. 427-436.

Jopling A.V., 1965, Hydraulic factors controlling the shape of laminae in laboratory deltas: JSP, v. 35, p. 777-791.

Krantzler, I., 1966, Origin of oil in lower member of Tyler Formation: AAPG Bull., v. 50, p. 2245-2259.

Maughan, E.K. 1984, Paleogeographic setting of Pennsylvanian Tyler Formation and relation to underlying Mississippian rocks in Montana and North Dakota: AAPG Bull., v. 68, p. 178-195.

Maughan, E.K., and A.E. Roberts, 1967, Big Snowy and Amsden Groups and the Mississippian–Pennsylvanian boundary in Montana: USGS Prof. Pap. 554-B, p. 27.

McDade, L.B., and J. Starkweather, 1969, Kelley Field: *in* 20th Ann. Conf., Eastern Montana Symp.: MGS, p. 153-158.

Miall, A.D., 1981, Analysis of fluvial depositional systems: AAPG Education Course Note Series 20, p. 75.

Miall, A.D., 1985, Architectural-element analysis: a new method of facies analysis applied to fluvial deposits: *in* R.M. Flores, ed., Recognition of Fluvial Depositional Systems and their Reservoir Potential, SEPM Short Course Notes No. 19., p. 33-81.

Mundt, P.A., 1956a, Heath-Amsden strata in central Montana: AAPG Bull., v. 40. p. 1915-1934.

Mundt, P.A., 1956b, The Tyler and Alaska Bench Formations, *in* Judith Mountains – Central Montana: 7th Ann. Field Conf. Guidebook, BGS, p. 46-51.

Nobel, R.A., 1984, Depositional environments and petrology of the Tyler Formation in central Montana: unpub. MS thesis, MT College of Mineral Science and Technology, Butte, Montana, 99 p.

Norton, G.H., 1956, Evidences of unconformity in rocks of Carboniferous age in central Montana: 7th Ann. Field Conf. Guidebook, BGS, p. 52-66.

Poole, L.E. and J. Starkweather, 1969, Hiawatha Field, Musselshell County, Montana, in 20th Ann. Conf., Eastern Montana Symposium: MGS, p. 145-150.

Scotese, C.R., R.K. Bambach, C. Baron, R. van der Voo, and A.M. Ziegler, 1979, Paleozoic base maps: Jour. Geol., v. 87, p. 217-277.

Scott, H.W., 1935, Some Carboniferous stratigraphy in Montana and northwestern Wyoming: Jour. Geol., v. 43, p. 1011-1032.

Silverman, M.R., 1985, Breed Creek Field, *in* J.J. Tonnsen, ed., 1985, Montana Oil and Gas Fields Symposium, MGS, p. 281-284.

Smith, D.G., 1983, Anastomosed fluvial deposits; modern examples from Western Canada, *in* J.D. Collinson and J. Lewin, eds., Modern and Ancient Fluvial Systems, IAS Spec. Pub. 6, p. 155-168.

Smith, D.G., 1986, Anastomosing river deposits, sedimentation rates and basin subsidence, Magdalena river, northwestern Columbia, South America: Sed. Geol., v. 46, p. 177-196.

Smith, D.G. and N.D. Smith, 1980, Sedimentation in anastomosed river systems: examples from alluvial valleys near Banff, Alberta: JSP, v. 50, p. 157-164.

Staggs, J.O., 1959, Stensvad Field, in Sawtooth-Disturbed Belt: 10th Ann. Field Conf. Guidebook, BGS, p. 124-128.

Stanton, P.T., 1986, Sedimentology, diagenesis and reservoir potential of the Pennsylvanian Tyler Formation, central Montana: unpub. MS thesis, Univ. of CO, Boulder, CO, 158 p.

Todd, D.F., 1959, The lower Tyler of central Montana, *in* Sawtooth-Disturbed Belt: 10th Ann. Field Conf. Guidebook, BGS, p. 69-74.

Tonnsen, J.J., ed., 1985, Montana Oil and Gas Fields Symposium, MGS, 1,202 p.

Varland, R.O., 1956, Big Wall Field, in Judith Mountains – Central Montana: 7th Ann. Field Conf. Guidebook, BGS, p. 113-115.

Williams, L.A., 1981, The sedimentational history of the Bear Gulch Limestone (middle Carboniferous), central Montana: unpub. PhD thesis, Princeton Univ., Princeton, NJ, 251 p.

Willis, R.P., 1959, Upper Mississippian-Lower Pennsylvanian stratigraphy of central Montana and Williston basin: AAPG Bull., v. 43, p. 1940-1966.

Wilson, M.D. and E.D. Pittman, 1977, Authigenic clays in sandstones: recognition and influence on reservoir properties and paleoenvironmental analysis: JSP, v. 47, p. 3-31.

Petrologic Character of a Morrowan Sandstone Reservoir, Lexington Field, Clark County, Kansas[1]

MARTIN EMERY[2]
PETER G. SUTTERLIN[3]

[1]Received August 15, 1988; Revised March 15, 1989
[2]Maxus Exploration Company
[3]Wichita State University

Lexington Field is located in the Hugoton Embayment of the Anadarko Basin, Clark County, Kansas. The primary reservoir for hydrocarbons at Lexington Field is a Lower Pennsylvanian Morrow-age sandstone, termed the Morrowan "A" sandstone for operational purposes. Morrowan "A" sandstones are glauconitic, pyritic quartz arenites to conglomeratic litharenites. Sedimentary rock fragments are a major component of the framework grains in conglomeratic units. Authigenic minerals include syntaxial quartz, calcite, ankerite (all as cements), kaolinite, illite, and mixed layer illite/smectite. The sandstone ranges from fine to coarse-grained and is well to poorly sorted.

The Morrowan "A" sandstone formed by aggradation in an estuary on a mesotidal coast. This occurred during a regressive or stillstand subcycle of the overall transgression that flooded the Mississippian strata during the Early Pennsylvanian. Four subfacies are present in the sandstone body: supratidal, intertidal, channel-bank, and tidal-channel.

The supratidal subfacies is predominantly shale with minor sandstone lenses and contains lenticular bedding, flame structures, load casts, boudins, and numerous heterogeneities that render the rocks impermeable and uneconomic as an oil reservoir. Only minor porosity is observed in the conglomeratic, poorly sorted tidal-channel subfacies, which is cemented extensively with poikilotopic calcite. The intertidal and channel-bank subfacies are the primary reservoir rock. Both contain reduced primary intergranular and dissolution (of carbonate cement) porosity. Pyritic shale laminae and thin, dessicated shale beds are present in the intertidal subfacies; the channel bank subfacies exhibits cross-stratification.

The petrologic character of the Morrowan "A" sandstone suggests that approximately 50% of the original oil-in-place (or 3,400,000 BO) ultimately will be produced. Cumulative production is 2,440,000 BO and 4.2 BCFG since discovery in 1978; gross ultimate recovery estimated from production decline curves is 3,3500,000 BO and 4.2 BCFG, in close agreement with the petrologic assessment.

INTRODUCTION

Lexington Field is located in northeastern Clark County, Kansas (Fig. 1), in the Hugoton Embayment of the Anadarko Basin. The discovery well (No. 1-19 Seacat, SW SE Sec 19 T31S R21W), drilled and completed by Mesa Petroleum Co. in 1977, initially produced 94 BOPD and 603 MCFGPD from porous, oolitic limestone of the Mississippian St. Louis Formation. In December of 1978, Mesa established production from a Pennsylvanian Morrowan sandstone in the No. 1-20 Moore well (SW SW Sec 20 T31S R21W) while attempting to extend Mississippian pro-

duction. The No. 1-20 Moore well initially flowed 984 BOPD and 374 MCFGPD (Paul and others, 1980). Following discovery of the Morrow reservoir, interest in the marginally economic Mississippian reservoir diminished, although 13 wells ultimately were completed in the St. Louis Limestone. Cumulative production from both reservoirs is 2,770,000 BO and 5.6 BCFG as of September, 1987.

This study reports the depositional history, petrography, and diagenetic history of the Morrowan sandstone reservoir of Lexington Field. Portions of this paper were published previously (Emery and Sutterlin, 1986). Data available include Morrow cores from

FIELD DATA:	Lexington Field
Producing Interval:	Morrowan "A" sandstone
Geographic Location:	Clark County, Kansas
Present Tectonic Setting:	Hugoton Embayment of the Anadarko Basin
Depositional Setting:	Tansgressive shoreline
Age of Reservoir:	Lower Pennsylvanian (Morrowan)
Lithology of Reservoir:	Glauconitic quartz arenite or cherty litharenite
Depositional Environment:	Estuary, mesotidal coast
Diagenesis:	Quartz cementation, carbonate cementation, dissolution of carbonate cement, kaolinization, pyritization
Porosity Types:	Intergranular, dissolution, minor intercrystalline
Porosity:	Maximum 27%, average 15%
Permeability:	Maximum 2,000+ md, average 275 md
Fractures:	Limited healed vertical fracturing
Nature of Trap:	Facies stratigraphic
Entrapping Facies:	Surrounding Morrow Shale
Source Rock:	Morrow Shale, Lower Pennsylvanian
Timing of Migration:	Late Pennsylvanian, early Permian
Discovered:	1977
Reservoir Depth:	Average 5,130 ft (1,683 m)
Reservoir Thickness:	8–37 ft (3–12 m)
IP (discovery well):	984 BOPD flowing
Areal Extent:	Approximately 1,000 acres (405 ha)
Cumulative Production (9/87):	2,770,000 BO and 5.6 BCFG
Estimated Oil in Place:	6,800,000 BO
Approximate Ultimate Recovery:	3,350,000 BO
Oil Gravity:	39.8° API
Minimum Water Saturation:	15%

five of the field wells and suites of geophysical well logs from 62 wells in and around Lexington Field. An understanding of the geology might be utilized to ascertain internal heterogeneities of the Morrowan sandstone and serve as a model for similar reservoirs in the region.

STRATIGRAPHY

The stratigraphic interval of interest in the Lexington Field area includes, in descending order, rocks of the Pennsylvanian Desmoinesian and Morrowan stages, and the Mississippian Meramecian stage (Fig. 2). The productive Morrow sandstone at Lexington Field, termed the "A" sandstone (an operational unit), is positioned between the Mississippian St. Louis Limestone (atop which a regional unconformity exists) and the Pennsylvanian Desmoinesian Krebs Formation. The thin limestone beds and intercalating radioactive shales which are characteristic of Atokan rocks to the south are absent in this portion of the Hugoton Embayment. The shale atop the Morrow sandstone may be Atokan (Emery and Sutterlin, 1986).

Upper Mississippian Series

The uppermost Mississippian strata encountered in wells at Lexington Field are Meramecian limestones of the St. Louis Formation. The uppermost boundary of the Mississippian strata is a regional unconformity that

developed prior to transgression of the early Pennsylvanian seas. Chesterian rocks were removed by pre-Pennsylvanian erosion.

Rocks of the St. Louis range from sublithographic limestones to porous calcarenites. Hydrocarbons are produced from the St. Louis Limestone where structural attitude is favorable and porosity is developed. The thickness of the St. Louis limestone exceeds 200 ft (67 m) in the deeper portions of the Hugoton Embayment (Zeller, 1968).

Lower Pennsylvanian Series

Morrowan rocks occupy the interval from the base of the Inola Limestone Member of the Krebs Formation down to the Mississippian unconformity. The Morrow interval ranges in thickness from 4 ft (1 m) to approximately 140 ft (47 m), conforming to the paleotopography developed on the Mississippian surface. Morrowan strata include pale–green to black, fissile shale and light–yellowish brown to light olive–gray, calcareous, medium to fine–grained quartz arenites. Thin siltstones, conglomeratic sandstones, and thin coal laminae also were observed in cores.

Cherokee rocks are alternating beds of limestone and shale (Zeller, 1968). The beds display uniform thickness across the area, in contrast to the variable Morrowan rocks. The Cabaniss and Krebs formations of the Cherokee Group are approximately 100 ft (33 m) thick.

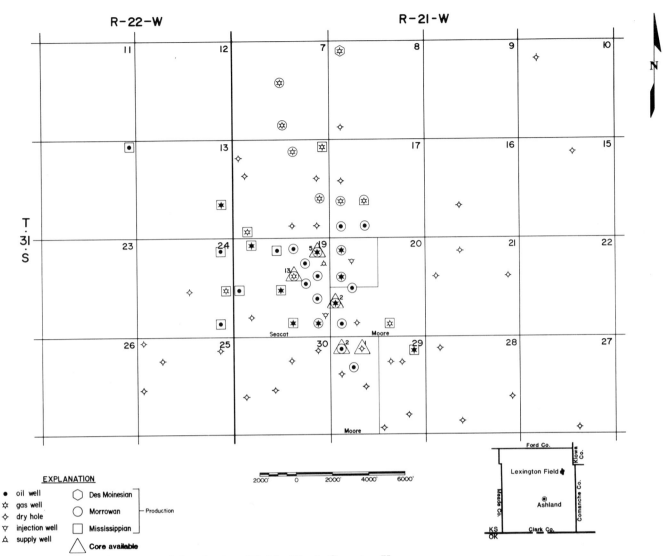

Figure 1. Location map of Lexington Field, Clark County, Kansas.

STRUCTURAL SETTING

The Anadarko Basin is an asymmetrical basin, the structural axis being situated parallel and adjacent to the Amarillo–Wichita Uplift, a feature that became positive during late Mississippian time. Bounding positive features of the Anadarko Basin during early Pennsylvanian time were the Amarillo–Wichita Mountain Front to the south, the Central Kansas Uplift to the north, the Cimarron–Sierra Grande Uplift to the west, and the Ozark Dome to the east (Fig. 3). Lexington Field is positioned on a broad, northwestern shelf that was transgressed by an epeiric sea during the Pennsylvanian, following a period of regional uplift and erosion near the close of Mississippian time (Moore, 1979).

Present regional dip in the Lexington area (Fig. 4), mapped on the base of the Inola Limestone, is about to the south, or basinward. Gently plunging synclinal and anticlinal features oriented approximately north–south are the most prominent disruptions in the local structure. Morrow sandstone production is related to a south-trending synclinal feature. The approximate

elevation of the original water–oil contact in the Morrowan A sandstone is −3065 ft. (−935 m).

LITHOFACIES AND DEPOSITIONAL ENVIRONMENTS

Early Pennsylvanian clastic sedimentation filled paleotopographic "lows" on the Mississippian surface during an overall transgressive cycle. Minor stillstands or regressions during the transgressive sequence allowed the aggradation of coarser clastic material which was at least partially preserved with renewed transgression and subsidence. The thickness of Morrow rocks (base of the Inola Limestone to the top of the Mississippian St. Louis Limestone) at Lexington Field reflects the pre–Morrow paleotopographic depression (Fig. 5).

The model that most closely reproduces the vertical sequence observed in Morrowan "A" sandstone cores is that of a migrating, sandy tidal channel in a valley-filling estuarine environment (Clifton, 1982) (Fig. 6). The model sequence consists of a basal, shell-bearing lag deposit overlain by either bidirec-

System	Series	Stage	Group	
PERMIAN	Lower	Leonardian	Nippewalla	
			Sumner	
		Wolfcampian	Chase	
			Admire	
			Council Grove	
PENNSYLVANIAN	Upper	Virgilian	Waubansee	
			Shawnee	
			Douglas	
		Missourian	Pedee	
			Lansing–Kansas City	
			Pleasanton	
	Lower	Des Moinesian	Marmaton	
			Cherokee	Cabaniss
				Krebs
				Inola Limestone Member ✿
		Morrowan		Morrow Sandstone ✳
MISSISSIPPIAN	Upper	Meramacian		St. Louis Limestone ✳
	Lower	Osagean		
		Kinderhookian		
ORDOVICIAN	Middle			Viola Limestone
	Lower	Simpson		
		Arbuckle		
CAMBRIAN	Upper			
				Reagan Sandstone
PRE-CAMBRIAN				Igneous Basement

Figure 2. Generalized stratigraphic column for northeastern Clark County.

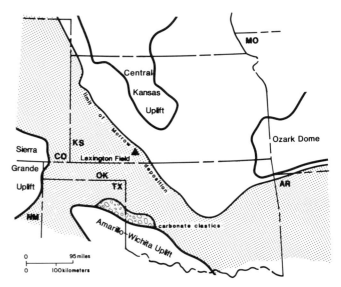

Figure 3. Early Pennsylvanian topography in the Mid–Continent U.S., with limits of Morrow deposition (after Rascoe and Adler, 1983).

tional crossbedded or ripple–bedded sandstone, depending on the magnitude of tidal variation. Structureless, burrowed intertidal deposits, grading upward into mudflat sediments, top the sequence.

The interpreted depositional environment for the Morrowan "A" sandstone is an estuary on a mesotidal coast. The geometry of the deposit is consistent with this interpretation (Figs. 7 and 8). The estuary was filled with sand possibly derived from the Central Kansas Uplift and was confined by Mississippian topography.

The vertical sequence in lithofacies in the Morrowan "A" is similar to the model sequence of Clifton. At the bottom of the sequence are conglomeratic tidal–channel sandstones having a reactivation surface at the base, and exhibiting horizontal–planar, undulatory, with lesser low angle cross–stratification,

lenticular bedding, convolute stratification, and load casts (Fig. 9). This glauconitic and pyritic sublitharenite is extensively cemented with carbonate, and contains fossil clasts and fragments of limestone, chert, and clay. Healed vertical fracturing is present. These deposits are structureless or horizontally laminated.

Overlying these deposits are quartz sandstones that form the reservoir for hydrocarbons. These are believed to have been laid down as intertidal bars and deposits at channel banks. The intertidal deposits are thin bedded, fine upward, and contain desiccation and reactivation surfaces. Low–angle (less than 15°) cross–stratification, trough cross–stratification, and planar and wavy horizontal bedding are present (Fig. 10). Structureless beds suggesting tidal–flat deposition (alternating suspension and bedload transportation) were noted. The sandstone generally qualifies as a quartz arenite and is glauconitic, pyritic, and weakly to moderately cemented with interparticulate carbonate and syntaxial silica.

The channel–bank subfacies contains low angle cross–stratification, possibly a remnant of tidal action. Horizontal–planar to undulatory sedimentary structures are present. Trough crossbedding is the result of tidal fluctuation along the flood ramps and in ebb channels (Fig. 11). The deepest portion of the estuarine inlet probably was dominated by ebb currents which oriented sediment in seaward–directed sand waves that were partially modified by flood tides, thus forming reactivation surfaces (Galloway and Hobday, 1983).

Overlying these rocks are supratidal deposits displaying interbedded shale, sandstone, and siltstone laminae; some shale laminae are mudcracked. Flame structures, load casts, and boudins indicate unequal loading and compaction between the various lithologies.

Atop the Morrowan "A" sandstone is dark–gray, fissile shale that represents sedimentation under condi-

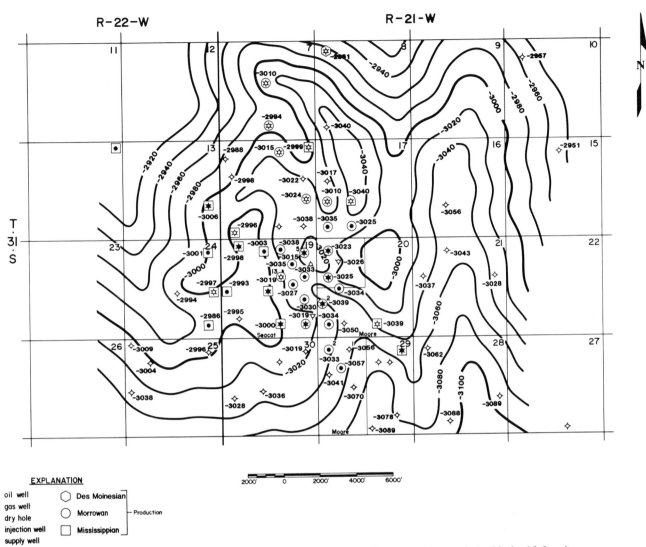

EXPLANATION

- oil well
- ☆ gas well
- ◇ dry hole
- ▽ injection well
- △ supply well

⬡ Des Moinesian
◯ Morrowan — Production
▢ Mississippian

Figure 4. Structural contour map of top of Morrow Shale. Contour interval is 20 ft (6.0 m).

tions of renewed transgression. The shale forms a top seal and probably was the source for hydrocarbons basinward.

PETROGRAPHY AND DIAGENESIS

Mineral percentages were determined by analysis of thin sections (Table 1). Sandstones range from quartz arenite to litharenite (Folk, 1974). Quartz dominates the framework grains in all but the conglomeratic subfacies, with 98% of quartz grains being monocrystalline. Other framework grains include feldspars; sedimentary rock fragments (including chert, shale, and limestone clasts); glauconite; and heavy minerals (Plate 1A). The authigenic minerals of the sandstone include: ankerite and calcite cements, syntaxial and chalcedonic silica cement, authigenic clays (kaolinite, illite, and mixed layer groups) (Robinson, 1983), pyrite, and insoluble material along stylolitic surfaces.

Cements and Clays

The Morrowan "A" sandstone exhibits subangular to well-rounded grains (Table 2) that range from

poorly to well sorted. Overall, grain–size distributions are symmetrical to positively skewed, and meso– to leptokurtic. The sandstone qualifies as submature to mature (Folk, 1974).

Silica cement occurs as syntaxial overgrowths on framework grains, and as "meniscus" cement (Scholle, 1979). The presence of syntaxial overgrowths is indicated by anhedral and euhedral quartz grains and underlying dust rims adjacent to the host framework grains (Plate 1B). Chalcedonic quartz cement was observed in trace amounts in sample 5–198.

Incomplete to almost total poikilotopic carbonate cement occurs in the Morrowan "A" sandstone. X-ray diffraction (XRD) analysis indicates that both calcite and ankerite are present. Ankerite ranges from approximately 20% to in excess of 80% of carbonate cement (Plate 1C). Poikilotopic carbonate cements probably were derived from Mississippian carbonates and from syndepositional shell debris. Subsequent leaching of carbonate cements enhanced porosity (Fig. 12).

Authigenic kaolinite is the dominant clay mineral in the Morrowan "A" sandstone, as determined by

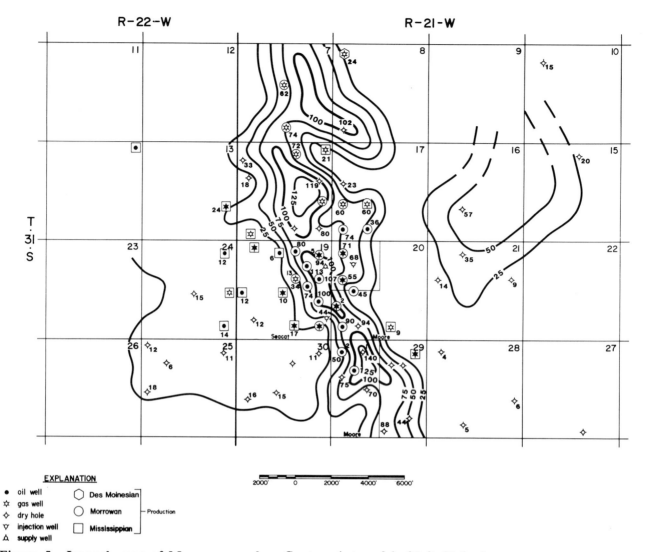

Figure 5. Isopach map of Morrowan rocks. Contour interval is 25 ft (7.6 m).

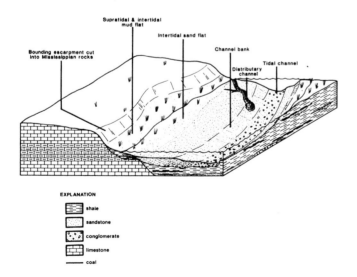

Figure 6. Estuarine depositional environment of Morrowan "A" sandstone; base of block diagram represents approximately 2 mi (3.2 km)

XRD and scanning electron microscopy (SEM) analyses. Authigenic, vermicular kaolinite lines pores (Fig. 13). Robinson (1983) performed a detailed analysis of the clay mineralogy of the Morrowan "A" sandstone and encasing shale, and identified authigenic illite, minor mixed layer illite/smectite, and trace amounts of chlorite. Overall, authigenic clay minerals comprise less than 2% of sandstones.

Replacement and Deformation Fabrics

Authigenic pyrite occurs in discontinuous masses generally less than 1 mm in diameter, as a replacement mineral completely occluding pore space. Pyritohedrons and amorphous pyrite replace carbonate cement and glauconite globules.

A fabric interpreted to reflect burial compaction was noted in Morrowan "A" sandstones. Strain shadows, Boehm lamellae, and concavo-convex grain contacts contribute to this compaction–deformation fabric (Scholle, 1979). Stylolites also were noted. Quartz grains exhibit abrupt truncation along stylolitic surfaces. Proximal to the stylolites, the sandstone is cemented primarily by silica interpreted to have been

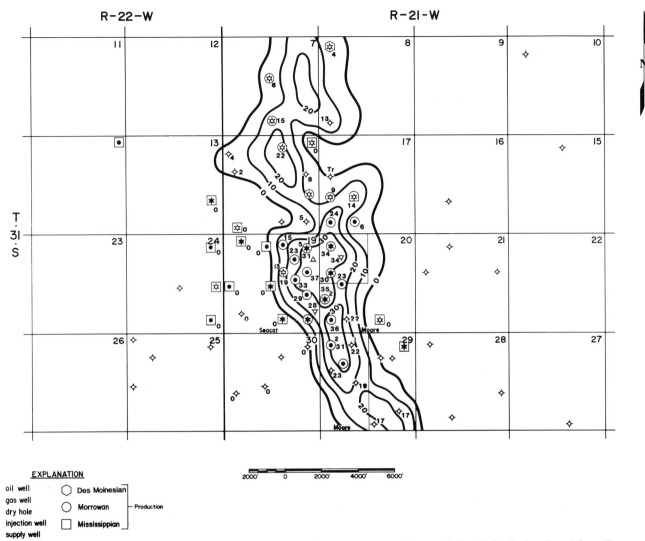

Figure 7. Gross thickness of Morrowan "A" sandstone. Contour interval is 10 ft (3.0 m). After Emery and Sutterlin (1986).

released by pressure solution of quartz along the stylolitic contact (Scholle, 1979).

Diagenetic History

The diagenetic history of the Morrowan "A" sandstone involves multiple episodes of cementation, followed by kaolinization and pyritization in conjunction with dissolution of carbonate cement (Robinson, 1983). Early minor grain–coating clays seemingly were deposited, as evidenced by dust rims underlying silica and carbonate cements. Next, compaction resulted in pressure solution of silica and development of deformation fabric and concavo–convex quartz grain contacts. Subsequent precipitation of carbonate cement was episodic. Complete pore occlusion by carbonate cement occurs where the sandstone is proximal to the Mississippian unconformity, suggesting an exchange of pore waters between the two formations.

Dissolution of carbonate cement allowed kaolinization in the resultant moldic porosity, and may have coincided with the dewatering of encasing shales and

the associated carbon dioxide front. Pyrite has replaced both silica and carbonate cements, suggesting pyritization was the latest diagenetic event (Robinson, 1983).

Petrographic Differences Between Subfacies

No thin sections were prepared from samples of the supratidal subfacies; petrologic attributes were ascertained by macroscopic examination of the core. The subfacies contains clay–sized particles to fine sand grains. Sandstone lenses are moderately well sorted and contain subangular to well–rounded grains. Some fining–upward, small scale (1–10 cm) bedding also is present. Silica is the principle cementing agent. The supratidal subfacies lacks sufficient porosity and permeability to be an economic reservoir.

Intertidal deposits contain fewer shale laminae than do supratidal rocks. Ankerite is the predominant carbonate cement. Quartz cement occurs as syntaxial overgrowths and "meniscus" grain contacts. Concavo–convex and sutured quartz-grain contacts suggest that compaction deformation preceded carbonate in-

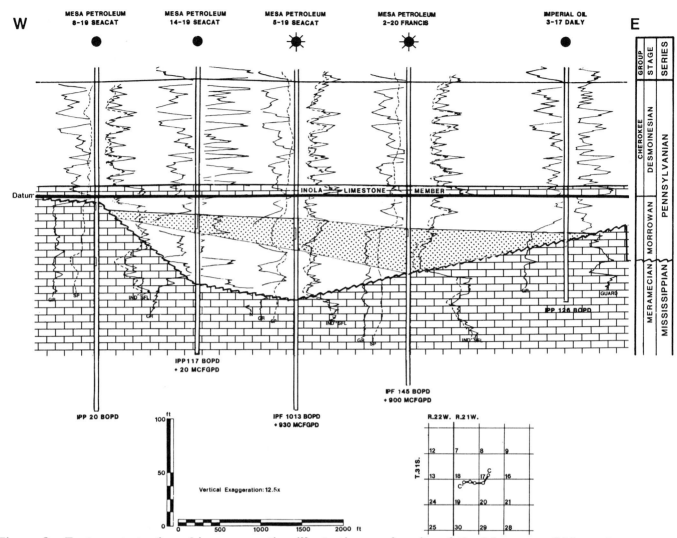

Figure 8. East–west stratigraphic cross–section illustrating conformity of the Morrowan "A" sandstone to the paleotopographic low.

duration. Intertidal sandstones are medium to fine grained and moderately to well sorted, with subangular to round, and spherical to elongate grains. Slight alignment of grains parallel to bedding was observed in vertically oriented thin sections. Intertidal sandstones contain reduced primary intergranular porosity and secondary porosity. Secondary pores include intercrystalline, oversize, and pores resulting from dissolution of carbonate cement (Schmidt, McDonald, and Platt, 1977). Secondary porosity accounts for approximately 25% of total pore volume in this subfacies (Plate 1D). Authigenic clay minerals occlude pore space and constrict pore throats, creating microporosity which can be important in well–log evaluation. Pyritic laminae, perhaps remnants of heavy mineral deflation surfaces, are common and cut transverse to core samples; they may present a barrier to fluid flow.

Ankerite is the dominant cement in channel-bank sandstones, in conjunction with syntaxial quartz overgrowths and "meniscus" grain contacts. Channel-bank sandstones are moderately to well sorted. Me-

dium-sized grains are equant and elongate, and subround to round. Secondary and reduced primary intergranular porosity were observed in channel-bank sandstones, pore networks being similar to those in the intertidal subfacies, but with fewer shale and pyritic laminae disruptions (Plate 1E). Minor amounts of secondary intercrystalline porosity (authigenic kaolinite) were observed. The pore network is relatively free of occluding authigenic cements and clay minerals (Fig. 14). Channel-bank sandstones are poor in detrital clay, probably a reflection of the winnowing effect of the tidal currents active in the estuary.

The conglomeratic tidal channel subfacies is indurated extensively with poikilotopic calcite cement. Limestone, shale, and chert clasts comprise approximately 7% of the framework grains. Stylolites are present, as are glauconite, shell debris, and laminae of pyritic shale. Grain orientation parallel to bedding occurs throughout tidal–channel sandstones. The sandstone is poorly sorted and framework grains are well-rounded to subangular. Framework grains range

Figure 9. Core of conglomeratic tidal-channel subfacies, showing horizontal laminae and lenticular bedding alignment of coarse grains and clasts.

Figure 11. Core of channel-bank subfacies. Note low angle cross-stratification and reactivation surface.

from silt to cobble sized. Poikilotopic carbonate cement has obliterated the primary, intergranular porosity. Minor secondary (moldic) porosity is related to dissolution of carbonate cements. Minor shrinkage porosity adjacent to shale clasts is exhibited (Plate 1F).

RESERVE ANALYSIS

Volumetric analyses indicate 6,800,000 STB of original OIP in the Morrowan "A" reservoir. Estimated ultimate recovery from the Morrowan "A" sandstone is 3,350,000 BO and 4.2 BCFG. Most of the hydrocarbons will be produced from the intertidal and channel bank subfacies; they have the greatest porosity and permeability (Fig. 15). These subfacies also display the least heterogeneity in the form of sedimentary disruptions which could impede fluid transmissibility.

Flow units (Hearn and others, 1984) are reservoir units that display similar bedding characteristics, stratigraphic position, porosity, and permeability. Flow units are generally similar and are in flow communication, but are not necessarily homogeneous. The intertidal and channel-bank facies probably behave as one flow unit, even though the subfacies do not necessarily form flow units because of varying degrees of diagenesis, different structural positions, variations in texture, etc.

Wardlaw and Cassan (1978) suggest that certain features of pore networks govern recovery efficiency: 1) pore-to-throat size ratio ("aspect ratio"), 2) throat-to-pore coordination number (or, roughly, the number of pore throats per pore), 3) non-random

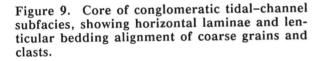

Figure 10. Core of intertidal subfacies. Note horizontal laminae and thin-bedded, dessicated siltstone (D).

Table 1A: Point-count mineral percentages (whole rock) of framework grains in thin-section samples. Subfacies (SF) include intertidal (In), channel bank (CB), and tidal channel (TC).

Sample			SF	FRAMEWORK							
				Qtz		Fld	Cht	Gla	Rk Frag		Hy
				M	P				SH	LS	
5-191	H	5231.8	In	50.0	3.1	0.4	2.7				Tr
5-192	H	5234.6	In	63.8	1.1		0.4	0.7			Tr
5-193	V	5234.6	In	64.0	2.6	Tr	0.3	0.8			Tr
5-194	H	5241.4	In	59.9	0.3	0.3	0.8	0.3			
5-195	H	5244.6	CB	61.7	0.3	Tr	0.8	0.5			Tr
5-196	V	5244.6	CB	65.5	0.2		0.5	0.5			Tr
5-197	V	5254.1	CB	48.3	0.7	0.2	Tr	0.2			Tr
5-198	V	5260.5	In	64.8	0.7	0.2	0.7	1.0			.2
13-192	H	5193.8	In	66.0	0.8	Tr	0.8	1.7		0.3	Tr
13-193	H	5196.1	CB	73.2	0.5		0.7	0.5			Tr
13-194	V	5196.1	CB	78.3	0.2		0.5	0.2			Tr
13-195	V	5200.5	CB	66.6	0.9	0.5	0.2	Tr	0.5		Tr
13-196	H	5205.1	CB	59.8	0.3		1.1	0.3	1.4		Tr
13-197	V	5205.1	CB	55.6	0.4		0.4	0.2	Tr		Tr
13-198	V	5208.4	TC	52.1	2.3	0.2	2.3	1.7	8.0	1.2	Tr
2-201	V	5158.2	In	65.3		Tr	1.3	0.8			Tr
2-202	H	5162.5	In	63.6	0.2	Tr	0.5	1.0			Tr
2-203	V	5162.5	In	68.9	0.4		0.9	0.2			Tr
2-204	H	5165.6	In	63.0	0.9	0.3		1.7	Tr		Tr
2-206	V	5168.5	CB	60.4	2.2		1.8	Tr			Tr
2-207	H	5175.0	CB	70.5	1.4		0.7	0.3	1.4		
2-209	H	5179.8	CB	62.9	1.4	0.7	0.5	0.7	0.2		Tr
2-2010	H	5184.3	CB	60.4	1.2	0.4	0.8	Tr			
2-2011	V	5192.7	TC	60.9	2.7	0.2	3.9	0.2			Tr
1-291	V	5228.2	TC	47.4	6.1	Tr	3.4	Tr	2.1	0.8	Tr
2-291	H	5126.7	In	58.1	1.1		0.7	1.1	0.9		Tr
2-292	H	5130.6	In	63.8	4.0		1.4	0.7			
2-293	V	5130.6	In	68.9	0.9		0.6	0.3			Tr
2-294	H	5137.8	In	58.4	0.8		1.6		0.3	0.5	Tr
2-295	H	5142.7	CB	66.3	2.0	0.3	0.3	0.7			Tr
2-296	V	5142.7	CB	67.5	1.3		0.8	0.3		0.3	Tr
2-297	V	5146.2	CB	64.3	1.0	Tr	1.3	0.5		0.2	Tr

M = monocrystalline quartz
P = polycrystalline quartz
Fld = feldspar
Cht = chert
Gla = glauconite
SH = shale clast
LS = limestone clast
Hy = heavy minerals

Sample Nomenclature Explanation

A-BBC D EEEE.E
A = well number
BB = section number
(T31S-R21W)
    Sec. 19 = Seacat
    Sec. 20, 29 = Moore
C = sample number
D = orientation   V = vertical
H = horizontal   EEEE.E = depth

Table 1B. Point–count mineral percentages (whole rock) of authigenic minerals in thin–section samples, with key petrophysical parameters. Subfacies and samples same as in Table 1A.

Sample			SF	AUTHIGENIC				Oth	Por	P:T	
				Carb	Si	Cl	Pyr				
5–191	H	5231.8	In	16.3	7.1	Tr	1.3		19.0	4.958	
5–192	H	5234.6	In	3.1	1.8	1.6	3.1		24.5	3.629	
5–193	V	5234.6	In	4.0	2.0	0.6	0.8		24.9	3.928	
5–194	H	5241.4	In	8.7	2.1	0.3			27.4	4.090	
5–195	H	5244.6	CB	8.0	3.1	0.3	Tr		25.4	3.350	
5–196	V	5244.6	CB	5.3	3.4	0.5	0.2		24.0	2.780	
5–197	V	5254.1	CB	20.3	2.4	Tr	3.5		24.4	2.722	*
5–198	V	5260.5	In	0.5	8.6	6.0	0.5	1.0	15.8	2.556	
13–192	H	5193.8	In	5.0	2.2	1.9	0.6	Tr	20.6	3.936	
13–193	H	5196.1	CB	4.9	2.0	0.7	0.2		17.3	3.263	
13–194	V	5196.1	CB	1.3	1.8	1.0	0.2	Tr	16.4	2.906	
13–195	V	5200.5	CB	6.8	1.6	0.7	11.0	Tr	11.2	4.312	
13–196	H	5205.1	CB	13.4	1.4	0.6	2.5		19.3	2.741	
13–197	V	5205.1	CB	18.0	3.4	0.6	2.2		19.1	2.673	
13–198	V	5208.4	TC	22.5	1.3	1.2	2.1	0.4	4.6	NA	
2–201	V	5158.2	In	12.3	3.1	Tr	Tr		17.2	2.515	
2–202	H	5162.5	In	10.1	3.4	0.2	0.8		20.2	2.393	*
2–203	V	5162.5	In	6.2	1.7	0.9	1.5		19.3	2.512	
2–204	H	5165.6	In	6.4	2.0	4.4	0.6		20.7	3.191	
2–206	V	5168.5	CB	12.6	5.9	0.4	0.7		15.9	3.726	*
2–207	H	5175.0	CB	5.5	2.7	0.3	0.3		16.8	2.874	*
2–209	H	5179.8	CB	5.5	3.1	1.0	5.5	0.1	18.4	3.152	
2–2010	H	5184.3	CB	30.3	0.8		Tr		6.0	NA	
2–2011	V	5192.7	TC	30.5	1.1	Tr	0.2	Tr	0.2	NA	
1–291	V	5228.2	TC	31.4	0.6				8.2	NA	
2–291	H	5126.7	In	7.4	3.0	0.2	10.6		16.8	3.327	
2–292	H	5130.6	In	7.1	2.6	3.1		0.5	16.8	3.687	
2–293	V	5130.6	In	4.4	2.7	1.2	Tr		21.0	2.884	
2–294	H	5137.8	In	14.1	2.7	0.3	3.2		18.3	3.544	
2–295	H	5142.7	CB	18.6	3.8	1.8	3.0	Tr	3.3	NA	
2–296	V	5142.7	CB	21.0	2.7	1.1	0.5	Tr	4.5	NA	
2–297	V	5146.2	CB	13.5	3.3	5.5	0.2		11.1	4.023	

Carb = carbonate cement
Si = silica cement
Cl = authigenic clay
Pyr = pyrite
Oth = other
Por = porosity
P:T = pore–to–throat size ratio

*poor thin section quality

Table 2. Textural analyses of thin-section samples. Subfacies and samples same as in Table 1.

Sample			SF	GRAIN SIZE		Std. Dev.	Skew.	Kurt.
				Med.	Mean			
5-191	H	5231.8	In	1.011	1.075	.765	.190	.956
5-192	H	5234.6	In	1.196	1.238	.560	.190	1.182
5-193	V	5234.6	In	1.179	1.148	.467	−.070	1.103
5-194	H	5241.4	In	1.700	1.678	.484	−.053	1.134
5-195	H	5244.6	CB	1.710	1.707	.650	.015	.984
5-196	V	5244.6	CB	1.820	1.864	.482	.147	1.214
5-197	V	5254.1	CB	1.750	1.750	.672	−.036	1.107
5-198	V	5260.5	In	1.663	1.656	.561	−.072	1.127
13-192	H	5193.8	In	1.829	1.867	.559	.168	1.072
13-193	H	5196.1	CB	1.675	1.699	.508	.130	1.011
13-194	V	5196.1	CB	1.952	1.990	.483	.114	1.014
13-195	V	5200.5	CB	1.868	1.880	.550	.071	1.033
13-196	H	5205.1	CB	1.733	1.752	.690	.076	1.443
13-197	V	5205.1	CB	1.851	1.878	.704	.096	1.259
13-198	V	5208.4	TC	1.846	1.878	1.714	.024	.619
2-201	V	5158.2	In	1.932	2.001	.572	.153	.931
2-202	H	5162.5	In	1.758	1.740	.667	−.030	.969
2-203	V	5162.5	In	1.800	1.770	.651	−.080	1.138
2-204	H	5165.6	In	1.618	1.554	.716	−.100	1.113
2-206	V	5168.5	CB	1.719	1.743	.666	.114	1.099
2-207	H	5175.0	CB	1.803	1.808	.602	.032	1.103
2-209	H	5179.8	CB	1.303	1.337	.715	.048	1.010
2-2010	H	5184.3	CB	1.609	1.581	.414	.007	.947
2-2011	V	5192.7	TC	1.394	1.385	.623	.009	1.080
1-291	V	5228.2	TC	1.286	1.200	1.021	−.196	.982
2-291	H	5126.7	In	1.661	1.686	.552	.011	.877
2-292	H	5130.6	In	2.066	2.020	.606	−.013	1.155
2-293	V	5130.6	In	1.808	1.827	.629	.043	1.136
2-294	H	5137.8	In	1.573	1.556	.640	.029	1.061
2-295	H	5142.7	CB	1.698	1.693	.610	−.011	1.299
2-296	V	5142.7	CB	1.756	1.782	.549	.124	1.042
2-297	V	5146.2	CB	1.762	1.759	.665	−.035	1.352

Sample Nomenclature Explanation

A–BBC D EEEE.E
A = well number
BB = section number
(T31S–R21W)
    Sec. 19 = Seacat
    Sec. 20, 29 = Moore
C = sample number
D = orientation   V = vertical
H = horizontal   EEEE.E = depth

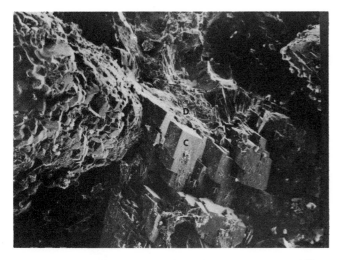

Figure 12. SEM image of carbonate cement (C) displaying evidence of dissolution. Scale bar is 10 microns.

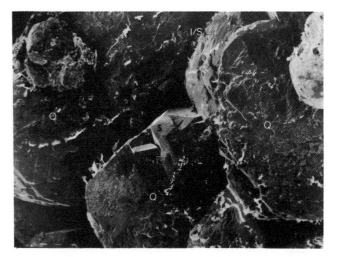

Figure 14. SEM image illustrating the typical pore detrital quartz grain (Q) relationship. Syntaxial quartz overgrowths (S) and minor, authigenic mixed layer illite/smectite (I/S). Scale bar is 10 microns.

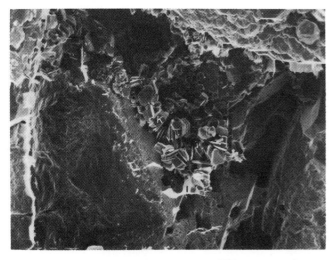

Figure 13. SEM image of pore-filling, pseudohexagonal kaolinite platelets (K) and minor illite (I). Scale bar is 100 microns.

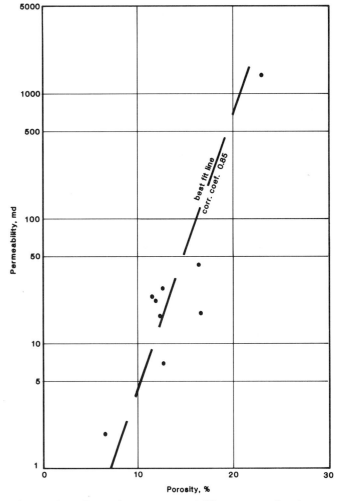

Figure 15. Porosity – permeability cross plot for Morrowan "A" sandstone, Lexington Field, Clark County, Kansas.

heterogeneities, and 4) pore-surface roughness. Aspect ratios correlate inversely to recovery efficiency; in water-wet reservoirs undergoing imbibition, hydrocarbons are displaced first from the smaller elements of the pore network, bypassing some of the oil in the larger pores and leaving isolated "ganglia" of residual oil.

The Morrow reservoir has been under waterflood since 1984, after primary production of 2,100,000 BO. Channel-bank and intertidal sandstones exhibit low means of aspect ratios in thin section. Channel-bank and intertidal subfacies display relatively high throat-to-pore coordination numbers (3.21 and 3.37, respectively), based on visual estimates from thin sections. The pore network is relatively "smooth". All of these factors imply good recovery efficiency. How-

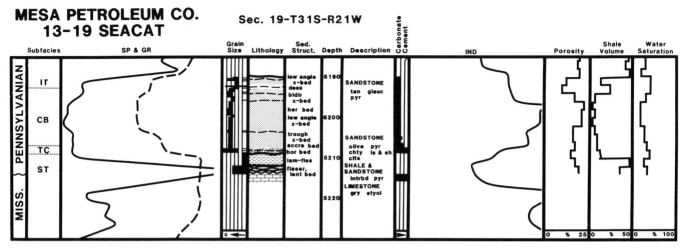

Figure 16. Example of a composite log relating well–log responses and calculations to core data.

ever, these sandstones also contain non–random heterogeneities in the form of dissolution porosity which, in a water–wet reservoir, should decrease recovery efficiency by capillary trapping of oil in oversize dissolution pores. By the criteria of Wardlaw and Cassan, the recovery factor for intertidal and channel bank subfacies should equal approximately 50% of the original OIP. (Supratidal and tidal channel subfacies were not evaluated as they are not economic reservoirs.)

Composite logs with data of well–log responses, pay calculations, and core descriptions were constructed for the cored wells (Fig. 16). These allowed the assessment of the thickness of productive intertidal and channel–bank sandstone in non–cored wells, and the construction of a net–pay isopach map (Fig. 17). Economic delimiters of 7% porosity, 30% shale volume, and 50% water saturation were applied in the net–pay calculation. The estimated volume of the reservoir is 1,634.5 ac–ft. This translates into approximately 6,800,000 STB of original OIP, assuming a formation volume factor of 1.3, and that 30% of the reservoir capacity is occupied by gas.

Discussion

The area of thickest pay is in the central portion of the field, a result of thicker intertidal and channel–bank deposits. Relatively homogeneous porosity is present in this portion of the reservoir. In the southern part of the field, the reservoir sandstone contains less pay, reflecting the downdip position and thicker tidal–channel deposits. The northern end of the field probably contains primarily supratidal and intertidal reservoirs.

Of the four subfacies, only the intertidal and channel–bank subfacies offer reservoir–quality sandstone. The shale intercalations and shale laminae in the intertidal subfacies might act as barriers to fluid migration. However, they do not seem to be areally continuous and probably do not divide the reservoir as a whole.

However, crossbedding in intertidal and channel–bank sandstones, especially where divided by pyritic laminae, might diminish fluid flow. The orientation of grains parallel to bedding noted in thin sections seems to a impart similar fabric to the pore network. There-

fore, where the reservoir is crossbedded, horizontal transmissibility might be adversely affected (Pettijohn, Potter, and Siever, 1973). Graded bedding probably introduces small heterogeneities that reduce sweep efficiency of the waterflood, especially where bedsets are separated by relatively impermeable, silty, pyritic laminae.

A production decline curve (Fig. 18) for the Morrow "A" reservoir indicates the gross ultimate recovery from the reservoir will be 3,350,000 STBO and 4.2 BCFG. This is in close agreement with the estimate arrived at by petrologic means.

CONCLUSIONS

Detailed geologic analysis of petroleum reservoirs is important in oil and gas field development by providing a more complete image of heterogeneities in the reservoirs. Rock characteristics affecting reservoir performance include: 1) textures; 2) mineralogy, especially those minerals that react with foreign gases and fluids to adversely affect the pore network; 3) geometry and sedimentary structures imparted by the environment of deposition; and 4) diagenetic history. Definition of heterogeneities aids in efficient recovery of hydrocarbons.

Potentially, reactions detrimental to Morrowan "A" reservoir quality can occur between the reservoir and foreign fluids introduced during drilling, completion, or improved recovery operations. For instance, vermicular kaolinite and mixed–layer illite/smectite, present as delicate crystals, could detach and migrate into pore throats during oil production. In addition, the smectite fraction of the mixed layer clay distends when introduced to fresh water. Fortunately, the intertidal and channel bank subfacies contain only relatively small amounts of authigenic clays. Acid-sensitive minerals include ankerite cement, glauconite, and pyrite, all iron–bearing minerals (Ali, 1981).

Intertidal and channel–bank sandstones exhibit the least heterogeneity of the four subfacies. Intertidal and channel–bank subfacies display low aspect ratios, apparently high throat–to–pore coordination numbers, relatively few non–random heterogeneities, and predominantly "smooth", unimpeded pores and pore throats.

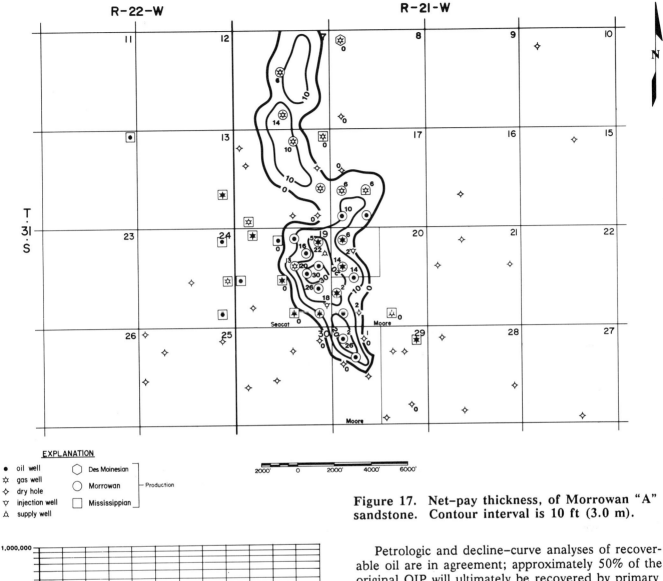

Figure 17. Net-pay thickness, of Morrowan "A" sandstone. Contour interval is 10 ft (3.0 m).

Petrologic and decline-curve analyses of recoverable oil are in agreement; approximately 50% of the original OIP will ultimately be recovered by primary and secondary methods. The advantage of predicting recovery with petrologic data is that the analyses can be performed early in the development of the field and, after a few years of production, can be adjusted with decline curve data. In addition, the efficiency of enhanced recovery techniques can be estimated.

The model ascribed to the Morrowan "A" sandstone at Lexington Field can be applied during exploring for and development of similar sandstone bodies. Recognition of the primary and secondary heterogeneities of the reservoir is imperative to optimize hydrocarbon recovery.

← **Figure 18.** Production decline curve, Morrowan "A" sandstone, Lexington Field, Clark Co., Kansas. Production increase in 1985 corresponds to initiation of waterflooding operations. Estimated remaining reserves are 911,000 BO, with an economic limit of 60 BO/month.

REFERENCES

Ali, S.A., 1981, Sandstone diagenesis – Applications to hydrocarbon exploration and production: unpub. manual, Gulf Oil Co., 214 p.

Clifton, H.E., 1982, Estuarine deposits, *in* P.A. Scholle and E. Spearing, eds., Sandstone Depositional Environments: AAPG, Tulsa, OK, p. 179–190.

Emery, M., and P.G. Sutterlin, 1986, Characterization of a Morrowan Sandstone reservoir, Lexington Field, Clark County, Kansas: Shale Shaker, Oklahoma City Geol. Soc., v. 37, no. 2, p. 18–33.

Folk, R.L., 1974, Petrology of Sedimentary Rocks: Hemphill Publ. Co., Austin, TX, 182 p.

Galloway, W.E., and D. Hobday, 1983, Terrigenous Clastic Depositional Systems: Springer-Verlag, NY, 423 p.

Hearn, C.L., W.J. Ebanks, R.S. Tye, and V. Ranganathan, 1984, Geological factors influencing reservoir performance of the Hartzog Draw Field Wyoming: JPT, v. 36, p.1335–1344.

Moore, G.E., 1979, Pennsylvanian paleotopography of the southern Mid-Continent *in* N.J. Hyne, ed., Pennsylvanian Sandstones of the Mid-Continent: Tulsa Geol. Soc. Spec. Pub. 1, p. 2–12.

Paul, S.E., J.T. Fish, J.S. Wells, R. Peters, D.L. Gordon, and J.J. Mosler, 1980, Oil and gas developments in north Mid-Continent: AAPG Bull., v. 64, p. 1437–1444.

Pettijohn, F.J., P.E. Potter, and R. Siever, 1973, Sand and Sandstone: Springer-Verlag, NY, 618 p.

Rascoe, B. Jr., and F.J. Adler, 1983, Permo-Carboniferous hydrocarbon accumulations, Mid-Continent, U.S.A.: AAPG Bull., v. 67, p. 979–1001.

Robinson, R.J., 1983, Geochemical investigation of diagenetic history of Pennsylvanian Morrowan sandstone, Lexington Field, Clark County, Kansas: unpub. MS thesis, KS State U., 61 p.

Schmidt, V., D.A. McDonald, and R.L. Platt, 1977, Pore geometry and reservoir aspects of secondary porosity in sandstones: Bull. Canadian Petroleum Geologists, v. 25, p. 271–290.

Scholle P.A., 1979, A color illustrated guide to constituents, textures, cements, and porosities of sandstones and associated rocks: AAPG Mem. 28, Tulsa, OK, 201 p.

Wardlaw, N.C., and J.P. Cassan, 1978, Estimation of recovery efficiency by visual observation of pore systems in reservoir rocks: Bull. Canadian Petroleum Geologists, v. 26, p. 572–585.

Zeller, D.E., 1968, The stratigraphic succession in Kansas: KS Geol. Survey Bull. 189, 81 p.

Authigenic illite growing on sheets of altered, expanded mica. Dakota Fm., sec 18 T33N R7W, La Plata Co., CO. Depth 7,899–7,901 ft (2,408 m). Photo donated by Bill Keighin.

The Weber Sandstone at Rangely Field, Colorado[1]

KENT A. BOWKER[2]
WILLIAM D. JACKSON[3]

[1]Received August 15, 1988; Revised April 4, 1989
[2]Chevron U.S.A. Inc., New Orleans, Louisiana
[3]Chevron U.S.A. Inc., Houston, Texas

The Permo–Pennsylvanian Weber Sandstone is the major producing horizon at the giant Rangely Field, Rio Blanco County, Colorado. The Weber is separated into three major lithotypes, the distribution of which is related to depositional environment. The Weber was deposited in two major depositional environments: fluvial and eolian. The fluvial deposits, derived from the ancestral Uncompahgre Uplift, are dominantly arkosic sandstones, siltstones, and shales. The arkosic lithofacies are not productive and act as intraformational permeability barriers. The eolian sediments were deposited in dune, interdune, and extradune environments as fine and very fine-grained subarkosic sand. They are either cross laminated (mostly wind-ripple laminae) or massively bedded (bioturbated). The cross-laminated lithofacies is the major productive lithofacies, with an average porosity of 12%. Permeability is highly directional on a small scale because of differential cementation related to grain sizes within inverse-graded laminae. Permeability along the laminae averages 2 md; permeability across the laminae averages 0.4 md. Massive sandstone has a mean porosity of 7.1% and mean permeability of 0.2 md.

The Raven Park Anticline provides the trap at Rangely. One major normal fault and several minor normal faults affect hydrocarbon production by displacing productive zones between injection and production wells, and by acting as water and carbon dioxide conduits or thief zones.

In the diagenetic history of the Weber, much of the original porosity was destroyed by early and late cementation, although some was subsequently restored by dissolution of detrital and authigenic minerals. Asphaltene, which appears as moveable oil on wireline logs, was precipitated near the end of diagenesis.

The Weber reservoir initially was water wet, with a water saturation of 27.5%; the current carbon dioxide flood could be altering wettability. The carbon dioxide flood should boost ultimate recovery from the Weber to 900,000,000 BO.

INTRODUCTION

The objective of this paper is to describe each of the three major lithotypes identified in the Permo–Pennsylvanian Weber Sandstone, emphasizing those petrophysical characteristics that affect oil and gas production. Core descriptions, core analyses, optical and scanning electron microscopy (SEM), and x-ray diffraction (XRD) and special core analyses were used to separate the Weber into three major lithotypes. Distribution of these lithotypes is controlled by depositional environments and is the major influence on hydrocarbon production in the field.

The giant Rangely Field (Fig. 1), in Rio Blanco County, Colorado, is one of the largest oil fields in the Rocky Mountain region, covering approximately 19,000 acres (7,689 ha) (Fig. 2). It lies at the northern end of the Douglas Creek Arch, which separates the Uinta and Piceance basins. Rangely Field is by far the largest of a trend of Weber Sandstone fields found along the northern Piceance Basin.

Petroleum migrated into the region during the Mesozoic, before the Late Cretaceous–Early Tertiary Laramide Orogeny (Campbell, 1955; Fryberger, 1979). Oil may have been trapped against impermeable Maroon rocks all along the southern terminus of Weber deposition. Asphaltene found in sandstones throughout the region may have precipitated at that time.

Shallow production from the Cretaceous Mancos Group shales was established at Rangely from 1901

FIELD DATA:	Rangely Field
Producing Interval:	Weber Sandstone
Geographic Location:	Centered in T2N R102W; Rio Blanco County, Colorado
Present Tectonic Setting:	Northwest edge of Piceance Basin
Depositional Setting:	Edge of sand sea, near margin of Uncompahgre fluvial system
Age of Reservoir:	Permo–Pennsylvanian
Lithology of Reservoir:	Subarkosic sandstone
Depositional Environment:	Erg and erg margin
Diagenesis:	Quartz, carbonate and clay cementation; dissolution of feldspars and carbonates; precipitation of asphaltene
Porosity Types:	Primarily intergranular and secondary, with some intragranular and fracture
Porosity:	Maximum 25%; average 12%
Permeability:	Maximum 200 md; average 2 md
Fractures:	Both local and extensive fractures
Nature of Trap:	Anticlinal closure
Entrapping Facies:	Tight siltstones and shales of the Permian State Bridge Formation
Source Rock:	Permian Phosphoria Formation(?)
Timing of Migration:	Jurassic or later
Discovered:	1933 (Weber production; Mancos production found earlier)
Reservoir Depth:	Average 6,500 ft (1,980 m)
Reservoir Thickness:	Average net 275 ft (84 m); average gross 650 ft (200 m)
IP (discovery well):	F 229 BOPD
Areal Extent:	19,153 acres (7,751 ha)
Original Reservoir Pressure:	2,750 psi
Cumulative Production (6/88):	722,000,000 BO, 4.10 BCFG
Estimated Oil in Place:	1,578,000,000 BO
Approximate Ultimate Recovery:	939,000,000 BO, 5.30 BCFG
Oil Gravity:	34° API
Water Saturation:	Minimum 27.5%
Sulfur Content:	0.7%

through 1933. Oil from the Weber Sandstone was discovered by the California Oil Company (Chevron) in 1933 with the drilling of the No. A–1 Raven (Sec 30 T2N R102W). Because of the remoteness of the discovery, development did not begin until the period of increased petroleum demand during World War II. By 1949, the field was fully developed by 478 wells drilled on 40–acre (16 ha) spacing. The Weber reservoir was unitized (termed the Rangely Weber Sand Unit) and a waterflood begun in 1957. In 1963, 20–acre (8 ha) infill drilling began, and the waterflood expanded. That infill program included all but the flank areas of the field. The current carbon dioxide injection program was initiated in October 1986. Currently, 0.1 BCFPD of carbon dioxide are being injected into the Weber. The flood will be expanded beyond the central portion of the field as processing facilities are constructed. There are over 650 active production and injection wells in the field at present. Secondary hydrocarbon production has been established from the Mancos Group and minor production from the Shinarump, Morrison, and Dakota formations. Chevron operates the field, with approximately 50% working interest. Other companies with substantial interest include Amoco, Exxon, Equity, Unical, Texaco, and Marathon.

REGIONAL STRATIGRAPHY

The Weber Sandstone, first named by Clarence King (1876), is underlain by the Pennsylvanian Ma-

roon Formation (Fig. 3). The eolian Weber interfingers with the fluvial Maroon from northwest to southeast across the Rangely area (Fryberger, 1979). Five mi (8 km) south of Rangely, the Weber is entirely absent by facies change (Koelmel, 1986). The nearest Weber outcrop is near Dinosaur National Monument, ten mi (16 km) northwest of Rangely. However, at Dinosaur the abundant intercalated siltstones and shales of the Maroon facies found at Rangely are absent. Overlying the Weber is the Permo–Triassic State Bridge Formation (DeVoto, et al., 1986), which acts as the reservoir top seal.

STRUCTURAL SETTING

During deposition of the eolian Weber Sandstone, arkosic sediments of the Maroon Formation were being shed off the ancestral Uncompahgre Uplift (Fig. 1). Koelmel (1986) defined a paleotectonic platform north of Rangely which may have impeded the northward progradation of Maroon arkosic sediments into the Rangely area. This platform could have permitted the southward movement of eolian sediment into the area.

The structural features shown on Figure 1 were formed during the Laramide Orogeny. The Uncompahgre Uplift and Front Range became positive structural elements again at that time. The Raven Park Anticline (Fig. 2) which forms the trap at Rangely Field is located on the hanging wall of the southernmost Uinta reverse fault (Fig. 1). The anticline is

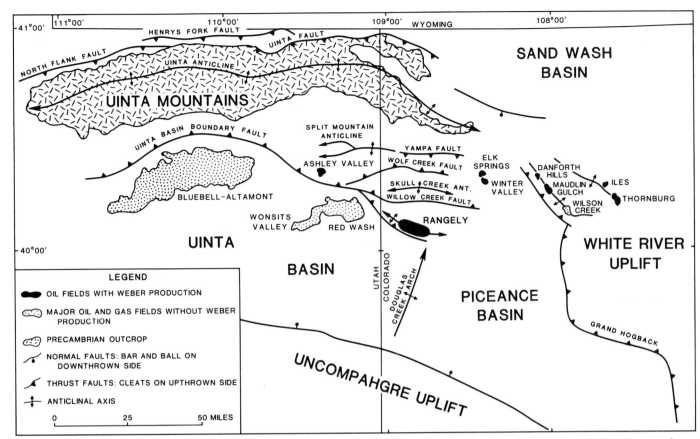

Figure 1. Regional tectonic and index map. Rangely Field lies at the north end of the Laramide–age Douglas Creek Arch, on the northwest margin of the Piceance Basin. (25 mi = 40.2 km)

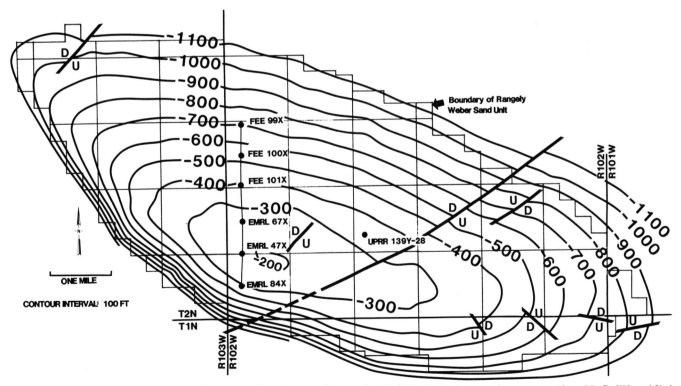

Figure 2. Structure map, top of Weber Sandstone (Rangely Field). The trace of cross section N–S (Fig. 12) is shown. The No. 139Y UPRR is the type well. Faults have a normal sense. (1 mi = 1.61 km)

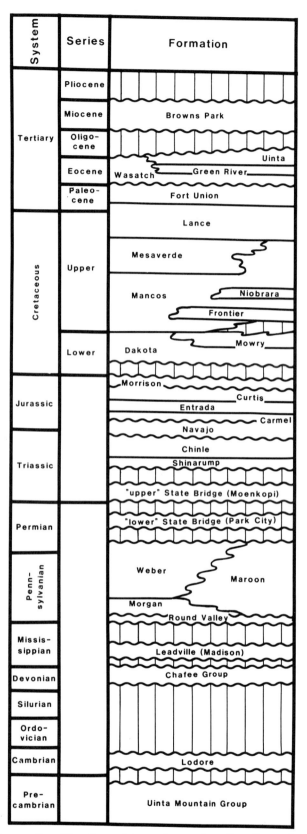

System	Series	Formation
Tertiary	Pliocene	
	Miocene	Browns Park
	Oligo-cene	
	Eocene	Uinta / Wasatch — Green River
	Paleo-cene	Fort Union
Cretaceous	Upper	Lance / Mesaverde / Mancos — Niobrara / Frontier
	Lower	Dakota — Mowry
Jurassic		Morrison / Curtis / Entrada / Carmel / Navajo
Triassic		Chinle / Shinarump / "upper" State Bridge (Moenkopi)
Permian		"lower" State Bridge (Park City)
Penn-sylvanian		Weber — Maroon / Morgan / Round Valley
Missis-sippian		Leadville (Madison)
Devonian		Chafee Group
Silurian		
Ordo-vician		
Cambrian		Lodore
Pre-cambrian		Uinta Mountain Group

Figure 3. Stratigraphic column for the Rangely area. Note interfingering of the Maroon and Weber formations.

doubly plunging and asymmetrical, with a steeper southwestern limb.

One major normal fault (the Main Field Fault) and several minor normal faults are mapped at the Weber level (Fig. 2). These faults, especially the Main Field Fault, affect production by displacing productive zones between injection and producing wells, and by acting as water and carbon dioxide conduits or thief zones. These faults probably are related to the thrust fault located beneath the Raven Park Anticline.

The occurrence of artificially induced earthquakes at Rangely illustrates the presence of stress. Overpressuring of the reservoir (over 3,500 psi) during flooding operations has caused the Main Field Fault to slip (Raleigh, et al., 1976). The reservoir pressure presently is maintained just above 2,700 psi, the pressure necessary to keep the injected carbon dioxide miscible.

LITHOFACIES AND DEPOSITIONAL ENVIRONMENTS

The depositional history of the Weber is discussed fully by Bissel (1964) and Fryberger and Koelmel (1986). Environments and lithofacies are outlined here, based on their work and on the authors' investigations.

Fluvial

Fluvial rocks (Fig. 4, Plate 1) in the Weber–Maroon are composed predominantly of arkosic sands, silts, and clays derived from the ancestral Uncompahgre Uplift and deposited in alluvial fans. Colors vary from gray and dusky red in siltstones and shales, to gray and orange-red in fluvial sandstones. Reworked eolian subarkosic sand was incorporated into portions of the fluvial sediments, especially during the deposition of the lower portion of the Weber.

These rocks occur in cyclic, fining-upward sequences: rippled sandstones grade upward into intercalated siltstones and shales (Fig. 5) which are sometimes burrowed. Overbank siltstones and shales are the most common fluvial lithofacies within the Weber. These cyclic sequences may be repeated several times within a single fluvial unit (Fig. 6).

Channel deposits are predominantly medium to very coarse arkosic sandstones. Laminated clasts (channel lag) are found occasionally at the base of coarse channel sandstones, indicating erosion of proximal banks (Fig. 6). Reworked eolian subarkosic sandstone, deposited as current-rippled cross strata is found in portions of some fluvial deposits. Both the arkosic and reworked subarkosic sandstones usually are barren of hydrocarbons.

Eolian

Eolian sediments, the reservoir facies, were deposited in three depositional subenvironments: dune, interdune, and extradune. Dune deposits are identified by bedding types (Fig. 4) and by vertical sequences (Fig. 5). Sedimentary characteristics include a preponderance of fine and very fine subarkosic sand; individual strata are well sorted and lack bioturbation. Three primary types of dune strata are present: 1) abundant high-angle (up to 25°), inverse-graded avalanche strata, 2) ripple laminae, and 3) rare grainfall

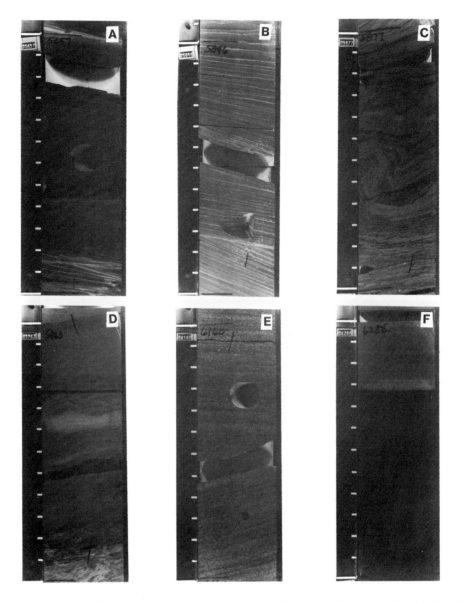

Figure 4. Cores of major lithofacies. The photographs are from various depths of the No. 139Y UPRR. One-in. (2.56 cm) tick marks are located to the left of each core for scale.

A. Cross-laminated facies. Dark material at the lower half of the center cross-bed set is asphaltene. Carbonate cements (white streaks) excluded asphaltene precipitation in portions of some laminae. Most of the laminations are wind ripples; grainflow deposits are located at the base of some of the dune sets. See Figure 8 for SEM and porosimeter data from this sample, and Plates 1A, 1B, and 1C for thin-section photomicrographs. 5,657 ft (1,724 m).

B. Cross-laminated facies. The laminae coarsen upward, suggesting that they were formed by the migration of wind ripples. Note that the carbonate cement in very fine-grained portions of the laminae (white layers) has excluded the hydrocarbon saturation seen in the remaining, fine-grained portions. White "spots" in rock are poikilotopic carbonate. 5,846 ft (1,781.9 m).

C. Contorted (laminated) facies. Laminae can be seen because of precipitation of asphaltene (dark) in the coarser-grained portions of the laminae and carbonate (lighter color) in the finer portions; moveable hydrocarbon stains the remaining rock. 5,877 ft (1,791.3 m).

D. Massive (bioturbated) facies. Asphaltene and carbonate emphasize moderate bioturbation. See also Figure 9 and Plates 1D, 1E and 1F, illustrations of this rock. 5,963 ft (1,817.5 m).

E. Core from the arkosic (fluvial) facies. The laminae in the upper half of the photograph appear to coarsen upward, which implies that eolian processes reworked this fluvial deposit. See also Figure 10 and Plates 1G and 1H, illustrations of this sample. 6,160 ft (1,877.6 m).

F. Shale (dark red), siltstone (medium red), and sandstone (light red) of the arkosic (fluvial) facies. 6,286 ft (1,916 m).

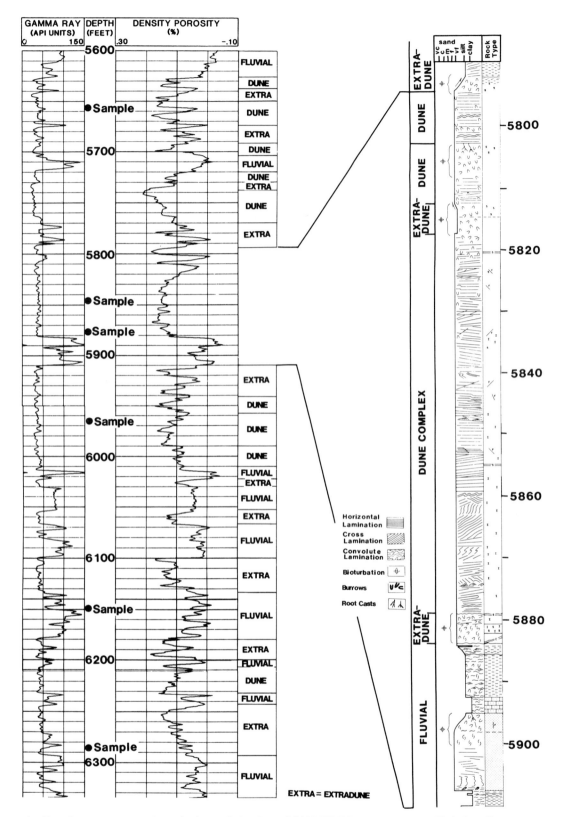

Figure 5. Wireline log and core description of the No. 139Y UPRR, the type well (Fig. 2). The core description shows one major cycle of Weber eolian deposition. Note the fluvial unit below the base of the cycle, the contorted beds at the base, and the upward progression from cross-laminated facies to massive (bioturbated) facies. Porosity decreases upward, allowing recognition of cycles on porosity logs. The fluvial zones generally have gamma-ray values greater than 50 API units. Depths of samples described elsewhere are shown in the depth column. (Depth increment = 10 ft, or 3.05 m)

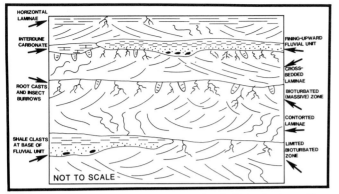

Figure 6. Stratigraphic model of lithofacies discussed in text. Notice the cyclic nature of the deposits.

strata. The cross-laminated facies of this paper includes all three types. The bedding attitude changes at one- to five-ft (0.3 to 1.5 m) thick intervals (Fig. 4), suggesting that small dunes, two to ten ft (0.6 to 3.0 m) high, probably located at the erg margin, were the primary deposits. Other features observed in the core are contorted bedding (Fig. 4C), ripple foresets, and granule ripples.

The bases of dunes are abrupt, usually overlying a well-cemented bioturbated sandstone or fluvial deposit. Basal strata consist of cross-laminated and contorted sandstone. The contorted laminae probably were influenced by a water table within the dune (Doe and Dott, 1980). These beds grade upward into laminated layers which, in turn, grade into bioturbated zones. The amount of bioturbation increases until there is an abrupt change to another dune sequence or fluvial zone. Root casts and insect burrows dominate the bioturbation types. The dune deposits were preserved by burial under fluvial sediments.

It is difficult to distinguish interdune from extradune rocks in core. Interdune deposits have been restricted in our study to those zones where 1) a dune sequence lies directly above and below, 2) the net thickness is less than one ft (0.3 m), and 3) the rock type is consistent. Interdune deposits are primarily gray-green and black shales and red, laminated siltstones; the siltstones are rippled in places. Thin, well-cemented, and bioturbated sand-sheet deposits also are found. Interdune zones are limited in lateral extent and most likely were deposited between coalescing dunes.

The extradune environment encompasses all other environments in the eolian system. These include playas (both carbonate and siliciclastic), sand sheets (vegetated or gravel pavement) and small, widely spaced dunes. The extradune depositional surface was characterized by low relief. Dunes acted as sediment traps; the extradune areas were a surface of sand transport. The presence of beds of highly bioturbated and carbonate-cemented eolian rocks up to ten ft (3 m) thick (Fig. 5; Plate 1) indicates that relatively long periods of time might have separated dune migrations over a particular area. The lithofacies referred to as massively bedded is the bioturbated facies of the sand-sheet and dune environments.

DIAGENESIS

The diagenetic history of the Weber Sandstone is complex. Much original porosity was lost because of precipitation of various cements; some secondary porosity was formed by dissolution of detrital and authigenic minerals. Texture, related to depositional environment, was an important factor.

Diagenetic Sequence

Superposition and cross-cutting relationships of cements provide evidence for the following diagenetic sequence (see also Koelmel, 1986):
1) Precipitation of poikilotopic calcite and sulfates, and microcrystalline calcite in the massive (bioturbated) and cross-laminated lithofacies through soil-forming processes. Illuviated clays may have coated grains. 2) Burial of sediments, and precipitation of quartz druse and quartz overgrowths. 3) Precipitation of dolomite and calcite cements with iron-rich outer rims. 4) Formation of authigenic clays (mostly illite, with some grain coating chlorite and mixed-layer illite/smectite). 5) Dissolution of authigenic and detrital minerals. 6) Migration of hydrocarbons and precipitation (deposition?) of asphaltene in porous sections of the Weber. 7) Further, limited dissolution of carbonate cements. 8) Migration of the producible hydrocarbons now present in the Weber.

Poikilotopic cements are found mostly in the cross-laminated (dune) facies, but are relatively rare overall. Microcrystalline carbonates are found in the massive (bioturbated) facies. Abundant bioturbation, and presence of fluvial deposits and contorted bedding (Doe and Dott, 1980) indicate that the Weber "desert" probably had a fluctuating, but relatively high water table. Evaporation rates were high, resulting in the formation of carbonates and perhaps sulfates. Clay may have filtered into the sediments by eluviation. Most of the clay is found in the poorly sorted massive (bioturbated) sandstones. Bioturbation destroyed the laminae and decreased the sorting. During burial, quartz precipitated as overgrowths and druse (Figs. 7 and 8). Very few detrital quartz grains have "dust rims," so the abundance of overgrowths cannot be quantified in thin section. However, SEM examination of the Weber shows that nearly every detrital quartz grain is coated by druse or overgrowths.

Most of the porosity loss is due to carbonate cements. Calcite and dolomite precipitation was followed by ferran calcite and ferran dolomite (found in iron-rich outer rims; Plate 1). Most dolomite is subhedral or euhedral. Both calcite and dolomite have replaced quartz (including overgrowths) and feldspar grains (Plate 1C). In the cross-laminated facies, most of the carbonate cement is found in the very fine-grained portion of the laminae (Fig. 4, Plate 1). Perhaps carbonate dust, which was deposited in the very fine-grained portion of the laminae, acted as nucleation sites for carbonate cement (Mayer and others, 1988).

About 90% of the clay is illite, with minor amounts of chlorite and mixed-layer illite/smectite (Plate 1 and

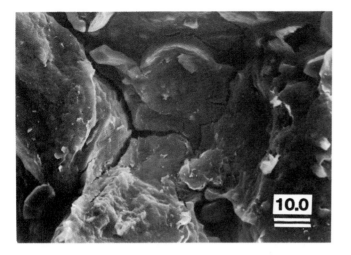

Figure 7. Asphaltene lining a pore in a cross-laminated sandstone (material in center of SEM image exhibiting shrinkage cracks). Quartz overgrowths are also present. No. 139Y UPRR, 5,657.7 ft (1,724.4 m); bar scale in microns.

Figs. 9, 10, and 11). Clay accounts for less than five percent of the reservoir rock; it is much more abundant in less porous portions of the Weber. Roger L. Burtner (pers. comm.) has dated the formation of illite at approximately 89 Ma, using the K/Ar technique.

Following the formation of clays, dolomite, calcite and feldspars were leached. Some feldspars were altered to illite (Fig. 11). Perhaps as much as a quarter of the Weber porosity is secondary, as indicated by oversized pores and "channel-like" porosity (Koelmel, 1986).

Subsequently, hydrocarbons migrated into the Rangely area, depositing (or precipitating) asphaltene. The asphaltene is concentrated in the lower portions of zones with cross lamination (Fig. 4A), where it lines pores (Fig. 7 and Plate 1), but rarely occludes porosity completely. Asphaltene may account for as much as 20 vol% of some cross-laminated sandstones.

Robert Carlson (pers. comm.) has identified the asphaltene as an NSO (for Nitrogen-Sulfur-Oxygen rich) compound. The asphaltene appears to be less mature than the oil presently being produced. It is not the product of thermal processes, but formed as a result of the loss of lighter fluid components. It is brittle and is insoluble in most organic solvents; it also appears as oil on wireline logs.

Another period of dissolution, less extensive than the previous episode, followed the precipitation of asphaltene. Only carbonates appear to have been affected.

Apparently, all diagenesis ceased with the migration of the hydrocarbons now being produced at the field. Fryberger and Koelmel (1986) show that this migration may have occurred before the Laramide Orogeny.

Distribution of Diagenetic Minerals

Examination of several hundred thin sections reveals that porosity generally decreases from the northwest portion of the field to the southeast; but the difference is smaller than is indicated by well logs. True effective porosity is less than log or apparent porosity in the northwest portion because asphaltene is concentrated in the northwest and central portions of the field. The amount of asphaltene decreases downsection because of a general decrease in porosity lower in the Weber (Fig. 12).

Dolomite concentrations are higher in the northwest; calcite concentrations are higher to the southeast. However, both increase in amount lower in the Weber. Koelmel (1986) has shown that the concentrations of quartz cement and overgrowths decrease from west to east across the Uinta and Piceance ba-

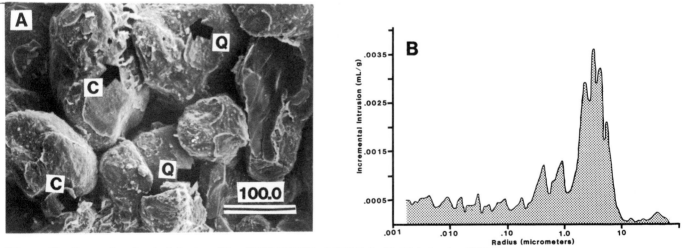

Figure 8. Cross-laminated facies, No. 139Y UPRR, 5657.7 ft (1,724.4 m). SEM image and porosimeter data from same rock sample.

A. SEM image of very fine to fine-grained sandstone. Note clay coats (mostly illite, C) and quartz overgrowths (Q). Bar scale in microns.

B. Mercury porosimeter-capillary pressure data, showing distribution of pore-throat sizes for this facies. Note abundance of pore throats 2-4 microns in radius.

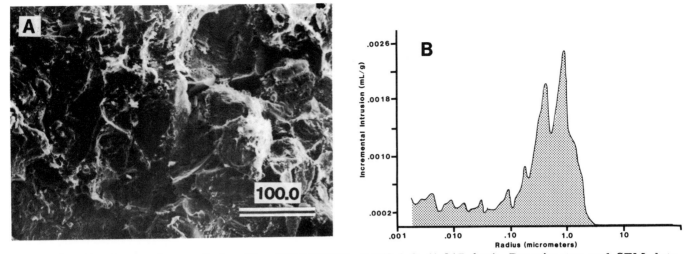

Figure 9. Massive sandstone facies, No. 139Y UPRR, 5,963.1 ft (1,817.6 m). Porosimeter and SEM data from same rock sample.

A. SEM image of tightly cemented very fine to fine-grained sandstone. Note paucity of visible pores. Bar scale in microns.

B. Mercury porosimeter-capillary pressure data reported as distribution of pore-throat sizes for this sample. Most of the porosity is not effective, because pore throats are smaller than one micron in radius.

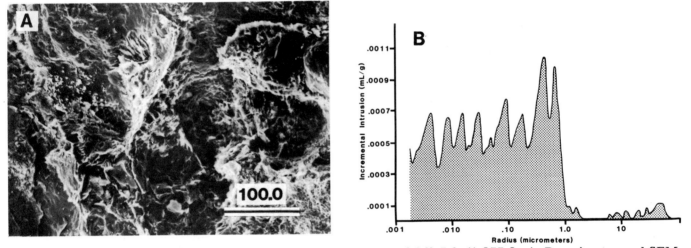

Figure 10. Fluvial, arkosic sandstone facies; No. 139Y UPRR, 6,160.7 ft (1,877.8 m). Porosimeter and SEM data from same rock sample.

A. SEM image of coarse-grained, tightly cemented sandstone. Even very coarse-grained sandstones of this facies rarely are saturated with hydrocarbons. Bar scale in microns.

B. Mercury porosimeter-capillary pressure data, showing distribution of pore-throat sizes for this sample of fluvial sandstone, which is typical of this facies. Most of the very small pore-throat radii are attributed to microporosity formed by alteration of detrital feldspar.

sins and, hence, decrease across the Rangely area from west to east.

Production data indicate that clay concentrations increase down-section and to the southeast. Clay concentrations average only about 5% in productive sandstones.

RESERVOIR QUALITY

Porosity and Permeability

Weber lithofacies were classified as cross laminated (mostly dune deposits), massively bedded (bioturbated eolian zones), and arkosic (fluvial sandstones, siltstones, and shales). Each lithofacies exhibits a

unique porosity/permeability distribution. Data from core from the No. 139Y UPRR well, located in the center of Rangely Field, approximate an "average" Weber section in this regard (Fig. 13). Data from several wells across the field were not used in the cross plot because important depositional influences on porosity and permeability would have been masked by the diagenetic trends discussed above. The data cluster around a best-fit line (correlation coefficient equals 0.76). However, each lithofacies has a different distribution along this line. The cross-laminated facies has the largest average porosity and permeability because a lack of early cementation allowed preservation of more original porosity and permeability (Fig.

73

Figure 11. Detrital feldspar grain partially altered to clay (probably mixed–layer illite), which forms part of the microporosity documented in mercury porosimeter data for this facies (see Fig. 8). Cross–laminated facies, No. 139Y UPRR, 5,657.7 ft (1,724.4 m). Bar scale in microns.

8A). Pore throats for a sample typical of this lithofacies are relatively large (Fig. 8B). There is a large directional component to permeability because of lamination and differential cementation (Fig. 14).

The more thoroughly cemented massive (bioturbated) facies contains a lower percentage of effective porosity (defined as porosity greater than 10% and permeability greater than one md) compared with cross–laminated sandstones. Porosimeter data from this facies confirm the smaller pore–throat sizes interpreted from the porosity–permeability cross plot and SEM data (Fig. 9).

The arkosic (fluvial) sandstones and siltstones are rarely effective as reservoirs (Figs. 10 and 13). Complete cementation of coarse–grained sandstone is common. What little porosity is seen in thin section (Plate 1) is ineffective. Pressure tests conducted at Rangely also show that the arkosic (fluvial) facies are permeability barriers when not fractured.

The rare carbonates and interdune/extradune mudstones and siltstones were not routinely sampled for PKS (porosity, permeability, and fluid saturation) analyses. However, these facies are always described as tight and barren in cores.

Distribution of Reservoir Facies

The subarkosic sandstone with cross–laminated structure is the reservoir facies of the Weber Sandstone at Rangely Field. The distribution of this facies is nearly the same as the distribution of the dune depositional environment within each zone. Therefore, the porosity and permeability distribution of the reservoir is correlatable and can be described by depositional facies maps.

A map of sandstone "quality" (Fig. 15), or the percentage of clean (gamma ray less than 50 API units) sandstone with porosity greater than 10% in Zone 5 indicates areas of high and low reservoir quality. A gamma–ray value of 50 API units usually corresponds to the change from eolian deposits (less than 50 API units) to fluvial deposits (50 API units and greater). There is a distinct northwest trend shown by these data, confirming that the prevailing wind direction could have been from the northeast (Fryberger, 1979). Interestingly, the isopach of the overlying fluvial zone (Fig. 16) shows an antithetic relationship to sandstone quality ratio. Again, there is a distinct northwest trend to the data. The high sandstone quality areas are interpreted by us as dunes that were anchored and then buried by fluvial sediments. Generally, the concentration of clean subarkosic sandstone in the Weber decreases to the south and east, and also down–section (Fig. 12). The patterns of reservoir facies distribution become less distinct in these directions and therefore the heterogeneity of the section as a whole is greater. The reason for this change is the dominance of the arkosic Maroon (fluvial) facies in these directions.

Distribution of Permeability Barriers

As in most reservoirs, permeability distribution controls the ultimate production of hydrocarbons at Rangely Field. Both intergranular and fracture permeability are present. The contribution of fracture permeability at Rangely is just now being appreciated, not as a benefit, but as a hindrance; fractures appear to act as carbon dioxide "thieves", decreasing the effectiveness of the current carbon dioxide flood.

The distribution and scale of permeability barriers in the Weber are controlled by depositional environments (Fig. 6). Partial barriers exist at the millimeter scale in the cross–laminated (dune) facies because of differential cementation of the laminae (Fig. 4, Plate 1). If the laminae are contorted, fluid movement will be disrupted. Contorted bedding (Plate 1C), which can be found in zones several feet thick (Fig. 4), converts what is commonly called "vertical permeability" into "horizontal permeability," and *vice versa*. Even if the laminae are not disturbed, the overall permeability of the wind–ripple facies is constrained by the low permeability perpendicular to the laminae. Due to rapid lateral changes in bedding attitude, fluid will have to move across the more thoroughly cemented, very fine–grained portion of the laminae. However, there is some benefit to this heterogeneity: increased tortuosity increases the effectiveness of the carbon dioxide flood (Warner, 1977). The massively bedded (bioturbated) facies, which can occur in beds up to ten ft (3.0 m) thick, acts as an intermediate-scale permeability barrier. Porosity and permeability data confirm the effectiveness of this facies as a barrier (Fig. 13C).

The lateral extent of the arkosic fluvial facies varies from hundreds of feet to tens of miles; five of the fluvial zones are used as field–wide markers. A stratigraphic cross section (Fig. 12) gives some indication of the distribution of this facies. Thicknesses can range from zero to tens of feet. The abundance of fluvial beds increases to the southeast across the field and also down–section. The behavior of fluids is quite different in the northwest portion of the field, where the Weber is 10% fluvial, compared with the southeast portion, where the section is 40% fluvial deposits. The fluvial sandstones, siltstones, and shales

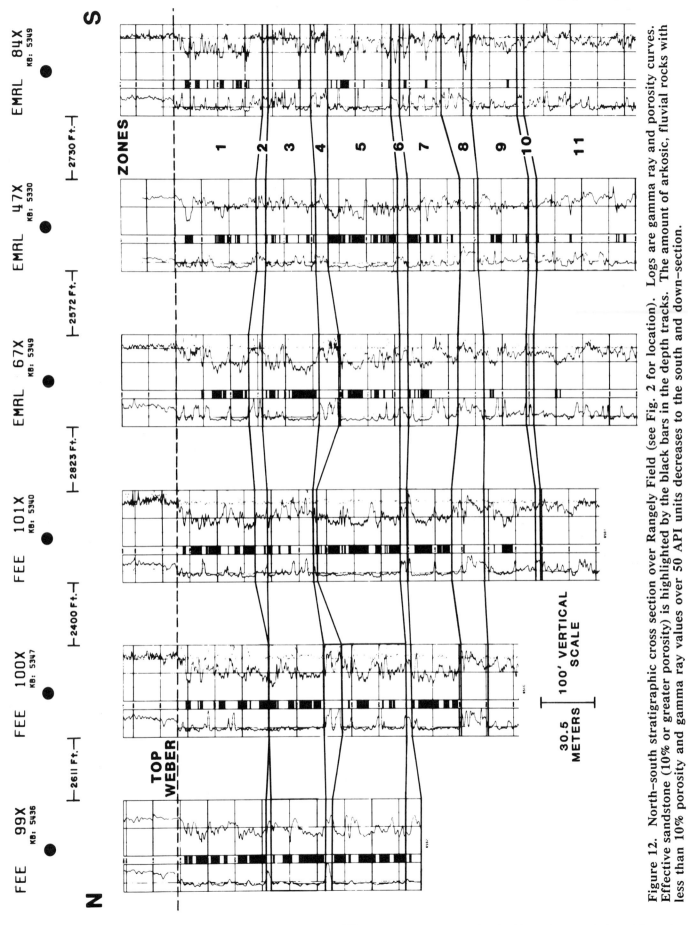

Figure 12. North-south stratigraphic cross section over Rangely Field (see Fig. 2 for location). Logs are gamma ray and porosity curves. Effective sandstone (10% or greater porosity) is highlighted by the black bars in the depth tracks. The amount of arkosic, fluvial rocks with less than 10% porosity and gamma ray values over 50 API units decreases to the south and down-section.

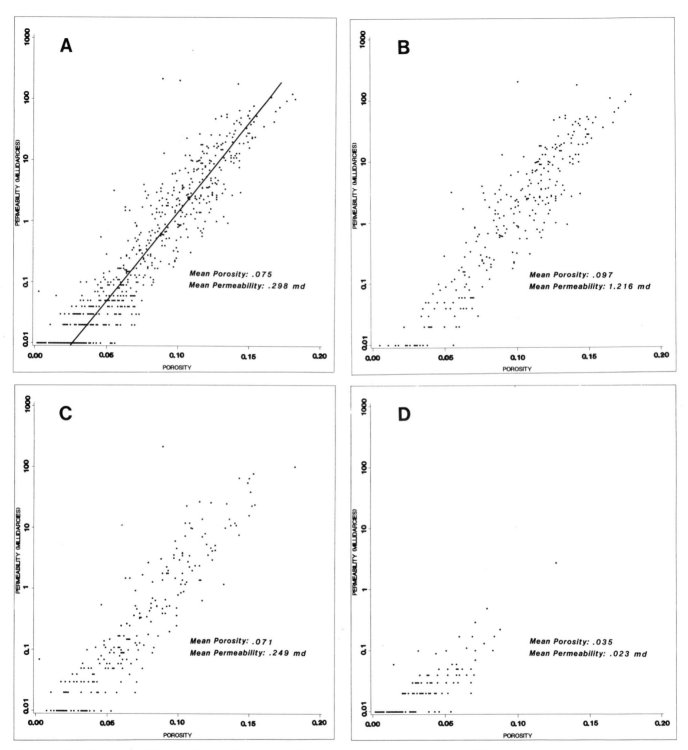

Figure 13.   Permeability and porosity data, Weber Sandstone.   Permeability is measured to air, with no Klinkenberg or overburden pressure corrections made; measurements made parallel to laminae, if present. Porosity measured by Boyle's Law (helium) method.   Arithmetic mean porosity and geometric mean permeability reported.   Data from No. 139Y UPRR well.

A.   Data from all three major lithologic facies (n=641).

B. Data from the cross–laminated facies only (n=275).   This is the most permeable facies.

C. Data from the massive (bioturbated) facies only (n=231).   Note trend toward lower permeabilities.

D. Data from the arkosic (fluvial) facies. Includes sandstones and siltstones; shales were not analyzed (n=135).   This is not reservoir rock.

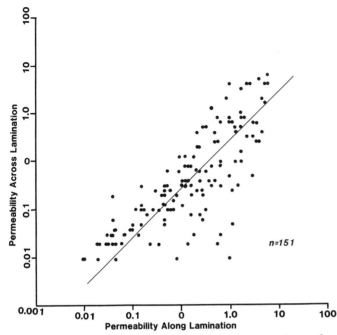

Figure 14. Graph of permeability across and parallel to laminae, cross–laminated facies. Permeability along the laminae in the effective (greater than one md) portions of the reservoir is approximately four times that across the laminae. Permeability is approximately the same along the "dip" and "strike" of the laminae. Correlation coefficient is 0.78. Data from No. 139Y UPRR.

are the most effective permeability barriers in the Weber.

Fluid Characteristics

The presumed source of the oil produced from the Weber is the Phosphoria Formation (Heffner and Barrow, in prep.). Central Utah is the only location near Rangely where the Phosphoria has a high enough concentration of organic carbon and where it reached the oil generative window. The oil, if this is the correct source, migrated some 175 mi (282 km) to Rangely.

The oil produced from the Weber has a 34° API gravity and contains 0.7 wt% sulfur. The initial gas/oil ratio was 300 CFG/STBO. The original gas/oil contact was at –330 ft (100 m) subsea. The oil/water contact was at –1,150 ft (351 m).

The Weber reservoir was initially water wet with a water saturation of 27.5%. A sample of cross–laminated sandstone used for relative permeability tests (Fig. 17) exhibited some hysteresis in the water curve, which is common in Weber samples. Water saturation must exceed 50% before equal water and oil relative permeabilities are obtained; this is a clear indication that the reservoir is water wet. However, there is some conflicting evidence that implies that the reservoir has mixed wettability: some "fresh–state" samples (i.e., unaltered samples from sponge core) of Weber will imbibe both oil and brine. The current carbon dioxide flood could be altering the wettability.

Production History

The decline curve of the Chevron No. 3 Fee (Fig. 18, Sec 29 T2N R102W), one of the first Weber wells

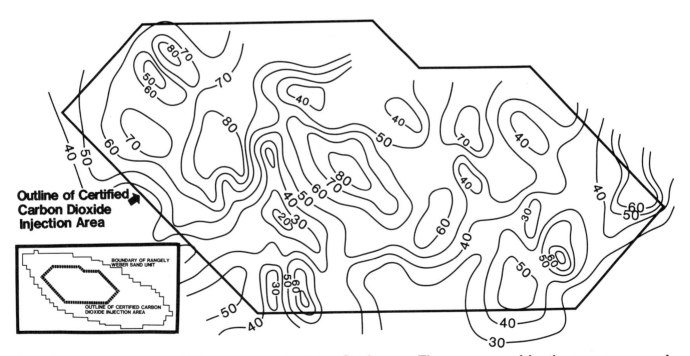

Figure 15. "Sandstone quality" map, Zone 5, Weber Sandstone. The area covered by the map corresponds with the carbon dioxide injection area. Sandstone quality is thickness of clean sandstone (gamma ray value less than 50 API units) divided into thickness of clean sandstone with porosity greater than 10%.

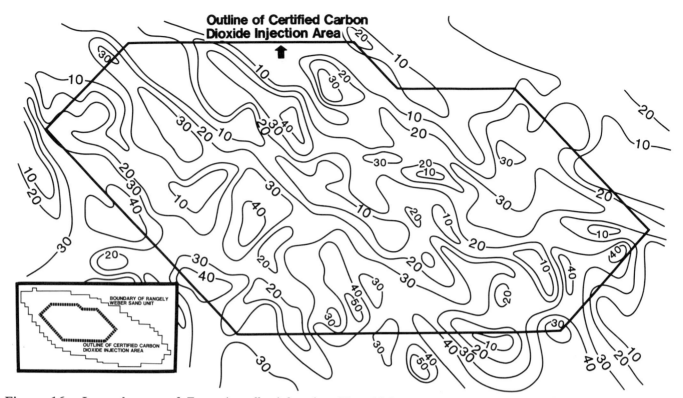

Figure 16. Isopach map of Zone 4, a fluvial unit. The thickness of this zone is inversely related to the sandstone quality map of the underlying eolian Zone 5 unit (Fig. 15). This map can be used to determine the distribution of permeability barriers (i.e., the fluvial deposits) and the underlying eolian reservoir facies.

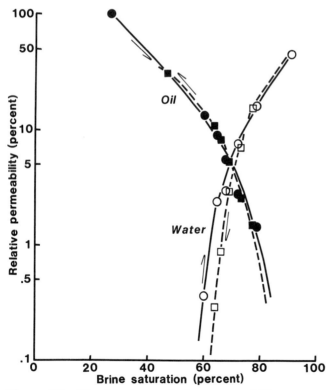

Figure 17. Steady-state relative permeability curve for a typical effective Weber sandstone. Fresh-state sample from No. 51AX-20 UPRR (Sec 20 T2N R102W), 6,015.5 ft (1,833 m). Oil permeability at 26.6% water saturation equals 38.4 md.

completed in the field, is typical of wells drilled near the crest of the anticline in the gas cap. Other wells within the carbon dioxide injection area exhibit a similar response to the tertiary recovery project; i.e., increased oil and natural gas production, and decreased water production.

CONCLUSIONS

The three major lithofacies described herein (cross laminated, massively bedded, and arkosic) are easily recognized in cores of the Weber. These deposits can be discerned on wireline logs and, hence, the various lithofacies can be mapped without the benefit of core. Distribution of the lithofacies is important because the arkosic fluvial units form extensive permeability barriers within the Weber. On a smaller scale, the tightly cemented massive (bioturbated) zones also form effective barriers to fluid flow.

Cross lamination, enhanced by differential cementation of the laminae, forms the smallest scale of reservoir heterogeneity. Permeability measurements of the cross-laminated facies vary depending on the orientation of the sample plug relative to the cross lamination. Fractures add to heterogeneity.

The Weber experienced a complex diagenesis, which included, late in diagenesis, precipitation of asphaltene. Asphaltene is found in other portions of the region. The asphaltene is solid and insoluble; however, it appears as moveable oil on conventional wireline logs.

A successful tertiary recovery project is now underway at Rangely. The carbon dioxide being injected into the Weber will add substantially to the ultimate

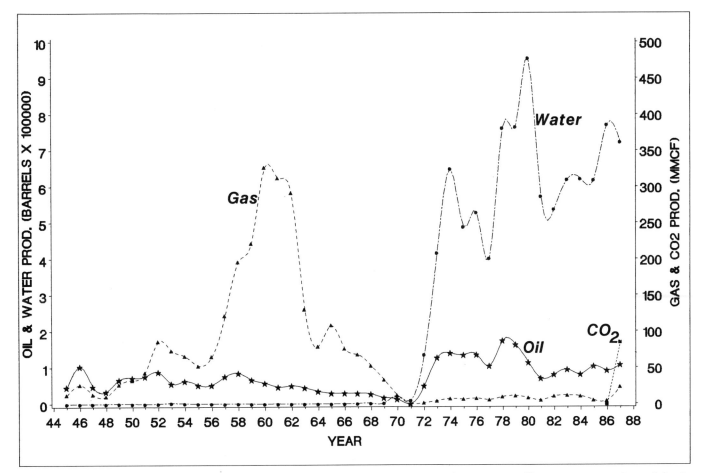

Figure 18. Yearly decline curve for the No. 3 Fee (Sec 29 T2N R102W). These well responses to the original waterflood and the current carbon dioxide flood are typical. Notice how increases in oil production after 1971 were accompanied by increases in water production, until the initiation of carbon dioxide flood in late 1986. The slight increase in oil production in 1987 compared to 1986 was accompanied by a decrease in water production. Natural gas production increased with carbon dioxide injection.

recovery from the field. The carbon dioxide, however, is affecting the Weber reservoir (Bowker and Shuler, 1989). Clay that coats the carbonate cements is released as the carbonate is dissolved by the low-pH, carbonated brine. Laboratory work indicates that the loss in permeability due to the migration of clay is offset by an increase due to carbonate dissolution. Chemistry changes in the produced water indicate that clays and feldspars also are being leached by the flood.

ACKNOWLEDGEMENTS

We thank the management of Chevron U.S.A., Inc., for permission to publish this study. Work done by Myron Smith, Bill Copeland, and Pat Flynn increased our understanding of the Weber, as did conversations with Tom Heffner, Ken Barrow, Mike Mendeck, Bob Ladd, Fred O'Toole, Jim Halvorsen, Terry Eschner, and Steve Cumella. We also thank Jim Castle, Steven Fryberger, and Ed Coalson for their editorial guidance during the preparation of this manuscript.

REFERENCES

Bissell, H.J., 1964, Lithology and petrography of the Weber Formation, (sic) in Utah and Colorado, in E.F. Sabatka, ed., Guidebook to the Geology and Mineral Resources of the Uinta Basin: IAPG, 13th Ann. Field Conf., p. 67–91.

Bowker, K.A., and P.J. Shuler, 1989, Carbon dioxide injection and resultant alteration of Weber Sandstone (Pennsylvanian-Permian), Rangely Field, Colorado [abs.]: AAPG Bull., v. 73, p. 336.

Campbell, G.S., 1955, Weber pool of Rangely Field, Colorado, in H.R. Ritzma and S.S. Oriel, eds., Guidebook to the Geology of Northwest Colorado: IAPG-RMAG, 6th Field Conf., p. 99–100.

DeVoto, R.H., B.L. Burtleson, C.J. Schenk, and N.B. Waechter, 1986, Late Paleozoic stratigraphy and syndepositional tectonism, northwest Colorado, in D.S. Stone, ed., New Interpretations of Northwest Colorado Geology: RMAG, p. 37–49.

Doe, T.W., and R.H. Dott, Jr., 1980, Genetic significance of deformed cross bedding–with examples from the Navajo and Weber sandstones of Utah: JSP, v. 50, p. 793–812.

Fryberger, S.G., 1979, Eolian-fluviatile (continental) origin of ancient stratigraphic trap for petroleum in Weber Sandstone, Rangely Oil Field, Colorado: Mtn. Geol., v. 16, p. 1–36.

Fryberger, S.G., and M.H. Koelmel, 1986, Rangely Field: eolian system-boundary trap in the Permo-Pennsylvanian Weber Sandstone of northwest Colorado, in D.S. Stone, ed., New Interpretations of Northwest Colorado Geology: RMAG, p. 123–149.

Gale, H.S., 1908, Geology of the Rangely oil district, Rio Blanco County, Colorado: USGS Bull. 350, 61 p.

Heffner, T.A., and K.T. Barrow, in prep., Rangely Field: AAPG special publication.

King, C., 1876, Paleozoic subdivisions on the 40th parallel: Am. Jour. Sci., 3 Ser., v. 11, p. 475–482.

Koelmel, M.H., 1986, Post-Mississippian paleotectonic, stratigraphic, and diagenetic history of the Weber Sandstone in the Rangely Field area, Colorado, *in* J.A. Peterson, ed., Paleotectonics and Sedimentation in the Rocky Mountain Region: AAPG Mem. 41, p. 371–396.

Mayer, L., L.D. McFadden, and J.W. Harden, Distribution of calcium carbonate in desert soils–a model: Geology, v. 16, p. 303–306.

Raleigh, C.B., J.H. Healy, and J.P. Bredenoeft, 1976, An experiment in earthquake control at Rangely, Colorado: Science, v., 191, p. 1230–1236.

Warner, H.R., 1977, An evaluation of miscible CO_2 flooding in waterflooded sandstone reservoirs: JPT, v. 29, p. 1339–1347.

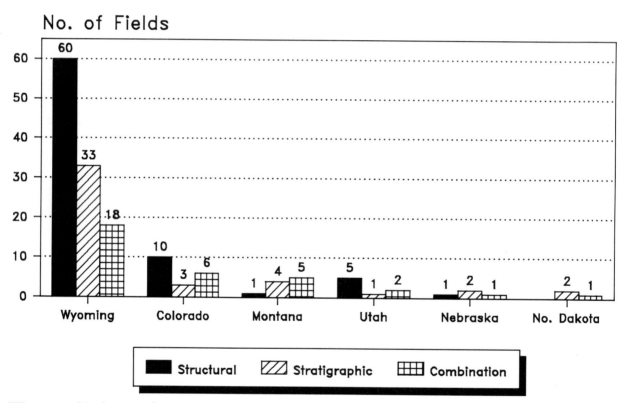

When considering the largest (>10,000,000 BOE) fields in the Rocky Mountains with sandstone reservoirs (n=155), Wyoming accounts for 72% of all fields and 78% of the structural fields. Numerous large gas fields in the San Juan Basin are not included in the dataset. Production data compliments of Petroleum Information. Compiled by John W. Robinson, 1989. See page 351ff for further information.

Diagenetic History and Reservoir Characteristics of a Deep Minnelusa Reservoir, Hawk Point Field Powder River Basin, Wyoming[1]

SUSAN W. JAMES[2]

[1]Received August 15, 1988; Revised February 15, 1989
[2]TOTAL Minatome Corporation, Houston, Texas

The Minnelusa "B" reservoir of Hawk Point Field, Campbell Co., Wyoming, is a massive to laminated, fine-grained, well-rounded, well-sorted sandstone deposit of eolian and sabkha environments. Avalanche facies, apron and flank deposits, sand sheets, and interdune deposits are identified by sedimentary structures and lithology. Poikilotopic crystals of early-formed anhydrite, the dominant cement, occlude 4 to 100% of the pore space. Porosity develops in areas where once-pervasive anhydrite cement has been removed by dissolution. The best production is associated with avalanche strata and massive sandstone intervals with minimal laminations. When found near the top the dune complex, these strata display maximum dissolution of anhydrite and creation of well-developed secondary porosity and permeability.

Dolomite cementation postdates anhydrite. The dolomite occurs as isolated well developed fine to very fine-crystalline rhombs that line pores, and as clusters replacing carbonate and feldspar grains. Clay content ranges from 2 to 5% and is composed of grain-coating illite and mixed-layer illite/smectite.

Reservoir sandstones at Hawk Point can be subdivided according to productivity, which is related to pore-throat radius and relative position in the reservoir. Pore-throat radii larger than 1 micron are necessary at Hawk Point for adequate relative permeability to oil. Capillary pressure data for the best reservoir sandstones indicate low clay contents and well-sorted pore-throat networks with low entry pressures and irreducible water saturations from 10 to 15 percent.

Evidence exists for two stages of oil migration. Emplaced in Late Jurassic time, the first-phase oil occurs as a nonthermal alteration product or bitument coats the diagenetic cements in the pores and pore throats. The second-stage, producible hydrocarbons migrated into the trap during Laramide development of the Powder River Basin.

Laboratory-measured saturation and cementation exponents were anomalously low. This may be due to wettability changes during coring and core cleaning and/or pore geometries. Evidence suggests a fractionally oil-wet reservoir at Hawk Point that would result in n values larger than those measured in the laboratory.

INTRODUCTION

Hawk Point Field was discovered in June, 1986, by the Total Petroleum, Inc. No. 41–30 Hawk Point Federal well (NE NE Sec 30 T47N R72W, Campbell County, Wyoming), completed flowing 754 BOPD. The reservoir is an eolian sandstone of the Permian Upper Minnelusa Formation. Production coincides with the crest of an anticlinal nose that trends northeast-southwest through the area; the trap is formed by the lateral pinchout of reservoir porosity and perme-

ability (Fig. 1). The Hawk Point Field discovery is significant because, at a depth of 11,450 ft (3,490 m), it is the largest and deepest Minnelusa field on the eastern side of the Powder River Basin.

The purposes of this study were to describe the eolian origins of the Minnelusa reservoir and to understand the diagenetic history responsible for the evolution of primary and secondary porosity. Additionally, the possibility of two-stage hydrocarbon emplacement and its control on production was

FIELD DATA:	Hawk Point Field
Producing Interval:	Upper Minnelusa "B" Sandstone
Geographic Location:	T47N R72W, Campbell Co., Wyoming
Present Tectonic Setting:	East flank of intracratonic Powder River Basin
Depositional Setting:	Arid coastal plain
Age of Reservoir:	Permian (Wolfcampian)
Lithology of Reservoir:	Anhydrite- and dolomite-cemented quartzarenites
Depositional Environment:	Dune fields and sabkhas
Diagenesis:	Anhydrite, dolomite, and limited clay cementation; dissolution of anhydrite
Porosity Types:	Secondary and primary intergranular; intercrystalline microporosity
Porosity:	Maximum 18%, average 13% (core)
Permeability:	Maximum 144 md, average 30 md (core)
Nature of Trap:	Stratigraphic pinchout with structural component
Entrapping Facies:	Tight Minnelusa anhydrites and dolomites
Source Rocks:	Pennsylvanian Middle Minnelusa
Timing of Migration:	Laramide
Discovered:	June, 1986
Reservoir Depth:	Average 11,350 ft (3,459 m)
Reservoir Thickness:	30 ft (9 m)
Areal Extent:	400 acres (162 ha)
Average IP:	475 BOPD
Drive Type:	Compaction/depletion
Cumulative Production (1/89):	1,330,000 BO, 0.26 BCFG
Approximate Oil Recoverable:	5,000,000 BO
Oil Gravity:	36° API at 60°F (15.6°C)
Average Temperature:	245°F (118°C)
Minimum Water Saturation:	23.6%

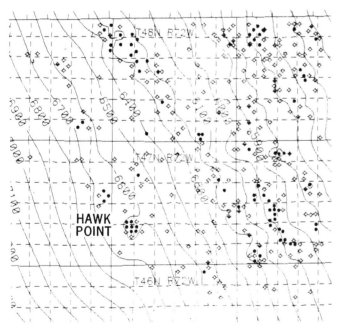

Figure 1. Structure, top of Minnelusa "B" Dolomite with location of Hawk Point Field.

addressed. This information will optimize reservoir description and prediction, and will aid in assessing both primary and secondary field development.

REGIONAL STRATIGRAPHY AND PALEOGEOGRAPHY

In eastern Wyoming, the Minnelusa Formation is divided into three members: upper, middle, and lower (Fig. 2). The upper member is Permian (Wolfcampian) in age while the middle and lower members are of Pennsylvanian age (Desmond, et al., 1984; Fryberger, 1984). In the Hawk Point Field area, the middle and lower members are predominantly tight carbonates while the upper member consists of alternating deposits of eolian sandstone with interbedded sabkha and marine dolomites and anhydrites. The dolomites lack effective porosity and permeability; production occurs only from the sandstones.

During Permo-Pennsylvanian time, eastern Wyoming was a broad coastal tidal flat, similar to the coastline along the present-day Persian Gulf (Shinn, 1973; Fryberger, 1984). An arid climate, abundant siliciclastic material, and restricted marine and supratidal evaporitic conditions resulted in the development of eolian dune, interdune, sand sheet, and sabkha sediments of the prograding Minnelusa sand sea (Fryberger, et al., 1983). Sand dunes, both isolated and coalesced, prograded southward across the sabkha surface in the direction of the prevailing wind (Jorgensen and James, 1988). Periodic storms and

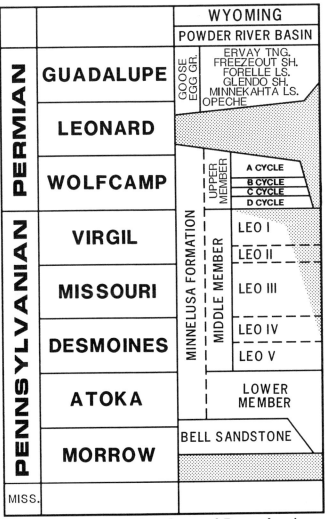

Figure 2. Stratigraphic column of Pennsylvanian and Permian rocks of eastern Wyoming. Stippling indicates unconformities.

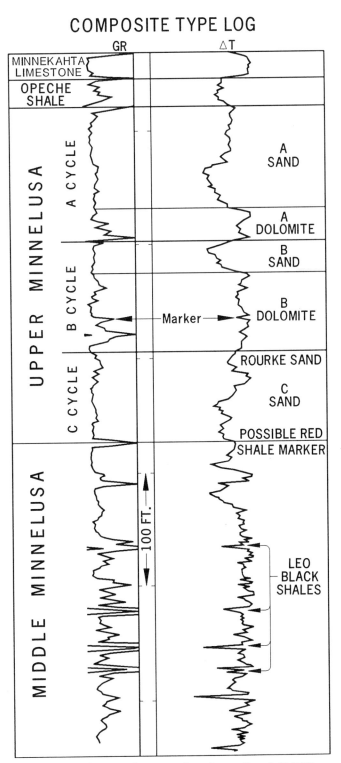

Figure 3. Composite type log from Sec 2 T47N R71W and Sec 25 T48N R71W, with "A", "B" and "C" cycles of the upper Minnelusa Formation (from George, 1984). (100 ft = 30.48 m)

minor marine transgressions inundated the coastal area, stabilizing the dunes and preserving them beneath marine carbonates and interdune evaporites. With the retreat of marine waters, the coastline returned to eolian deposition and progradation of the next sand cycle.

The Upper Minnelusa Formation chronicles four of these regressive/transgressive cycles (George, 1984). These are informally designated in descending order, "A", "B", "C", and "D" (Fig. 2). Locally, the cycles can be correlated (Fig. 3); on a semi–regional scale, cycle–correlation becomes more difficult. Each cycle consists of a transgressive evaporite/carbonate unit overlain by a regressive sandstone.

Lateral and vertical intercalation of porous and permeable eolian sands with impermeable marine carbonates and sabkha evaporites resulted in the development of abundant stratigraphic traps within the Upper Minnelusa Formation. These reservoirs remain some of the most prolific in the Powder River Basin.

Hawk Point produces from a sandstone of the "B" cycle. An extensive transgression of the Wolfcampian sea onto the broad coastal sabkha marked the begin-

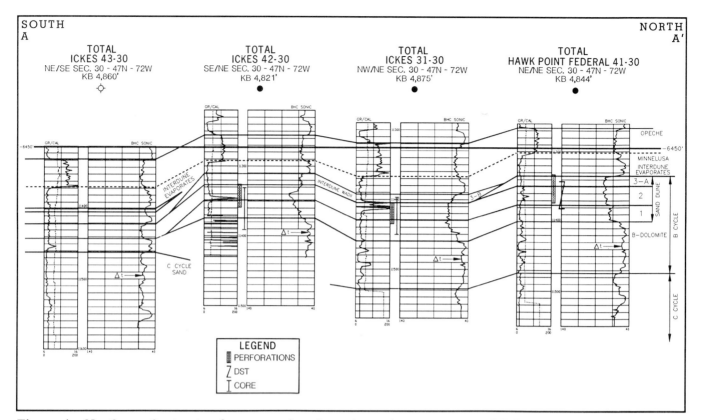

Figure 4. North–south structural cross section through southwestern part of field. Location of section shown on Figure 5. Logs are sonic logs. Depth divisions on logs are 10 ft (3.05 m) apart.

ning of the "B" cycle. The basal carbonate, the "B" Dolomite, is a shallow–subtidal deposit of impermeable anhydrite and dolomite. The extensive continuity of this unit documents the widespread nature of this transgressive event. Because the "B" dolomite is an excellent internal marker, it was chosen as the structural mapping horizon (Fig. 1). Completing the "B" cycle is the overlying, regressive, "B" Sandstone.

At Hawk Point Field, the thickness of the "B" cycle exceeds 125 ft (38.1 m). North–south cross section A–A' (Fig. 4) shows "B"–cycle correlations and the structural position of wells across the field.

DATA AND METHODOLOGY

Three wells at Hawk Point Field, two of them productive, were cored (Total No. 42–30 Ickes, Total No. 31–30 Ickes, and Total No. 32–30 Ickes); six were logged with dipmeter surveys (Fig. 5). Thin–section and scanning electron microscopy (SEM), and energy–dispersive spectrometry (EDS) were applied to samples selected from the three cored wells to determine mineralogic and lithologic variations and sandstone diagenesis. Stratigraphic correlations were based on lithologic examinations of core material, on resistivity and porosity logs, and on dipmeter data.

Figure 5. Map of locations of all wells drilled, Hawk Point Field. Location of structural cross section A–A' (Fig. 4) shown. Cored wells indicated by asterisks. Wells with dipmeter data designated with stars. (1000 ft = 304.8 m)

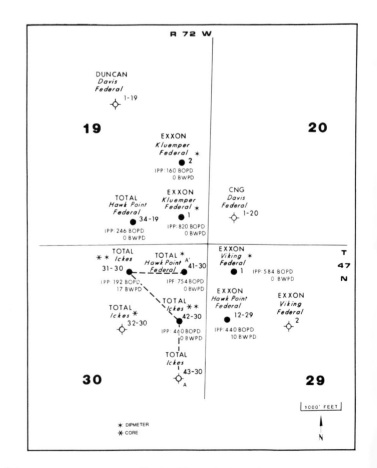

Special analyses were performed on cores from the two producing wells. A six-in. (15.2 cm) sample from each foot of core in the two producing wells was cleaned with toluene injected under pressure by CO_2. Boyle's Law (helium injection) porosity and air permeability values were obtained from full-diameter core measurements. For formation factor and cementation exponent determinations, four samples from each well were saturated with simulated formation brine (57,900 ppm total dissolved solids); resistivities were measured at ambient and effective overburden pressure.

Capillary pressures were measured by mercury injection methods on four samples from each core. Pore-throat radii were calculated from mercury injection data using standard values for the air-mercury system (140° contact angle, 480 dynes/cm interfacial tension).

Samples for water-oil imbibition relative permeability determinations were selected from cleaned core pieces. Refined mineral oil and simulated formation brine were utilized.

LITHOFACIES, POROSITY, AND DEPOSITIONAL MODEL

A depositional model (Fig. 6) was developed, based on examinations of the Hawk Point Field cores and logs (see below) and on descriptions of modern eolian sedimentary structures (Fryberger et al., 1983). The most common sedimentary features observed are those formed on dune slip faces. These features include avalanche strata with fadeout laminae; wavy laminae; sandflow or avalanche toes; and ripple strata with fine, inverse graded laminations and pin-stripe laminae (Fryberger and Schenk, 1988). Other common slipface characteristics include apron deposits characterized by gently dipping ripple strata, sandflow toes, and climbing ripples.

Interdune deposits consist of two types in the Hawk Point cores: wet-evaporitic and wet-non-evaporitic. Evaporitic interdunes are composed of laminated anhydrite, flat ripple strata, and salt-ridge

features. Wet-nonevaporitic interdune deposits contain subaqueous-ripple, point-bar, and fining-upward sequences deposited by ephemeral streams or wadii. Both types of interdune deposits are well cemented with anhydrite.

Lithofacies in the No. 42-30 Ickes and No. 31-30 Wells

Eolian facies are distinguishable from core and log data in these wells (Figs. 7 and 8). The shallow-reading resistivity logs that were run have vertical resolutions of about six inches (15.2 cm) and are good tools for correlation in these eolian rocks. Dipmeter data show a predominantly southward dip direction for cross-bedding. Unfortunately, the four-arm dipmeter tool could not resolve small-scale cross-bed dips, allowing only generalized dip interpretations in these wells.

The cored interval was divided into distinct units based on sedimentary structures and textures. Porosity and permeability values were grouped and averaged for each unit. Differences in core porosity and permeability between units are due to distinct stratigraphic changes and related diagenetic evolution.

Interdune Units

Interdune sequences occur in both wells (Figs. 7 and 8). Numerous fining-upward sequences occur in the upper 9 to 13 ft (3 to 4 m) of the interdune intervals, each sequence with a sharp base and capped by a thin (3 to 5 mm) shale. These are interpreted as interdune wadi deposits. The scattered dips from the dipmeter support the sedimentary structures observed. Porosity and permeability values are low in these intervals.

The lower five ft (1.5 m) of interdune deposits in the No. 42-30 Ickes core are horizontal interbeds of shale, sandstone, and banded anhydrite, interpreted as interdune pond deposits. Porosity and permeability range from 2.7 to 6.5% and from 0.4 to 2 md. The average radius of pore throats (PTR) is less than 0.5 microns (see discussion of petrophysics below). Within this nonproductive rock unit, abundant spotty and banded anhydrite with minor dolomite cement occludes porosity and reduces permeability.

Sand-Sheet Units

Both wells contain interpreted sand-sheet deposits. These massive sandstones are nearly featureless, although in places they are ripple laminated; have minor deflationary coarse sand lags; and have minor, spotty anhydrite cement throughout. The variable strikes and shallow dips shown by the dipmeter are characteristic. Dolomite, the dominant cement, occurs as fine to very fine-crystalline rhombs that line the pores. Porosity and permeability are slightly better in this facies (8-10% and 1.5-13 md). Minimal production is attributed to these sandstones. The sand-sheet facies in the No. 31-30 Ickes core contains minor deflationary coarse-sand lags and horizontal ripple laminae with porosity and permeability of 10.3% and 13 md.

Dune-Complex Units

Again, both wells contain sandstones of this facies. These sandstones are of two types: cross-bedded ava-

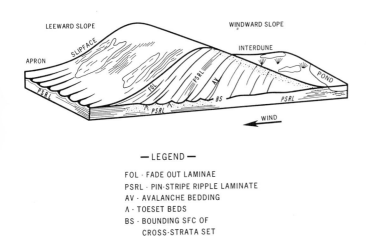

LEEWARD SLOPE   WINDWARD SLOPE
SLIPFACE   INTERDUNE
APRON   POND
PSRL   FOL   PSRL   AV   BS   PSRL   WIND
PSRL

— LEGEND —

FOL - FADE OUT LAMINAE
PSRL - PIN-STRIPE RIPPLE LAMINATE
AV - AVALANCHE BEDDING
Λ - TOESET BEDS
BS - BOUNDING SFC OF
    CROSS-STRATA SET

Figure 6. Schematic block diagram of a barchan dune with depositional position of commonly observed sedimentary structures located.

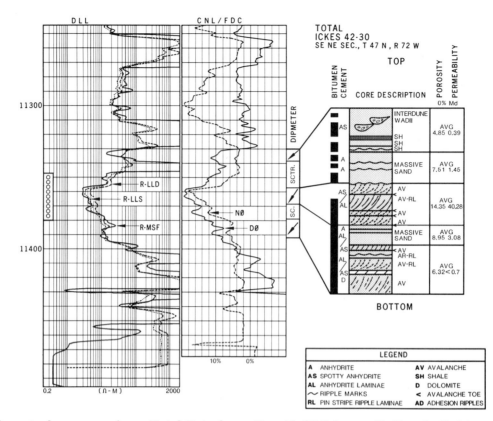

Figure 7. Core–to–log comparison, Total Petroleum No. 42–30 Ickes well. Depth divisions on logs are 10 ft (3.05 m) apart. DLL = dual laterolog, CNL/FDC = neutron/density log (sandstone matrix). Note superior porosity of avalanche deposits. R–MSF = microspherically focused log.

lanche deposits and massive sandstones of reworked dune fronts. Avalanche deposits display sets of cross strata that have sandflow toes at the base, high dip angles (greater than 25°), and fadeout and inter-bedded pin–stripe ripple laminae (Plate 1). The greatest core porosity, permeability, and PTR's occur in this facies; the maximum porosity and permeability measured, 18% and 104 md, occur in the top foot of this lithofacies in the No. 42–30 Ickes well.

The best reservoir in the No. 31–30 Ickes well also occurs in avalanche–produced deposits of high angle cross–strata and massive sandstones in which porosity averages 10.7% and permeability 26.3 md (5 microns PTR). Anhydrite is present as spotty cement and in minor anhydrite–cemented ripple laminae.

A massive sandstone occurs between 11,369 ft (3,465.3 m) and 11,375 ft (3,467.1 m) depths in the No. 42–30 Ickes core. The dipmeter shows scattered azimuths compatible with the lack of sedimentary structures. An increased concentration of anhydrite cement, as a banded unit in the top two ft (6 m) and as spotty concentrations elsewhere, results in diminished porosity and permeability. Average porosity and permeability are 9.0% and 3.1 md (2 microns PTR).

In the No. 42–30 Ickes core, anhydrite cementation increases downward in the interval from 11,375 ft (3,467.1 m) to the base of the core. In the top four

ft (1.2 m) of this interval, gently dipping (less than 10o), fine, climbing–ripple laminations are color–enhanced by alternating dolomite and anhydrite cement. The remaining 11 ft (3.3 m) of the core are predominantly high–angle avalanche strata with abundant ripple and fadeout laminae. The increased occurrence of anhydrite in this interval has resulted in low porosity and permeability (averaging 6.3% and less than 0.7 md).

Increasing concentrations of anhydrite cement are also observed in the last 10 ft (3 m) of the No. 31–30 Ickes cores. Avalanche crossbed sets from one to six ft (0.3 to 1.8 m) in thickness are characterized by intercalated thin sets of ripple laminae that decrease in angle toward the base and terminate in toeset beds. These generally white, anhydrite–cemented sandstones are specked with black dead oil stain, evidence of minor remnant porosity. Permeability averages 2.7 md for this interval.

PETROGRAPHY

In general, detrital grains in the "B" Sandstone are fine grained, well–rounded, well–sorted, and equant quartz grains, with lesser amounts of feldspar. The dominant diagenetic minerals are anhydrite and dolomite with lesser quantities of clays, quartz, and pyrite (Table 1). MINERALOG (registered trademark of

TOTAL
ICKES 31-30
NW NE SEC. 30, T 47 N - R 72 W

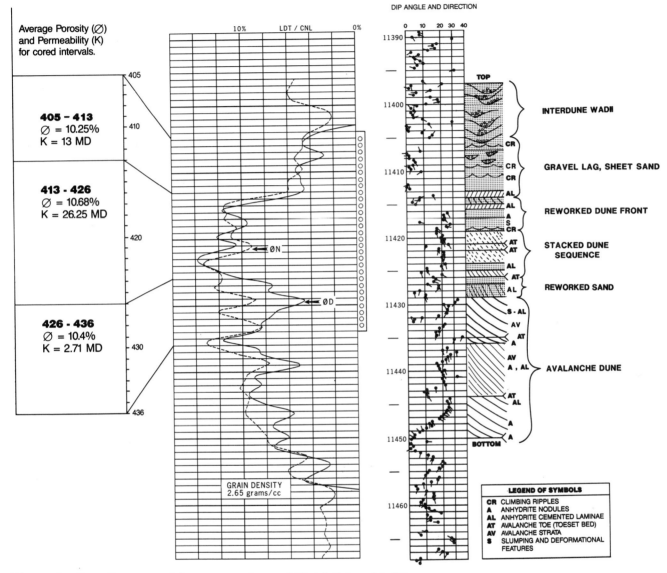

Figure 8. Detail core and log comparison of Total Ickes 31–30.

Core Laboratories), an analytical method for identification of common minerals based on infrared spectroscopy, identifies the same suite of minerals, although quartz is 20% greater in the No. 42-30 Ickes well (Table 2) because MINERALOG does not include porosity in the percent calculations.

Anhydrite Cement

Anhydrite is the predominant cement in each core (Fig. 7 and 8), occurring as intergrowths of poikilotopic crystals. Toward the base of the sandstone, poikilotopic anhydrite completely occludes the pore space. Where anhydrite occurs adjacent to porosity (usually stratigraphically high in the dune com-

plex), isolated patches of poikilotopic cement are in optical continuity and display crystal–cleavage alignment with cement in adjacent tight rock. Anhydrite that was once a single crystal is now fragmented by dissolution (Schenk and Richardson, 1985; Schenk, 1988). Additional evidence for dissolution includes oversized pores (Plate 2), irregular birefringence zonation ("dissolution fringe" of Schenk and Richardson, 1985) along the edges of optically continuous anhydrite remnants, high intergranular porosities adjacent to tightly packed laminae with little or no visible porosity, and anhydrite crystals with ragged shapes that begin at grain boundaries and extend along the cleav-

Table 1. Petrographic analysis of sandstone thin sections from Total Petroleum No. 31–30 Ickes well (NW NE Sec 30 T47N R72W), Campbell County, Wyoming.

Sandstone Components	11,408–409'	11,412–413'	11,415–416'	11,421–22'
Quartz Grains	64%	55%	55%	62%
Dolomite Cement	9	2	5	2
Anhydrite Cement	8	15	4	4
Dead Oil	4	20	25	26
Clay Minerals	2	tr	1	tr
Heavy Minerals	tr	tr	tr	tr
Secondary Intergranular Pores	12%	8%	10%	5%

Table 2. Mineralog* (registered trademark of Core Laboratories, Inc.) analyses, in wt %, Total Petroleum No. 42–30 Hawk Point Fed (SE NE Sec 30 T47N, R72W), Campbell County, Wyoming.

MINERALOG* DATA (WEIGHT PERCENT)													
Sample Depth (ft)	QTZ	PLG	KSP	CAL	DOL	PYR	ANH	BAR	CLAY	KAO	ILL	CHL	SMC
11354.7	87	0	5	0	7	0	0	0	1	A	P	A	A
11357.7	78	0	4	0	9	0	2	0	7	A	P	A	P
11373.0	83	0	0	0	8	0	6	0	3	A	P	A	P

*Core Laboratories   A=Absent   P=Present

QTZ – Quartz	KSP – K–Feldspar	DOL – Dolomite	ANH – Anhydrite	KAO – Kaolinite	CHL – Chlorite
PLG – Plagioclase	CAL – Calcite	PYR – Pyrite	BAR – Barite	ILL – Illite	SMC – Smectite

ages. These observations are similar to those made at Mellot Field by Schenk (1988).

Early precipitation of calcium sulfate is evidenced by less compaction and open packing in anhydrite-cemented parts of the reservoir than in laminae cemented with dolomite. Early precipitation of gypsum is well documented in coastal sabkha environments (Kinsman, 1969; Bush, 1973; Butler, 1973; Shinn, 1973; Fryberger, et al., 1983).

Partial dissolution of anhydrite is pervasive. White patches of remnant anhydrite cement exist in sharp contrast to adjacent brown and black, oil-saturated secondary porosity (Plate 2).

Dolomite Cement

Dolomite is the second most abundant intergranular cement in the reservoir, ranging from 2 to 19 wt%. Dolomite occurs as aggregates of small euhedral rhombs (Plate 2) that line pores, forming intercrystalline pore throats. Dolomite is the major cement in finer-grained ripple-laminated beds that exhibit no evidence of anhydrite. In areas of partial anhydrite dissolution, dolomite rhombs postdate the anhydrite. Aggregate clusters of dolomite also are present as replacement products of carbonate and feldspathic grains (Plate 2).

Authigenic Clay

The sandstones in the No. 42–30 Ickes core contain 2 to 5% clay, mostly illite (80% of clay minerals)

and mixed-layer illite/smectite (20%). Illite occurs as highly crenulated grain-coating masses and as elongate laths projecting into intergranular pores (Plate 2). Mixed-layer illite/smectite occurs as "honeycomb" crenulated platelets.

DISTRIBUTION OF POROSITY

The best porosity and permeability are found in avalanche strata where they are located in the upper portion of the dune complex. Anhydrite-dissolving fluids could circulate through well sorted avalanche strata where laminations are poorly developed. Core data reveal that only at the top of the dune complex did porosity and permeability develop. Laterally continuous ripple laminae, typically cemented in alternating bands by anhydrite and dolomite, are vertical permeability barriers and also may limit the radius of drainage away from the drillhole. In all cases, the basal portions of the "B" Sandstone have remained thoroughly cemented with anhydrite, regardless of internal sedimentary structures. All sandstones deposited in interdune environments are pervasively cemented with anhydrite and dolomite, and therefore are not productive.

In the ripple-laminated portions of the reservoir, original inhomogeneity in the distribution of anhydrite can be observed. Finer-grained (0.09 mm to 0.21 mm) laminae display tight packing, planar and concavo-convex grain contacts, mechanical- and chemical compaction features, and little or no porosity.

These are interbedded with medium-grained (0.33 mm to 0.42 mm) laminae with loosely packed grains, tangential and planar grain contacts, and high intergranular porosity. Lack of anhydrite cement left the finer-grained rocks subject to compaction, pressure solution, and dolomite cementation. The coarser-grained laminae probably were cemented early by anhydrite; later dissolution of anhydrite left loosely packed grains with secondary porosity (Plate 2).

OIL MIGRATION

Two types of petroleum substances occur in the Hawk Point reservoir. One is an insoluble, immobile, black solid that coats pores and pore throats. This bitumen is most common in the smallest pores and microporosity. Analysis of a sample of the bitumen was performed by Core Laboratories in Dallas, Texas. TOC was 1.02 wt%. Elemental composition was (in wt%):

C	H	S	O	N	Ash	H/C
75.48	5.21	4.40	1.31	0.70	10.29	0.82

Also present in the reservoir is low in sulphur (0.47 wt%) producible crude. It is possible that the hydrocarbons represent a two-stage migration into the reservoir.

Processes that may alter reservoir hydrocarbons to bitumen include thermal alteration by increasing temperatures, gas deasphalting, and near surface water-washing degradation and biodegradation (Rogers, McAlary, and Bailey, 1974). Thermal alteration of the Hawk Point bitumen is suggested by its H/C ratio and insolubility in toluene.

However, a thermal origin alone does not explain the presence of both bitumen and mobile crude in the same reservoir. The maximum depth of burial for Hawk Point probably is the present depth. Because the present reservoir temperature of 256°F (124°C) has not adversely affected the producible hydrocarbons, then gas deasphalting, water washing, or biodegradation would have to be invoked to explain the bitumen.

Oil from maturing Pennsylvanian and Permian source rocks (Meissner, Woodward, and Clayton, 1984; Peterson, 1984) migrated into eastern Wyoming in Late Jurassic time (Sheldon, 1967; Momper and Williams, 1984), and could have been trapped in shallow structural and stratigraphic traps formed in response to Ancestral Rockies tectonics. Later loss of seal or influx of meteoric waters could have facilitated both anhydrite dissolution and nonthermal alteration of early oil; evidence of influx of meteoric fluids is provided by Late Jurassic and Early Cretaceous dissolution of salt beds in the Permian Goose Egg Formation (Rasmussen and Bean, 1984). Oils degraded by these processes could have been converted to bitumen with increased temperature and burial (Connan and Van Der Weide, 1978; Hunt, 1979).

The producible hydrocarbons at Hawk Point Field may have been sourced locally from radioactive black shales of the middle Minnelusa (Clayton and Ryder, 1984). This oil migrated into structural and stratigraphic traps that developed as a result of Laramide development of the basin.

PETROPHYSICS

In interpreting petrophysical data, the characteristics of secondary porosity must be considered. Secondary pores and pore throats have a greater diversity in size and shape than do primary intergranular pores. As observed in core the Hawk Point cores, the distribution of secondary porosity is much less uniform then is typically the case with primary porosity, although it still is related to facies.

Porosity-Permeability Relationships

H.D. Winland developed an empirical relationship between porosity, permeability, and r_{35}, or pore-throat determined from mercury injection-capillary pressure testing, at 35% mercury saturation (Kolodzie, 1980; cf. Pittman, this volume):

$$\log r_{35} = 0.732 + 0.588 \log Ka - 0.864 \log \phi$$

where Ka = core air permeability (md)
and ϕ = core porosity (percent)

In the No. 42-30 Ickes core, three clusters of points identify three pore-throat sizes in the reservoir (Fig. 9). The reservoir interval with the largest pore throats (3-6 microns) makes the greatest contribution to fluid flow. Rocks with pore-throat radii of two microns probably contribute to fluid production. Wet-interdune rocks found at the top of the core, have porosity occluded by anhydrite and dolomite cement display an average pore throat radius of 0.5 microns; this is not large enough to be a fluid conduit. Of the 33 ft (10.2 m) of reservoir perforated in this well, the top nine ft (2.8 m) have small pore throats and should not have been perforated. By plotting permeability vs. porosity while accurately noting depth, the clustered relationships can be easily detected.

A similar plot for the No. 31-30 Ickes core (not illustrated) revealed a relatively great thickness of rocks with small pore throats in the lower part of the perforated interval. A high relative permeability to water in these rocks might be expected and is in fact observed in production from this well (IPP 192 BOPD, 17 BWPD).

Capillary Pressures

Capillary pressures are a measure of pore volume controlled by pore throats greater than a given size. These curves may be used to estimate displacement pressures, immobile water saturations, the thickness of the hydrocarbon-water transition zone, and pore-throat size and sorting (Schowalter, 1979). The capillary pressure curves (e.g., Figs. 10A and 11A) reflect reservoir rock that is low in clay content and has well-sorted pore throats with r_{35} values of 2.08 to 4.39 microns. This is congruent with sizes predicted from Winland's equation.

Rocks with smaller pore throats, and consequently lower permeability, require greater pressures to permit initial entry of hydrocarbons into the pore spaces; this critical pressure is termed "displacement pressure". Pressures needed to achieve 10% mercury saturation are roughly equal to displacement pressures (Schowalter, 1979). These vary in the Ickes wells between 17 and 35.4 psia, indicating a variable pore-throat network between samples and low displacement pres-

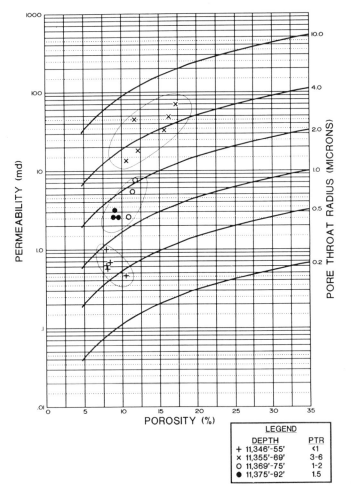

LEGEND

DEPTH	PTR
+ 11,346'–55'	<1
× 11,355'–69'	3–6
O 11,369'–75'	1–2
● 11,375'–92'	1.5

Figure 9. Plot of porosity versus permeability. Lines indicate values of r35, or pore-throat radius at 35% mercury saturation, derived from mercury injection test by the equation of Winland (Kolodzie, 1980). Total Petroleum No. 42–30 Ickes core.

sures. Because porosity in this reservoir is secondary, samples with similar porosity and permeability can vary considerably in displacement pressure.

Pore-throat sorting (PTS) was calculated for each sample with capillary pressure data by the method of (Jennings, 1987) (Table 3). On a scale of 1.0 (perfect sorting) to 8.0 (no sorting), the No. 42–30 Ickes well has an average PTS of 1.72; the No. 31–30 Ickes average PTS is 1.66. This indicates that, once displacement pressure has been exceeded, very little additional pressure is required to greatly increase oil saturation and fill almost all the porosity with oil.

The inflection points on both capillary pressure curves have sharp curvature, indicating relatively few small pore throats. The steep portions of the curves are measures of immobile water saturations in a water wet reservoir; at 2,000 psi mercury injection pressure (equivalent to 800–1,000 ft, or 247–305 m, of oil column), immobile water saturation varies from 10 to 15% of pore space. At 100 ft (30.5 m) in the oil column (250 psi), immobile water saturations range from 15% in the best rock to 30% in the rocks with smaller pore throats.

Table 3. Indices of pore-throat sorting (Jennings, 1987), based on capillary pressure data, Minnelusa "B" Sandstone, Hawk Point Field.

PORE THROAT SORTING (PTS)						
Depth	Perm, md	Por, %	Swi	75% MSP	25% MSP	PTS
No. 31–30 Ickes						
11,414	26	11.0	11%	60	22	1.65
11,421	20	13.1	12%	76	28	1.65
11,427	7.9	12.5	15%	120	42	1.69
					Average	1.66
No. 42–30 Ickes						
11,358	100	18.7	10%	40	20	1.41
11,361	61	17.3	10%	60	23	1.61
11,366	29	12.4	12%	110	22	2.23
11,377	3.0	11.6	12%	180	65	1.66
					Average	1.72

PTS = [75% MSP/25% MSP]$^{1/2}$ where:
PTS is Pore Throat Sorting
MSP is mercury saturation pressure at 25% saturation and 75% saturation
1.0 = perfect sorting
8.0 = no sorting

Height above free water level was calculated for each injection pressure in the two producing cores (Table 4) using values of 30° for contact angle (Core Laboratory Standard, and Berg, 1975) and 21 dynes/cm for interfacial tension (Schowalter, 1979). A minimal transition zone where both water and oil would be produced is documented by the plateau of the capillary pressure curves. To date, water has not been produced in any appreciable quantities at Hawk Point Field. A small amount of connate water (less than 1 barrel per day) is produced from the No. 31–30 Ickes well (resistivity = 0.017 at 245°F, or 118°C).

Electrical Properties

Electrical properties were determined from the two productive cores, with interesting results. The cementation exponent "m" (Archie, 1942) is related to pore structure. In most clean sandstones, "m" is close to a value of 2. Values of "m" measured in both wells from the best portions of the reservoir range from 1.82 to 1.84 at overburden pressures of 7,175 and 7,230 psi (Table 5). These low values could represent pore variations caused by differential anhydrite dissolution, dolomite cementation, and compaction.

The saturation exponent "n" (Archie, 1942), as a measure of electrical conductivity through the reservoir when it is partially oil saturated, is very sensitive to wetting state. In water-wet rocks, formation water is located in the small pores and as a continuous layer on grain surfaces in the large pores. In clean, normal water-wet systems, the saturation exponent maintains

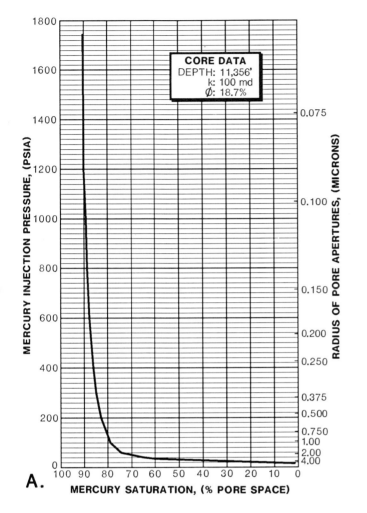

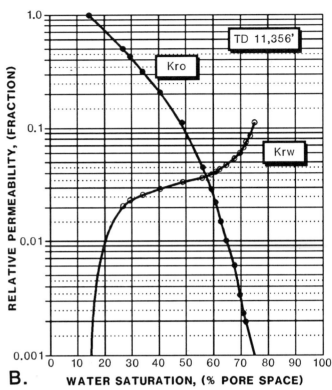

Figure 10. Mercury injection–capillary pressure (A) and relative permeability (B) curves for the Total Petroleum No. 42–30 Ickes 42–30.

Table 4. Calculations of height above free water, Minnelusa "B" Sandstone, Hawk Point Field.

No. 31–30 Ickes			
Sample Depth	11414	11418	11421
Subsea Depth	−6538	−6542	−6545
Perm, md	26	1.9	20
Porosity, %	11.0	9.8	13.1
Sat. Oil, %	78.3	75.0	80.6
Height above FWL, ft	105.1	123.9	105.1
No. 42–30 Ickes			
Sample Depth	11356	11359	11364
Subsea Depth	−6535	−6542	−6547
Perm, md	100	61	29
Porosity, %	18.7	17.30	12.40
Sat. Oil, %	85.8	82.49	79.36
Height above FWL, ft	135.2	112.65	135.20

a nearly constant value of 2. Values larger than 2 are documented for oil–wet and mixed–wettability core, in which oil preferentially wets grain and crystal surfaces, thereby decreasing conductivity. (Highly resistive organic compounds such as coal, bitumen, and asphalt can cause irregular "n" values that can exceed 10; see Anderson, 1986b). Low "n" values can result from bound water in clay– or dolomite–related microporosity.

In the Hawk Point cores, extremely low saturation exponent values were measured, ranging from 1.19 to 1.53 at ambient conditions (Table 5). While overall clay percentage is low, dolomite content ranges from 2 to 19% (Tables 1, 2), which may be sufficient to yield slightly lower "n" values.

These low values may not be representative of the formation. In plugs where thin laminations occur, saturation equilibrium may not be achieved during the time of the test. Also, if laboratory measured "n" values are to be meaningful, measurements must be made on samples at reservoir wetting conditions (Anderson, 1986b). The anomalously low "n" values measured could reflect wettability alteration during core retrieval and processing. A contact–angle measurement made on a Minnelusa oil sample from the Rock Creek Field, one mi (1.6 km) northwest of Hawk Point Field, indicated oil–wet behavior. U.S.

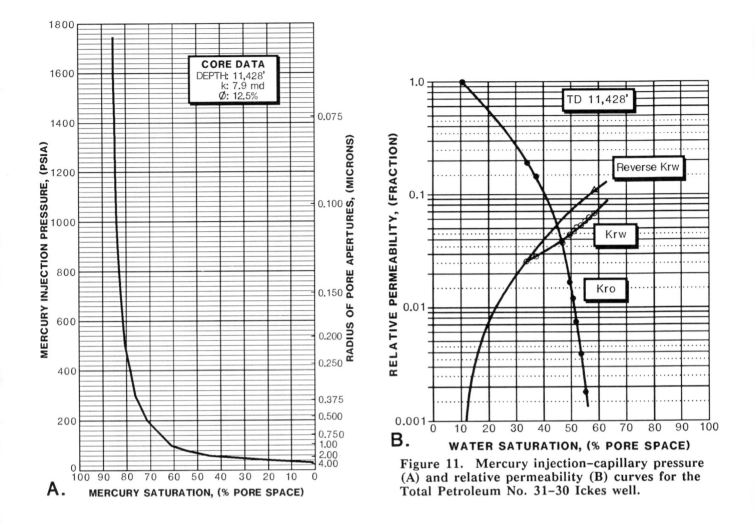

Figure 11. Mercury injection–capillary pressure (A) and relative permeability (B) curves for the Total Petroleum No. 31–30 Ickes well.

Table 5. Laboratory measurements of electrical properties, Minnelusa "B" Sandstone, Hawk Point Field.

No. 31–30 Ickes

Cementation Exponent		
Pressure, psi	"a"	"m"
0	1.00	1.59
400	1.00	1.69
7230	1.00	1.84

Saturation Exponent (Ambient Pressure)	
Depth	"n"
11418–11419	1.50
11421–11422	1.46
11421–11422	1.62
11427–11428	1.55
Composite	1.53

No. 42–30 Ickes

Cementation Exponent		
Pressure, psi	"a"	"m"
0	1.00	1.65
400	1.00	1.70
7175	1.00	1.82

Saturation Exponent (Ambient Pressure)	
Depth	"n"
11356–11357	1.26
11359–11360	1.33
11364–11365	1.08
11374–11375	1.15
Composite	1.20

Bureau of Mines and Amott Wettability studies of restored state core material from this field further support an oil–wet reservoir in sandstones with either high or low bitumen content. As with the Hawk Point samples, low "n" values (1.07 to 1.25) were measured on the cleaned core material prior to restoration. In situations of oil–wet behavior, the observed "n" values are lower than is reasonable.

In the Hawk Point area, immobile bitumen lines all the pores and pore throats. The producible oil probably contains polar surface active (surfactants) agents that would cause the oil to adsorb to the bitumen, causing the rocks to be partially oil wet and partially water wet. Thus, the observed "n" values are lower than is reasonable. The core material was subjected to chemical cleaning before routine porosity and permeability measurements were made. Anderson (1986b) demonstrated that core cleaning will transform naturally oil–wet rock to the water–wet state, with an accompanying decrease in the saturation exponent. Wettability also can be altered by: 1) drilling fluid invasion, especially in cases where the fluid contains surfactants or has a pH different from that of the reservoir fluids; 2) pressure and temperature changes between the reservoir and the surface; and 3) improper core handling and preservation that allows oxidation and evaporation of hydrocarbon light ends (Anderson, 1986a).

Relative Permeability

Relative permeability is a measure of the ability of a fluid to flow through porous rock when more than one fluid is present. Relative permeabilities are dependent on wettability, pore size distribution and geometry, and saturation, and may be used to evaluate recovery efficiency. For instance, during waterfloods of water–wet rock, water imbibes into small and medium–sized pores, displacing oil into the larger pores and pushing oil ahead of the flood front. Good recoveries are expected in this case. On the other hand, in oil–wet or marginally water–wet reservoirs, waterfloods still displace the non–wetting fluid into the larger pores but, that fluid is water. Recovery efficiencies are lower in these reservoirs. Relative permeability data are useful in quantifying these phenomena.

It is postulated that oil–wet Hawk Point cores might have been rendered water–wet by cleaning. If true, and if these relative permeability data are used to predict waterflood behavior, the net result will be too–high predictions of recovery efficiencies and early breakthrough of flood water (Anderson, 1987). The observed relative permeability data might be adjusted to represent the oil wet case, but such an approach depends on theoretical considerations beyond the scope of this paper.

STRATIGRAPHIC MAPPING

Core–to–log correlations allow stratigraphic interpretations in non–cored wells at Hawk Point Field. Despite abrupt lateral and vertical stratigraphic changes that occur between wells, three correlative intervals emerge throughout the reservoir. These are designated Sequences One through Three from oldest to youngest.

Sequence One

Sandstone of Sequence One directly overlies the "B" Dolomite. The interval is thickest in the center of the field (Fig. 12A). Total–magnitude dip vectors of cross–bedding from dipmeter logs imply a south-southwestward wind direction (Jorgensen and James, 1988). The earliest Sequence One sand accumulation was affected by a large subjacent "C" Sandstone buildup. This "C" Sandstone buildup was not mapped because of inadequate well penetration in the field, but is reflected in thicknesses of the overlying "B" Dolomite (Fig. 13); "B" Dolomite thicknesses are antithetic to "C" Sandstone topography (Fig. 4).

Sequence One is composed of eolian cross–bedded fine grained sandstones that are pervasively cemented by anhydrite (Fig. 7). Excellent examples of steeply dipping avalanche strata can be observed in core and dipmeter data. Since anhydrite dissolution did not penetrate these rocks, no wells are productive from this horizon.

Sequence Two

This interval includes the lower part of the field pay. The sandstones are thickest slightly east of the Sequence One "thick" (Fig. 11B). Dip vectors show a predominance of south dips, with continued sand deflection implied into and around the subjacent "C" Sandstone buildup. In the No. 42–30 Ickes core (Fig. 7), Sequence Two is composed of several stacked dune sets that range from two to five ft (0.60–1.52 m) in thickness. The upper nine ft (3.0 m) of Sequence Two in the this well consist of massive sandstone, interpreted as a reworked portion of the advancing dune front. The best porosity and permeability in the No. 42–30 Ickes are from this interval. The base of Sequence Two corresponds to the approximate base of the dissolution front that created secondary porosity in the No. 42–30 Ickes.

Sequence Three

Sequence Three can be divided into two mappable units on the basis of core data: Sequence Three–A, the top of the prograding dune (Fig. 12C; Fig. 5) and Sequence Three–B, the interdune wadi and pond sabkha deposits. Sequence Three–A is characterized by excellent porosity and permeability, a reflection of the pervasive anhydrite dissolution that occurred in this zone. Dipmeter data (Jorgensen and James, 1988) indicate high–angle cross–strata, as well as the scattered dips characteristic of reworked sands. The thickest part of this interval lies in the same position as that of Sequence Two, but is reduced in area. None of the wells cored Sequence Three–A.

Sequence Three–B (Fig. 12D) includes the non-productive wadi and pond deposits of the interdune sabkha. These units are made up of finely graded sandstone and shale that are highly cemented with anhydrite and dolomite. Dipmeter data support the lack of sedimentary structures that typify these deposits.

CONCLUSIONS

Eolian sandstones can form thick, widespread, "blanket" reservoirs with homogeneous properties. However, reservoir characteristics of the "B" Sand-

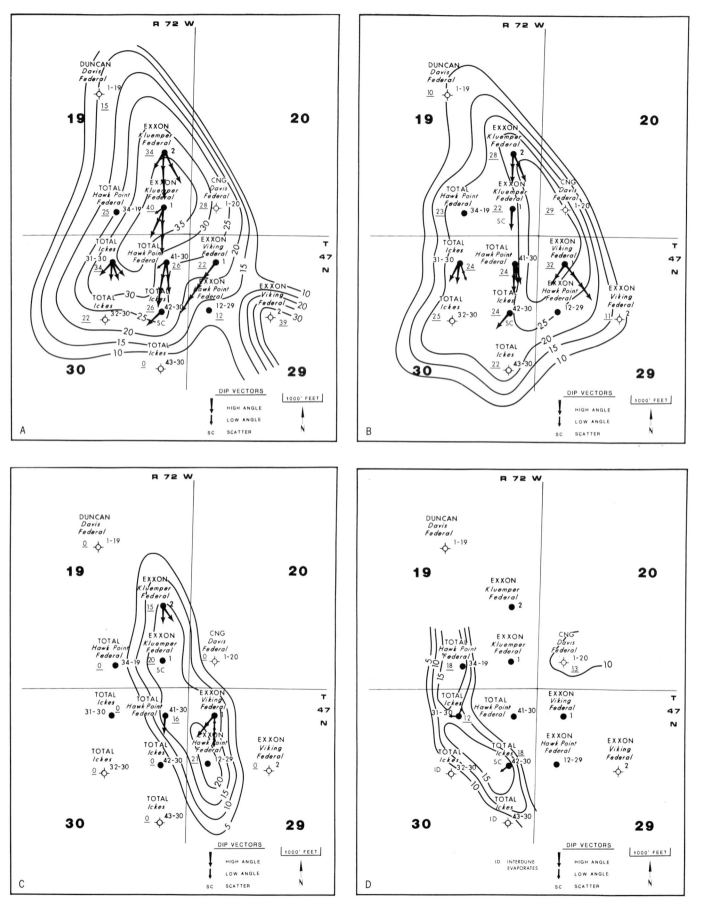

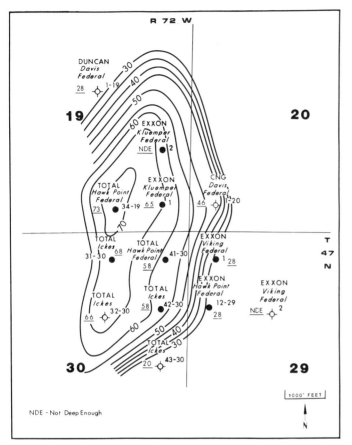

Figure 13. Area of thick "B" Dolomite closely approximates the position of a thin area in the underlying "C" Sandstone.

stone reservoir at Hawk Point Field are highly variable, and are a function of heterogeneous pore geometry caused by depositional facies variations and post–consolidation diagenetic changes. Consequently, water saturation and production quality are variable within the sandstone body.

In the coarser–grained sands, primary porosity and permeability were higher than in the finer–grained sediments; permeabilities may have differed by a factor of 100 between the end–member grain sizes. Growth of cements such as quartz, dolomite, anhydrite, and clay significantly reduced the primary porosity and permeability. The reduction affected all facies to a similar extent. Therefore, the facies with the best primary pore quality remained the best reser-

voir after diagenesis (D.J. Hartmann, 1989, pers. comm.).

The onset of oil migration terminated cementation. However, the emplaced oil further modified the pore system. The bitumen in the pores suggests that either changes in oil properties with time, or two stages of oil migration were responsible.

Effective porosity in the reservoir is directly proportional to the amount of anhydrite remaining in the pore space. Secondary porosity created by the partial dissolution of early pore–filling anhydrite is responsible for the reservoir at Hawk Point Field.

Dissolution of anhydrite is common (Schmidt and McDonald, 1979). However secondary porosity development in the Minnelusa Formation has been recognized only recently (Market and Al–Shaieb, 1984; Schenk and Richardson, 1985; Schenk, et al., 1988; Schenk, 1988). The existence of secondary porosity at Hawk Point is significant because of the depth of the reservoir; it is possible that compaction, pressure/solution, and other processes would have significantly decreased primary porosity not protected by poikilotopic anhydrite.

The extent to which anhydrite has been dissolved in the reservoir is problematical. It is possible that anhydrite–dissolving fluids were better able to invade and circulate through well–sorted avalanche strata than alternating tight and porous laminations typical of ripple strata. Thus, stratigraphy played a major role in determining sandstone bodies most likely to have secondary porosity development. However, the extent of dissolution is impossible to predict for a given reservoir.

The authigenic clays present may effect relative permeability, immobile water saturation, and electrical properties. Even in small amounts, the observed illite and mixed layer illite/smectite are sensitive to salinity and pH changes (John Kullman, Core Laboratories, personal communication) which, can result in drilling, stimulation, or production problems. Any drilling or cement filtrates that exceed a pH of 9.5 will decrease formation integrity and result in fines migration, swelling clays, and internal clay filters for trapping particles from dirty fluids. Rapid production of these rate–sensitive clays is not recommended. Smectite is naturally attracted to organic chemicals or surfactants that, if added to the fluid system, can alter wettability and decrease rock permeability to oil. Exotic surfactants, dispersants or emulsifiers should be avoided. An API fluid loss of not less than 6 cc's per 30 min-

← Figure 12. Thicknesses of correlative stratigraphic facies from well logs and core data. (1000 ft = 304.8 m)

A. Sequence One, basal "B" Sandstone, represents initial sand deposition, as well as a portion of the dune still cemented with anhydrite.

B. Sequence Two, middle "B" Sandstone, is the reservoir for producing wells in the central portion of the buildup.

C. Sequence Three–A, uppermost "B" Sandstone, is the uppermost portion of the prograding dune. Wells with thick Sequence Three–A sandstones are the most prolific producers.

D. Sequence Three–B is a separate unproductive facies not to be confused with Three–A despite the relative position at the top of the sand cycle. Three–B represents tight interdune sandstone and evaporites laid down contemporaneously with Sequence Three–A sands.

utes and strict maintenance of fluid pH at 8.0 to 9.0 will help to maintain formation integrity.

The question of the validity of "n" values measured on these cores is significant. In using Archie's (1942) equation for water saturation, utilization of an "n" value that is too low will result in the creation of pay zones when, in reality, those zones are wet or of marginal quality. Clearly, if wetting changes are responsible for low "n" values such as these, and if the acquisition of a native state core is not possible due to physical or economic prohibitions, an attempt must be made to restore the core material back to reservoir conditions. In any case, the "n" used for this reservoir should be 2 plus or minus 0.1

ACKNOWLEDGMENTS

I am grateful to Ben Hull, Dan Hartmann, Steve Fryberger, and Gray James for their many helpful comments and suggestions. I also thank the management of Total Petroleum, Inc. and TOTAL Minatome Corporation for permission to publish this paper.

REFERENCES

Anderson, W.G., 1986a, Wettability literature survey–Part I: rock/oil/brine interactions and the effects of core handling on wettability: JPT, v. 38, p. 1125–1144.

Anderson, W.G., 1986b, Wettability literature survey–Part 3: the effects of wettability on the electrical properties of porous media: JPT, v. 38, p. 1371–1378.

Anderson, W.G., 1987, Wettability literature survey–Part 5: the effects of wettability on relative permeability: JPT, v. 39, p. 1453–1468.

Archie, G.E., 1942, The electrical resistivity log as an aid in determining some reservoir characteristics: Trans. AIME, v. 146, p. 54–62.

Berg, R.R., 1975, Capillary pressures in stratigraphic traps: AAPG Bull., v. 59, p. 939–956.

Bush, P., 1973, Some aspects of the diagenetic history of the sabkha in Abu Dhabi, Persian Gulf, in B.H. Purser, ed., The Persian Gulf: Springer-Verlag, NY, p. 395–407.

Butler, G.P., 1973, Strontium geochemistry of modern and ancient calcium sulphate minerals, in B.H. Purser, ed., The Persian Gulf: Springer-Verlag, NY, p. 423–452.

Clayton, J.L. and R.T. Ryder, Organic geochemistry of black shales and oils in the Minnelusa Formation (Permian and Pennsylvanian), Powder River Basin, Wyoming, in Hydrocarbon Source Rocks of the Greater Rocky Mountain Region: RMAG, p. 231–253.

Connan, J. and B.M. VanderWeide, 1978, Thermal evolution of natural asphalts, in G.V. Chilingarian and T.S. Yen, eds., Bitumens, Asphalts, and Tar Sands: Elsevier, NY, p. 27–55.

Desmond, R.J., J.R. Steidtmann, and D.F. Cardinal, 1984, Stratigraphy and depositional environments of the middle member of the Minnelusa Formation, central Powder River Basin, Wyoming, in WGA Guidebook: 35th Ann. Field Conf., p. 213–239.

Fryberger, S.G., 1984, The Permian Upper Minnelusa Formation, Wyoming: Ancient example of an offshore-prograding eolian sand sea with geomorphic, facies, and system boundary traps for petroleum, in WGA Guidebook: 35th Ann. Field Conf.

Fryberger, S.G., A.M. Al-Sari, and T.J. Clisham, 1983, Eolian dune, interdune, sand sheet and siliclastic sabkha sediments of an offshore prograding sand sea, Dhahran area, Saudi Arabia: AAPG Bull., v. 67, p. 280–312.

Fryberger, S.G. and C.J. Schenk, 1988, Pin-stripe lamination: A distinctive feature of modern and ancient eolian sediments: Sed. Geol., n. 55, p. 1–15.

George, G.R., 1984, Cyclic sedimentation and depositional environments of the Upper Minnelusa Formation, central Campbell County, Wyoming, in WGA Guidebook: 35th Ann. Field Conf.

Hunt, J.M., 1979, Petroleum Geochemistry and Geology: W.H. Freeman and Co., San Francisco, 617 p.

Jennings, J.B., 1987, Capillary pressure techniques: application to exploration and development geology: AAPG Bull., v. 71, p. 1196–1209.

Jorgensen, S.D. and S.W. James, 1988, Integration of stratigraphic high resolution dipmeter into the development of the Minnelusa "B" sand reservoir in Hawk Point Field, Campbell County, Wyoming, in WGA Guidebook: 39th Ann. Field Conf., p. 105–ff.

Kinsman, D.J.J., 1969, Modes of formations, sedimentary associations and diagnostic features of shallow-water and supratidal evaporites: AAPG Bull., v. 53, p. 830–840.

Kolodzie, S., 1980, The analysis of pore throat size and use of the Waxman-Smits equation to determine OOIP in Spindle Field, Colorado: SPE-AIME 55th Ann. Fall Tech. Conf. and Exhibition, Paper SPE-12191, 8 p.

Market, J.C. and Z. Al-Shaieb, 1984, Diagenesis and evolution of secondary porosity in Upper Minnelusa sandstones, Powder River Basin, Wyoming, in D.A. McDonald and R.C Surdam, eds., Clastic Diagenesis: AAPG Mem. 37, p.367–389.

Meissner, F.F., J. Woodward, and J.L. Clayton, 1984, Stratigraphic relationships and distribution of source rocks in the greater Rocky Mountain region, in Hydrocarbon Source Rocks of the Greater Rocky Mountain Region: RMAG, p. 1–34.

Momper, J.A. and J.A. Williams, 1984, Geochemical exploration in the Powder River Basin, in G. Demaison and R.J. Murris, eds., Petroleum Geochemistry and Basin Evaluation: AAPG Mem. 35, p. 181–191.

Peterson, J.A., 1984, Permian stratigraphy, sedimentary facies, and petroleum geology, Wyoming and adjacent area, in The Permian and Pennsylvanian Geology of Wyoming: WGA Guidebook, 39th Ann. Field Conf., p. 25–64.

Rasmussen, D.L. and D.W. Bean, 1984, Dissolution of Permian salt and Mesozoic syndepositional trends, central Powder River Basin, Wyoming, in The Permian and Pennsylvanian Geology of Wyoming: WGA Guidebook, 39th Ann. Field Conf., p. 281–294.

Rogers, M.A., J.D. McAlary, and N.J.L. Bailey, 1974, Significance of reservoir bitumens to thermal-maturation studies, Western Canada Basin, v. 58, p. 1806–1824.

Schenk, C.J., 1988, Diagenesis of sandstones from the Permian Upper Minnelusa Formation, Powder River Basin, Wyoming, in S.G. Fryberger, L.S. Krystinick, and C.J. Schenk, eds., Modern and Ancient Eolian Deposits: Petroleum Exploration and Production: RMS-SEPM Field Seminar, Sec. 14.1–14.20.

Schenk, C.J. and R.W. Richardson, 1985, Recognition of interstitial anhydrite dissolution: a cause of secondary porosity, San Andres Limestone, New Mexico, and Upper Minnelusa Formation, Wyoming: AAPG Bull., v. 69, p. 1054–1076.

Schenk, C.J., J.W. Schmoker, and R.M. Pollastro, 1988, Diagenesis of sandstones in Permian Upper Minnelusa Formation, West Mellott Field, Powder River Basin, Wyoming [abs.].: AAPG Bull., v. 72, p. 244–245.

Schmidt, V. and D.A. McDonald, 1979, Secondary reservoir porosity in the course of sandstone diagenesis: AAPG Cont. Ed. Course Note Series No. 12, 124 p.

Schowalter, T.T., 1979, Mechanics of secondary hydrocarbons migration and entrapment: AAPG Bull., v. 63, p. 723–760.

Sheldon, R.P., 1967, Long-distance migration of oil in Wyoming: Mtn. Geol., v. 4, p. 53–65.

Shinn, E.A., 1973, Sedimentary accretion along the leeward, southeast coast of Qatar Peninsula, Persian Gulf, in B.H. Purser, ed., The Persian Gulf: Springer-Verlag, NY, p. 199–209.

Sedimentary Facies and Reservoir Characteristics of the Nugget Sandstone (Jurassic), Painter Reservoir Field, Uinta County, Wyoming[1]

LAURA E. TILLMAN[2]

[1]Received August 30, 1988; Revised February 15, 1989
[2]Chevron U.S.A, Inc., Denver, Colorado

Painter Reservoir Field is one of a number of fields producing from the Jurassic Nugget Sandstone in the Thrust Belt Province of southwest Wyoming and northeast Utah. The field is an asymmetric anticlinal structure located on the hanging wall near the leading edge of the Absaroka Thrust Plate. Original oil in–place (OIP) is estimated to be 138,000,000 barrels. Painter Reservoir Field has produced over 30,000,000 BO since its discovery in 1977.

The Nugget Sandstone is a stratigraphically complex and heterogeneous unit deposited primarily by eolian processes in an extensive sand sea. Dune and interdune/sand sheet facies have been identified during studies of over 5,000 ft (1,500 m) of core from 13 Painter Reservoir wells. The dune foreset facies is the best reservoir rock and consists of dipping avalanche and wind–ripple strata. The interdune facies has the poorest reservoir quality and consists of flat–lying wind–ripple strata, with zones of bioturbation and wavy lamination. The dune facies comprises approximately 75% of the cores examined, and the interdune facies approximately 25%. A high degree of heterogeneity results from variations in grain size, sorting, mineralogy, and thickness between cross strata. Porosity ranges from 1.5 to 21.5%. Air permeability measured on core plugs ranges from hundredths to thousands of millidarcies.

Nugget reservoir characteristics are strongly influenced by depositional environment. Porosity and permeability variations between facies and their arrangement in stacked vertical sequences result in stratigraphic layering of the reservoir. Consistent Nugget dune orientations result in directional permeability trends. The maximum permeability direction is parallel to dune slipfaces, which trend northwest to southeast. However, facies discontinuity, fracturing, and faulting offset permeability trends in parts of the field. The stratigraphic layering and directional permeability of the Nugget Sandstone are reflected in Painter Reservoir field history.

INTRODUCTION

Painter Reservoir Field is located in the Fossil Basin of southwest Wyoming, and is one of a series of fields on the hanging wall of the Absaroka Thrust Plate in the Thrust Belt Province (Fig. 1). Hydrocarbon production is from the Jurassic Nugget Sandstone, the principal reservoir for several fields located along the trend. The hydrocarbons were generated in Cretaceous source rocks in the footwall of the Absaroka Thrust (Warner, 1980). The Painter structure was first mapped with geophysical data and was confirmed in 1977 by the drilling of the discovery well, PRU 22–6A. Painter Reservoir Field is operated by Chevron USA with other working interests owned by Amoco Production Company and Union Pacific Resources. The field was developed on 40–acre (16 ha) spacing. Nitrogen and produced hydrocarbon gas were injected to balance withdrawals and to maintain reservoir pressure, until a tertiary recovery program was initiated in January, 1983. The tertiary program utilized nitrogen injection to increase reservoir pressure, and to cause miscible displacement of oil by gas–cap fluids. Initial response to the program was good; production peaked in 1983 at 14,000 BOPD. However, reservoir pressure was reduced in 1987 due to premature nitrogen breakthrough and increasing gas/oil ratios (GOR's). The current pressure–maintenance program once again utilizes nitrogen and produced hydrocarbon gas.

STRUCTURE

Painter Reservoir Field is trapped by a northeast-trending, doubly–plunging, asymmetric anticline located on the hanging wall near the leading edge of

FIELD DATA:	Painter Reservoir Field
Producing Interval:	Nugget Sandstone
Geographic Location:	Uinta County, Wyoming
Present Tectonic Setting:	Utah–Wyoming Thrust Belt
Depositional Setting:	Eolian sand sea just east of a shallow sea (Kocurek and Dott, 1983)
Age of Reservoir:	Jurassic
Lithology of Reservoir:	Very fine to coarse-grained, moderately to well-sorted quartz arenite to subarkosic arenite
Diagenesis:	Compaction; quartz, dolomite, and calcite cements; grain-coating and pore-bridging illite; fracturing
Porosity Types:	Intergranular, rare secondary porosity
Porosity:	1) dune maximum 21.5%, average 13.6%, 2) interdune/sand sheet maximum 18.0, average 9.7%
Permeability:	1) dune maximum 1,450 md, arithmetic average 16.5 md; 2) interdune/ sand sheet maximum 120 md, arithmetic average 1.5 md
Fractures:	Abundant fractures
Nature of Trap:	Structural
Entrapping Facies:	Gypsum Springs anhydrite member of Twin Creek Limestone
Source Rocks:	Subthrust Cretaceous shales
Timing of Hydrocarbon Migration:	Eocene or later (60 Ma or less)
Discovered:	1977
Reservoir Depth:	9,500–10,200 ft (2,850–3,060 m)
Reservoir Thickness:	850–950 ft (255–285 m)
IP (discovery well):	410 BOPD, 859 MCFGPD
Areal Extent:	About 1,700 acres (688 ha); 3.5 by 1 mi (5.6 by 1.6 km)
Original Reservoir Pressure:	4,130 psi
Cumulative Production (1/89):	30,900,000 BO, 274 BCFG
Estimated Oil in Place:	138,000,000 BO, 502 BCFG
Oil Gravity:	45–58° API
Minimum Water Saturation:	Dune 10%, interdune/sand sheet 14%

the Absaroka Thrust (Figs. 2 and 3). The structure has a gently dipping west flank, with a relatively undisturbed stratigraphic section. The east flank is structurally more complicated; wells generally penetrate numerous imbricate splays of the Bridger Hill Thrust and steeply dipping or overturned Nugget Sandstone. The structure has approximately 1,150 ft (345 m) of closure above the oil–water contact.

STRATIGRAPHY

The Nugget Sandstone overlies red beds of the Triassic Ankareh Formation and is unconformably overlain by marine limestones, anhydrites, and shales of the Middle Jurassic Twin Creek Formation (Fig. 4; Jordan, 1965; Picard, 1975; Fox, 1979). The Gypsum Springs Anhydrite, the lowermost member of the Twin Creek, serves as the top seal for the Nugget reservoir. The Twin Creek interval is overlain by clastic rocks of the Stump and Preuss formations. Salt beds up to 200 ft (60 m) thick are common in the lowermost Preuss Formation and serve as a detachment surface for the Bridger Hill Thrust. The nonmarine Lower Cretaceous Gannett and Bear River units unconformably overlie the Stump interval and are, in turn, separated from the Cretaceous–Paleocene Evanston Formation by an angular unconformity (Lamb, 1980). The Tertiary (Eocene) Wasatch Formation is present at the surface and is separated from

the Evanston Formation by another unconformity (Lamb, 1980; Frank, et al., 1982). Although the Nugget Sandstone is currently the only productive unit in the field, oil and/or gas shows have been encountered in the Thaynes Formation, various Twin Creek members, and the lowermost Ephraim Conglomerate Member of the Gannett Formation.

The Nugget Sandstone is areally extensive and was deposited primarily by eolian processes in a coastal to inland sand sea or erg (Hunter, 1981; Kocurek and Dott, 1983; Lindquist 1983, 1988). It extends from south–central and southwestern Wyoming to southeastern Idaho and northern Utah, increasing in thickness from less than 100 ft to over 2,000 ft (30–600 m) from east to west (Jordan, 1965). Nugget rocks are stratigraphically equivalent to the Navajo Sandstone of Colorado, Utah, and Arizona, and to the Aztec Sandstone of southern Nevada (Jordan, 1965; Doelger, 1981; Marzolf, 1982; Kocurek and Dott, 1983). The Nugget type section is located near Nugget Station on the Oregon Shortline Railroad 15 mi (24 km) west of Kemmerer, Wyoming (Veatch, 1907). The section is poorly exposed and small, as are most Nugget Sandstone outcrops in southwestern Wyoming near the producing trend. The best outcrops of sandstones comparable to those at Painter Reservoir Field Navajo sandstone are found along the south flank of the Uinta Mountains.

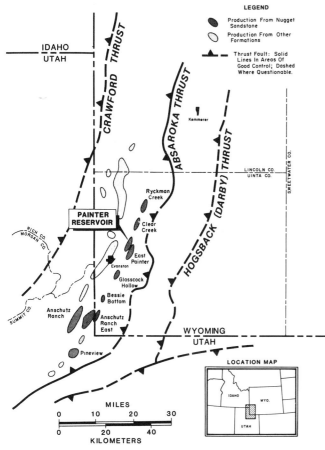

Figure 1. Location map of southwest Wyoming showing Thrust Belt fields and trends of major thrust faults (after Royse and Warner, 1987; reprinted with permission of the AAPG).

SEDIMENTARY FACIES

The Nugget Sandstone in Painter Reservoir Field is very fine to coarse grained, moderately to well sorted, and ranges in composition from quartz arenite to sub-arkosic arenite. Dune and interdune/sand sheet facies similar to those described by Lindquist (1983, 1988) have been identified during studies of over 5,000 ft (1,500 m) of core from 13 Painter Reservoir wells and are described in the following sections. These facies are the product of complex eolian processes occurring in a large sand sea.

Dune Facies

Dune deposits are the most abundant rock type, comprising 75% of the Nugget core examined. The facies is characterized by dipping (up to 25°), laminated to thin-bedded strata ranging in thickness from less than 0.1 in. (0.25 cm) to over 1.0 in. (2.5 cm) (Fig. 5). Individual dunes range in thickness from less than one ft (0.3 m) to almost 50 ft (15 m), and consist of either one set of cross strata formed by the migration of a simple dune, or of multiple cosets formed by the migration of superimposed dunes. Burrow traces locally disrupt stratification of dune deposits in the lower half of the formation.

Cross-strata provide clues to the origin of Nugget dunes. Thicker strata (typically thicker than 0.4 in., or 1.0 cm) are interpreted as grainflow deposits of avalanches on the slipfaces of migrating dunes. Thinner laminae (typically thinner than 0.4 in. or 1.0 cm), are interpreted as translatent strata (Hunter, 1977) formed by the migration of wind ripples across the dune slipfaces. Grainfall deposits have not been identified in cores, possibly due to their poor preservation potential in large dunes; they tend to form in the upper slipface regions, which commonly avalanche and are beveled (Hunter, 1981).

The "avalanche subfacies" consists primarily of avalanche strata, although interbedded wind-ripple laminae usually are present (Fig. 5, Plate 1A). It is the most abundant subfacies, comprising 45% of the Nugget core examined. Bedding is either distinct or indistinct. Flame structures and fadeout laminae are present. Dunesets composed primarily of avalanche strata are thickest and most common in the upper two-thirds of the Nugget Sandstone. Avalanche strata make the best Nugget reservoir. This is due to coarser grain sizes, better sorting, and thicker bedding, which lend better transmissibility to the rocks (Fig. 6).

The "mixed" subfacies, or dune deposits consisting of repetitive interbeds of thin avalanche deposits and wind-ripple laminae, comprises 30% of the Nugget cores. Dunes composed of mixed strata are thickest and most common in the lower half of the Nugget section. Both foreset and toeset deposits are present in this subfacies, but are difficult to differentiate in core. Toeset deposits can be recognized in some sequences by a gradual upward increase in bedding angle, from horizontal interdune laminae below to steeper dipping dune foreset beds above (Fig. 5). Toesets are characterized by concave-upward strata, and by almost tangential contacts with underlying interdune laminae. Characteristic "toeing out" or pinching out of strata also is present in some sequences. Mixed-subfacies dunes have poorer reservoir properties than do avalanche-subfacies dunes. Porosity and permeability are lower, and horizontal/vertical permeability ratios higher, in this subfacies than in the avalanche subfacies (Figs. 6 and 7) because of the greater abundance of finer-grained, poorer-sorted, and thinner wind-ripple strata.

Interdune/Sand Sheet Facies

The interdune/sand sheet facies comprises 25% of the core examined. Individual units range in thickness from less than one ft (0.3 m) to over 30 ft (10 m). The facies is thicker and more common in the lower half of the Nugget. Two subfacies are recognized. The "dry" interdune subfacies comprises 20% of cores examined. It is characterized by moderate sorting and horizontal lamination typically less than 0.4 in. (1 cm) thick (Fig. 5, Plate 1B). Preserved ripple forms can be identified locally. These rocks are interpreted as translatent strata formed by the migration of wind ripples across a relatively dry interdune or sand sheet environment. Reservoir quality is poorer in the dry interdune/sand sheet subfacies than in the dune facies (Figs. 6 and 7) due to finer grain sizes, poorer sorting, and thinner strata; higher hori-

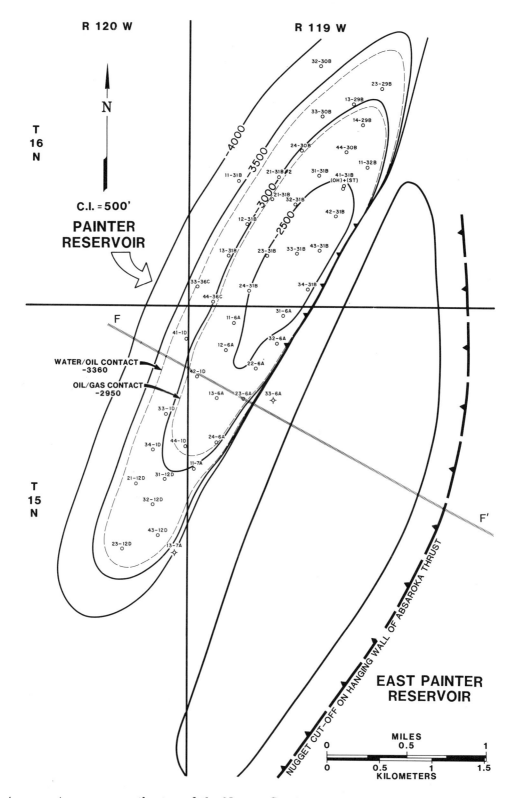

Figure 2. Structure contour map on the top of the Nugget Sandstone, Painter Reservoir Field. Datum is sea level. The location of East Painter Reservoir Field is outlined.

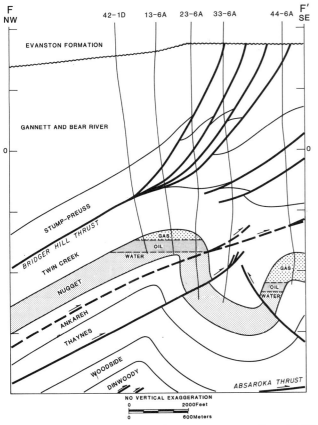

Figure 3. Northwest–southeast cross section F–F' across Painter Reservoir Field, interpreted by T. A. Heffner, 1984, and revised by R.L. O'Neill, 1988. Line of section is shown in Figure 2.

zontal permeabilities in rocks of this subfacies are associated with thicker laminae and coarser grain sizes. The horizontal/vertical permeability ratio is highest in this subfacies because of the thin and texturally variable strata.

The "damp" interdune subfacies composes 5% of cores examined. It is identified by burrowed, mottled, wavy, and/or contorted wind–ripple laminae (Plate 1C). These structures are inferred to result from a damp environment, as moisture in the sediment tends to stimulate organic activity and to reduce the competency of the sand (Ahlbrandt and Fryberger, 1981; Kocurek, 1981). The damp interdune facies is most common in the lower half of the Nugget Sandstone. Rocks of damp–interdune origin have the poorest reservoir properties of any Nugget facies (Figs. 6 and 7), because of the tendency for finer grains to become trapped in a moist environment (Ahlbrandt and Fryberger, 1981). The ratio of horizontal to vertical permeability is lowest in this facies because of bioturbation.

DIAGENETIC AND TECTONIC FEATURES

Diagenetic features seen in the Nugget Sandstone at Painter Reservoir Field include compaction, pressure solution, quartz overgrowths, poikilotopic carbonate cements (Plate 1D), molds after quartz and feldspar, and grain–coating and pore–bridging illite. Tec-

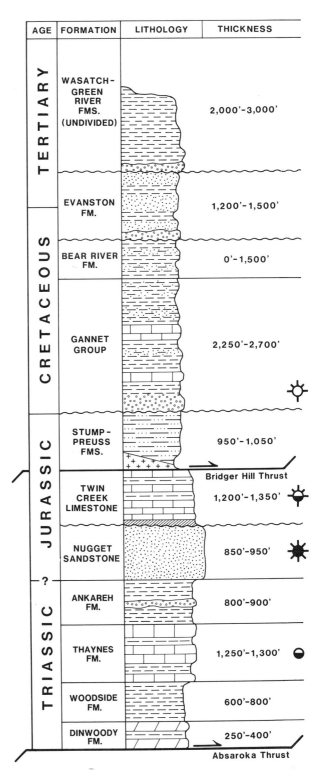

Figure 4. Schematic columnar section of Painter Reservoir Field. Productive and "show" zones in the field indicated by symbols at right of column.

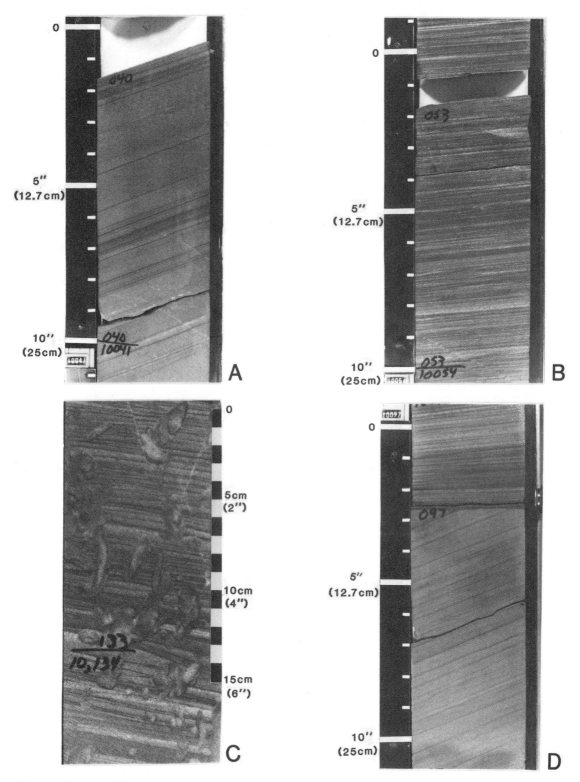

Figure 5. Cores of major Nugget reservoir facies.

A. Dune facies composed primarily of avalanche strata, with interbedded wind–ripple strata. PRU 31–31B, 10,040 ft (3,060 m).

B. Dry interdune/sand sheet subfacies composed of flat–lying wind–ripple translatent strata. PRU 31–31B, 10,053 ft (3,064 m).

C. Damp interdune subfacies, with burrows disrupting bedding. PRU 42–31B, 10,133 ft (3,089 m).

D. A typical facies sequence. Dipping foreset strata are truncated and overlain by relatively flat–lying wind ripple strata of a dune toeset. PRU 31–31B, 10,097 ft (3,078 m).

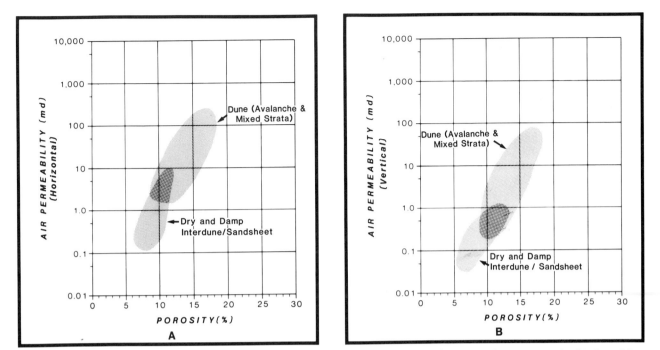

Figure 6. Porosities and air permeabilities measured on core plugs from major reservoir facies, Nugget Sandstone. Horizontal permeabilities (A) are markedly greater than vertical permeabilities (B) for any given porosity. Cores from wells PRU 31–31B and 42–31B.

tonic features include both open and closed fractures. Although these features affect the reservoir, productive characteristics are controlled principally by depositional processes.

Diagenetic processes most responsible for reduction in reservoir quality are compaction and illite formation. Compaction has reduced both porosity and permeability, particularly in finer–grained and more poorly sorted strata (Plate 1B; Fox, 1979). Illite is ubiquitous, coating grains, bridging pores, and reducing permeability (Fig. 8), especially in the finer–grained strata. The presence of pore–bridging illite does not reduce porosity as much as it does permeability, which causes scatter of data on plots of porosity versus permeability (Fig. 6).

Linear or anastomosing, high–angle fractures are abundant in the Nugget Sandstone and significantly affect the reservoir. They typically are filled with finely ground quartz gouge and cemented by quartz (Plate 1D). The gouge is created by limited movement, typically less than two in. (5 cm), along the fracture. As in East Painter Field (Lindquist, 1983), permeability measured in fractured and non–fractured core plugs in Painter Field indicates that fractures reduce horizontal permeability and may redirect fluid flow through the dune facies. However, permeability in the interdune/sand sheet facies generally is not reduced by the presence of gouge–filled fractures. Open fractures are observed less commonly in core than are closed fractures, possibly because core is lost more often from rocks in which the fractures are not cemented. Therefore, the importance of open fractures in the reservoir is difficult to quantify.

PALEOGEOGRAPHY

The Nugget stratigraphic sequence at Painter Reservoir is similar to that described at Anschutz Ranch East Field (Lindquist, 1988). Porosity tends to increase upward, reflecting the gradual buildup and migration of eolian sediments in an extensive sand sea or erg (Fig. 9). Core studies confirm Lindquist's interpretation that the depositional environment in the lower third of the Nugget was one of small, isolated dunes surrounded by extensive low–relief interdune areas and sand sheets. The depositional environment in the upper two–thirds of the Nugget in Painter Field was characterized by large dunes and dune complexes in a vast sand sea. Sediment supply and aridity increased through time during Nugget Sandstone deposition. Structural complications make measurement of Nugget stratigraphic thickness difficult; however, restorations indicate that the formation is between 850 and 950 ft (255–285 m) thick in Painter Field

STRATIGRAPHIC FACTORS IN RESERVOIR BEHAVIOR

Stratigraphic Layering

Nugget stratigraphy is characterized by stacked facies sequences, which are fairly well defined in cores and on wireline logs (Lindquist 1983, 1988). The marked difference in porosity and permeability between facies results in stratigraphic layering of the reservoir that directs fluid flow. Effects of stratigraphic layering in the Nugget reservoir have been observed in producing wells (Fig. 10). For instance, the PRU

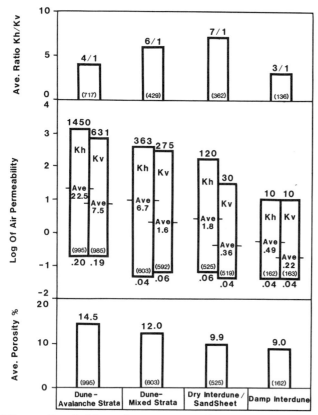

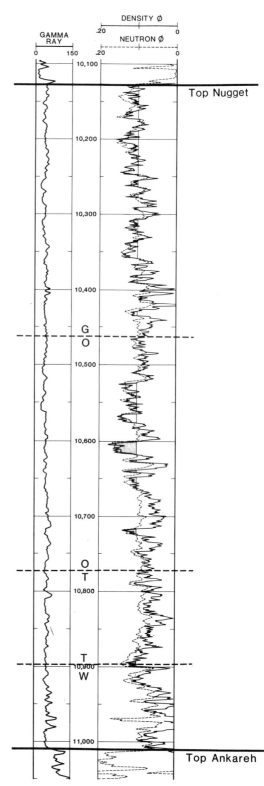

PRU 11-6A

Figure 7. Arithmetic averages of porosity, permeability, and horizontal/vertical permeability ratios, by facies. Permeability ranges also are shown. Permeabilities are measured in millidarcies. The number of samples (n) used for calculation is shown. Measurements were made on core plugs from same wells as in Figure 6.

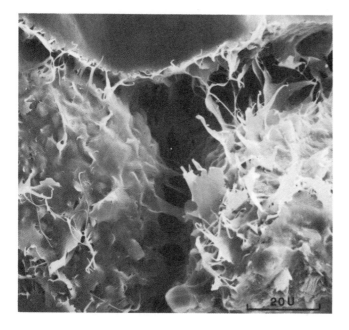

Figure 8. SEM image of grain-coating and pore-bridging illite. Magnification 1,000x. PRU 21-12D, 10,359 ft (3,157.4 m).

Figure 9. Compensated neutron/formation density log with gamma ray, showing the upward increase in Nugget Sandstone porosity. (100 ft = 30.5 m)

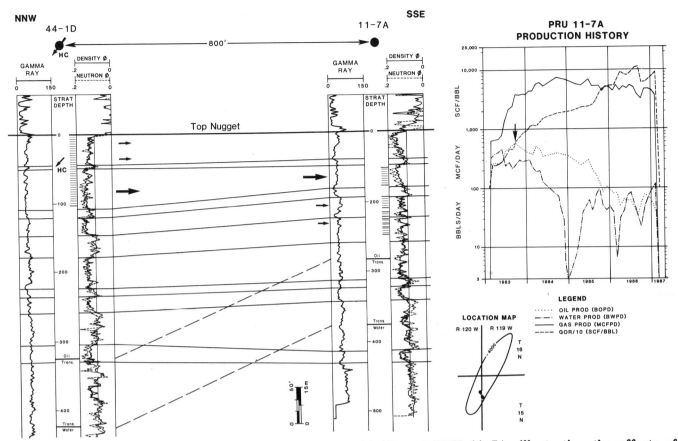

Figure 10. Stratigraphic cross section between PRU 44-1D and PRU 11-7A, illustrating the effects of stratigraphic layering on reservoir behavior. Logs display true stratigraphic thickness and are hung on the top of the Nugget. Most of the gas injected into the PRU 44-1D was entering the Nugget reservoir at the stratigraphic horizon shown by a heavy arrow; most of the gas produced from the PRU 11-7A was out of the correlative zone (also shown by a heavy arrow). See text for detailed discussion.

44-1D was converted from oil production to hydro-carbon-gas injection in February, 1983. One month after the conversion, the PRU 11-7A, which had previously been shut in due to high water cuts, was put back on production at a rate of 270 BOPD and 350 BWPD, with a GOR of 2,500 CFG/BO. Within seven months, oil production had increased to over 600 BOPD with a GOR of 6,500 CFG/BO. However, by January of 1987, oil production had fallen to 60 BOPD with a GOR of almost 80,000 CFG/BO, the highest in the field. Production logs indicated that almost half of the gas injected into the PRU 44-1D was entering a porous zone near the top of the reservoir and channelling to the PRU 11-7A well through the same zone. Thus, the injection zone in the PRU 44-1D well and the uppermost perforated zone in the PRU 11-7A appear to be in direct stratigraphic communication. The PRU 11-7A well was subsequently shut in. This type of behavior is common in Painter Field, but typically is more subtle than this example. Lateral discontinuity of facies, variable dune geometry, and the possible presence of faults and fractures in the Nugget Sandstone make prediction of these occurrences, and their magnitude, difficult.

Gas production also increased in the deeper producing intervals of the PRU 11-7A while gas was being injected into the PRU 44-1D well, despite apparent stratigraphic separation from the injection interval. Thus, the interdune deposits in the upper Nugget between these two wells are not barriers to flow, but they do tend to direct flow through more-permeable dune facies. Where pressure gradients are small, flow is controlled primarily by permeability layering. Where pressure gradients are large, vertical flow across the lower-permeability interdune facies can be significant, as between the perforated stratigraphic layers in the PRU 11-7A. Large pressure differentials also occur between injection and production perforations in dual injection/production wells.

Directional Permeability

Depositional attitudes of Nugget cross strata at Painter Reservoir have been determined from dipmeter logs, after rotation to remove structural dip components (Fig. 11). Data from several wells indicate dip azimuths between 215° and 225°. This southwesterly trend coincides well with other regional dip azimuths reported in the literature on the Nugget and Navajo formations (Jordan, 1965; Picard, 1975;

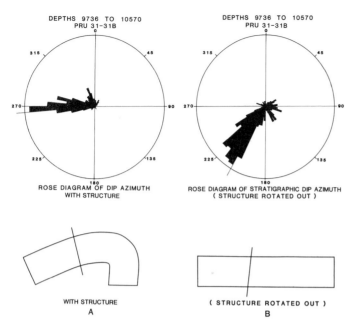

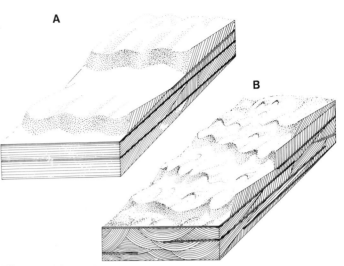

Figure 11. Present Nugget structural dip azimuth (A), and Nugget stratigraphic dip azimuth, with structural attitude rotated out (B). Note the unimodal distribution of laminae.

Doelger, 1981; Kocurek and Dott, 1983; Lindquist, 1983). The unimodality of the trend suggests that Nugget dunes were predominantly straight–crested transverse, barchanoid, or oblique dunes (Hunter, 1981; McKee, 1979; Lindquist, 1983, 1988). Wider scatter of rotated dip data in some wells indicate that an incorrect structural dip was used or that other Nugget dune morphologies are present, although minor.

The consistent depositional dip orientations and the straight–crested dune morphologies inferred for the Nugget at Painter Reservoir suggest that directional permeability should exist. Based on the geometry of modern transverse dunes, the maximum permeability should be parallel to the internal stratification and dune axis, because this is the direction in which fluids can travel the farthest before encountering flow–inhibiting boundaries (Fig. 12A). In the Nugget, the direction of maximum permeability should be northwest–southeast.

This permeability anisotropy is supported by production history in the field, particularly during pressurization of the gas cap from 1983 to 1985. During this period, nitrogen and hydrocarbon–gas injection rates were increased in the gas cap to elevate field pressure and to cause miscible displacement of the oil in the oil "leg". Pressure response and subsequent gas breakthrough occurred more rapidly along northwest–southeast trends, rather than longitudinally up and down the field (Fig. 13A). The trend is parallel to the inferred dune axes and maximum–permeability direction.

The field deviates from this trend on its northern end, possibly a result of geologic factors. First, downwind migration and lateral truncation of Nugget dunes have altered their original geometries, perhaps affecting permeability trends (Fig. 13B). Variation in the

Figure 12. Block diagrams illustrating idealized Nugget Sandstone transverse/barchanoid dunes (A), the possible complexity of the depositional environment (B), and the resulting stratigraphic sequences. Transverse/barchanoid dune morphologies are inferred from unimodal depositional dip orientations (A). The direction of maximum permeability parallels dune axes, which are oriented predominantly in a southeast–northwest direction. However, directional permeability is influenced by relict dune geometry, which may be more complex than the idealized transverse/barchanoid dune geometry (B).

orientations of fractures and faults also can affect permeability trends. Thus, prediction of field–wide trends in directional permeability is difficult, given that the factors influencing these trends are hard to extrapolate beyond the borehole. Study of reservoir performance is essential in determining the significance and direction of permeability trends at any particular location in the field.

CONCLUSIONS

The Nugget Sandstone in Painter Reservoir Field is a stratigraphically heterogeneous reservoir. This heterogeneity is inherited primarily from eolian depositional processes. It is observed on many different scales in cores and field performance. Finer–scale heterogeneity results from variations in grain size, sorting, mineralogy, and bed thickness. Larger–scale heterogeneity results from porosity and permeability variations between dune and interdune facies, and from the geometry of these facies. Diagenetic and tectonic processes such as illite formation, fracturing, and faulting also affect reservoir properties.

Stratigraphic layering of the reservoir results from porosity and permeability variations between facies and their arrangement in stacked vertical sequences. Directional permeability resulting from consistent dune orientations and internal stratification is confirmed by field performance. The trend is altered in some locations by fracturing, faulting, and/or variations in dune geometries. Stratigraphic heterogeneity, combined with other complexities such as structure and hydro-

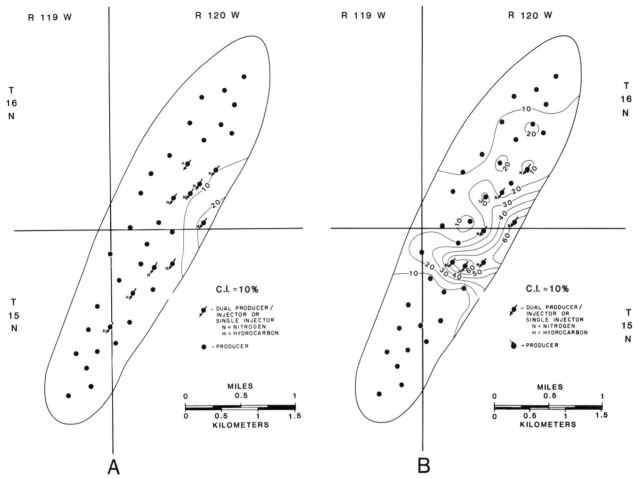

Figure 13. History of nitrogen migration during reservoir pressurization, shown by contours of produced nitrogen cuts. Wells near the crest and on the east flank of the field typically produce from the lower Nugget porosity zone; wells on the west flank and plunge ends typically produce from the upper Nugget zone. In January 1983, at the onset of reservoir pressurization, high nitrogen cuts in the central portion of the field were produced from the deep production perforations in the dual wells, and indicate vertical flow from the injection intervals to the production intervals (A). During January 1985, two years after the onset of reservoir pressurization, nitrogen production increased in a northwest–southeast trend in the central portion of the field. Note the deviation from this trend in the north plunge end (B).

carbon composition make exploitation of Painter Reservoir Field challenging.

ACKNOWLEDGEMENTS

The information presented in this paper is a synthesis of work performed by many Chevron geologists over several years. Jim Frank and Jim Robertson performed detailed core studies at Chevron Oil Field Research Center in La Habra, California. Chris Peterson and Dan Wallem first recognized the significance of stratigraphic layering and directional permeability in the Nugget. Jim Halvorson quantified the relationships between facies and reservoir quality. Toni Stathopoulos of Chevron Geosciences built the nitrogen cut maps. Kerry Miyoshi calculated the rock statistics. I thank Pat Flynn and Myron Smith for the thin–section and SEM photomicrographs and descriptions; Steve Petersen for the core photographs; and Nancy Angle, Glenda Jackson, and George Martinez for their superior drafting work. My fellow employees at Chevron and the RMAG editors greatly improved the quality of this manuscript. I thank Chevron U.S.A., Inc. for permission to publish this paper.

REFERENCES

Ahlbrandt, T.S. and S.G. Fryberger, 1981, Sedimentary features and significance of interdune deposits, *in* F.G. Ethridge, and R.M. Flores, eds., Recent and Ancient Non-marine Depositional Environments: SEPM Spec. Pub. 31, p. 293-314.

Doelger, N.M., 1981, Depositional environment of the Nugget Sandstone, Red Canyon Rim, Fremont County, Wyoming: unpub. MS thesis, U. of WY, 188 p.

Fox, L., 1979, Porosity and permeability reduction in the Nugget Sandstone, southwestern Wyoming: unpub. MA thesis, U. of MO, 117 p.

Frank, J.R., S. Cluff, and J.M. Bauman, 1982, Painter Reservoir, East Painter Reservoir and Clear Creek Fields, Uinta County Wyoming, *in* R.B. Powers, ed., Geologic Studies of the Cordilleran Thrust Belt: RMAG Guidebook, p. 601-611.

Hunter, R.E., 1977, Terminology of cross-stratified sedimentary layers and climbing-ripple structures: Jour. Sed. Pet., v. 47, p. 697-706.

Hunter, R.E., 1981, Stratification styles in eolian sandstones: some Pennsylvanian to Jurassic examples from the western interior U.S.A., *in* F.G. Ethridge and R.M. Flores, eds., Recent and Ancient Nonmarine Depositional Environments: SEPM Spec. Pub. 31, p. 315–329.

Jordan, W., 1965, Regional environmental study of the early Mesozoic Nugget and Navajo Sandstones: unpub. PhD diss., U. of WI, 206 p.

Kocurek, G., 1981, Significance of interdune deposits and bounding surfaces in aeolian dune sands: Sedimentology, v. 28, p. 753–780.

Kocurek, G., and R.H. Dott, Jr., 1983, Jurassic paleogeography and paleoclimate of the central and southern Rocky Mountains region, *in* M.W. Reynolds and E.D. Dolly, eds., Mesozoic Paleogeography of West-central United States: RMS-SEPM, p. 101–116.

Lamb, C.F., 1980, Painter Reservoir Field–Giant in Wyoming thrust belt: AAPG Bull., v. 64, p. 638–644.

Lindquist, S.J., 1983, Nugget Formation reservoir characteristics affecting production in the Overthrust Belt of southwestern Wyoming: JPT, p. 1355–1365.

Lindquist, S.J., 1988, Practical characterization of eolian reservoirs for development: Nugget Sandstone, Utah–Wyoming thrust belt: Sed. Geol., v. 56, p. 315–339.

Marzolf, J.E., 1982, Paleogeographic implications of the early Jurassic (?) Navajo and Aztec Sandstones, *in* E.G. Frost and D.L. Martin, eds., Mesozoic–Cenozoic Tectonic Evolution of the Colorado River Region, California, Arizona and Nevada: Cordilleran Publishers, p. 493–501.

McKee, E.D., 1979, Ancient sandstones considered to be eolian, *in* E.D. McKee, ed., A Study of Global Sand Seas: USGS, Prof. Paper 1052, p. 187–238.

Picard, M.D., 1975, Facies, petrography, and petroleum potential of Nugget Sandstone (Jurassic), southwestern Wyoming and northeastern Utah, *in* D.W. Bolyard, ed., Deep Drilling Frontiers of the Central Rocky Mountains: RMAG Field Conf. Guidebook, p. 109–127.

Royse, F., and M.A. Warner, 1987, Thrust faulting and hydrocarbon generation: Discussion, AAPG Bull., v. 71, p. 882–889.

Veatch, A.C., 1907, Geography and geology of a portion of southwestern Wyoming: USGS, Prof. Paper 56, 178 p.

Warner, M.A., 1980, Source and time of generation of hydrocarbons in Fossil Basin, western Wyoming Thrust Belt [abs.]: AAPG Bull., v. 64, p. 800.

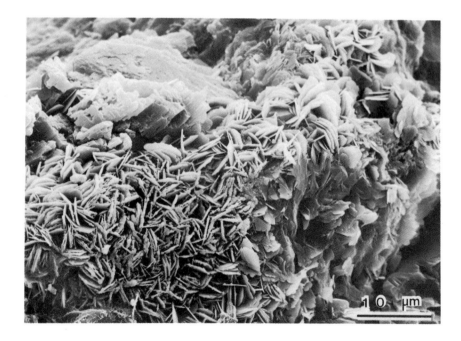

Authigenic chlorite forms a partial coating on a detrital framework grain. Surface sample of Point Lookout sandstone, La Plata Co., CO. Photo donated by Bill Keighin.

Performance of Lower–Porosity Nugget Reservoirs, Anschutz Ranch East, Bessie Bottom, and North Pineview Fields, Utah and Wyoming[1]

WILLIAM J. SERCOMBE[2]

[1]Received November 9, 1989; Revised February 5, 1989
[2]Amoco Production Co., Denver, Colorado

Gas deliverability from Triassic–Jurassic Nugget Sandstone reservoirs of the Overthrust Belt of Wyoming and Utah is strongly affected by the nature of natural fracturing. Fractures in higher–porosity Nugget reservoirs generally reduce permeability because they are gouge–filled (Lindquist, 1983). However, the fractures seen in Nugget reservoirs with porosity less than 15% generally do not have gouge filling; reservoirs with these open fractures can have in situ permeabilities an order of magnitude greater than matrix permeabilities measured on cores in the laboratory. By contrast, reservoirs with no open fractures typically have in situ effective permeabilities much lower than permeabilities measured in the laboratory. (In situ permeability may be approximated with suitable corrections.) Directional permeability related to eolian dune facies has less influence on deliverability than does the presence or absence of open fractures.

Deliverability also is related to original water saturations. Wells with the lowest water saturation and highest structural elevation have the highest flow rates.

INTRODUCTION

This investigation was initiated in order to explain poor production from Nugget reservoirs in some fields in the Thrust Belt of southwestern Wyoming and eastern Utah (Figs. 1 and 2). The Bessie Bottom, Anschutz Ranch East, and North Pineview fields are asymmetric hanging–wall anticlines on the Absaroka Thrust sheet.

Initial production from the Bessie Bottom discovery, drilled by Amoco in 1983, was 2,400 MCFGPD. This rate was significantly lower than the initial flow rates of 5,000 to 20,000 MCFGPD from wells in the nearby Anschutz Ranch East Field (Fig. 3). Neither acid treatment nor fracture stimulation improved flow rates or tubing pressure (320 psi). Production differences could not be explained by conventional core or facies analyses, although gouge–filled fractures were initially blamed for poor deliverability. This factor was discounted when it was found that cores from highly productive wells in the east "lobe" of Anschutz Ranch East Field contained pervasive gouge–filled fractures. Paradoxically, wells with the best production had lower porosity and permeability (average values of 6% and 0.43 md, respectively), and contained more gouge–filled fractures than did the less–productive Bessie Bottom well (average porosity of 8.5% and average matrix permeability of 0.64 md).

Effective permeability within the zone of completion in the Bessie Bottom well, determined by Horner analysis of pressure buildup tests, was only 0.05 md. The geometric average of "k_{90}" permeabilities measured on the Bessie Bottom core was 0.64 md, where k_{90} is the lesser of two whole–core permeability measurements taken at 90° to each other. The greater permeability value is referred to as "k max". The k_{90} value was chosen for averaging as it represents a minimum, and probably is more representative of deliverability from a heterogeneous reservoir. Explaining this discrepancy became the point of the study. Understanding the poor deliverability from the Bessie Bottom well was considered important to the economic viability of the Bessie Bottom Field and to other, similar exploration objectives.

PREVIOUS WORK

Eolian sedimentation and the geology of the Paleozoic and Mesozoic sand seas (ergs) of the western U.S. is summarized by Picard (1975) and Kocurek and Dott (1981). Relationships between Nugget reservoir characteristics and reservoir performance are discussed by Lindquist (1983), who related reservoir characteristics to depositional environment, diagenesis, and fracturing.

METHODS

The Bessie Bottom well was compared to wells in the nearby Anschutz Ranch East–East Lobe and North Pineview fields (Table 1). The nearby fields had both high– and low–deliverability wells, including

REGIONAL DATA:

Producing Interval:	Nugget Sandstone
Geographic Location:	Uinta County, Wyoming; Summit County, Utah
Present Tectonic Setting:	Wyoming–Utah Thrust Belt
Depositional Setting:	Continental pediment
Age of Reservoir:	Triassic–Jurassic
Lithology of Reservoir:	Quartz arenite
Depositional Environment:	Eolian dune fields
Diagenesis:	Quartz overgrowths; fracturing; and illite and pyrobitumen grain–coatings
Porosity Types:	Intergranular
Porosity:	6 to 8.5%
Permeability:	0.05 to 8 md
Minimum Sw in Pay:	21%
Fractures:	Vertical; open or gouge–filled
Nature of Traps:	Anticlines on thrust–sheet hanging walls
Drive Type:	Gas expansion
Source Rocks:	Mesozoic, Permian
Timing of Migration:	Post–Laramide
FIELD DATA:	Bessie Bottom Field
Discovered:	1983
Reservoir Depth:	15,000 ft (4,572 m)
Reservoir Thickness:	300 ft (91 m)
IP (discovery well):	2,400 MCFGPD, 181 BCPD
Areal Extent:	1,100 acres (445 ha)
Original Reservoir Pressure:	6,227 psia
Cumulative Production (1/89):	0.50 BCFG, 65,000 BO
Oil Gravity:	Retrograde condensate
FIELD DATA:	Anschutz Range East–East Lobe Field
Discovered:	1981
Reservoir Depth:	14,000 ft (44,67 m)
Reservoir Thickness:	1,000 ft (305 m)
IP (discovery well):	1,000 MCFGPD, 101 BCPD (restricted)
Areal Extent:	860 acres (348 ha)
Original Reservoir Pressure:	5,902 psia
Cumulative Production (1/89):	17.2 BCFG, 739,000 BO (total for Anschutz Ranch East field)
Oil Gravity:	Retrograde condensate
FIELD DATA:	North Pineview Field
Discovered:	1982
Reservoir Depth:	13,000 ft (3,962 m)
Reservoir Thickness:	400 ft (122 m)
IP (discovery well):	8,000 MCFGPD, 700 BCPD
Areal Extent:	1,200 acres (486 ha)
Original Reservoir Pressure:	FTP 2,000 psia
Cumulative Production (1/89):	6.44 BCFG, 568,000 BO
Oil Gravity:	Retrograde condensate

wells with several times the flow capacity of the Bessie Bottom discovery, even though their porosity was lower (8.5% vs. 5.6%, Table 2). The objectives of the study were met by comparing deliverabilities of completed zones to porosity, permeability, and water saturation in each zone.

NUGGET SANDSTONE FACIES AND ROCK PROPERTIES

When the investigation was initiated, dune litho-facies were considered to be the principal control of

Nugget permeability (Lindquist, 1983). It was desirable, therefore, to determine any relationship between deliverability and porosity and permeability values as influenced by dune lithofacies.

Dune–forming depositional processes produce two major reservoir lithofacies which are characterized either by centimeter–scale bedding or by millimeter–scale bedding. Nonreservoir interdune facies were deposited as subaqueous ripple–laminated sand, or hardpan interdune playas.

Centimeter–scale bedding is a result of gravity deposition on the lee face of dunes. Gravity deposi-

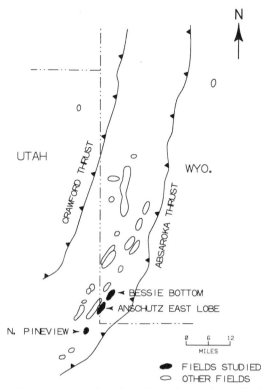

Figure 1. Index map showing location of studied (black) and nearby Triassic-Jurassic Nugget Sandstone fields. Bessie Bottom, Anschutz Ranch East, and North Pineview are hanging-wall anticlines in the southern part of the Absaroka Thrust Sheet. (6 mi = 9.7 km)

AGE		FORMATION OF GROUP		LITHOLOGY
TERTIARY		SALT LAKE GRP.	GREEN RIVER GRP.	
		WASATCH GRP.		
CRETACEOUS	UPPER	ADAVILLE FM.		
		HILLIARD FM.		
		?		
		FRONTIER FM.		
	LOWER	ASPEN FM.		
		BEAR RIVER GRP.		
		GANNETT GRP.		
		? STUMP ?		
JURASSIC		PREUSS		
		TWIN CREEK FM.		
JR.	UPPER	☼ NUGGET GRP.		
TRIASSIC		ANKAREM		
	MIDDLE	THAYNES		
	LOWER	WOODSIDE		
		DINWOODY		
PERMIAM		PHOSPHORIA		
PENNSYLVANIAN		WEBER-WEELS	TENSLEEP AMSDEN	
MISSISSIPPIAN		BRAZER	MADISON	
		LODGEPOLE		
DEVONIAN		THREE FORKS	DARBY	
		JEFFERSON		
SILURIAN		LAKETOWN		
ORDOVICIAN		FISH HAVEN	BIGHORN	
		SWAN PEAK		
		GRADEN CITY		
CAMBRIAN		ST. CHARLES	GALLATIN	
		WORM CREEK		
		NOONAN		
		BLOOMINGTON	GROSVENTRE	
		BLACK SMITH		
		UTE		
		LANGSTON		
		BRIGHAM	FLATHEAD	
PRE-CAMBRIAN		SEDIMENT & METASEDIMENT		
PRE-CAMBRIAN		GRYSTALLINE BASEMENT		

☼ **RESERVOIR STUDIED**

Figure 2. Stratigraphic column for the Wyoming-Idaho-Utah Fold and Thrust Belt. The Triassic-Jurassic Nugget Formation is an eolian sandstone and one of the principal reservoirs in the Wyoming Thrust Belt.

tion includes both grainflow and avalanche-slump deposition. Grainflow deposits exhibit parallel laminations and inverse-graded bedding due to shear sorting as sand slides down the dune face. Avalanche-slump deposits are comparable to grainflow, except that bedding is non-parallel or contorted.

The principal millimeter-scale bedding includes grainfall and wind-rippled sand, although subaqueous and interdune-playa deposits also are millimeter-scaled. Grainfall laminae are deposited as sand blows over a dune crest onto the lee slope. However, grainfall bedding is not encountered often in the geologic record because dune crests are rarely preserved. Wind-rippled sand laminae form as sand is reworked at the base of the lee face of a dune; they exhibit translation ripples. Wind ripples account for most of the millimeter-scale bedding found in preserved dunes.

For the purpose of graphing, dune lithofacies were grouped into avalanche-slump, grainflow, wind-ripple, grainfall, and interdune facies. This allowed distinguishing major lithologic effects on permeability. Facies with centimeter-scale bedding consistently had permeabilities an order of magnitude greater than those in millimeter-scale beds. Interdune deposits had very low permeabilities.

However, although the relationship between scale of bedding and permeability was clear, the question of deliverability was not answered. The average effective permeability in the Bessie Bottom well as determined

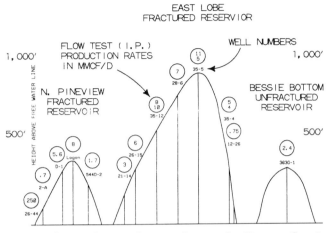

Figure 3. Heights of gas columns in Nugget Sandstone reservoirs, Bessie Bottom, Anschutz Ranch East, and North Pineview fields, Wyoming. The deliverability of gas increases with height above free water. Deliverability also is impacted by the relative permeability effects associated with increasing connate water saturations. (500 ft = 152 m)

Table 1. Principal wells studied (core available).

Well	Location
Bessie Bottom	7-13N-120W
1. Champlin 363G-1	Uinta Co., WY
North Pineview	25-3N-7E
2. Champlin 544D-2	Summit Co., UT
Anschutz Ranch East– East Lobe	
3. E35-5	35-13N-121W
(Champlin 404-1c)	Uinta Co., WY
3. E26-15	26-13N-121W
	Uinta Co., WY
All other uncored field wells were included in the study.	

from pressure buildup data was an order of magnitude less than the average core permeability of any facies (Table 3). On the other hand, wells in the Anschutz East Lobe Field exhibited the opposite relationship; effective permeability was an order of magnitude greater than the matrix permeabilities measured on cores in the laboratory.

FRACTURES

Open natural fractures were observed in cores from the Anschutz Ranch–East Lobe and North Pineview fields. However, no open natural fractures were observed in cores from the Bessie Bottom well. Gouge-filled fractures were pervasive in the Anschutz cores, but only about one gouge-filled fracture per foot of core was seen in the Bessie Bottom well. Unfortunately, fracture intensity was unpredictable for the Anschutz reservoir.

Table 2. Summary of well deliverabilities

Perforated Interval Ft.	Gas MMCFPD	Conden-sate BPD	Fm. Water BPD	FTP psi	Effective Perme-ability
Bessie Bottom 363G-1					
Acid, Frac					
15100-15148	1.8	144		300	5.2 md-ft or 0.058 md/ft.
15120-15190					
I.P.	2.45	180		320	
Anschutz Ranch East Lobe E26-15					
Acid					
14604-14613	5.7	0	19	1800	875 md-ft. or 2.2 to 2.9 md-ft.
14593-14597					
14587-14590					
14572-14582					
14544-14564					
I.P.	5.8	11.6	18	1350	
E35-5					
Acid					
14210-14304	11	427		3050	4060 md-ft.
14324-14405	11.3	123		3020	6867 md-ft. 5145 md-ft. 8.12 md-ft. 13.7 md-ft. 10.29 md-ft.
I.P.	5.7	528	34		
Champlin 544D-2					
12974-13180	1.2	9	22	550	No buildup data
Frac	1.1	43	2	560	
	1.8	129	104		
I.P.	1.757	99	40	1050	

The relatively high effective permeability in Anschutz East wells appeared to be due to the presence of open natural fractures. These fractures are extensional and cross-cut the gouge-filled fractures.

OTHER FACTORS INFLUENCING PERMEABILITY

Matrix permeability typically decreases with increasing net confining stress, especially in low-permeability rocks (Thomas and Ward, 1972); this proved true for Nugget sandstones (Fig. 4). Corrections were made to routine core permeabilities to more closely approximate reservoir conditions of stress and saturation.

Table 3. Core data differentiated by facies.

Facies	K max	K 90	K vert	Plug K	Corepor	Plugpor	90/Max	Vert/Max
Bessie Bottom								
Permeability Averages Geometric								
Slump	5.3	3.61	2.7	5.41	10.99	11	.67	.5
Grain Flow	4.2	2.65	1	4.2	10.6	10.6	63	.63
Wind Ripple	.45	.33	.13	.45	6.63	6.66	.73	.29
Wind Dune	.79	.39	.19	.83	6.71	6.72	.49	.24
Anschutz E26–15								
Permeability Averages Geometric								
Slump	2.38	1.98		1.2	6.97	6.81	.83	
Grain Flow	3.35	1.3		3.72	7.41	7.43	.38	
Wind Ripple	3.69	.189		2.74	6.77	6.82	.51	
Inter Dune	.79	.22		.25	5	4.74	.27	
Anschutz E35–5								
Permeability Averages Geometric								
Slump	2	1.62	1.23	8.25	6.85	7.85	.81	.61
Grain Flow	3.48	2.65	.49	9.63	8.34	9.54	.76	.14
Wind Ripple	3.25	2.08	.54	14.56	7.26	8.45	.64	.16
Inter Dune	.22	.2	.2	4.3	4.44	6.66	.91	.91
North Pineview 544D–2								
Permeability Averages Geometric								
Slump	3.32	1.79		1.2	9.91	10.17	.54	
Grain Flow	8.19	1		3.72	8.78	8.15	.12	
Wind Ripple	6.12	1.36		2.74	7.8	6.9	.22	
Inter Dune	3.55	1.08		.25	7.68	7.15	.3	

Klinkenberg Effect

The "Klinkenberg correction" for variations in mean free path of gas molecules is needed when calculating the permeability to gas of most tighter reservoirs (Jones and Owens, 1980). Mean free path is influenced by factors which include pressure, temperature, and the nature of the gas. As mean free path decreases, gas flow approaches liquid flow, and permeability also decreases. The Klinkenberg correction for the Bessie Bottom reservoir reduces routine permeability by 30%. This loss is, however, insufficient to account entirely for the discrepancy between core and effective permeabilities.

Relative Permeability and Water Saturation

Production tests indicate that deliverability and gas saturation decrease with increasing depth in each field investigated (Fig. 3). The effect of increasing water saturation as the gas/water contact are approached became a possible explanation for reduced deliverability.

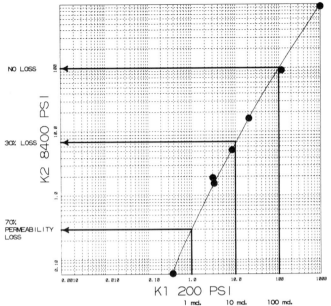

Figure 4. Effect of increased overburden pressure on matrix permeability, Nugget Sandstone, Bessie Bottom, Anschutz Ranch East, and North Pineview fields, Wyoming. Laboratory permeabilities less than one md. are reduced by over 70% when corrected for net overburden pressure.

To assess the effects of changing water saturation on well performance, it is necessary to know both the relative permeability characteristics and the actual water saturation (Sw) of the reservoir. Archie–type calculations of water saturation (Sw) were made from open–hole logs and core porosities (Table 4); Sw profiles were generated for each well in order to relate the position of each completed zone in the gas column to Sw. Capillary pressure data provided a theoretical Sw profile against which logs could be compared (Fig. 5). Irreducible Sw was estimated as about 20% at 1,200 ft (366 m) of gas column. A transition zone (less than 40% Sw) was present, and determined to extend 250 ft (76.2 m) above the gas/water contact (Fig. 5).

If differences in relative permeabilities were a cause of variation in deliverability, this was expected to be reflected in the relationship between Sw and

Table 4. Archie parameters, the variables in the Archie equation used to calculate water saturation (Archie, 1947).

	Bessie Bottom	Anschutz East Lobe	North Pineview
Ωm	.075 @ 240 F	.055 @ 215 F	.19 @ 220 F
a	1	1	1
m	1.88	1.9	1.84
n	1.9	1.97	1.9
Rt	ILD	LLD, ILD	ILD

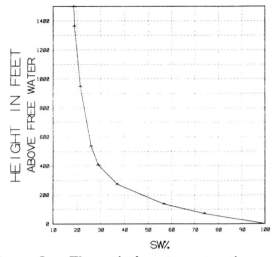

Figure 5. Theoretical water–saturation profile based on mercury injection–capillary pressure data for Nugget Sandstone, Bessie Bottom, Anschutz Ranch East, and North Pineview fields, Wyoming. The reservoir exhibits a moderately long transition zone.

deliverability from each completed zone. When flow rates from each zone were plotted against average Sw (Fig. 6), two domains became apparent. With similar Sw values, fractured zones in the Anschutz Ranch wells have greater deliverabilities than do nonfractured zones in the Bessie Bottom well. Deliverability from zones in the North Pineview wells is variable. When deliverability is plotted against height above free water (Fig. 7), a similar pattern emerges. Because Sw is a function of gas column, it is possible to establish the relationship between deliverability and column height. It is also clear that even where permeability in Nugget reservoirs is enhanced by open fractures, the permeability also is strongly influenced by relative permeability effects.

In order to make a quantitative correction for relative permeability, it is necessary to prepare a gas–water drainage curve. The process modelled by drainage curves is gas displacing water in the reservoir rock as gas is produced. Permeability to gas is determined for decreasing increments of Sw. Permeability at irreducible Sw is said to be 100% of the "total" permeability. When permeabilities at decreasing values of Sw are plotted as a percentage of total permeability, permeability to gas will be zero when Sw equals 100%.

Because no laboratory drainage relative–permeability curves were available, an empirical curve was calculated from the relationship of deliverability to water saturation. The relationships observed were the same for both fractured and nonfractured zones (Fig. 8). The data indicate that at 60% Sw, only 30% of the permeability which exists at irreducible Sw (20% Sw) would be effective.

RESULTS OF CORRECTIONS

Application of the necessary corrections to core permeability in the Bessie Bottom well gave a permeability value very similar to the value for effective per-

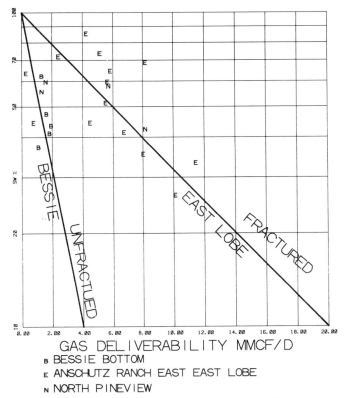

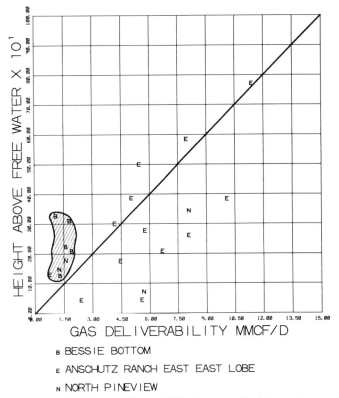

Figure 6. Effect of water saturation on deliverability on Nugget Sandstone, Bessie Bottom, Anschutz Ranch East, and North Pineview fields, Wyoming. Test intervals with no natural open fractures exhibit much lower deliverability. Deliverability is impacted by higher connate water saturations, independent of fractures.

Figure 7. Gas deliverability versus height above free water, Nugget Sandstone, Bessie Bottom, Anschutz Ranch East, and North Pineview fields, Wyoming. Higher connate water saturations reduce deliverability.

meability determined from pressure buildup data. This may be shown as:

$$Ke = A \cdot B \cdot C \cdot Kc$$

where: Ke = effective permeability
Kc = routine laboratory permeability from cores, = 0.64 md
A = permeability loss due to net confining pressure, = 0.15
B = permeability loss due to relative permeability, = 0.6
C = Klinkenberg correction, = 0.7

The permeability calculated in this manner is 0.04 md, essentially identical to that determined by analysis of pressure buildup data (0.05 md).

CONCLUSIONS

This study is an example of how *in situ* reservoir behavior may not be predictable from routine and permeability determinations. Open natural fractures can improve effective reservoir permeability by an order of magnitude over matrix permeability measured in the laboratory. Therefore, pressure data should be analyzed for effective permeability and compared to matrix permeabilities from core analysis when reservoir performance is under consideration. Reservoirs with effective permeabilities far in excess of matrix permeabilities may indicate the presence of open frac-

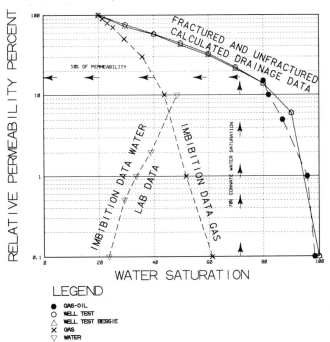

Figure 8. Theoretical relative permeability curve, Nugget Sandstone, Bessie Bottom, Anschutz Ranch East, and North Pineview fields, Wyoming. The best–fit linear equations from Figure 6 were used to derive this drainage relative permeability curve, allowing correction of lab permeabilities for connate water saturation.

tures. Fracture types and their distribution should be determined in all wildcat discoveries. Any investigator of well performance also should consider a number of other factors. Effective permeability is influenced by net overburden pressure as well as by water saturation. Increasing water saturation reduces flow capacity; therefore deliverability tends to be best at the top of a hydrocarbon accumulation, where water saturation is lowest. Determination of accurate water saturations and relative permeabilities is necessary to characterize the performance of a reservoir under a variety of subsurface conditions.

REFERENCES

Hayes, K.H., 1976, A discussion of the geology of the southeastern Canadian Cordillera and its comparison to the Idaho-Wyoming–Utah fold and thrust belt, *in* J.G. Hill, ed., Symposium on Geology of the Cordilleran Hingeline: RMAG, p. 59–82.

Jones, F.O., and W.W. Owens, 1980, A laboratory study of low–permeability gas sands: JPT, v 32, p. 1631–1640.

Kocurek, G., and R.H. Dott, 1981, Distinction and uses of stratification types in the interpretation of eolian sand: JSP, v. 51, p. 579–595.

Lindquist, S.J., 1983, Nugget Formation reservoir characteristics affecting production in the overthrust belt of southwestern Wyoming: JPT, v. 35, p. 1355–1365.

Picard, M.D., 1975, Facies, petrography, and petroleum potential of Nugget Sandstone (Jurassic), southwestern Wyoming and northeast Utah, *in* D.W. Bolyard, ed., Symposium on Deep Drilling Frontiers in the Central Rocky Mountains, RMAG, p. 109–127.

Thomas, R.D., and D.C. Ward, 1972, Effect of overburden pressure and water saturation on gas permeability in tight sandstone cores: JPT, v. 24, p. 120–124.

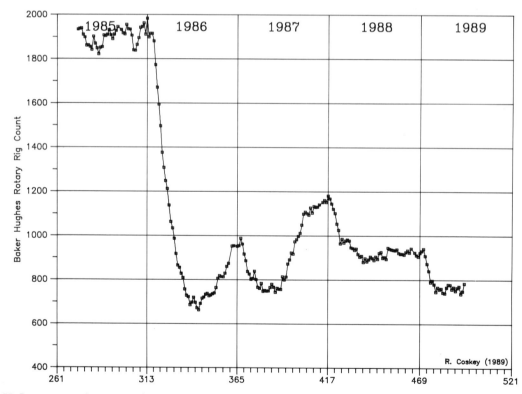

Total U.S. rotary rig count for the period 1985 through June 19, 1989. Week numbers begin at January 7, 1980. Data collected weekly from Oil and Gas Journal. Figure donated by R.J. Coskey, Rose Exploration.

Petrography, Diagenesis, and Reservoir Properties of the Dakota Sandstone of West Lindrith Field, Rio Arriba County, New Mexico[1]

STANLEY P. FRANKLIN[2]
THOMAS T. TIEH[2]

[1]Received August 7, 1988; Revised February 15, 1989
[2]Department of Geology, Texas A&M University, College Station, TX

The upper portion of the Cretaceous Dakota Sandstone at West Lindrith Field on the eastern margin of the San Juan Basin consists of a series of coarsening–upward, shallow–marine sandstones interstratified with marine shale. Petrographic and SEM analyses indicate that the sandstones are very fine to medium–grained litharenites that have been pervasively altered by the diagenetic processes of compaction, authigenesis, and dissolution.

The course of diagenesis varied spatially and temporally within the sandstones because of variations in primary composition and texture related to depositional environment. Diagenetic alterations have profoundly affected the development of secondary rock properties such as porosity, permeability, and water saturation (Sw). Each of the resulting "diagenetic facies" contains a unique authigenic mineral assemblage and a dominant secondary porosity type, reflecting specific sequences of diagenetic alterations.

Q–mode multivariate factor analyses of petrographic data were used to delineate three compositional end members, and to relate depositional environments, diagenesis, and reservoir quality. End Member 1 consists of clean, quartzose, sandstones that are silica cemented and contain relatively high porosity, permeability, and low Sw. End Member 2 sandstones, adjacent to interbedded shales, are tightly carbonate cemented and have little or no reservoir potential. End Member 3 sandstones are shaly, low energy, fine to very fine–grained, bioturbated deposits, and have low porosity, very low permeability, and high Sw. Graphs of resistivity, Sw, and porosity for intervals of known end–member composition provide a means of correcting log values for the effects of authigenic mineral phases in non–cored intervals.

Variations in sandstone reservoir properties can be ascribed to both primary lithologic contrasts and subsequent diverging diagenetic histories. Factor analysis provides a promising approach to quantifying the relationship between siliciclastic depositional environments, diagenesis, and reservoir properties.

INTRODUCTION

The Dakota Sandstone of the San Juan Basin consists of intertonguing marine and nonmarine sandstones deposited near the southwestern margin of the Late Cretaceous epicontinental sea (Owen, 1969). This study concentrates on the marine sandstone members that form the upper portion of the Dakota Sandstone along the eastern flank of the basin. Cored intervals from three wells in West Lindrith Field were used to interpret the depositional environment and diagenetic history of the sandstone. A total of 356 ft (109 m) of core, representing a depth inter-

val of 663 ft (202 m), from 7,167 to 7,830 ft (2,185–2,387 m), were studied in detail.

The West Lindrith Gallup–Dakota Field is located in northwest New Mexico in the southeastern portion of Rio Arriba County, approximately 25 mi (40 km) northwest of Cuba and 75 mi (120 km) southeast of Farmington, New Mexico (Fig. 1). The field is situated on the southeastern flank of the basin in a transition zone between gently dipping strata of the Chaco Slope to the southwest and steeply dipping strata of the Hogback Monocline to the northeast.

The Dakota Sandstone has undergone a complex burial history. The primary compositional and tex-

FIELD DATA:	West Lindrith Gallup–Dakota Field
Producing Interval:	Dakota Sandstone
Geographic Location:	T24–25N, R2–3W, Rio Arriba County, New Mexico
Present Tectonic Setting:	Southeastern flank, San Juan Basin
Depositional Setting:	Delta and marine shelf
Age of Reservoir:	Upper Cretaceous (Cenomanian)
Lithology of Reservoir:	Massive to laminated sandstones capping coarsening–upward sequences
Depositional Environments:	Upper to middle shoreface turbidites
Diagenesis:	Compaction; cementation by quartz, then carbonates, then clays; dissolution
Porosity Types:	Fracture, intergranular, intragranular, microporosity
Porosity:	Maximum 18%, average 8%
Permeability:	Maximum 2.5 md, average 0.05 md
Water Saturation:	Minimum 8%, average 38%
Nature of Trap:	Stratigraphic and permeability pinchouts
Entrapping Facies:	Marine shale of the Lower Mancos Shale
Source Rock:	Lower Mancos Shale
Discovered:	Johnston & Shear No. 1-1 Jicarilla
Reservoir Depth:	7,300 ft (2,226 m)
Pay Thickness:	40 ft (12 m)
Reservoir Morphology:	Stacked series of discontinuous sandstone lenses, strike–trending to the northwest–southeast
Areal Extent:	6,240 acres (2,225 ha), or 39 wells on 160-acre (64.8 ha) spacing
IP:	Average 80 BOPD, 380 MCFGPD
Bottom Hole Pressure:	3,100 psi
Temperatures:	160°F (71°C) BHT; 1.5 F°/100 ft (2.7 C°/km) gradient
Cumulative Production:	2,300,000 BO, 14.3 BCFG
Approximate Primary Recovery:	4,680,000 BO, 9.75 BCFG
Oil Gravity:	45.6° API
Drive Type:	Solution gas and fluid expansion
Completion Procedure:	Sand–oil fracture with KCl water, acidize

tural changes produced during diagenesis have profoundly affected the magnitude and distribution of the secondary rock properties; porosity, permeability, and fluid saturation. Analysis of the composition and texture of the detrital and authigenic mineral assemblages is essential in order to understand the diagenetic history and its effect on reservoir rock properties. Therefore, the objectives of this study were to determine: 1) the depositional environment of the sandstones, 2) the texture and mineralogy of the detrital and authigenic assemblages, 3) the sequence of diagenetic alterations, and 4) the effects of diagenesis on reservoir rock properties.

REGIONAL GEOLOGIC SETTING

Structure

The San Juan Basin is a structural and sedimentary basin in the southeastern portion of the Colorado Plateau, in northwestern New Mexico and southwestern Colorado. The central basin is roughly circular in map view and strongly asymmetric in cross–section with a steep, fault bounded northeastern flank and a broad gently dipping southern margin (Rice, 1983). The outer basin borders the central basin on the west and south and contains gently dipping strata of the Chaco Slope (Fig. 1). The San Juan Basin is

bounded on all sides by uplifts resulting from Late Cretaceous and Early Tertiary (Laramide) deformation (Kelly, 1957).

The study area is located in a transition zone between the central and outer basins approximately 20 mi (32 km) west of the northern extent of the Nacimiento Uplift (Fig. 1). The area contains numerous northwest–plunging, *en echelon*, open folds and northeast–trending, high–angle faults associated with the Nacimiento Uplift. Approximately 6,500 ft (1,982 m) of structural relief exists across the Hogback Monocline between the study area and El Vado Dome, 18 mi (29 km) to the east.

Stratigraphy

The San Juan Basin contains as much as 15,000 ft (4,573 m) of sedimentary rocks ranging in age from Cambrian to Quaternary. Peterson, et al. (1965) recognized ten major events in the sedimentary history of the area. These include transgressions in Cambrian, Devonian, Permian, and Cretaceous times, with major uplifts and regressions in the Ordovician–Silurian, Mississippian, and Tertiary. Cretaceous rocks are as much as 6,000 ft (1,829 m) thick in the San Juan Basin (Peterson, et al., 1965; Rice, 1983). In addition to the initial transgression, three major transgressive–regressive episodes combined with several less

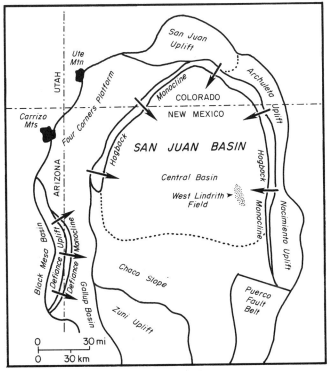

Figure 1. Tectonic map of the San Juan Basin showing the major bounding structural features and the location of West Lindrith Field on the southeastern flank of the basin (after Kelley, 1957).

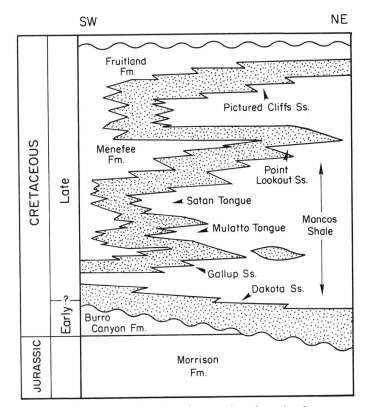

Figure 2. Stratigraphic column showing the interfingering relationship of the Upper Cretaceous strata of the San Juan Basin. The sequence consists of intertonguing marine deposits to the northeast and regressive sandstone tongues to the southwest. The Dakota Sandstone rests unconformably on the Jurassic Morrison Formation and Lower Cretaceous clastic units.

extensive cycles occurred during the Late Cretaceous (Young, 1960). The resulting Upper Cretaceous clastic sequence consists of intertonguing marine and non-marine sediments of the Dakota Sandstone, Mancos Shale, and the Mesaverde Group deposited along a fluctuating northwest–southeast trending shoreline (Fig. 2).

The Upper Cretaceous Dakota Sandstone is of probable Cenomanian age. It represents the initial transgression across a vast erosional surface formed on the Lower Cretaceous Burro Canyon Formation, the Upper Jurassic Morrison Formation, and progressively older rocks westward across the southern margin of the Colorado Plateau (Fassett, 1974). Local subsidence and major uplifts to the west resulted in eastward tilting and erosion of the pre-Cretaceous non-marine sediments and deposited the debris as braided stream complexes of the Burro Canyon Formation and the lower portion of the Dakota Sandstone.

Along the eastern margin of the basin, nearshore and marine sandstones of the upper Dakota Sandstone form a complex, intertonguing sequence with the overlying neritic strata of the lower Mancos Shale. The sequence has been divided into four formal sandstone members and two intervening shale tongues based on surface mapping (Owen, 1969). In the Chama Basin, a northeastern re-entrant of the San Juan Basin, Owen (1969) differentiated the Dakota into a lower nonmarine conglomeratic sandstone, a middle transitional shale, and an upper unit composed of regularly interstratified, laterally persistent marine

strata intertonguing with the Mancos Shale. This sequence is highly variable laterally across the basin and generally grades from fluvial deposits in the west-northwest to marine sediments toward the south-southeast (Grant and Owen, 1974). Apparently, there were interruptions in the transgression of the Dakota sea over the area with subsequent minor unconformities and local regressive depositional features (Deischl, 1973).

WEST LINDRITH FIELD

The Dakota Sandstone of the San Juan Basin has been a prolific oil and gas producer since discovery of the Basin Dakota Gas Field in the 1940's. The central portion of the basin contains an estimated 3–4 TCFG while the fields on the periphery of the basin produce both oil and gas. West Lindrith Field is an extension of the Lindrith B Unit located in T24N R2W. The field was discovered in 1959 with the Johnston and Shear No. 1-1 Jicarilla which initially flowed 1,914 MCFGPD on a 3/4" choke (Attebury, 1978). An accelerated infill program was initiated in 1980 with 10 wells, and completed on 160-acre spacing in 1986 with 39 wells. Primary yields are on the order of 120,000 BO and 250,000 MCFG per well.

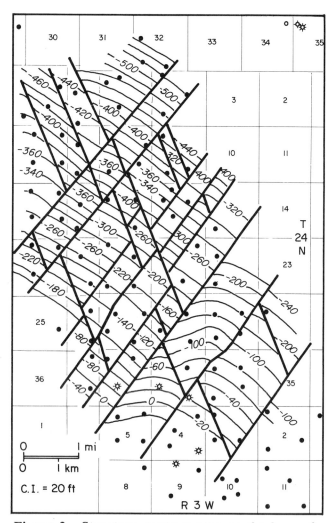

Figure 3. Structure contour map on the base of the Greenhorn Limestone, which reflects Dakota Sandstone structure. The low-angle northeast dip is interrupted by numerous faults with minor offset. Contour interval is 20 ft (6.1 m).

The field has produced 2,300,000 BO and 14.3 BCFG from 39 wells.

The structure at West Lindrith Field is a relatively uniform 1° dip to the northeast (Fig. 3). The field contains a number of small northeast-trending, high-angle faults and northwest-plunging, open folds (J. Jensen, pers. comm.; Rice, 1983). These are thought to be related to right-lateral movement along the Puerco and Nacimiento fault zones (Woodward and Callender, 1977). While structural closure does not control production, fractures associated with faults and flexures significantly increase the productivity of the reservoir.

In West Lindrith Field, the Dakota Sandstone, at depths of 7,000 to 8,500 ft (2,134 to 2,591 m), consists of a stacked series of sandstone members with an aggregate thickness of 180 to 260 ft (55 to 79 m) (Fig. 4). These lenticular sandstone bodies are encased in marine shale that acts as both source and seal for hydrocarbons. Local thinning of the lenses combined with increased shaliness and a loss of per-

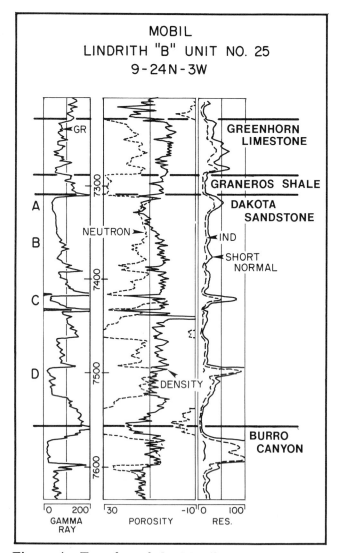

Figure 4. Type log of the Mobil No. 25 Lindrith "B" Unit (Sec 9 T24N R3W) showing the gamma ray, neutron-density porosity, and resistivity logs of the marine members of the Dakota Sandstone at West Lindrith Field. Note the coarsening-upward nature of each sandstone member. Depth divisions on log are 100 ft (30.48 m) apart.

meability provide the trap. Downdip hydrodynamic flow is thought to contribute to the trapping of gas within the Basin Dakota Gas Field and may also be important in fields situated near the flanks of the basin such as West Lindrith (Deischl, 1973).

Of the four marine sandstone members that locally comprise the Dakota, the dominant producers are the "A" and "B" zones and the more laterally continuous "D" zone. Net sandstone thickness for all members as measured from gamma ray (GR) logs (GR less than 40 API units) ranges from 26 ft (8 m) to 43 ft (13 m), and averages 32 ft (10 m). Net sandstone makes up 12 to 14% of the overall Dakota interval. Porosity values are low, ranging from 3–12%, and averaging about 8%. Permeability values range from 0.01 to 2.30 md, averaging 0.1 md. Water saturation (Sw) varies widely, ranging from 8% to 50% in productive zones. An extensive system of natural vertical fractures combined with artificially induced fracture stimulation is necessary to maintain commercial flow rates.

MATERIALS AND METHODS

Slabbed conventional cores of the No. 3 Cullins Federal (CF3), No. 1 Hughes Federal (HF1), and the No. B–7 Lindrith (B7) were examined, photographed (Figs. 5 and 6), correlated with logs, and sampled for laboratory analyses. Thin sections of 85 samples taken from the cores were studied to characterize the detrital composition and texture, determine the extent, nature and sequence of diagenetic alteration, and delineate the magnitude of secondary porosity development (Plates 1 and 2). Composition was determined by counting two hundred points per thin section (Table 1). Cements and authigenic clays were differentiated from detrital grains and reported as bulk rock percentages. All thin sections were stained with Alizarine Red–S to allow differentiation of calcite and dolomite. For texture, the apparent long axis of 50 monocrystalline quartz grains per thin section were measured and the arithmetic mean and standard deviation used as a measure of grain size and sorting. Petrographic porosity was determined and categorized by separately counting 100 points. The criteria of Schmidt and McDonald (1979) were used to identify secondary porosity.

Twelve samples from the three cores were analyzed for clay minerals. X–ray diffraction (XRD) data of magnesium–saturated, magnesium/ethylene glycol–saturated, and potassium–saturated clay samples at 25°C and heated to 300°C and 550°C were obtained. The mineralogy of the clays was determined by analysis of interlayer spacing and changes due to saturation and heat treatment. Scanning electron microscopy (SEM) was used to observe textural characteristics of the clays.

Q–mode factor analysis was performed on petrographic data obtained from thin sections. The nine petrographic variables, all in percent of bulk rock, include: 1) monocrystalline quartz, 2) polycrystalline quartz, 3) total feldspars, 4) total rock fragments, 5) detrital matrix, 6) authigenic clay, 7) silica cement, 8) carbonate cement, and 9) petrographic porosity. The factor–analysis program calculates the number of end–member populations sufficient to account for the majority of the cumulative variance within the data set. This was accomplished by analyzing an 85 X 9 matrix of all samples to determine the significant number of distinctive populations. The technique is designed to delineate end–member populations and to calculate the relative contribution of each to any given independent variable.

DEPOSITIONAL ENVIRONMENT AND SANDSTONE DISTRIBUTION

The marine portion of the Dakota, the focus of this study, consists of an alternating sequence of sandstones and shales with an overall thickness of about 260 ft (79 m). Four locally persistent units have informally been termed in descending order, the "A", "B", "C", and "D" members. The sandstone members have gradational lower contacts, coarsen upward, and are abruptly overlain by black marine shale of the overlying member (Fig. 4).

The "D" sandstone member is composed of two gradational units. The lower "D" unit coarsens upward from highly bioturbated, silty mudstones to clean, massive, and laminated sandstone (Figs. 5L–G). Individual bedsets range from 2.5 to 8.5 ft (0.8 to 2.6 m) in thickness, but often have disconformable lower contacts (Fig. 5K). The lowermost mudstone unit is bioturbated by horizontal burrowing and mottled by sand–filled burrow tubes in a silty clay matrix (Fig. 5L). Ripple laminae and discontinuous planar laminae impart a faint horizontal aspect to the bedding. The overlying sandstone is massive, containing wispy, discontinuous laminae and abundant carbonaceous fragments (Figs. 5J and 5K). The massive sandstone is overlain by clean, quartzose sandstone containing trough cross–bedding and horizontal laminae (Figs. 5G–I). The coarsening–upward sequence represents an upward increase in flow regime and sand content.

The upper unit of the "D" member contains thin, discontinuous bedsets of massive sandstone grading upward into rippled and bioturbated sandstone (Figs. 5A–F). Each bedset is capped by an intensely bioturbated, silty sandstone with a truncated upper surface (Figs. 5B, 5C). Some textural grading is present within individual bedsets of the upper sandstone. The abundance and diversity of bioturbation (Fig. 6) increases upward in the "D" sandstone indicating the development of a normal shallow marine environment. Numerous disconformable contacts are evidence of rapid, episodic sand deposition and intervening periods of clay accumulation and bioturbation. This pattern may be indicative of alternating storm and fair weather deposition.

According to Berg (1979), the upward transition from marine siltstone to sandstone is typical of deposition within a prograding sand body. Berg (1979) interpreted a deltaic and fluvial origin for the Dakota "D" sandstone at Lone Pine Field, about 18 mi (29 km) to the southwest. Within the study area, the "D" sandstone exhibits a sequence of sedimentary structures indicative of a deltaic to shallow marine origin, probably as distributary–mouth bars. However, variable sedimentary structures within equivalent sandstones indicate a high degree of lateral variability within the depositional environment. The presence of clean, horizontally laminated and massive sandstone suggests the presence of upper shoreface deposition lateral to the distributary–mouth bars. A net sandstone isopach map of the "D" sandstone member displays both dip–trending and strike–trending components (Fig. 7A). To the west, the sandstone has a moderately sinuous morphology characteristic of distributary–mouth bar deposits. To the east the sandstone has linear, strike–trending morphology typical of sediments deposited in an upper to middle shoreface (bar) environment. The "D" sandstone has a greater lateral extent than do the "A", "B", or "C" members. However its productive limits are not continuous. In cross–section, the "D" sandstone member is typically blocky to massive and does not display the distinct coarsening–upward trend seen in the upper three sandstone members (Fig. 8).

Table 1: Petrographic data of Dakota Sandstone, West Lindrith Field, San Juan Basin, New Mexico

Depth Interval (ft.)	Number of Samples	Grain Size (mm)			Detrital Composition[a] (%)					Authigenic Minerals[b]			Perm[c] (md)	Porosity[c] (%)
		Mean	Max.	St.D.	Qtz	Feld	Rx	Oth	Mx	Sil	Carb	Clay		
CF3														
AB 7638–7665	9	0.20	0.39	0.06	55.1	2.5	22.4	4.2	15.9	<1	7.2	1.8	0.06	5.1
C 7718–7737	10	0.23	0.44	0.08	53.4	2.4	25.6	3.7	11.8	2.5	8.7	2.6	0.14	4.3
D 7802–7828	10	0.22	0.43	0.07	56.3	6.3	29.7	4.8	2.9	6.7	7.9	2.8	0.40	8.6
B7														
AB 7167–7225	21	0.27	0.49	0.08	63.5	2.8	26.0	3.5	4.2	6.0	5.4	5.2	0.20	6.0
C 7287–7298	6	0.27	0.45	0.07	65.8	3.1	23.9	3.0	4.4	7.6	2.5	3.7	0.25	3.1
D 7381–7398	8	0.14	0.25	0.04	61.7	9.8	23.8	3.6	1.1	5.0	2.1	5.2	0.08	11.2
HF1														
AB 7213–7239	10	0.23	0.42	0.07	62.0	2.6	27.7	2.0	5.7	5.4	4.8	4.9	0.25	5.4
C 7312–7333	5	0.10	0.21	0.04	47.1	4.1	28.3	6.0	14.5	1.3	20.3	9.8	0.10	2.4
D 7404–7419	6	0.07	0.12	0.02	49.0	5.2	38.0	5.2	2.8	5.4	10.7	10.3	0.10	3.2
Means of All Samples:		0.22	0.36	0.07	58.4	4.0	26.8	3.8	6.6	4.7	6.9	4.7	0.19	5.8

[a] Qtz = quartz; Fd = feldspars; Rx = rock fragments; Ot = others; Mx = matrix
[b] Sil = silica; Carb = carbonates. All authigenic minerals are in percent of bulk rock
[c] Perm = permeability data from core analysis; porosity from point counting of thin sections

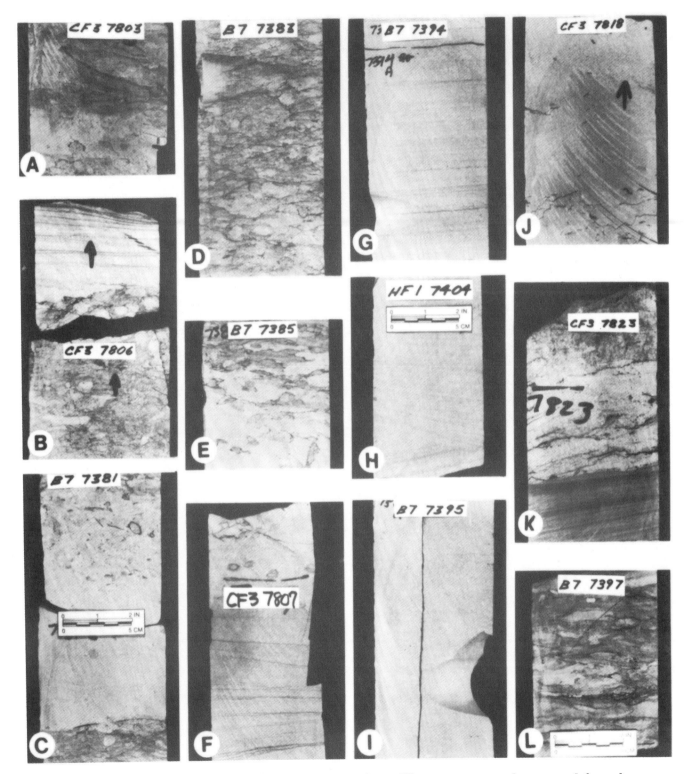

Figure 5. Core photographs of the "D" sandstone member. The sequence grades upward from lower right to upper left (L to A). Note the upward gradation from massive and laminated sandstone (G, H, I) to highly bioturbated sandstone (A, B, D). Individual bedsets consist of fining-upward sequences with disconformable lower contacts (B, C, K). Open vertical fractures are common (I).

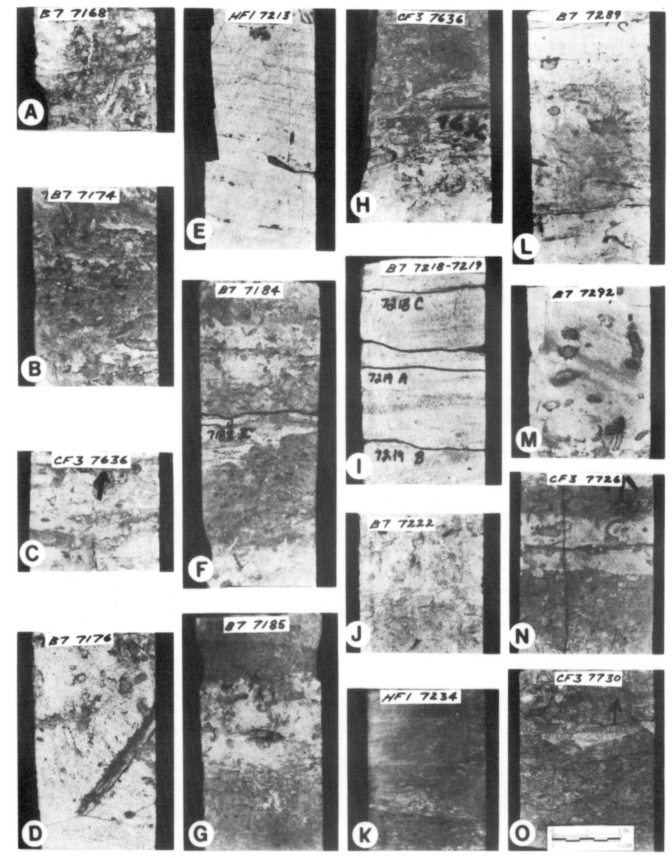

Figure 6. Core photographs of the "A", "B", and "C" sandstone members. The "C" member grades upward from lower right to upper right (O to L). The "A–B" grades upward from K to A. Intense bioturbation, including abundant *Ophiomorpha* burrows (M, L), has destroyed most of the original sedimentary structures.

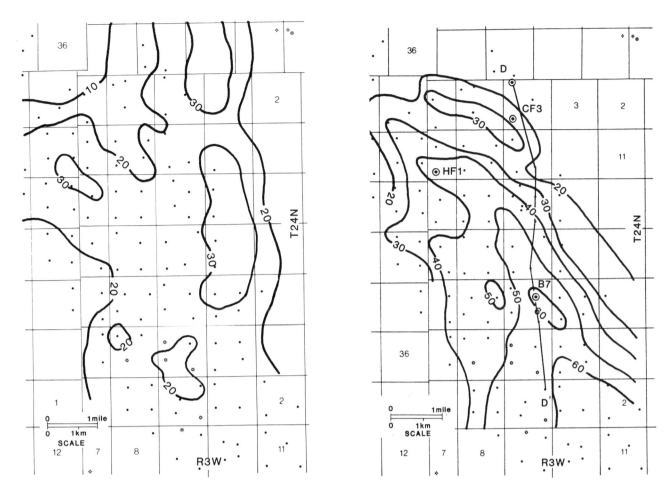

Figure 7. Net sandstone isopachs.

A. Net-sandstone thicknesses of the "D" unit. The "D" member displays a dip-trending morphology to the west and a strike-trending morphology toward the east-northeast.

B. Net-sandstone thickness of the combined "A" and "B" members, which show a strong northwest-southeast, strike-trending. The cored wells used in this study (CF3, HF1, and B-7) are circled.

The "A", "B", and "C" sandstone members coarsen upward, grading uniformly from silty marine shale to bioturbated, massive, and laminated sandstones (Figs. 6L–O). Although the sequences coarsen upward, close examination reveals that they are composed of thin, fining-upward bedsets that increase in both shale content and bioturbation upward. Individuals bedsets are 1.5 to 2.5 ft (0.45 to 0.75m) thick, and consist of a basal unit of massive sandstone grading upward into highly bioturbated and rippled sandstone (Figs. 6M–6K). The rippled, bioturbated sandstone is often truncated by massive sandstone of the overlying bedset. Massive sandstones contain abundant *Ophiomorpha* and other burrows along with shale clasts up to 1 in (2.5 cm) in diameter near the base (Fig. 6M). Thin zones of medium-grained sandstone display plane, parallel, even, and continuous laminae which dip 0 to 8° (Figs. 6E, 6I). The majority of the sandstone is highly bioturbated and churned with local variations in silt and clay content producing a mottled appearance (Figs. 6A, 6B, 6F, 6H).

Compositional and textural evidence indicates that the "A", "B", and "C" sandstone members were de-posited as sand ridges on a marine shelf. The abundance and diversity of bioturbation suggest deposition in a shallow to middle-neritic environment. The fining-upward and truncated nature of individual bedsets indicates that the sandstones probably were deposited by storm currents and locally redistributed by tidal or longshore currents. The presence of disconformable lower contacts indicates that some scouring may have occurred as the sands were rapidly deposited onto underlying shelf sediments. Waning currents and decreasing flow regime upward in each bedset produced sedimentary structures such as wavy and climbing ripples (Fig. 6H). The rippled zones were subsequently reworked by burrowing organisms during periods of low sediment influx.

The increase in sand content and grain size upward in the "A", "B", and "C" sequences indicates local or regional progradation of one or more clastic wedges. The extent of progradation was dependent on the relative rates of subsidence and sediment influx in localized areas. Regressive or stillstand episodes that deposited sandstone were punctuated by short periods of rapid transgression with deposition of ma-

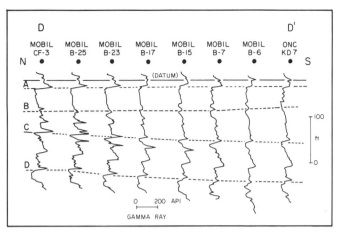

Figure 8. North–south stratigraphic cross–section across West Lindrith Field, showing the nature of the Dakota Sandstone members. Note that the "B" member shales out toward the south. The cross–section location is shown in Figure 7B. No horizontal scale. (100 ft = 30.48 m)

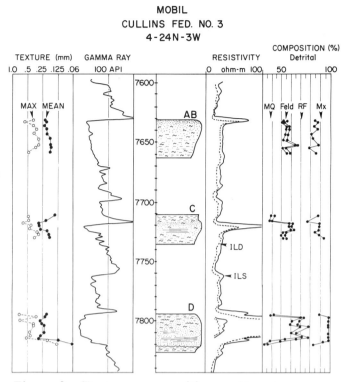

Figure 9. Texture, composition, sedimentary structures, and log character of the Dakota Sandstone from cores of the Mobil No. 3 Cullins Federal (Sec 4 T24N R3W). Detrital composition is divided into monocrystalline quartz (MQ), feldspar (Feld), rock fragments (RF), and detrital clay (Mx). ILD = deep induction curve. ILS = shallow–reading resistivity log. Minor depth divisions are 10 ft (3.05 m) apart.

rine siltstone and shale. Net sandstone "thicks" in the "A" and "B" members (Fig. 7B) strike linearly northwest–southeast, have lengths of about 25 mi (40 km)(Edwards, 1989), and are about five mi (8.05 km) in width. These sandstone bodies are lenticular and laterally discontinuous, grading into shale at the outer margins of the field (Fig. 8).

TEXTURE AND MINERALOGY OF THE DAKOTA SANDSTONE

The Dakota Sandstone is fine to very fine–grained with an average grain size of 0.22 mm, and a range of less than 0.06 mm to 0.46 mm (Table 1). Monocrystalline quartz grains are subangular to well rounded, the roundness increasing with grain size and sorting. The standard deviation averages 0.07 mm, indicating a moderately well sorted sand (Folk, 1974). Each sandstone member displays a distinct coarsening–upward trend (Fig. 9). The coarsening–upward trend is present throughout the Dakota interval.

The average detrital composition of the Dakota Sandstone is that of a lithic arenite, with individual samples ranging from sublitharenite to subarkose (Folk, 1974). Framework grains average 58% quartz, 4% feldspar, 27% rock fragments, 4% other minerals and 7% detrital matrix (less than 10 microns). Feldspar content is consistently low; the abundance of monocrystalline quartz and rock fragments vary widely.

Monocrystalline quartz is the most abundant mineral in these sandstones. Quartz content increases upward with grain size, ranging from a low of 33% in very fine–grained sandstone to 83% in medium–grained sandstone (Fig. 9). The increase in quartz is interpreted to be due to winnowing of detrital matrix with increasing current velocities. Approximately equal amounts of undulose and non–undulose quartz grains are present. Feldspar is a volumetrically minor constituent of detrital grains, comprising only 3 to 4% of the detrital composition. There is a slight decrease

in feldspar upward through the sequence, from an average of 7% in the lower "D" member, to 3% in the "C" zone, and less than 3% in the "A" and "B" zones. Plagioclase and alkali feldspar commonly occur as slightly altered grains to skeletal dissolution remnants, although occasionally grains appear fresh and unaltered.

Rock fragments represent the other dominant detrital constituent, averaging 27% of the detrital grain population. Rock fragments are igneous, sedimentary, and metamorphic. Polycrystalline quartz is dominant, comprising 58% of the total rock fragments. Volcanic rock fragments average 14% and were identified by a glassy to "chert–like" appearance combined with the presence of opaque granules as an alteration product. Sedimentary rock fragments average 17%. Shale clasts (2 to 6 mm) and chert predominate, with trace amounts of detrital carbonate particles, mostly foraminifera tests. Shale clasts are often deformed between more rigid detrital grains and appear as pseudomatrix. Chert fragments are present in all samples and were identified by the presence of numerous crystallites 2 to 7 microns in size. Well–rounded chert pebbles up to 1.0 mm in diameter are present in the clean, laminated sandstones. Metamorphic rock fragments make up an average of 11% of the total rock fragment population and consist mainly of schistose grains and foliated polycrystalline quartz.

The remainder of the detrital fraction is composed of accessory minerals, organic matter, and detrital matrix. The accessory species identified include well-rounded zircon and tourmaline; opaque minerals; biotite and muscovite; and glauconite pellets. Carbonaceous debris occur as fragments, pellets, and stringers. Material smaller than 10 microns includes dispersed detrital matrix, shale fragments, and shale laminae. These modes of occurrence are modified or obliterated where allogenic clays are reworked and homogenized by burrowing organisms (Wilson and Pittman, 1977). Detrital clay contents range from 0 to 33% of the detrital fraction, averaging 7%. Laminated and massive sandstones contain an average of 2 to 3% matrix, while the highly bioturbated sandstones average 10 to 14% detrital matrix. The high clay content of the bioturbated sands undoubtedly represents the churning and redistribution of shale laminae into dispersed detrital matrix and biogenic pellets.

The dominance of stable sedimentary and metasedimentary detritus in the detrital fraction indicates derivation from the weathering of older sedimentary rocks. The accessory–mineral suite, consisting almost entirely of rounded zircon and tourmaline grains, also is indicative of multicyclic detritus. The source of much of the clastic material was probably the Morrison Formation and other exposed clastic units.

DIAGENESIS OF THE DAKOTA SANDSTONE

Quartz and carbonate are the most common cementing minerals, averaging 5% and 7% of the bulk rock. Minor amounts of anhydrite, pyrite, and siderite also are present. Authigenic clays comprise an average 5% of the bulk rock, ranging up to 17% (Table 1).

Compaction

Fuchtbauer (1974) believed that grain slippage and rotation constitute the principal mechanism of compaction of quartzose sands down to depths of 3,000–4,000 ft (915–1,220 m). In the Dakota Sandstone, brittle framework grains such as quartz and feldspar typically display evidence of fracture, slippage, and rotation. The Dakota contains a relatively large amount of deformed labile grains including micas, glauconite pellets, and pelitic rock fragments. These highly deformed grains often form pseudomatrix. Early cementation of clean sands by carbonate and/or silica arrested compaction at very shallow depths, as dramatically illustrated by floating framework grains observed in several highly cemented samples.

Authigenesis

Silica cement is present in the form of optically continuous overgrowths on detrital quartz grains, varying from 0 to 16% of the bulk rock. Overgrowths form either euhedral crystal terminations or anhedral aggregates of coalescing crystals. Although overgrowths usually were identifiable by the presence of dust rims and euhedral terminations, petrographic

analysis probably represents a minimum value. Silica cement is much more abundant in clean massive sandstones and laminated sandstones with relatively high quartz content. The amount of silica cement varies inversely with detrital matrix content. High concentrations of pore–lining and pore–filling clays of both detrital and authigenic origin prohibited the precipitation of silica cement locally (Plate 1A).

Silica cementation began very early, perhaps contemporaneously with deposition. However, observations indicate multiple phases of quartz precipitation. This suggests that the source of silica and the precipitation mechanism probably varied through burial. Silica precipitation was more pervasive in well–sorted quartzose sandstones for several reasons: 1) well–sorted sandstones have the highest initial permeability and thus can act as conduits for fluid migration, 2) the sandstones contain very little allogenic clay matrix to prohibit nucleation of quartz overgrowths, 3) the higher quartz content provided increased surface area for overgrowth nucleation, and 4) the importance of pressure solution is greater in quartzose sandstones containing mainly brittle framework grains.

Carbonate cement, dominantly calcite and dolomite, occurs in all samples and ranges up to 41% of the bulk rock. The abundance of carbonate cement varies widely between samples, increasing abruptly in sandstones directly adjacent to interstratified marine shale. Carbonate cement also displays a patchy distribution in individual thin sections. Poikilotopic calcite is present locally, forming a continuous cement that supports floating framework grains. Calcite also etches quartz grains and replaces less stable framework grains such as feldspar (Plate 1B), glauconite, and biotite.

Textural relations indicate that precipitation of calcite cement occurred after an initial stage of silica cementation (Plate 1C). The calcite cementation decreases abruptly with increasing distance from the sandstone–shale boundary, forming a "diagenetic aureole" (Füchtbauer, 1974). This phenomenon is best illustrated in the "D" zone of the CF3 core (Fig. 10). The zone displays remarkable symmetry, with carbonate cement occurring near the sandstone–shale boundaries, and silica cement dominating the central portion of the unit. From this relationship it is inferred that shale dewatering was responsible for calcite cementation. Local concentrations of shell material in the shales provide a source of calcite. Pervasive calcite cementation reduced permeability, restricted pore water flux, and in many places precluded the development of later authigenic phases.

Dolomite occurs as coarse, euhedral crystals in pore–filling or replacive textures; and as minute crystallites nucleated in pore–filling clays and shale fragments (Plate 1D). Nonferroan dolomite precipitation postdated both calcite and silica cementation (Plate 1C). The abundance of fine–grained dolomite associated with pore–filling allogenic clays and shale rock fragments indicates that the Mg^{+2} was derived directly from the fine–grained materials. It is probable that local concentrations of calcareous material incorporated the Mg^{+2} mobilized by illitization of allogenic clays to produce dolomite during moderate to deep burial.

Mobil
Cullins Federal No. 3
4 - 24N - 3W

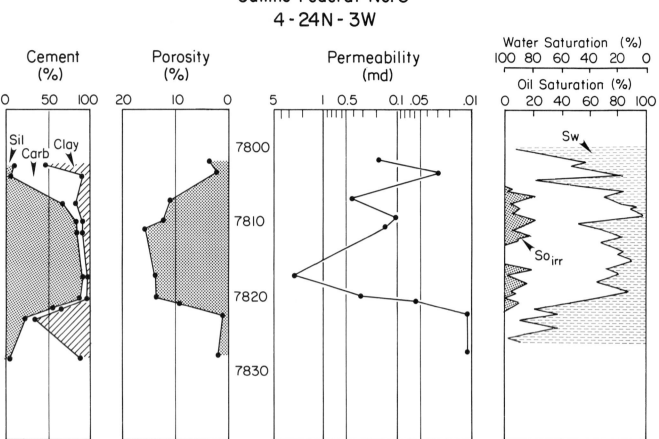

Figure 10. Relationship between cement type, porosity, and permeability for the "D" sandstone of the No. 3 Cullins Federal well. Cements include silica (Sil), carbonate (Carb), and clay of detrital and authigenic origin (Clay). Note that the silica-cemented zone contains greater porosity and permeability than the surrounding carbonate-cemented zones. Also the silica-cemented zone yielded the greatest amount of mobile oil and had the lowest Sw. (10 ft = 3.05 m)

Minor amounts of authigenic pyrite, siderite, and anhydrite are locally important as cementing minerals. Pyrite occurs as botryoidal nodules filling pores and replacing both framework grains and authigenic cements. A few samples contain large pyrite nodules. Pyrite also is very common as an alteration product of iron-rich grains such as glauconite, biotite, and volcanic rock fragments. Siderite occurs locally as euhedral, pore-filling crystals, usually with a brownish-yellow iron oxide coating. Poikilotopic anhydrite occurs as stringers between loosely packed framework grains and is replaced by calcite and dolomite locally.

Authigenic clay minerals comprise an average 5% of the bulk volume of these sandstones, occurring as pore-filling, pore-lining, and replacive minerals. The dominant clay minerals identified by XRD analyses include illite, kaolinite, chlorite, vermiculite, and mixed-layer clays (Franklin, 1986). Most sandstone samples contain fine-grained, pore-filling material of both detrital and authigenic origin interspersed within the pore network. Furthermore, at least some of the

original detrital matrix has recrystallized in response to changing chemical conditions.

The presence of randomly interstratified illite/smectite and/or illite/vermiculite was inferred from the presence of a broad, asymmetrical 12 angstrom peak on the diffractogram for the magnesium-saturated coarse and fine clay fractions (Fig. 11). Mixed-layer clays have morphologic characteristics that may appear similar to layered clays, depending on the relative amount of each constituent. If illite-rich, the structure may be essentially indistinguishable from illite and take the form of sheets with short lath-shaped digitate edges (Fig. 12A). A smectite-rich mixed-layer clay may resemble the crinkly form of smectite and differ only in the presence of spiny projections (Fig. 12B). The detrital clay matrix is dominantly mixed-layer illite/smectite, and typically displays evidence of minor recrystallization, with the development of curled, digitate edges (Fig. 12C).

The presence of discrete illite, chlorite, and kaolinite in both fractions is indicated by XRD (Fig. 11). Illite commonly forms a network of pore-bridg-

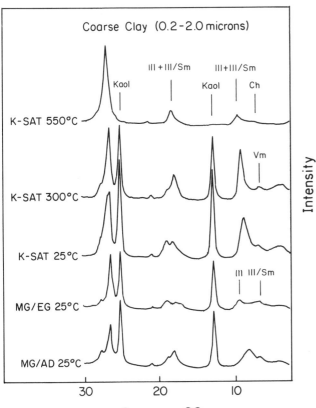

Figure 11. X-ray diffractograms of the coarse clay fraction showing the various clays: chlorite (ch), kaolinite (kaol), illite (ill), and illite/smectite (ill/sm). The patterns were obtained after various treatments: K-SAT = potassium-saturated; MG/EG = magnesium ethylene glycol saturated.

ing, lath-shaped fibers (Fig. 12C). Chlorite is typically more abundant in the coarse clay fraction, although it makes up only a few percent of the sandstone. Chlorite most commonly develops as grain coats oriented normal to the grain surface. Kaolinite is more abundant in the coarse clay fraction (Franklin, 1986). Kaolinite is often associated with authigenic illite (Fig. 12D).

Authigenic clays formed by the alteration of unstable detrital phases and by direct precipitation from pore fluids. Chlorite grain coats precipitated at an early phase of burial. Pore-filling and replacive kaolinite formed both from direct precipitation and as an alteration product of feldspar, possibly in several stages during burial. The K+ released by the reaction facilitated the smectite to illite transformation of detrital mixed-layer clays and the precipitation of discrete illite. The presence of illite fibers on pore-filling kaolinite indicates the later precipitation of illite or the alteration of kaolinite to illite (Fig. 12D).

Dissolution and Secondary Porosity

Diagenetic processes have modified the size, distribution, and geometry of pores within the Dakota Sandstone. The present porosity appears to be dominantly secondary in origin, by the criteria of Schmidt

and McDonald (1979). Secondary porosity resulted primarily from dissolution of feldspar, micas, and carbonate cement. The total petrographic porosity, excluding fractures, is composed of three major porosity types: intergranular, intragranular, and microporosity. Each type possesses distinct permeability, Sw, and capillary pressure characteristics associated with pore size, pore geometry and the degree of interconnection between pores (Pittman, 1979).

Intergranular porosity occurs sporadically and is of local importance in the Dakota reservoir. These pores are usually isolated, but occasionally exhibit a well-developed pore network connected by fractures (Plate 1E). The dissolution of early pore-filling carbonate cement may have enhanced the development of intergranular porosity. Intragranular porosity developed through the dissolution of feldspar, biotite, and other unstable detrital grains (Plate 1F). Intragranular pores typically are isolated, with essentially no interconnected pore throats. Microporosity may be defined as pores with pore-aperture radii smaller than 0.5 microns (Pittman, 1979). Micropores are typical among pore-filling clay minerals; the high ratio of surface area to volume, and the tight packing of clay minerals segment pores into a large number of micropores (Fig. 11B). Clay-rich samples commonly have significant microporosity, regardless of whether the clays are detrital or authigenic in origin.

Both microscopic and macroscopic fractures are present and provide the permeability necessary for commercial production. Open and mineralized fractures were observed in cores (Fig. 5I) and thin section. Fracture porosity is important on a microscopic scale because it increases the interconnection between isolated pore spaces, thereby increasing the effective porosity (Plate 1E).

FACIES, DIAGENESIS, AND RESERVOIR PROPERTIES

Facies Control on Diagenesis

Factor analysis of petrographic data shows that there are three end members in the sample set that can be defined as "diagenetic facies". Each end member is uniquely defined by its detrital composition, authigenic composition, and porosity (Plate 2). End Member 1 is characterized by relatively high contents of monocrystalline quartz, polycrystalline quartz, silica cement, feldspar, and porosity, and by little or no detrital matrix and carbonate cement. End Member 2 is composed of samples which are very high in carbonate cement and low in silica cement, with virtually no porosity. End Member 3 is characterized by having relatively high contents of rock fragments, detrital matrix, and authigenic clays, with no silica cement and low porosity values. Each diagenetic facies is the end product of a unique diagenetic pathway resulting from pre- and post-burial processes.

The high degree of sorting and low matrix content of End Member 1 sandstones produced initially very high permeabilities. These clean, quartzose sandstones acted as conduits for fluid migration during burial. The authigenic minerals formed in these conditions include quartz, carbonates, anhydrite, and kaolinite. The sample most typical of End Member 1

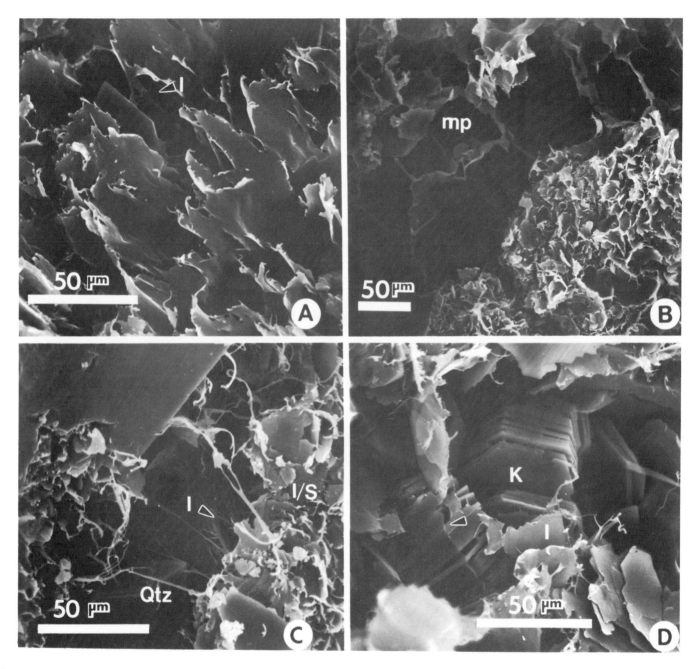

Figure 12. SEM images showing the morphology and textural relationships of various authigenic clays of the Dakota Sandstone.

A. Flaky morphology of illite composed of coalescing subparallel fibers (I). Scale bar represents 50 microns.

B. Microporosity (mp) associated with pore-filling smectitic mixed-layer clay. Note recrystallized detrital clay at lower right. Scale bar represents 50 microns.

C. Fibrous illite (I) bridging pore and coprecipitated with quartz overgrowth (Qtz). Note the recrystallized mixed/layer clay (I/S). Scale bar represents 50 microns.

D. Pore-filling kaolinite (K) with fibrous illite (I, arrow) developed on its surface. Scale bar represents 50 microns.

displays 11% porosity, permeability of 0.44 md, and Sw of 6%. This group of samples represents the reservoir diagenetic facies.

End Member 2 sandstones represent a relatively small number of samples that are extensively cemented by carbonate cement, irrespective of composition and texture. End Member 2 sandstones are intercalated with shale, and therefore experienced extensive carbonate cementation by fluids derived from shale dewatering. Carbonate cements fill virtually all of the framework porosity and have replaced a significant volume of detrital grains. The pervasive early cementation of End Member 2 sandstone precluded the development of later authigenic phases. End Member 2 samples contain virtually no intergranular porosity. They are somewhat variable, but typically have 2 to 4% porosity, permeability less than 0.1 md, and Sw of 20% or higher. This is a nonreservoir diagenetic facies.

The clay-rich sediments represented by End Member 3 samples were deposited in low-energy conditions. These sandstones had much lower initial permeability and underwent less pore-fluid flux. This inhibited the early nucleation of quartz overgrowths. Authigenic phases formed in these sandstones include early authigenic pyrite and dolomite that precipitated within the pore-filling matrix. Much of the matrix apparently recrystallized and donated cations for precipitation of illite and chlorite. End Member 3 sandstones contain very low porosity and permeability due to the abundance of clay minerals. The sample most typical of End Member 3 has 4% porosity, permeability of 0.04 md, and Sw of 33%. These sandstones are a nonreservoir diagenetic facies because of the exceedingly small average pore-throat size.

Thus, the diagenetic pathways of End Members 1 and 3 were determined primarily by the initial composition and texture of the sandstone as determined by depositional environment. The diagenetic pathway of End Member 2 was determined primarily by stratigraphic position adjacent to shale beds.

Diagenetic Controls on Reservoir Properties

The heterogeneity of reservoir properties in the Dakota Sandstone can be ascribed to both primary lithological contrasts and divergent diagenetic histories. Mechanical compaction, cementation, dissolution, and precipitation of authigenic clays all played important roles in determining the present reservoir quality. Mechanical compaction was a dominant physical process during early diagenesis. Authigenic cements also have greatly reduced the porosity and permeability of the sandstone where they persist in significant amounts, because cements are preferentially precipitated at pore throats. The type of cement greatly influences the reservoir properties of the sandstone. Sandstone directly adjacent to shale layers displays 1 to 4% porosity and permeability of less than 0.05 md (Fig. 10). Silica-cemented sandstones have porosities greater than 10% and permeability up to 2.3 md (Fig. 10), constitute the reservoir facies.

Authigenic clays create microporosity and drastically reduce permeability without significantly reducing porosity (Hayes, 1979). The high surface area of

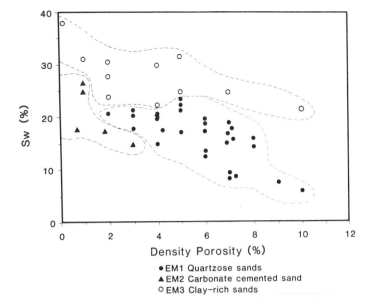

Figure 13. Graph of Sw against density porosity for sandstones of the three diagenetic facies. The sandstones show an overall decrease in Sw with increasing porosity. Each compositional end member displays a unique field of Sw - porosity values. Clay-rich sandstones have high Sw; quartzose sandstones have relatively low Sw; and carbonate-cemented sandstones display low Sw and low porosity.

authigenic clays such as illite/smectite also significantly reduces permeability (Almon and Schultz, 1979). The precipitation of authigenic clays and cements has significantly reduced average pore-throat radius and reservoir quality. The relative abundance of clays within the pore system of a reservoir also affects the electrochemistry and resistivity (Rt) of the sandstone (Wescott, 1983).

The petrophysical properties of the three diagenetic facies vary significantly and can be recognized by cross-plotting porosity, Rt, and Sw. Quartz-rich End Member 1 sandstones display lower Sw and higher density-log porosity than either the carbonate-cemented or clay-rich sandstones (Fig. 13). The low Sw is due to the low clay content and high oil saturation; high density-log porosity reflects the lack of relatively dense, pore-filling carbonate cements. End Member 2 sandstones have high Sw values and low density-log porosity values (Fig. 13). End Member 3 sandstones display relatively high Sw and variable density-log porosity as compared to the other end members (Fig. 13), due to having high irreducible Sw in microporosity.

End Member 1 sandstones display higher Rt than the other two diagenetic facies because of the relative paucity of clay minerals and their higher oil saturation (Fig. 14). The high porosity, permeability, and Rt of a few End Member 1 samples suggests that a relatively small number of highly porous, permeable zones are responsible for a significant portion of the production (Fig. 15). End members 2 and 3 display low porosity

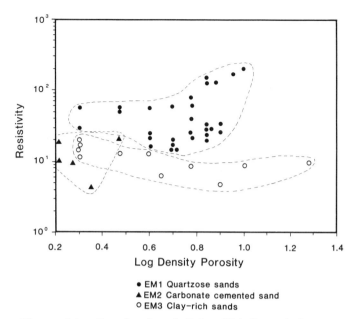

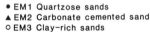

● EM1 Quartzose sands
▲ EM2 Carbonate cemented sand
○ EM3 Clay-rich sands

Figure 14. Graph of resistivity (Rt) from induction log against density–log porosity for sandstones of different diagenetic facies. Sandstones of different compositions form well-defined resistivity – porosity fields due to the compositional controls on reservoir properties. Quartzose sandstones are highly resistive. Clay-rich sandstones are highly conductive. Carbonate-cemented sandstones display low resistivity and low porosity.

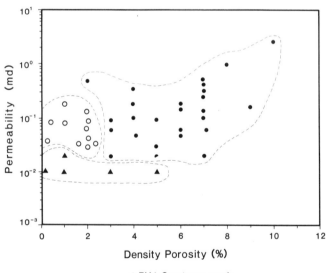

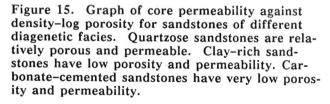

● EM1 Quartzose sands
▲ EM2 Carbonate cemented sand
○ EM3 Clay-rich sands

Figure 15. Graph of core permeability against density–log porosity for sandstones of different diagenetic facies. Quartzose sandstones are relatively porous and permeable. Clay-rich sandstones have low porosity and permeability. Carbonate-cemented sandstones have very low porosity and permeability.

and permeability values due to the abundance of authigenic cements and clay minerals.

CONCLUSIONS

The upper Dakota Sandstone of the San Juan Basin is composed of a series of regressive sandstones deposited in an overall transgressive sequence. The "D" sandstone member was deposited as distributary-mouth bar and strandplain sediment in a deltaic to upper shoreface environment. The "A", "B", and "C" sandstone members were deposited in a shallow marine environment and reworked locally by storm, tidal, or longshore currents to produce a series of northwest–southeast trending sand ridges.

The diagenetic processes of compaction, authigenesis, and dissolution have pervasively altered the composition, texture, and reservoir properties of the sandstone. Divergent diagenetic pathways were created by differences in original composition, texture, and stratigraphic position of the sandstones.

End Member 1 sandstones display a wide range in petrophysical properties, but include the only reservoir-quality rocks. End Member 2 sandstones generally display low Sw, but also have low porosity and permeability. End Member 3 sandstones may be capable of producing gas, but generally have low permeability. Fracture porosity greatly enhances the permeability of the sandstone by interconnecting isolated dissolution pore spaces.

Graphical methods are a valuable tool in relating diagenetic and reservoir facies in productive intervals, and may be employed to recognize diagenetic facies and delineate the compositional and textural controls on petrophysical properties. Once the reservoir facies are identified, this technique may be used to recognize and correct for anomalous log responses, and direct the selection of pay zones for perforation. However, the technique must be used only in conjunction with adequate knowledge of the composition, texture, and depositional environment of the sandstone. By combining these factors with an understanding of the diagenetic history of the rocks, it is possible to fully characterize any sandstone reservoir.

ACKNOWLEDGEMENTS

The authors thank Gordon K. Baker and Mobil Producing Texas and New Mexico, Inc., for providing the cores and the financial assistance necessary to complete this study. We thank Dr. Robert R. Berg for discussions concerning the environmental interpretation of cored intervals and Dr. John H. Spang for financial and moral support. We gratefully acknowledge Pat O. Edwards for providing sandstone isopach maps and cross-sections. In addition, the authors would like to thank the AAPG Grant in Aid Committee, the Texas A & M University Center for Energy and Minerals Research and the Texas Mining and Minerals Resources Research Institute of Austin, Texas for providing financial support which made this study possible.

REFERENCES

Almon, W.R., and A.L. Schultz, 1979, Electric log detection of diagenetically altered reservoirs and diagenetic traps: Trans.-GCAGS, v. 29, p. 1-10.

Attebury, R.T., 1978, Lindrith Gallup-Dakota, West: *in* J.E. Fassett, ed., Oil and Gas Fields of the Four Corners Area, FCGS, p. 381 -384.

Berg, R.R., 1979, Oil and gas in delta-margin facies of Dakota Sandstone, Lone Pine Field, New Mexico: AAPG Bull., v. 63, p. 886-904.

Deischl, D.G., 1973, The characteristics, history, and development of the Basin Dakota gas field, *in* Cretaceous and Tertiary Rocks of the Southern Colorado Plateau: FCGS Mem., p. 168-173.

Edwards, P.O., 1989, Depositional environment of the Dakota Sandstone, West Lindrith Field, Rio Arriba County, New Mexico: unpub. MS thesis, Texas A&M U., in preparation.

Fassett, J.E., 1974, Cretaceous and Tertiary rocks of the eastern San Juan basin, New Mexico and Colorado, *in* Ghost Ranch: NMGS, 25th Field Conf. Guidebook, p. 225-230.

Folk, R.L., 1974, Petrology of Sedimentary Rocks: Hemphill, Austin, TX, 182 p.

Franklin, S.P., 1986, Diagenesis and clay mineralogy of the Dakota Sandstone, West Lindrith Field, Rio Arriba County, New Mexico [abs]: GSA Ann. Mtg., Abstracts with Programs, v. 18, p. 196.

Füchtbauer, H., 1974, Sediments and Sedimentary Rocks, 1: Part II; Halstead Press, NY, 464 p.

Grant, K., and D.E. Owen, 1974, The Dakota Sandstone (Cretaceous) of the southern part of the Chama basin, New Mexico - A preliminary report on its stratigraphy, paleontology, and sedimentology, *in* Ghost Ranch: NMGS, 25th Field Conf. Guidebook, p. 239-249.

Hayes, J.B., 1979, Sandstone diagenesis - the hole truth: in SEPM Spec. Pub. 26, p. 127-140.

Kelley, V.C., 1957, Tectonics of the San Juan Basin and surrounding areas, in Geology of Southwestern San Juan Basin: NMGS, 2nd Field Conf. Guidebook, p. 44-52.

Owen, D.E., 1969, The Dakota Sandstone of the eastern San Juan and Chama basins and its possible correlation across the Southern Rocky Mountains: Mtn. Geol., v. 6, p. 87- 92.

Peterson, J.A., A.J. Loleit, C.W. Spencer, and R.A. Ullrich, 1965, Sedimentary history and economic geology of San Juan basin: AAPG Bull., v. 49, p. 2076-2119.

Pittman, E.D., 1979, Porosity, diagenesis, and productive capability of sandstone reservoirs: SEPM Spec. Pub. 26, p. 159-174.

Rice, D.D., 1983, Relation of natural gas composition to thermal maturity and source rock type in San Juan basin, northwestern New Mexico and southwestern Colorado: AAPG Bull., v. 67, p. 1199-1218.

Schmidt, V., and D.A. McDonald, 1979, The role of secondary porosity in the course of sandstone diagenesis, in SEPM Spec. Pub. 26, p. 175-207.

Wescott, W., 1983, Diagenesis of the Cotton Valley Sandstone (Upper Jurassic), east Texas: Implications for tight gas sand pay recognition: AAPG Bull., v. 67, p. 1012-1023.

Wilson, M.D., and E.D. Pittman, 1977, Authigenic clays in sandstones: Recognition and influence of reservoir properties and paleoenvironmental analysis: JSP, v. 47, p. 3-31.

Woodward, L.A., and J.F. Callender, 1977, Tectonic framework of the San Juan Basin: in San Juan Basin III, NMGS, 28th Field Conf. Guidebook, p. 209-212.

Young, R.G., 1960, Dakota Group of the Colorado Plateau: AAPG Bull., v. 44, p. 156-194.

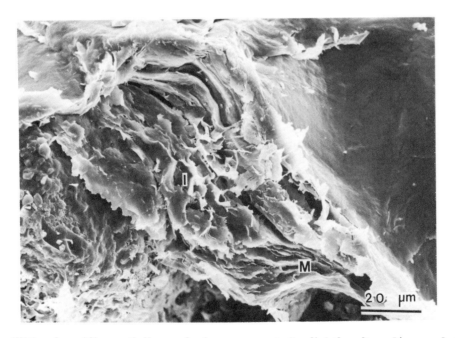

Authigenic illitic clay (C) partially replacing compacted, slightly altered/expanded detrital mica (M). Dakota Fm., sec 18 T33N R7W, La Plata Co., CO. Depth 7,899—7,901 ft (2,408 m). Photo donated by Bill Keighin.

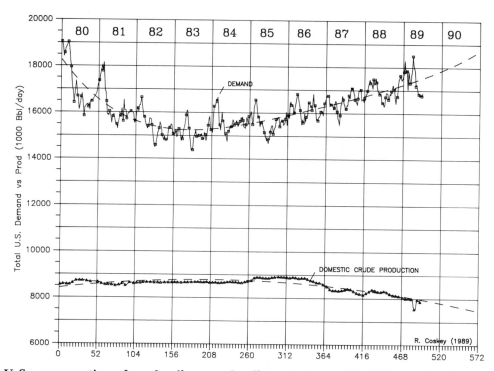

Trends in U.S. consumption of crude oil an crude oil products, and in U.S. crude oil production for the period January 7, 1980 through June 19, 1989. Data collected weekly from the Oil and Gas Journal. symbols are posted at four-week intervals. Production data do not include natural gas liquids (approximately 1.64 million barrels). Demand data do not include crude and crude product exported by the United States (approximately 600,000 to 700,000 barrels/day). Figure donated by R.J. Coskey, Rose Exploration.

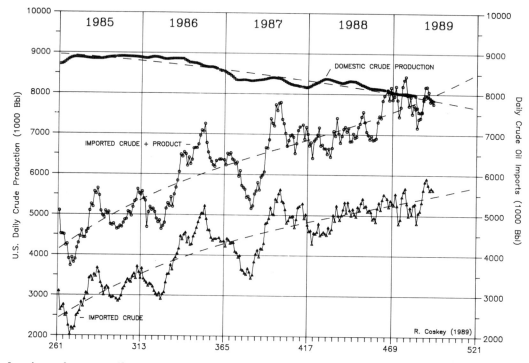

U.S. production of crude oil, imports of crude oil, and imports of crude oil plus refined products, for the period 1985 through June 19, 1989. Week numbers begin January 17, 1980. Data collected weekly from Oil and Gas Journal. Production data do not include natural gas liquids (approximately 1.64 million barrels). Figure donated by R.J. Coskey, Rose Exploration.

Paleostructural Control of Dakota Hydrocarbon Accumulations on the Southern Moxa Arch, Southwest Wyoming and Northeast Utah[1]

K.D. REISSER[2]

STEVE J. BLANKE[2]

[1]Received September 9, 1988; Revised March 29, 1989
[2]Oryx Energy, Dallas, Texas

The Lower Cretaceous Dakota Formation has produced large volumes of oil and gas from fluvial and deltaic sandstones along the southern Moxa Arch in southwest Wyoming and northeast Utah. The Dakota fields in this area are not distributed evenly across the structural crest of the Moxa Arch, but rather tend to be found on the eastern margin. Some sandstone units are productive over only a limited area. Gas/oil ratios in the fields vary greatly from south to north. These anomalies are explained by the depositional, structural, diagenetic, and thermal histories of the Dakota Formation.

Development of the Western Overthrust Belt and its foreland basin largely controlled the orientation of Dakota fluvial and deltaic systems. Differences in sandstone trends between the upper and lower Dakota resulted in different migration pathways and locations of oil and gas accumulations. The onset of major structural growth of the Moxa Arch began contemporaneous with deformation in the Overthrust Belt, during Late Cretaceous (Campanian) time. After early migration of hydrocarbons into structural/stratigraphic traps, diagenesis of the Dakota sandstones, most effective in the downdip water legs of the reservoirs, sealed the accumulations in their initial paleostructural positions. Paleocene and Eocene structural compression reversed the original northward plunge of the arch and rotated it slightly to the east into its present structural configuration. Hydrodynamically driven, convective water flow increased temperature gradients along the crest of the arch, locally increasing thermal maturation of trapped hydrocarbons, while cooling the southern portion of the arch and retarding thermal maturation.

INTRODUCTION

The Moxa Arch is an elongate, north–south trending anticlinorium located approximately 25 mi (40 km) east of the Western Overthrust Belt in southwestern Wyoming's Green River Basin. This feature extends more than 120 mi (190 km) from the north flank of the Uinta Mountains to the Labarge Platform, where it plunges under the Overthrust Belt. The topic of this study is the Dakota Formation along the southern portion of the Moxa Arch, an area including Church Buttes, Butcherknife Springs, Henry, Taylor Ranch, Luckey Ditch, and Bridger Lake fields (Fig. 1).

Production from the Dakota Formation was first established on the Moxa Arch at Church Buttes field in 1945. Twenty years later, Bridger Lake was discovered. The area saw little exploration activity until the discovery of Butcherknife Springs Field in 1978. This was soon followed by discoveries at Henry and Taylor Ranch fields, culminating with the discovery of Luckey Ditch Field in 1985.

During the evolution of this play, a number of apparent anomalies became evident. While these fields are located near the crestal portion of the Moxa Arch, the best production is obtained from wells located east of the structural crest. Some crestal wells have been plugged after testing water or non-commercial amounts of hydrocarbons from the Dakota. Hydrocarbon–water contacts do not follow structural contours consistently. While oil production from the lower Dakota sandstone has only been found south of Butcherknife Springs Field, the upper Dakota produces gas and condensate from traps all along the length of the arch. Gas/oil ratios (GOR's) of Dakota reservoirs show a progressive increase northward, ranging from a low of 800:1 at Bridger Lake Field to over 200,000:1 at Church Buttes Field. This paper will attempt to explain some of these anomalous patterns.

Producing Interval:	"D" & "D–1" sandstones of lower Dakota Formation
Geographic Location:	Uinta and Sweetwater Counties, Wyoming; Summit County, Utah
Present Tectonic Setting:	Moxa Arch, southwest Green River Basin
Depositional Setting:	Alluvial/coastal plain southeast of the Western Interior Foreland Basin
Age of Reservoir:	Early Cretaceous (Albian)
Lithology of Reservoir:	Fine to medium–grained sublitharenite
Depositional Environments:	Fluvial, marginal–marine, and associated environments
Diagenesis:	Silica overgrowths, pore–filling kaolinite, chlorite rims
Porosity Types:	Primary intergranular, microporosity associated with clays
Porosity:	Maximum 23%; average 14%
Permeability:	Maximum 713 md; average 60 md
Fractures:	Not significant
Nature of Traps:	Combination structural/stratigraphic
Entrapping Facies:	Floodplain and interdistributary–bay shales; dia- genetically altered sandstone in downdip water legs
Source Rock:	Overlying Cretaceous Mowry/Aspen shales
Timing of HydrocarbonMigration:	Emplacement of Absaroka Thrust Sheet (70 Ma)

FIELD DATA:	Luckey Ditch Field
Discovered:	1985
Reservoir Depth:	13,250–15,750 ft (4,039– 4,800 m)
Reservoir Thickness:	10–35 ft (3–11 m)
Areal Extent:	Presently 12,800 acres (5,180 ha); 4 by 5 mi (6.4 by 8.0 km)
IP (discovery well):	Flowing 887 BOPD, 7,500 MCFGD
Original Reservoir Pressure:	7,200 psi
Cumulative Production (1/89):	4,270,000 BO; 21.0 BCFG
Estimated Oil in Place:	68,000,000 BO; 228 BCFG
Approximate Ultimate Recovery:	11,500,000 BO; 164 BCFG (primary)
Oil Gravity:	39–46° API
Minimum Water Saturation:	26%

REGIONAL STRATIGRAPHY

Although production on the Moxa Arch has been obtained from reservoirs ranging in age from Mississippian through Tertiary, in the study area the only reservoir of commercial significance to date is the Lower Cretaceous Dakota Formation. The Dakota is overlain by the Cretaceous Mowry Shale and underlain by the Jurassic Morrison Formation (Fig. 2). Good outcrops of the Dakota sandstone can be found on both flanks of the Uinta Mountains, with the closest being near Manila, Utah (Fig. 1).

The Dakota in the area of the southern Moxa Arch averages 350 ft (107 m) in thickness and represents approximately 15 million years of time. It is correlative to the "Rusty Beds", the Thermopolis Shale, and the Muddy Sandstone to the north and northeast, and the Bear River and Kelvin formations of the Western Overthrust (Ryer, et al., 1987). Generally, it records the initial transgression of the Cretaceous seaway into southwestern Wyoming and northern Utah.

The Dakota in outcrops and subsurface cores contains a variety of fluvial and marginal–marine lithofacies, discussed more fully below. These can be generally grouped into a lower, predominantly fluvial sequence and an upper, restricted- to marginal-marine member. On the southern Moxa Arch, oil

geologists historically have divided the Dakota into lithostratigraphic units in ascending order from the base of the formation. However, the obscure nature of the Dakota/Morrison contact and the common practice of limited penetration of this sequence make a nomenclature of descending order more practical. In this paper, seven lithostratigraphic units are designated, labeled from A through G, with subunits used where the multistoried nature of some of the units have made it necessary (Fig. 2). Most of the production in Bridger Lake Field has come from the G sandstone, while the major pay at Luckey Ditch is the D–1 interval. Henry Field produces from the D, D–1, and B–1 sandstones (Fig. 3). In general, pay zones occur stratigraphically higher to the north.

Henry Field appears to be the northern limit of commercial lower Dakota production on the southern Moxa Arch (Fig. 4). Although a number of wells in Church Buttes Field were completed open–hole in the entire Dakota interval, it does not appear that the lower Dakota has contributed significantly to production. The lower Dakota interval is characterized by very high sandstone/shale ratios, ranging from 35% to almost 100%. Sandstone isolith maps of individual lithostratigraphic units show northerly to northeasterly trends (e.g. Fig. 5). Stratigraphic dipmeter patterns trend in the same direction.

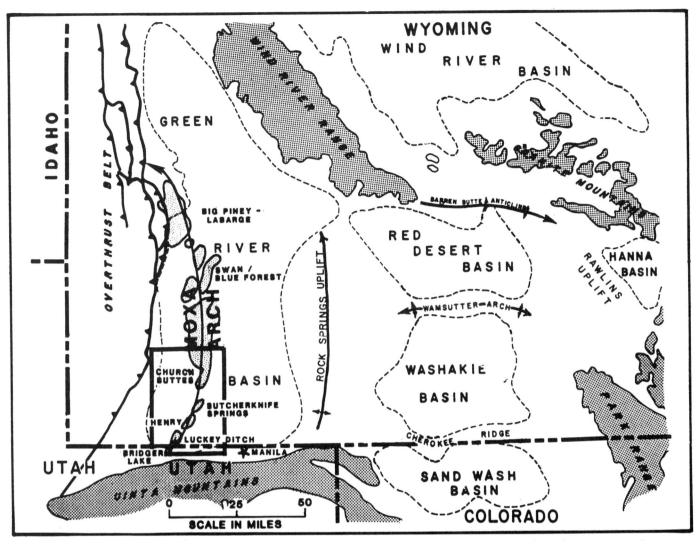

Figure 1. Location map, southwestern Wyoming, showing outline of area covered in this paper, major structural features, and Moxa Arch fields that produce from the Dakota Formation. (25 mi on map = 40.2 km)

Individual sandstones show varying degrees of lateral continuity. The E, F, and G sandstones of Bridger Lake Field are ribbon–like and discontinuous, although it is difficult to correlate sandstones between wells drilled on 320–acre (129.5 ha) spacing. The D and D–1 pays of Luckey Ditch, Taylor Ranch, and Henry fields, however, can be traced throughout the fields and for more than 30 mi (48 km) northward along the Moxa Arch. North of T18N, they become more marine in character and display funnel–shaped (coarsening upwards) gamma ray signatures. Some upward aggradation of the D–1 stratigraphic interval into the D interval is apparent from electrical logs in the Henry Field area, probably reflecting a lateral shift of the local depocenter.

Lithofacies and Depositional Environments

Most of the lithologic and petrophysical observations and conclusions presented in this paper were derived from study of approximately 670 ft (204 m) of Dakota cores from nine wells in and near Luckey Ditch Field. Based on lithofacies observed in cores, four major environments of deposition appear to have been present along the southern Moxa Arch during lower Dakota time. These are channel lags, point and longitudinal bars, floodplains and coastal plains, and interdistributary bays.

Channel Lags

This lithofacies commonly is found at the bases of sandstones, although it also occurs in thin beds within massive sandstones or as discrete units up to 20 ft (6.1 m) thick. It consists of clasts of chert, quartzite, and shale up to 1.2 in (3 cm) in diameter, in some places supported by a matrix of fine to medium–grained sandstone. Sharp, erosional contacts often show the steeply inclined surfaces characteristic of erosional cut and fill (Plate 1A). Grain size usually decreases upward, being transitional with the overlying point–bar lithofacies. This lithofacies is moderately indurated. Porosity values rarely exceed 10%. The primary cementing agent is calcite. Permeability is not sufficient to allow production.

The common association of this lithofacies with bases of sandstone units or directly above truncated

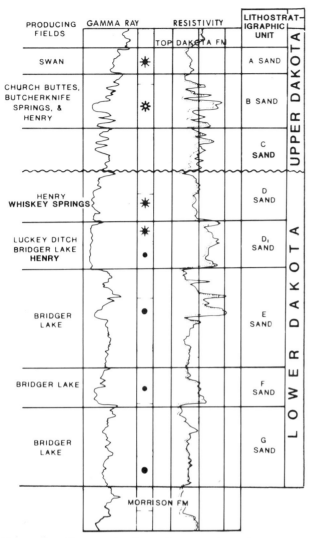

Figure 2. Composite log of the Dakota Formation in the Moxa Arch area, annotated with lithostratigraphic nomenclature used in this paper and fields productive from different stratigraphic horizons.

cross laminae implies channel lag deposition within a braided channel environment. Thick conglomerate beds seen in some cores suggest that these channels had episodic high-energy flows that deposited coarse-grained longitudinal bars.

Point and Longitudinal Bars

This lithofacies comprises the bulk of lower Dakota reservoirs on the Moxa Arch. Varying in thickness from 10 to 40 ft (3 to 12 m), these sequences consist of multiple cross-bedded fining-upward sequences. Cross-bed types range from planar to trough, with individual moderate-angle cross-bed sets averaging 4 to 6 in (10 to 15 cm) in thickness. Occasional planar laminae and ripple-drift cross-laminae occur near the tops of individual fining-upward sequences. In many cases, thin cross-laminae are rich in carbonaceous debris, imparting a "salt and pepper" appearance to cores (Plate 1B). Stylolites bounding some of these organic-rich horizons indicate pressure solution.

Cross-sets commonly are separated by lags of shale rip-up clasts, and display abrupt changes in cross-bed orientations (Plate 1C). These sandstones are characterized on electric logs by blocky gamma ray, spontaneous potential, and resistivity responses (Figs. 3 and 4), although multiple fining-upward sequences are apparent in core. Apparently, these individual sequences, averaging 3 ft (0.9 m) in thickness, are too thin to be resolved by logs. Original stratification is in places distorted by soft-sediment deformation (Plate 1D), particularly in basal beds of individual fining-upward sequences. Deformation commonly is restricted to individual cross sets, suggesting very early origin due to slumping, coupled with rapid deposition of overlying bedsets.

These sandstones are moderately well sorted, fine to medium-grained sublitharenites containing 77–89% monocrystalline quartz, 5–12% rock fragments and 2–3% feldspar (Plate 2A). Authigenic clays make up 2–8% of rock volume, occurring as chlorite rims and intergranular pore filling kaolinite. Kaolinite represents the predominant cementing agent within producing zones (Fig. 6A). Thin-section and scanning electron microscopy of highly permeable sandstones show local concentrations of intergranular kaolinite approximately 3–5 mm (0.12–0.20 in.) in width with all intergranular porosity occluded (Fig. 6B; Plates 1E and 2B). Porosity, permeability, and relative permeability tests for this lithofacies (Figs. 7A and 8) show excellent reservoir quality. Oil staining is ubiquitous within this lithofacies at Luckey Ditch, imparting a light yellow-gray color to high-permeability sandstones. Isolated zones rich in kaolinite, found most commonly on the western margin of the field, exhibit dark colors and mottling (Plate 1F). This coloration is due to tarry, dead oil coating of the grains (Plate 2C; Figs. 6C and D). This suggests the possibility of bacterial degradation or tilting of an old oil/water contact.

Coastal Plain

Capping the point bar lithofacies at Luckey Ditch Field is a less massive, finer-grained lithofacies that does not exhibit the excellent reservoir quality of field pay. Composed of interbedded light to medium-gray siltstone and very fine to fine-grained sandstone, it exhibits low-amplitude ripple-drift laminae and commonly is bioturbated. Rooting is evidenced by an abundance of irregular, subvertical carbonaceous streaks. Thin-section photomicrographs show the pores to be extensively filled by silica and carbonate cements (Plate 2D). The rocks contain as much as four times the kaolinite, chlorite, and illite content of point-bar sandstones. Consequently, permeabilities in these rocks are much lower than those in point-bar sandstones of similar porosity (Fig. 7).

Coastal-plain deposits are widespread and exceed 50 ft (15.2 m) in thickness in Luckey Ditch Field. Where good permeability develops, such as immediately west of Luckey Ditch in the Texaco No. 1 Whiskey Springs Unit (Sec 1 T12N R115W), these sandstones are capable of commercial flow rates. Good permeability also is found in thin beds of this lithofacies in Luckey Ditch, where it is commingled with point-bar sandstone production in three wells. These isolated high-permeability zones probably repre-

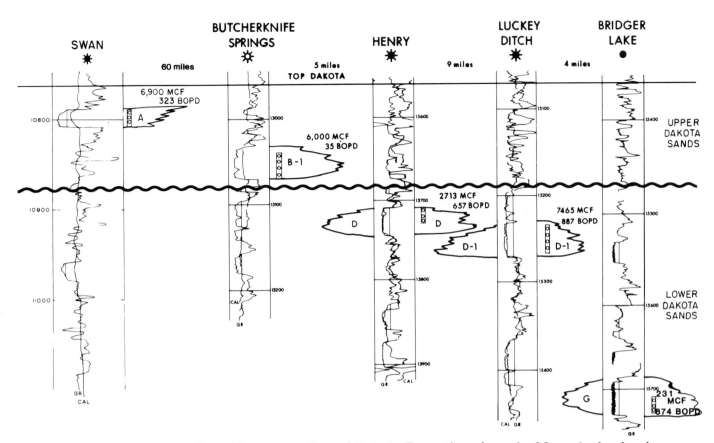

Figure 3. North–south stratigraphic cross section of Dakota Formation along the Moxa Arch, showing general upward progression of field pays to the north. Each major depth division on log =100 ft (304.8 m)

sent either crevasse splays or other proximal–overbank deposits of the coastal plain environment.

Flood Plain/Interdistributary Bay

Intervals of dark gray to black shale and argillaceous siltstone up to 40 ft. (12 m) thick commonly separate beds of usually massive, slightly calcareous, and micaceous sandstone containing abundant burrows and vertical root traces. Fossiliferous horizons thinner than 2 in. (5 cm) and containing thin-walled pelecypods, and thin zones of coal and carbonaceous debris were noted in many cores. Pyrite nodules are present in the black shales in trace amounts, suggesting a reducing environment of deposition. Red and green mottling is common in lighter colored shales, which are generally thinner and more restricted in areal extent than their darker colored counterparts.

The thin, mottled shales are interpreted as alluvial floodplain and levee deposits. The black shales were deposited in interdistributary bay settings during minor marine transgressions.

Paleogeography

Crustal loading of central Utah and western Idaho by the advancing Paris–Willard thrust sheet created a pronounced asymmetrical foreland basin prior to Dakota deposition, as suggested by thicknesses of Lower Cretaceous rocks (Fig. 9). The area of interest lay immediately east of this foredeep, which exerted a great influence upon sediment distribution (Young,

1970; Ryer, et al., 1987). Although the Paris–Willard Thrust Sheet could have been a source of clastic sediments, this would require transportation across a foredeep now filled with up to 4,000 ft (1,200 m) of age–equivalent shale and siltstone. A southerly source seems necessary to explain both the northerly trend of sandstone bodies (Fig. 5) and the paleocurrent directions derived from outcrops along the flanks of the Uinta Mountains (Vaughn and Picard, 1976). This source has been postulated by MacKenzie and Poole (1962) and Young (1970) to lie in southern Utah. However, the thicknesses and large clasts of the chert–pebble conglomerates seen in Luckey Ditch suggest that the source may have been closer. Trends of lower Dakota sandstone bodies suggest fluvial transportation perpendicular to a generally east–west trending shoreline, probably due to reactivation of the Uinta Mountain allocogen.

Regardless of the distance to the sand source, it appears that a delta system developed along the southern Moxa Arch in early Dakota time under conditions of relatively rapid base–level rise, depositing the G, F, and E sandstones of Bridger Lake Field. Sediment supply increased through time, while distributary channels became less sinuous and carried more bedload as this system extended to the north. This led to the formation of a series of braid deltas during the deposition of the D and D–1 sandstone. These deltas are characterized by sand–rich, con-

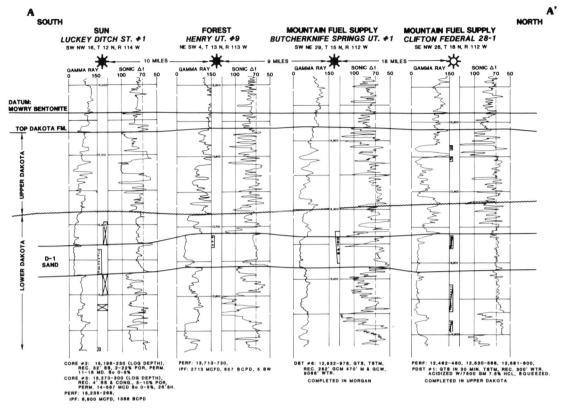

Figure 4. South–north stratigraphic cross section (A–A') showing northward decrease in reservoir quality of lower Dakota sandstones on the Moxa Arch. See Figure 13 for location. Each major depth division on logs = 100 ft (304.8 m).

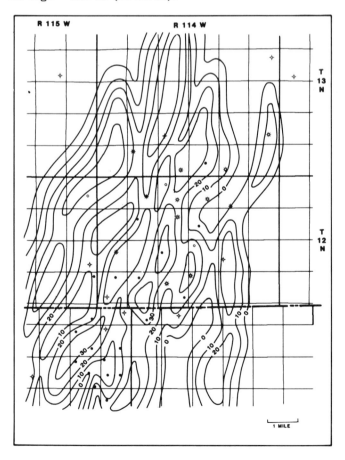

glomeratic braid plain and distributary mouth bars lacking a muddy matrix and exhibiting "sheet" geometry (McPherson et al., 1987). Thin channel-abandonment deposits present at the top of most channels, and finer-grained coastal plain sediments represent loss of sediment supply due to upstream avulsion to another portion of the actively forming braid delta plain. This sequence of deposits is reflected in the lower Dakota sequence in the Luckey Ditch area (Fig. 10).

Upper Dakota lithostratigraphic units are considerably thinner and exhibit much lower sandstone/shale ratios than do the sandstones of the lower Dakota. They are productive at Henry, Butcherknife Springs, and Church Buttes fields, where they have northwesterly trends and show less continuity than do lower Dakota sandstones.

By upper Dakota time, the Mowry Seaway had transgressed southward and the western foredeep had migrated further eastward, causing a rapid rise in base level and major reorientation of the shoreline. The Mowry interval reflects this new shoreline, thickening markedly from southeast to northwest (Fig. 11). Sandstone bodies in the upper Dakota resemble low-

◄—— Figure 5. Net sandstone (porosity greater than 12%) isolith map of Dakota D–1 lithostratigraphic unit, Bridger Lake/Luckey Ditch area. Contour interval = 10 ft (3 m). Well control current to September of 1988. Grid is one-mi (1,609 km) square sections.

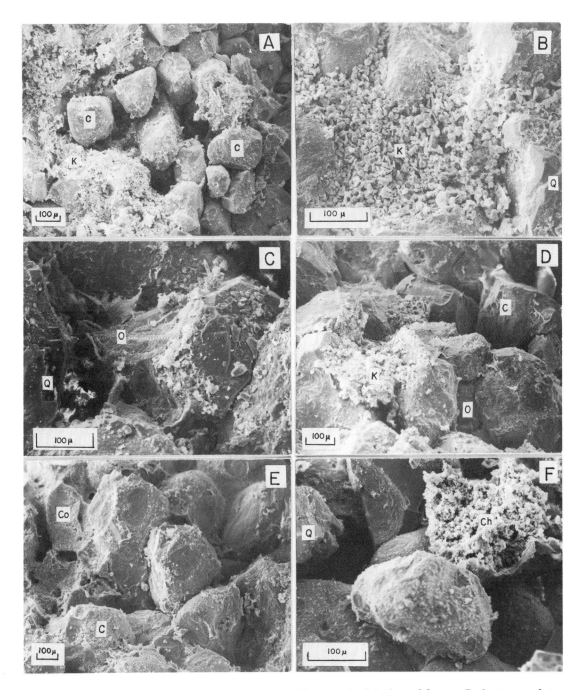

Figure 6. SEM images illustrating cement types and diagenetic fabrics of lower Dakota sandstones.

A. Overview of reservoir-quality point-bar sandstone with good porosity, limited kaolinite cement (K), and thin chlorite grain coatings (C). Sun No. E-7 Luckey Ditch Federal (14,603 ft; 4,503.6 m). 75x magnification.

B. Close-up of kaolinite "patch", with limited quartz overgrowths (Q) and all intergranular porosity occluded by kaolinite booklets (K). Sun No. I-11 Luckey Ditch Federal (15,648 ft; 4,825.8 m). 200x magnification.

C. Tarry, dead oil coating grains (O), and limited quartz overgrowths (Q) in a point-bar reservoir sandstone. Sun No. I-11 Luckey Ditch Federal (15,648 ft; 4,825.8 m). 200x magnification.

D. Overview of general area of Figure 6C, showing dead oil (O) lining pore throat, kaolinite cement (K), and chlorite rims (C). Sun No. I-11 Luckey Ditch Federal (15,648 ft. 4,825.8 m). 100x magnification.

E. Chlorite grain coatings (C) and collophane cement (Co) possibly formed by re-precipitation of bone material. Sun No. G-9 Luckey Ditch Federal (15,559.3 ft; 4,798.49 m). 75x magnification.

F. Limited quartz overgrowths (Q) and leached chert fragment (Ch). Sun No. E-7 Luckey Ditch Federal (14,603 ft; 4,503.6 m). 200x magnification.

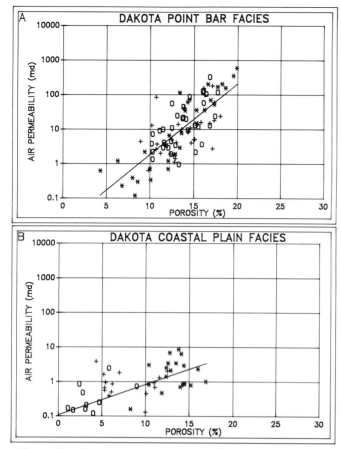

Figure 7. Porosity vs. permeability graphs of (A) point bar lithofacies and (B) coastal plain lithofacies, lower Dakota sandstone, Luckey Ditch producing complex.

energy, highly constructive deltaic distributary channels in their distribution and areal extent. Aside from the basal conglomerates, grain size generally is very fine to fine, with a high percentage of silt. Sandstone thickness maps suggest that channels flowed from southeast to northwest, perpendicular to the new shoreline, depositing isolated point–bar sandstones. North of the study area, destructional marine processes reworked these into northeast–trending bar sandstones that produce oil and gas in Swan and Blue Forest fields.

STRUCTURAL TIMING

Although considerable evidence suggests movement of the Moxa Arch as early as the upper Paleozoic, the major pulse of growth was during early Campanian time, after the deposition of the Rock Springs Formation and prior to deposition of the Ericson member of the Mesaverde Formation (Wach, 1977; Miller, 1977), when up to 2,500 ft (762 m) of Mesaverde and Hilliard sediments were eroded from the crest of the arch (Fig. 12). The erosional nature of this thinning is well illustrated by a seismic survey in the vicinity of Henry Field (Fig. 13). The Moxa Arch at this time was a north–plunging anticlinorium with its highest point in the vicinity of Bridger Lake Field.

Further compression during Paleocene and Eocene times, reflected by movement on the Darby and Prospect thrusts and the Labarge Platform (McDonald, 1973; Wiltschko and Dorr, 1983) resulted in two episodes of movement on the Moxa Arch. The first compressional event is evidenced by thinning of the Ericson and Almond members of the Mesaverde, especially along the northern portion of the arch. At this time, the previous northward structural plunge was reversed to the southward plunge seen today. An ad-

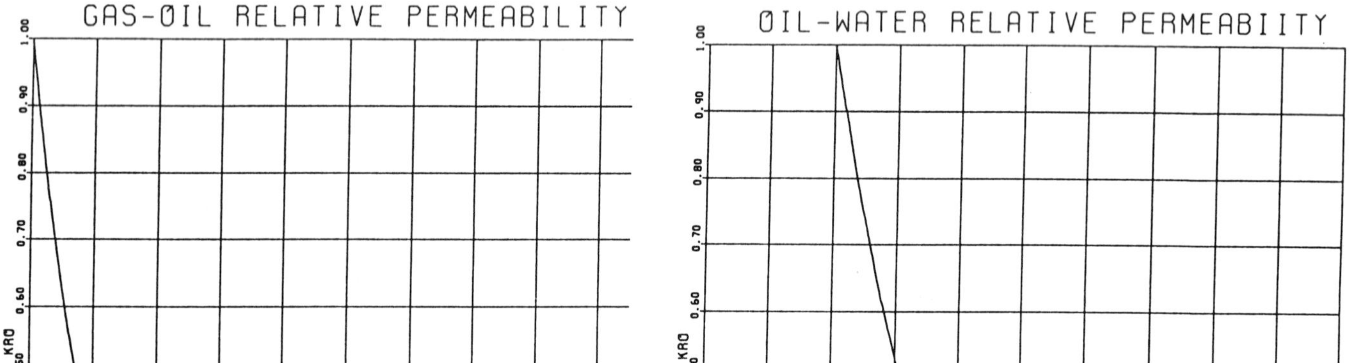

Figure 8. Relative permeability data for Luckey Ditch D-1 sandstone reservoir, southern Moxa Arch. Gas-oil drainage relative permeability on left, oil-water drainage relative permeability on right.

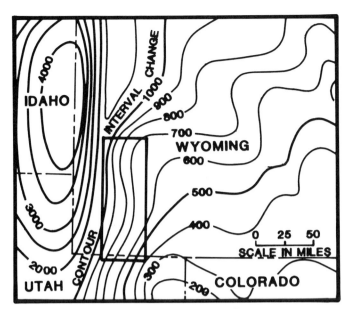

Figure 9. Isopach map of Lower Cretaceous strata illustrating the Lower Cretaceous Foreland Basin. Study area outlined. Adapted from Young (1970) and reprinted with permission of the Wyoming Geological Association. (25 mi =40.2 km)

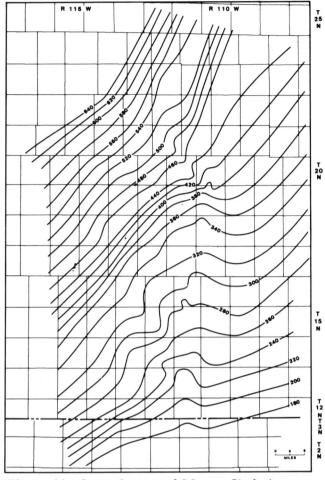

Figure 11. Isopach map of Mowry Shale in study area. Contour interval = 20 ft (6 m). Grid is one-mi (1.609 km) square sections.

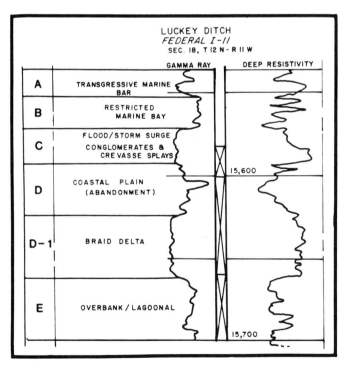

Figure 10. Representative electric log of Luckey Ditch producing complex, from Sun No. I-11 Luckey Ditch Federal well. Annotated with inferred depositional environments and lithostratigraphic nomenclature used in this study. Cored intervals indicated in depth track. Depth divisions on log are 50 ft apart (15.2 m).

ditional component of eastward rotation is evidenced by the essentially symmetrical thickness of the interval from the base of the Ericson to the Mowry (Fig. 12); this is in contrast to the markedly asymmetrical structure seen at the Dakota level today (Fig. 14).

A final, relatively minor episode of structural growth is suggested by thinning of the Paleocene Fort Union Formation, and further depression of the southern terminus of the arch as the Uinta Mountains were thrust northward. Though subsequently buried beneath great thicknesses of Eocene sediment, the present structural configuration of the Moxa Arch was essentially established by the end of this third episode of growth, approximately 55 Ma.

DIAGENESIS

Diagenesis of lower Dakota point-bar sandstones is one of the most important controls on the distribution of hydrocarbons in the southern Moxa Arch. Diagenetic events characteristic of Dakota reservoirs observed in Luckey Ditch cores were, in approximately chronological order:

1) Generation of rare collophane cement, probably as a result of a mobilization of bone material (Fig. 6E).

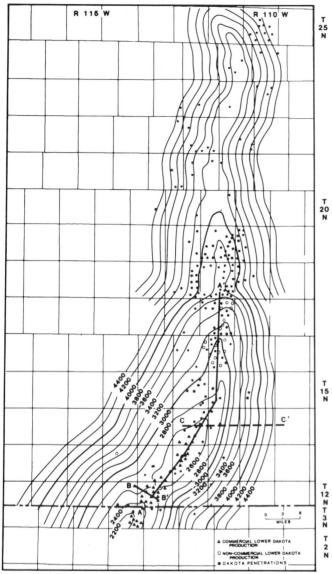

Figure 12. Isochore map of interval from the base of the Ericson unconformity to the top of the Mowry Shale, showing the structural configuration of the Moxa Arch after the first major pulse or growth. Contour interval = 200 ft (61 m). Wells with commercial and non-commercial lower Dakota production are noted. Note location of cross sections A–A' (Fig. 4), B–B' (Fig. 16), and seismic line C–C' (Fig. 14). Grid is one-mi (1.609 km) square sections.

2) Precipitation of calcite and dolomite cements, predominantly within high-permeability zones such as coarse channel lags. In places, carbonate cements replace framework grains, leading to the development of secondary porosity by preferential dissolution of less stable framework grains such as lithic fragments and feldspar (Fig. 6F).

3) Deposition of chlorite as thin grain coatings. This was a common feature of samples (Fig. 6A). Chlorite seldom occurs in sufficient volume within point-bar sandstones to reduce effective porosity by

occluding pore throats, but is quite common in coastal plain deposits.

4) Precipitation of silica overgrowths on quartz grains. This was ubiquitous in the samples (Figs. 6B, C, and F). The overgrowths formed an interlocking structure that prevented extensive compaction and pressure solution, even at the substantial burial depths at which the Dakota reservoirs now exist. The overgrowths do not significantly reduce pore space and are not well developed in samples that exhibit considerable chlorite grain coating (Fig. 6A).

5) Precipitation of pore-filling kaolinite. This also was seen in nearly all the Dakota samples. Kaolinite occurs both disseminated through the pore space and in locally high concentrations, yielding a "patchy" or spotted appearance to sandstones stained dark gray by oil (Plates 1E, 1F, and 2B). The kaolinite precipitated preferentially around nuclei, perhaps alumina-rich feldspar grains. These high concentrations of kaolinite result in patches of very low permeability within permeable reservoir rocks.

6) Rare late-stage precipitation of barite cement, and pyrite replacement of shale clasts.

HYDROCARBON GENERATION, MIGRATION, AND THERMAL ALTERATION

Liquid hydrocarbons produced from Dakota reservoirs on the Moxa Arch are similar to most Cretaceous oils of the Rocky Mountain states. They are high-gravity, low-sulfur crude oils and condensates with similar gas chromatography profiles (Exlog/Brown & Ruth Laboratories, 1988). However, upper and lower Dakota reservoirs produce very different GOR's, even in the same field. Lower Dakota GOR's also vary along the arch from field to field.

Shales with widespread distribution and adequate organic content to be considered source candidates (greater than 1% TOC) include the Cretaceous Mowry, Aspen, Frontier, Hilliard, and Mesaverde formations. The Frontier, Hilliard, and Mesaverde shales generally are believed to contain largely gas-prone continental kerogens with little potential for generation of liquid hydrocarbons. However, the Mowry Shale and its western equivalent, the Aspen Shale, were deposited during a major transgression, when organic matter consisted largely of marine organisms (Kauffman, 1977; Rice and Gautier, 1983). During Mowry/Aspen deposition, currents may have created an oxygen-minimum zone within the foreland basin, enhancing preservation of oil-prone kerogen (Dean et al., 1988). The most likely potential source beds, therefore, would seem to be the Mowry and Aspen Shales.

Model of Hydrocarbon Generation and Migration

Although some studies place hydrocarbon generation in the vicinity of the Moxa Arch at 50–55 Ma (Exlog/Brown & Ruth Laboratories, 1988), earlier generation and migration is necessary to explain the entrapment of hydrocarbons in lower Dakota sandstones along the southern part of the arch, which was

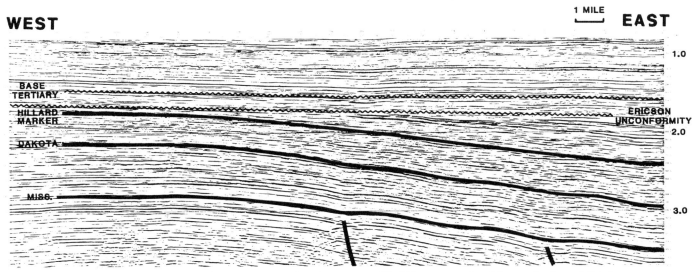

WEST   1 MILE   EAST

Figure 13. Portion of a regional west–east seismic survey (C–C') across the Moxa Arch exhibiting erosional truncation of Upper Cretaceous beds by the Ericson unconformity. See Figure 13 for location. Printed with permission of Professional Geophysics Incorporated. Vertical scale is in seconds. Horizontal scale is in miles (1.609 km).

structurally depressed relative to the north by this time. The best candidate for source area seems to be the footwall of the Absaroka Thrust, where Warner (1982) placed hydrocarbon generation from the Mowry/Aspen shales as early as 70 Ma. The emplacement of the Absaroka Thrust Sheet would have provided a thick, insulating overburden, maturing and expelling hydrocarbons, as well as waters enriched in alumina and organic acids, from the Mowry/Aspen source beds.

From 70 to 60 Ma, a likely migration pathway out of the foreland basin would be to the east, toward the developing Moxa Arch. As discussed earlier, the lower Dakota is believed to have been deposited along a wide east–west trending alluvial/coastal plain. Though the western extent of this depositional system is not definitely known, the Exxon No. 1 Mumford Ridge Unit, located near the footwall of the Darby Thrust (Sec 21 T13N R117W), encountered a thick section of lower Dakota sandstone. Thus, a relatively continuous conduit of clean, porous lower Dakota sandstone could have been present from the Absaroka footwall to the Moxa Arch during oil expulsion. These sandstones would be expected to trap hydrocarbons at the apex of the nearest major structure present along the migration pathway, i.e., the then north–plunging paleo-Moxa Arch.

Charging of the lower Dakota sandstones occurred long before the Mowry Shale reached thermal maturity in the vicinity of the Moxa Arch, approximately 50 Ma. However, upper Dakota sandstones, being more laterally discontinuous, did not receive hydrocarbons during this early migration. Rather, they were charged during a later migration event, based on the difference in GOR's seen between upper and lower Dakota reservoirs. For instance, Henry Field produces oil and associated gas from the lower Dakota at a GOR of 4,000:1, but gas and condensate from the upper Dakota at a GOR of 40,000:1.

Anomalous Hydrocarbon–Water Contacts

There are numerous examples of anomalous hydrocarbon/water contacts in the area. An apparently tilted oil/water contact occurs in the Luckey Ditch Field, where production has been established in the No. 2 Luckey Ditch Federal, 13 ft (4 m) low to a wet Dakota sandstone in the Texaco No. 1 Whiskey Springs Unit well (Fig. 15). Although fault or stratigraphic isolation is one explanation, there are no seismic or production data suggesting such gross reservoir inhomogeneity in this part of the field. Also, the western limits of the majority of fields are defined by a loss in reservoir-quality sandstone, apparently due to cementation by clays.

An explanation for these anomalous contacts involves differential diagenesis. After initial migration of oil into the traps, diagenesis continued in the downdip portions of the reservoirs (Plate 2F), while porosity and permeability were preserved by the presence of hydrocarbons within the structural traps (Plate 2E). Upon structural inversion and eastward rotation, the accumulations were diagenetically sealed in their present configuration and prevented from remigration.

Thermal Alteration of Hydrocarbons

In lower Dakota reservoirs, API gravities and GOR's vary dramatically along the arch. In the Church Buttes/Bruff producing area, GOR's approach 200,000:1. Bridger Lake and Luckey Ditch fields exhibit GOR's as low as 800:1. Such uniform source rocks as the Mowry and Aspen shales would not be expected to yield this wide variance in hydrocarbons. If the Mowry/Aspen is indeed the source of hydrocarbons found in the Dakota, some other factors must have played a role in altering their character.

Law and Smith (1983) found a marked increase in temperature gradients along the crest of the Moxa Arch (Fig. 16). This phenomenon is seen often over

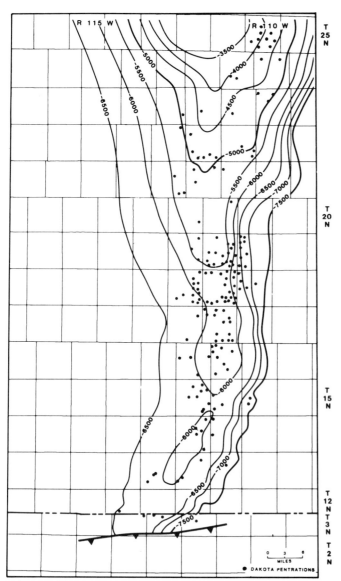

Figure 14. Structure map, datum top of Dakota Formation, showing present–day structural configuration of the Moxa Arch. Contour interval = 500 ft (152 m). Grid is one–mi (1.609 km) square sections.

regional uplifts and usually is explained by conductive heat flow sourced by basement uplift. However, Kilty and Chapman (1980) proposed an alternative mechanism, one of hydrodynamically driven heat advection.

Following this model, water from surface recharge was warmed in the depths of the Western Foreland Basin and deflected upwards by the Moxa Arch, carrying the absorbed heat with it (Fig. 17). Conversely, waters descending along the bounding faults on north flank of the Uinta Mountains may have created the observed "chilled" thermal margin noted by Law and Clayton (1987). The Sun No. 1 Wadsworth Fee well, located on the east flank of the arch six miles (9.7 km) from the North Flank Thrust (Sec 6 T12N R112W), recovered fresh water from an upper Dakota sandstone at a depth of 14,600 ft (4,450 m), suggesting at least local groundwater influx.

If this mechanism is responsible for the observed geothermal regimes along the Moxa Arch, it should have been much more active during the early history of the arch, when fluid expulsion from the Western Thrust Belt was at a peak. Recent geochemical studies show an abrupt increase in vitrinite reflectance within the Hilliard Formation along the crest of the arch (Exlog/Brown & Ruth Laboratories, 1988).

Regardless of the mechanism driving the observed geothermal gradients, an increase in background heat flow would be expected to thermally alter any hydrocarbon accumulation, providing the easiest explanation for the wide range in GOR's in the lower Dakota along the Moxa Arch. Among the highest observed gradients is in the Church Buttes/Bruff producing area, where GOR's also are very high. The relatively cool Bridger Lake and Luckey Ditch fields are not as thermally altered, and exhibit low GOR's.

CONCLUSIONS

Our paleostructural hypothesis of hydrocarbon accumulation in the Dakota Formation helps to explain some of the puzzling irregularities in distribution and character of Dakota fields in the area. The hypothesis also has implications for future exploration.

The concentration of commercial lower Dakota production along the southern terminus of the Moxa Arch supports hydrocarbon migration into primary structural traps as early as 70 Ma, where they were diagenetically sealed in place before structural inversion of the arch approximately 50 Ma. Thick sandstones in the lower Dakota can be correlated far to the north and updip of established production, but have tested water or lacked sufficient reservoir quality to produce at commercial rates. The limited lower Dakota production found north of Henry Field is from stratigraphic traps in the more distal portions of the delta system, where thinner sandstones and higher clay contents reduce reservoir quality to noncommercial levels.

The more discontinuous nature of the upper Dakota sandstones protected them from diagenetic fluids expelled from the footwall of the Absaroka Thrust. Consequently, these sandstones retained their reservoir quality until filled by lighter hydrocarbons that migrated vertically from traps in the lower Dakota or laterally from Mowry/Aspen source beds closer to the arch. This is one of the factors that made it possible for Dakota fields along the Moxa Arch to produce at widely different GOR's.

The other factor appears to be post–migrational thermal alteration of trapped hydrocarbon accumulations. A hydrodynamically driven convective heat–flow model applied to the arch suggests that the most liquid–rich hydrocarbon accumulations are likely to be found either within the chilled thermal margin along the Uinta Mountains or in stratigraphic traps off the east flank of the arch. The best example of the latter case is the recent development drilling in the Swan/Blue Forest area flanking the northern Moxa Arch, where GOR's are as low as 30,000:1 adjacent to fields along the crest of the arch which produce at GOR's exceeding 200,000:1.

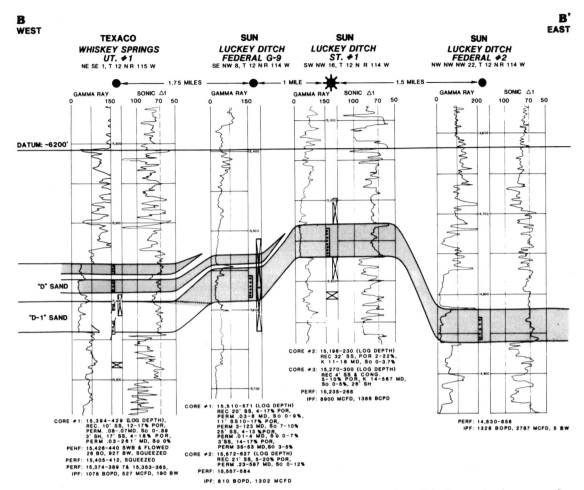

Figure 15. West–east structural cross section (B–B') across the Luckey Ditch producing complex, showing an apparent tilted oil/water contact in the lower Dakota D–1 reservoir. See Figure 13 for location. Depth divisions on logs mark 50–ft (15.2 m) intervals.

The gently dipping western flank of the arch has a multitude of small structural closures that would seem to be prospective, but to date have not contained sandstone of reservoir quality or more than non–commercial shows. Whether these diagenetic effects exhibit eastward asymmetry due to hydrodynamic tilting of original fluid contacts, post–diagenetic eastward rotation of the structure, or a combination of both requires further well control and investigation.

Though no eastern fluid contacts have been documented in upper Dakota channel–sandstone reservoirs, asymmetric fluid contacts and productivity could be expected in these units as well, though their stratigraphic variability introduces considerably more exploration risk than do the more continuous lower Dakota sandstones.

Fluvial–channel sandstones overlying structural closures constitute virtually all important Dakota oil and gas reservoirs in this area. However, success may be expected in prospecting for lower Dakota point–bar pinchouts or crevasse splays where they were deposited parallel to structural strike, as appears to be the case in Texaco's Whiskey Springs Field. Unfortunately, this type of play carries a great deal of inherent risk. Despite much steeper dips, exploration plays

along the eastern flank of the arch seem to be more prospective from the standpoint of diagenesis, especially where the eastern boundary of a field remains undefined.

ACKNOWLEDGMENTS

The authors wish to express their sincere thanks to those without whose assistance this paper would not have been possible: Howard White of Sun's Geological Services Group for his extensive petrographic studies and depositional environment interpretations; Alice Cameron and the Reservoir Simulation staff for their contributions to reservoir characterization; and Sun's Northern Region management staff for their support in allowing this work to be published.

REFERENCES

Dean, W.E., M.A. Arthur, and L.M. Pratt, 1988, Inorganic and organic geochemical cycles in petroleum source rocks of the Cretaceous western interior seaway–records of paleoceanographic change [abs.]: USGS Circ. 1025, p. 10–13.

Exlog/Brown & Ruth Laboratories, 1988, Evaluation of liquid hydrocarbon potential: Green River Basin/Moxa Arch: Exclusive report.

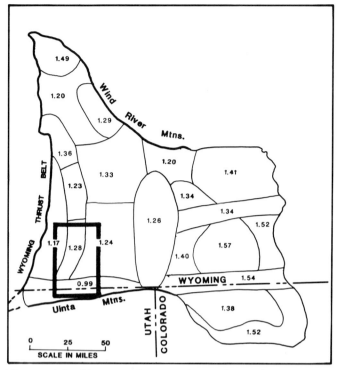

Figure 16. Present–day geothermal gradients (F°/100 ft), Green River Basin. Study area outlined. Adapted from Law and Smith (1983). Reprinted with permission of USGS. (25 mi = 40.2 km)

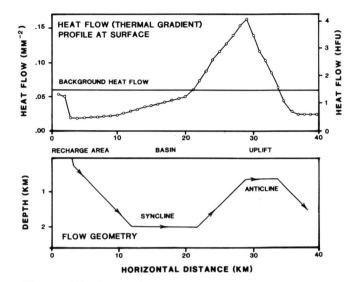

Figure 17. Two–dimensional model showing a hypothetical hydrodynamic system and the resultant heat–flow profile. Adapted from Kilty and Chapman (1980). Reprinted with permission of Ground Water Magazine.

Kauffman, E.G., 1977, Geological and biological overview; western interior Cretaceous basin: Mtn. Geol., v. 14, p. 75–99.

Kilty, K., and D.S. Chapman, 1980, Convective heat transfer in selected geologic situations: Ground Water, v. 14, p. 75–99.

Law, B.E., and J.L. Clayton, 1987, A burial, thermal, and hydrocarbon source rock evaluation of Lower Cretaceous rocks in the southern Moxa Arch area, Utah and Wyoming [abs.]: WGA, 38th Ann. Field Conf. Guidebook, p. 357.

Law, B.E., and C.R. Smith, 1983, Subsurface temperature map showing depth to 180° F of the greater Green River Basin of Wyoming, Colorado, and Utah: USGS Misc. Field Studies MF-1504.

MacKenzie, D.B., and D.M. Poole, 1962, Provenance of Dakota Group sandstone of the western interior: Symposium on Early Cretaceous Rocks of Wyoming and Adjacent Areas, WGA, 17th Ann. Field Conf. Guidebook, p. 62–71.

McPherson, J.G., G. Shanmugam, and R.J. Moiola, 1987, Fan-deltas and braid deltas: varieties of coarse-grained deltas: GSA Bull., v. 99, p. 331–340.

McDonald, R.E., 1973, Big Piney-Labarge producing complex, Sublette and Lincoln counties, Wyoming: WGA, 25th Ann. Field Conf. Guidebook, p. 57–77.

Miller, F.X., 1977, Biostratigraphic correlation of the Mesaverde Group in southwestern Wyoming and northwestern Colorado, *in* H.K. Veal, ed., Exploration Frontiers of the Central and Southern Rockies: RMAG, 28th Ann. Field Conf. Guidebook, p. 117–137.

Rice, D.D., and D.L. Gautier, 1983, Patterns of sedimentation, diagenesis and hydrocarbon accumulation in Cretaceous rocks of the Rocky Mountains: SEPM Short Course No. 11 Notes, unpaginated.

Ryer, T.A., J.J. McClurg, and M.M. Muller, 1987, Dakota-Bear River paleoenvironments, depositional history and shoreline trends-implications for foreland basin paleotectonics, southwestern Green River Basin and southern Wyoming Overthrust Belt: WGA, 38th Ann. Field Conf. Guidebook, p. 79–206.

Vaughn, R.L., and M.D. Picard, 1976, Stratigraphy, sedimentology, and petroleum potential of Dakota Formation, northeastern Utah: RMAG, 27th Ann. Field Conf. Guidebook, p. 267–279.

Wach, P.H., 1977, The Moxa Arch, an overthrust model?: WGA, 25th Ann. Field Conf. Guidebook, p. 651–664.

Warner, M.A., 1982, Source and time of generation of hydrocarbons in the Fossil Basin, western Wyoming Thrust Belt: RMAG, Geologic Studies of the Cordilleran Thrust Belt, v. 2, p. 805–815.

Webb, J.E. 1975, Sedimentology and clay cementation, Dakota Formation, Bridger Lake Field, Utah: RMAG Symposium, p. 217–224.

Wiltschko, D.V., and J.A. Dorr, Jr., 1983, Timing of deformation in the Overthrust Belt and foreland of Idaho, Wyoming, and Utah: AAPG Bull., v. 67, p. 1304–1322.

Young, R.G., 1970, Lower Cretaceous of Wyoming and the southern Rockies: WGA, 22nd Ann. Field Conf. Guidebook, p. 147–160.

Diagenetic and Petrophysical Variations of the Dakota Sandstone, Henry Field, Green River Basin, Wyoming[1]

MARGARET M. MULLER[2]
EDWARD B. COALSON[3]

[1]Received July 21, 1988; Revised May 7, 1989
[2]Houston, Texas
[3]Bass Enterprises Production Co., Denver, Colorado

The predominantly sublithic Early Cretaceous Dakota sandstones of the southwestern Green River Basin were deposited in a fluvial to coastal plain setting. Three sandstone lithofacies are recognized in the vicinity of Henry Field: fluvial channel, restricted marine, and overbank. Petrographic evidence, facies relationships, and log responses indicate an unconformity within the Dakota which is used to divide the formation into lower and upper members.

There is a clear relationship between the percentage of matrix clay (chlorite, mixed layer illite/smectite, and microcrystalline kaolinite), and permeability. Matrix clay reduces permeability to a greater degree than do comparable percentages of quartz overgrowths and authigenic kaolinite. Clay content in turn relates to depositional environment and stratigraphic position. Samples from overbank and restricted marine lithofacies or those found immediately below the unconformity contain more matrix clay than do fluvial channel samples. As a result, fluvial channel sandstones have the greatest permeability and porosity of the reservoir lithofacies.

Mineralogy and diagenesis not only affect permeability, but also impact log calculations. Log–derived water saturations can be in error on the high side. At Henry Field, the cementation exponent ("m") has been measured as approximately 1.5 for those sandstones with the highest permeability. Such low "m" values in sandstones normally are caused by high clay content, which implies the presence of microporosity and low permeability. However, the high permeability sandstones at Henry Field lack significant matrix clay. Petrographic analysis suggests that interconnected moldic and vuggy porosity combined with interconnected intergranular macro– to mesoporosity may contribute to these low cementation values.

INTRODUCTION

Henry Field is located on the southern plunge of the Moxa Arch in the Green River Basin of southwestern Wyoming in Uinta County (Fig. 1). The field was discovered by Forest Oil Corporation in October, 1980. Production is from the Dakota Formation, which is bounded below by the Cedar Mountain Formation and above by the Mowry Formation (Hansen, 1965; Kinney, 1955; Ryer, et al., 1987) (Fig. 2). This discovery spurred exploration for other combination stratigraphic, structural, and diagenetic traps in the Dakota in that region because the wells produced condensate and light oil at rates up to 2,000 BPD,

and gas at rates up to 10 MMCFPD, with profitable economics.

There are approximately 150 ft (46 m) of anticlinal closure in Henry Field (Fig. 3). From Upper Paleozoic through Early Tertiary time, the arch experienced periodic uplifts (Wach, 1977). During Early Cretaceous time, the Moxa Arch served as the eastern hinge of the foreland basin (Ryer, et al., 1987). However, the major folding and bulging of the Moxa Arch occurred during the Late Cretaceous (Thomaidis, 1973).

Eighteen wells from the vicinity of Henry Field were selected for study (Muller, 1986). Sixteen

FIELD DATA:

Producing Interval:	Henry Field
Geographic Location:	Dakota Formation
Geographic Location:	T13–14N, R113–114W, Uinta County, Wyoming
Present Tectonic Setting:	Southern Moxa Arch, western Green River Basin
Depositional Setting:	Southern part of Cretaceous foreland basin
Age of Reservoir:	Lower Cretaceous (Albian)
Lithology of Reservoir:	Sublithic arenites
Depositional Environments:	Fluvial and shallow marine
Diagenesis:	Kaolinite, chlorite, illite/smectite, quartz overgrowths, calcite, and saddle dolomite cementation; dissolution of carbonate
Pore Types:	Intergranular to intercrystalline macro to mesoporosity; intercrystalline microporosity; moldic to vuggy macroporosity (often interconnected pores)
Porosity:	Maximum 20%, average 14%
Permeability:	Maximum 300 md, average 43.4 md
Water Saturation:	Minimum 20%, average 30%
Nature of Trap:	Stratigraphic pinchouts, structural closure, and diagenetic changes
Entrapping Facies:	Lower Cretaceous Mowry Shale
Source Rock:	Mowry Shale (see Reisser and Blanke, this volume)
Discovered:	1980
Reservoir Depth:	13,665 ft (4,165 m)
Reservoir Thickness:	19 ft (5.8 m)
Areal Extent:	5,950 acres (2,408 ha)
Cumulative Production (1/89):	2,620,000 BO, 22.3 BCFG
Estimated Oil and Gas in Place:	4,500,000 BO, 50 BCFG
Oil Gravity:	23–60° API (average 50°)
Drive Type:	Solution gas

Dakota cores and 106 thin sections were examined. Subsurface well logs and outcrops also were studied.

REGIONAL SETTING

The closest Dakota outcrop is the Manila road cut, approximately 29 mi (47 km) southeast of Henry Field. At this location, the Dakota Formation is approximately 350 ft (107 m) thick. The lower Dakota consists of alternating layers of mudstone and sandstone with some epsilon cross-stratification or lateral accretion surfaces of a point bar. It is overlain by a sheet-like, sandy fluvial-channel sequence in the upper Dakota.

Crossbedding in fluvial sandstone outcrops of the Dakota on the north and south flanks of the Uinta Mountains record a general northward transport of sediment (Webb, 1975; Vaughn and Picard, 1976). Environments of deposition in both the upper and lower Dakota change from dominantly fluvial in the southern Moxa Arch to more marine north of T18N (Ryer, et al., 1987).

LOCAL STRATIGRAPHY

The lower Dakota consists predominantly of fluvial strata on the southern part of the Moxa Arch. These sandstones have a characteristic blocky gamma-ray log response and account for most of the production at Henry Field. The upper Dakota consists predominantly of coarsening-upward sandstones less than 15 ft (4.5 m) thick that were deposited in a low-energy restricted-marine environment. These strata were deposited during transgression of the Shell Creek-Mowry Sea (Ryer, et al., 1987).

Unconformity

Petrographic evidence, facies relationships, and log responses indicate an unconformity within the Dakota which divides the formation into lower and upper members (Fig. 4). The unconformity is believed to be equivalent to that which separates the Muddy Sandstone from the Skull Creek Shale in the Wind River and Powder River Basins (Ryer, et al., 1987). Most of the uppermost sandstones in the lower Dakota have low resistivities due to the abundance of matrix clay associated with the unconformity (Fig. 4). The term "matrix clay" here refers to detrital clay, authigenically altered detrital clay, and authigenically precipitated pore-filling clay. Microcrystalline kaolinite identified by X-ray diffraction (XRD) methods is referred to as matrix clay. However, clearly authigenic, equant, vermiform booklets of kaolinite are not included in this category. XRD analyses of two samples from near the upper/lower Dakota contact indicate that the microcrystalline matrix clay which completely fills the intergranular areas is predominantly kaolinite and chlorite (Table 1, Plate 1A). Some of the clay in the wackes may be authigenic, based on a distinctly bimodal texture; there are clay-sized particles with medium-grained sand (Plate 1A).

These clay-choked sandstones were subaerially exposed during the Muddy lowstand of sea level. Layers of volcanic air-fall ash are interpreted to have covered these exposed surfaces, providing a ready

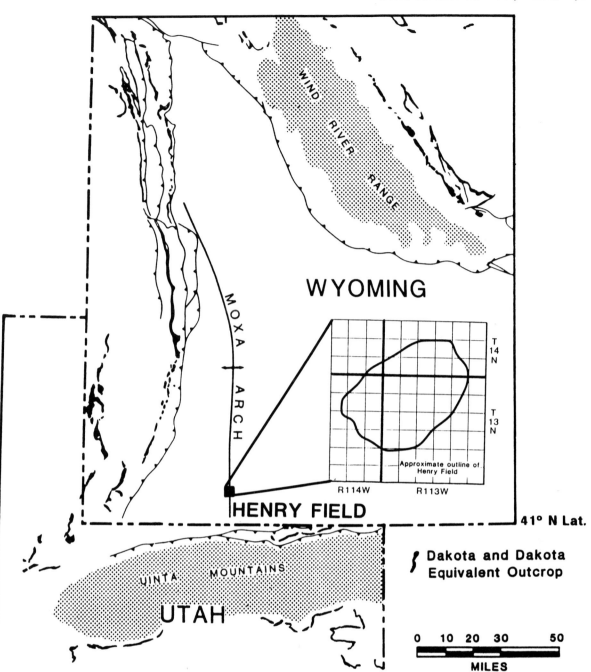

Figure 1. Location of Henry Field on the Moxa Arch, Uinta County, Green River Basin, Wyoming. (10 mi = 16.1 km)

source of ions to form the predominantly kaolinitic and chloritic clay matrix in the uppermost sandstone of the lower Dakota.

LITHOFACIES

Three sandstone lithofacies are recognized in Henry Field: fluvial channel, restricted marine, and overbank. Rocks present include sandstones, siltstones, shales, mudstones, and thin coals.

Fluvial Channel

Fluvial-channel sandstones comprise the best reservoir rock in Henry Field. Fluvial channels primarily

contain low to medium angle, large scale trough cross-stratification, and moderately well-sorted, fine to medium-grained sandstone (Plate 1B). Small scale ripple-drift cross-lamination was observed in some of the sandstones. Carbonaceous debris that accentuate laminae are common, as are concentrations of granule- to pebble-sized fragments and shale rip-up clasts at the base of individual channels. Lower bed boundaries typically are sharp or scoured with some upward decrease in bed thickness. Logs patterns in many of the channel sandstones in Henry Field appear more blocky than fining upward; the upper bed

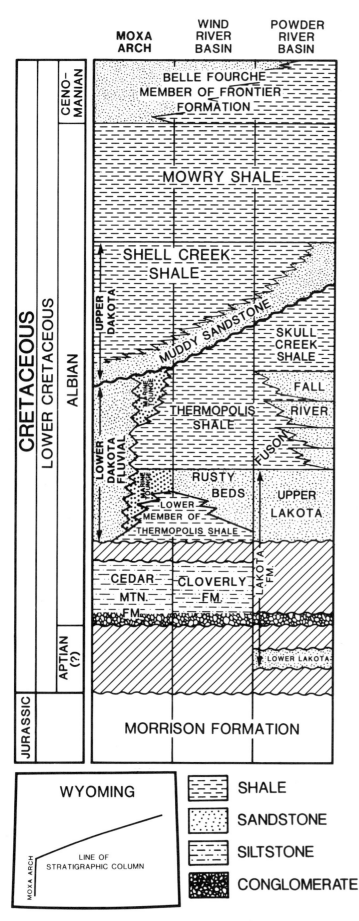

WYOMING

	SHALE
	SANDSTONE
	SILTSTONE
	CONGLOMERATE

boundaries can be abrupt as well. Average thickness of channel sandstones is 30 ft (9 m).

Most of these sandstones are sublitharenites, although some are quartz arenites (Fig. 5A). The porosity classification scheme developed by Coalson, et al., (1985) was used to identify porosity types because of the postulated relationships between their pore classes and petrophysical parameters. Using this system, one classifies porosity mainly by geometry and pore size. The pore geometry categories are: intergranular, intercrystalline (rocks composed of angular particles, e.g., euhedral quartz overgrowths or clay particles), vuggy, and fracture (Fig. 6). Fluvial sandstones are characterized by low contents of matrix clay and by intergranular, intercrystalline, and vuggy macro- to mesoporosity (Plate 1C, 1D). Secondary porosity is inferred to have been created primarily by dissolution of carbonate cement, as well as by some dissolution of quartz and matrix clay. Evidence of dissolution includes patches of partially dissolved carbonate cement (Plate 1E, 1F), detrital quartz grains with irregular and corroded margins (Plate 2A, 2B), and a dispersed fabric of framework grains with relatively little compaction (Plate 1D). These pores are termed vuggy because they are larger than the surrounding sand grains. The pores, whether intergranular, intercrystalline, or vuggy, have good to excellent connectivity.

Overbank

Overbank or alluvial/delta plain deposits consist of clay-rich, very fine-grained sandstone and siltstone, silty shale, carbonaceous shale, coal, and mudstone. These commonly are rooted or convoluted (Plate 2C), which may be the result of soft-sediment deformation or burrowing. Silty and, less commonly, sandy deposits contain ripples and probably were deposited as levees and overbank splays.

Overbank sandstones are primarily lithic wackes and sublithic arenites (Fig. 5B). The pore geometry present in samples from alluvial/delta plain rocks is intercrystalline microporosity resulting from the presence of abundant matrix clay (chlorite, kaolinite, or mixed layer illite/smectite) (Plate 2D).

Restricted Marine

Most of the restricted-marine deposits occur in the upper Dakota and are associated with a sea-level rise following the Muddy regression. These sandy bay-fill deposits typically are less than 15 ft (4.5 m) thick. They commonly coarsen upward from black shale, to shale interbedded with very fine-grained ripple-drift laminated sandstone (Plate 2E), to intensely bioturbated, massive, or laminated sandstone. Rooted siltstones or silty shales typically cap the sequence. The low diversity of trace fossils present in these deposits, primarily Planolites and Diplocraterion, suggest that salinities were low and perhaps highly variable.

The detrital composition of the restricted marine sandstone is very similar to that of overbank sand-

◄—Figure 2. Generalized Lower Cretaceous stratigraphic column for Wyoming (modified from Ryer, et al., 1987). Cross-hatching indicates unconformities.

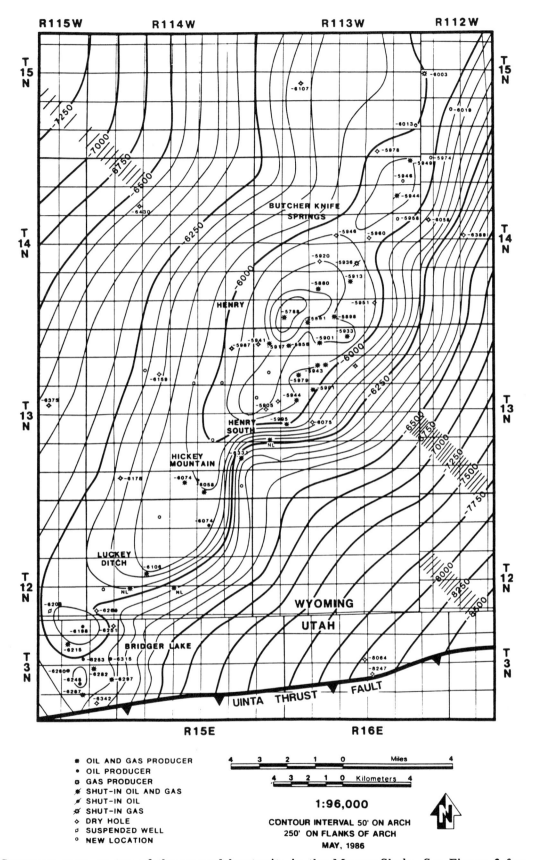

Figure 3. Structure map on top of the second bentonite in the Mowry Shale. See Figure 2 for stratigraphic location of datum. Variable contour interval: 50 ft (15.2 m) on the top of the arch; 250 ft (76.2 m) on the flanks.

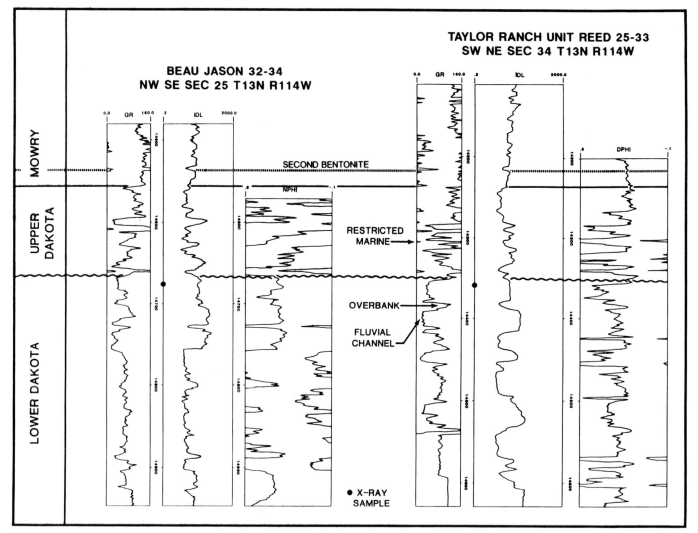

Figure 4. Logs showing unusual low resistivities immediately below the unconformity, caused by the presence of kaolinite and chlorite clay matrix. XRD sample (Table 1) locations are indicated on the logs. Log responses are typical for the three lithofacies.

stones: primarily sublitharenite or lithic wacke (Fig. 5C). Because of the quiet water setting, most of the deposition was suspended load, resulting in very clay-rich deposits with intercrystalline microporosity (Plate 2F).

PETROPHYSICAL VARIATIONS

Porosity and permeability in Henry Field are related to pore geometry, depositional environment, and stratigraphic position. The presence of solution porosity affects the interpretation of log data.

Porosity and Permeability

Fluvial-channel sandstones, the primary reservoir lithofacies at Henry Field, have the highest average core porosity and permeability of all sandstone types, at 11.3% and 43.4 md (Table 2). These are higher permeabilities than any from restricted-marine or overbank sandstones (Fig. 7).

The relative abundance of several authigenic cements and their subsequent dissolution contributes significantly to the differing porosity and permeability values observed. The presence of kaolinite and authigenic silica in sandstone reservoirs commonly does not have a major effect on permeability. Neasham (1977) suggested that sandstones containing "discrete particle" clays such as kaolinite retain relatively high permeabilities for a given porosity. However, small amounts of "pore-lining" and "pore-bridging" clays, usually mixed-layer clays, can significantly lower permeabilities, even in sandstones with high porosities; high porosities in these clay-rich sandstones result from intercrystalline microporosity. Similar effects of clay minerals on porosity and permeability have been found by other authors (Stalder, 1973; Ruhovets and Fertl, 1982). Their results also indicate that pore lining, pore bridging, and illitic clay decrease permeability more than do vermiform booklets of kaolinite.

The presence of chlorite, mixed-layer illite/smectite, and finely crystalline kaolinite in these Dakota reservoirs appears to degrade permeability (Fig. 8).

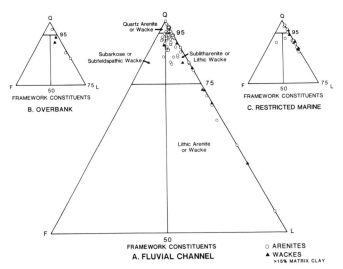

Figure 5. Ternary (QFL) diagrams for the various sandstone lithofacies. The sandstone classification is based on a scheme modified from Folk (1974). Arenites and wackes are plotted on the same diagram and are indicated by different symbols. Wackes contain 15% or more matrix clay. This matrix clay may be detrital or authigenic. However, it does not include clearly authigenic, equant, vermiform booklets of kaolinite, which were categorized as authigenic cement.

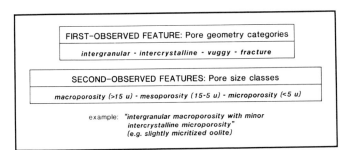

Figure 6. Coalson et al., (1985) porosity classification scheme based on pore geometry and pore size.

At 10% porosity, sandstones containing 0–9% matrix clay have an average permeability of 1.7 md, whereas sandstones containing more than 10% matrix clay have average only 0.09 md. Thus, moderately kaolinite–rich, quartzose Dakota sandstones typically have good permeability, in part due to the presence of large percentages of well-connected vuggy porosity.

Log Interpretations

Log-derived water saturations (Sw's) can be misleading in the study area because differences in pore geometry affect tortuosity, and therefore also affect resistivity. Commonly observed pore geometry types listed in order of decreasing tortuosity and resistivity (other factors being equal) are: unconnected vuggy

Table 1. X–ray diffraction (XRD) data for selected samples from the Dakota Formation at Henry Field. The two samples with abundant chlorite are from immediately below the unconformity between the lower and upper Dakota.

WELL NAME	LOCATION	DEPTH (feet)	CHLORITE	KAOLINITE	ILLITE
Taylor Federal	W1/2 SW 35–T13N–R114W	14,248	A	Mod	—
Reed 2	NW SE 9–T13N–R114W	13,914	—	Mod	M
Henry 14	NE SW 28–T14N–R113W	13,392	M	Mod	M
Reed 22-33	NW SE 25T–13N–R114W	14,358	Mod	A	—
Beau Jason	SW NE 34T–13N–R114W	14,676	A	M	—

(column header: 5 MICRON GRAIN SIZE FRACTION)

Table 2. Average rock compositions, listed by environment for all point–counted thin sections (n = 88).

CONSTITUENTS	ENVIRONMENT		
	FLUVIAL CHANNEL, n=67	RESTRICTED MARINE, n=16	OVERBANK n=5
Rock Fragments QFL	8.3% 10.8%	5.1% 6.8%	6.1% 7.9%
Authigenic Silica	3.3%	6.8%	7.9%
Matrix Clay	7.6%	10.8%	14.5%
Kaolinite	2.2%	3.3%	0.1%
Carbonate Cement	3.2%	0.1%	0.1%
Total Cement	17.0%	20.4%	23.4%
Thin Section Porosity	5.5%	2.%	0.7%
Core Porosity	11.3%	11.5%	8.3%
Core Permeability	43.4 md	5.3 md	0.3 md

and moldic porosity; intergranular and intercrystalline porosity; and fracture porosity (Asquith, 1985).

Water saturations were calculated for wells in Henry Field where thin sections were available from the producing zone, using the method of Archie (1942). Calculations were done with "a" (tortuosity) equal to 1.0, so that the value "m" (cementation exponent) would reflect variations in cementation or pore geometry. Generally, "m" varies from 1.5 to 1.9 in shaly sandstone with intercrystalline microporosity and increases from 2.0 to or higher in sandstone with unconnected vuggy or moldic macroporosity. The presence of fracture porosity or preferential alignment of porosity decreases the "m" value to as low as 1.0.

"M" values were determined by direct measurement (Core Laboratories, proprietary report for Forest Oil) for 43 rock samples from seven cored wells. "M" values varied from 1.47 to 2.18. When plotted along with porosity and permeability (Fig. 9), "m" values appear to be associated with distinct porosity and permeability ranges. Samples with lower "m" values (1.5–1.9) have porosities of 12 to 19% and permeabilities of 35 to 555 md (Fig. 9). Thin sections indicate that these sandstones are generally free of clay matrix and contain connected vuggy macro- to mesoporosity. Sandstones with higher "m" values

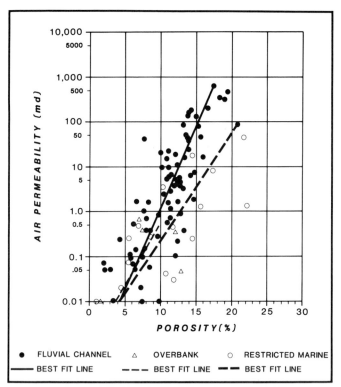

Figure 7. Graph of core porosity vs. permeability for fluvial channel, restricted marine, and overbank sandstone lithofacies for all analyzed thin sections (n = 106). Restricted-marine sandstones have lower permeabilities than do other rocks.

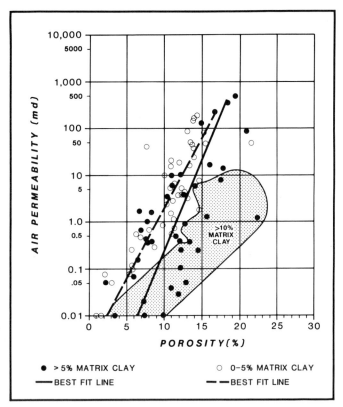

Figure 8. Graph of core porosity vs. permeability as a function of matrix clay for all point-counted thin sections (n = 88). Clay-rich sandstones have lower permeabilities than do other rocks.

(1.92–1.96) have porosities from 11 to 14% with permeabilities from 1 md to 10 md. In short, the better reservoir rocks have lower "m" values, the opposite from the expected relationship in sandstones.

An Application

Recognition of the different rock/porosity types in the Dakota may alleviate significant problems in formation evaluation. The Woods Petroleum No. 1 Leo Unit II (SE NW Sec 20 T15N R111W) was an unsuccessful wildcat well drilled east of Henry Field. The well encountered two sandstone "benches" in the Dakota. A drill-stem test (DST) indicated that both sandstone intervals were tight and/or barren of hydrocarbons, although there were indications that the DST might have been a partial misrun. The DST results seemed to contradict log calculations (Fig. 10B). Using conventional "m" and "n" values, the upper bench (zone 1) appears to be a potential producing interval, with porosity and Sw similar to those in the No. 1 Henry (NE SW Sec 5 T13N R113W) well, a prolific gas producer (Fig. 10A). The lower bench (zone 2) in the Woods well calculates porous, but wet. (Resistivity readings in zone 3 of the lower bench are considered unreliable and too high due to bed-averaging effects; therefore the low calculated Sw is discounted.) Seemingly, the upper bench (zone 1) should have produced gas during the DST, and/or the lower bench water, yet the only recovery was drilling

mud. This is the kind of well that often is interpreted as a bypassed producer.

Examination of core and conventional core analyses of the Woods well, and drawing of analogies to Henry Field, at least reduces the ambiguity of interpretation. A plot of porosity versus permeability (Fig. 10C) and visual examination of the cores indicate that the Woods well contains two of the major porosity types present in Henry Field: interconnected vuggy and moldic quartz sandstone in zones 2 and 3; and chlorite-rich sandstone in zone 1. As a result, Sw values in the lower bench of the Dakota should be calculated using m = 1.5 (Table 3). This recalculation indicates that zone 2 actually has mediocre Sw (48%), probably too low to produce water and too high to produce gas, assuming reasonable relative permeability characteristics. The upper bench (zone 1), on the other hand, apparently does not need to be recalculated. However, while Sw values are low enough to indicate that hydrocarbons are present, low permeabilities preclude gas production without stimulation. The well can be discounted as a bypassed producer, at least in the Dakota sandstones. The hydrocarbon shows on logs, however, are of interest; a structurally higher location might yield gas production from Zone 2.

CONCLUSIONS

The percentage of matrix clay present in the Dakota sandstone at Henry Field relates to depositional environment and to stratigraphic position; the re-

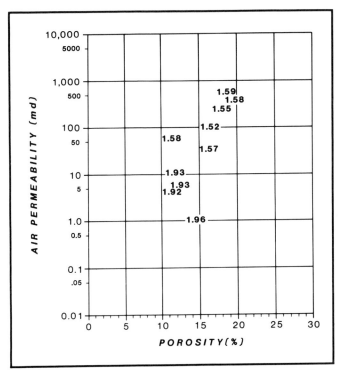

Figure 9. Graph of core porosity vs. permeability with corresponding "m" values plotted for the 1.50-1.59 and the 1.90-1.99 ranges (see text for discussion). "M" values were determined by Core Laboratories

Table 3. Comparison of water saturation calculations for the upper and lower benches in the Woods Petroleum No. 1 Leo Unit II. "M" value of 2.0, while appropriate for chloritic rocks in upper bench, is not appropriate for the lower bench, as it consists of rocks with abundant secondary porosity.

INTERVAL	POROSITY	Rt	Sw (m=2)	Sw (m=1.5)
Upper Bench	Zone 1 0.15	40	38	Didn't need recalculation
Lower Bench	Zone 2 0.13	14	77	48
	Zone 3 0.13	90	30	18

Rw = 0.15   n=2

stricted marine and overbank lithofacies contain abundant matrix clay, as do fluvial sandstones from just below the unconformity between the upper and lower Dakota. Abundant matrix clay typically inhibits the producibility of the sandstone because it fills larger pores with intercrystalline microporosity. Porosity, permeability, and "m" also relate closely to depositional environment, stratigraphic position, and porosity type. The fluvial channel sandstones typically have the best porosity and permeability, with pore geometries ranging from intergranular/intercrystalline macro- to mesoporosity, to connected vuggy macro- to mesoporosity. Samples with connected solution porosity commonly have excellent porosities, permeabilities, and anomalously low "m" values.

Diagenesis and dissolution have created pore geometries in Henry Field that result in potentially misleading log interpretations. Pore geometries should be analyzed to determine the effects they may have on log calculations, prior to condemning southwestern Wyoming Dakota tests.

ACKNOWLEDGEMENTS

Thanks are due RPI International and Forest Oil Corporation for permission to publish these data. Tom Ryer and Jon McClurg (both formerly of RPI International) contributed significant time and effort in unraveling the regional Dakota correlations in the vicinity of the Moxa Arch. Gus Gustason of RPI International provided stimulating conversation and insight into the stratigraphic relationships of the Dakota Formation in Wyoming. Many thanks to Robin Lockart, Grant Morrison, and Martin Wright of RPI's Graphics Department for their drafting support. Bob Pfister of Amoco Production Company also was very helpful with last-minute drafting changes.

REFERENCES

Archie, G.E., 1942, Electrical resistivity as an aid in determining some reservoir characteristics: Trans. AIME, v. 146, p. 54-62.

Asquith, G.B., 1985, Handbook of log evaluation techniques for carbonate reservoirs: Methods in Exploration Series No. 5, AAPG, Tulsa, OK, 47 p.

Coalson, E.B., D.J. Hartmann, and J.B. Thomas, 1985, Productive characteristics of common reservoir porosity types: South Texas Geol. Soc. Bull., v. 25, no. 6, p. 35-51.

Folk, R.L., 1974, Petrology of Sedimentary Rocks: Hemphill Publ. Co., Austin, TX, 182 p.

Hansen, W.R., 1965, Geology of the Flaming Gorge area, Utah-Colorado-Wyoming: USGS Prof. Paper 490, 196 p.

Kinney, D.M., 1955, Geology of the Uinta River-Brush Creek area, Duchesne and Uinta Counties, Utah: USGS Bull. 1007, 185 p.

Muller, M.M., 1986, Petrography, diagenesis, and petrophysical variations of the Dakota Sandstones, Henry Field, Green River Basin, Wyoming: unpub. MS thesis, U. of CO, Boulder, 185 p.

Neasham, J.W., 1977, The morphology of dispersed clay in sandstone reservoirs and its effect on sandstone shaliness, pore-space, and fluid flow properties: SPE, Paper SPE-6858, 8 p.

Ruhovets, N., and W.H. Fertl, 1982, Digital shaly sand analysis based on Waxman-Smits model and log-derived clay typing: Log Analyst, May-June, p. 7-23.

Ryer, T.A., J.J. McClurg, and M.M. Muller, 1987, Dakota-Bear River Paleoenvironments, depositional history and shoreline trends-implications for foreland basin paleotectonics, southwestern Green River Basin and southern Wyoming overthrust belt, *in* WGA, 38th Ann. Field Conf. Guidebook: p. 179-206.

Stalder, P.J., 1973, Influence of crystallographic habit and aggregate structure of authigenic clay minerals on sandstone permeability: Geologie en Mijnbouw, v. 52, no. 4, p. 217-220.

Thomaidis, N.D., 1973, Church Buttes Arch, Wyoming and Utah, *in* WGA, 25th Ann. Field Conf. Guidebook: p. 35-39.

Vaughn, R.L., and M.D. Picard, 1976, Stratigraphy, sedimentology, and petroleum potential of Dakota Formation, northeastern Utah, *in* J.G. Hill, ed., Symposium on the Geology of the Cordilleran Hingeline: RMAG Field Conf. Guidebook, p. 267-279.

Wach, P.H., 1977, The Moxa Arch, an overthrust model?, *in* E.L. Heisey, D.L. Lawson, E.E. Norwood, P.H. Wach, and L.A. Hale, eds., Rocky Mountain Thrust Belt Geology and Resources: WGA, 29th Ann. Field Conf. Guidebook, p. 651-664.

Webb, J.E., 1975, Sedimentology and clay cementation, Dakota Formation, Bridger Lake Field, Utah, *in* Symposium on Deep Drilling Frontiers in the Central Rocky Mountains: RMAG. Field Conf. Guidebook, p. 217-224.

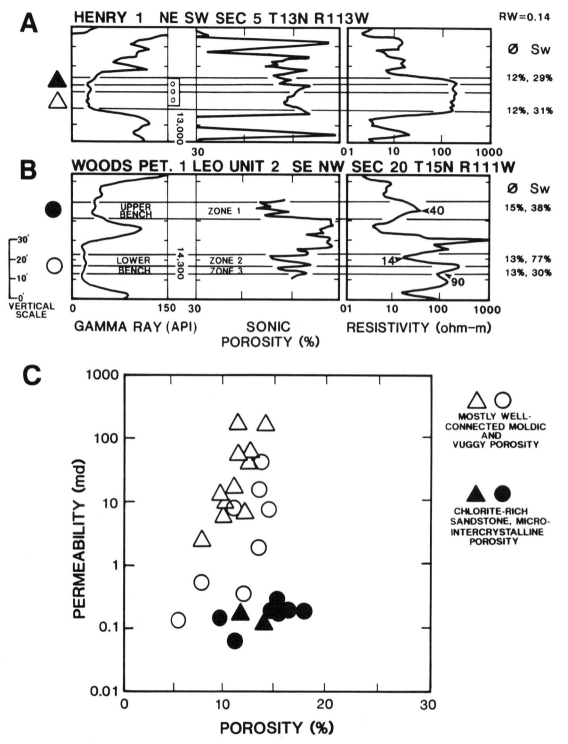

Figure 10: Example of petrophysical evaluation of Dakota reservoirs.
A. Log suites and water saturation calculations for the No. 1 Henry well, a prolific producer of gas. (10 ft = 3.05 m)
B. Similar data for Woods Petroleum No. 1 Leo Unit II Unit well. Samples identified by solid symbols are chloritic sandstones having intercrystalline microporosity. Sandstones identified by open symbols are quartzose and clay–poor, and have interconnected vuggy, moldic, and intergranular/intercrystalline porosity.
C. Graph of conventional core porosity against permeability, illustrating the effect of two rock/porosity types on reservoir quality. No. 1 Henry data shown with triangles; No. 1 Leo Unit II data shown with circles.

Geological and Engineering Evaluation of Barrier Island and Valley–Fill Lithotypes in Muddy Formation, Bell Creek Field, Montana[1]

MICHAEL SZPAKIEWICZ[2]
RICHARD SCHATZINGER[2]
MATT HONARPOUR[2]
MIN THAM[2]
RODERICK TILLMAN[3]

[1]Received July 15, 1988; Revised December 15, 1988
[2]National Institute for Petroleum and Energy Research, Bartlesville, Oklahoma
[3]Consulting Sedimentologist, Tulsa, Oklahoma

The Lower Cretaceous Muddy Formation produces oil from barrier–island and overlying valley–fill deposits at Unit "A" of Bell Creek Field, Montana. A combined geological/engineering study was made of the depositional, diagenetic, and architectural aspects of the barrier–island and valley–fill deposits; the classification and scaling of geological heterogeneities that affect production; and the petrophysical and production characteristics of the Muddy reservoir rocks. Data were from both Muddy-Formation cores from Unit "A" and outcrops around the Powder River Basin

The productive interval consists of stacked, upward–shallowing barrier–island sandstones. They are confined on the basinward side by valley fills and on the landward side by nonproductive lagoon or estuarine facies. Non–barrier sediments form a large part of the valley fill, generally have low permeability, and contribute little to total oil production. An unconformity separates valley–fill and barrier–island reservoirs. Erosion removed a significant portion of the barrier–island sequence, the best reservoir sandstone.

Depositional, diagenetic, and structural heterogeneities at a variety of scales define the geometry, continuity, and transmissivity of flow units. Large scale heterogeneities include fluid properties, depositional features, and structural framework. Among medium and small scale features are diagenesis and faults. Depositional trends such as sequence of facies, rock textures, and distribution of detrital clays are the most predictable heterogeneities in the barrier–island facies. The least predictable heterogeneities are diagenetic, erosional, and fault–related features.

INTRODUCTION

This study was undertaken as part of continuing research by the National Institute for Petroleum and Energy Research (NIPER) to characterize geological and production behavior of barrier–island reservoirs. The objectives were to predict the fluid flow and residual oil saturation in interwell areas. Few published geological models of ancient barrier–island reservoirs contain sufficient detail to predict reservoir heterogeneities and to explain variations of reservoir properties present at different scales.

The barrier–island reservoir selected for detailed analysis is located in Unit "A" of Bell Creek Field, Carter and Powder River counties, Montana, on the northeastern flank of the Powder River Basin (Fig. 1). Bell Creek Field consists of six hydraulically independent and stratigraphically trapped producing units named "A" through "E" and Ranch Creek. The largest and most productive is Unit "A". Since 1976, two tertiary oil–recovery pilot projects have been completed in Unit "A". This study concentrated on the four mi² (10.4 km²) area of Unit "A" located in Secs 22, 23, 26 and 27 T8S R54E. How-

REGIONAL DATA:

Producing Interval:	Muddy Sandstone
Present Tectonic Setting:	Eastern flank of intracratonic Powder River Basin
Depositional Setting:	Cretaceous interior seaway
Age of Reservoir:	Lower Cretaceous
Depositional Environments:	Marginal marine barrier–island complex and nonmarine valley–fill
Nature of Traps:	Stratigraphic pinchout
Source Rock:	Marine shale of Lower Cretaceous Mowry Formation
Timing of Hydrocarbon Migration:	Laramide

FIELD DATA:

	Bell Creek Field, Unit "A"
Discovered:	1967
Geographic Location:	T8S R54E, Powder River County, Montana
Lithology of Reservoir:	Very fine to fine–grained, moderately to well sorted, illitic and kaolinitic quartz arenites and subarkoses
Diagenesis:	Dissolution of feldspar, chert, and sedimentary rock fragments; precipitation of siderite; compaction; formation of quartz overgrowths; precipitation of poikilotopic calcite; dissolution of calcite cement and pseudomatrix; kaolinization; emplacement of oil
Porosity Types:	Intergranular and intercrystalline porosity; intragranular microporosity
Porosity:	Range 6–36%, average 28.5%
Matrix Density:	Range 2.60–2.64 gm/cc, average 2.62 gm/cc
Permeability:	Range 0.1–13,000 md; arithmetic mean 2,250 md; geometric mean 915 md
Wettability:	Water wet, possibly mixed or intermediate
Initial Water Saturation:	Range 20–35%, average 26%
Temperature:	110°F (43°C)
Original Reservoir Pressure:	1,204 psia at –800 ft (–244 m) (coincidentally equal to the bubble point pressure)
Drive Types:	Primary solution–gas drive; secondary line–drive waterflood initiated in 1970; tertiary micellar–polymer pilots installed in 1975 and 1981
Oil Type:	Paraffinic
Solution GOR:	200 SCFG/BO (360 std m3/m3)
Formation Volume Factor:	1.112 vol/vol (1.05 vol/vol at start of waterflood)
Oil Gravity:	Range 31.5–40° API; average 32.5° API
Oil Viscosity:	2.76 cp at original reservoir pressure and temperature
Formation Water Resistivity:	1.08 ohm–m at 68°F (20°C); 6,400–7,400 ppm TDS
Reservoir Depth:	Average 4,500 ft (1,373 m)
Areal Extent:	7,219 acres (2,922 ha)
Pay Thickness:	Average gross 25.7 ft (7.8 m); average net 22.9 ft (7 m)
Bulk Volume of Productive Area:	86,189 acre–ft
Spacing:	Primary and secondary spacing 40 acres (16 ha)
Original Oil in Place:	127,000,000 BO
Cumulative Production (8/87):	69,930,000 BO (21,960,000 primary; 46,600,000 secondary; 1,370,000 tertiary)
Approximate Ultimate Recoverable:	Not reported

ever, core and log data from adjacent areas aided in the geological interpretation.

The Muddy Formation and Bell Creek Field have been the subject of many geological studies during the last two decades (Berg and Davies, 1968; McGregor and Biggs, 1969; Stone, 1972; Almon and Davies, 1979; Weimer, 1981; Weimer et al., 1982, 1988). Major geological characteristics of the Muddy Formation in Bell Creek Field and the influence of geological factors on tertiary oil production were discussed by Szpakiewicz and others (1987).

The succession of lithology, sedimentary structures, and textures identified in the Muddy Formation barrier–island complex is similar to that observed in Holocene barrier–island deposits near Galveston, Texas, and in other barrier–island reservoirs (Reinson, 1984). The Muddy barrier system differs from many previously described in that it is, at least in part, a transgressive barrier (cf. Demerest and Kraft, 1987). Characterization of the field using abundant log, well-test, production, and core data may shed light on heterogeneities encountered in similar deposits.

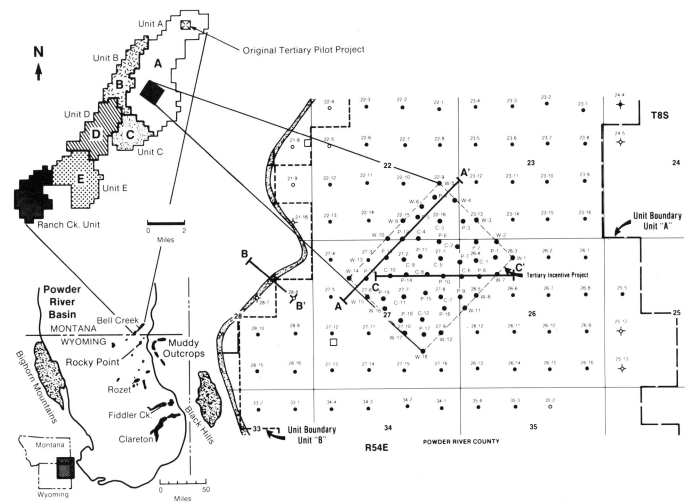

Figure 1. Location map of Bell Creek Field and study area within Unit "A". Locations of cross-sections and general area of studied outcrop also shown. (1 mi = 1.609 km)

PRODUCTION HISTORY

Bell Creek Field is the northernmost major oil field in the Powder River Basin and has produced 125,000,000 BO through 1987 (Weimer, et al., 1988). The field was discovered in June, 1967 and was developed rapidly on 40-acre spacing. Primary production was by solution gas drive; drive from hydraulically isolated aquifers in the downdip portion of reservoir was limited. Initially there were several gas wells in the field. However, the gas accumulation was local. Primary performance indicated no significant gas-cap drive. Original oil-in-place (OOIP) for the field was 242,900,000 STBO with an ultimate primary recovery of 48,400,000 STBO, or 19.9% of the OOIP. Unit "A" accounts for approximately one-half of the OOIP at Bell Creek Field. Primary production from Unit "A" was 22,000,000 STBO (Honarpour, et al., 1988).

Line-drive waterflooding of Unit "A" started in August, 1970, at the northwestern (downdip) edge of the unit. In 1978, an additional line of injectors was located in the eastern part of the unit. Injection pushed oil into the updip part of the barrier-island

facies where it interfingers with back barrier and lagoonal facies. Waterflooding succeeded in recovering more than 35% of the OOIP. Total primary and secondary production exceeded 55% of the OIP (Honarpour et al., 1988).

In June, 1976, a 160-acre, tertiary micellar-polymer pilot project was implemented in the watered-out northern portion of Unit "A". This project recovered 28% of the OIP at the beginning of the tertiary preflush in February, 1979. In 1980, a second tertiary project was undertaken. This micellar-polymer tertiary incentive project (TIP) covered 179 acres near the center of the Unit "A" reservoir, in the watered-out portion of the line-drive waterflood. It consisted of 12 injector-centered, 20-acre five-spot patterns, nine of which were chemical injectors. The other wells were designed for pattern waterflooding. The project was surrounded by 18 water-injection wells. It is estimated that the micellar-polymer TIP project recovered 39% of the remaining oil in place at the start of the preflush (Hartshorne and Nikonchik, 1984). This project was technically more successful because the earlier tertiary project encountered unanticipated geological complexity.

GEOLOGICAL SETTING

In Bell Creek Field, oil is produced from the Lower Cretaceous Muddy Formation (Fig. 2) at an average depth of 4,500 ft (1,373 m). The Muddy Formation dips west toward the axis of the Powder River Basin. Outcrops with facies analogous to the reservoir rocks are exposed in northeastern Wyoming on the flank of the Black Hills Uplift approximately 30 mi (48 km) southeast of the field.

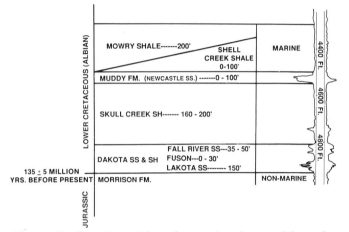

Figure 2. Stratigraphic column showing position of Muddy Formation in the Lower Cretaceous sequence. (100 ft = 30.5 m)

The Muddy Formation near Bell Creek Field ranges in total thickness from less than 60 ft (18.3 m) to almost 100 ft (30.5 m) (Stone, 1972). However, the maximum documented thickness of stacked barrier-island sandstones in Unit "A" does not exceed 30 ft (9.2 m). The thickest sequence of stacked barrier-island sandstone present in outcrops is found near New Haven, Wyoming, about 30 mi (48 km) southeast of Bell Creek Field. Here barrier-island sandstones are 28.4 ft (8.6 m) thick.

Previous workers interpreted the Bell Creek-Muddy reservoirs as barrier-bar sandstones. Stratigraphic traps in Unit "A" were formed by updip (eastward) pinchouts from barrier-island sandstones into lagoonal rocks. Multiple oil-water contacts are known on the western downdip margin (Berg and Davies, 1968; Burt et al., 1975; Vargo, 1978). Other workers have recognized at least two sandstone intervals with significantly different production characteristics, separated by a "shale barrier" in each of the waterflood units (Burt et al., 1975; Gary-Williams, 1982; Hartshorne and Nikonchik, 1984). The lower sandstone is the most favorable reservoir (Vargo, 1978; Gary-Williams, 1982), and is very fine- to fine-grained quartz sandstone that is clean, moderately sorted, and partly consolidated. Clay and silt fractions range from two to eight wt% (Berg and Davies, 1968; Gary-Williams, 1982). In most areas, this sandstone is a barrier-island deposit. Much of the upper sandstone has been interpreted as a valley-fill deposit.

The Muddy barrier-island and related deposits (lagoon, estuary, tidal flat, tidal channel, alluvial valley fill, and others) are underlain and overlain by marine shales of the Skull Creek and Shell Creek/Mowry formations, respectively. The basal contact of the Muddy in the outcrop and at Bell Creek is unconformable. The upper contact is interpreted to be a transgressive ravinement surface.

STRUCTURAL CHARACTERISTICS

The Muddy Formation in Unit "A" generally dips northwest at 100 ft/mi (19 m/km). Detailed structural analyses reveal several previously unrecognized faults in the TIP and adjacent areas. These discontinuous faults commonly strike N50E and N40W (Fig. 3), generally parallel to regional lineaments (Slack, 1981; Weimer, et al., 1982). The direction of principal stress in the area near the Wyoming, Montana, and South Dakota border is northeast-southwest (Zoback and Zoback, 1980). Major linear features mapped from Landsat imagery in Hilight Field, 80 mi (128 km) south of Bell Creek Field, reveal azimuths of 50-55° and 145-150° (Michael and Merin, 1986). Similarity of directions obtained from this variety of sources and from different locations in the northeastern part of the Powder River Basin strongly suggests that one structural framework is common to the entire area.

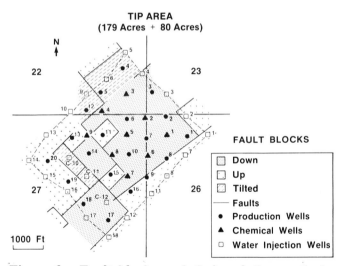

Figure 3. Fault blocks and their relative vertical positions. Tertiary incentive project (TIP) area also shown. Note positions of production, chemical, and water injection wells. (1,000 ft = 305 m)

Vertical displacement of post-depositional faults (i.e., those that cut both the base and the top of the Muddy Formation) commonly are from 10 to 20 ft (3 to 6 m), although displacements greater than 40 ft were identified in Section 27 (Fig. 4). The ratio of vertical displacement to net pay thickness varies from 0.5 to 1.5, suggesting the possibility of local restriction or disconnection of fluid flow. Fault separation of the barrier-island reservoir resulted in locally anomalous sweep efficiencies in five-spot EOR patterns. In part of the TIP area, where gently tilted blocks contain

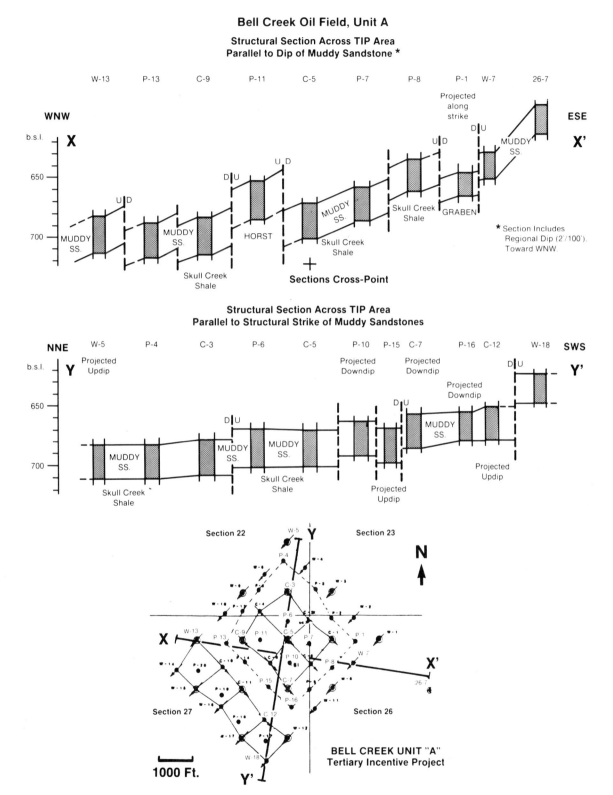

Figure 4. Structural stick sections of Muddy Formation across TIP area, oriented parallel to dip (X–X') and to strike (Y–Y').

several wells, faulting has not complicated hydraulic communication.

Natural fractures were not obvious in the 16 cores from the TIP area. However, outcrop observations near New Haven (Szpakiewicz et al., 1988) and elsewhere in the Muddy Formation indicate that the density of natural fractures decreases abruptly away from fault planes; subsurface fractures may be present at Bell Creek, but may not have been detected in wells located some distance from a fault zone.

As expected, downthrown fault blocks produce less oil but higher total fluids because of the natural tendency of oil to concentrate in structurally high blocks. Well P–14 (Fig. 5), which is structurally low due to faulting, produced 76,000 BO and more than 2.5 million bbl of total fluids during the 1980–87 period. Adjacent well P–11 (Fig. 4), located in an upthrown fault block, produced 40% more oil and 35% less total fluid during the same period.

Pressure–pulse tests and falloff tests were conducted in the TIP area before the initiation of tertiary micellar–polymer flooding. When pressure–transient information is superimposed on a fault map, it is evident that faults did not completely sever fluid commu-nication between adjacent wells. The preferential direction of flow along some faults is from northwest to southeast, as indicated by the advancement of the water fronts (Honarpour et al., 1988).

DEPOSITIONAL HISTORY

Regional paleogeographic and paleotectonic reconstructions of the Muddy Formation (McGregor and Biggs, 1969; Forgotson and Stark, 1971; Stone, 1972; Slack, 1981; Weimer, et al., 1982, 1988) show continental (delta channel and deltaic plain), brackish marine (lagoon, estuary, and tidal flat), and coastal marine (barrier–island) sedimentation in the northeastern Powder River Basin. At least four different interpretations of stratigraphic frameworks for the Bell Creek area are extant:

1) The barrier–island deposits lie stratigraphically above an unconformity at the top of the Skull Creek Shale (Stone, 1972; Almon and Davies, 1979).

2) The barrier–island and valley–fill deposits are, in part, synchronous within a deltaic system (McGregor and Biggs, 1969).

3) Valleys and their subsequent "fills" are incised into barrier–island deposits and are stratigraphically

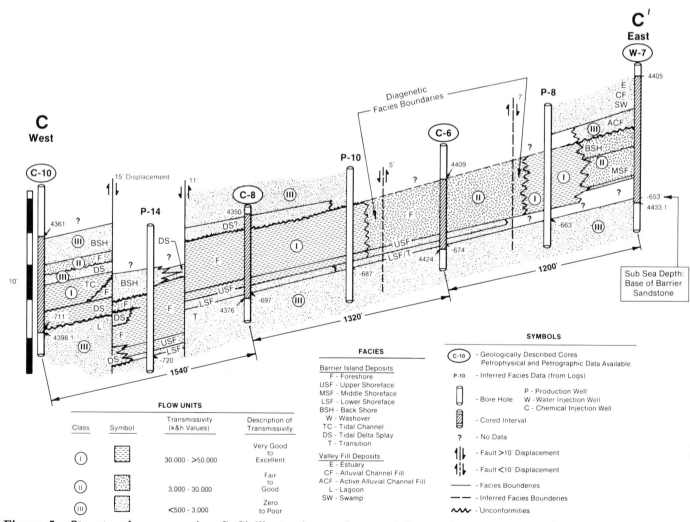

Figure 5. Structural cross section C–C' illustrating geology and flow units across central part of TIP area. For location of cross section, see Figure 1.

younger. In this view, the barrier–island deposits are generally conformable with the Skull Creek Shale (Weimer, 1981).

4) The barrier–island deposits lie unconformably on the Skull Creek Shale and partly on lagoonal or estuarine deposits. Two periods of valley cut–and–fill have incised the barrier–island deposits. The earlier valleys are distributed over a large portion of the barrier. The second set of channels were narrow and are filled with marine shale (this study).

In some cores from Unit "A", lower shoreface barrier–island rocks overlie the marine Skull Creek Shale. However, lagoonal deposits are found beneath other barrier–island sandstones, as they are in outcrops exposed near New Haven. D. Dailey (pers. comm.) confirms that foraminifers from interpreted lagoonal deposits are distinct from those in the Skull Creek Shale. In outcrop (Fig. 6), lenses of rounded marine shale clasts separate lagoonal Muddy Formation deposits from the Skull Creek Shale. Incision of valley fill into the top of barrier–island deposits is, however, commonly observed in Bell Creek cores (Szpakiewicz et al., 1988), strongly supporting the chronology of Weimer (1981).

The influence of relative sea level changes on sandstone distribution, erosional cuts, and infilling of valleys with brackish and non–marine sediments in the Bell Creek area is still in question. Albian stratigraphy can be correlated to periods of deposition and erosion during postulated high and low sea–level stands (Fig. 7). Stacked Muddy barrier–island sandstones were deposited at a time of minor fluctuations in sea level (T5). During a sea level drop (T6), valleys are inferred to have been incised into the top of the barrier islands. The accumulation of valley–fill sediments took place during a subsequent sea level rise (T7), completing deposition of the Muddy Formation. Continued transgression resulted in deposition of the Shell Creek Shale.

BARRIER ISLAND AND VALLEY FILL SEDIMENTATION

Method of Study

Detailed investigation of the stratigraphy, lithology, sedimentary and biogenic structures, grain–size distribution, and cement distribution in various facies is based on examination of 26 complete or partial cores from the northern part of Bell Creek Field (Fig. 8). In addition, 21 outcrops in the New Haven area representing a variety of analogous facies were described and interpreted (e.g., Fig. 6). Some of the outcrops (e.g., 22 and 1/86) offered almost continuous lateral exposure for thousands of feet, comparable to inter-well distances in Bell Creek Field. Four of the outcrops studied (22a, 22, 23, and 3/86) were cored in order to characterize the petrophysical properties of exposed barrier–island facies (Honarpour, et al, 1988).

The inferred depositional setting for the Bell Creek area (Fig. 8) is based on geological analyses of available cores and logs from wells located in and near units "A", "B", "C", and "D". A similar interpretation was done for the outcrop area (Fig. 9). Similarity in depositional patterns between the subsurface and

outcrops (Fig. 10) leads us to conclude that details regarding facies distribution, stacking pattern, and continuity of sandstone units observed in outcrops can be applied to the subsurface in Unit "A".

Gamma ray (GR), spontaneous potential (SP), and resistivity wireline log signatures from 16 wells and core descriptions from six wells were used for geological correlation of the major lithologic units (Fig. 11). Log responses were related to cored genetic units. "Calibration" of major facies changes and observed unconformities was done with core–gamma logs where available, and subsurface GR logs.

The tops of barrier–island sandstones in most cores are disconformable with the overlying valley–fill deposits. Although this contact is not always readily identifiable on logs, electric logs commonly show an upward decrease in resistivity in the valley–fill deposits in contrast to the usually high resistivity (oil–rich) barrier–island complex. Separation of these two genetic units is almost impossible based on SP and GR log shapes. For example, the resistivity log from cored well W–10 (Fig. 10) shows similar responses in barrier–island and valley–fill sandstones. The sonic log, however, indicates a significant decrease of average porosity in the valley–fill section, allowing separation of the two lithologic units.

Identification and distribution of facies within the Muddy valley–fill can be determined only in wells with core control. Interpretation of lateral continuity and vertical distribution of individual facies in non–cored wells requires a more comprehensive method of log analyses than attempted in this study.

Interpretation of Depositional and Erosional Features

A typical stratigraphic cycle of prograding barrier–island facies exhibits predictable characteristics (Table 1). Stacking of several barrier–island cycles is recognized in Bell Creek cores. For example, in well W–16, 21 ft (6.4 m) of shoreface and foreshore facies are underlain by 2.8 ft (1.0 m) of barrier–washover facies, which is, in turn, overlain by another 2.4 ft (0.8 m) of possible barrier–washover facies. Local thickening therefore results from deposition of more than one barrier–island cycle.

Total barrier thickness seldom is preserved, because of erosion. The eolian deposits that commonly occur at the top of modern barrier–island sequences are very susceptible to erosion; these are represented only by thin beds overlying foreshore facies in some Bell Creek cores (e.g., well C–8). Shoreface facies have better reservation potential and compose most of the producing interval.

Stacking of foreshore and shoreface sequences at Bell Creek resulted from small changes in relative sea level. During periods of regression, the older barrier–island sequences were partially eroded. During subsequent transgressions, new barrier islands buried the remnants. Subsequent to and independent of barrier building, valley "cuts" locally removed significant portions of the upper part of the barrier complex. Locally, only remnants of the original barriers are preserved. In extreme cases, the entire barrier was removed (Figs. 12, 13). There is evidence of two stages of valley incision during late Muddy deposition:

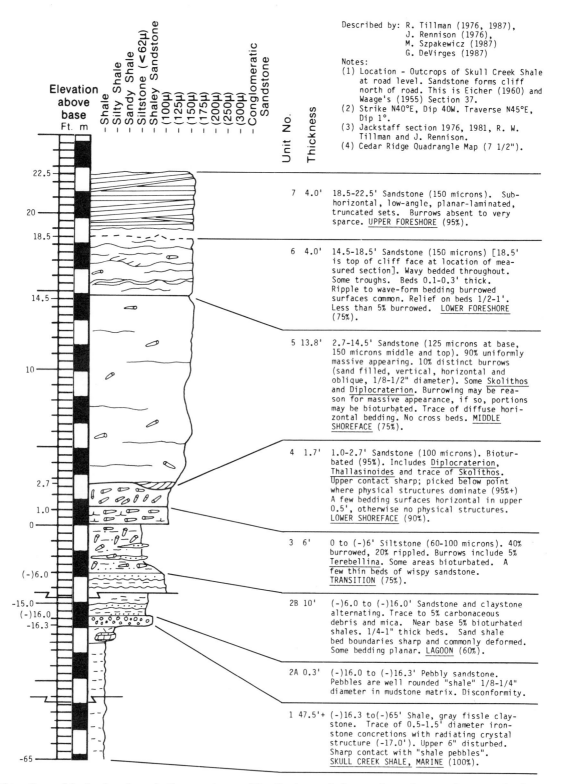

Figure 6. Stratigraphic facies description, outcrop 22. Outcrop is located at the southern end of a continuous exposure of barrier–island sandstones nearly 2,150 ft (655 m) long (Fig. 9). Cementation by calcite and ferruginous minerals is characteristic for top part of the exposure, mostly in upper foreshore and tidal channel facies. The barrier island rests on alternating lagoonal sandstones and claystones. Pebbly sandstone marks the base of a nearly 40–ft (12 m) thick section of Muddy Formation, and lies just above the disconformity with the underlying Skull Creek Shale. Outcrop was sampled horizontally and vertically for measurement of petrophysical properties.

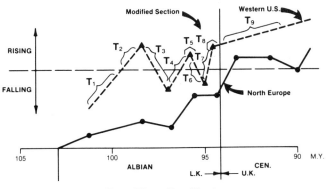

Time of Deposition / Erosion

T₁ - Inyan Kara Group (Lakota and Fall River Sandstones)

T₂ - Skull Creek Shale

T₃ - Lower Muddy Valley incisions (in topographic lows)

T₄ - Lower Muddy Valley filling (accumulation in topographic lows) (Newcastle Type)

T₅ - Barrier Islands formed (Middle Muddy) on topographic highs (Bell Creek, New Haven type)

T₆ - Valley incisions into Barrier Islands (Bell Creek, New Haven area)

T₇ - Valley infill (Upper Muddy) brackish marine and continental (Bell Creek)

T₈ - Shell Creek / Mowry Shale

T₉ - Belle Fourche Shale

Figure 7. Relationship of deposition and erosion to inferred sea-level changes during Lower Cretaceous in northeastern Powder River Basin. Based on lithostratigraphy of Muddy Formation in Bell Creek Field and from Weimer et al., 1982.

an earlier, low relief event affecting in most cases only barrier-island deposits; and a later, narrow, deep cut affecting barrier-island and older sequences of valley-fill deposits.

Erosional thinning or removal of barrier-island sandstone strongly affects reservoir storage capacity and transmissivity. Complete hydraulic disconnection of the reservoir may occur, as is the case between units "A" and "B" (Fig. 14). A ribbon-like channel incision, filled with very low energy shaley and silty sediments (well 28-11, Fig. 14) of the second stage of erosion, cuts about 35 ft (10.7 m) into the Muddy (almost to or below the base) and creates a steep, narrow hydraulic obstruction about 500 ft (153 m) wide. Different pressure regimes and positions of water-oil contacts on opposite sides of the hydraulic barrier reflect effective isolation of the two production units. Thicknesses of sandstone units are similar on either side of the incision, suggesting that the front of the barrier island lies west of Unit "A" (Fig. 15). No significant faulting between units "A" and "B" is known.

There is no evidence of whether the cut resulted from subaerial processes or from subsea currents. Superposition of the deep bifurcating cuts provides analogy to the position of Unit "A" in the Bell Creek system. The cut on the left-hand side corresponds to the western limit of Unit "A". The cut on the right-

hand side may belong to the valley system documented east of Unit "A" in a dry hole, the Superior Oil No. 1 Lornegan (NE NE Sec 24 T8S R54E).

Several types of valley-fill deposits are known (Fig. 12, Table 2). Most of the valley fills in Unit "A" are of non-marine origin, have very fine mean grain size (75 to 125 microns), and contain abundant clay matrix. X-ray diffraction (XRD) analyses of barrier-island and valley-fill sandstones from the subsurface and outcrops reveal that they contain significantly different clay assemblages (Table 3).

Valley-fill sandstone may immediately overlie barrier-island sandstone, as in well W-7 or, more commonly, may be separated by lagoonal, estuarine, or alluvial channel deposits. The juxtaposition of valley-fill sandstone on barrier-island sandstone suggests that local hydraulic communication between these two types of Muddy sandstone exists, in contrast to earlier interpetations.

Cross section A-A' (Fig. 11), constructed along the northwest side of the TIP area, illustrates only small variation (20%) in barrier-island thickness parallel to the general elongation of the barrier (Table 4). The top part of the Muddy along the trend of the cross section consists of silty and clayey valley-fill facies. The average thickness of valley-fill sandstones in this area is 8 ft (2.4 m), with variations as great as 65% and significantly lower values toward the northeast. However, the total thickness of the Muddy is relatively constant (42.5-49.0 ft, 12.9-14.9 m) due to compensating thicknesses between barrier-island and valley-fill deposits. Relief on the disconformity at the top of the barrier-island facies apparently is minimal. However, narrow, deep incisions between interpreted wells cannot be ruled out.

PETROGRAPHIC CHARACTERISTICS

Mineralogy of Sandstones

Foreshore, shoreface, and washover facies have similar petrographic characteristics, although lower shoreface and some washover samples tend to contain more clay cement and matrix. These deposits are moderately to well sorted, very fine to fine-grained quartz arenites and subarkoses. Individual barrier-island facies cannot be distinguished by either framework mineralogy or clay content alone.

Barrier-island and valley-fill sandstones from the subsurface and analogous outcrops display high quartz contents and differentiation of clay assemblages (Table 3). Barrier-island sandstones exhibit a 2:1 ratio between kaolinite and illite; clays comprise less than 15 wt%. In valley-fill sandstones and mudstones, smectite and kaolinite dominate the clay assemblage. In a regional study of the Muddy Formation, Stone (1972) concluded that the clays in the shales are dominantly illite and montmorillonite (smectite group), whereas clays in sandstones are almost exclusively kaolinite. This generalization does not entirely apply to the valley-fill sandstones. Most clay in barrier-island sandstones is diagenetic kaolinite derived from decomposition of feldspars and other unstable grains such as rock fragments. Chert is the most common surviving lithic fragment. Potassium feldspars are virtually the only type of feldspar represented. Based on thin sec-

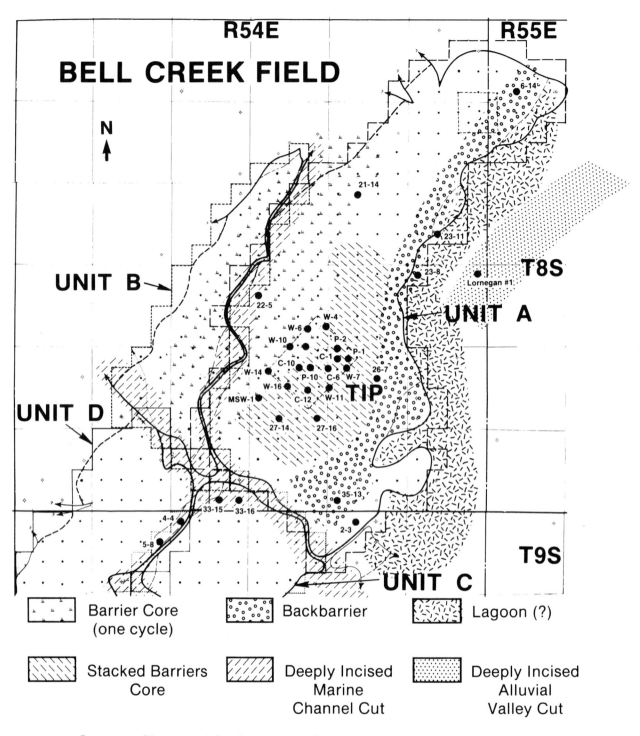

Figure 8. Sketch map of the inferred depositional setting and facies distribution based on cores and logs in northern part of Bell Creek Field. Range is six mi (9.6 km) wide.

tion studies, feldspars generally account for no more than two to three percent of total rock volume.

Diagenesis

Early diagenesis, particularly leaching, is important to modification of the pore space in the Bell Creek reservoir; virtually all of the later diagenetic phases reduced reservoir quality. Feldspars and chert show

the most obvious effects of leaching. All degrees of corroded feldspar and polycrystalline quartz are associated with the collapse of surviving silt–size remnants. Leached chert and polycrystalline quartz are microporous. Leaching of sedimentary rock fragments also was seen in most samples from throughout the field. The leaching of unstable grains, particularly sedimen-

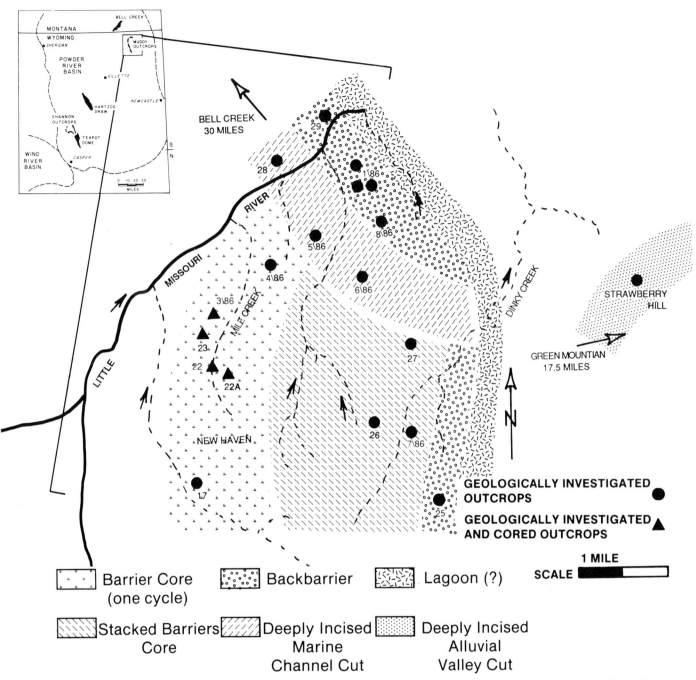

Figure 9. Sketch map of inferred depositional setting and facies based on Muddy outcrops in New Haven area, Wyoming. Location of outcrops shown. (1 mi = 1.61 km)

tary rock fragments, is believed to be responsible for creation of the numerous oversized pores (Plate 1). We infer that substantial early leaching of the barrier-island facies was controlled by infiltrating fresh water and the establishment of one or more meteoric lenses. The net result of early leaching was twofold. First, it created abundant secondary interparticle and intraparticle porosity, enhancing the fluid-storage capacity of the reservoir. Second, partial leaching resulted in kaolinization of some feldspars which collapsed, locally blocking pore throats.

Siderite precipitated early. It is not abundant in cores from the barrier-island facies and generally does not occur where mineralogical cross-cutting relationships could establish its exact timing. Siderite locally replaced matrix and rock fragments or precipitated as a void-filling cement shortly after the first (significant) stage of leaching.

The major results of early compaction included grain reorientation and collapse of surviving remnants of leached grains. As burial continued, chemical compaction by a solution-reprecipitation process in-

Figure 10. Muddy Formation barrier–island sandstones, as seen in outcrops 26 and 27, New Haven area, Wyoming. For location, see Figure 9.

A. Measured section in outcrop 26: transition sandstones and siltstones (7.8 ft, or 2.4 m), interbedded with gray shale.

B. Measured section in outcrop 27: transition sandstone intercalated with silty and sandy shale (1); lower shoreface with traces of shale drapes, hummocky cross–stratification (HCS), and pebbly layer in upper 1.5 ft. (0.5 m) interbedded with silty shale (2); middle shoreface sandstone, with beds 0.5 and 1.5 ft (0.15 and 0.5 m) thick (3).

C. Close–up of lower shoreface facies from profile in B. Just above contact with transition facies (1) is hummocky cross–stratified layer (arrow) and pebbly layer (arrows at hammer level) indicating high energy events.

D. Three–ft (1 m) diameter, highly calcite–cemented patch (arrow) in lower shoreface sandstone, outcrop 23, about 24 ft (8 m) east of measured profile.

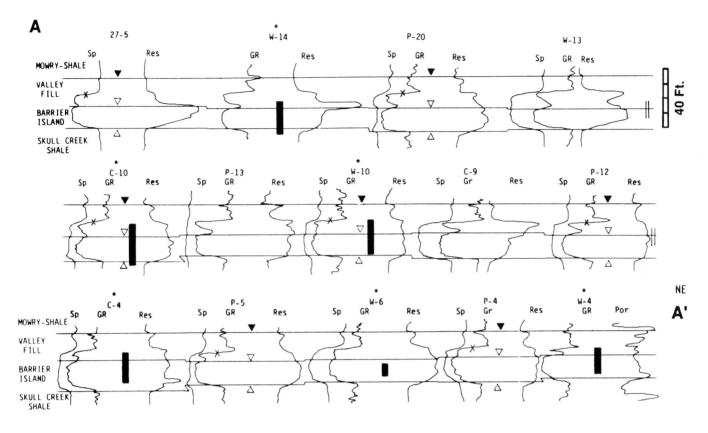

|| break in cross-section
* Core control in these wells.
∆ base of Muddy formation and barrier island unit.
▽ top of barrier island unit.
X top of Muddy sandstones complex (barrier island and valley fill).
▼ top of Muddy formation

█ Core control

Figure 11. **Stratigraphic cross section A–A', oriented in a southwest–northeast direction, parallel to the structural strike of the Muddy Formation. (40 ft = 12 m)**

creased the breadth of grain contacts and the interpenetration of grains to a moderate extent. Grain shape eccentricity was enhanced by compaction, and grain sphericity decreased.

Diagenetic silica occurs as syntaxial overgrowths on relatively few detrital grains. Fine "dust rims" of clay rarely separate the host grains from this authigenic cement. Euhedral overgrowths or those that formed on all sides of detrital grains are rare. The onset of quartz cementation preceded the main phase of clay precipitation. However, because clays are trapped within younger portions of some quartz overgrowths, some clay precipitation was concurrent with later stages of overgrowth formation.

Calcite comprises medium to coarse-crystalline, subhedral to euhedral, poikilotopic cement. Calcite also replaced a small amount of the margins of detrital grains. Calcite cementation postdates compaction; well C–6 at 4,423.5 ft (1,349.2 m) illustrates this by the packing of detrital grains adjacent to calcite, and

by the presence of calcite between bent, splayed-open books of compacted micas. Because clay generally is not present in calcite-cemented pores, the calcite probably preceded the second and most important stage of clay precipitation. Although calcite cement is present only sporadically in the reservoir, where it does occur, it has greatly reduced porosity and permeability.

Late-stage leaching is indicated by four lines of evidence. First, the outer margins of calcite cements are locally corroded. Second, primary pore spaces filled by poikilotopic calcite cement are found surrounding secondary pores that contain remnants of feldspar. Third, compacted siliceous framework grains are present around oversize pores (e.g., well C–8 at 4,370.5 ft, or 1,319.9 m). Fourth, in sandstones with a compacted framework, pseudomatrix and oversize pores are the same size (Plate 1), and both are significantly larger than the other detrital components. Undoubtedly, portions of the pseudomatrix that

Table 1. Dominant features identified in barrier island sandstones, Muddy Formation (Bell Creek cores and New Haven outcrops).

Upper Foreshore   Sandstone, 150–200 μ, swash deposit. Moderately to well sorted. Low angle to subhorizontal stratification. Trace to 5% burrowed (*Skolithos, Corophioides Diplocraterion*). Trace of shale (rip-up clasts) and siltstone. Interruptions in sedimentation (subunits), poorer sorting, more burrowing, and local bio-turbation may indicate backshore deposit.

Lower Foreshore   Sandstone, 125–150 μ, intertidal deposit. Moderately to well sorted. Subhorizontally laminated to low angle troughs. Wavy bedded, not swash laminated. Less than 10% burrowed. Trace of shale laminae.

Washover   Sandstone, 100–175 μ, storm overwash deposit. Poor to fair sorting. Massive or subhorizontally to horizontally laminated planar beds. Possible ripple–form bedding. Typically nonburrowed and clean.

Upper Shoreface   Sandstone, 125–175 μ, fairweather current and/or wave deposit (subtidal). Occurs only rarely. Fair sorting. Cross–bedded or massive appearing, swaly cross–stratification (SCS), wave and current ripples. Hummocky cross–stratification (HCS) absent. Few burrows (*Diplocraterion, Rosellia, Ophiomorpha*). Shaley siltstone up to 25%.

Middle Shoreface   Sandstone, 100–175 μ, wave–dominated deposits at depth into which longshore bars and trough ridges have migrated. Poor to good sorting. Mostly massive due to burrowing (up to 60%) or bioturbation (>75%). Very low relief troughs to subhorizontal lamination. Shale drapes common but discontinuous.

Lower Shoreface   Sandstone, 100–150 μ. Poor sorting. Shale and siltstone 25–60% increasing downward. Low angle to subhorizontal stratification. Hummocky cross–stratification (HCS), rippled. Commonly bioturbated, burrowed 10–90% (*Thallasinoides, Asterosoma, Rosellia, Corophioides*).

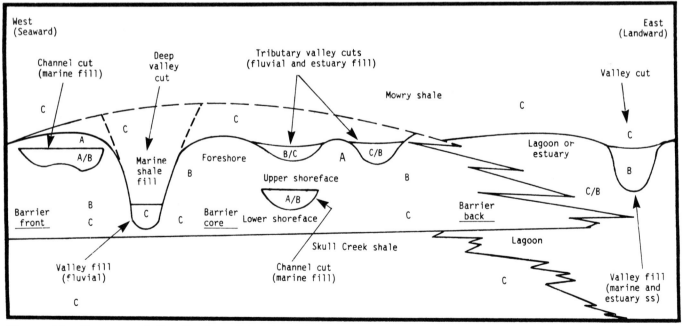

Figure 12. Conceptual distribution of barrier–island and genetically associated non–barrier facies observed in cores at Bell Creek Field. Categories of reservoir quality explained in Table 5. Note varying styles of erosion on top of barrier island.

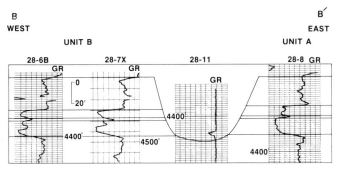

Figure 13. Stratigraphic cross section B–B', showing geometry of deep incision where only 4 ft (1.2 m) of barrier–island or inlet–fill sandstone remain. Thick barrier–island sandstones continue on opposite sides of the erosional cut. Location shown in Figure 1. (20 ft = 6 m)

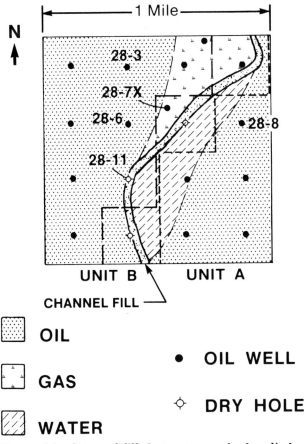

CHANNEL FILL

OIL

GAS

WATER

● OIL WELL

◇ DRY HOLE

Figure 14. Channel fill that acts as a hydraulic barrier, western limit of Unit "A". Note positions of oil, gas, and water contacts on opposite sides of barrier. (1 mi = 1.609 km)

survived compaction subsequently were leached to create the oversized pores.

Clay cement found in the barrier–island sandstone is dominantly kaolinite (Table 3). The secondary, authigenic nature of kaolinite and minor illite cement was established by petrographic and SEM analysis of textures. Clay cement in Unit "A" mostly precipitated after compaction, precipitation of siliceous overgrowths, calcite cementation, and late stage leaching.

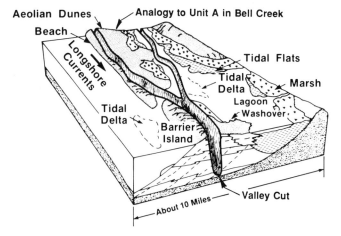

Modified from Reinson, 1984

Figure 15. Model of deep erosional cuts and barrier–island deposits, showing analogies to separate production units in Bell Creek Field.

Kaolinite cement commonly forms 5– to 30–micron–thick coatings on detrital grains. Individual crystals often are oriented perpendicular to the surface of the substrate. Less common pore–filling kaolinite cement is microporous, monomineralic, and consists of coarsely crystalline masses. Kaolinite and illite vary in abundance throughout the TIP area from 0% to more than 15%.

Distribution of Clay

Most of the clay in the middle and upper–shoreface and foreshore facies of the barrier–island complex appears to be diagenetic. The distribution of these diagenetic clays (Fig. 16) is controlled in part by faulting that may have provided pathways for diagenetic fluids; in the unfaulted eastern portion of the TIP area, diagenetic clay is less abundant. Clay abundance also relates to both average horizontal air permeability and to residual oil saturation obtained from routine core analysis (Honarpour et al., 1988).

Oil Migration and Entrapment

The presence of oil in microporosity between diagenetic clay particles indicates that it was the last phase to enter the reservoir rock. The water remaining after oil entrapment in the reservoir was only sufficient for diagenesis to continue at greatly reduced rates (Feazel and Schatzinger, 1985).

PETROPHYSICAL PROPERTIES

Facies from Bell Creek cores can be grouped into three classes according to decreasing turbulence of the depositional environment, and reservoir quality (Table 5). Class "A" sediments, where not severely affected by diagenesis, have the best reservoir properties and have permeabilities in the range of hundreds to thousands of millidarcies. In contrast, class "B" deposits have permeabilities that rarely exceed hundreds of millidarcies. Nonproductive sediments of class "C" usually have permeabilities ranging from near zero to tens of millidarcies.

Table 2. Sedimentologic division of typical valley fill sandstones associated with barrier island deposits, Muddy Formation—dominant features identified in Bell Creek cores and New Haven outcrops.

Continental

Fluvial Channel Fill (High Energy)
Sandstone, 100–200 μ, alluvial deposit. Fair to moderately well sorted. Abundant troughs, horizontally or subhorizontally laminated in thin sets; massive appearing where thoroughly rooted, sometimes recognizably rooted or burrowed; 5–10% current ripples associated with shale. Carbonaceous (5%). Trace of shale as rip–up clasts or drapes on ripples. Lower boundaries erosional and abrupt.

Brackish Marine

Sandy Estuary Open Lagoon
Sandstone, 75–125 μ interlaminated with siltstone (30%) and shale (30%). Carbonaceous (15%). Very poorly sorted. Massive appearing or horizontally to subhorizontally very finely laminated; subordinate wavy bedding; low amplitude current ripples; common soft sediment deformation. Burrowed (5–50%); locally thoroughly bioturbated or rooted.

Tidal Channel and Delta
Sandstone, 150–175 μ, current deposit. Poorly sorted. Cross–bedded or low–relief planar tabular laminations. Poorly burrowed (*Skolithos*).

Table 3. Quantitative XRD determination of mineralogy for subsurface samples from Bell Creek Field and a nearby outcrop.

Well	Depth (ft)	Depositional Setting	Q	F	C	D	A	B	P	K	I	Sm	I/S	Si
Subsurface														
C–8	4351	Lagoon	76	3	–	4	–	–	–	7	8	tr	–	2
27–16	4303.3	Washover	88	2	tr	tr	–	–	–	6	4	–	tr	tr
W–14	4309.3	U/L/Shoreface	89	3	tr	tr	–	–	tr	5	3	tr	–	–
27–14	4309.5	U. Shoreface/foreshore	94	tr	tr	tr	–	–	–	4	2	tr	–	–
27–14	4331.5	U. Shoreface/foreshore	90	2	–	2	–	–	tr	4	2	tr	1	–
W–16	4308.6	Foreshore	91	2	1	1	–	tr	–	3	2	1	–	–
W–16	4318	U. Shoreface	88	2	1	1	–	tr	–	5	3	tr	–	–
W–7	4405.5	Estuarine	88	4	–	tr	–	–	–	2	tr	6	–	–
W–7	4410.0	Estuarine	79	4	–	–	–	–	–	2	tr	15	–	–
W–7	4417.5	Swamp	92	3	–	–	–	–	–	3	tr	2	–	–
W–7	4418.9	Alluvial channel	96	1	–	–	–	–	–	3	tr	tr	–	–
W–7	4419.5	U. Shoreface	94	2	–	–	–	–	–	2	2	tr	–	–
W–7	4431.3	U. Shoreface	91	3	–	–	–	2	–	2	2	tr	–	–
Outcrop (Green Mountain)														
GM	0	Fluvial channel ss	93	2	–	tr	1	–	–	3	1	tr		
GM	10	Fluvial channel ss	97	tr	–	–	–	–	–	2	tr	1		
GM	52	Continental slts.	96	tr	–	tr	tr	–	–	2	tr	2		
GM	65	Fluvial ss	97	tr	–	tr	tr	–	–	1	tr	22		

Q = Quartz	D = Dolomite	P = Pyrite	Sm = Smectite
F = Feldspar	A = Anhydrite	K = Kaolinite	I/S = Ill./Smectite
C = Calcite	B = Barite	I = Illite	Si = Siderite

Table 4. Comparison of stratigraphic thicknesses along cross–section A–A' based on interpretation of gamma ray, SP, and resistivity logs and available cores (in feet).

	Well No.	Barrier–Island Sandstone	Valley–Fill Sandstone	Total Valley Fill	Total Muddy Formation
SW	27.5	17.5	9.0	25.0	42.5
	W–14[1]	18.0	10.0	25.5	43.5
	P–20	20.0	8.0	25.5	45.5
	W–13	18.0	10.0	28.0	46.0
	C–10[1]	20.0	11.0	29.0	49.0
	P–13	20.5	7.0	25.0	45.5
	W–10[1]	21.0	10.0	24.0	45.0
	C–9	20.0	7.0	24.0	44.0
	P–12	19.5	6.0	25.0	44.5
	C–4[1]	21.0	5.5	26.0	47.0
	W–9	20.5	7.5	24.0	44.5
	P–5	21.0	7.5	21.5	43.5
	W–6[1]	20.0	9.5	23.0	43.0
	C–3	22.0	5.0	20.0	44.0
	P–4	21.5	5.5	22.0	43.5
NE	W–4[1]	21.0	4.0	21.5	42.5

[1]Core control on these wells.

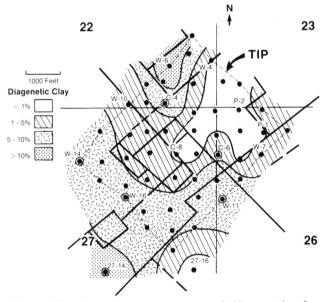

Figure 16. Average percentages of diagenetic clay in middle and upper shoreface and foreshore facies in barrier–island strata. Thin sections were available from numbered wells. Circled wells have values greater than 10% authigenic clay. (1,000 ft = 305 m). Percentages of total clay (not illustrated) display very similar patterns.

Table 5. Classification of productive and non-productive facies of Muddy Formation sediments in Bell Creek reservoir. B = barrier island deposit. NB = non–barrier island deposit

Class		Facies		
A	PRODUCTIVE	<u>Foreshore</u>[1]	(Upper/Lower)	– B
		Aeolian		– B
		Aeolian Flat		– B
		<u>Upper Shoreface</u>		– B
		<u>Middle Shoreface</u>		– B
		<u>Washover</u>	(Tail & Core)	– B
		Channel Cut Fill	(High Energy)	– NB
		Marine Valley Fill	(High Energy)	– NB
B		<u>Lower Shoreface</u>		– B
		Washover		– B
		Marine Valley Fill	(Low Energy)	– NB
		Channel Cut Fill	(Low Energy)	– NB
		Alluvial Valley Fill	(High Energy)	– NB
		<u>Estuary Fill</u>		– NB
		Windblown Sand in Lagoon		– NB
C	NON-PRODUCTIVE	<u>Lagoon Fill</u>		– NB
		Alluvial Valley Fill	(Low Energy)	– NB
		Swamp & Marsh		– NB
		Marine Transition to the Barrier		– NB

[1]Dominant facies are underlined.

The lateral extent and continuity of these facies classes can be predicted by analogy to modern depositional models. In the TIP area, class "B" and class "C" facies are significantly thinner than are class "A" facies. The central portion of barrier–island deposits has better reservoir potential than the back barrier, where thinner sandstones are intercalated with non-productive members of adjacent depositional environments. Thus, oil productivity should be directly pro-portional to the total thickness of barrier–island deposits because class "A" and high energy class "B" rocks predominate. Barrier–island deposits may be underlain by class "C" Skull Creek Shale or lagoonal siltstone. Barrier–island deposits are locally unconformably overlain by class "B" and "C" continental brackish and shallow marine valley–fill or by class "B" marine deposits.

Net pay in Unit "A" was determined from porosity, permeability, wireline logs, and from detailed core descriptions. Arbitrary "cutoff" values of 50 md and 5% oil saturation were used. Zones with permeability lower than 50 md do not contribute significantly to total fluid conductivity.

Net pay up to 26 ft (7.9 m) thick is present in the area where the barrier island is thickest. Thicknesses of both barrier sandstones and net pay decrease eastward, toward the lagoonal side of the barrier (Fig. 17). Average core porosities and permeabilities of sandstones also reflect the distribution of barrier-island deposits (Figs. 18 and 19).

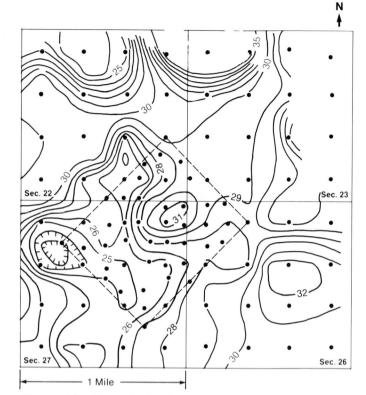

Figure 18. Core-derived average percentage porosity in barrier-island and valley-fill deposits. Contour interval is 1%. Areas of high porosity coincide with presence of thicker and cleaner foreshore facies. (1 mi = 1.61 km)

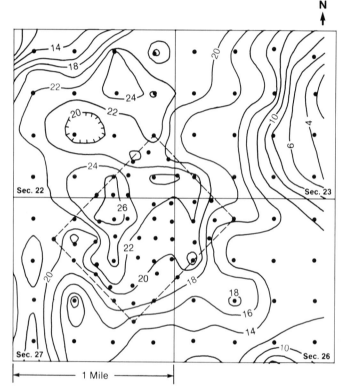

Figure 17. Net pay map of Muddy Formation, Unit "A" of Bell Creek Field. Contour interval is 2 ft (0.6 m). TIP area outlined by dashed line. (1 mi = 1.61 km)

In Bell Creek Field, a trend exists between air permeability and porosity for all facies (Fig. 20, Table 6). Reservoir and outcrop samples show parallel but offset trends in permeability/porosity data from barrier-island subfacies (Fig. 21), suggesting that subaerial exposure of the outcrops did not significantly alter the petrophysical properties of those rocks. There is, however, a significant difference in permeability/porosity ranges between lower shoreface and higher energy barrier-island facies.

Comparison of petrographic data with permeabilities suggests that authigenic clay content and compaction locally may be the dominant control on permeability, and that the variations in permeability may not necessarily reflect depositional facies. This is illustrated by data from wells C-1 and W-16, located

less than 1 mi (1.6 km) apart. Reservoir sandstones in well W-16 are highly clay-cemented and have 80% less permeability than analogous "clean" (non-cemented) sandstones in well C-1. However, porosity contrasts are significantly less than 80%; the more clay-filled rocks display porosities 18% less in foreshore and 10% less in washover sandstones.

Structural cross-section C-C' (Fig. 5) across the central part of the TIP area reveals the distribution of depositional, diagenetic and structural factors which govern the distribution of flow units. A flow unit is here defined as a section of reservoir rock with a transmissivity coefficient (kh) that is significantly different from the kh of adjoining intervals. The continuity of flow units on cross-section C-C' is actually less than would be expected from the stratigraphic distribution of barrier-island and valley-fill facies alone, because of diagenetic and tectonic factors. On the periphery of barrier islands, a subdivision of flow units results in interfingering with less permeable facies.

A low ratio of vertical to horizontal permeability (0.3-0.6) is characteristic of valley-fill deposits (Fig. 22). Barrier-island sandstones have a ratio of about 0.7 for upper and middle shoreface and about 1.0 for foreshore facies. These numbers indicate restriction of vertical fluid flow by valley-fill deposits.

Because of the similar log characteristics and comparable horizontal permeability values, the upper

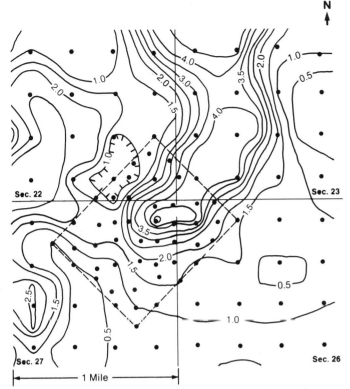

Figure 19. Arithmetic averages of horizontal air permeabilities measured on core samples of barrier-island and valley-fill deposits. Contour interval is 0.5 darcy. Areas of high permeability coincide with presence of thicker and cleaner foreshore facies. (1 mi = 1.61 km)

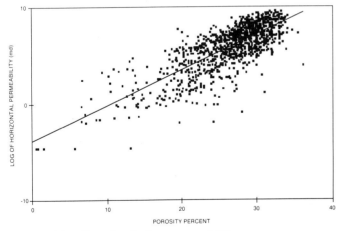

Figure 20. Graph of air permeability versus porosity. Both barrier-island and valley-fill deposits are present but not differentiated.

shoreface and foreshore barrier-island facies have been characterized as one flow unit. However, the kv/kh ratio in well 26-7 indicates significant differences in flow potential between these facies. Also, portions of the barrier island immediately underlying the unconformity at the base of the valley fill are strongly affected by diagenetic processes, at least locally.

Samples with a large permeability range (20 to 4,500 md) show little sensitivity to brine or distilled water (Honapour et al., 1988). This is because expandable clay generally is absent from the barrier-island sandstones.

A good correlation has been found between air permeability and irreducible water saturation from air-brine drainage capillary pressure curves at 100 psi displacement pressure (Fig. 23). As the air permeability of the samples increases, the irreducible water saturation decreases.

GEOLOGICAL HETEROGENEITIES IN THE MUDDY FORMATION

An attempt was made to scale depositional, diagenetic, and tectonic heterogeneities of the Muddy Formation in the Unit "A" TIP area (Table 7). The large scale heterogeneities are depositional and fluid-related, and include facies changes, valley erosion and infilling, and sandstone-shale boundaries. Intermediate scale heterogeneities relate mostly to distribution of detrital and authigenic clays, high-permeability channels, and faults. For instance, faulting and clay cementation in the southwestern portion of TIP area created the most unfavorable conditions for oil recovery (Honarpour et al., 1988). In this area, volumetric sweep efficiency was low and residual saturation was high after 10 years of waterflooding. The effects of these heterogeneities combine with the effects of large scale heterogeneities to control EOR patterns and govern reservoir performance.

The most influential small scale heterogeneities include effects of leaching, grain compaction, and local cementation. These diagenetic phenomena generally divert the direction of fluid flow rather than provide flow barriers.

Predictability of heterogeneities varies. Depositional trends are most predictable in interwell areas where the facies are confidently identified in cored wells. Knowledge of depositional trends enables spatial interpretation of unit thickness and rock textures affecting porosity and permeability. Least predictable are erosional, fault, and diagenetic features which govern net pay, disturb continuity of depositional flow units, and may strongly affect their local transmissivity. Further improvement of predictability at the field and interwell scale could be obtained by reconstruction of crucial stages in reservoir history. This will lead to better understanding of resulting processes and distribution of their products during burial history, changing hydrodynamic conditions, hydrogeochemical alteration, and tectonic development.

PRODUCTION CHARACTERISTICS

Primary Production

Production has been obtained both from upper Muddy sandstones (in most cases valley-fill deposits) and from barrier-island sandstones. It is estimated that about one eighth of the total production is from the upper sandstone (Gary-Williams, 1982).

Primary reserves calculated for wells in Sections 22, 23, 26, and 27 in Unit "A" vary from 70,000 to 500,000 STBO (Sharma et al., 1987). Primary reserves were calculated from decline curves of all the

Table 6. Relation of porosity and permeablity to modal grain size and sorting for individual facies in well W-16. Muddy formation, Bell Creek Field, Unit "A," TIP area.

UNIT NUMBER	ENVIRONMENT OF DEPOSITION	$\bar{K}$(md)	$\bar{K}$(md) "NON-CEMENTED" ONLY	$\bar{\phi}$(%)	MODAL GRAIN SIZE (μ)	SORTING
6	"LAGOON"	247	—	18	60	POOR
5	SUBTIDAL SANDSTONE	507	—	26	150	FAIR
4	BACKBARRIER WASHOVER	1189	—	27	150	POOR
3	FORESHORE (BEACH)	746	823	24	175	FAIR TO MODERATE
2	MIDDLE SHOREFACE	182	494	20	100	POOR
1	BACKBARRIER WASHOVER	1070	—	28	125	FAIR

producing wells, extrapolated to 1 STBO/D. The decline rate was exponential at 0.1/month. The region of greatest primary reserves is elongated and parallel to the depositional strike of the barrier island. Regions of high cumulative primary production (180-210,000 STBO) correspond to regions with highest average porosity and permeability (Gary-Williams, 1982). Wells near the eastern extremity of Unit "A" have lower reserves (less than 100,000 BO) because net pay, porosity, and permeability all decrease toward the lagoon. Thus, the internal stratigraphy and geometry of the barrier-island and associated facies are the dominant geological aspects that influenced cumulative primary performance in the TIP area. However, diagenetic effects (mainly clay cementation) also influence the overall production performance. The influence of structural factors is low or negligible.

Secondary Production

Unlike primary production, secondary production was highly influenced by the structural dip of the reservoir. Water injected into the western part of Unit "A" through January 1981 advanced at rates of 0 to 14 ft/day (0 to 4.3 m/D) in a northwest to southeast direction (Honarpour et al., 1988). Wells located updip of the water-injection line-drive pattern showed greater cumulative production toward the south and east. Locally, as observed in Sections 23 and 27, faulting has some detectable influence on the directions of water advancement. In Section 23, the front movements were rapid; during several years, a significant amount of water moved south following the high permeability trend.

Diagenesis greatly reduced reservoir quality in barrier-island sandstones in the southwestern corner of the TIP area. This effect was magnified by the downdip position of wells in this region, resulting in

lower than expected secondary production. A similar diagenetic effect, combined with significant removal of barrier facies by a valley erosion, occurred southeast of the TIP area. However, the productivity of this area was greatly enhanced by its updip structural position.

Tertiary Production

Primary and secondary production is expected to recover 55% of OOIP in Unit "A", leaving more than 55,000,000 BO as a tertiary target. A combination of 20-acre (8 ha) infill drilling and five-spot pattern has been estimated as being capable of recovering 16% of the remaining OIP after line-drive waterflooding. The 20-acre spacing overcomes some of the intermediate scale geological heterogeneities between wells in areas where substantial stratification exists and allows mobilization of some of the trapped oil.

A micellar-polymer flood was initiated under the DOE tertiary incentive project (TIP) in February, 1981, and encompassed 179 ac (71 ha) in the central part of the barrier-island complex. Until mid-1987, the TIP micellar-polymer flood appeared to be most effective in areas where reservoir quality was superior and geological heterogeneities were absent, or where the presence of the heterogeneities such as faulting favored EOR recovery (Fig. 24). High levels of production were obtained from wells such as P1 and P8 because of their upthrown structural positions. However, in highly heterogeneous areas, infill drilling and pattern waterflooding were most effective in recovery of trapped oil.

CONCLUSIONS

Our detailed sedimentological analysis of available cores confirms earlier observations that the Muddy Formation in Unit "A" is composed of barrier-island

Table 7. Summary of reservoir heterogeneities in cores and fluid samples from Unit "A" of Bell Creek Field. Muddy Formation (barrier island and valley fill).

			SCALE[1]
A.	**DEPOSITIONAL HETEROGENEITIES**		
	(1)	Laterally changing facies patterns:	L/M
		– within one complete barrier sedimentary cycle	L
		– between stacked incomplete sedimentary barrier–cycles	M
	(2)	Variation in petrophysical (log) properties and net pay caused by:	M
		– distribution of sedimentary structures (bedding types, bioturbation, clay laminations)	M/S
		– variation of grain size and sorting	L/M
		– variation of detrital clay content and type	L/M
		– variation of sandstone mineralogy	M
		– position of sand–shale boundaries	L
	(3)	Modification of reservoir geometry and net pay by erosion of barrier island deposits:	L
		– variation in depths of cuts	M
		– variation widths of cuts	L/M
		– variation in petrophysical properties of infills (sandstones, siltstones, and shales)	M
B.	**DIAGENETIC HETEROGENEITIES**		
	(4)	Distribution of diagenetic clays:	M
		– kaolinite "cement" dominant	M/S
		– coatings on framework grains and blocking pore throats	M
		– amplified by compaction	S
		– control of ϕ and k in barrier sandstone	L/M
	(5)	Under–compacted zones:	S/M
		– process poorly understood; diagenetic origin explains 1–2 foot thick intervals with as much as 11,000 md permeability; lateral extent not yet documented	U
		– can reverse expected ϕ and k trends	S
	(6)	Non–clay cementation	S/M
		– thin calcite-cemented zones provide local and interwell blockage of fluid flow	S/M
		– dolomite, quartz overgrowths create local hindrances to fluid flow	S
C.	**STRUCTURAL (TECTONIC) HETEROGENEITIES**		
	(7)	Influence of faulting offset along faults causes decreases or cessation of fluid flow between wells	U/M
		– different vertical displacement and tilting of tectonic blocks	M
		– decrease in offset of faults over a short distance	M/S
		– fault–related fracturing of Muddy reservoir	U
D.	**FLUID HETEROGENEITIES**		
	(8)	Lateral changes in oil gravity	L
	(9)	Variable wettability	U
	(10)	Variable characteristics of formation fluids	L
	(11)	Variable reservoir pressure	L
	(12)	Position of water/oil and oil/gas contacts	L/M

[1]L – Large scale, affect large areas of field or productive unit (in miles).
M – Medium scale, affect predominately the interwell areas among a group of wells (hundreds to thousands of feet).
S – Small scale, affecting local fluid flow pattern in interwell area (in feet or tens of feet).
U – Unknown scale, to date.

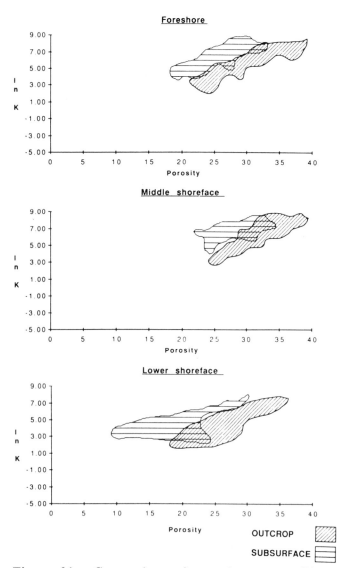

Figure 21. Comparison of porosity-permeability relationships in core versus outcrop samples. Note higher porosities of outcrop samples.

and valley-fill deposits. At least 18 barrier and valley-fill facies were identified in the 26 cores studied. Stratigraphic compensation between those two environments of deposition is a primary factor defining productivity potential of the Muddy.

If the Bell Creek barrier islands were deposited on a tectonic "high" as suggested by Forgotson and Stark (1971) and by Weimer et al., (1988), then independent periods of valley erosion and fill would be possible. In the Bell Creek area, we postulate one such event predating, and one postdating, deposition of the barrier islands and associated sediments. Many recent analogues are observed along the Texas Gulf Coast and elsewhere; multiple encisements should be considered normal for this type of nearshore sandstone deposit.

Hydrocarbon production from the Muddy Formation in Unit "A" of Bell Creek Field is controlled by at least five geological factors, including; stratigraphic

relation of the barrier-island sandstone to the valley-fill deposits; development and architecture of the barrier-island facies in one or more sedimentary cycles; depth, width, and infilling of erosional cuts; distribution, type, and degree of diagenesis (clay filling, compaction); and local faulting. Lateral changes of facies in the barrier-island suite define continuity of fluid-flow units unless disruptions resulting from faults or diagenetic facies occur. Internal subdivision of flow units is controlled by depositional and diagenetic layering, and offset by faults.

Two major diagenetic effects are recognized in reservoir-quality sandstone. First, strong leaching occurred very early in the diagenetic sequence and significantly increased porosity. Early and late stage leaching removed less stable components, such as feldspar and sedimentary rock fragments. The effect of all other diagenesis was to reduce porosity and permeability. Second, the distribution and magnitude of late stage clay cementation in the barrier-island sandstone is the most crucial limiting diagenetic factor relative to fluid flow paths and ultimately to well performance.

Superior reservoir properties were documented for shoreface, foreshore, and washover sandstones. Storage capacity and flow capacity tend to decrease toward the back-barrier side of the buildup, but are highly variable within the barrier. Better petrophysical properties and reservoir quality have been found in the central part of the barrier island rather than in distal parts, where thinner sandstones intercalate with non-productive depositional environments. Average porosities and permeabilities depend largely on clay distribution in the TIP and surrounding areas. Permeability trends reflect the strike of the barrier in the study area, and depend on position in the barrier. Restrictions in vertical flow of fluids are created by valley-fill deposits.

Based on data from Unit "A", primary production was most strongly influenced by depositional heterogeneities and less so by diagenetic heterogeneities. Secondary production was affected most by structural dip and distribution of diagenetic heterogeneities. Tertiary production was more influenced by depositional and diagenetic heterogeneities as well as by faulting. Predictability of geological features in the interwell area is high for depositional and textural trends, and low for erosional, diagenetic, and fault-related features.

The greatest tertiary recovery occurred in areas of: 1) favorable development of barrier-island sandstone; 2) negligible diagenetic effects; 3) good sedimentary and structural continuity; and 4) well patterns which allow balanced sweep by the four chemical injectors surrounding a producing well. Only one well in the TIP area fulfilled all of those requirements, well P-6. This well had an exceptionally good tertiary oil recovery (1,800,000 BO).

ACKNOWLEDGMENTS

This work was performed for the U.S. Department of Energy under Cooperative Agreement DE-FC22-83FE60149. Special thanks are due to John Nikonchik from Gary-Williams Oil Producers Inc. for providing laboratory and field data. The authors also

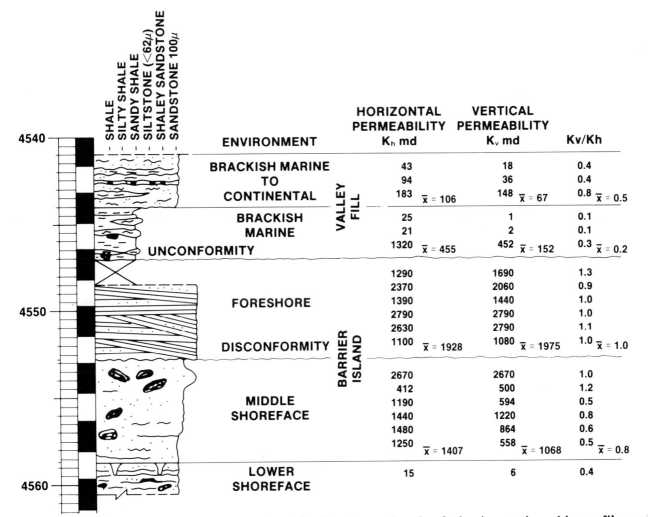

Figure 22. Petrophysical properties of barrier-island and non-barrier facies in stratigraphic profile, well 26-7.

thank E.B. Nuckols of the DOE Bartlesville Project Office for his guidance. Special thanks are given to Susan Jackson, Liviu Tomutsa, Bijon Sharma, and Guy deVerges of NIPER for their assistance in data gathering, data analysis, and illustrating the results. Our appreciation to Paul Stapp, Aaron Cheng, and Bill Linville, also of NIPER, for their valuable suggestions. Thanks are also due to Mrs. Edna Hatcher for typing the manuscript. Authors also wish to thank NIPER management, especially Herbert B. Carroll, Jr. for their encouragement and support.

REFERENCES

Almon, W.R. and D.K. Davies, 1979, Regional diagenetic trends in the Lower Cretaceous Muddy sandstone, Powder River Basin, *in* P.A. Scholle, and P.R. Schluger, eds., Aspects of Diagenesis: SEPM Spec. Pub. 26, p. 379–400.

Berg, R.R., and D.K. Davies, 1968, Origin of Lower Cretaceous Muddy sandstone at Bell Creek Field, Montana: AAPG Bull., v. p. 1888-98.

Burt, R.A., F.A. Haddenhorst, and J.C. Hartford, 1975, Review of Bell Creek waterflood performance—Powder River County, Montana: SPE-AIME Paper SPE 5670, Ann. Tech. Conf. and Exhib., Dallas (Sept. 28-Oct. 1).

Demerest, G.M., and G.C. Kraft, 1987, Stratigraphic record of Quaternary sea-levels; implications for more ancient strata, *in* D. Nummedal, O.H. Pilkey, and G.D. Hovard, eds., SEPM Spec. Pub. 41, p. 223-240.

Feazel, C.T., and R.A. Schatzinger, 1985, Prevention of carbonate cementation in petroleum reservoirs, *in* N. Schneiderman and P.M. Harris, eds., Carbonate Cements: SEPM Spec. Pub. 36, p. 97-106.

Forgotson, J.M. Jr., and P.H. Stark, 1971, Well data files and the computer a case history from Northern Rocky Mountain: AAPG Bull., v. 56, p. 1114-1217.

Gary-Williams Oil Producers Inc., 1982, Bell Creek field micellar-polymer pilot demonstration: Final Report, June 1976-March 1982, contract no. DOE/SF/01802-61, U.S. DOE.

Hartshorne, J.M., and S.J. Nikonchik, 1984, Micellar polymer flood success in Bell Creek Field: SPE-AIME Ann. Tech. Conf. and Exhib. (Houston), Paper SPE 13122.

Honarpour, M.M., 1988, Refined engineering model of Unit "A", Bell Creek Field, Montana; A barrier island deposystem: Topical Report, NIPER-343, p. 1-49.

Honarpour, M.M., M. Szpakiewicz, R.A. Schatzinger, L. Tomutsa, H.B. Carroll, Jr., and R. Tillman, 1988, Integrated geological/engineering model of barrier island deposits in Bell Creek Field, Montana: SPE/DOE Enhanced Oil Recovery Symposium (Tulsa), SPE/DOE Paper 17366.

McGregor, A.A., and C.A. Biggs, 1969, Bell Creek Field, Montana: A rich stratigraphic trap: AAPG Bull., v. 52, p. 1869-1887.

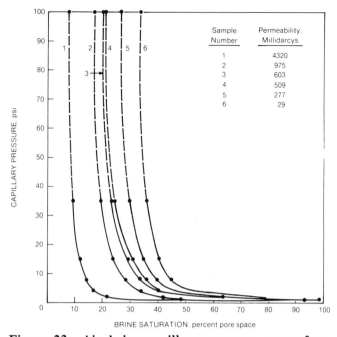

Figure 23. Air–brine capillary pressure curves for six samples from well 22–9, illustrating direct relationship between irreducible water saturation and air permeability.

Michael, C.R., and E.S. Merin, 1986, Tectonic framework of Powder River Basin, Wyoming and Montana from Landsat imagery: AAPG Bull., v. 70, p. 453–455.

Reinson, G.E., 1984, Barrier island and associated strand plain system, in R.G. Walker, ed., Facies Models: Geoscience Canada, Reprints Series, No. 1., p. 119–140.

Sharma, B., M. Szpakiewicz, M.M. Honarpour, R. Schatzinger, and R. Tillman, 1987, Critical heterogeneities in a barrier island deposit and their influence on primary, waterflood, and chemical EOR operations: SPE-AIME Ann. Tech. Conf. and Exhib. (Dallas), SPE paper 16749.

Slack, P.B., 1981, Paleotectonics and hydrocarbon accumulation, Powder River Basin, Wyoming: AAPG Bull., v. 65, p. 730–743.

Stone, W.D., 1972, Stratigraphy and exploration of the Lower Cretaceous Muddy Formation, northern Powder River Basin, Wyoming and Montana: The Mountain Geologist, v. 9, p. 355–378.

Szpakiewicz, M., K. McGee, and B. Sharma, 1987, Geological problems related to characterization of clastic reservoirs for enhanced oil recovery: presented at 5th SPE/DOE Symposium on EOR (Tulsa), 1986, SPE/DOE paper 14888, and SPE Formation Evaluation, Dec. 1987, p. 449–460.

Szpakiewicz, M., R. Tillman, S. Jackson, and G. deVerges, 1988, Sedimentologic description of barrier island and related deposits in the Bell Creek cores, Montana and analogous outcrops near New Haven, Wyoming: NIPER open file. Available from the authors.

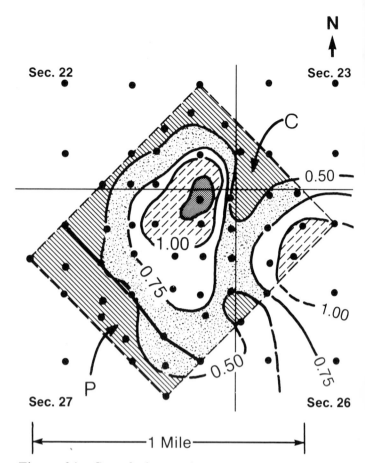

Figure 24. Cumulative tertiary oil production, December 1980 to mid–1987, TIP area, Unit "A" of Bell Creek Field. "C" indicates location of micellar-polymer floods. "P" indicates the location of pattern waterfloods. (1 mi = 1.61 km)

Vargo, J.J., 1978, Site selection, reservoir definition and estimation of tertiary target oil for the Bell Creek unit, a micellar-polymer project: Paper SPE 7071 presented at the SPE Symposium on Improved Methods for Oil Recovery, Tulsa, April 16–19.

Weimer, R.J., 1981, New age interpretation of Bell Creek sandstone, Powder River Basin, Montana and Wyoming: AAPG Bull., v. 69, p. 870.

Weimer, R.J., J.J. Emme, C.L. Farmer, L.O. Anna, T.L. Davis, and R.L. Kidney, 1982, Tectonic influence on sedimentation, Early Cretaceous, East flank Powder River Basin, Wyoming and South Dakota: CSM Quarterly, v. 77, 61 p.

Weimer, R.J., C.A. Rebne, and T.L. Davis, 1988, Geologic and seismic models, Muddy sandstone, Lower Cretaceous, Bell Creek – Rocky Point area, Powder River Basin, Montana and Wyoming [abs.]: AAPG Bull., v. 72, p. 883–884.

Zoback, M.L., and M. Zoback, 1980, State of stress in the coterminous United States: Jour. Geophy. Res., v. 85, p. 6113–6156.

Influence of Depositional Environment and Diagenesis on Regional Porosity Trends in the Lower Cretaceous "J" Sandstone, Denver Basin, Colorado[1]

DEBRA K. HIGLEY[2]

JAMES W. SCHMOKER[2]

[1]Received September 26, 1988; Revised March 9, 1989.
[2]U.S. Geological Survey, Denver Federal Center, Denver, Colorado.

Regional distribution of median core porosity in the Lower Cretaceous "J" Sandstone was mapped and compared to median core permeability, present depth, and thermal maturity in 135 widely distributed Denver Basin drillholes. "J" Sandstone porosity relationships were detailed for drillholes in Wattenberg and Kachina fields.

Median core porosity in the "J" Sandstone decreases from 24% at depths of about 4,000 ft (1,220 m) to 7 to 10% at depths of 9,000 ft (2,740 m). This decrease in porosity is exponential with increasing depth of burial, and a power function of increasing thermal maturity. The correlation coefficient between porosity and thermal maturity is −0.88, a closer fit than the porosity–depth correlation of −0.79; thermal maturity reflects the effects of increased pressure and temperature due to burial, as well as local heat–flow variations. Permeability is a rough logarithmic function of porosity.

The influence of depositional environment on porosity distribution is suggested by: 1) higher median porosities in channel sandstones than in other sandstone lithofacies; 2) vertical trends in sediment textures and inferred depositional energy in marine and nonmarine sandstones that relate to porosity; and 3) an area of high porosity in the eastern third of the basin that corresponds to a major incised drainage system and valley–fill sandstone sequence.

Diagenesis of "J" Sandstone reservoirs is reported for drillholes in two Denver Basin fields. Wattenberg Field, which straddles the axis of the basin, produces gas from low porosity and permeability delta–front sandstone in which hydrocarbons are trapped by depositional and diagenetic processes. Kachina Field, located on the eastern flank, produces oil from highly porous and permeable distributary–channel sandstone in which primary porosity was enhanced by dissolution of lithic grains and quartz cement; hydrocarbons are trapped by structure, hydro–dynamics, and overlying mudstone.

INTRODUCTION

The Denver Basin of Colorado, Kansas, Nebraska, and Wyoming is a structural basin with a gently dipping eastern flank and a steeply dipping western flank (Fig. 1). The two deepest parts of this 60,000 mi^2 (155,400 km^2) basin are located near Denver, Colorado and Cheyenne, Wyoming. The structural axis lies on a line connecting these two cities.

The informal economic unit known as the "J" Sandstone is part of the Lower Cretaceous Dakota Group (Fig. 2). This sandstone is present beneath the entire eastern flank of the basin. Outcropping Muddy ("J") Sandstone units are well exposed near the Front Range, along most of the section from southwest of Denver to Wyoming.

The "J" Sandstone consists of sandstone, siltstone, and shale of nearshore–marine, deltaic, and valley–fill origin (Haun, 1963; MacKenzie, 1965, 1971; Matuszczak, 1973; Clark, 1978; Land and Weimer, 1978; Weimer, et al., 1986). Muddy ("J") Sandstone nomenclature (Fig. 2) includes subdivision into the Fort Collins and Horsetooth Members of MacKenzie (1971). "J" Sandstone will be used herein as a general term which includes the Muddy Sandstone and its members.

Approximately 90% of the 800,000,000 BO and 1.2 TCFG produced from the Denver Basin has been

REGIONAL DATA:

Producing Interval:	Muddy ("J") Sandstone of Dakota Group
Present Tectonic Setting:	Denver Basin of Colorado, Nebraska, and Wyoming
Depositional Setting:	Eastern shelf of Cretaceous seaway
Age of Reservoir:	Lower Cretaceous (Albian)
Depositional Environments:	Nearshore–marine, deltaic, and valley–fill
Nature of Traps:	Primarily stratigraphic; influenced by paleostructures, hydrodynamics, and unconformities
Source Rock:	Marine shale of Cretaceous Skull Creek, Mowry, Graneros, Carlile, and Pierre Formations, and Cretaceous Greenhorn Limestone
Timing of Hydrocarbon Migration:	Late Cretaceous to Tertiary

FIELD DATA[1]**:** Wattenberg Field

Discovered:	1970
Geographic Location:	T1N R67W, Weld County, Colorado
Reservoir:	Fort Collins and Horsetooth Members of "J" Sandstone
Nature of Trap:	Stratigraphic
Lithology of Reservoirs:	Fort Collins – very fine–grained, moderately sorted, quartz arenite and sub-litharenite
Depositional Environments:	Mainly delta front and nearshore marine (Fort Collins), with valley–fill (Horsetooth)
Diagenesis:	Compaction, chlorite rims, quartz overgrowths, calcite cementation and contemporaneous dissolution of feldspar and lithic fragments, calcite dissolution, illite–smectite, late fracturing (Weimer, et al., 1986)
Porosity Types:	Intergranular with minor matrix microporosity and secondary dissolution porosity (Weimer, et al., 1986)
Porosity:	8–12%
Permeability:	0.05–0.005 md
Water Saturation:	Average 44%
Temperature:	Average 260°F (112°C)
Drive Type:	Gas expansion
Reservoir Depth:	Average 7,600 ft (2,316 m)
Reservoir Thickness:	Average 20 ft (6 m)
Areal Extent:	627,000 acres (253,700 ha)
IP:	100–3,600 MCFGPD
Cumulative Production (1/89):	15,500,000 BO, 566.2 BCFG
Approximate Ultimate Recovery:	0.9–1.2 TCFG

FIELD DATA[1]**:** Kachina Field

Discovered:	1974
Geographic Location:	T3S R52W, Washington County, Colorado
Reservoir:	"J" Sandstone
Nature of Trap:	Combination structural and stratigraphic
Lithology of Reservoir:	Fine to medium–grained, poorly– to moderately–sorted quartz arenite
Depositional Environments:	Nearshore–marine and deltaic; distributary–channels
Diagenesis:	Compaction, quartz and feldspar overgrowths, calcite cementation and contemporaneous dissolution of feldspar and lithic fragments, calcite dissolution, illite–smectite and other matrix clays, and kaolinite
Porosity Types:	Intergranular with minor to extensive dissolution porosity and minor microporosity
Porosity:	16–28%
Permeability:	19–1,520 md
Temperature:	128°F (39°C)
Drive Type:	Edge water
Oil Gravity:	22° API
Reservoir Depth:	Average 4,284 ft (1,306 m)
Reservoir Thickness:	Average 2 ft (0.7 m)
Areal Extent:	360 acres (146 ha)
IP:	Average 93 BOPD
Cumulative Production (1/89):	1,130,000 BO
Approximate Ultimate Recovery:	1,500,000 BO

[1]Matuszczak (1973, 1976); Nylund (1978); Petroleum Information Corporation's WHCS well history and PDS petroleum systems field databases (to 12/1986); NRG Associates Significant Oil and Gas Fields of the United States database (to 12/1985); Clayton and Swetland (1980); Gautier, et al. (1984); Meyer and McGee (1985); Weimer, et al. (1986).

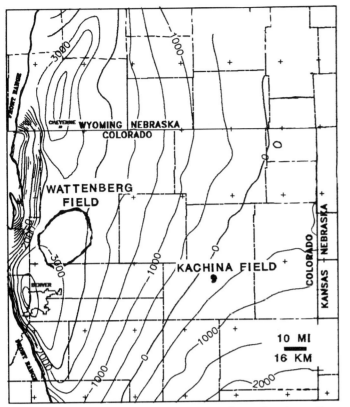

Figure 1. Structure map contoured on the top of the Lower Cretaceous "J" Sandstone in the Denver Basin. Contour interval is 1,000 ft (305 m). Shown are locations of the Wattenberg and Kachina Fields.

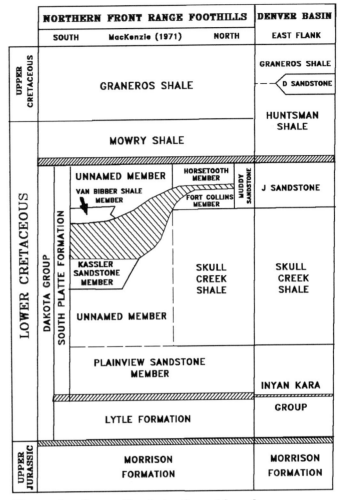

Figure 2. Generalized stratigraphic column showing nomenclature and correlations for the "J" Sandstone and associated units, including subdivision of the Muddy Sandstone into the Fort Collins and Horsetooth Members, Front Range area (modified from MacKenzie, 1971). Unconformities are indicated by the cross-hatched patterns.

from the "J" Sandstone (Land and Weimer, 1978; Tainter, 1984). The "J" Sandstone produces from deposits of tributary and distributary channel, crevasse–splay, delta–front, and nearshore–marine depositional environments. Production is from sandstones equivalent to the Fort Collins and Horsetooth Members of the Muddy ("J") Sandstone.

In this paper, the regional distribution of median porosity in the "J" Sandstone is mapped using 135 widely scattered Denver Basin drillholes. Data of core porosity and permeability from these drillholes represent the primary "J" sandstone producing facies. The cores are available for study at the U.S. Geological Survey core library near Denver.

The purpose of this study is to show regional trends in "J" Sandstone porosity and to indicate how the trends were influenced by diagenesis and by depositional environment. Porosity was compared to: 1) permeability; 2) present depth; 3) thermal maturity as determined by vitrinite reflectance, Rock–Eval pyrolysis, and time–temperature models; and 4) generalized sandstone depositional environments.

Local porosity distribution and sandstone diagenesis will be illustrated for two drillholes. The No. 1 G. W. Steiber Unit (SW SW Sec 24 T1N R67W) and the No. 6 Sheetz (SW SW Sec 23 T3S R52W) drillholes contain rocks that are representative of producing li-

thologies in the Wattenberg and Kachina fields, respectively (Table 1).

REGIONAL GEOLOGIC SETTING

"J" Sandstone thickness ranges up to approximately 150 ft (46 m) in the Denver Basin, although it generally is less than 100 ft (30 m) thick. The basal "J" Sandstone contact is transitional or erosional with shale and siltstone of the marine Skull Creek Shale (Albian). The upper contact is sharp and erosional, with the overlying beds being marine Mowry Shale (Albian) in the Wattenberg Field area, and either the "D" Sandstone or the Graneros Shale over the rest of the basin. Where the "D" Sandstone is present, the lower part of the Graneros is locally called the Huntsman Shale.

Table 1. "J" Sandstone point-count data from Wattenberg and Kachina fields, showing mineral percentages. Tabulated data represent analysis of 300 counts per thin section. Thin sections from hydrocarbon-stained or productive intervals are labeled with an asterisk. Glauconite was included with matrix mudstone because of similar ductile behavior. Total matrix clays include both detrital and authigenic clays. "Matrix MS" refers to intergranular soft sediments, not clasts.

Field Name, Sample Location	Core Depth (ft)	Grain Size	Framework Grains Mono. Qtz.	Other Lithics	Feld-spars	Matrix MS., Other	Total Matrix Clays	Chl. Cem.	Qtz. Cem.	Calcite Cement and Replc.	Poly. Qtz., Chert Cem.	Kao. Cem.	Intergr. Porosity	Minus Cement Por.
KACHINA FIELD AREA														
Gibson Oil Co.														
No. B-1 Sheetz														
SE SW Sec 14 T3S														
R52W														
4,629.8 *	33	49	6.0	1.1	4.5	6.4	0	5.0	0	1.4	4.3	22	FSS
4,279.8 *	37	50	4.0	1.7	2.0	6.0	0	17	0	0	0	20	F-MSS
4,283.8 *	38	53	2.3	1.3	3.3	2.3	0.3	9.3	11	2.0	1.3	14	F-MSS
4,288.5 *	36	51	4.0	0.9	4.0	3.3	0.3	15	0	0.3	0.7	20	F-MSS
Gibson Oil Co.														
No. 6 Sheetz, SW														
SW Sec 23 T3S R52W														
4,279.3 *	29	48	16	1.0	1.0	4.3	3.0	9.7	0	0	0	17	F-MSS
4,283.5 *	34	38	0.6	0.7	13	14	0	11	0	1.7	8.7	13	F-MSS
4,284.9 *	43	51	1.3	0.7	0	4.3	1.0	21	0	5.0	1.3	14	F-MSS
Gibson Oil Co.														
R. Thomas No. 1														
NE NE Sec 23 T3S														
R52W														
4,302.1 *	26	57	2.9	2.9	3.3	8.0	1.5	3.7	0	0.7	0.4	19	FSS
4,308.0	27	61	0.3	0.6	2.6	6.1	0	9.4	0	0.6	2.6	17	FSS
4,312.6 *	28	62	1.2	1.9	0.9	6.2	0	8.4	0	0.9	1.2	17	F-MSS
4,322.9 *	34	55	1.3	1.6	0.6	7.0	0	14	0	0.3	1.0	10	FSS
4,328.0 *	34	53	1.3	3.0	1.3	6.7	0.7	17	0	1.3	1.3	14	FSS
WATTENBERG FIELD														
Amoco Prod. Co.														
No. 1 George W.														
Steiber Unit,														
SW SW Sec 24														
T1N R67W														
8,032.6	26	59	3.6	0	8.3	3.6	1.3	3.3	0	20	0	1.0	VFSS
8,044.0 *	32	40	11	0	6.6	9.7	13	15	0	1.5	0	1.8	VFSS
8,061.8 *	21	58	4.7	1.0	1.7	14	7	4.3	0.7	4.0	0	4.6	VFSS
8,069.7 *	25	55	6.0	0.7	12	2.0	0.3	4.7	2.0	11	0	6.7	VFSS
8,083.7	25	59	2.7	0.4	3.2	9.5	9.6	0.9	4.5	7.3	0.4	2.3	VFSS
Amoco Prod. Co.														
E. Max Serafini														
C SW Sec 16														
T2N R68W														
7,866.0	38	57	2.7	0	1.3	1.0	0.7	15	18	2.0	0.7	1.7	FSS
7,872.8	37	50	2.3	0.3	4.3	6.0	0	14	0	3.0	15	5.3	VF-FSS
7,885.1 *	33	54	2.7	1.7	4.0	4.7	2.3	14	0	4.7	4.0	8.7	VF-FSS
7,895.6 *	35	52	4.7	0	4.1	5.3	0	25	0	0.9	0.9	4.4	VF-MSS

"J" Sandstone Depositional Environments and Lithofacies

The "J" Sandstone consists of shale, siltstone, and very fine to medium-grained sandstone. Generally, sandstones and shales deposited under nearshore-marine, delta-front, and delta-plain conditions are separated from valley-fill clastics by a basin-wide unconformity. The basin-wide subdivision of the Muddy ("J") Sandstone into the Fort Collins and Horsetooth Members by Weimer, et al. (1986) is based on the presence of this unconformity.

The Fort Collins Member in the western third of the basin is composed primarily of bioturbated, very fine to fine-grained, coarsening-upward sandstone of delta-front, shoreline, and nearshore marine origin. In the rest of the basin, "J" Sandstone strata equivalent to this member are mainly coarsening-upward delta-front and delta-plain sandstones, siltstones, and shales which were deposited following a marine regression at the end of Skull Creek time.

Fine to medium-grained nonmarine rocks of the Horsetooth Member rest unconformably on Fort Collins strata. A pre-Horsetooth drop in sea-level resulted in erosion of Fort Collins strata; the Fort Collins Member is completely removed in some areas. Horsetooth valley-fill sediments subsequently were deposited within the incised drainages (Weimer, et al., 1986). Regional trends in "J" Sandstone thickness (Fig. 3) show the location of pre-Horsetooth tributary channels.

A marine transgression followed deposition of the Horsetooth Member. A thin marine shale, representing a condensed section, may separate Fort Collins and Horsetooth strata from a thin, bioturbated, laterally discontinuous, transgressive upper sandstone which is nonproductive (Weimer and Land, 1972; Land and Weimer, 1978).

"J" Sandstone Burial History

Burial depths of the "J" Sandstone through Cenozoic and Late Mesozoic time (Fig. 4) reflect deposition and erosion of overlying strata related to tectonics in the Denver Basin and the Front Range Uplift. The "J" Sandstone was deposited 99-97 Ma, during a regression of the Cretaceous epicontinental seaway (Kauffman, 1977; Tainter, 1984). The unconformity at 97 Ma is the result of eustatic sea-level drop, erosion, and subsequent deposition of valley-fill sediment prior to marine transgression and deposition of the overlying marine Mowry and Graneros Shales. Eustatic sea-level changes were the primary factors causing unconformities at 95, 90, and 81-80 Ma (Weimer, 1984).

The steep slope of the burial curve at 81-69 Ma represents deposition of 6,400 ft (1,900 m) of marine Pierre Shale. Relatively rapid deposition of this thick shale indicates basin subsidence prior to the dated onset of the Laramide Orogeny; the Laramide Orogeny reached peak activity during Paleocene time and ended approximately 50 Ma. There was a decreased rate of sedimentation at about 68 Ma, showing that basin subsidence slowed with the onset of the orogeny. During this time, basin structure was estab-

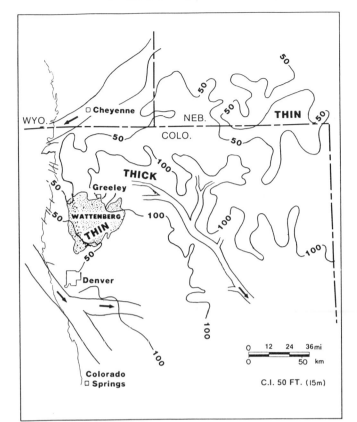

Figure 3. "J" Sandstone regional isopach map showing the distribution and direction of flow of pre-Horsetooth incised drainages (arrows) (Weimer, et al., 1986). Isopach "thin" in area of Wattenberg Field is indicated by stippling.

lished. The "J" Sandstone in Wattenberg Field subsided to its present structurally low position.

Reconstruction of the thermal history using Lopatin's time-temperature indices (TTI) model (Waples, 1980) indicates that the source rocks for "J" Sandstone hydrocarbons lying in the deeper parts of the Denver Basin reached oil-generative maturity during Late Cretaceous to early Tertiary time. Gas-generative maturity in the source rocks for the Wattenberg Field area probably was reached during middle to late Tertiary time (Higley and Gautier, 1988). Many vitrinite reflectance values obtained in the Wattenberg Field are greater than the lower value for thermogenic-gas generation of 1.35%. Values range from 1.10% to 1.51% (Higley, 1988). Vitrinite reflectance is 1.14% at the No. 1 G. W. Steiber Unit location.

Included in the burial history is an estimate of 1,400 ft (427 m) of upper Tertiary sediment deposition and subsequent removal. This conservative estimate is based on the present thickness of Tertiary strata near the No. 1 G. W. Steiber Unit well and on reported thicknesses in other parts of the basin. As much as 4,000 ft (1,220 m) of additional upper Tertiary strata may have been eroded from the basin during the time period from 7 Ma to present. The Denver Basin currently is undergoing extensional tectonism, contributing to present-day sediment erosion

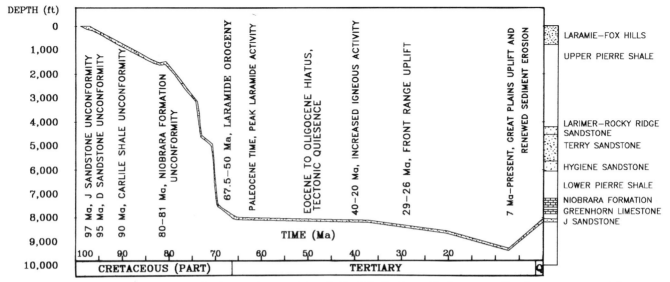

Figure 4. "J" Sandstone burial history in the No. 1 G. W. Steiber Unit gas well, Wattenberg Field. Shown are Lower Cretaceous unconformities of Weimer et al. (1986) and major periods of Denver–Basin and Front–Range tectonism. Summarized from Cobban, personal communication; Brown (1943); Obradovich and Cobban (1975); Tweto (1975, 1980); Irwin (1977); Kauffman (1977); Trimble (1980); Zoback and Zoback (1980); Porter and Weimer (1982); Tainter (1984); and Weimer (1984). (1,000 ft = 304.8 m)

and measured high subsurface heat flows in parts of the basin (Lachenbruch and Sass, 1977; Lachenbruch, 1979; Zoback and Zoback, 1980; Meyer and McGee, 1985).

PATTERNS IN "J" SANDSTONE POROSITY

Regional Trends

Median porosity for "J" Sandstone cores from 135 drillholes (Higley, 1988) was mapped and compared to data of generalized lithofacies, depth, median permeability, and thermal maturity. Median, rather than mean, porosity and permeability were used in order to minimize potentially large effects of anomalous samples on averages. Map areas of sparse data were filled with median porosity calculated from geophysical logs from 19 additional drillholes. Core was sampled at one–ft (0.3 m) intervals for porosity and permeability analyses. Sampled sandstones range in thickness from 10 to 65 ft (3 to 20 m) and in depth from 4,000 to 9,000 ft (1,220 to 2,745 m). Porosity and permeability measurements for sandstones from all 135 tested wells, excluding measurements of non-sandstone porosity and fracture porosity as identified on core reports, will be called the "porosity database".

A subset of median porosities and permeabilities was built for tributary and distributary channel sandstones from 27 drillholes. Identification of channel lithofacies was based on core and wireline–log studies and on published reports. The channel sandstones are characterized generally as fine to medium–grained, massive to trough and planar cross–bedded sequences that are normally graded and have erosional bases. This subset will be called the "channel–sandstone subset", or just "channel sandstones".

Porosity decreases approximately linearly with the log of permeability in both the porosity database and the channel sandstone subset (Fig. 5). In most cases, median porosity and permeability are greater for channel sandstones than for all sandstones in the same drillhole. The correlation coefficient of the least-squares fit of porosity with the log of permeability (r) for the porosity database is 0.42. For the channel sandstone subset, r is 0.78. The correlation coefficient is considerably higher when only one type of facies is considered. However, neither correlation can be used as a predictive model, mainly because of scatter in the data.

Porosity in all sandstones decreases approximately exponentially with increasing depth (Fig. 6). The r for the least–squares fit of the log of porosity to depth is −0.79 for the porosity database and −0.69 for the channel–sandstone subset. Greater median porosity is seen for the channel–sandstone portion than for all sandstones in most drillholes, regardless of depth.

Because present–day, not maximum, burial depth was plotted against porosity, considerable scatter may result where variable degrees of erosion are present across the basin. Another reason for the high degree of scatter is that depth influences porosity loss through several processes, including diagenetic effects associated with increased pressure and temperature, and mechanical compaction. Porosity also is dependent on sand–grain shape, size, and sorting (Beard and Weyl, 1973), factors that are related to depositional energy conditions and sediment source.

The influence of burial depth on porosity is shown by the approximate alignment of isoporosity contours (Fig. 7) roughly parallel to basin structural contours (Fig. 1). The median porosity of the "J" Sandstone reaches a high of about 24% on the eastern flank of the basin, and decreases to 7 to 10% in the deepest

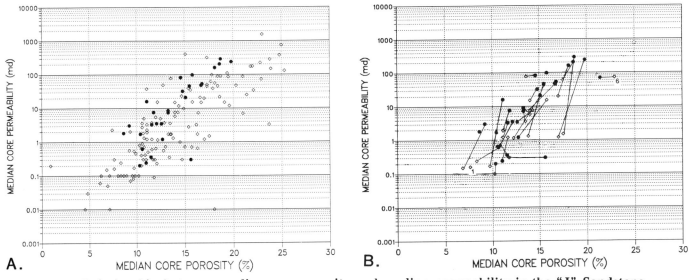

A.   B.

Figure 5.   Relationship between median core porosity and median permeability in the "J" Sandstone.

A.   Open diamonds represent median values from the porosity database; dots are median values for the channel–sandstone subset.   Note generally greater permeabilities within the channel sandstones.

B. Data for the channel–sandstone subset.   Lines link porosity values from the same drillholes.   The No. 1 G. W. Steiber Unit (7.6 %) and Sheetz No. 6 (23%) data points are labeled "1" and "6", respectively.

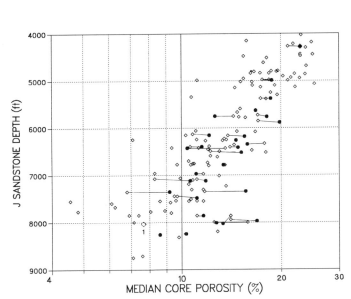

Figure 6.   Relationship between median core porosity and depth to the top of the "J" Sandstone across the Denver Basin.   Open diamonds represent data from the porosity database; dots represent values for the channel–sandstone subset. Lines link porosity values from the same drillholes.   The No. 1 G. W. Steiber Unit and No. 6 Sheetz No. 6 data points are labeled "1" and "6", respectively.

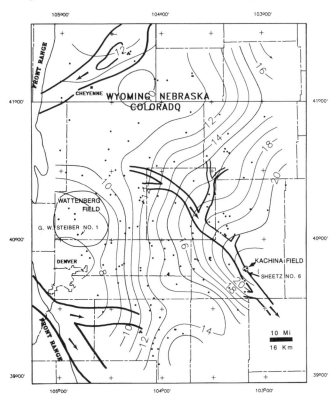

Figure 7.   "J" Sandstone isoporosity map covering most of the Denver Basin. Superimposed are the incised drainage systems of Weimer, et al. (1986).   Dots are drillhole locations.   Contour interval is 1% porosity.   The No. 1 G. W. Steiber Unit and No. 6 Sheetz drillholes are labeled. The contour grid has been smoothed with a moving average statistical manipulation to illustrate regional porosity trends.

parts of the basin. On the eastern flank of the basin, an area of high porosity coincides with thick "J" sandstones found within a major incised drainage system, associated with thick valley–fill and delta–plain sediments. Effects of tributary systems located in the southwestern and northwestern flanks of the basin are undefined because of limited well control.

Schmoker and Gautier (1988) have modeled the relationship between porosity and burial diagenesis for several Rocky Mountain sandstone formations, including the "J" Sandstone in the Denver Basin. They hypothesize that porosity loss in studied sandstones was the result of thermal stress associated with burial diagenesis, and that the porosity–thermal maturity relationship can be characterized by a power function of the form:

$$\emptyset = a(M)^b$$

where $\emptyset$ is porosity and M is a measure of integrated time–temperature history such as vitrinite reflectance, TTI, or Tmax from Rock–Eval pyrolysis. The petrologic coefficient "a" in the above equation combines net effects of depositional and diagenetic factors. The exponent "b", a negative number, reflects rate–limiting steps in porosity loss.

The r of the least–squares fit of the logs of porosity and vitrinite reflectance is –0.76 for the porosity database (Fig. 8). The r, using the above equation, is –0.88, a better fit. (Vitrinite reflectance and porosity were not correlated for the channel–sandstone subset). Thus, thermal maturity may better characterize regional porosity relationships than does depth. Thermal maturity values reflect diagenetic changes resulting from pressure and thermal effects associated with maximum burial depths and with variations in basin and local heat flows.

Porosity Relationships in "J" Sandstone Reservoir Lithotypes

"J" Sandstone reservoirs can be classified as deltaic and nearshore–marine sandstones, of which Wattenberg Field is an example (Matuszczak, 1973; Weimer, et al., 1986), and distributary–channel sandstones, of which Kachina Field is an example (Nylund, 1978). Sandstones from both fields were sampled and examined by thin–section microscopy (Table 1). Vertical trends in core porosity and permeability seen in each type of producing sandstone reservoir are related to depositional environment, which controls grain size, shape, and sorting, bedforms, and biologic activity. In general, "J" Sandstone porosity and permeability increase upward in marine and progradational delta–front sequences, and decrease upward in most fluvial sandstone sequences.

Delta–front and nearshore–marine sandstones in Wattenberg Field are characterized generally as matrix– or grain–supported, very fine–grained, moderately sorted quartz arenite and sublitharenite. Wattenberg Field Horsetooth Member production (E. Max Serafini well, Table 1) is from delta–front and higher–energy distributary channel sandstone. The diagenetic sequence in the Wattenberg tight gas sandstone was: 1) sediment compaction; 2) growth of chlorite rims; 3) formation of quartz overgrowths;

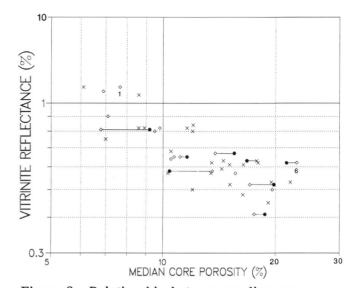

Figure 8. Relationship between median core porosity and vitrinite reflectance for the "J" Sandstone across the Denver Basin. Open diamonds represent porosity database values. Dots represent channel–sandstone subset values. Crosses denote data values estimated from "J" sandstone porosity, depth, and degree of thermal maturity across the basin. These were added to aid in visual identification of trends and were not used in statistical analyses. Lines link porosity values from the same drillholes. The No. 1 G. W. Steiber Unit (1.14% R_O) and No. 6 Sheetz (0.62% R_O) data points are labeled "1" and "6", respectively. Vitrinite reflectance values based on measured reflectances and on Rock–Eval analyses of 2–4 core samples of shale per drillhole (Higley et al., 1985).

4) calcite cementation and contemporaneous dissolution of feldspar and lithic fragments; 5) calcite dissolution; 6) growth of illite–smectite; and 7) late fracturing (Weimer, et al., 1986). Late–stage chert and polycrystalline quartz cement (after calcite dissolution) may be present in some sections, especially those containing abundant intergranular mud and mudstone laminae. Generally–minor amounts of pore–filling authigenic kaolinite (postdating growth of illite–smectite) also may be present. Kaolinite is more common in distributary–channel than in delta–front sandstone (E. Max Serafini well, Table 1), possibly because of greater permeability and intergranular porosity in these sediments.

Samples from Kachina Field are mainly grain-supported, fine to medium–grained, poorly to moderately sorted quartz arenite. Although Kachina Field sandstone has not been buried as deep or been subject to the high heat flows found in the Wattenberg area, the diagenetic sequences in the two fields are very similar: 1) sediment compaction; 2) formation of syntaxial quartz and feldspar overgrowths; 3) calcite cementation and contemporaneous dissolution of feldspar and lithic fragments; 4) calcite dissolution; 5) growth of illite–smectite, chlorite, and other matrix clays; and 6) growth of kaolinite. Very minor and localized chert and polycrystalline quartz cementation followed calcite dissolution.

Wattenberg samples generally have less intergranular, and about the same minus–cement porosity as Kachina samples. Finer grain size, higher concentration of detrital mudstone and clays, and greater burial depths in the Wattenberg area result in more complete porosity reduction through compaction and ductile deformation of soft sediment. Wattenberg porosity was further reduced through formation of quartz overgrowths (where chlorite rims were absent or minor); locally large amounts of calcite, chert, and polycrystalline quartz cements; and precipitation of later clays. Porosity reduction in Kachina Field occurred through compaction, growth of syntaxial quartz and feldspar overgrowths, and pore–filling by authigenic clay. Corrosion of lithic grains by calcite resulted in slightly enhanced porosity in the Wattenberg area and minor to extensive porosity enhancement in the Kachina area. Current calcite concentrations are greater in Wattenberg Field; formation waters in the permeable Kachina Field sandstones were more efficient at removing calcite cement.

Late–stage kaolinite cements in Kachina Field often are associated with corroded feldspar grains, and result partly from feldspar destruction by meteoric waters. Late–stage kaolinite present in several Wattenberg samples may also result from meteoric water influx. "J" sandstone outcrops along the Front Range are recharge areas for the Dakota aquifer (Ottman, 1981; Belitz, 1985).

Porosity Relationships in Wattenberg Field (Amoco Production Co., No. 1 G. W. Steiber Unit, NE SW SW Sec 24 T1N R67W, Weld Co., Colorado)

The "J" Sandstone in this drillhole consists of a coarsening–upward sequence of bioturbated, medium–gray siltstone and very fine–grained quartz arenite and sublitharenite (Figs. 9 and 10). Upward–increasing energy in this predominantly marine unit is reflected by upward increases in core porosity and permeability (Fig. 9). The "J" Sandstone at this location consists of Fort Collins Member strata; the Horsetooth Member of the Muddy ("J") Sandstone is absent.

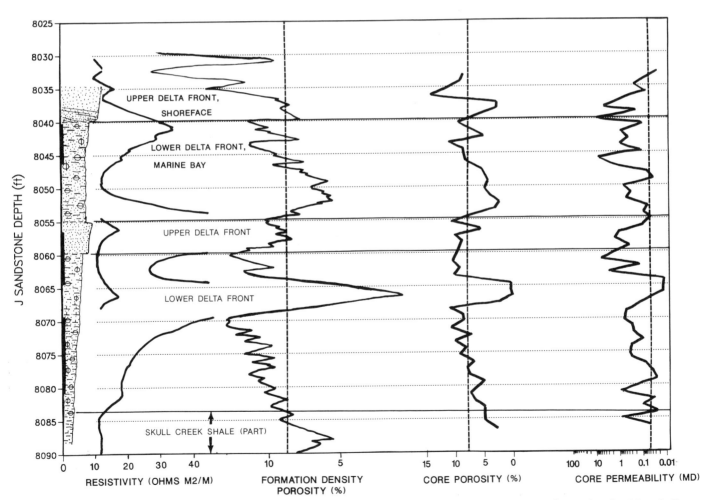

Figure 9. "J" Sandstone lithology, producing intervals, well log curves, and core analyses in the No. 1 G. W. Steiber Unit drillhole (NE SW SW Sec 24 T1N R67W), Wattenberg Field. Vertical bars represent producing intervals. ⊖ and ⊕ symbols indicate horizontal and vertical burrows, respectively. Dashed lines are reservoir quality porosity and permeability "cutoffs".

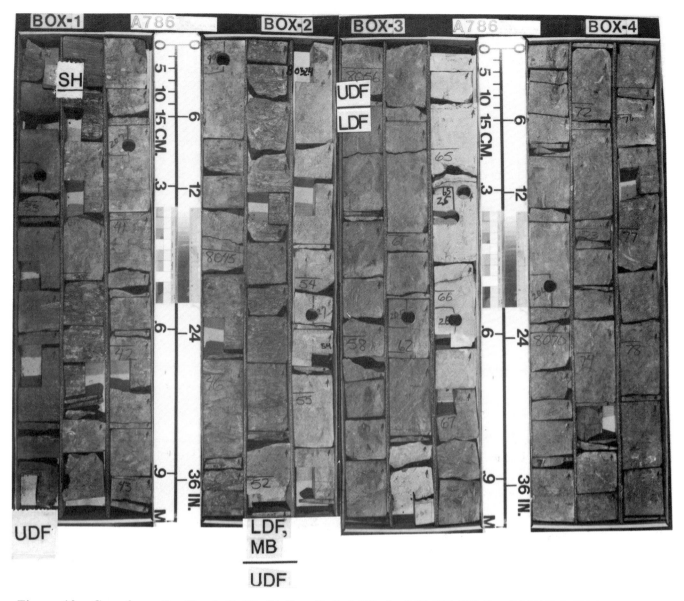

Figure 10. Core from the No. 1 G. W. Steiber Unit drillhole (NE SW SW Sec 24 T1N R67W). Abbreviations are: upper delta front (UDF), lower delta front (LDF), marine bay (MB), and upper shoreface (SH).

The upper Skull Creek contact (8,084 ft, or 2,466 m, Fig. 9) is transitional with overlying Fort Collins lower delta-front sediments. Lower delta-front sediments are medium gray, very fine-grained, and extensively burrowed. Burrows are mainly *Asterosoma-Teichichnus*, with *Skolithos* and *Arenicolites* burrows increasing up-section. Relict bedding is laminar to ripple laminated. A low-porosity zone from 8,063–8,067 ft (2,459–2,460 m) is nonproductive, very fine-grained, burrowed, lower delta-front sandstone in which pervasive calcite cement has totally occluded porosity. This is the only interval that has abundant calcite cement, although lithic grains in other intervals exhibit evidence of extensive dissolution and replacement by calcite.

A thin marine sandstone at 8,055–8,059 ft (2,457–2,458 m) (Fig. 10) has a transitional contact with underlying lower delta-front sandstone and siltstone. This thin marine sandstone is oil stained, medium gray, very fine grained, and appears massive, with only subtle tabular bedding. Porosity and permeability in this interval decrease upward slightly, although sand-grain size increases upward. The low-porosity and -permeability zone at 8,056 ft (2,457 m) traps hydrocarbons in the underlying productive interval.

This thin marine sandstone is overlain by a lower delta-front or marine bay sequence of coarsening-upward, very fine to fine-grained sandstone at 8,039–8,055 ft (2,452–2,457 m). Most bedding is destroyed by horizontal and minor vertical burrowing, but relict laminar and ripple-laminated sandstone bedding is present. Porosity and permeability increase upward. A beach deposit at the top of the cored interval (8,035–8,039 ft, 2,451–2,452 m) is a coarsening-upward, fine-grained sandstone. Internal bedding consists of a five-in. (13-cm) thick, low angle, planar-laminar (swash) bed that is overlain by fine-grained, upper shoreface massive sandstone. No burrows were noted in these sandstones. Core and formation-density porosity generally increase upward, but permeability appears to decrease upward. Extensive quartz cementation results in low porosity and very low permeability, which trap hydrocarbons in the underlying productive interval. Thin sections of a gas-productive, bioturbated, very fine-grained delta-front unit found at 8,044 ft (2,453 m) show a moderately sorted, matrix-supported sandstone with mudstone laminae and hydrocarbon-filled solution seams (Plate 1A, 1C, and 1E). Only 2% of clean, intergranular porosity is present; many of the pore spaces are partly occluded by chlorite, kaolinite, and other detrital and authigenic clays. Core-plug porosity in this interval is 6.9%, indicating that most of the porosity is partly-occluded intergranular and microporosity. Early-emplaced chlorite blades are oriented perpendicular to rims of lithic rock fragments. Authigenic chlorite in a later-stage clay matrix is oriented perpendicular to corroded quartz grains (Plate 1E). Quartz grains have minor syntaxial overgrowths where earlier chlorite rims are absent or minor (Plate 1C, 1E). Dust rims generally are indistinct.

Quartz overgrowths preceded calcite emplacement. Calcite is minor and very localized, but where it is present, poikilotopic cement totally occludes porosity (Plate 1C). Extensive dissolution of quartz overgrowths and grains, as well as other lithic fragments, and replacement by calcite has enhanced porosity. Original quartz-grain dust rims are preserved within some calcite-replacement areas. Dissolution of lithic rock fragments is indicated by corroded grain bounda-

ries, sutured grain contacts, and mottled and honeycombed grains. Features of later lithic-grain dissolution are visible where calcite borders a pore space (Plate 1C). Pore spaces resulting from calcite and lithic-grain dissolution were usually filled with illite-smectite, chlorite, and kaolinite. Hydrocarbons are present in pores and in late-stage solution seams (Plate 1A) which are oriented approximately parallel to horizontal and low-angle bedding planes. Open porosity in seams would not be present at depth.

Porosity Relationships in Kachina Field (J. W. Gibson Co., No. 6 Sheetz, SW SW Sec 23 T3S R52W, Washington Co., Colorado)

The "J" Sandstone in this drillhole is a coarsening-upward sequence of bioturbated delta-front mudstone and very fine-grained sandstone (Fort Collins Member or facies equivalent), overlain by fine to medium-grained, heavily oil-stained sandstone and interbedded mudstone of mainly channel and channel-margin origin (Horsetooth Member or equivalent) (Figs. 11 and 12). Mudstone of the overlying Graneros Shale (found above 4,226 ft, or 1,289 m, core depth) is the primary reservoir seal. Bioturbated prodelta mudstone and siltstone of the Skull Creek Shale grade upward into lower delta-front rocks of the Fort Collins Member. A thin marine shale at 4,304.3 ft (1,313 m) core depth marks the Skull Creek–"J" Sandstone contact.

The delta-front rocks are mainly medium-gray mudstone and very fine-grained sandstone; bedding commonly is destroyed by bioturbation, including *Teichichnus* burrows, but minor relict horizontal and ripple-laminated bedding is present. Porosity and permeability show overall upward increases, reflecting

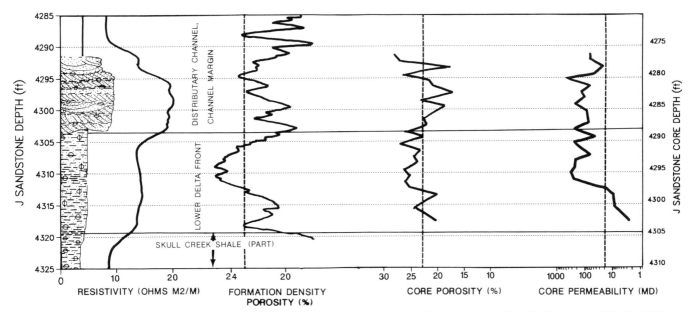

Figure 11. "J" Sandstone lithology, well log curves, and core analyses in the No. 6 Sheetz drillhole (SW SW Sec 23 T3S R52W), adjacent to Kachina Field. The trough- and planar cross-bedded sandstone at 4,288–4,302 ft (1,308–1,312 m) resistivity log depth is oil stained and laterally equivalent to the productive horizon in Kachina Field. ⊖ and ⊕ symbols indicate horizontal and vertical sediment burrowing, respectively. Dashed lines are reservoir quality porosity and permeability "cutoffs". (Five ft = 15.2 m)

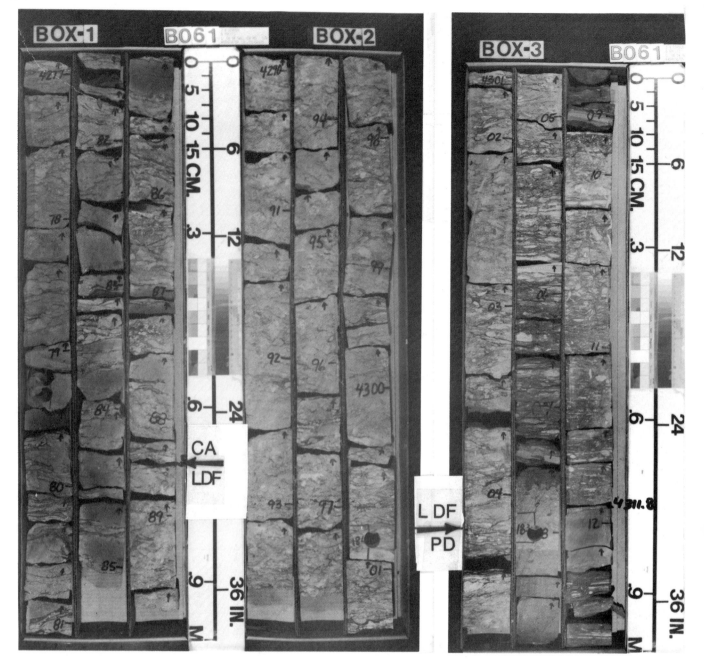

Figure 12. Core photographs of the No. 6 Sheetz drillhole (SW SW Sec 23 T3S R52W). Sandstone at 4,277–4,288.5 ft (1,304–1,308 m) is oil stained, fine to medium grained, and mainly trough cross bedded. Deformation structures result primarily from dewatering and slumping. Interbedded mudstones contain some horizontal burrows. Underlying delta-front, very fine-grained, bioturbated sandstone is located at 4,288.5– 4,311.8 ft (1,308–1,315 m). Abbreviations are: distributary channel, channel margin, and partially abandoned channel (CH); lower delta front (LDF); and prodelta (PD).

the upward-increasing depositional energy conditions related to delta progradation.

An erosional contact at 4,288.3 ft (1,308 m) core depth separates the delta-front interval from overlying fining-upward sandstone of distributary-channel environments. This sandstone is oil stained but nonproductive. The unit is laterally equivalent and lithologically very similar to a productive sandstone found in the adjacent Kachina Field. These sandstones were deposited in channel, channel-margin,

and partially-abandoned channel environments. They are characterized by numerous thin-bedded, planar-tabular and trough cross-bedded sandstones that are light gray to brown and fine to medium grained. These sandstones do not contain burrows, although interbedded mudstone laminae contain some horizontal, sand-filled burrows. Abundant soft-sediment deformation features are present and are due to dewatering and slumping.

Individual cross–bedded sandstones are normally graded. Core porosity decreases upward in the channel sandstone. Although significant porosity is present, it is less than effective Kachina reservoir porosity in most of the interval. Oil–stained sandstones are 60 to 80% water saturated, although core water saturations probably are too high. The formation density trace is irregular. This is due partly to the presence of numerous thin sandstones and to the influence of interbedded mudstone, which does not affect the core porosity plot because the mudstone was not sampled.

Photomicrographs were prepared of thin sections from an oil–stained, trough cross–bedded, distributary–channel sandstone from 4,279 ft (1,305 m) core depth in the Sheetz No. 6 drillhole (Plate 1B, 1F) and 4,283.8 ft (1,306 m) in the No. B–1 Sheetz drillhole (Plate 1D). These show porous and permeable, grain–supported, subrounded, fine to medium–grained sandstone. Intergranular porosity is 17% for the No. 6 Sheetz channel sandstone. Porosity is almost entirely primary and secondary intergranular, with minor microporosity present in matrix clays and late–stage kaolinite. Kaolinite frequently is found located adjacent to or within corroded feldspar grains. Calcite is absent in most Kachina samples. Feldspar is very minor. Thin clay coatings are present as dust rims on some quartz grains. Syntaxial quartz overgrowths are abundant and well developed. Extensive dissolution of quartz and feldspar grains by calcite (Plate 1D) contributed to porosity development. Features created by dissolution of lithic rock fragments and quartz overgrowths are present: corroded grain and overgrowth boundaries, mottled grains, and grain fragments (Plate 1D, 1F). Secondary porosity development is indicated by these features, by "floating grains" in pore spaces, by intragranular pores, and by oversized, irregular shaped pores (Plate 1D, 1F). Hydrocarbons (Plate 1D) and kaolinite were deposited later in primary pore spaces and those enlarged by dissolution of silica cement and lithic grains (Plate 1F).

CONCLUSIONS

"J" Sandstone diagenesis in Wattenberg Field is complex and far advanced. The recovery of gas is affected by low porosity and permeability in reservoir rocks; by fractures; by the presence of hydrocarbon traps within the vertical section; and by the types and amounts of clays and other cements present. The primary reservoir seals are interbedded mudstones and sandstones cemented by quartz, chert, polycrystalline quartz, calcite, and authigenic clays. Pore throats frequently are bridged by illite and kaolinite. Pores are filled with chlorite and other clays, quartz overgrowths, chert cements, and detrital material.

At Kachina Field, "J" Sandstone reservoirs are much less cemented and more porous and permeable. However, there is a surprising amount of complexity to diagenetic events, including creation of significant dissolution porosity.

For the basin as a whole, channel–sandstone sequences generally have higher median porosity and permeability than do sandstones of all facies. The effect of depositional environment on porosity is indicated by the influence of depositional energy on vertical porosity trends, and by the area of high porosity and permeability located in the eastern Denver Basin that corresponds in size and location to an incised drainage and Horsetooth Member distributary channel system. The porosity database and channel subset show similar trends with depth, permeability, and thermal maturity. Sandstone porosity loss correlates to loss of permeability, to increasing burial depth, and to thermal maturity of hydrocarbon source rocks.

REFERENCES

Beard, D.D., and P.K. Weyl, 1973, Influence of texture on porosity and permeability of unconsolidated sand: AAPG Bull., v. 57, p. 349–369.

Belitz, K., 1985, Hydrodynamics of the Denver basin: an explanation of subnormal fluid pressures: unpub. PhD diss., Stanford U., 186 p.

Brown, R.W., 1943, Cretaceous–Tertiary boundary in the Denver Basin, Colorado: GSA Bull., v. 54, p. 65–86.

Clark, B.A., 1978, Stratigraphy of the Lower Cretaceous J sandstone, Boulder County, Colorado: A deltaic model, in J.D. Pruit and P.E. Coffin, eds., Energy Resources of the Denver Basin: RMAG, p. 237–244.

Clayton, J.L., and P.L. Swetland, 1980, Petroleum generation and migration in the Denver Basin: AAPG Bull., v. 64, p. 1613–1633.

Gautier, D.L., J.L. Clayton, J.S. Leventhal, and N.J. Redden, 1984, Origin and source rock potential of the Sharon Springs Member of the Pierre Shale, Colorado and Kansas, in J. Woodward, F.J. Meissner, and J.L., Clayton, eds., Hydrocarbon Source Rocks of the Greater Rocky Mountain Region: RMAG, p. 369–386.

Haun, J.D., 1963, Stratigraphy of Dakota Group and relationship to petroleum occurrence, northern Denver Basin, in Geology of the Northern Denver Basin and Adjacent Uplifts: 14th Ann. Field Conf. Guidebook, RMAG, p. 119–134.

Higley, D.K., 1988, Core porosity, permeability, and vitrinite reflectance data from the Lower Cretaceous J sandstone in 141 Denver basin coreholes: USGS Open–File Report 88–527, 6 p., 2 diskettes.

Higley, D.K., and D.L. Gautier, 1988, Burial history reconstruction of the Lower Cretaceous J sandstone in the Wattenberg Field, Colorado, "hot spot" [abs.], in L.M.H. Carter, ed., USGS Research on Energy Resources: USGS Circ. 1025, p. 20.

Higley, D.K., M.J. Pawlewicz, and D.L. Gautier, 1985, Isoreflectance map of the J sandstone in the Denver basin of Colorado: USGS Open–File Report 85–384, 98 p., 1 pl.

Irwin, D., 1977, Subsurface cross sections of Colorado: RMAG Spec. Pub. 2, 39 p., 24 pl.

Kauffman, E.G., 1977, Geological and biological overview: Western Interior Cretaceous basin: Mtn. Geol., v. 14, p. 75–99.

Lachenbruch, A.H., 1979, Heat flow in the Basin and Range province and thermal effects of tectonic extension: Pure and Applied Geophysics, v. 117, p. 35–50.

Lachenbruch, A.H., and J.A. Sass, 1977, Heat flow in the United States and the thermal regime of the crust, in J.G. Heacock, ed., Geophysics Monograph Series 20, AGU, p. 626–675.

Land, C.B., and R.J. Weimer, 1978, Peoria Field, Denver Basin, Colorado–J sandstone distributary channel reservoir, in J.D. Pruit, and P.E. Coffin, eds., Energy Resources of the Denver Basin: RMAG, p. 81–104.

MacKenzie, D.B., 1965, Depositional environments of Muddy Sandstone, western Denver Basin, Colorado: AAPG Bull., v. 49, p. 186–206.

MacKenzie, D.B., 1971, Post–Lytle Dakota Group on west flank of Denver Basin, Colorado: Mtn. Geol., v. 8, p. 91–131.

Matuszczak, R.A., 1973, Wattenberg Field, Denver Basin, Colorado: Mtn. Geol., v. 10, p. 99–105.

Matuszczak, R. A., 1976, Wattenberg Field: A Review, in R.C. Epis and R.J. Weimer, eds., Studies in Colorado Field Geology: CSM Prof. Contrib., no. 8, p. 275–279.

Meyer, H.J., and H.W. McGee, 1985, Oil and gas fields accompanied by geothermal anomalies in Rocky Mountain region: AAPG Bull., v. 69, p. 933-945.

Nylund, J.W., 1978, Kachina Field, T3S-R52W, Washington County, Colorado, *in* J.D. Pruit, and P.E. Coffin, eds., Energy Resources of the Denver Basin: RMAG, p. 105-112.

Obradovich, J.D., and W.A. Cobban, 1975, A time scale for the Late Cretaceous of the western interior of North America: Geological Association of Canada Special Paper, no. 13, p. 31-54.

Ottmann, J.D., 1981, Hydrodynamic entrapment of petroleum in the "J" sandstone of the Denver Basin, northeastern Colorado: unpub. MS thesis, U. of Houston, 109 p.

Pittman, E.D., 1988, Diagenesis of Terry Sandstone (Upper Cretaceous), Spindle Field, Colorado: JSP, v. 58, p. 785-800.

Porter, K.W., and R.J. Weimer, 1982, Diagenetic sequence related to structural history and petroleum accumulation: Spindle Field, Colorado: AAPG Bull., v. 66, p. 2543-2560.

Schmoker, J.W., and D.L. Gautier, 1988, Sandstone porosity as a function of thermal maturity: Geology, v. 16, p. 1007-1010.

Stonecipher, S.A., R.D. Winn, Jr., and M.G. Bishop, 1984, Diagenesis of the Frontier Formation, Moxa Arch: a function of sandstone geometry, texture and composition, and fluid flux, *in* D.A. McDonald, and R.C. Surdam, eds., Clastic Diagenesis: AAPG Mem. 37, p. 289-316.

Tainter, P.A., 1984, Stratigraphic and paleostructural controls on hydrocarbon migration in Cretaceous D and J sandstone of the Denver Basin, *in* J.F. Woodward, F. Meissner, and J.

Clayton, eds., Hydrocarbon Source Rocks of the Greater Rocky Mountain Region: RMAG, p. 339-354.

Trimble, D.E., 1980, Cenozoic tectonic history of the Great Plains contrasted with that of the southern Rocky Mountains; a synthesis: Mtn. Geol., v. 17, p. 54-67.

Tweto, O., 1975, Laramide (Late Cretaceous-Early Tertiary) orogeny in the southern Rocky Mountains, *in* B. Curtis, ed., Cenozoic Geology of the Southern Rocky Mountains: GSA Mem. 144, p. 1-44.

Tweto, O., 1980, Summary of the Laramide Orogeny in Colorado, *in* H. Kent, and K. Porter, eds., Colorado Geology: RMAG, p. 129-134.

Waples, D.W., 1980, Time and temperature in petroleum formation: application of Lopatin's method to petroleum exploration, AAPG Bull., v. 64, p. 916-926.

Weimer, R.J., 1984, Relation of unconformities, tectonics, and sea-level changes, Cretaceous of western interior, U.S.A., *in* J.S. Schlee, ed., Interregional Unconformities and Hydrocarbon Accumulations: AAPG Mem. 36, p. 7-35.

Weimer, R.J., and C.B. Land, 1972, Field guide to Dakota Group (Cretaceous) stratigraphy Golden-Morrison area, Colorado: Mtn. Geol., v. 9, p. 241-267.

Weimer, R.J., S.A. Sonnenberg, and G.B. Young, 1986, Wattenberg Field, Denver Basin, Colorado, *in* C.W. Spencer and R.F. Mast, eds., Geology of Tight Gas Reservoirs: AAPG Studies in Geology no. 24, p. 143-164.

Zoback, M.L., and M. Zoback, 1980, State of stress in the conterminous United States: Journal of Geophysical Research, v. 85, no. B11, p. 6113-6156.

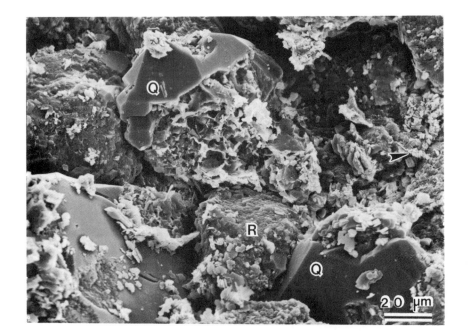

Quartz overgrowths (Q) are well-developed, but do not significantly reduce porosity in this sample. Arrow marks location of isolated booklets of kaolinite. Much porosity in this sample is due to partial leaching of framework grains. "R" indicates rock fragment. Surface sample of Turner Fm., sec 23 T36N R62W, Niobrara Co., WY. Photo donated by Bill Keighin.

Sequence Stratigraphic Analysis of Muddy (J) Sandstone Reservoir, Wattenberg Field, Denver Basin, Colorado[1]

ROBERT J. WEIMER[2]
STEPHEN A. SONNENBERG[3]

[1]Received November 9, 1988; Revised May 5, 1989
[2]Professor Emeritus, Department of Geology and Geological Engineering, Colorado School of Mines, Golden, Colorado
[3]Bass Enterprises Production Company, Denver, Colorado

The Wattenberg Field, located north of Denver, is a large gas accumulation that straddles the synclinal axis of the Denver Basin. Estimated reserves are in the order of 1 TCFG from the Lower Cretaceous Muddy (J) Sandstone from an area of 600,000 acres (242,000 ha); production is from depths of 7,600 to 8,400 ft (2,310 to 2,560 m); net pay thickness varies from 10 to 50 ft (3 to 15 m); porosity ranges from 8 to 12%; permeability varies from 0.1 to 0.05 md (Matuszczak, 1973, 1976).

Three stratigraphic sequences are identified in the Lower Cretaceous of the Denver Basin. Petroleum production is largely from the Muddy (J) Sandstone in sequences 2 and 3. The sequence boundary, a regional unconformity, occurs within, at the top of, or at the base of the Muddy (J) Formation. Where present, deltaic and marine sandstones beneath the surface of erosion are included in the Fort Collins Member; fluvial and estuarine strata above the unconformity belong to the Horsetooth Member. The gas production at Wattenberg is from the Fort Collins Member, a widespread delta front sandstone deposited during a highstand regression of the Skull Creek seaway. Fluvial channel sandstones form stratigraphic traps in the incised valley fills and are productive in fields marginal to the Wattenberg field.

Sequence stratigraphic analysis places new emphasis on the role of the regional unconformity in trapping hydrocarbons in Wattenberg Field. A drop in sea–level caused subaerial exposure and a lower base level with valley incisement and interstream divide erosion. The amount of erosion into older deposits is estimated to be from 20 to 100 ft (6 to 30 m). In general, paleovalleys drained to the southeast, and valley deepening occurs in that direction. Paleosol development initiated early diagenesis that reduced porosity and permeability. The lowstand surface of erosion (LSE) truncates the pay sandstone on all margins of Wattenberg Field, and this truncation, together with early diagenetic minerals, forms the seal that prevents gas from escaping from the synclinal area of the Denver Basin. Paleostructure controls the distribution of the reservoir, the magnitude of erosion, and may have contributed to early gas accumulation.

With a sea level rise, coastal onlap filled the incised valleys and covered the interstream divide (paleostructure) areas with coastal plain deposits. As the shoreline moved over the coastal plain, a transgressive surface of erosion (TSE) truncated 10 to 30 ft (3 to 10 m) of sediment. In some portions of paleostructural (topographic) highs, the LSE and TSE merge and the Muddy (J) is thinner than elsewhere in the basin.

INTRODUCTION

The purpose of this paper is to discuss the geology of the tight petroleum reservoir, the Fort Collins Member of the Muddy (J) Sandstone in the Wattenberg Field. In addition, the general stratigraphic setting is described for typical Muddy (J) Sandstone fields producing from channel sandstones in the

For Reservoir Summary, see Higley and Schmoker, this volume.

Horsetooth Member. The relationship of production to regional unconformities is analyzed by use of sequence stratigraphy. Most Muddy (J) Sandstone production in the area is classed as from stratigraphic traps, but subtle paleostructure and unconformities have also controlled the petroleum accumulations.

Since 1970, petroleum fields have been found over an area of one million acres in the deeper portion of the Denver Basin (Fig. 1). The activity started with the discovery of the Wattenberg gas field by drilling to the Muddy (J) Sandstone at depths of 7,600 to 8,400 ft (2,300 to 2,500 m) (Fig. 2). More than 600,000 acres are now productive from the Fort Collins Member of the Muddy (J) Sandstone with total producible gas estimated to be about 1 TCF.

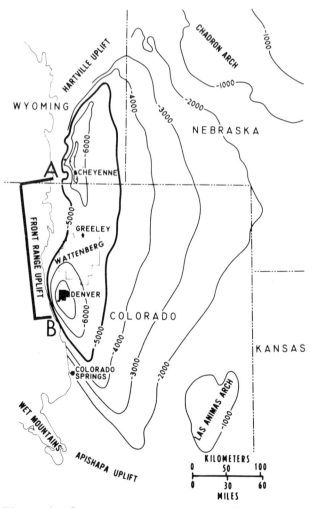

Figure 1. Structure contour map of Denver Basin on top of Precambrian with Wattenberg study area. After Matuszczak, 1973.

STRUCTURAL AND PALEOSTRUCTURAL ANALYSIS

Wattenberg Field straddles the axis of the Denver Basin (Fig. 3). The basin is asymmetric, with a gently dipping east flank and a steeply dipping west flank. The basin axis lies close to and parallels the Front Range. Laramide uplift of the Front Range along basement faults has dominated the overall structural style. Small drape folds over basement faults form sharp anticlines which are productive along the west margin of the Denver Basin (e.g., Fort Collins, Wellington, Loveland, and Berthoud fields). Minor changes in regional strike or dip within the Denver Basin result principally from small scale subtle warping of strata over basement fault blocks. Two trends of fold axes are present: northwest and east–northeast.

Although presently in a structural low, the Wattenberg area was a structural high at the start of deposition of the Pierre Shale. A key to understanding the paleostructure and configuration of basement fault blocks is to analyze the origin of the thinning in the Dakota Group and Niobrara Formation. An isopach map from the top of the Muddy (J) Sandstone to the top of the Niobrara Formation (Fig. 4) indicates a thin area of less than 700 ft (213 m) with thickening southward to more than 900 ft (273 m) and northward to 800 ft (246 m). The thinning is related to what is interpreted as an east–west trending anticline (horst block). After the Niobrara was deposited, structural movement occurred during the time of early Pierre deposition, resulting in an uplifted shoal area on the sea floor. This area was subjected to beveling by marine processes, or possibly by subaerial processes, although no evidence for subaerial exposure is found. The erosion may have occurred during a drop in sea level, with the top of the paleostructure subjected to more intense wave or current action than the flank areas (Weimer, Sonnenberg, and Young, 1986). After the period of erosion, marine shales of the lower Pierre were deposited.

If the lower Pierre Shale was deposited in a nearly horizontal attitude (Fig. 2), then the isopach map can be used as a paleostructure contour map (Fig. 4) (Weimer, et al., 1986). The isopach map shows greatest thinning in an east–west trending area 10 mi (16.1 km) wide and 50 mi (80.5 km) long. This paleostructure probably persisted during the deposition of several thousand feet of the lower half of the Pierre Shale. Natural gas, which was free to migrate in the Muddy (J) Sandstone during this sequence of events, accumulated in a combined structural, stratigraphic, and unconformity trap. This trap was subsequently warped into the present low structural position at the bottom of the Denver Basin.

Uncertainty exists as to whether or not the Wattenberg gas is thermogenic, or a mixture of both thermogenic and biogenic. Because of above–normal heat

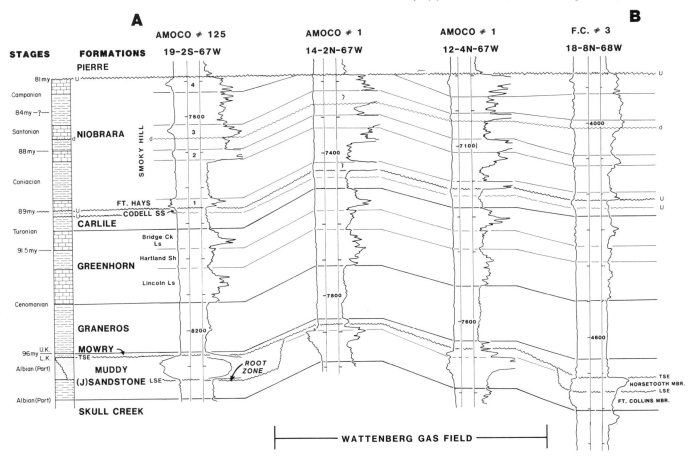

Figure 2. Surface stratigraphic section and north–south electric log section of the lower 900 ft (275 m) of Cretaceous strata drilled in general Wattenberg area. Refer to Figure 20 for section location. Radiometric age dates are taken from Fouch, et al. (1983) and correlated to Denver Basin section.

flow (Myer and McGee, 1985) and isotopic composition in the Wattenberg area, Momper (1981) and Rice and Threlkeld (1982, 1983) believe the gas is thermogenic. However, Clayton and Swetland (1980, p. 1631) state that "methane gases from the Wattenberg field near Denver are isotopically too light to have formed by late–mature thermal cracking." If significant quantities of the gas are biogenic, and therefore of early origin, then the early paleostructure played an important role in the accumulation.

The relationship of the Wattenberg paleohigh to other paleostructural elements in the Denver Basin is described by Sonnenberg and Weimer (1981). Comparison of regional isopachs of the Niobrara and the Skull Creek–Muddy (J) Sandstone intervals in the Denver Basin show a correspondence of thin areas of deposition. Moreover, valley–fill deposits are best developed in thick areas between paleostructural high areas. These observations suggest structural movement during deposition of the Muddy (J) Sandstone. In addition, extensional fracturing associated with paleodrape folds, along the margin of the basement blocks, probably developed a natural open fracture system in the Muddy (J) Sandstone. The regional fracture trends are east–west, northwest and northeast.

The influence of paleostructure on the location and magnitude of erosion associated with unconformities will be discussed in later sections.

REGIONAL STRATIGRAPHY

The stratigraphic section for the lower portion of the Cretaceous of the Denver Basin is well known from outcrop, core, and electric log data (Fig. 2). The lower 900 ft (275 m) of the Cretaceous stratigraphic section drilled in the general Wattenberg area contains mainly marine shale, siltstone, sandstone and limestone. However, the Dakota Group in the lower one–fourth of the interval is both marine and nonmarine in origin. Although outcrop and core data have assisted in stratigraphic studies, the main data base is from mechanical well logs. The electric log patterns for the mappable formation (or members) are illustrated by the log sections accompanying this report. More than 400 wells were analyzed in an area 60 mi (96.5 km) long and 40 mi (64 km) wide. Detailed thickness studies of these units were undertaken to determine if paleostructural movement influenced deposition and final distribution. Regional unconformities which influence thicknesses have been identified within the Muddy (J) Sandstone, the base of the

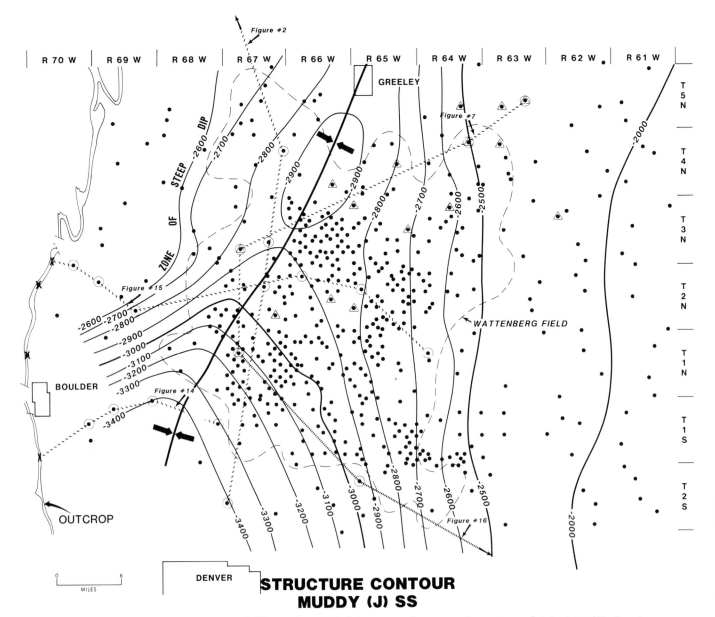

STRUCTURE CONTOUR MUDDY (J) SS

Figure 3. Structure contour map of Wattenberg Field area. Contoured on top of Muddy (J) Sandstone. Contour interval is 100 ft (30.5 m). Solid dots are control wells; those with triangles have cores from Muddy (J) Sandstone. Circles indicate wells in lines of section.

Codell Sandstone, and the base and top of the Niobrara Formation (Fig. 2). These unconformities are major sequence boundaries.

Skull Creek Shale

The thickness and distribution of units within the marine Skull Creek Shale are critical to interpreting the origin of the Muddy (J) Sandstone. The Skull Creek is dominantly marine shale and varies in thickness from 50 to 200 ft (15 to 61 m). The greatest thickness is in the area of Wattenberg Field, where the upper contact is transitional with the overlying Muddy (J) Sandstone. The thinnest sections are south of Wattenberg in the Boulder to Morrison area where only the lower Skull Creek is present because erosion, prior to deposition of the Muddy (J) Sand-

stone, cut out the upper part of the Skull Creek. In addition, in this thin area the marine shale changes to largely bioturbated marine sandstone.

Muddy (J) Sandstone

Over the Wattenberg Field area, the Muddy (J) Sandstone ranges in thickness from less than 75 to more than 150 ft (23 to 46 m) (Fig. 5). Thickest sections are to the northeast and to the southwest of Wattenberg.

Two types of sandstone bodies comprising the Muddy (J) Sandstone in the Denver Basin were described by MacKenzie (1965) from outcrops along the west margin of the basin. He formally named them the Fort Collins and Horsetooth Members of the

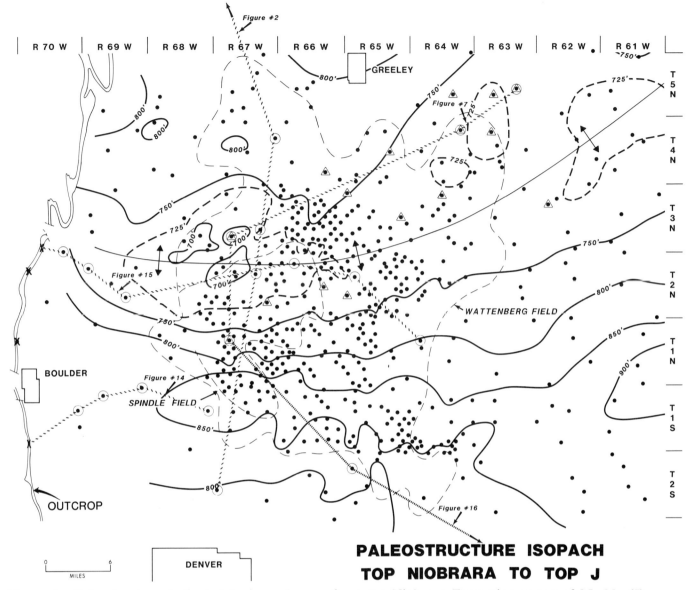

PALEOSTRUCTURE ISOPACH TOP NIOBRARA TO TOP J

Figure 4. Paleostructure indicated by isopach map from top Niobrara Formation to top of Muddy (J) Sandstone. Contour interval is 50 ft (15.2 m).

Muddy Sandstone, which is the "J" Sandstone of the subsurface.

The older Fort Collins Member is a very fine to fine-grained sandstone containing numerous trace fossils and is interpreted to be delta front sandstones deposited during rapid regression of the shoreline of the Skull Creek sea. Sandstones of the younger Horsetooth Member are fine to medium-grained, well sorted, cross-stratified, and contain carbonized wood fragments. Productive sandstones are intercalated with siltstone and mudstone and are interpreted to be channels deposited as part of valley-fill deposits of fresh and brackish-water origin. The first use of the term "valley-fill deposits" and associated productive sandstones in the Denver Basin (Nebraska portion) was by Harms (1966). He described two sandstone units in the Muddy (J) Sandstone that have similar

lithologies to the Fort Collins and Horsetooth members of the Muddy (J) Sandstone. Production is from channel sandstones of the valley-fill in the Horsetooth Member.

Benton Group and Niobrara Formation

From 400 to 500 ft (120 to 150 m) of black shale and gray limestone between the Muddy (J) Sandstone and the Niobrara Formation has been mapped in outcrop as the Benton Shale along the west flank of the basin. Based on characteristic log patterns, the Benton can be subdivided in the subsurface into four formations, which in ascending order are the Mowry Shale, the Graneros Shale, the Greenhorn Formation, and the Carlile Shale (Fig. 2). The Greenhorn has three members, the Lincoln Limestone, Hartland

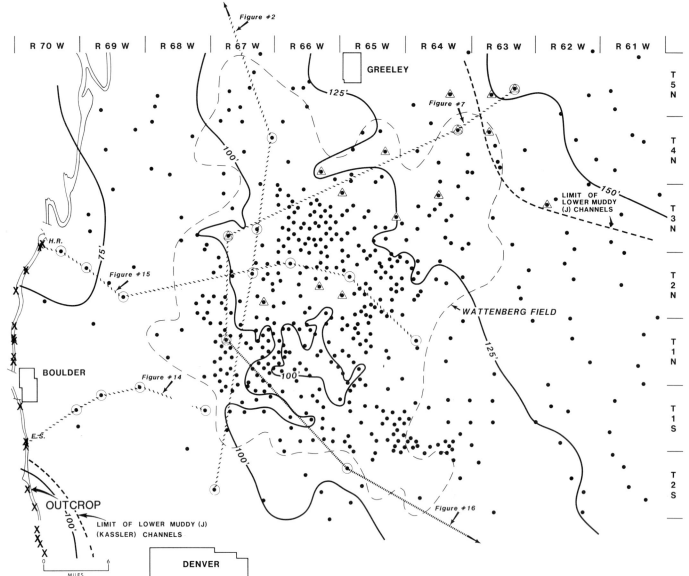

ISOPACH MUDDY (J) SANDSTONE

Figure 5. Isopach map of Muddy (J) Sandstone. Contour interval is 25 ft (7.6 m). Triangular symbols indicate wells used for core study.

Shale and Bridge Creek Limestone; the Carlile has the Codell Sandstone Member in the upper part.

Regional thickness patterns and descriptions for these four formations throughout the Denver Basin were published by Weimer (1978) and in the Wattenberg Field area by Weimer, et al. (1986). The Benton Group contains source beds for the oil and gas found in Lower Cretaceous sandstones in the Denver Basin (Clayton and Swetland, 1980).

The Niobrara Formation consists of four regional limestone units with intercalated dark gray to black shale and bentonite. The thickness varies from 250 to 400 ft (76 to 122 m). The lowermost limestone is the Fort Hays Member and the overlying three limestones with intervening shales are designated the Smoky Hill member (Fig. 2). The limestone and

shale layers contain abundant marine molluscan and trace fossils.

Recognition of the distinctive lithologies of the thin Mowry Shale is important in the study of the underlying Muddy (J) Sandstone. The Mowry Shale is widespread in Wyoming, but thins southward into Colorado and pinches out southeast of Wattenberg Field (Haun, 1963; Rojas, 1980). Across the field area, thicknesses vary generally between 10 and 20 ft (3 to 6 m) with local areas greater than 20 ft (6 m) (Fig. 6). The lithology is interbedded shale, siltstone, and very fine–grained sandstone in repetitive layers that are 1 to 2 in. (2.5 to 5 cm) thick. The thin ripple–laminated or parallel–laminated sandstone layers commonly have sharp bases with underlying shales, and grade upward to siltstone and then black shale.

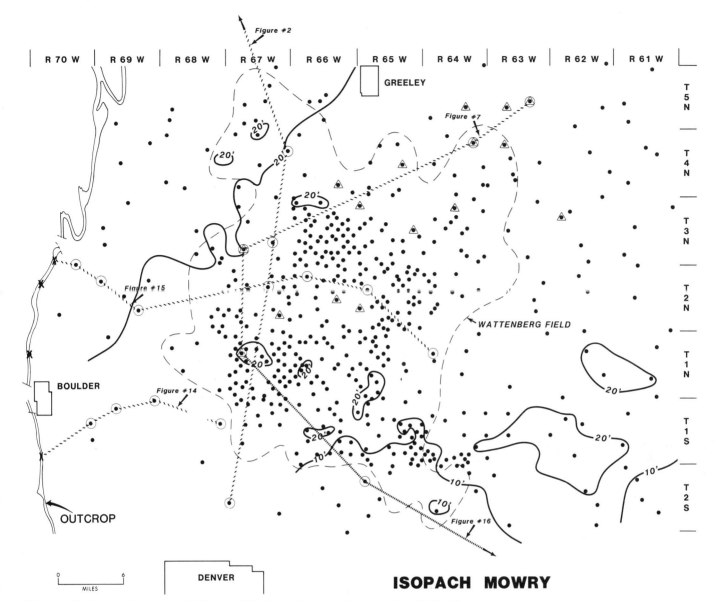

Figure 6. Isopach map of Mowry Shale. Contour interval is 10 ft (3 m).

The combination of these lithologies gives a characteristic pattern on electric logs, with a slightly higher resistivity than the overlying marine Graneros Shale. Some of the black shale layers have abundant fish scales. The Mowry is interpreted as a marine anoxic deposit with thin sandstone and siltstone layers deposited by density currents, followed by quiet water clay deposition from suspension.

LITHOLOGIES AND RESERVOIR PARAMETERS

Muddy (J) Sandstone

The Muddy (J) Sandstone reservoir in Wattenberg Field is productive over an area of 600,000 acres, at depths of 7,600 to 8,400 ft (2,310 to 2,560 m). Reservoir parameters were summarized by Matuszczak (1973) as follows: net pay thickness varies from 10 to 50 ft (3 to 15 m); porosity ranges from 8 to 12%; and permeability ranges from 0.1 to 0.05 md; reservoir pressure and temperature average 2,750 psig and 260°F (176°C); and average water saturation is 44%. Regional porosity and permeability maps for the J Sandstone have been published by Higley and Gautier (1986, 1987, and this volume).

Over the Wattenberg Field, the Muddy (J) Sandstone ranges in thickness from approximately 75 to 150 ft (22.8 to 45.7 m) (Fig. 5). The majority of the gas production comes from fine-grained sandstone of the Fort Collins Member (delta front sandstone, Figs. 7, 8, and 9), which ranges in thickness from a wedge edge to greater than 80 ft (24.4 m) (Fig. 10). However, the main pay section in the upper portion of the Fort Collins averages between 10 and 20 ft (3 and 6 m). Thin areas, or areas where the Fort Collins Member is absent, are caused by erosion during an incisement of drainage prior to deposition of valley-fill

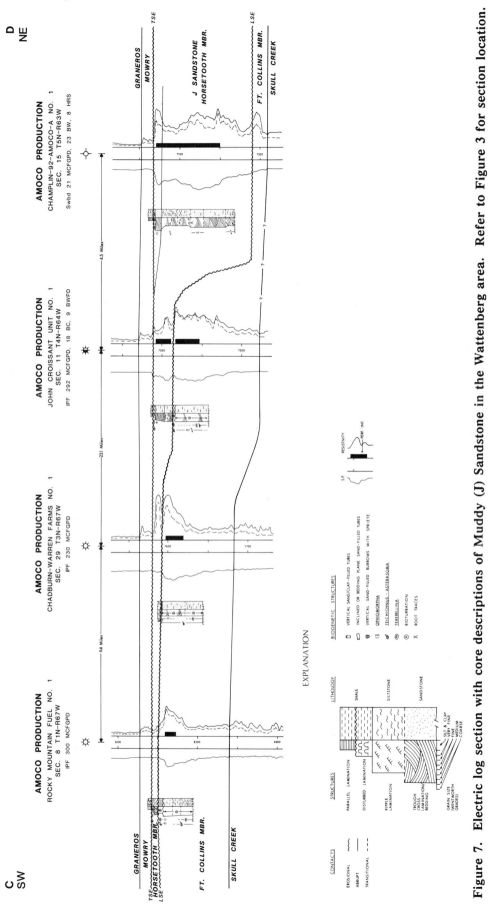

Figure 7. Electric log section with core descriptions of Muddy (J) Sandstone in the Wattenberg area. Refer to Figure 3 for section location.

AMOCO ≠ 1 ROCKY MTN FUEL
Nw Sw Sec. 8-T1N-R67W

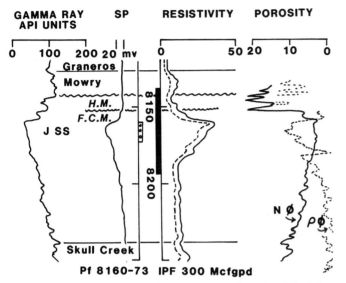

GAMMA RAY SP RESISTIVITY POROSITY
API UNITS

Graneros
Mowry
H.M.
F.C.M.
J SS
8150
8200
Skull Creek

N∅
P∅

Pf 8160-73 IPF 300 Mcfgpd

Figure 8. Mechanical log patterns for the Muddy (J) Sandstone from a typical well in Wattenberg Field. H.M. is Horsetooth Member; F.C.M. is Fort Collins Member. Refer to Figures 10A and B for core photographs and Figure 7 for core description.

deposits of the Horsetooth Member, or by truncation by the transgressive surface of erosion (TSE) near the top of the Muddy (J) Sandstone.

Because of the widespread distribution of the marine Fort Collins Sandstone, the log character of the Muddy (J) Sandstone appears to be fairly uniform across Wattenberg Field. A normal log suite consists of resistivity, spontaneous potential, gamma ray, neutron, and density logs (Fig. 8). For the Fort Collins Member, the gamma ray and spontaneous potential curves have funnel shapes, indicating a textural coarsening-upward sequence (i.e., more sand and less shale). The log response is typical for delta front sandstones in Wattenberg Field. The resistivity curve is almost a mirror image of the gamma ray and SP curves. The highest resistivities occur in the upper portion of the delta front sandstones, and are caused by gas being present in the reservoir. Porosity values from the neutron and density logs through the upper delta front are 3% and 6 to 10% respectively. The neutron-density crossover is a gas effect.

Fort Collins Member

The Fort Collins Member is a very fine to fine-grained sandstone composed of approximately 80% quartz, 10% argillaceous matrix, 5% rock fragments, and 5% feldspar. The sand grains are subrounded to rounded and the sandstones are poorly to well sorted. Clay is the main matrix material which results both from bioturbation and diagenesis. Bioturbation, in a complete section, decreases vertically in abundance. The decrease in the clay matrix is due to higher en-

ergy conditions which winnowed out the clay fraction and also to a change from deposit-feeding to suspension-feeding organisms. The lithologies of outcrop sections described by Clark (1978) and Suryanto (1979) west of Wattenberg Field are similar to cores from producing wells (Figs. 7, 8, and 9A and B).

The porosity is mainly intergranular with minor amounts of microporosity found in the matrix material, and secondary interparticle porosity associated with leached feldspars and lithic rock fragments. The order of the normal diagenetic processes in the sandstone is as follows: compaction; growth of clay rims (chlorite); formation of quartz overgrowths; calcite cementation and contemporaneous feldspar and lithic rock fragment solution; subsequent calcite solution; growth of illite/smectite; and late stage fracturing.

One of the most important diagenetic events in the Fort Collins Member is the formation of quartz overgrowths (Fig. 11A and 11B). The euhedral overgrowths are separated from the detrital quartz grains by a clay rim and show crystal faces directed into pores, which generally results in triangular pore shapes. The percentage of overgrowths appears to diminish as matrix content increases. Near the subaerially exposed surface at the top of the Fort Collins Member, pore-filling kaolinite follows early quartz overgrowths.

Capillary pressure data (Fig. 12A) and porosity and permeability data (Fig. 12B) for the Amoco No. 1 Rocky Mountain Fuel well indicate characteristics of a "tight gas sand reservoir". Note on Figure 12A the high irreducible water saturation and displacement pressure (Pd) typical of low porosity and permeability reservoirs. The shape of the curve also suggests poor sorting of pores.

Horsetooth Member

Sandstones of the Horsetooth Member are fine to medium-grained, well sorted, and well rounded. They are composed of 75 to 80% quartz, 5 to 10% rock fragments, and 5% feldspar. The porosity is mainly intergranular, with minor microporosity and intraparticle porosity. The Horsetooth ranges in thickness from less than 20 ft (6.1 m) to greater than 140 ft (42.6 m) (Fig. 13). The Horsetooth Member with its vertically stacked channel sandstone complexes is thickest in the northeast and southwest portions of the mapped area. Graphic descriptions of the Horsetooth Member are presented for the outcrop and four wells in Wattenberg Field (Fig. 7).

In the No. 1 Rocky Mountain Fuel well (Figs. 7, 8, and 9), the Horsetooth Member consists of alternating shaly sandstone and laminated sandstone and shale. A bioturbated interval in the upper 2 ft (0.7 m) is interpreted as a transgressive marine sandstone (Fig. 9B) that formed during the marine Mowry transgression related to sea level rise. The low spontaneous potential, high gamma ray, and low resistivity reflect the abundance of clay in the sandstone. In other areas of the field, cleaner sandstones are present in the Horsetooth Member and the log response changes accordingly (Fig. 7).

The diagenetic processes affecting the Horsetooth Member are similar to those of the Fort Collins Member, with the exceptions of more intense silica cemen-

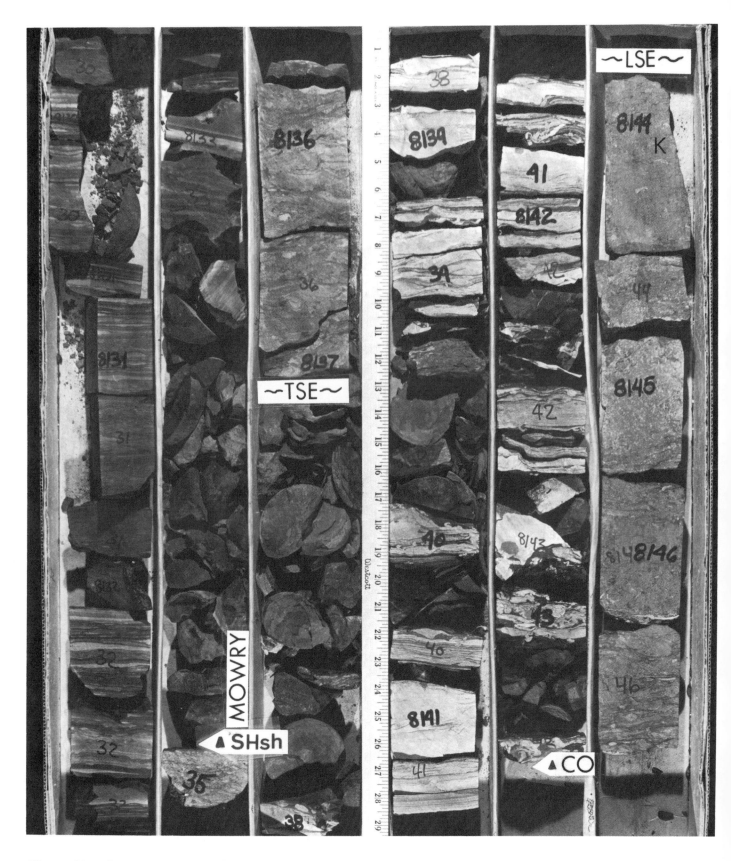

Figure 9A. Core photograph of upper portion of core. Refer to Figures 7 and 8 for log patterns related to core. LSE = lowstand surface of erosion; CO = coastal onlap of coastal plain strata; TSE = transgressive surface of erosion overlain by 2 ft (0.7 m) of transgressive marine sandstone; SH8H = marine shale (Mowry).

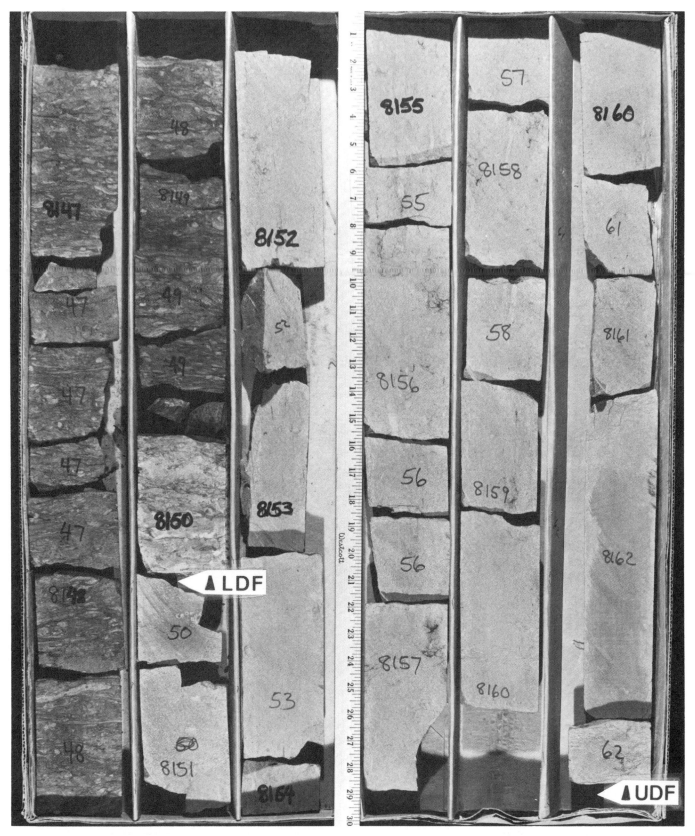

Figure 9B. Core photograph of pay sandstone interval from Amoco No. 1 Rocky Mountain Fuel well
(NW SW Sec 8 T1N R67W) in Wattenberg Field. Environments of deposition are: UDF = upper delta front;
LDF = lower delta front.

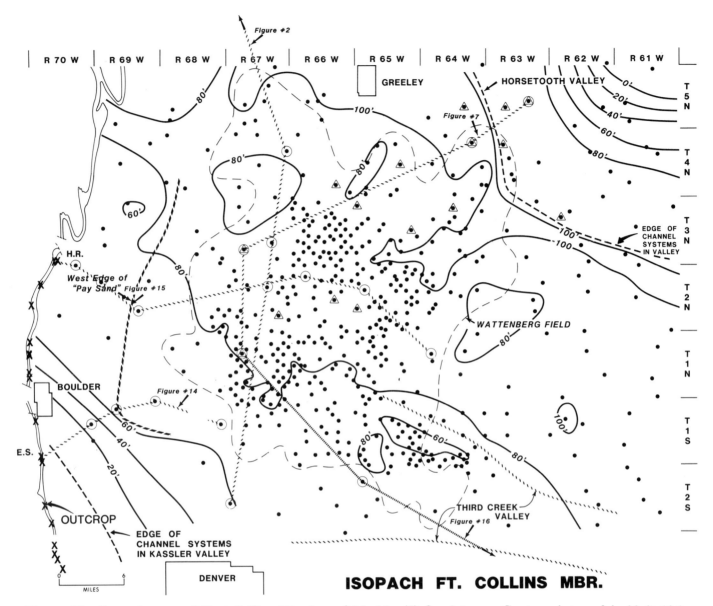

Figure 10. Isopach map of Fort Collins Member of Muddy (J) Sandstone. Contour interval is 20 ft (6.1 m).

tation and the presence of smectite, chlorite, and kaolinite clay pore filling. This combination of silica overgrowths and clay cement may totally occlude primary porosity. These cements in the Horsetooth Member may help trap the gas in the Fort Collins Member and, therefore, appear to be the seal (in part) on the eastern side of Wattenberg Field.

SEQUENCE STRATIGRAPHY— UNCONFORMITIES AND DEPOSITIONAL MODELS FOR RESERVOIRS

Sequence stratigraphy is the study of genetically related strata which are bounded by unconformities or their correlative conformities (Vail, et al., 1977; Vail, 1987). An unconformity is defined as a sedimentary structure of regional occurrence in which two groups

of rocks are separated by an erosional surface; the erosion may be by subaerial or submarine processes.

Three sequences bounded by unconformities can be observed in the Lower Cretaceous of the Denver Basin (Figs. 14, 15, and 17). Sequence 1 is the non-marine Lytle Formation. Sequence 2 includes the coastal plain deposits of the Plainview Sandstone, the overlying marine Skull Creek Shale, and the overlying deltaic and marine sandstone genetically related to the Skull Creek. This latter interval for mapping purposes is placed in the Muddy (J) Formation. Sequence 3 usually includes incised valley fill deposits (Fig. 16) or coastal onlap deposits of the Muddy (J) Formation, along with the overlying marine Mowry Shale, Graneros Shale, Greenhorn Limestone, and that portion of the Carlile Shale underlying the erosional sur-

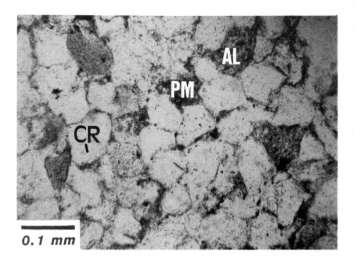

Figure 11A. Thin–section photomicrograph of Muddy (J) Sandstone (Fort Collins Member) showing clay rims and quartz overgrowths, argillaceous lithic fragments (AL), and pseudomatrix (Pm) resulting from diagenetic pore filling.

Figure 11B. SEM photomicrograph of J Sandstone. Quartz overgrowths (Q) are abundant; authigenic smectite (S) lines pores.

MERCURY INJECTION
CAPILLARY PRESSURE CURVE

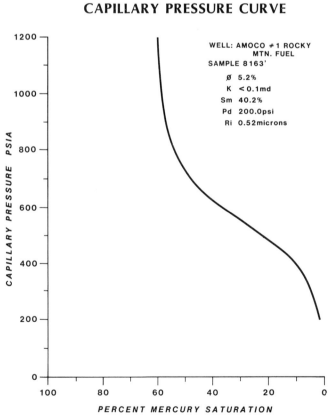

WELL: AMOCO #1 ROCKY MTN. FUEL
SAMPLE 8163'

Ø 5.2%
K <0.1md
Sm 40.2%
Pd 200.0psi
Ri 0.52microns

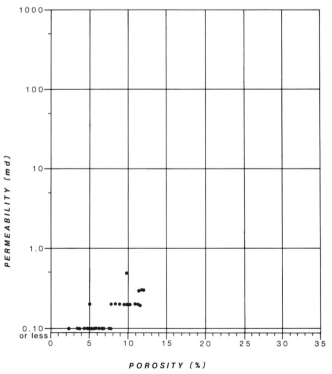

Figure 12A. Capillary pressure curve for Muddy (J) Sandstone, Amoco No. 1 Rocky Mountain Fuel well (refer to Figure 8 for log patterns). φ = porosity, K = permeability; Swi = irreducible saturation; Pd = displacement pressure; Ri = pore radii.

Figure 12B. Plot of porosity and permeability for Amoco No. 1 Rocky Mountain Fuel well.

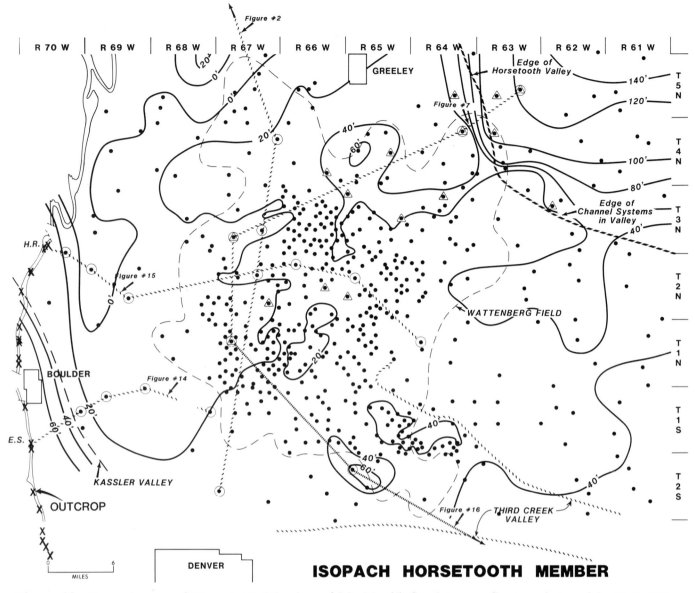

Figure 13. Isopach map of Horsetooth Member of Muddy (J) Sandstone. Contour interval is 20 ft (6.1 m). The Kassler paleovalley, observed in outcrop and subsurface, is named for the fluvial Kassler Sandstone Member of the South Platte Formation (MacKenzie, 1971).

face at base of the Codell Sandstone. All strata above the Mowry are designated as Upper Cretaceous.

Two types of major erosional surfaces are observed either within or at the formation contacts of the Muddy (J) Sandstone. Each is associated with major changes of relative sea level but the magnitude of erosion may be influenced by local tectonic events. One type, a sequence boundary called a lowstand surface of erosion (LSE), is related to a lowering of base level which causes subaerial exposure and incisement of drainages into older deposits. The subaerial exposure causes chemical changes in the strata by oxidation, etc. The second type is a transgressive surface of erosion (TSE) related to shoreline and shoreface (marine) erosion, caused by rising sea level and deepening water. The unconformity associated with the TSE occurs within a depositional sequence.

Studies of the late Quaternary history of coastal areas of the eastern and gulf coast U.S. give insight as to the origin and processes related to these two types of erosional surfaces (Demarest and Kraft, 1987; Nummedal and Swift, 1987). A sequence boundary placed at the base of the Holocene is a lowstand surface of erosion (LSE) caused by a lowering of sea level during Pleistocene glaciation. Coastal plain sedimentation with coastal onlap occurred during the post–glacial rise of sea level. A transgressive surface of erosion (TSE) (ravinement surface of some authors) developed as shoreface erosion moved over coastal plain deposits during shoreline retreat, a process still active today.

A third type of surface sometimes can be identified that is related to nondeposition with possible minor erosion. If present, it occurs within a condensed ma-

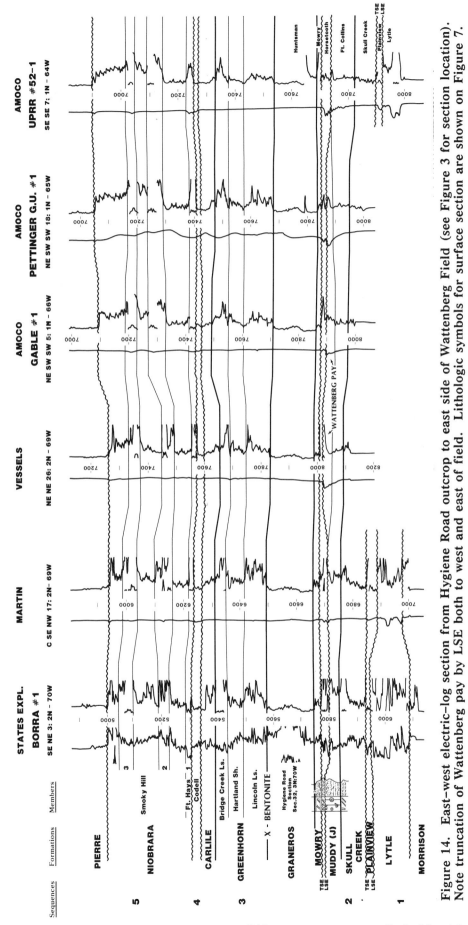

Figure 14. East-west electric-log section from Hygiene Road outcrop to east side of Wattenberg Field (see Figure 3 for section location). Note truncation of Wattenberg pay by LSE both to west and east of field. Lithologic symbols for surface section are shown on Figure 7.

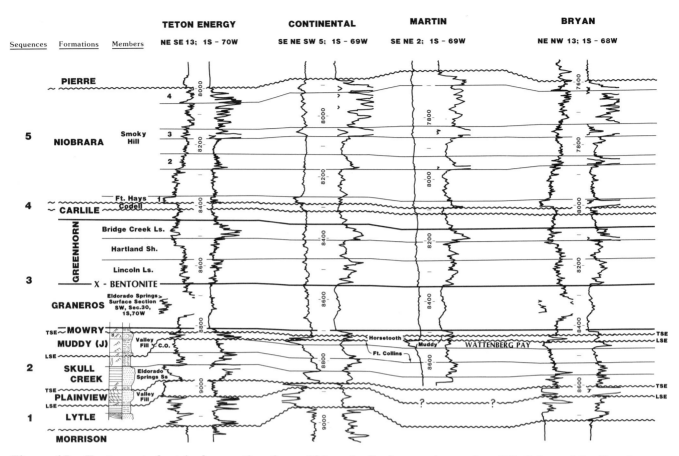

Figure 15. East–west electric–log section from Eldorado Springs outcrop (modified from MacKenzie, 1971) to east side of Wattenberg Field (see Figure 3 for section location). Lithologic symbols for surface section are shown on Figure 7.

rine section that generally has a high total organic content (e.g., the middle Skull Creek Shale or in the lower Graneros Shale). Minor scour may concentrate lags of shells, or glauconite and phosphate grains. Bentonite may occur in shale layers above or below the surface. In sequence stratigraphy such a surface has been called: the surface of maximum transgression; surface of maximum flooding; or, surface of maximum starvation (Vail, 1987). Minor erosional surfaces associated with depositional processes within environments of deposition are called diastems (e.g., scour at the base of a channel).

The erosional surfaces related to sea–level changes have been mapped regionally for the three sequences in the Lower Cretaceous. Sequence 2 is defined by analysis of outcrop and nearby subsurface data (Fig. 17). The marine Skull Creek Shale and genetically related underlying and overlying sandstones are interpreted as highstand deposits (HSD). The lower and middle Skull Creek Shale (Unit A, Fig. 17) are dominantly transgressive shale deposits (TD) related to deeper water conditions. A condensed section (CS) with a high total organic content (source bed) occurs in the upper 10 to 20 ft (3 to 6 m) of Unit A. The upper Skull Creek (Units B and C) and the overlying Fort Collins Member of the Muddy (J) Sandstone are dominantly regressive shale and sandstone deposits (RD) related to water shoaling and progradation. For

convenience and accuracy in subsurface mapping, the marker horizon (M) at the base of Unit C was chosen by Amoco Production Co. (Matuszczak, 1976) as the base of the Muddy (J) Sandstone in the Wattenberg Field area. This definition is followed in this paper in preparing maps and sections, although the Muddy (J)–Skull Creek contact in outcrop is placed at the top of Unit C (base of the Fort Collins Member, Fig. 17). The marker horizon (M) at the top of Skull Creek Unit B, is an important reference to determine the depth of incisement related to valley–cutting during the sea–level lowstand (LSE) between sequences 2 and 3. In the outcrop area south of Boulder, Unit C and most of Unit B were removed by erosion prior to deposition of the incised valley fill deposits (IVF) of the Horsetooth Member of the Muddy (J). In addition, black fissile shales of Unit A change southward to marine sandstones (Eldorado Springs Sandstone, Fig. 17) and bioturbated sandstones, siltstones, and shales in the I–70 and Turkey Creek areas.

A paleontologic summary for the Skull Creek Shale was reported by Waage and Eicher (1960). The middle part of the Skull Creek (upper of Unit A and the lower part of Unit B, Fig. 17) is the only interval of the Dakota Group that contains common and useful fossils. The megafossils are the *Inoceramus comancheanus* fauna and the microfossils are the *Ammobaculites euides* and the *Verneuilinoides kansasen-*

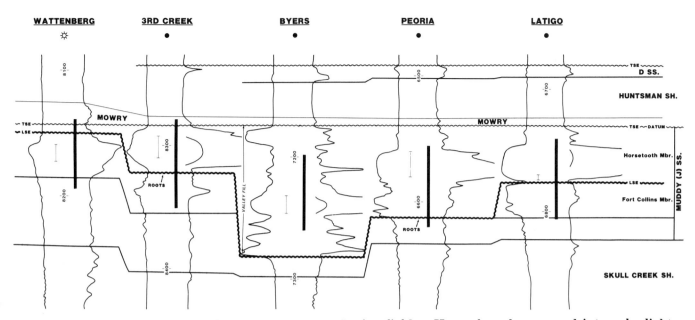

Figure 16. Electric–log section from Wattenberg to Latigo fields. Heavy bar shows cored intervals; light bar shows perforated intervals. Wattenberg well is Amoco No. 1 Rocky Mountain Fuel well (300 MCFGPD); Third Creek well is Amoco no. 117–6 Champlin, Sec 7 T2S R65W (72 BOPD); Byers well is UPRR No. 41–11 Jefferies, Sec 11 T4S R62W (225 BOPD, 188 MCFGPD); Peoria well is Midwest Oil No. 1–A Baughman Farms, Sec 32 T4S R60W (292 BOPD); Latigo well is Amoco No. 3 UPRR, Sec 13 T5S R61W (31 BOPD, 1,575 MCFGPD). Location shown on Figure 20.

sis biofacies of the *Haplophragmoides gigas* zone. MacKenzie (1971) and Chamberlain (1976) described trace fossils from the Dakota Group. Foraminifera and biostratigraphy of the Mowry and Graneros shales were described by Eicher (1965). All these data support the marine interpretation for the Skull Creek, Mowry, and Graneros.

Interpretation of the Origin of Muddy (J) Sandstone Reservoirs

Following the highstand transgressive deposits (HSD) of the Skull Creek Shale, a regressive event deposited deltaic shoreline and shallow marine sandstones that have a transitional contact with the underlying Skull Creek Shales (Fig. 18). Depositional patterns over basement fault blocks, where slight fault block movement influenced topography and sedimentation, depended on the rates of submergence and sediment supply. Rivers and associated deltas positioned themselves in structural and topographically low areas (i.e., grabens), whereas delta margin or interdeltaic sedimentation occurred along an embayed coast over structural horst blocks. Delta front and shoreface sands extended seaward from the shoreline a distance controlled by effective wave base. The shoreline prograded seaward to position T2 and a sheet–like sand body was deposited over a large area (Fort Collins Member, the pay sandstone of Wattenberg). These depositional patterns are highstand regressive deposits that developed during a stillstand or slightly lowered sea level.

A drop in sea level (T3 in Fig. 19) occurred during which a large portion of the depositional basin (Skull Creek seaway) was drained. River drainages were incised into older strata, especially in topo-

graphic lows which correspond with the graben fault block areas (Figs. 17 and 19). Over much of the Denver Basin, the base of the incisement is on the T1 or T2 sandstone complex (Fort Collins Member). Locally, the erosional surface cut into the Skull Creek Shale. The depth of valley incisement in the Denver Basin varies from 20 ft (6 m) to more than 130 ft (40 m). This drop in sea level is related to the worldwide low sea level reported by Vail, et al. (1977) as occurring approximately 97 to 98 Ma, although the dating is uncertain because of limited information. The geographic distribution of the major incised valleys during the lowstand is shown on a paleodrainage map for the Muddy (J) Sandstone (Fig. 20) and in the outcrop restored section (Fig. 17). The paleovalleys are interpreted from isopach maps of the Muddy (J) Sandstone as occurring in those areas where the formation is greater than 100 ft (30 m) in thickness and erosion can be observed into the upper Skull Creek Shale.

A rise in sea level occurred (T4 on Fig. 21) during which the incised valleys were modified and filled with fluvial and estuarine sandstone, siltstone, and shales. The incised valley fill deposits may be zoned, with more fresh–water deposits in the lower part and brackish to marine rocks in the upper part. The zoning reflects aggradational fill and landward movement of the shoreline (transgression) associated with coastal onlap on the lowstand surface of erosion (LSE).

With a continued rise in sea level, the coastal plain deposits were transgressed by shoreline and shoreface environments and an associated erosional surface formed over a large area (TSE). In some outcrop sections, a thin (1 ft, or 0.3 m) lenticular bed of fine to coarse–grained conglomeratic sandstone is observed at the top of the Muddy (J) Sandstone (MacKenzie,

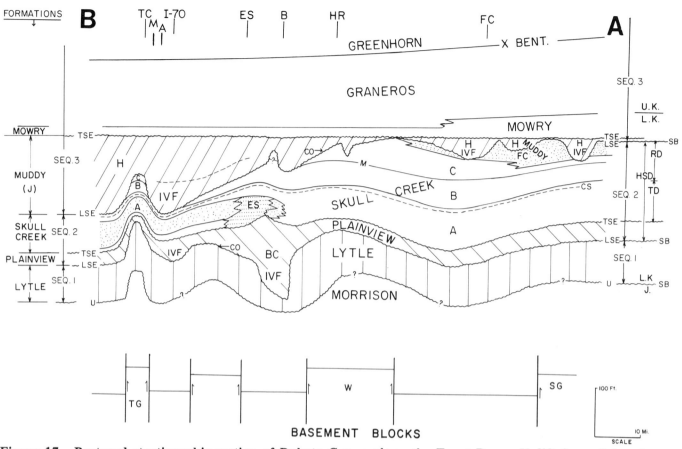

Figure 17. Restored stratigraphic section of Dakota Group along the Front Range Uplift from Colorado-Wyoming state line to south of Morrison, Colorado; from outcrop sections and nearby subsurface (modified after MacKenzie, 1971 and Weimer, 1984). Legend for the letters is as follows: for formations – Muddy Formation, Fort Collins (FC), and Horsetooth (H) members; Skull Creek – Units A, B and C, regional marker horizon (M), Eldorado Springs sandstone (ES); Bear Canyon sandstone (BC) of Plainview. Sequence stratigraphy terms are: sequence (SEQ.), highstand deposits (HSD), transgressive deposits (TD), regressive deposits (RD), condensed section (CS), sequence boundary (SB), lowstand surface of erosion (LSE), transgressive surface of erosion (TSE), incised valley fill (IVF) coastal onlap (CO); basement fault blocks – Turkey Creek (TC), Wattenberg (W), and Skin Gulch (SG); geographic localities – Fort Collins (FC), Hygiene Road (HR), Boulder (B), Eldorado Springs (ES), Interstate Highway 70 (I-70), Alameda (A), Morrison (M), and Turkey Creek (TC).

1965). Although included in the Muddy (J) Sandstone, the layer is a relict or palimpsest sandstone genetically related to the Mowry transgression (Rojas, 1980). The conglomeratic sandstone occurs in minor scour depressions associated with the transgressive surface of erosion (TSE). Where the coarse materials are absent, the transgressive deposit is a thin fine-grained sandstone, intensively burrowed by marine organisms.

This record of sediment reworking during the transgression of the sea over shoreline and coastal plain deposits, and the widespread thin nature of the Mowry Shale (Fig. 6) indicate rapid and uniform water deepening in this area during the transgression. No significant structural movement occurred, although local 20% thinning might suggest minor movement of fault blocks (Fig. 6). The convergence of the lowstand and transgressive surfaces over interstream divides (structural highs) suggests that more erosion occurred in those areas by shoreline and shoreface

erosion than in the valley areas (Figs. 7, 14, 15, 16, and 17).

Following time T4, the entire region received laminated marine silt and mud deposits (Mowry and Graneros shales). These organic-rich black shales were deposited under anoxic bottom conditions during which time detrital input was slower, so that concentration of organic matter increased. The resultant condensed section has a high total organic carbon content in shale layers.

Muddy (J) Sandstone Reservoirs and the Unconformities

Recognition of the stratigraphic position of reservoirs relative to the two surfaces of erosion establishes age relationships more accurately than does correlation based on stratigraphic position. Three stratigraphic settings for reservoirs can be determined which are independent of stratigraphic level. First, the Fort Collins Member, the main productive reser-

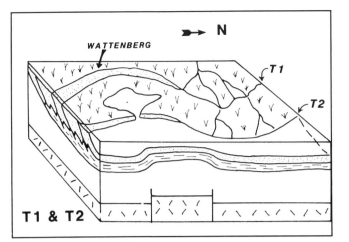

Figure 18. Depositional and tectonic model for highstand regression over basement fault blocks with penecontemporaneous fault movement. T1 = Time 1; T2 = Time 2. Rate of sediment supply exceeds rate of subsidence or submergence. Not to scale (from Weimer, 1984).

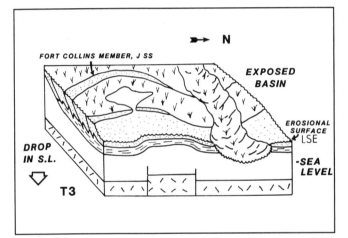

Figure 19. Lowstand sea level (T3 = Time 3) recorded as basin-wide erosional surface (LSE) resulting from subaerial exposure (major sequence boundary). Root zones form on exposed marine shales and sandstones. Not to scale (from Weimer, 1984).

voir in Wattenberg Field, is the oldest part of the Muddy (J) Sandstone. Generally this reservoir occupies a high stratigraphic level (Figs. 2, 7, and 21). Second, reservoirs of the Horsetooth Member, between the lowstand surface of erosion (LSE = sequence boundary) and the transgressive surface of erosion (TSE), are younger but may be at a lower stratigraphic level than the Fort Collins Member. Examples of this relationship are indicated by the channel sandstone reservoirs in the Byers, Peoria, and Latigo fields (shown by the electric-log section, Fig. 16), (Land and Weimer, 1978; Weimer, et al., 1986). Although younger than the Fort Collins Member, the Horsetooth channel production at Fort Col-

lins (Fig. 2) and Third Creek (Fig. 16) (Reinert and Davies, 1976) fields is at the same stratigraphic level as the upper Fort Collins.

A third type of production occurs from thin marine sandstone bars above the transgressive surface of erosion (TSE). The sandstones are narrow, elongated, and have trends different from the valley-fill channel systems. These sandstones are marine bars related genetically to the transgressive deposits overlying the TSE. An example of production from these youngest sandstones is reported for the Scotts Bluff trend in Nebraska (Silverman, 1988), in Poncho Field (Ethridge and Dolson, 1988 and this volume), and in other fields (Dolson, et al., 1989).

In the western portion of the Wattenberg study area, the two surfaces of erosion (LSE and TSE) converge and the Mowry Shale rests on the Fort Collins Member; the Horsetooth Member is absent (Fig. 6). Over much of Wattenberg Field the Horsetooth varies from 10 to 30 ft (3 to 9 m), and forms a thin interval over the Wattenberg paleostructure because of onlap onto high topography and possibly because of a greater magnitude of erosion related to the transgressive surface. Where this interval is thin, uncertainty exists in log interpretation as to whether these coastal plain deposits are genetically related to the Fort Collins member as a delta plain deposit, below the surface of erosion, or if the deposits are above the surface of erosion and related to the coastal onlap of the Horsetooth Member. The latter interpretation is followed in this report.

In summary, the sequence boundary (LSE) may be within, at the base, or at the top of the Muddy (J) Formation. Regardless of stratigraphic position, the sandstone reservoirs above the LSE, primarily in the incised valley fill, are younger than the Fort Collins Member below the unconformity.

The sea level changes described for the Denver Basin are recorded as basin-wide events. Descriptions of fields in the Powder River Basin, using similar terminology, have been reported by Weimer (1984), Weimer, et al. (1988), and Dolson, et al. (1989).

TRAPPING MECHANISMS

Seals for traps in Muddy (J) Sandstone fields are changes in porosity and permeability at the unconformity, facies changes of channel sandstones within the valley fill, and impermeable rocks along valley walls. By use of sequence stratigraphic analysis, the role of the unconformity (sequence boundary) in trapping becomes clear.

The Wattenberg accumulation belongs to the class of "deep basin traps" described by Masters (1979) and Gies (1981). This type of trap has no downdip water, and may not have updip sandstone equivalents that produce water. The Muddy (J) Sandstone is a "tight sand" productive from a large area that lies across the axis of the Denver Basin. No water is produced from the reservoir in the structural low areas of the field. The seals on the present traps appear to be a combination of stratigraphic, unconformity, and related diagenetic changes, with the unconformity above

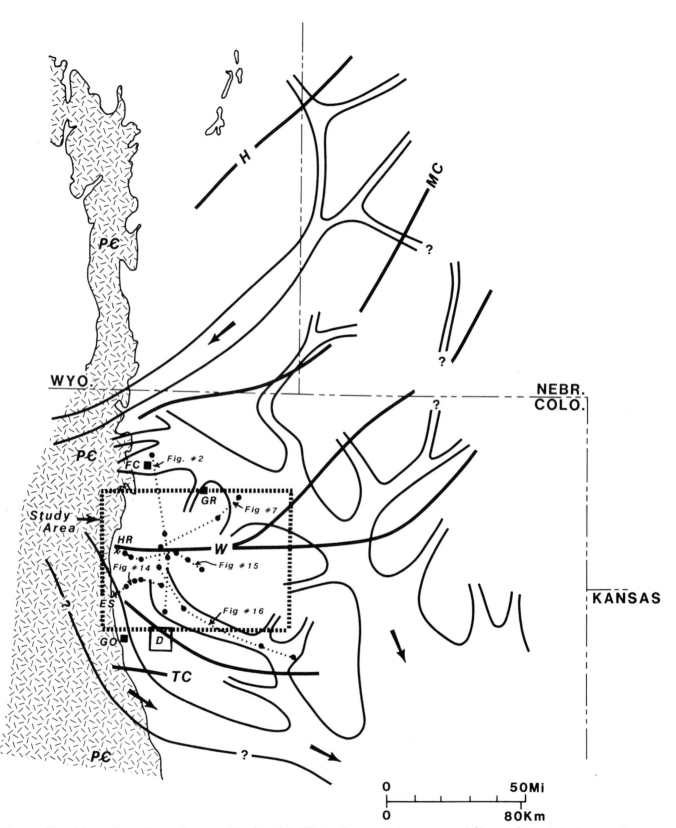

Figure 20. Map of northern Denver Basin with Wattenberg study area and lines of electric log sections (Figs. 2, 7, 14, 15, and 16). Measured surface sections are: HR = Hygiene Road; ES = Eldorado Springs. The major paleovalleys, of the Muddy (J), with direction of flow, are indicated. Paleostructural highs influencing drainage patterns and thickness of Muddy (J) Sandstone are: W = Wattenberg; TC = Turkey Creek; MC = Morrow County; H = Hartville. PC = present Precambrian outcrop of Front Range. Geographic locations are: D = Denver; Gr = Greeley; FC = Fort Collins; Go = Golden.

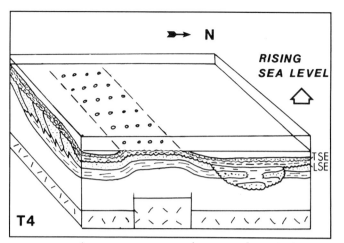

Figure 21. Rising sea level during Time 4 (T4) with fill of incised valley and deposition of marine shale and sandstone. A thin transgressive lag generally less than 1 ft (0.3 m) thick, sometimes with coarse-grained material, occurs on a surface of erosion (transgressive surface) at top of sequence. Lowstand surface of erosion (LSE) and the transgressive surface of erosion (TSE) are labeled. Not to scale (from Weimer, 1984).

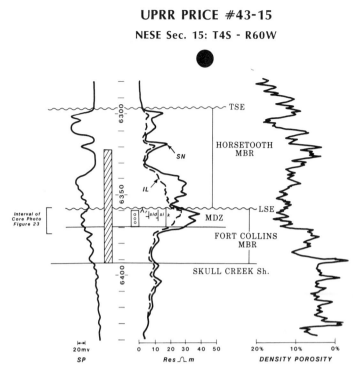

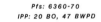

Figure 22. Electric log of Muddy (J) Sandstone in North Peoria Field. Cored interval indicated by diagonal ruling (depth correction: 6,366 ft in core = 6,359 ft on log). LSE = lowstand surface of erosion (regional unconformity with subaerial exposure); R = root zone; sid = siderite as blebs or all-pervasive; si = all-pervasive silica; K = kaolinite. Range of cements in 10 ft (3 m) Maximum Zone of Diagenesis (MZD) is indicated on log. Bars represent solid cementation.

the pay sandstone playing the dominant role in trapping.

Unconformity and Diagenesis

The Wattenberg pay sandstone is truncated on the west flank of the Denver Basin forming a seal between the axis of the basin and the outcrop (Figs. 7, 14, 15, and 16). Impermeable shales, siltstones, and sandstones are in contact with impermeable bioturbated sandstones and shales of the lower Fort Collins Member. The truncation is either by the lowstand surface of erosion (LSE) or the transgressive surface of erosion (TSE), or both.

The seal across the north and east side of Wattenberg Field also appears to be related to the unconformity, either by truncation of the pay sandstone at the valley walls (Figs. 10, 20, and 21) or by chemical changes caused by early cementation in the upper part of the pay sandstone (Fort Collins Member) that formed during subaerial exposure. The chemical changes, possibly related to paleosol development, are not everywhere present, either because of lack of original development, or later removal by diastems (erosion) at the base of channel sandstones in the lower Horsetooth Member.

Silica cementation of the Horsetooth Member channel sandstones also may contribute to trapping along the northeast margin of the field (Matuszczak, 1973). Some channel sandstones that have retained porosity and permeability and that have fluid continuity across the valley wall, produce minor amounts of gas.

Chemical changes (paleosols) under the surface of erosion (LSE) are present in the Hygiene Road section (Fig. 14). A well-developed root zone occurs in

a 3 ft (1 m) sandstone that has a concentration of silica by quartz overgrowths. Kaolinite is present in an underlying bioturbated shaley sandstone.

Typical development of the diagenetic minerals in the subsurface is shown in the Muddy (J) Sandstone core from the UPRR No. 43-15 Price well (NE SE SW Sec 15 T4S R60W) at North Peoria Field. The position of the unconformity between the Fort Collins and Horsetooth members of the Muddy (J) Sandstone is shown on electric logs from the well (Fig. 22). A core across the unconformity shows the development of a root zone overlain by carbonaceous shale on the surface of erosion (LSE). Associated with the root zone is an interval 10 ft (3 m) thick representing a paleosol that has kaolinite, siderite, and silica as pore-filling minerals that block porosity and permeability. Kaolinite appears throughout the interval; silica overgrowths and siderite occur either in small concentrations or as solid bands (Fig. 23). Primary depositional fabric is obliterated in the upper 3 ft (1 m).

Figure 23. Photo of core interval 6,366 ft (upper left) to 6,380 ft (lower right) with minerals in Maximum Zone of Diagenesis (MZD) indicated by symbols. Refer to Figure 22 for legend and range of cementing minerals.

GEOTHERMAL GRADIENTS AND THERMAL MATURITY

Geothermal gradients change from less than 2.0 to more than 2.5 F°/100 ft (3.6–4.6 C°/100 m) across the Denver Basin (Fig. 24). These gradients are important when considering where petroleum generation has occurred. The minimum burial depth needed to initiate thermal petroleum generation depends on the burial history and geothermal gradients of the source rocks. In the majority of Rocky Mountain basins, petroleum generation generally is thought to have occurred in the deeper portions (Meissner, 1978, 1981; Momper, 1981; Clayton and Swetland, 1980; MacMil-

lan, 1980; Tainter, 1984; Higley and Gautier, 1988). Areas of high geothermal gradients in these deeper parts may be the areas of most intense generation.

A geothermal gradient map of the Denver Basin was constructed using bottom hole temperatures from over 500 wells that penetrated the Muddy (J) Sandstone. Gradients were calculated by a method of Meissner (1978).

Areas of mature source rocks are restricted to the deeper portions of the Denver Basin (Fig. 24). Petroleum generation is thought to have occurred along the basin axis beginning in late Paleocene time, expanding outwards toward the basin flanks with time (MacMillan, 1980; Tainter, 1984).

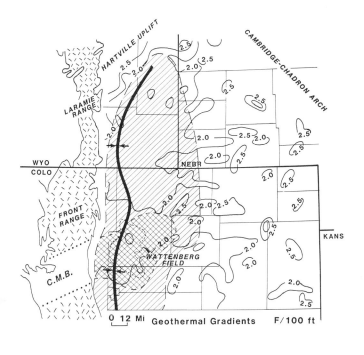

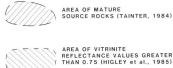

AREA OF MATURE SOURCE ROCKS (TAINTER, 1984)

AREA OF VITRINITE REFLECTANCE VALUES GREATER THAN 0.75 (HIGLEY et al., 1985)

Figure 24. Geothermal gradients in northern portion of Denver Basin, in F° per 100 ft. C.M.B. is Colorado Mineral Belt, a Precambrian structural trend with a zone of Tertiary intrusions, exposed in the Front Range Uplift.

Geothermal gradients indicate that Wattenberg Field is positioned over a geothermal anomaly. Across much of the deeper portions of the basin, geothermal gradients are less than 2 F°/100 ft (3.6 C°/100 m). In the area of Wattenberg Field, gradients are greater than 2 F°/100 ft, and in some cases exceed 2.5 F°/100 ft (4.6 C°/100 m) (Myer and McKee, 1985). The geothermal anomaly coincides with the projection into the basin of the Colorado Mineral Belt, a northeast–trending zone of Tertiary mineralization in the Rocky Mountains. The increase of geothermal gradients may be related to heat being dissipated along northeast–trending fracture systems. Higley, et al. (1985, 1988, and this volume) noted anomalously high vitrinite reflectance values for the Wattenberg Field area as compared to areas of similar depth in the basin. The geothermal gradient map and vitrinite reflectance data suggest that the area of most intense petroleum generation in the basin may have been in the general Wattenberg area. The east flank of the Denver Basin is abnormally hot in terms of geothermal gradients. However, vitrinite reflectance data suggest that source rocks on the east flank are thermally immature.

A subnormal formation pressure regime exists throughout the Denver Basin (Pruit, 1978). The original reservoir pressure for the Muddy (J) Sandstone in Wattenberg Field was 2,750 psi (Matuszczak,

1973). This pressure converts to a 0.34 psi/ft gradient; normal hydrostatic pressure gradient is 0.465 psi/ft. Belitz and Bredehoeft (1988) interpret the subnormal pressures in the basin as a result of hydraulic insulation of strata within the basin from their recharge zones as compared to their discharge zones.

CONCLUSIONS

Hydrocarbon production in Wattenberg Field is from delta front regressive sandstones in the Muddy (J) Sandstone. Sequence stratigraphic analysis shows a regional unconformity, or sequence boundary, truncates the pay section in all directions around the field. In addition, chemical changes associated with weathering during subaerial exposure of the unconformity caused early diagenesis, reducing porosity and permeability. Thus, the trap in the structurally low portion of the Denver Basin is a combination unconformity and diagenetic trap. Penecontemporaneous structural movement controlled topographic relief on the unconformities, the positions of paleovalleys, and the thicknesses and facies distribution of the reservoir rocks.

ACKNOWLEDGMENTS

This paper is a revision of a manuscript on the Wattenberg Field submitted to the AAPG in 1983 and published in 1986. Barbara Brockman typed the manuscript and drafting was provided by Bass Enterprises. This assistance in the preparation of the paper is gratefully acknowledged.

REFERENCES

Belitz, K., and J.D. Bredehoeft, 1988, Hydrodynamics of Denver Basin: explanation of subnormal pressures: AAPG Bull., v. 72, p. 1334–1359.

Clark, B.A., 1978, Stratigraphy of the J Sandstone (Lower Cretaceous) Boulder County and southwest Weld County, Colorado: unpub. MS thesis, CSM, Golden, Colorado, 190 p.

Clayton, J.L., and P.J. Swetland, 1980, Petroleum generation and migration in Denver Basin: AAPG Bull., v. 64, p. 1613–1633.

Demarest, J.M., and J.C. Kraft, 1987, Stratigraphic record of Quaternary sea levels: implications for more ancient strata, *in* D. Nummedal, O.H. Pilkey, and J.D. Howard, eds., Sea–level Fluctuation and Coastal Evolution: SEPM Spec. Pub. 41, p. 223–240.

Dolson, J.C., D.S. Muller, M.J. Evetts, and J. Stein, 1989, Regional paleostratigraphic trends and production, Muddy Sandstone (Lower Cretaceous), Rocky Mountain Basins: AAPG Bull. (in press).

Eicher, D.L., 1965, Foraminifera and biostratigraphy of the Graneros Shale: Jour. Paleontology, v. 39, p. 875–909.

Ethridge, F., and J.C. Dolson, 1988, Unconformities and valley–fill reservoirs at Lonetree and Poncho fields, Denver Basin, Colorado [abs]: AAPG Bull., v. 72, p. 183.

Fast, C.R., G.B. Holman, and R.J. Covlin, 1977, The application of massive hydraulic fracturing to the tight Muddy "J" Formation, Wattenberg Field, Colorado: JPT, v. 29, p. 45–51.

Fouch, T.D., D.L.T. Nichols, W.B. Cashion, and W.A. Cobban, 1983, Patterns of synorogenic sedimentation in Upper Cretaceous rocks of central and northeastern Utah, *in* M.W. Reynolds, E.D. Dolly, and D.A. Spearing, eds., Mesozoic Paleogeography of West-central United States: RMS-SEPM Spec. Pub., p. 305–336.

Gies, R.M., 1981, Lateral trapping mechanisms in deep basin gas trap, Western Canada [abs]: AAPG Bull., v. 65, p. 930.

Harms, J.C., 1966, Stratigraphic traps in a valley-fill, western Nebraska: AAPG Bull., v. 50, p. 2119–2149.

Haun, J.D., 1963, Stratigraphy of Dakota Group and relationship to petroleum occurrence, northern Denver Basin, *in* P.J. Katich and D.W. Bolyard, eds., Geology of the Northern Denver Basin and Adjacent Uplifts: RMAG, p. 119–134.

Higley, D.K. and D.L. Gautier, 1986, Median-permeability contour maps of the J Sandstone, Dakota Group, in the Denver Basin, Colorado, Nebraska and Wyoming: USGS Misc. Field Studies Map MF-1837.

Higley, D.K., and D.L. Gautier, 1987, Median-porosity contour maps of the J Sandstone, Dakota Group, in the Denver Basin, Colorado, Nebraska, and Wyoming: USGS Misc. Field Studies Map MF-1982.

Higley, D.K., M.J. Pawlewicz, and D.L. Gautier, 1985, Isoreflectance map of the J Sandstone in the Denver Basin of Colorado: USGS Open File Report 85-384, 9 p.

Higley, D.K., and D.L. Gautier, 1988, Burial history reconstruction of the Lower Cretaceous J Sandstone in the Wattenberg Field, Colorado, "Hot spot": USGS Circ. 1025, p. 20-21.

Land, C.B., and R.J. Weimer, 1978, J Sandstone distributary channel reservoir, *in* J.D. Pruit and P.E. Coffin, eds., RMAG Symposium, Energy Resources of the Denver Basin, p. 81-104.

LeRoy, L.W., and N.C. Schieltz, 1958, Niobrara-Pierre boundary along Front Range, Colorado: AAPG Bull., v. 42, p. 2444-2464.

Lowman, B.M., 1977, Stratigraphy of the upper Benton and lower Niobrara Formations (Upper Cretaceous), Boulder County, Colorado: unpub. MS thesis, CSM, Golden, Colorado, 94 p.

MacKenzie, D.B., 1965, Depositional environments of Muddy Sandstone, western Denver Basin, Colorado: AAPG Bull., v. 49, p. 186-206.

MacKenzie, D.B., 1971, Post-Lytle Dakota Group on west flank of Denver Basin, Colorado: Mtn. Geol., v. 8, p. 91-131.

MacMillan, L., 1980, Oil and gas of Colorado: a conceptual view, *in* H. Kent and K.W. Porter, eds., Colorado Geology: RMAG, p. 191-198.

Masters, J.A., 1979, Deep basin gas trap, Western Canada: AAPG Bull., v. 63, p. 152-181.

Matuszczak, R.A., 1973, Wattenberg Field, Denver Basin, Colorado: Mtn. Geol., v. 10, p. 99-105.

Matuszczak, R.A., 1976, Wattenberg Field: a review, *in* R.C. Epis and R.J. Weimer, eds., Studies in Colorado Field Geology: CSM Prof. Contrib. No. 8, p. 275-279.

Meissner, F.F., 1978, Patterns of source-rock maturity in nonmarine source rocks of some typical western interior basins, *in* Non-marine Tertiary and Upper Cretaceous Source Rocks and the Occurrence of Oil and Gas in West-central U.S.: RMAG Cont. Ed. Lecture Notes, January.

Meissner, F.F., 1981, Where oil and gas come from and how they get to where we find them: unpub. CSM Petroleum Geology Course Notes, 128 p.

Momper, J.A., 1981, Denver Basin, Lower Cretaceous, J Sandstone, tight reservoir gas potential, AAPG Short Course Notes, Geochemistry for Geologists, February 23-26, p. 1-15.

Myer, H. J., and H. W. McGee, 1985, Oil and gas fields accompanied by geothermal anomalies in Rocky Mountain Region: AAPG Bull., v. 69, p. 933-945.

Nummedal, D., and D.J.p. Swift, 1987, Transgressive stratigraphy at sequence-bounding unconformities, *in* D. Nummedal, O.H. Pilkey, and J.D. Howard, eds., Sea-level Fluctuation and Coastal Evolution: SEPM Spec. Pub. 41, p. 241-260.

Porter, K.W., and R.J. Weimer, 1982, Diagenetic sequence related to structural history and petroleum accumulation: Spindle Field, Colorado: AAPG Bull., v. 66, p. 2543-2560.

Pruit, J.D., 1978, Statistical and geological evaluation of oil production from the J Sandstone, Denver Basin, Colorado, Nebraska and Wyoming, *in* J.D. Pruit, and P.E. Coffin, eds., Energy Resources of the Denver Basin: RMAG Symposium, p. 9-24.

Reinert, S.L., and D.K. Davies, 1976, Third Creek Field, Colorado: a study of sandstone environments and diagenesis: Mtn. Geol., v. 13, p. 47-60.

Rice, D.D., and C.N. Threlkeld, 1982, Occurrence and origin of natural gas in ground water, southern Weld County, Colorado: USGS Open File Report OF82-496, 6 p.

Rice, D.D., 1983, Character and origin of natural gas from upper Cretaceous Codell Sandstone, Denver Basin, Colorado, *in* Mid-Cretaceous Codell Sandstone Member of Carlile Shale Eastern Colorado: RMS-SEPM Field Trip Guidebook, p. 96-100.

Rice, D.D., and D.L. Gautier, 1983, Patterns of sedimentation, diagenesis, and hydrocarbon accumulation in Cretaceous rocks of the Rocky Mountains: SEPM Short Course No. 11 Notes, 10 p.

Rojas, I., 1980, Stratigraphy of the Mowry Shale (Cretaceous), Western Denver Basin, Colorado: unpub. MS thesis, CSM, Golden, Colorado, 148 p.

Silverman, M.F., 1988, Petroleum geology, paleotectonics and sedimentation of the Scotts Bluff trend, northeastern Denver Basin: Mtn. Geol., v. 25, p. 87-102.

Smith, M.B., G.B. Holman, C.R. Fast, and R.J. Covlin, The azimuth of deep, penetrating fractures in the Wattenberg Field: SPE Paper 6092, p. 24-35.

Sonnenberg, S.A., and R.J. Weimer, 1981, Tectonics, sedimentation and petroleum potential, northern Denver Basin, Colorado, Wyoming and Nebraska: CSM Quarterly, v. 76, no. 2, 45 p.

Suchecki, R.K., G.R. Baum, S. Phillips, and J.S. Hewlett, 1988, Role of stratigraphic discontinuities in development of reservoir quality, Muddy and Skull Creek sandstones, Denver Basin, *in* D.p. James and D.A. Leckie, eds., Sequences, Stratigraphy, Sedimentology: Surface and Subsurface: Proceeding of Can. Soc. of Petrol. Geologists Tech. Mtg., Calgary, Alberta, Sept. 14-16, p. 585.

Suryanto, U., 1979, Stratigraphy and petroleum geology of the J Sandstone in portions of Boulder, Larimer and Weld Counties: unpub. MS thesis, CSM, Golden, Colorado, 173 p.

Tainter, P.A., 1984, Stratigraphic and paleostructural controls on hydrocarbon migration in Cretaceous D and J Sandstones of the Denver Basin, *in* J. Woodward, F.F. Meissner, and J.L. Clayton, eds., Hydrocarbon Source Rocks of the Greater Rocky Mountain Region, RMAG: p. 339-354.

Vail, P.R., R.M. Mitchum, Jr., and S. Thompson III, 1977, Seismic stratigraphy and global sea level changes, Part 3: AAPG Mem. 26, p. 63-82.

Vail, P.R., 1987, Seismic stratigraphy interpretations procedure, *in* A.W. Bally, ed., Atlas of Seismic Stratigraphy, v. 1, AAPG Stud. in Geol. No. 27, p. 1-10.

Waage, K.M., and D.L. Eicher, 1960, Dakota Group in the northern Front Range area, *in* R.J. Weimer and J.D. Haun, eds., Guide to the Geology of Colorado: RMAG, p. 230-237.

Weimer, R.J., 1978, Influence of Transcontinental arch on Cretaceous marine sedimentation: a preliminary report, *in* J.D. Pruit and P.E. Coffin, eds., RMAG, Energy Resources of the Denver Basin: Symposium, p. 211-222.

Weimer, R.J., 1980, Recurrent movement on basement faults-a tectonic style for Colorado and adjacent areas, *in* H.C. Kent and K.W. Porter, eds., Colorado Geology: RMAG, p. 23-35.

Weimer, R.J., 1984, Relation of unconformities, tectonics, and sea level changes, Cretaceous of Denver Basin and adjacent areas, *in* M. Reynolds and E. Dolly, eds., Mesozoic Paleogeography of West-central United States: RMS-SEPM Spec. Pub., p. 359-376.

Weimer R.J., and S.A. Sonnenberg, 1982, Wattenberg Field, paleostructure-stratigraphic trap, Denver Basin, Colorado: OGJ., v. 80, March 22, p. 204-210.

Weimer, R.J., and S.A. Sonnenberg, 1983, Codell Sandstone, new exploration play, Denver Basin: OGJ, v. 81, May 30, 1983, p. 119-125.

Weimer, R.J., K.W. Porter, and C.B. Land, 1985, Depositional modeling of detrital rocks with emphasis on cored sequences of petroleum reservoirs: SEPM Core Workshop No. 8, 252 p.

Weimer, R.J., S.A., Sonnenberg and G.B.C. Young, 1986, Wattenberg Field, Denver Basin, Colorado, *in* C.W. Spencer and R.F. Mast, eds., AAPG Stud. in Geol. No. 24, p. 143-164.

Weimer, R.J., C.A. Rebne, and T.L. Davis, 1988, Geologic and seismic models, Muddy Sandstone, Lower Cretaceous, Bell Creek-Rocky Point area, Powder River Basin, Montana and Wyoming, *in* Field Conf. Guidebook, Eastern Powder River Basin-Black Hills: WGA, p. 161-177.

Young, G.B.C., 1987, Stratigraphy and petrology of the Lower Cretaceous J Sandstone, Wattenberg gas field, Weld County, Colorado: unpub. MS thesis, CSM, Golden, Colorado, p. 369.

Unconformities and Valley–Fill Sequences –
Key to Understanding "J" Sandstone (Lower Cretaceous)
Reservoirs at Lonetree and Poncho Fields, D–J Basin, Colorado[1]

FRANK G. ETHRIDGE[2]

JOHN C. DOLSON[3]

[1]Received August 3, 1988; Revised January 25, 1989
[2]Dept. of Earth Resources, Colorado State University, Fort Collins, CO
[3]Amoco Production Company, Denver, CO

Previous workers suggest that the Lower Cretaceous "J" Sandstone in the D–J Basin is divisible into three conformable genetic units: a lower delta–front (J–3) unit, a middle delta–plain (J–2) unit, and an upper destructional marine–bar (J–1) unit. However, the presence of root casts and siderite cement at the upper contact of the J–3 sandstone suggests that J–2 deposits are separated from the underlying J–3 sandstone by a regional unconformity. J–2 deposits are here reinterpreted as point bar, crevasse splay, and floodplain sequences of a meander–belt complex.

Thin–section and SEM analyses reveal that the principal cements in both fluvial and marine–bar sandstones are quartz overgrowths, calcite, kaolinite, and chlorite. The bulk of the porosity is secondary and is related to dissolution of carbonate cement and feldspar grains. Delta–front (J–3) deposits that underlie the unconformity are tightly cemented by siderite and do not produce in either field. J–2 sandstones are productive from northwest–trending meander belt deposits in both fields, and from laterally equivalent crevasse–splay deposits at Lonetree Field. Overlying J–1 sandstones form three northeast–trending marine bars. Two echelon bars are present at Poncho, but only the western one is productive; the eastern marine bar at Poncho and the bar at Lonetree are wet. Fluvial deposits of the J–2 interval at Lonetree and Poncho fields probably were deposited by tributary channels that flowed southwest through the Peoria Field area to join a major trunk stream represented by the valley–fill deposits of the Kassler Sandstone.

INTRODUCTION

Lonetree and Poncho fields are located on the gently dipping eastern flank of the D–J Basin (Fig. 1). Structural dip is about 0.5° northwest, with no obvious structural controls on the location of these fields (Fig. 2). Reservoirs are the Lower Cretaceous (late Albian) "J" Sandstone (Fig. 3), which is equivalent to the Muddy Formation in outcrop. Subdivisions of the "J" in the area include (from top to bottom) the J–1, J–2 (Horsetooth Member in outcrop), and J–3 (Ft. Collins Member in outcrop). These fields are typical of most of the 1–5 million BO–sized fields in the southern D–J Basin that produce from "J" sandstones.

Previous interpretations of the "J" Sandstone in the D–J Basin (Haun, 1963; Ecker, 1971; Land and Weimer, 1978; Miyazaki and Dolson, 1982; Zeigler, 1982), including those by the authors, suggested that the J–2 sandstones were deposited in delta–

distributary channels contemporaneous with J–3 delta–front sandstones. Weimer and Sonnenberg (1982) and Weimer (1983, 1984), building on the work of Harms (1966) and MacKenzie (1971), presented the first comprehensive documentation of erosional unconformities within the "J" Sandstone in the D–J Basin.

The objectives of this study were to re–evaluate and determine: the depositional environments of the three major units of the "J" Sandstone in the field areas; the major diagenetic events and their effects on reservoir and nonreservoir rocks; the presence of unconformities and their effect on hydrocarbon accumulation; the size, distribution, and orientation of major reservoir units; and the relationship of the channel deposits at Lonetree/Poncho to regional Muddy drainage systems.

The data base for the study consists of wireline logs from 118 wells, continuous cores from 11 wells (six shown on Fig. 2), and 29 thin sections, 57 SEM

REGIONAL DATA:

Producing Interval:	"J" Sandstone
Geographic Location:	Adams and Arapahoe Counties, Colorado
Present Tectonic Setting:	Eastern flank of Denver Basin
Depositional Setting:	Eastern side of Cretaceous foreland basin
Age of Reservoirs:	Lower Cretaceous
Lithology of Reservoir:	Well–sorted, very fine to fine–grained quartz arenites to sublithic arenites
Depositional Environments:	Marine bar, alluvial valley fill, and deltaic
Diagenesis:	Clay skins; quartz overgrowths; calcite, kaolinite, and chlorite cements; feldspar and calcite dissolution
Porosity Types:	Reduced intergranular, intragranular, and micro-porosity
Source Rock:	Lower Cretaceous Benton Group
Timing of Hydrocarbon Migration:	Eocene
Nature of Trap:	Stratigraphic
Entrapping Facies:	Shales of "J" Sandstone and overlying shales of the Benton Group
Drive Type:	Solution gas

FIELD DATA:	Lonetree Field[1]
Reservoir:	J–2 sandstone
Discovered:	1974
Reservoir Depth:	6,210 ft (1,915 m)
Pay Thickness:	Average 14 ft (4.3 m)
Areal Extent:	960 acres (389 ha)
IP:	Average 138 BOPD, 119 MCFGPD
Cumulative Production (1/89):	2,720,000 BO, 3.96 BCFG
Oil Gravity:	41° API
Porosity:	Average 15%
Permeability:	Maximum 350 md, average 57 md
Water Saturation:	Average 51%

FIELD DATA:	Poncho Field[1]
Reservoir:	J–1 sandstone
Discovered:	1971
Reservoir Depth:	6,029 ft (1,859 m)
Pay Thickness:	Average 8 ft (2.4 m)
Areal Extent:	908 acres (367 ha)
IP:	Average 264 BOPD
Cumulative Production (1/89):	1,530,000 BO, 2.03 BCFG (combined with J-2)
Approximate Ultimate Recovery:	3,900,000 BO
Oil Gravity:	40° API
Porosity:	Maximum 26%, average 21%
Permeability:	Maximum 118 md, average 28 md
Water Saturation:	Average 39%

FIELD DATA:	Poncho Field[1]
Reservoir:	J–2 Sandstone
Discovery Date:	1971
Reservoir Depth:	6,042 ft (1,863 m)
Pay Thickness:	Average 15 ft (4.5 m)
Areal Extent:	456 acres (185 ha)
IP:	Average 264 BOPD
Cumulative Production:	1,530,000 BO, 2.03 BCFG (combined with J-1)
Approximate Ultimate Recovery:	3,300,000 BO
Oil Gravity:	40° API
Porosity:	Maximum 21%, average 16%
Permeability:	Maximum 526 md, average 88 md
Water Saturation:	Average 31%

[1]In part from Clayton and Swetland, 1980; Miyazaki and Dolson, 1982; and Ziegler, 1982

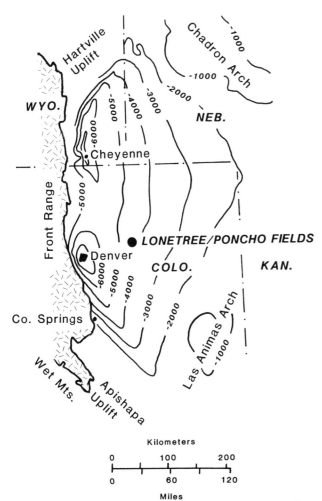

Figure 1. Location of Lonetree and Poncho fields, south-central D-J Basin. Structure contours on top of Precambrian basement.   Contour interval is 1,000 ft (310 m).

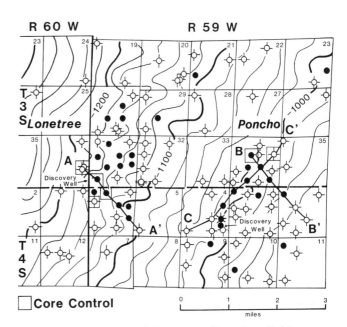

Figure 2.   Map of Lonetree/Poncho field area, showing well and core control, location of stratigraphic cross-section (Fig. 13), and structure contoured on top of J-1 sandstone.   Contour interval is 20 ft (6 m).   (One mi = 1.609 km)

images, and porosity and permeability data from 189 core plugs. Detailed graphic logs were prepared for each core. Thin sections were examined for composition, texture, and diagenetic features. Samples were examined under the SEM to determine the nature and types of cements and pores, which was documented with 57 SEM images.

DEPOSITIONAL ENVIRONMENTS

Detailed vertical sequences seen in two of the 11 cores examined (Figs. 4 and 5) provide data for interpreting depositional environments of the "J" Sandstone. The J-1 sandstone is relatively thin, widespread, and ubiquitously bioturbated. The unit ranges from matrix-free sandstone to muddy sandstone (Fig. 6A) with rare low-angle planar beds (swash laminae?) and erosional contacts. Recognizable trace fossils include *Ophiomorpha* and *Teichichnus*. The thin, widespread, nature of this bioturbated sandstone and its occurrence above a fluvial sequence and below a marine shale suggest that it was deposited as a transgressive, nearshore, marine-bar sand.

The J-2 unit varies from a thick, cross-bedded sandstone with an erosional base to a sequence of thin-bedded, burrowed, and rooted sandstones interbedded with organic-rich shales. Thick sandstones generally have an erosional basal contact and trough cross-bedded sandstones (Fig. 6C) grading upward into ripple-drift cross-stratified sandstone (Fig. 6B) and interbedded bioturbated sandstones and shales (Fig. 4). The lower part of this sequence is typical of point-bar deposits of meandering channels. Interbedded sandstones and rooted and burrowed shales at the top of some point-bar sequences probably represent natural levee deposits. In areas adjacent to thick sandstones, the J-2 interval is characterized by thin, rippled, and lenticular-bedded sandstones, interbedded with bioturbated shales and bioturbated muddy sandstones (Fig. 5). These sequences are interpreted as crevasse splay and floodplain deposits. Some rooted intervals within the J-2 unit may represent paleosol horizons (Fig. 6D).

The J-3 sandstone interval is characterized by a coarsening-upward sequence of intensely bioturbated, muddy sandstone with occasional ripple cross-stratification that grades upward into horizontal to low-angle planar-bedded sandstones with ripples. Identifiable trace fossils include *Ophiomorpha* and *Terebellina*. The J-3 interval is typical of delta front deposits of a wave-dominated shore or delta system. The top of the J-3 commonly contains siderite cement and rootlets extending downward from overlying J-2 deposits.

TEXTURE, COMPOSITION AND DIAGENESIS

Based on measurements of the apparent long axes of monocrystalline quartz grains in thin section, the

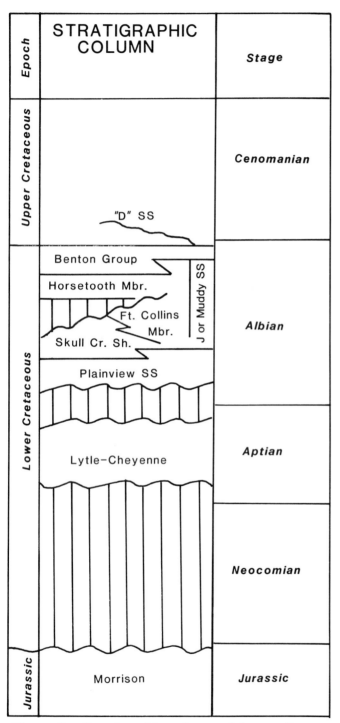

Figure 3. Stratigraphic column of Lower Cretaceous rocks, D–J Basin, Colorado (modified from Dolson, et al., in press).

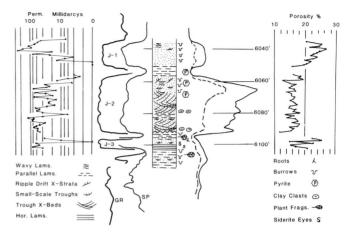

Figure 4. Vertical sequence of sedimentary structures, accessories, permeability, and porosity in Amoco Production Co. No. 5 Poncho (SE NW Sec 34 T3S R59W), Poncho Field. Also shown are well–log curves. (20 ft = 6.096 m)

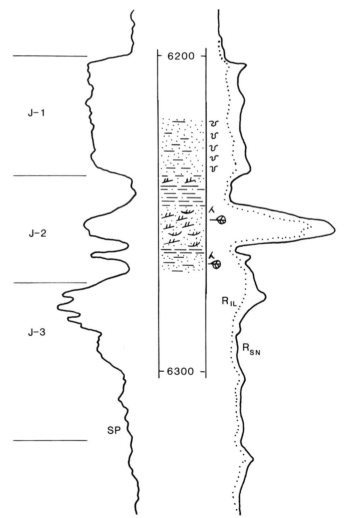

Figure 5. Vertical sequence of sedimentary structures, lithologies, and accessories in Midwest Oil No. 1 Healey (NE NW Sec 6 T4S R59W), Lonetree Field, with electric–log curves. See Figure 4 for key. (100 ft = 30.48 m)

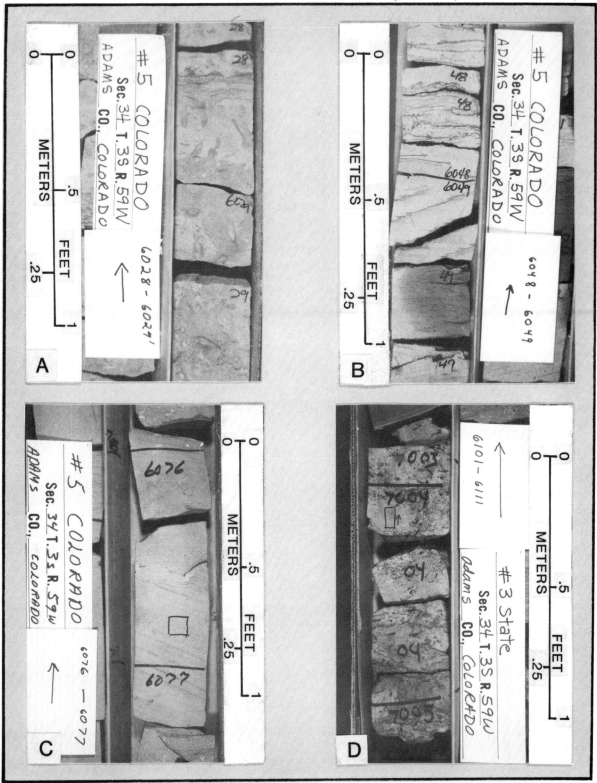

Figure 6. Core photographs, "J" Sandstone, Poncho Field.

A. Burrowed sandstones of J–1 marine-bar sequence. Core is from No. 5 Poncho well. Depths are 6,028–29 ft (1,859.0–1,859.3 m).

B. Ripple–drift cross-stratification at the top of J–2 point bar sequence in No. 5 Poncho well. Depths are 6,048–49 ft (1,865.2–1,865.5 m).

C. Trough cross-beds at the base of J–2 point-bar sequence in No. 5 Poncho well. Depths are 6,076–77 ft (1,873.8–1,874.1 m).

D. Rooted siltstone in J–2 overbank deposits in Amoco No. 3 State well (Sec 34 T3S R59W). Depths are 6,101–6,111 ft (1,881.5–1,881.8 m).

"J" sandstones at Lonetree and Poncho fields are mature and well sorted. Sand grades range from very fine to fine, and average fine.

The "J" sandstones are compositionally mature, varying from quartz arenites to sublithic arenites. The most abundant framework mineral is monocrystalline quartz which ranges from 82 to 97%. Second in abundance are polycrystalline rock fragments, which range from 0 to 17%. These fragments include clay galls derived locally from penecontemporaneous deposits, and chert derived from older sedimentary rocks in a western source area (Beckham, 1978). Feldspars constitute 0 to 3% of framework grains. Other grains present in minor percentages include glauconite in the J-1 marine bar sandstones, and muscovite.

Diagenetic cements include quartz overgrowths, kaolinite, chlorite, chert, siderite, and calcite. Quartz overgrowths are the most common cement present and are easily recognized in SEM images by their flat crystal faces (Fig. 7A). Kaolinite, the second most abundant cement, is recognizable as discrete particles made up of booklets of pseudohexagonal crystals (Fig. 7E). Kaolinite is present in samples from all environments but is slightly more abundant in J-2 channel sandstones. Chlorite is a minor cement that occurs as clay rims in samples from all environments, but is more abundant in J-1 marine-bar sandstones (Fig. 7F). Other minor cements include framboidal pyrite; calcite in channel sandstones (Fig. 7C); siderite in small, circular patches in nonproductive J-3 sandstones (Fig. 7B); and fine-grained quartz, including chert found with diagenetic clays in tight, nonproductive fringe areas of J-1 marine-bar sandstones.

POROSITY AND PERMEABILITY

Porosity types include reduced-intergranular and intragranular, and microporosity. Most of the porosity in the productive sandstones is secondary, as indicated by the presence of elongate pores, oversized pores, and partially dissolved feldspar grains (Fig. 7D) and calcite cement. Microporosity is present in significant amounts in samples from channel sandstones with large percentages of kaolinite cement (Fig. 7E). Small amounts of reduced, primary, intergranular porosity are present in samples with significant amounts of quartz overgrowths (Fig. 7A).

Patterns of porosity and permeability variation seen in the Amoco Production Co. No. 5 Poncho well (Fig. 4) are representative of the various "J" Sandstone sequences in the entire study area. In this well, porosity is consistently higher in the J-1 marine bar, averaging 21% compared to 16% in the J-2 point-bar sandstone. Permeability also is higher in the marine-bar sandstone, averaging 88 md as compared to 28 md in the point-bar sandstone. Permeability in the marine-bar sandstone increases upward through about three-fourths of the sequence, with a systematic decrease toward the top. Vertical variations in permeability are much greater and less systematic in the point-bar deposits, but generally are greatest in the lower one-third of the deposit. Permeability probably is more uniform horizontally in the marine-bar sandstone than in the point-bar deposit.

Based on analyses of 189 core plugs with permeabilities of 0.1 md or more, a rather systematic decrease in permeability and porosity can be seen from marine-bar to channel and crevasse-splay and finally to delta-front sandstones (Fig. 8).

SEQUENCE OF DIAGENETIC EVENTS

In marine-bar and delta-front sandstones, diagenesis began with bioturbation (Fig. 6A; Fig. 9). The remaining events were almost identical for fluvial and marine-bar sandstones, and include: 1) the early development of thin clay skins, as evidenced by their presence between original grain boundaries and quartz overgrowths; 2) quartz overgrowth; 3) patchy to pervasive calcite cementation, which filled pores not occluded by quartz overgrowths; 4) partial dissolution of feldspars and calcite cement; 5) partial occlusion of secondary pores by authigenic kaolinite and chlorite clay coats; and 6) hydrocarbon emplacement in fluvial and marine-bar sandstones. This inferred diagenetic sequence is grossly similar to sequences described for "J" sandstones at nearby Third Creek Field (Reinert and Davies, 1976) and at Peoria Field (Beckham, 1978). Fine grain size, early development of siderite "eyes" (as evidenced by the floating grain packing within the eyes), and lack of secondary porosity precluded delta-front sandstones from becoming hydrocarbon reservoirs in the area.

EVIDENCE FOR A MAJOR UNCONFORMITY

Evidence for recognition of an unconformity within the Muddy Sandstone in outcrops northwest of Lonetree and Poncho Fields includes the presence of root zones and coaly deposits near the base of meander-belt sequences in the Horsetooth Member (J-2). Horsetooth-Member deposits fill paleo-valleys that cut 60 ft (18 m) into and rest directly on partially eroded, lower shoreface sandstone of the Fort Collins Member (J-3) (Dolson and Nibbelink, 1985).

In the Lonetree and Poncho field areas, evidence that suggests an unconformity between the J-2 and J-3 intervals includes: 1) the presence of abundant root casts and siderite in the upper portion of J-3 middle to lower shoreface sandstones; 2) the presence of rooted horizons in the lower portions of J-2 sequences, 3) channel deposits of the J-2 that both truncate and overlie J-3 shoreface deposits; 4) correlation of logs and lithofacies from 118 wells and 11 cores with regional drainage networks and unconformities (Weimer, 1983; Dolson, et al., 1988, and in press). Root casts and siderite in middle to lower shoreface sandstones are unusual and support the hypothesis that J-3 sandstones were subaerially exposed and partially eroded before deposition of J-2 sediments. The presence of diagenetic siderite suggests reducing and slightly acidic conditions and high concentrations of carbonate ions (Schroeder, 1978). These conditions are not common in shallow marine sandstones. Downward-percolating, CO_2-bearing meteoric waters could have mixed with decaying organic matter and humic acids derived from continental (meander belt) deposits above the unconformity, provid-

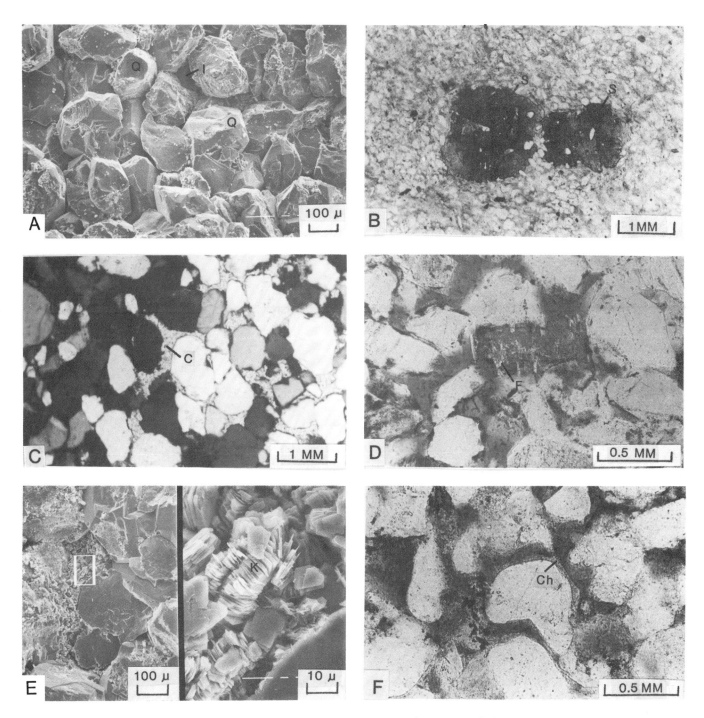

Figure 7. Petrographic investigations, "J" Sandstone, Poncho/Lonetree fields.

A. SEM image showing quartz overgrowths (Q) and reduced intergranular porosity (I), UPRR No. 42-9 Hanks (6,094 ft; 1,879.4 m). This is excellent reservoir rock.

B. Thin-section photomicrograph of siderite eyes (S) in eroded delta-front deposits, No. 6 Poncho (6,141 ft; 1,893.9 m).

C. Thin-section photomicrograph of pervasive, poikilotopic, calcite cement (C) in No. 8 Poncho well (6,075 ft, 1,873.5 m). Reservoir quality is nil. Crossed nicols.

D. Photomicrograph of partially dissolved feldspar grain (F) in No. 2 Poncho well (6,057 ft; 1,868.0 m). This process can improve permeability as well as create microporosity.

E. SEM image showing kaolinite pore-filling cement (K) in No. 1 Price 31-3 well (6,075 ft, 1,873.5 m). Note microporosity between kaolinite crystals. Image at right is a magnification of the area outlined in white on the left-hand image.

F. Photomicrograph of chlorite grain coatings (Ch) in No. 5 Poncho well (6,086 ft, 1,876.9 m).

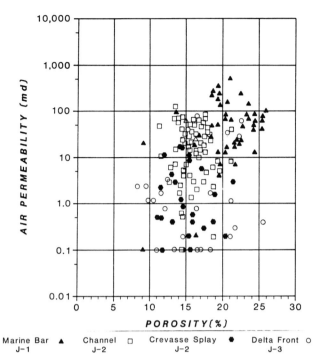

Marine Bar ▲   Channel □   Crevasse Splay ●   Delta Front ○
J-1   J-2   J-2   J-3

Figure 8. Bivariate plot of core porosity versus air permeability for major reservoir lithofacies, Lonetree/Poncho fields. Marine-bar sandstones have the best reservoir quality, although there is considerable scatter to the data.

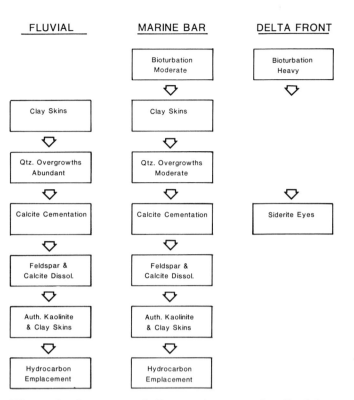

Figure 9. Sequence of diagenetic events for fluvial, marine-bar, and delta-front sandstones, Lonetree/Poncho fields. Note the close parallelism of events occurring in fluvial and marine-bar sandstones, and the much simpler history of delta-front sandstones.

ing the necessary diagenetic environment (Al-Gailani, 1981).

This unconformity probably is the same age as the one documented in outcrop between the Horsetooth and Fort Collins members along the western margin of the basin. If so, it is part of the 97 ma (late Albian) sea-level change that affected the entire Western Interior Cretaceous Basin (Weimer, 1984; Dolson and Nibbelink, 1985; Dolson, et al., 1988; Dolson et al., in press).

LOCAL GEOMETRY AND TREND OF SANDSTONE FACIES

Stratigraphic relationships and the geometry and trend of producing sandstones at Lonetree and Poncho Fields are shown by isolith maps and cross-sections (Figs. 10-13). Net-sandstone maps in the J-2 interval (Fig. 10) depict the northwesterly trend of productive channel sandstones, the complex geometry of productive crevasse-splay sandstones at Lonetree, and a southwest-oriented, nonproductive channel complex west of Lonetree Field, located downdip of the oil/water contact. Maximum thicknesses of channel deposits are 40-50 ft (12.2-15.2 m) (Table 1). Thickest crevasse-splay deposits are 10-20 ft (3-6.1 m) thick. These channel complexes form sinuous, belt-type deposits.

The presence of multiple oil/water contacts in the same channel systems in two fields can be explained by the presence of permeability barriers, seen by mapping "net porous sandstone" thicknesses (Fig. 11).

Barriers are inferred between productive crevasse-splay deposits and wet channel deposits in (Sec. 21), and between downdip, productive channel sandstones and updip, wet sandstones in Secs. 4, 5, 28, and 29.

Pressure testing of wells at Lonetree Field indicated the existence of common pressure systems between productive channel and splay sandstones. Secondary porosity may be partially responsible for creating a continuous J-2 reservoir at Lonetree, despite varying depositional environments.

All reservoirs in both fields are underpressured (0.26 psi/ft original pressure gradient), typical of this portion of the D-J Basin. Solution gas is the drive mechanism.

The J-1 sandstone contains a series of three northeast-oriented, elliptical marine bars (Fig. 12). Only one is productive. Since the area is outside the oil-generation window of the D-J Basin (Tainter, 1984), it is reasonable to assume that the J-2 channel systems acted as regional conduits for the migration of hydrocarbons. The productive bar at Poncho could have been in hydraulic communication with these channel sandstones at the time of hydrocarbon migration, although no direct evidence is available.

"J" sandstones vary in lateral continuity from highly continuous to very discontinuous (e.g. Fig. 13). Discontinuities in the J-1 and J-2 intervals result from

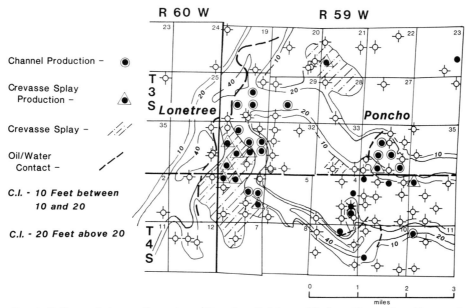

Figure 10. Map of net J-2 sandstone, Lonetree/Poncho fields, with location of wells producing from channel and crevasse–splay deposits. Variable contour interval: 10 ft (3.05 m) for thicknesses between 10 and 20 ft; and 20 ft (6.10 m) for thicknesses greater than 20 ft. (One mi = 1.609 km)

Table 1. Dimensions and width/thickness ratios of J-2 channel and J-1 bar complexes at Lonetree and Poncho fields, D-J Basin, Colorado.

Sandstone Trend	Maximum Thickness Ft (m)	Maximum Width Ft (m)	Minimum Length Ft (m)	Width/ Thickness Ratio
northern productive channel (J-2) Poncho/Lonetree	49 (15)	3,500 (1,070)	26,400 (8,050)	71
southern productive channel (J-2) Poncho/Lonetree	37 (11)	2,600 (793)	35,100 (10,700)	70
western non–Productive channel (J-2) Lonetree	49 (15)	4,400 (1,340)	26,400 (8,050)	90
western non–Productive bar (J-1) Lonetree	38 (12)	19,300 (5,880)	25,500 (7,770)	508
western productive bar (J-1) Poncho	18 (6)	5,280 (1,610)	15,000 (4,570)	293
eastern non–Productive bar (J-1) Poncho	30 (9)	8,750 (2,670)	29,000 (8,840)	291

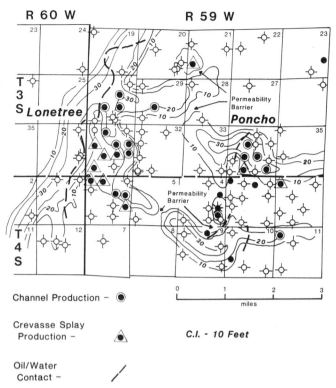

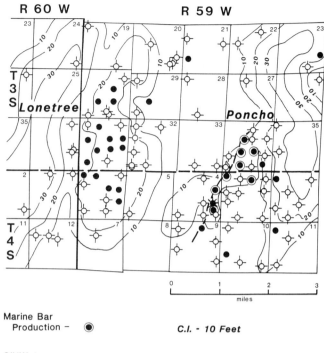

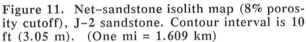

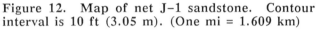

Channel Production – ◉

Crevasse Splay
Production – △

Oil/Water
Contact – ╱

C.I. - 10 Feet

Marine Bar
Production – ◉

Oil/Water
Contact – ╱

C.I. - 10 Feet

Figure 11. Net–sandstone isolith map (8% porosity cutoff), J–2 sandstone. Contour interval is 10 ft (3.05 m). (One mi = 1.609 km)

Figure 12. Map of net J–1 sandstone. Contour interval is 10 ft (3.05 m). (One mi = 1.609 km)

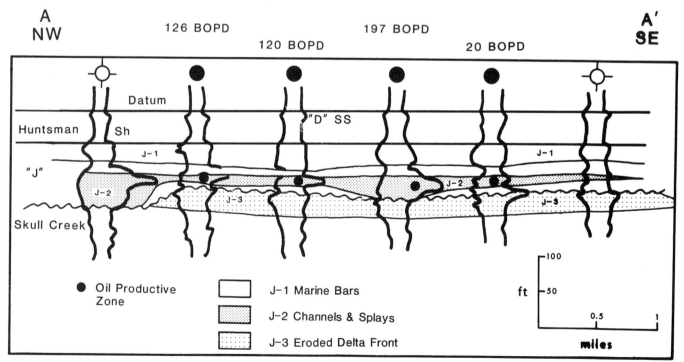

Figure 13. Stratigraphic cross–section A–A', Lonetree Field, showing the distribution and lateral continuity of the J–1, J–2, and J–3 sandstones and the inferred unconformity between the J–2 and J–3 intervals. Line of section shown on Figure 2. (50 ft = 15.2 m; 1 mi = 1.609 km)

stratigraphic pinchouts and imbrications of sandstones. J–3 discontinuities mostly are caused by truncation.

RELATIONSHIP TO REGIONAL PALEOGEOGRAPHY

Regional isopach mapping of the total Muddy interval in most of the D–J Basin (Fig. 14) reveals major "thicks" in southeastern Wyoming and in the southwestern and southeastern portions of the basin. These thicks reflect, respectively, the southeastern–Wyoming, eastern D–J, and Kassler–trunk J–2 valley fill drainages (Fig. 15). A major "thin" is seen to coincide with the Wattenberg Field paleostructural high (Fig. 15; Weimer et al., 1986). J–2 channel deposits at Lonetree and Poncho Fields are interpreted as deposits of streams tributary to higher–order tributaries that ultimately drained southward into the major Kassler drainage.

Regional stratigraphic cross–sections (Figs. 16, 17) depict the major trunk drainages (valley–fills) and paleotopographic highs (drainage divides) in the J–2 interval. The J–3 sandstone on these sections represents an erosional remnant of the thicker marine sandstones of the Wattenberg high. The J–1 interval was deposited during an onlap cycle accompanying the Benton Group marine transgression.

SUMMARY

Three genetic units are recognized in the "J" Sandstone at Lonetree and Poncho Fields: J–3

erosional remnants of a former delta front; J–2 point–bar, crevasse–splay, and floodplain deposits; and J–1 marine bar deposits. Root casts and siderite cement along the upper surfaces of J–3 marine sandstones and channel sandstones that truncate the J–3 sandstones suggest that the top of the J–3 sandstone marks a subaerial unconformity, an interpretation that is consistent with regional correlations. The unconformity is believed to be correlative with one seen in outcrop between the Horsetooth and Fort Collins Members of the Muddy Sandstone along the western margin of the basin and, if so, is part of the 97 Ma sea–level change that affected the entire Western Interior Cretaceous basin (Weimer, 1984).

J–3 marine sandstones are tightly cemented and do not produce in either field. J–2 point–bar deposits probably were deposited by northwesterly–flowing tributaries to southwest–oriented streams that flowed through the Peoria Field area and eventually emptied into a major trunk valley–fill system represented by the Kassler Sandstone.

J–2 point–bar sandstones are productive in both fields. However, laterally equivalent crevasse–splay deposits produce only at Lonetree Field, where splay and point–bar sandstones form a common reservoir.

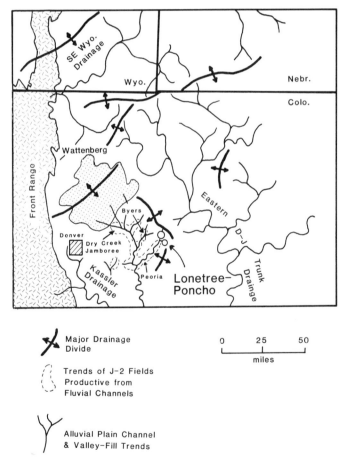

Figure 15. Interpreted major "J" Sandstone) drainages in D–J Basin, northeastern Colorado, southeastern Wyoming, and southwestern Nebraska. Stippling indicates location of isopach thin in area of "Wattenberg high" of Weimer et al. (1986). (25 mi = 40.2 km)

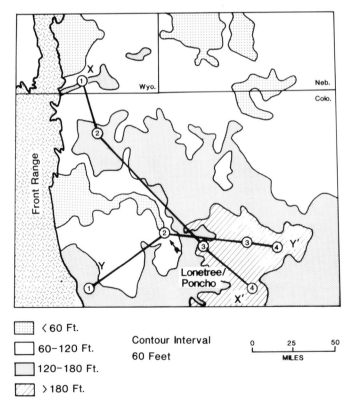

< 60 Ft.

60–120 Ft.

120–180 Ft.

> 180 Ft.

Contour Interval
60 Feet

Figure 14. Map of thickness of total Muddy (J) interval in a portion of the D–J Basin in northeastern Colorado, southeastern Wyoming, and southwestern Nebraska. Based on computer contouring of operator well tops. (25 mi = 40.2 km)

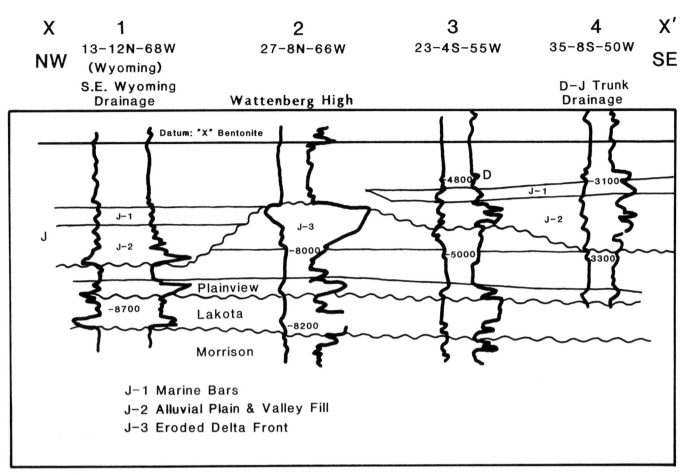

Figure 16. Stratigraphic cross-section X–X' from southeast-Wyoming paleodrainage, across Wattenberg high, to D-J trunk drainage. Line of section shown in Figure 14.

Northeast-trending J-1 marine-bar sandstones are seen in both field. Two of these bars are present at Poncho and one at Lonetree. Only the western bar at Poncho, which may have been in hydraulic communication with underlying productive J-2 channel sandstones at the time of hydrocarbon migration, is productive.

ACKNOWLEDGMENTS

Thanks are due to Amoco Production Company for access to cores and logs from Poncho and Lonetree fields and for permission to publish this manuscript, as well as to Mike Mellor who took the SEM photographs. The authors are especially grateful to Ed Coalson, Randi S. Martinsen, and Thomas A. Ryer for much-needed constructive criticism of an earlier version of the manuscript.

REFERENCES

Al-Gailani, M.B., 1981, Authigenic mineralizations at unconformities: implications for reservoir characteristics: Sed. Geol., v. 29, p. 89–115.

Beckham, E., 1978, Diagenesis of the Muddy Sandstone (Cretaceous), Peoria Field Denver Basin, Colorado: unpub. MS thesis, U. of TX, Austin, 109 p.

Clayton, J.L. and P.J. Swetland, 1980, Petroleum generation and migration in Denver Basin: AAPG Bull., v. 64, p. 1613–1633.

Dolson, J.C. and K.A. Nibbelink, 1985, Cretaceous depositional systems, northern D-J (Cheyenne) Basin - examples from the Dakota Group and Laramie-Fox Hills Formations, *in* D.L. Macke and E.K. Maughan, eds., RMS-SEPM Field Trip Guide: RMS-AAPG, RMS-SEPM, and NEMD-AAPG, p. 1–40.

Dolson, J.C., et al., 1988, Regional paleotopographic trends and production, Muddy Sandstone (Lower Cretaceous), MT, WY, CO [abs.]: The Outcrop, Newsletter of the RMAG, v. 37, p. 5.

Dolson, J.C. et al., in press, Regional paleotopographic trends and production, Muddy Sandstone (Lower Cretaceous), Rocky Mountain basins: AAPG Bull.

Ecker, G.D., 1971, Peoria Field, Arapahoe County, Colorado: Mtn. Geol., v. 8, p. 141–150.

Harms, J.C., 1966, Stratigraphic traps in a valley fill, western Nebraska: AAPG Bull., v. 50, p. 2119–2149.

Land, C.B. and R.J. Weimer, 1978, Peoria Field, Denver Basin, Colorado - J Sandstone distributary channel reservoir, *in* J.D. Pruit and P.E. Coffin, eds., Energy Resources of the Denver Basin: RMAG, p. 81–104.

MacKenzie, D.B., 1971, Post-Lytle Dakota Group on west flank of Denver Basin, Colorado: Mtn. Geol., v. 8, p. 91–131.

Miyazaki, B. and J.C. Dolson, 1982, Lonetree Field, T3S, R59W Adams County, Colorado and T4S, R59W Arapahoe county, Colorado, *in* M.C. Crouch III, ed., Oil and Gas Fields of Colorado/Nebraska & Adjacent Areas: RMAG, p. 304–309.

Reinert, S.L. and D.K. Davies, 1976, Third Creek Field, Colorado - A study of sandstone environments and diagenesis: Mtn. Geol., RMAG, v. 13, p. 47–60.

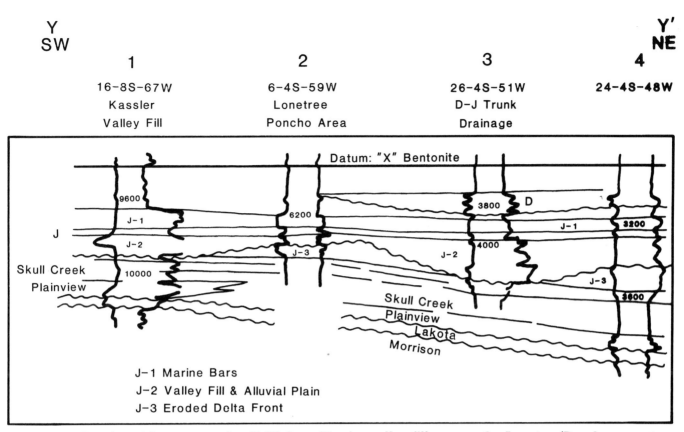

Figure 17. Stratigraphic cross-section Y-Y' from Kassler valley fill, across the Lonetree/Poncho area, to D-J trunk drainage. Line of section shown in Figure 14.

Schroeder, J.H., 1978, Cementation, in R.W. Fairbridge and J. Bourgeois, eds., The Encyclopedia of Sedimentology: Dowden, Hutchinson & Ross, Inc., Stroudsburg, PA, p. 110–115.

Tainter, T.A., 1984, Stratigraphic and paleostructural controls on hydrocarbon migration in Cretaceous D and J sandstones of the Denver Basin, in J. Woodward, F.F. Meissner, and J.L. Clayton, eds., Hydrocarbon Source Rocks of the Greater Rocky Mountain Region: RMAG, p. 339–354.

Weimer, R.J. and S.A. Sonnenberg, 1982, Wattenberg Field, paleostructure-stratigraphic trap, Denver Basin, Colorado: OGJ, March 22, p. 204–210.

Weimer, R.J., 1983, Relation of unconformities, tectonics and sea level changes, Cretaceous of the Denver Basin and adjacent areas, in M.W. Reynolds and E.D. Dolly, eds., Mesozoic Paleogeography of West-Central United States: RMS-SEPM Spec. Pub., p. 359–376.

Weimer, R.J., 1984, Relation of unconformities, tectonics, and sea-level changes, Cretaceous of Western Interior, U.S.A., in J.S. Schlee, ed., Interregional Unconformities and Hydrocarbon Accumulation: AAPG Mem. 36, p. 7–35.

Weimer, R.J., S.A. Sonnenberg, and G.B. Young, 1986, Wattenberg Field, Denver Basin, Colorado, in C.W. Spencer and R.F. Mast, eds., Geology of Tight Gas Reservoirs: AAPG Stud. in Geol. 24, p. 143–164.

Ziegler, J.R., 1982, Poncho Field, "J" Sandstone, T3&4S, R59W, Adams and Arapaho Counties, Colorado, in M.C. Crouch III, ed., Oil and Gas Fields of Colorado/Nebraska & Adjacent Areas: RMAG, p. 400–405.

Field of view consists entirely of authigenic minerals, primarily chlorite (Ch), which line a pore in a fine grained sandstone. Point Lookout sandstone, sec 30 T33N R13W, La Plata Co., CO. Depth 1032 ft (315 m). Photo donated by Bill Keighin.

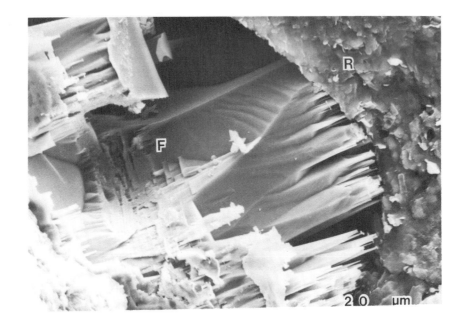

Delicate remnant of partially leached feldspar (F) which is enclosed in slightly compacted rock fragment (R). Sample from a medium-grained sandstone in the Turner Fm., sec 30 T46N R63W, Weston Co., WY. Depth 454 ft (138 m). Photo donated by Bill Keighin.

Petrography and Petrophysics of the Upper Cretaceous Turner Sandy Member of the Carlile Shale at Todd Field, Powder River Basin, Wyoming[1]

DAWADUEN CHAROEN-PAKDI[2]

JAMES E. FOX[2]

[1]Received October 10, 1988; Revised May 5, 1989
[2]Dept. of Geology and Geological Engineering, SD School of Mines and Technology, Rapid City, South Dakota

Petroleum-productive marine shelf sandstone bars of the lower Turner Sandy Member of the Carlile Shale at Todd Field are poorly sorted and texturally and compositionally immature sublitharenites, litharenites, and quartz arenites. Minor lithic arkoses, feldspathic litharenites, and subarkoses are also present. Detrital grains comprise about 60% of the bulk rock volume and include medium to coarse-grained particles of quartz, carbonate rock fragments, chert, shale, feldspar, phosphatic fossil fragments, and minor biotite, muscovite, garnet, zircon, and tourmaline, derived from a mixed igneous, sedimentary, and metamorphic source terrane. The rock matrix, averaging about 8% of the bulk volume, consists primarily of randomly oriented tiny grains of clay and detrital quartz. Authigenic quartz overgrowths, calcite, and clay make up about 23% of the bulk volume; the remainder is pore volume.

Diagenesis began with burial compaction and precipitation of quartz overgrowths on detrital quartz grains, reducing much of the original porosity. This was followed by carbonate precipitation. Fluids subsequently partially dissolved and removed some of the unstable grains as well as carbonate cement, significantly enlarging the pores in which oil accumulated in an early phase of oil migration. Authigenic minerals including kaolinite, illite, and chlorite formed after this, through alteration of unstable grains. A second phase of carbonate precipitation was followed by a second phase of partial dissolution which created and enlarged pores. Simultaneously, they were filled with oil during the final phase of oil migration.

Secondary porosity was derived mainly by partial dissolution of detrital feldspar grains, rock fragments, phosphatic fossil fragments, and authigenic cements. Secondary pores also originated through dissolution and enlargement of primary pores, which are less abundant. Minor pores developed from corrosion around the rims of detrital grains. Whereas primary pores are concavo-convex, secondary pores are crescentic, equant, or irregular spaces between noncompressible grains such as quartz, feldspar, and some rock fragments.

Pay zone thicknesses of sandstone bars range from 2 to 12 ft (0.6 to 3.6 m) and average about 6 ft (1.8 m). Permeability ranges from less than 0.01 to 17 md. Zones of highest porosity occur in the central region of the bars. Oil and a minor amount of gas are produced primarily by solution drive. Oil-in-place is calculated to be about 3,600,000 BO (460 BO per ac-ft). Primary recovery is estimated to be about 15%.

INTRODUCTION

The Powder River Basin, the largest intermontane basin of Laramide origin in the northern Rocky Mountains, occupies a large area of northeastern Wyoming and a small area of southeastern Montana (Fig. 1). The axis of this deep, north-trending, asymmetric, mildly deformed basin lies close to the western margin. The basin is defined on the west, south, and east by the Bighorn Mountains, the Hartville Uplift, and the Black Hills Uplift, respectively. The northern margin is the subtle northwest-trending Miles City Arch. Todd Field, on the eastern

FIELD DATA:	Todd Field
Producing Interval:	Turner Sandy Member, Carlile Shale
Geographic Location:	Weston County, Wyoming
Present Tectonic Setting:	East flank of Powder River Basin
Age of Reservoir:	Upper Cretaceous (Upper Turonian)
Lithology of Reservoir:	Sublitharenites, litharenites, quartzarenites
Depositional Environment:	Shallow marine shelf sandstone bars
Diagenesis:	Calcite, clay, and quartz overgrowth cementation; dissolution of detrital feldspar, rock fragments, and cements
Porosity Type:	Primary and secondary intergranular porosity
Porosity:	Maximum 18%; average 10%
Permeability:	Maximum 17.1 md; average 3 md
Nature of Traps:	Stratigraphic pinchouts
Entrapping Facies:	Marine shales of the Carlile Shale (Pool Creek and Sage Breaks Members)
Source Rocks:	Unknown
Timing of Hydrocarbon Migration:	Unknown
Discovered:	1974
Reservoir Depth:	Average 7,000 ft (2,310 m)
Reservoir Thickness:	6 ft (2 m)
IP (discovery well):	Davis Oil No. 1 Bacon Creek Federal (NE NW Sec 1 T44N R68W) 181 BOPD, 190 MCFGPD, 4 BWPD
Areal Extent:	1,440 acres (582.8 ha)
Original Reservoir Pressure:	719 psi (DST)
Cumulative Production:	1,510,000 BO
Estimated Oil in Place:	3,600,000 BO
Approximate Ultimate Recovery:	Unknown
Oil Gravity:	39–43° API
Minimum Water Saturation:	18%

flank of the basin, is located at T44–45N, R67–68W in Weston County, Wyoming, about 40 mi (64.4 km) southwest of Osage, Wyoming.

The present form of the basin is primarily the result of Laramide deformation. Major thrusting along the west and south sides of the basin began during the late Paleocene followed by renewed uplift, downwarping, and regional tilting as late as the Miocene (Blackstone, 1981; Gries, 1983; Jenkins, 1986). The eastern side of the basin is less deformed than the western and southern sides.

The Powder River Basin is filled by a thick sequence of predominantly clastic Phanerozoic strata. At least 8,000 ft (2,425 m) of these strata are non-marine Upper Cretaceous and lower Tertiary clastics associated with Laramide orogenesis.

UPPER CRETACEOUS STRATIGRAPHY AND SEDIMENTATION

The focus of this study is the Upper Cretaceous Turner Sandy Member of the Carlile Shale. Upper Cretaceous rocks thicken from about 5,000 ft (1,515 m) at the northern margin of the basin to about 9,000 ft (2,730 m) at the southern margin. They are more coarsely clastic in the southwestern part of the basin near the sedimentary source, reflecting their general distribution as a clastic wedge that prograded eastward into the Western Interior seaway.

Marine shale predominates in the eastern part of the basin; the only significant sandstone is the Turner Sandy Member of the Carlile Shale and discontinuous sandstone bars of the Shannon Sandstone Member of the Pierre Shale.

Sedimentary rocks of early Late Cretaceous age along the eastern flank of the Powder River Basin are, from older to younger, the Belle Fourche Shale, Greenhorn Formation, and Carlile Shale (Fig. 2). These shales, sandstones, siltstones, limestones, and bentonites have an aggregate thickness of 1,214 ft (370 m) near the town of Osage (Merewether, 1980). At this location, the Carlile Shale is about 540 ft (165 m) thick and includes, in ascending order, the Pool Creek, Turner Sandy, and Sage Breaks Members.

Todd Field occupies an area of about 1,440 acres (582 ha). Thirty wells have been drilled into the Upper Cretaceous Turner Sandy Member of the Carlile Shale since 1974 (Fig. 3). Cores of the Turner from five of these wells were studied, including: No. 1–8 Cities Service Federal, No. 3–5 Todd Federal, No. 1–4 Bruce Federal, Davis No. 4 Bacon Creek Federal, and Cities Service No. A–2 Matthewson Federal (Fig. 3).

Depositional Environment

The Turner sandstone at the Todd Field is divided into upper and lower sandstone units separated by interbedded shale and siltstone (Fig. 4). This study is restricted to the lower sandstone.

Stratigraphic correlation of well logs of the Turner Sandy Member and detailed study of cores substanti-

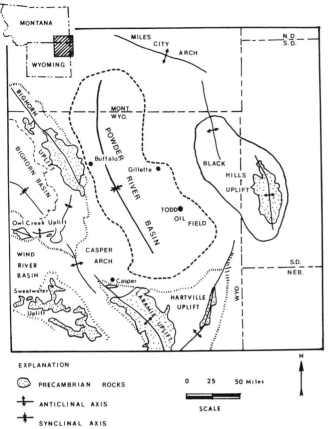

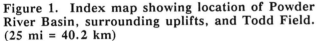

Figure 1. Index map showing location of Powder River Basin, surrounding uplifts, and Todd Field. (25 mi = 40.2 km)

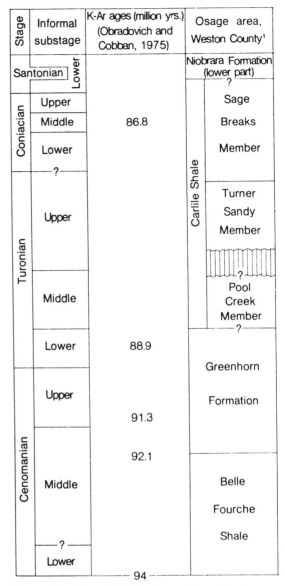

[1]Age of basal contact of Niobrara Formation from Evetts (1976, p.121).

Figure 2. Correlation of the lower Upper Cretaceous formations at selected localities in northeastern Wyoming (from Merewether, 1980).

ate the interpretation that the lower Turner sandstone unit is a shallow marine shelf sandstone bar deposited during a marine regression. This interpretation is based on: 1) coarsening–upward sandstones in the lower Turner Sandy Member (Figs. 4, 5, and 6); 2) marine fossil fish fragments; 3) hummocky cross-bedded sandstone and siltstone (Fig. 6), formed under the influence of storm processes; and 4) stratigraphic correlation (Fig. 4) revealing two major regressive marine cycles during which the lower and the upper Turner sandstones were deposited, separated by transgressive marine shale and siltstone.

This interpretation is consistent with that of correlative strata of the upper Frontier Formation ("First Wall Creek" or "First Frontier") on the west side of the Powder River Basin. Here, sandstone bars also are part of a regressive sequence of clastics derived from the west (Haun, 1958; Goodell, 1962; Barlow and Haun, 1970; Winn, et al., 1983). Farther to the west of these shelf sandstones, in central and western Wyoming, deltaic facies of equivalent age have been identified. To the east, in the eastern Powder River Basin and in the Black Hills of South Dakota, shelf sandstone becomes thinner.

Generally, sandstone in the lower Turner sandstone unit (Figs. 5, 6, and 7) is medium to coarse–grained, subrounded, poorly sorted, bioturbated, and contains minor greenish–gray mud clasts and black shale laminae. Minor fine–grained sandstone containing wavy discontinuous black shale laminae and shale partings also occurs. Upward–coarsening sequences were deposited as the energy level increased (Fig. 8).

PETROGRAPHY

Modal analyses of 300 points on each of 50 thin sections of lower Turner sandstone reveal the primary

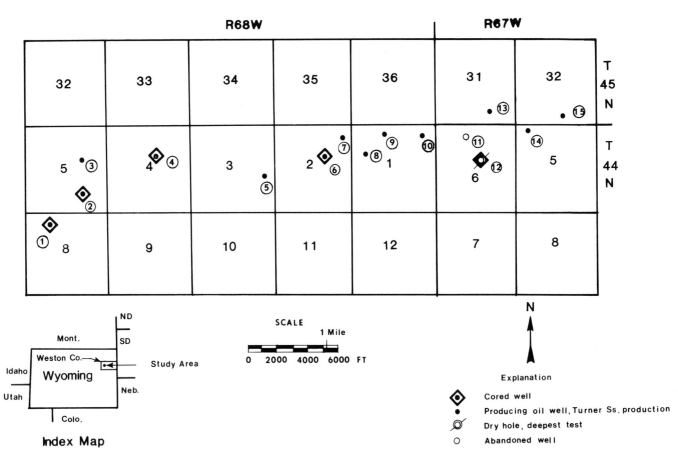

Figure 3. Location map of wells, Todd Field, Weston County, Wyoming. Well numbers: 1 = No. 1–8 Cities Service Federal; 2 = No. 3–5 Todd Federal; 3 = No. 2–5 West Todd; 4 = No. 1–4 Bruce Federal; 5 = No. 1 Sun Federal; 6 = Davis No. 4 Bacon Creek Federal; 7 = Davis No. 3 Bacon Creek Federal; 8 = Davis No. 2 Bacon Creek Federal; 9 = Davis No. 1 Bacon Creek Federal; 10 = No. 1 Conley Federal; 11 = No. 3–6 Federal; 12 = Cities Service No. A–2 Matthewson Federal; 13 = No. 2 Gordon Federal; 14 = Davis No. 2 EST; 15 = Todd Federal.

and authigenic mineral composition, texture, fabric, and diagenetic sequence. Pores were included in the point count, and were classified as primary or secondary by criteria of Schmidt, et al. (1977). Pore–system geometry also was identified, using petrographic and scanning electron microscopy (SEM).

Based on Folk's (1980) compositional classification scheme, 48% of the rock samples studied are sublitharenites, 24% are litharenites, and 10% are quartzarenites (Fig. 9). Of minor abundance are lithic arkoses, feldspathic litharenites, and subarkoses. These are texturally immature, poorly sorted rocks of complex mineralogy.

Detrital Grains

Source terrane for the Turner Sandstone at Todd Field was mixed igneous, sedimentary, and metamorphic as inferred from the composition of constituent grains. Grains consist of quartz, chert, carbonate rock fragments, shale, dolomite, siltstone, minor metamorphic rock fragments, detrital feldspar, and fossil fragments.

Quartz grains are mostly monocrystalline and show straight to slightly undulant extinction, suggesting a granitic source terrane. Polycrystalline quartz grains

are much less abundant, implying metamorphic rocks were minor contributors to the sediment. In general, quartz grains are subangular to subrounded and range from very fine to coarse–grained. Feldspar grains (Plate 1), most of which exhibit albite twinning, are much less abundant than quartz grains, comprising less than 8% of the rock constituents. Feldspar is often altered to clay minerals which precipitated in adjacent pores.

Carbonate rocks and chert grains are the most abundant sedimentary rock fragments in the Turner. Carbonate rock fragments (Plate 1A) are colorless to light brown under plane–polarized light and are composed of tiny angular crystals. Chert grains are colorless to dark brown and are as abundant as the carbonate rock fragments. Detrital chert grains generally have a uniform dark microcrystalline quartz fabric and behave as noncompressible detrital grains. Many of the carbonate and chert grains exhibit dissolution, with oil filling the molds.

Other clasts include shale and siltstone fragments, trace amounts of zebraic chalcedony, metamorphic rock fragments, biotite, hornblende, pyroxene, garnet, zircon, tourmaline, and organic matter. Shale fragments (Plate 1B) are brown to dark brown, composed

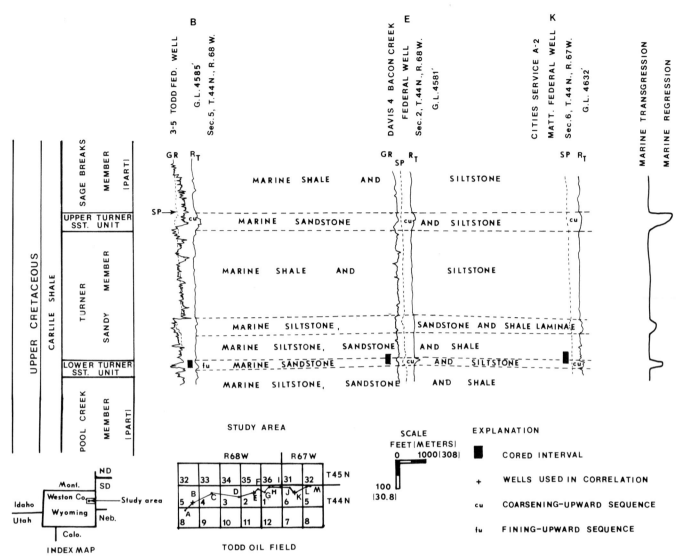

Figure 4. Stratigraphic correlation of the Turner Sandy Member, Carlile Shale, Todd Field, Weston County, Wyoming. SP = spontaneous potential, GR = gamma-ray, Rt = formation resistivity. See Figures 5, 6 and 7 for a detailed description of the lithology.

of finely crystalline clay minerals, and have dark brown rims of authigenic clay minerals. Detrital siltstone clasts are brown and composed mostly of tiny quartz crystals. Oil droplets fill dissolution enhanced pores.

Phosphatic fossil fish fragments (Plate 1C) are abundant in the Turner Sandstone. They are colorless to green and generally fragmented. Most of the fossil fragments were at least partially dissolved; many of the resulting pore spaces contain oil droplets (Plate 1C).

Matrix and Authigenic Minerals

Matrix, which comprises an average of about 8% of the bulk rock volume, consists of randomly oriented clay minerals, which may have originated as tiny shale clasts ("pseudomatrix"), and tiny grains of quartz. Quartz overgrowths, carbonate, and clay minerals comprise the authigenic constituents, which aver-

age about 23% of the bulk rock volume. Quartz overgrowths (Plate 1D) formed during the first stage of diagenesis on the free surfaces of detrital quartz grains that originally were rounded to well rounded. Their sharp crystal facets project into pore spaces but rarely fill intergranular pores completely. The overgrowths significantly reduce porosity.

Authigenic calcite (Plates 1A and B) is colorless, commonly shows a uniform extinction, and has twin lamellae. In many instances, authigenic calcite has been dissolved leaving tiny pores which subsequently were filled with oil.

Authigenic clay cements consist mostly of kaolinite and illite, precipitated as a result of dissolution of feldspar and rock fragments. Kaolinite (Plate 1E), the most abundant clay mineral in the Turner, occurs as vermicular crystals filling the pores and greatly reducing permeability. Green to greenish-brown authigenic chlorite is present as pore-lining.

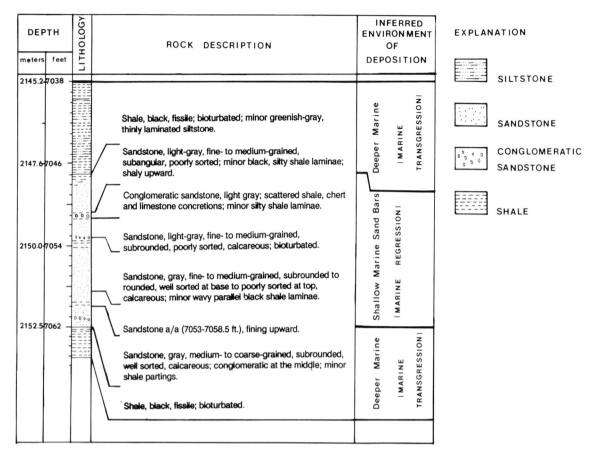

Figure 5. Lithologic description of the core samples from No. 3–5 Todd Federal well (Sec 5 T44N R68W), Todd Field, Weston County, Wyoming.

Figure 6. Lithologic description of the core samples from the Davis No. 4 Bacon Creek Federal well (Sec 2 T44N R68W), Todd Field, Weston County, Wyoming.

Figure 7. Lithologic description of the core samples from Cities Service No. A–2 Matthewson Federal well (Sec 6 T44N R68W), Todd Field, Weston County, Wyoming.

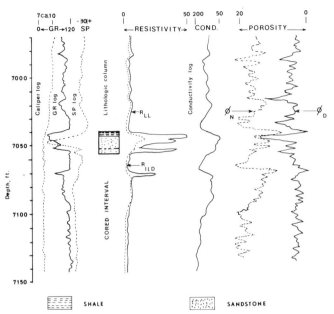

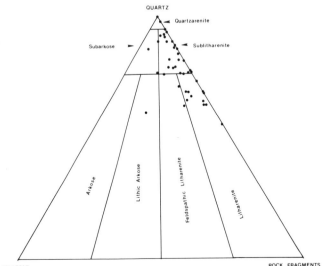

Figure 8. Well–log correlation of the No. 1–8 Cities Service Federal well (Sec 8 T44N R68W), Todd Field, Weston County, Wyoming. Cored interval of the lower Turner Sandstone unit is shown. GR = gamma–ray (API), SP = spontaneous potential (mv), Rll = resistivity reading from laterolog (ohm–m), Rild = resistivity reading from deep induction log (ohm–m), cond. = conductivity (mmho–m), n = neutron porosity (%), d = density porosity (%), ca. = caliper log (inch).

Figure 9. QFR classification of sandstones from the Turner Sandy Member of the Carlile Shale, Todd Field, Weston County, Wyoming (after Folk, 1980).

Porosity

Porosity of the Turner sandstone at Todd Field ranges from 1% to 28% and averages about 9%. The majority of pore spaces are secondary; primary porosity contributes only about 2% to the bulk rock volume. Some of the secondary porosity originated through dissolution of primary pores. Secondary porosity in the Turner includes the following types (Schmidt et al., 1977); 1) P1, or partial dissolution, 2) P2, or recognizable molds, 3) P3, or pores resulting from inhomogeneity of packing, 4) P4, oversized pores and "floating grains", 5) P5, or elongated pores, and 6) P6, or pores developed around corroded grains.

Primary pores in Turner sandstones are concavoconvex (Fig. 10), while secondary pores have several different shapes. P1 pores, the most common secondary pores (Plates 1C and F; Fig. 11), are mainly crescentic, equant, or irregular spaces between noncompressible grains such as quartz, feldspar, and rock

Figure 10. SEM image of triangular primary pore spaces. Note the reduction of primary pore space by quartz overgrowths.

Figure 11. SEM image of irregularly shaped secondary pore spaces developed by the process of partial dissolution.

fragments. P1 pores result from dissolution of detrital grains such as feldspar and rock fragments, or dissolution of authigenic cements such as carbonate and clay minerals. P6 pores that developed as a result of corrosion of detrital grains are the second most abundant pore type. They occur as irregular margins around detrital grains, and usually are small when compared to the P1 pore type. P2 pores are highly variable in shape and are not very abundant. In general, P3 and P4 pores are very large and irregular, have similar shape, are very difficult to distinguish, and are not very abundant. Pores classified as P4 contain "floating grains". P5 pores are usually elongate and probably formed due to the shrinkage of clay minerals along shale laminae. They are typically best developed where the lithology changes from sandstone to shale.

Diagenesis

A complex diagenetic sequence is proposed. Diagenesis began with burial and associated compaction by overburden pressure (Fig. 12, stage I). Detrital grains were squeezed together reducing the primary porosity. Quartz overgrowths (Fig. 12, stage II) formed at this time through precipitation from solutions expelled from shale during compaction and from pressure solution. Subsequently, precipitation of calcite filled primary pores (Fig. 12, stage III) and fractures. Thin sections show that this calcite was subsequently penetrated by authigenic kaolinite.

Following the precipitation of calcite, the rocks were invaded by acidic water and complexing agents. The source of these agents is not well understood, but may be adjacent shales. At this stage (Fig. 12, stage IV), relatively unstable detrital grains such as feldspar (Plate 1F), siltstone, metamorphic rock fragments, shale, fossil fragments (Plate 1C), and carbonate rock fragments were partially dissolved. This process is the "Framework Grain Dissolution (FGD)" of Seibert, et al. (1984). Calcite cement also was dissolved at this stage of diagenesis. FGD, as well as solution of calcite cement, resulted in a significant increase in porosity. Later during this stage, the more stable detrital grains such as chert and quartz were partially dissolved. Thin sections show partially dissolved chert and quartz grains embedded in carbonate cement. Detrital chert often has tiny pores filled with black oil. This stage (Fig. 12, stage IV) probably represents the first phase of oil migration.

Stage V began simultaneously with the FGD process. At this stage, the mass derived from dissolution of grains was precipitated as authigenic kaolinite, illite, and carbonate in the surrounding pore system (Plate 1E). The pores may have been partially or totally filled by these authigenic minerals. This stage is the "Framework Grain Alteration (FGA)" process (Seibert et al., 1984) and represents the second phase of calcite precipitation.

Subsequently, secondary pores developed as these authigenic cements were dissolved (Fig. 12, stage VI). A second phase of oil migration immediately filled these newly developed pores, representing the final phase of reservoir diagenesis recognized in this study.

RESERVOIR PROPERTIES

Twenty-three core plugs were taken from the following wells: No. 1-8 Cities Service Federal, No. 3-5 Todd Federal, No. 1-4 Bruce Federal, Davis No. 4 Bacon Creek Federal, and Cities Service No. A-2 Matthewson Federal. Laboratory analyses of these core plugs included air permeability, helium porosity, and grain density tests (Table 1). Figure 13 shows the relationship between air permeability and helium porosity in these cores. Cored sandstone with the greatest porosity occurs in the central part of the oil field, which is thought to represent a narrow east-west trending shelf sandstone bar.

Formation water saturations (Sw) were obtained from plots of true resistivities versus bulk densities (not shown in this report). A cutoff point of 60% for formation water saturation was used in the oil reserve calculation.

OIP calculated by the volumetric method, was estimated to be about 3,600,000 BO. Cumulative hydrocarbon production of the Todd Field is about 1,500,000 BO, which accounts for about 42% of the total oil reserve in the reservoir. A significant amount of oil and gas remains to be recovered from the Todd Field.

CONCLUSIONS

Strata of the lower part of the Turner Sandy Member of the Carlile Shale at Todd Field are interbedded sandstone, sandy shale, siltstone, and shale deposited as shallow marine shelf sandbars. Petrographic analyses of cores of the lower part of the Turner Sandy Member reveal texturally immature, poorly sorted rocks of complex mineralogy. Detrital grains, making up an average of about 60% of the bulk rock volume, are quartz, carbonate rock fragments, chert, shale, feldspar, phosphatic fossil fragments, and minor biotite, muscovite, garnet, zircon, and tourmaline. Feldspar grains comprising as much as 12% of the bulk volume were mostly altered. Authigenic clay minerals that filled pores between noncompressible grains may have been partially derived from altered feldspar grains. Much of the porosity occurs as the "ghosts" of these feldspar grains.

Sharp facets of quartz overgrowths on subrounded to rounded quartz grains project into open pores. Much of the original porosity was reduced by these overgrowths.

Secondary porosity was derived primarily from partial dissolution of detrital feldspar grains, rock fragments, and cementing materials. Minor pores were developed as a result of corrosion around the rims of detrital grains. Trace amounts of primary pores are also present. It is apparent that many of the secondary pores may have originated through enlargement of primary pores. High porosity zones are concentrated in the central part of the marine shelf sandstone bar complex. This bar complex has a pay zone thickness that averages about 6 ft (1.8 m).

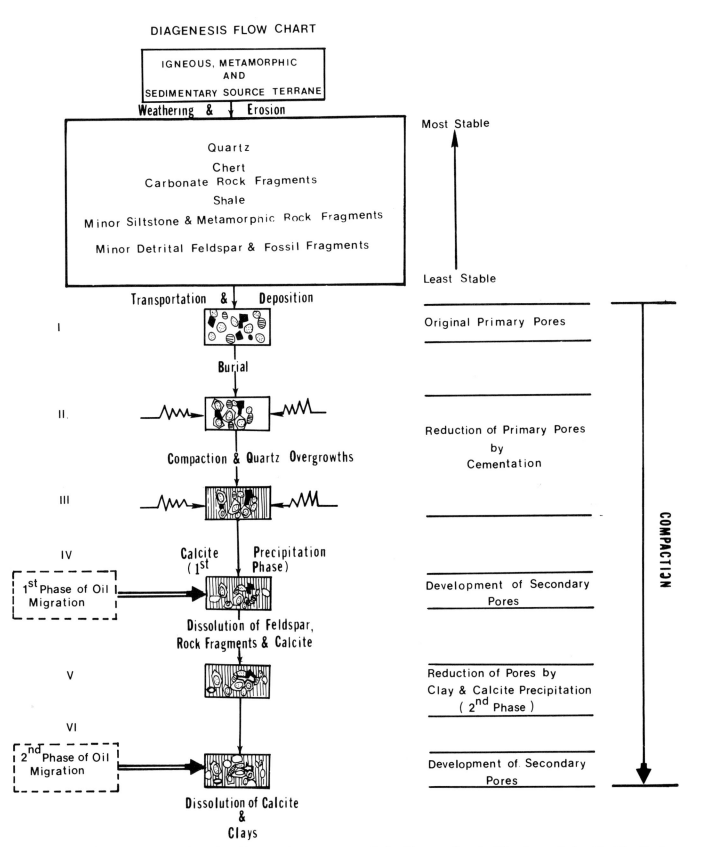

DIAGENESIS FLOW CHART

IGNEOUS, METAMORPHIC
AND
SEDIMENTARY SOURCE TERRANE

Weathering & Erosion

Quartz
Chert
Carbonate Rock Fragments
Shale
Minor Siltstone & Metamorphic Rock Fragments
Minor Detrital Feldspar & Fossil Fragments

Most Stable

Least Stable

Transportation & Deposition

I

Burial

II.

Compaction & Quartz Overgrowths

III

IV   Calcite   Precipitation
         (1st Phase)

1st Phase of Oil
Migration

Dissolution of Feldspar,
Rock Fragments & Calcite

V

VI

2nd Phase of Oil
Migration

Dissolution of Calcite
&
Clays

Original Primary Pores

Reduction of Primary Pores
by
Cementation

Development of Secondary
Pores

Reduction of Pores by
Clay & Calcite Precipitation
(2nd Phase)

Development of Secondary
Pores

COMPACTION

Figure 12. Flow chart showing the diagenetic sequence of the Turner Sandy Member of the Carlile Shale, Todd Field, Weston County, Wyoming.

Table 1. Data of routine core analyses, Turner Sandstone, Todd Field, Wyoming

Sample	Depth (ft)	Permeability (horizontal) (K_{air}, md)	Porosity (helium) (%)	Grain Density (gm/cc)
WELL: 1-8 CITIES FEDERAL				
*1	7048.2	–	18.7	2.66
*2	7052.0	–	6.1	2.64
WELL: 3-5 TODD				
3	7048.0	.11	7.0	2.65
4	7051.0	1.58	9.8	2.65
5	7055.7	21.1	13.9	2.64
6	7061.0	6.34	11.7	2.68
WELL: 1-4 BRUCE FEDERAL				
7	6991.7	.02	6.9	2.67
8	6993.0	<.01	7.4	2.67
9	6995.5	<.01	7.4	2.68
10	7017.0	4.91	11.1	2.65
11	7022.0	.35	5.7	2.66
12	7029.0	.05	4.6	2.67
WELL: DAVIS 4 BACON CREEK FEDERAL				
13	6742.3	1.42	10.9	2.65
14	6744.8	<.01	2.3	2.70
15	6746.0	.05	6.0	2.67
+16	6748.4	.04	1.7	2.68
17	6750.6	17.1	15.0	2.64
18	6753.6	1.14	9.1	2.65
19	6754.7	.44	10.0	2.65
20	6756.7	.02	2.2	2.68
WELL: CITIES SERV. A-2 MATT. FEDERAL				
21	6513.0	.02	8.4	2.67
22	6531.0	<.01	3.1	2.67
23	6538.0	.16	7.3	2.66

Notes: + Permeability measured along a fracture.
         * Sample unsuitable for analysis.
           Tests were conducted by Core Lab
           (Aurora, Colo.) in June 1987.

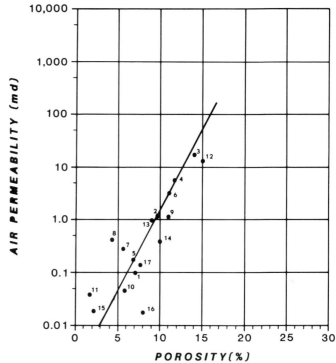

Figure 13. Graph of air permeability and helium porosity of sandstone samples from the Turner Sandy Member of the Carlile Shale, Todd Field, Weston County, Wyoming. Note that permeabilities less than 0.01 md are not included on the plot. Key is as follows: No. 3–5 Todd Federal well: 1 = sublitharenite at 7,048.0 ft (2,148.2 m), 2 = litharenite at 7,051.0 ft (2,149.1 m), 3 = litharenite at 7,055.7 ft (2,150.6 m), 4 = litharenite at 7,061.0 ft (2,149.1 m). No. 1–4 Bruce Federal well: 5 = sublitharenite at 6,991.7 ft (2,131.1 m), 6 = sublitharenite at 7,071.0 ft (2,155.2 m), 7 = quartzarenite at 7022.0 ft 2,140.3 m), 8 = sublitharenite at 7,029.0 ft (2,142.4 m). Davis No. 4 Bacon Creek Federal well: 9 = litharenite at 6,742.3 ft (2,055.1 m), 10 = sublitharenite at 6,746.0 ft (2,056.2 m), 11 =litharenite at 6,748.4 ft (2,056.9 m), 12 = sublitharenite/litharenite at 6,750.6 ft (2,057.6 m), 13 = litharenite at 6,753.6 ft (2,058.5 m), 14 = feldspathic litharenite at 6,754.7 ft (2,058.8 m), 15 = sublitharenite/litharenite at 6,756.7 ft (2,059.4 m). Cities Service No. A–2 Matthewson Federal well, 16 = quartzarenite at 6,513.0 ft (1,985.2 m), 17 = litharenite at 6,538.0 ft (1,92.8 m).

REFERENCES

Barlow, J.H., and J.D. Haun, 1970, Regional stratigraphy of the Frontier Formation and its relation to Salt Creek Field, *in* M.T. Halbouty, ed., Geology of Giant Petroleum Fields: AAPG Mem. 14, p. 147–157.

Blackstone, D.L., Jr., 1981, Compression as an agent in deformation of the east-central flank of the Bighorn Mountains, Sheridan and Johnson Counties, Wyoming: Cont. to Geol., U. of WY, v. 19, no. 2, p. 105–122.

Folk, R.L., 1980, Petrology of Sedimentary Rocks: Hemphill Publ. Co., Austin, TX, 131 p.

Goodell, H.G., 1962, The stratigraphy and petrography of the Frontier Formation of Wyoming, 17th Ann. Field Conf. Guidebook, WGA, p. 173– 210.

Gries, R., 1983, Oil and gas prospecting beneath Precambrian of Foreland thrust plates in Rocky Mountains: AAPG Bull., v. 67, p. 1–28.

Haun, J.D., 1958, Early Upper Cretaceous stratigraphy, Powder River basin, Wyoming: 13th Ann. Field Conf. Guidebook, WGA, p. 84–89.

Jenkins, C.D., 1986, Tectonic analysis of the northeastern flank of the Bighorn Mountains; Buffalo to Dayton, Wyoming: unpub. MS thesis, SD School of Mines and Technology, 121 p.

Merewether, E.A., 1980, Stratigraphy of mid-Cretaceous formations at drilling sites in Weston and Johnson Counties, northeast Wyoming: USGS Prof. Pap. 1186-A, p. 1–25.

Schmidt, V., D.A. McDonald, and R.L. Platt, 1977, Pore geometry and reservoir aspects of secondary porosity in sandstones: Bull. of Canadian Petroleum Geology, v. 25, p. 271–290.

Seibert, R.M., G.K. Moncure, and R.W. Lahann, 1984, A theory of framework grain dissolution in sandstones, *in* D.A. McDonald and R.C. Surdam, eds., Clastic Diagenesis: AAPG Mem. 37, p. 163–176.

Winn, R. D., S.A. Stonecipher, and M.G. Bishop, 1983, Depositional environments and diagenesis of offshore sand ridges, Frontier Formation, Spearhead Ranch Field, Wyoming: Mtn. Geol., v. 20, no. 2, p. 41–58.

Nature of the Terry Sandstone Reservoir, Spindle Field, Colorado[1]

EDWARD D. PITTMAN[2]

[1]Received August 5, 1988; Revised January 19, 1989
[2]Amoco Production Co., Tulsa, Oklahoma

The Upper Cretaceous Terry Sandstone Member of the Middle Pierre Shale is the chief reservoir for Spindle Field, which has recoverable reserves of 29,200,000 BO. The Terry is subdivided into two facies. The reservoir consists of high-energy, cross-bedded, fine to medium-grained sandstone interpreted as being deposited in the crestal position on an offshore marine bar. The nonreservoir is lower-energy, extensively bioturbated, very fine to fine-grained sandstone interpreted as originating on the flanks or margins of the bar. Reservoir and nonreservoir rocks are, in places, thinly interbedded, and constitute a third, nonreservoir facies. Dark gray mudstones occur as thin interbeds in the sandstone.

Three sandstones in the Terry are productive; two others are nonproductive. Production is limited to northwest-southeast trending "pods" of reservoir sandstone encased in nonreservoir sandstone. The reservoir sandstone facies has mean porosity and permeability of 14.3% and 1.38 md, compared to 12.9% and 0.41 md for nonreservoir sandstone. The reservoir sandstone has larger pore-entry sizes, better sorted pore apertures, and coarser pore apertures than does the nonreservoir sandstone. An empirical equation that relates porosity, permeability, and pore-aperture radius is useful for delineating the stratigraphic trap at Spindle Field.

The reservoir facies is lithic subarkose and feldspathic litharenite. Mechanical compaction is the chief cause of porosity loss in the reservoir facies because of the abundance of ductile lithic material. The most volumetrically important cements are chlorite (5.7 vol%), calcite (up to 33 vol% in concretions), and quartz (3.0 vol%). Plagioclase feldspars are essentially completely albitized below a depth of 5,000 ft (1,520 m).

Porosity in the reservoir sandstone facies consists of approximately 4% primary intergranular macroporosity, 4% secondary intergranular and intragranular macroporosity, and 6% microporosity, which is predominantly associated with clays and lithic fragments.

INTRODUCTION

The purpose of this paper is to discuss the reservoir distribution, origin and nature of the porosity, petrophysical characteristics, and diagenesis of the Terry Sandstone in a major Colorado oil field. This paper is based on study of 213 thin sections from 11 wells, supported by extensive X-ray diffractometry and scanning electron microscopy. For more-detailed information on the diagenesis, see Pittman (1988).

Spindle Field is in Weld County, Colorado, in the deep part of the Denver Basin, which has a shallowly dipping eastern flank and a sharply uplifted western margin (Fig. 1). Precambrian granite crops out in the Front Range Uplift about 20 mi (32 km) west of Spindle Field, and was encountered at a depth of 10,425 ft (3,180 m) in the Rocky Mountain Arsenal well drilled about seven mi (11 km) south of the field.

Spindle Field produces from the Upper Cretaceous Terry and Hygiene members of the Middle Pierre Shale (Fig. 2), commonly referred to as the Sussex and Shannon "sands", respectively, within the oil industry; however, they are not equivalent to the better known sandstones with the same names in Wyoming. The Terry is the major pay in Spindle Field, with 1,315 completions as compared to 312 for the Hygiene. Discussion in this paper is limited to the Terry, which lies approximately 400 ft (120 m) stratigraphically above the Hygiene, but there is only slight petrographic difference between the sandstones (Treckman, 1960; Porter, this volume).

The Terry sandstone at Spindle Field forms a stratigraphic trap lying primarily on the western flank of the Denver Basin, although the field crosses the basin axis (Fig. 3). Small faults occur within the field, but do not appear to affect production.

For Reservoir Summary, see Porter, this volume.

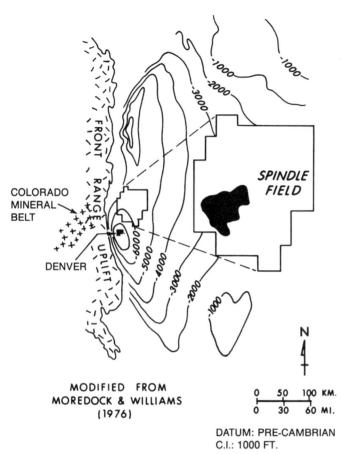

Figure 1. Location map showing Spindle Field and the asymmetrical geometry of the Denver Basin. Modified from Moredock and Williams (1976). By permission of the Colorado School of Mines Press.

MODIFIED FROM
MOREDOCK & WILLIAMS
(1976)

DATUM: PRE-CAMBRIAN
C.I.: 1000 FT.

FORMATION OR EVENT		LITHOLOGY	AGE, mybp	DEPTH, ft.
PRESENT –			0	
END LARAMIDE OROG. –			38	
START LARAMIDE OROG. –			65	
			66	SFC. –
LARAMIE AND FOX HILLS				
			68	1400
UPPER PIERRE				
			72	4000
MIDDLE PIERRE	LARIMER–ROCKY RIDGE			
			74	4650
	TERRY		75	5100
	HYGIENE		76	5400
LOWER PIERRE				
			81	7000
NIOBRARA			89	7500
BENTON			97	8000
DAKOTA GROUP			110	8300
MORRISON				

Figure 2. Representative Cretaceous columnar section for Spindle Field, which produces from the Upper Cretaceous Terry and Hygiene Members of the Middle Pierre Shale.

Previous Work

The first discovery in the Terry Sandstone in the deep Denver Basin was at Singletree Field in June, 1971, followed by Spindle and Surrey fields in January and February of 1972, respectively (Moredock and Williams, 1976). Later, the three fields were combined under the Spindle name. Information on field production occurs in Roundtree (1978) and Kolodzie (1980). Papers by Porter (1976 and this volume) and Porter and Weimer (1982) provide information on sedimentation, petrology, and diagenesis for the Terry and Hygiene members of Spindle Field. Hays and Tieh (1986) studied the diagenesis of the Terry Sandstone.

Warner (1980) made the interesting observation that the oil fields in the Denver region, including Spindle Field, align with the trend of mines in the mountains to the west (Fig. 1). According to Romberger (1980), most of the mineral deposits in the Colorado Mineral Belt of the Front Range are Late

Cretaceous–Early Tertiary (70–63 Ma), whereas a few are Middle Tertiary (about 39–26 Ma). Perhaps heat from these igneous events provided the thermal energy needed to generate hydrocarbons and account for the high temperatures (255° F at 8,100 ft; 124° C at 2,470 m) at the Dakota level in the deep part of the Denver Basin. Weimer and Sonnenberg (this volume)

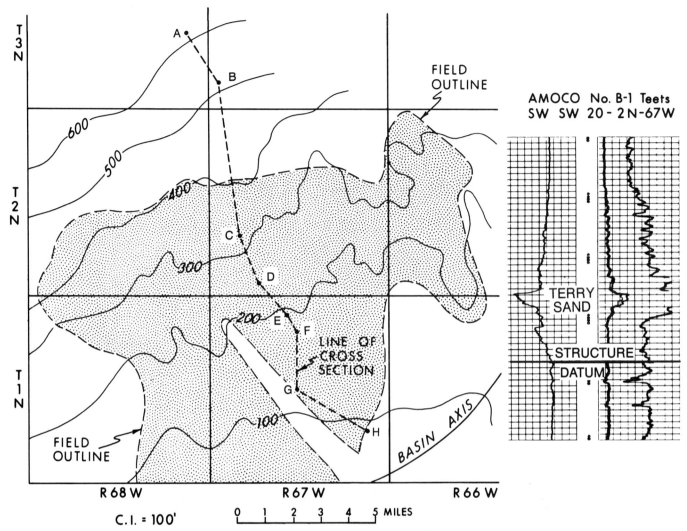

Figure 3. Structure map using the electric log pick shown in the log insert as a datum. The irregular field area (stippled) is the result of Terry stratigraphy. Production is found on both sides of the basin axis, with dips less than 1°. Contours from Moredock and Williams (1976), by permission of the Colorado School of Mines Press. Line of stratigraphic cross sections A – H (Figs. 5 and 6) shown. Contour interval = 100 ft (30.5 m). (1 mi = 1.61 km)

express a similar viewpoint and present data suggesting that a geothermal anomaly coincides with Spindle Field.

Source of Hydrocarbons

Clayton and Swetland (1980) showed that oils produced from the Muddy "D" and "J", Hygiene, and Terry reservoirs are all of the same type and are from a common source. Oil-to-source rock correlation (Amoco proprietary data) suggests that the shales of the Lower Cretaceous Dakota and Benton groups and the chalk of the Upper Cretaceous Niobrara Formation are the sources of oil produced from Cretaceous reservoirs. The Lower Pierre Shale, except at the base, is chemically dissimilar from the underlying source rocks in that it contains relatively more cyclic compounds than are found in the produced oil. The shale interbedded with the Terry has a mean vitrinite reflectance of only 0.65% (based on 5 samples); oil may have been generated but not expelled from the

Lower Pierre Shale, which would explain the oil-to-source rock correlation results.

According to Rice and Gautier (1983), the shales associated with the nonmarine Muddy "J" Sandstone contain Type III kerogen, whereas the other Lower Cretaceous shales and the chalk of the Niobrara Formation contain Type II kerogen. The oil source beds for all of the Denver Basin lie near the basin axis, where they have been buried deeply enough to reach maturity (Tainter, 1984). This implies a minimum vertical migration of 2,200 ft (670 m) from the top of the Niobrara to the Terry at Spindle Field. Gas in the Terry Sandstone at Spindle Field has been interpreted as thermogenic based on chemical and isotopic composition (Rice and Gautier, 1983).

SEDIMENTARY FACIES

The Terry was subdivided into two sandstone lithofacies: reservoir (Facies No. 1) and nonreservoir (Facies No. 2). A third, nonreservoir assemblage consisting of thinly interbedded Facies No. 1 and No. 2 also was mapped as a separate entity. Minor mudstone occurs within the bar complex.

Facies No. 1 consists of high–energy sandstone interpreted as being deposited in a crestal or central position of a marine bar (Fig. 4). This is Porter's (1976 and this volume) "central bar" facies. The sandstone is light gray and ranges from very fine to medium grained, but is typically fine grained. Sandstones in this facies usually are cross–bedded in shallow troughs with moderate dip and tangential relationship of foresets to lower bounded surfaces. Current ripples are common along the top of sets. Burrowing is essentially nonexistent within cross–beds, but *Asterosoma* do occur in thin, rippled, shaly sandstone interbeds.

Facies No. 2 consists of lower–energy, extensively bioturbated, very fine–grained sandstone interpreted as being deposited on the flanks or margins of bars (Fig. 4). This is equivalent to Porter's (1976 and this volume) bar-margin facies. Ripple–laminated sandstone and mudstone interbeds were extensively bioturbated to produce a light to dark gray, poorly bedded sandstone with abundant, non–definitive burrow types, although *Terebellina* and *Siphonites* do occur. The sand content often increases upward, which is reflected in the shape of SP curves (Fig. 5). Facies 2 normally is not perforated, but where it has been perforated separately, it produces slight, if any hydrocarbons, and can be considered nonreservoir.

Facies No. 1 and No. 2 commonly are interbedded as beds up to six in. (15 cm) thick (Fig. 4), suggestive of an environment that often shifted laterally. This interbedded facies is distinguishable on logs (Fig. 5) and can be considered nonreservoir.

Dark gray mudstones occur as thin interbeds in the Terry, although one mudstone is as thick as six ft (two m) (Fig. 6). This facies is interpreted to have formed in deeper water near the bars.

DISTRIBUTION OF SANDSTONE BODIES

There are three separate sandstone bodies that comprise the Terry and are productive in Spindle Field. Two other, nonproductive sandstones can be distinguished. The lowermost productive sandstone is cleaner and thicker than the other productive zones and is limited to the northeastern part of the field. This sandstone has a poorly defined northwest–southeast trend. The other two productive zones occur over most of the field. However, they thin to the east and merge in the western and northwestern portions of field. These two zones, which were used for this study, have a pronounced northwest–southeast orientation.

Log and core characteristics were correlated from study of several wells (Figs. 5 and 6). Log character was used to interpret the distribution of lithofacies types beyond cored intervals. Production is essentially limited to the pod of Facies No. 1, which is encased in Facies No. 2.

Figure 4. Representative core segments showing the high energy cross–bedded reservoir sandstone (Facies No. 1, left); low energy, highly bioturbated, argillaceous, nonreservoir sandstone (Facies No. 2, center); and interbedded Facies No. 1 and No. 2 (right), which also is nonreservoir. (1 ft = 0.30 m)

RESERVOIR CHARACTERISTICS
Physical Properties

Sandstones of the reservoir facies have slightly better permeability for a given porosity than do nonreservoir sandstones (Fig. 7). However, the porosity ranges and means are approximately the same for both facies: mean porosity and permeability of 14.3% and 1.38 md in the reservoir, compared to 12.9% and 0.41 md for the nonreservoir argillaceous sandstone facies.

Core-analysis data for Interbedded Facies No. 1 and No. 2 are misleadingly high (mean of 16.0% and 1.25 md) because sampling for plugs was strongly biased toward the high-energy reservoir sandstone interbeds, to the total exclusion of nonreservoir sandstones. This bias led to some problems in completion of wells. For example, one well (Well B, Fig. 6) had a biased core analysis that made the formation look as attractive (mean of 16.1% and 2.2 md) as any producer. The well was given five fracture treatments without recovering all of the load water or any oil. Inspection of the core would have revealed the extreme heterogeneity and sampling problem.

Mercury injection-capillary pressure data for 12 samples show that Facies No. 1 (reservoir) and Facies No. 2 (nonreservoir) fall into separate groups that do not overlap (Fig. 8). Reservoir sandstones have larger pore-entry sizes, better sorted pore-aperture sizes, and more pore space occupied by mercury at the limits of the test, indicating a coarser pore-aperture geometry compared to the nonreservoir argillaceous sandstone. This explains why one sandstone type produces, while the other does not.

Petrology

Sandstone Composition

Compositional data were derived from point counts (minimum of 300 points) for 20 samples of Facies No. 1 (reservoir) and seven samples of Facies No. 2 (nonreservoir). Alizarin Red-S and sodium cobaltinitrite were used to stain calcite and potassium feldspars.

The sandstones are lithic subarkoses and feldspathic litharenites, according to the McBride (1963) classification. The QFL proportions are 53:15:32 for Facies No. 1 (reservoir). Monocrystalline quartz (mean = 32.1 vol%) and chert/polycrystalline quartz (mean = 5.4 vol%) comprise the quartz component. The feldspar component is dominated by plagioclase (mean = 9.7 vol%) with potassium feldspars contributing less than 1 vol%. The plagioclase has undergone albitization (Pittman, 1988). Lithic fragments constitute 13.8 vol% (mean) and include slate, phyllite, volcanic and plutonic rocks, chert, shale, sandstone, and siltstone. Glauconite has a mean of 8.6 vol%, but ranges from a trace to 26.7 vol%. Glauconite pellets are most common, but glauconitized biotite is also present. For classification purposes, glauconite was included with lithic fragments because of its similar ductile behavior. The greater abundance of feldspar in Facies No. 2 probably reflects mineral partitioning by grain size because Facies No. 2 is finer grained than Facies No. 1.

Diagenesis

Compaction is an important process in the Terry because of the abundance of sedimentary lithics, phyllite, and altered volcanics, which are prone to ductile deformation. Glauconite, which may constitute over half of the rock volume in thin zones, also is highly ductile. Glauconite-rich sandstones typically have essentially no macroporosity because of loss of porosity by compaction (Plate 1A). Evaluation of minus cement porosity (MCP) provides a technique for estimating the amount of compaction. A glauconitic sandstone with 26.7 vol% glauconite has MCP of 8.9% because of porosity loss due to ductile deformation. For comparison, some of the better reservoir rock in Facies No. 1 has MCP of 26.6%. Assuming an initial porosity of 40%, then 31.1% of the intergranular volume was lost by compaction in the glauconite-rich sample, compared to 13.4% in the reservoir sandstone.

The generalized post-compaction diagenetic sequence is: 1) alteration of lithic fragments to provide cations for clays; 2) precipitation of chlorite, which occurs in pore-lining and pore-filling morphologies; 3) precipitation of quartz overgrowths; 4) precipitation of dolomite followed by and perhaps overlapping with calcite; 5) partial dissolution of carbonates and feldspars to form secondary porosity; 6) precipitation of kaolinite; and finally, 7) precipitation of feldspar overgrowths.

Pyrite occurs in traces as a replacement component. Tourmaline, which also occurs in trace amounts, appears to have formed late because it sometimes occurs in secondary pores; however, these minerals could not be fit reliably into the diagenetic sequence. Illite and mixed-layer illite/smectite occur as soil-derived cutans, which have been authigenically modified. Illite also occurs as an alteration product of kaolinite, suggesting that illitization is a relatively late event (Fig. 9). Albitization of plagioclase occurs with increasing depth of burial. The process is essentially complete at burial depths below approximately 5,000 ft (1,640 m).

The most volumetrically important cements are chlorite (mean = 5.7 vol%) and calcite (up to 33 vol%). Quartz (mean = 3.0 vol% for reservoir facies) is the most important of the other authigenic minerals, which individually contribute less than 1 vol%. Only the more abundant cements will be discussed further.

Chlorite probably formed from cations released by relatively early alteration of lithic grains. Chlorite occurs as a pore-lining form, as well as in a subsequent pore-filling morphology (Fig. 10 and Plate 1B, C). Where pore-lining chlorite formed on detrital quartz grains, quartz overgrowths were blocked from potential nucleation sites. This does not prevent quartz from nucleating elsewhere on the quartz grain and spreading to engulf the earlier formed chlorite (Fig. 11).

Calcite is pervasive in concretions (Plate 1D), but has a mean of only 3.9 vol% in the reservoir facies. Textural evidence suggests that some calcite was dissolved, creating secondary intergranular porosity. Calcite commonly replaced feldspars and may be the precursor of intragranular secondary porosity associated with feldspars.

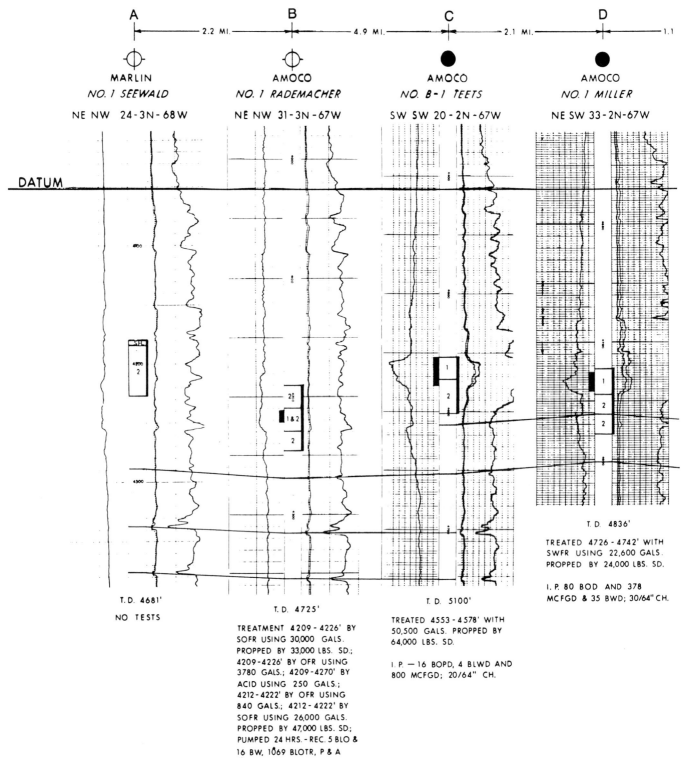

Figure 5. Stratigraphic cross section across Spindle Field (same wells as Fig. 6), using electrical logs. →

Formation of Secondary Porosity

Some intergranular secondary porosity formed by the partial dissolution of calcite and to a lesser extent, dolomite. However, most of the intergranular porosity is considered to be primary. Intragranular secondary porosity formed by partial dissolution of lithic fragments, feldspars (Fig. 12), and replacement calcite. It is not clear whether replacement calcite was the precursor of secondary intragranular porosity in all cases. Silicate minerals certainly can dissolve directly in carboxylic acids (Surdam, Boese, and Crossey, 1984) and perhaps in response to carbon dioxide (Al–Shaieb and Shelton, 1981).

Porosity in the Terry reservoir consists of approximately 4% primary intergranular macroporosity, 4% secondary macroporosity (inter– and intragranular),

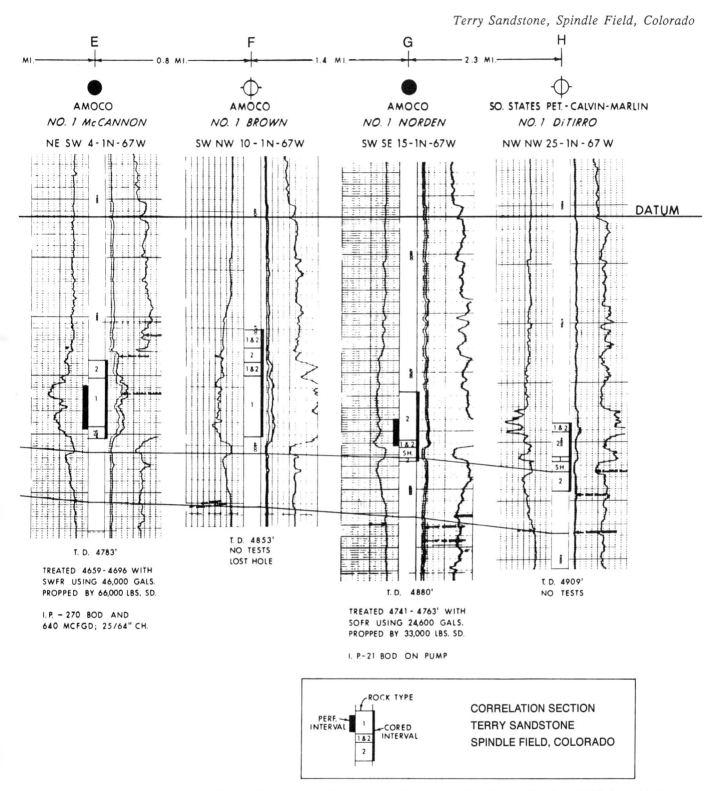

CORRELATION SECTION
TERRY SANDSTONE
SPINDLE FIELD, COLORADO

Location of section shown on Figure 3. Datum is a bentonite bed in the Pierre Shale. (100 ft = 30.5 m)

and 6% microporosity, which is mostly associated with clay minerals and lithic fragments. Microporosity was determined by subtracting point–count derived macroporosity from porosity measured on cores in the laboratory. The interpretation of intergranular macroporosity is subjective. It is not possible to determine the origin of each intergranular pore. A petrologist relies on petrographic criteria such as those developed by Schmidt and McDonald (1979), which leads to a qualitative, subjective appraisal regarding the origin of porosity.

Porosity in nonreservoir argillaceous sandstone has a patchy development because of bioturbation (Plate 1E). The very fine grain size, coupled with the patchy argillaceous matrix and abundance of lithic material leads to extensive microporosity (Plate 1F). Thus, the porosity is not as low as one might expect from a casual inspection. The pore–aperture size is

251

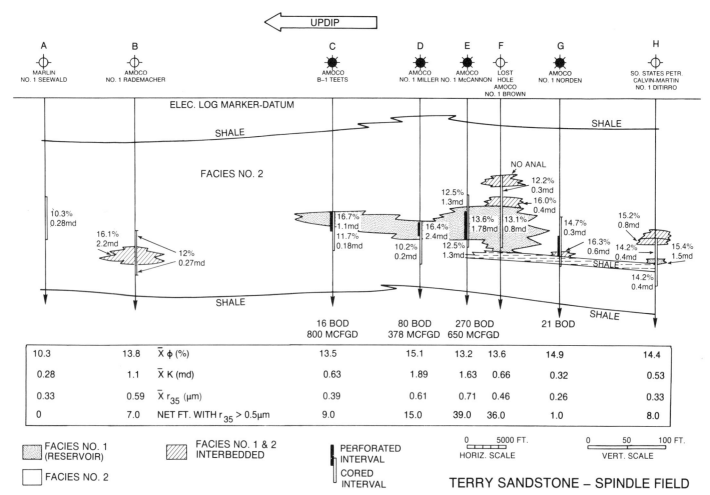

Figure 6. Diagrammatic cross-section showing the distribution of facies based on core descriptions. Datum is a bentonite bed in the Pierre Shale (Fig. 5). Cores were available for the Terry in each well. Log character was used to extend lithology types beyond the cored intervals. Key data from core analyses are posted beneath each well. Location of section shown on Figure 3. (5,000 ft = 1,524 m; 50 ft = 15.2 m)

quite small, however, as shown by mercury injection-capillary pressure tests.

Maps of thicknesses of sandstone with r_{35} greater than 0.5 microns were useful for delineating the trap. The best producing well (Well E, Fig. 6) contains 39 ft (13 m) of net sandstone. The poorest producer (Well G) has only one ft (0.3 m) of net sandstone, because sandstone of Facies No. 1 pinches out in the updip direction. The updip dry hole (Well A), which contains only Facies No. 2, has no net sandstone. Well B, containing interbedded sandstones of Facies No. 1 and No. 2, contains seven net ft (2.3 m). Again, this is a misleading indication of reservoir quality because the footage is distributed among beds ranging in thickness from 1.5 to 6 in. (3.8 to 15.2 cm) and because the clean sandstones were preferentially sampled.

TRAPPING CONDITIONS

Kolodzie (1980) published an empirical relationship developed by H.D. Winland, which showed that porosity, permeability, and mercury injection pore-aperture radius at the 35th percentile (r_{35}) are interrelated by:

$$\log r_{35} = 0.732 + 0.588 \log K_a - 0.864 \log \phi$$
where K_a = air permeability (md)
and ϕ = porosity (percent)

Winland also showed in an Amoco in-house publication that r_{35} values could be used to define the trap for the Terry in Spindle Field.

Means of porosity, permeability, and r_{35} were determined from core analyses (Fig. 6), including data for four wells used by Winland. A dry hole (Well A, Fig. 6) drilled updip from Spindle has smaller mean pore apertures than do the producing wells. Only one producer (Well G, Fig. 6), which lacks Facies No. 1 and was a marginal oil well, has a smaller mean pore aperture size (0.26 mm). A well with an Interbedded Facies No. 1 and Facies No. 2 sequence (Well B, Fig. 6) has an anomalously large mean pore aperture size because of the biased sampling discussed above.

SUMMARY

The Terry reservoir at Spindle Field is comprised of five offshore bars, three of which are productive. The oldest bar has better reservoir characteristics than

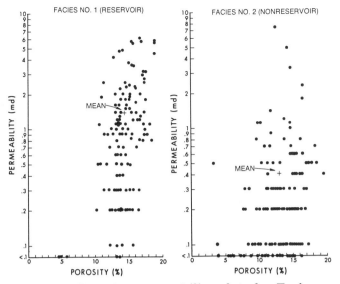

Figure 7. Porosity-permeability plots for Facies No. 1 reservoir sandstone (left) and Facies No. 2 nonreservoir sandstone (right) for wells on the cross-sections (Figs. 5 and 6). Mean porosity and permeability are 14.3% and 1.38 md for the reservoir facies and 12.9% and 0.41 md for the nonreservoir facies.

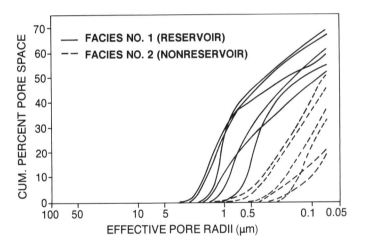

Figure 8. Mercury injection-capillary pressure data for reservoir and nonreservoir sandstones. The reservoir sandstone has larger pore-entry sizes, better sorted pore apertures, and a coarser pore-throat network than do the nonreservoir sandstones.

the other bars, but is limited to the northeastern portion of the field. The other bars have a pronounced northwest-southeast trend and cover most of the field.

The reservoir consists of high-energy, cross-bedded, glauconitic sandstone that occupied the crestal portion of the offshore bars. Nonreservoir rock includes highly bioturbated, argillaceous sandstone, which formed on the flanks or margins of the bar complex. Thin interbeds of Facies No. 1 and No. 2 are also nonreservoir, although the core analyses are

Figure 9. SEM image showing illitization (fibers) of authigenic kaolinite (plates).

Figure 10. Two stages of authigenic chlorite are recognizable under the scanning electron microscope. Pore-filling chlorite rosettes overlie pore-lining chlorite plates.

deceiving because of biased plug sampling of the better quality sandstone.

The reservoir facies has a mean porosity and permeability of 14.3% and 1.38 md, respectively, compared to 12.9% and 0.41 md for the nonreservoir facies. The reservoir and nonreservoir facies have distinctly different distribution, size, and volume of pore apertures.

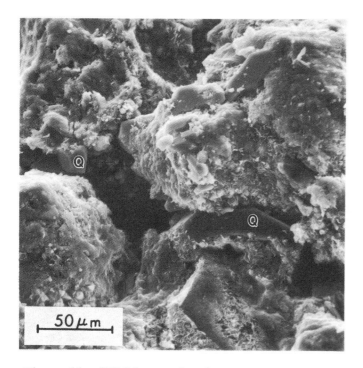

Figure 11. SEM image showing sparse quartz overgrowths (Q) with some pore–lining chlorite visible.

Figure 12. A partially dissolved grain of feldspar as viewed by scanning electron microscopy.

Calcite, chlorite, and quartz are important cements, but compaction is the chief cause of porosity loss in Terry sandstones at Spindle. Porosity in reservoir sandstone consists of approximately 4% primary intergranular macroporosity, 4% secondary intergranular and intragranular macroporosity, and 6% microporosity, which is associated with clays and altered lithic fragments.

Net sandstone values derived from the Winland equation are useful for delineating the updip limit of the stratigraphic trap in the Terry Sandstone at Spindle Field. Net sandstone maps defined in the usual way, with porosity "cutoffs", probably would not delineate the margins of the field as well.

REFERENCES

Al-Shaieb, Z. and J. Shelton, 1981, Migration of hydrocarbons and secondary porosity in sandstones: AAPG Bull., v. 65, p. 2433–2436.

Clayton, J.L. and P.J. Swetland, 1980, Petroleum generation and migration in Denver Basin: AAPG Bull., v. 64, p. 1613–1633.

Hays, P.D. and T.T. Tieh, 1986, Diagenesis in the Terry Sandstone Member of the Pierre Shale, Denver Basin, Colorado [abs]: GSA 99th Ann. Mtg., Abstracts with Program, p. 632.

Kolodzie, S., Jr., 1980, Analysis of pore throat size and use of the Waxman–Smits equation to determine OOIP in Spindle Field, Colorado: SPE-AIME, 55th Ann. Fall Tech. Conf. and Exhibition, Paper SPE-9382, 10 p.

McBride, E.F., 1963, A Classification of common sandstones: JSP, v. 33, p. 664–669.

Moredock, D.E. and S.J. Williams, 1976, Upper Cretaceous Terry and Hygiene Sandstones – Singletree, Spindle, and Surrey Fields, Weld County, Colorado, in R.C. Epis and R.J. Weimer, eds., Sandstone Reservoirs of the Rocky Mountains: CSM Contrib. No. 8, p. 264–274.

Pittman, E.D., 1988, Diagenesis of Terry Sandstone (Upper Cretaceous), Spindle Field, Colorado: JSP, v. 58, p. 785–800.

Porter, K.W., 1976, Marine shelf model, Hygiene Member of Pierre Shale, Upper Cretaceous, Denver Basin, Colorado, in R.C. Epis and R.J. Weimer, eds., Sandstone Reservoirs of the Rocky Mountains: CSM Prof. Contrib. No. 8, p. 251–263.

Porter, K.W. and R.J. Weimer, 1982, Diagenetic sequence related to structural history and petroleum accumulation – Spindle Field, Colorado: AAPG Bull., v. 66, p. 2543–2560.

Rice, D.D. and D.L. Gautier, 1983, Patterns of sedimentation, diagenesis, and hydrocarbon accumulation in Cretaceous rocks of the Rocky Mountains: SEPM Short Course No. 11 Lecture Notes, 332 p.

Romberger, S.B., 1980, Metallic mineral resources of Colorado, in H.C. Kent and K.W. Porter, eds., Colorado Geology: RMAG, p. 225–236.

Roundtree, R., 1978, Spindle Field became second largest field in Colorado eight years after discovery: Western Oil Reporter, May, 1978, p. 37–40.

Schmidt, V. and D.A. McDonald, 1979, Texture and recognition of secondary porosity in sandstone, in P.A. Scholle and P.R. Schluger, eds., Aspects of Diagenesis: SEPM Spec. Pub. No. 26, p. 209–225.

Surdam, R.C., S.W. Boese, L.J. Crossey, 1984, The chemistry of secondary porosity, in D.A. McDonald and R.C. Surdam, eds., Clastic Diagenesis: AAPG Mem. 37, p. 127–149.

Tainter, P.A. 1984, Stratigraphic and paleostructural controls on hydrocarbon migration in Cretaceous D and J Sandstones of the Denver Basin, in J. Woodward, F.F. Meissner, and J.L. Clayton, eds., Hydrocarbon Source Rocks of the Greater Rocky Mountain Region: RMAG, p. 339–354.

Treckman, J.F., 1960, Petrography of the Upper Cretaceous Terry and Hygiene Sandstones in the Denver Basin: unpub. MS thesis, U. CO, Boulder.

Warner, L.A., 1980, The Colorado lineament, in H.C. Kent and K.W. Porter, eds., Colorado Geology: RMAG, p. 11–22.

Structurally Influenced Stratigraphic and Diagenetic Trapping at Spindle Field, Colorado[1]

KAREN W. PORTER[2]

[1]Received June 1, 1988; Revised March 1, 1989
[2]Independent Geologist, Bozeman, MT

Production at Spindle Field is obtained from the Upper Cretaceous (Campanian) Hygiene and Terry members of the middle Pierre Shale. The reservoirs are marine sandstones enclosed in finer-grained rocks. Hygiene and Terry sediments were deposited in response to western interior sea-level fluctuations that affected water depths, energy levels, and sediment distribution across structurally controlled sea-floor topography. Hygiene and Terry sandstones consist of three facies distinguished by energy-related physical and biogenic sedimentary structures and lithologies. Vertical and lateral relations of these three facies define a sandy marine-shelf environment.

Reservoir sandstones are fine-grained, originally well sorted, feldspathic, glauconitic litharenites. Early diagenesis effectively occluded the primary porosity. Subsequent dissolution of calcite cement in the field area created secondary porosity. Emplacement of oil and gas occurred between development of secondary porosity and occlusion of that porosity by authigenic kaolinite.

Production from these sandstones is limited to the area of secondary porosity development. This area overlies a subtle paleostructure and excludes a large area where sandstones are thicker and lie structurally updip from the field. Thus, Spindle Field represents a combined stratigraphic and diagenetic trap influenced by paleostructure.

INTRODUCTION

Since its discovery in 1971, Spindle Field (Fig. 1) has produced more than 49,000,000 BO and 236 BCFG. Production is from the Hygiene ("Shannon") and Terry ("Sussex") sandstone members of the Pierre Shale (Fig. 2) lying at depths of 4,300 to 5,000 ft (900 to 1,500 m) near the structural axis of the Denver Basin. The field is now under infill drilling on 40-acre spacing. There are over 1,300 fracture-stimulated wells in the field.

Field boundaries have not changed significantly since 1976, when the first published information on the field appeared (Moredock and Williams, 1976; Porter, 1976). Moredock and Williams summarized the exploration history of the Hygiene and Terry sandstones and discussed the unconventional exploration and evaluation methods that led to the discovery of the field 70 years after this interval first produced oil from Boulder Field in 1901. Pittman (1988 and this volume) summarized field data and reservoir petrographic characteristics. The regional biostratigraphy of these units is summarized by Scott and Cobban (1959, 1965) and by Gill and Cobban (1973).

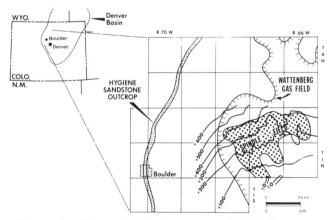

Figure 1. Map showing location of Spindle Field, structurally low in the Denver Basin. Structure contours drawn on marker horizon below Terry Sandstone (modified from Moredock and Williams, 1976). Outline of Wattenberg Field, which produces gas from "J" Sandstone of Dakota Group, shown by cross-hatched line (Porter and Weimer, 1982; reprinted by permission of AAPG).

FIELD DATA:	Spindle Field
Producing Interval:	Hygiene and Terry Sandstone Members, Pierre Shale
Geographic Location:	Adams, Boulder, and Weld Counties, Colorado
Present Tectonic Setting:	Denver Basin
Depositional Setting:	Marine shelf (Late Cretaceous seaway) with fluctuating sea levels
Age of Reservoir:	Upper Cretaceous
Lithology of Reservoir:	Glauconitic feldspathic litharenite
Depositional Environment:	Offshore marine bars
Diagenesis:	Chlorite, quartz, and calcite cements; dissolution of feldspars, lithic fragments, and calcite; kaolinite
Porosity Types:	Primary intergranular, secondary intergranular, and microporosity (cf. Pittman, this volume)
Porosity:	Maximum 19%; average 14%
Permeability:	Maximum 17 md; average 2 md
Water Saturation in Pay:	Range 25–80%; 60% average
Fractures:	Insignificant
Nature of Trap:	Stratigraphic and diagenetic
Entrapping Facies:	Shaly sandstones and marine shales of Pierre
Source Rock:	Benton Group shales
Timing of Hydrocarbon Migration:	Paleocene
Discovered:	June 10, 1971
Reservoir Depth:	4,300 ft (Terry)–5,000 ft (Hygiene) (1,370–1,550 m)
Reservoir Thickness:	25 ft (Terry)–20 ft (Hygiene) (6.2–7.7 m)
Areal Extent:	63,400 acres (25,658 ha)
Average IP:	125 BOPD
Original Reservoir Pressure:	1,450 psi
Drive Type:	Solution gas
Cumulative Production (1/89):	49,200,000 BO, 236 BCFG
Estimated Oil in Place:	500,000,000 BO
Oil Gravity:	42° API
Minimum Water Saturation:	30%

Surface and subsurface correlation of the units in the northern Denver Basin is presented by Kiteley (1978).

The type section for the Hygiene Sandstone Member is in Sec 34 T3N R70W, Boulder County, Colorado, where a prominent, east–dipping sandstone ridge occurs immediately south of Hygiene Road, 1.5 mi (2.4 km) west of the town of Hygiene. Good exposures of this sandstone occur intermittently along the Front Range from just north of Boulder, Colorado nearly to the Wyoming state line (Fig. 1). The Terry Sandstone Member generally is best developed east of the Front Range. A limited outcrop at Terry Lake (north of Fort Collins, Colorado) has ceded to urban development.

Sandstones of the middle Pierre are coarsening-upward marine shelf sequences recording several events of shoaling associated with the regressive phase of Mesaverde sedimentation in the western interior (Fig. 3). Lateral and vertical facies relationships suggest deposition as relatively clean, high-energy, cross-stratified central–bar sands and adjacent lower-energy, muddier bar-margin and sandy shelf (or interbar) deposits in an offshore shelf environment. Lithofacies seen in cores are typical of these environments (Fig. 4).

These deposits are equivalent in age to the Parkman delta deposits found in south-central Wyoming, although stratigraphic continuity is lost across the Hartville Uplift (Fig. 5). Similarly, the Colorado Front Range isolates these shelf sandstones from age-equivalent shoreline deposits in western Colorado. Equivalent strata in Middle Park consist of thin marine sandstones and shales.

OBJECTIVES OF PAPER

The occurrence of oil and gas in the Hygiene and Terry at Spindle Field raises questions about the timing and mechanism of hydrocarbon migration and entrapment. The field presently is structurally low in the Denver Basin. Sandstones outside the field commonly are both thicker and structurally higher, but also are tight and nonproductive. Objectives of this paper are to present interpretations of: 1) depositional environments, time stratigraphy, regional structural setting, and diagenetic history of the Hygiene and Terry intervals; 2) the timing and mechanism of hydrocarbon emplacement in Spindle Field; and 3) petrophysics of the reservoirs.

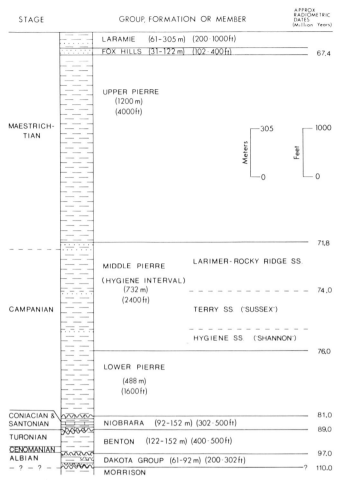

Figure 2. Cretaceous formations, Denver Basin, Colorado. Radiometric age dates from Fouch and others (1983) (Porter and Weimer, 1982; reprinted by permission of AAPG).

LITHOFACIES

The Hygiene and Terry sandstones seen in outcrop and in the subsurface display coarsening–upward sequences consisting of 1) bioturbated (*Asterosoma-Teichichnus* association) sandy mudstones and muddy sandstones; 2) burrowed to nonburrowed, thin–bedded, rippled to cross–stratified sandstones; and 3) fine to medium–grained, nonburrowed, cross–stratified, feldspathic, glauconitic litharenites (Porter and Weimer, 1982; Pittman, this volume), having rippled tops and burrowed mudstone drapes (Fig. 4). *Inoceramus sp.* shell fragments occur rarely in all facies. Reservoir sandstones interfinger laterally with lower energy sandstones and mudstones. These sandy sequences are completely enclosed by deep–marine, lower–energy mudstones of the Pierre Shale (Porter, 1976).

The sandstone bars in both intervals have a somewhat blanket–like distribution. However, Hygiene outcrop data suggest that individual bars may be on the order of one to two mi (1.6 to 3.2 km) in length and one half mile (0.8 km) in width.

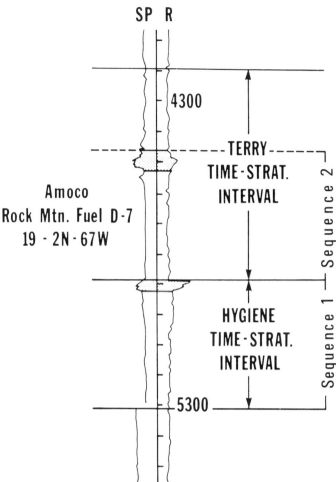

Figure 3. Typical electrical log of Hygiene and Terry sandstone members of Pierre Shale, which are coarsening–upward marine–shelf deposits. Time–stratigraphic intervals relate to isopach data discussed in text. Scale is in feet (Porter and Weimer, 1982; reprinted by permission of AAPG). Log from Amoco Production Co., No. D-7 Rocky Mountain Fuel, Sec 19 T2N R67W.

DEPOSITIONAL ENVIRONMENTS

The Hygiene and Terry intervals generally have been interpreted as offshore shelf deposits of storms (Porter, 1976) and/or tidal currents (unpublished observation of E. Mutti, personal communication, J. Warme). Alternatively, Moredock and Williams (1976) consider the Hygiene Sandstone to be the subaqueous edge of a small prograding delta, and the overlying Terry Sandstone to be nearshore tidal sand ridge deposits. However, on a regional scale Terry and Hygiene sediments are enclosed in marine shales and lack the associated fresher water deposits expected in deltaic and nearshore environments. Hence, the shelf environment seems more likely.

Sandstone facies of the Terry-Hygiene are designated sandy–shelf, bar–margin, and central–bar. De-

Figure 4. Core samples that typify the three sandy and one shaly lithofacies of the Hygiene and Terry. Six-in. (15.2 cm) rule for scale (Porter and Weimer, 1982; reprinted by permission of AAPG).

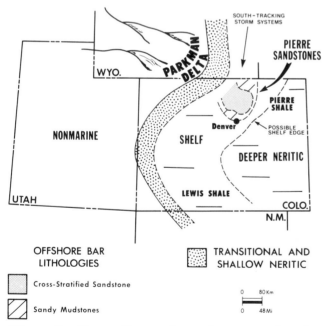

Figure 5. Upper Campanian paleogeography of central western interior (modified from Porter, 1976). Shoreline position based on Scott and Cobban (1959) and on Gill and Cobban, (1973) (Porter and Weimer, 1982; reprinted by permission of AAPG).

tails of the depositional model are presented by Porter (1976).

At the top of the Hygiene Sandstone at the type section locality, there is possible evidence of subaerial exposure in flat, angular structures that may be mud-chip imprints, as well as what appear to be mudcrack fillings later altered by surface case hardening. In the same area, central-bar sandstones reach their greatest thickness. Because the locality coincides with a paleostructural feature (discussed below), it is possible that this portion of the sandy shelf was briefly sub-aerially exposed during a relative sea level lowering. However, no other outcrops nor any Hygiene cores apparently indicate subaerial exposure.

SEDIMENT SOURCE

Hunter (1955) postulated that the Hygiene sands may have been shed from a positive feature in the approximate position of the present Front Range. However, Porter and Weimer (1982) suggest that Hygiene and Terry sediments were derived from the time-equivalent Parkman delta of south-central Wyoming (Scott and Cobban, 1959; Gill and Cobban, 1973), and accumulated on a broad, relatively shallow portion of the sea floor overlying the northeast-trending Transcontinental Arch. This paper suggests further that this arch may have controlled the position of the mid-Campanian shoreline (Fig. 6).

TIME STRATIGRAPHY

Along the Colorado Front Range the Hygiene interval contains the *Baculites gregoryensis* and *B. scotti* ammonite zones (Scott and Cobban, 1965), making it

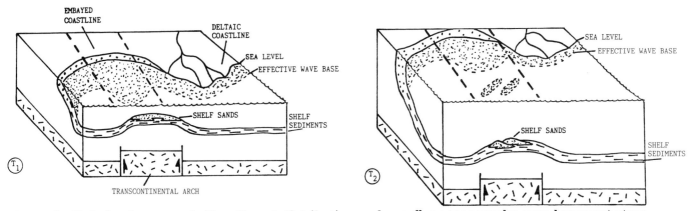

Figure 6. Relation between shelf–sediment distribution and sea–floor topography over basement structural blocks. Hygiene and Terry sediments initially reflect shelf deposition across Transcontinental Arch under relative lowstand conditions (T1); coarse–grained sediments move seaward, where shelf is relatively shallow over positive structural element. Later (T2), reworking and/or rapid burial occurred during transgression, caused either by sea–level rise as shown here, or by subsidence of basement block; sands on top of high are redistributed by shelf processes as long as transport energy touches bottom. Deltaic progradation would have occurred in structurally controlled topographic lows while an embayed coastline developed over the positive structural block.

age equivalent to the regressive Parkman Sandstone (lower Mesaverde) in south–central Wyoming. The Terry interval contains *Exiteloceras jennyi* in Colorado (Scott and Cobban, 1965), which suggests it to be slightly younger than its *Didymoceras stevensoni* association in southern Wyoming (Kiteley, 1978). A regional unconformity found in nonmarine Mesaverde rocks in southern Wyoming (Gill and Cobban, 1973) may coincide with a drop in sea level and shoaling of the eastern Colorado sea floor during Terry time. Extensive sediment reworking is suggested by abundant glauconite found in the Terry.

The upper and lower boundaries of the Terry and Hygiene intervals as defined on well logs (Fig. 3) are presumed time surfaces, either bentonites or laterally persistent silty shales. Regionally in the subsurface, the Hygiene Sandstone does not appear to cross time surfaces; hence the top of the sandstone is taken as the top of the time–stratigraphic interval. By contrast, the Terry Sandstone does cross time surfaces and does not occur at the same stratigraphic position everywhere within the Terry time–stratigraphic interval.

A marked reversal in depositional patterns occurred between Hygiene and Terry times; the Hygiene interval thickens westward, while the Terry interval thickens to the east (Figs. 7 and 8). Implications of this reversal are unclear, but the change may reflect structural movement of the sea floor.

SANDSTONE DISTRIBUTION

The distribution of central–bar reservoir sandstone can be mapped from electric logs (Figs. 7 and 8). The limits of sandstone deposition for both sandstone intervals in the field area are known from the work of Moredock and Williams (1976). Sandstone thicknesses generally coincide with thicknesses of time–stratigraphic intervals.

STRUCTURAL SETTING

Presently the Hygiene and Terry at Spindle Field lie structurally low on the western flank of the Denver Basin, at depths of 4,300 to 5,000 ft (920 to 1,500 m), with no evidence of structural closure (Fig. 1). Davis and Weimer (1976) describe basement faults and basement–controlled listric faults in the Benton, Niobrara, and Pierre intervals on the western flank of the Denver Basin in the area of Wattenberg and Spindle fields. Tensional faults in Wattenberg Field area are reported by Moredock and Williams (1976), who cite common normal faulting in the marine shale sequences above the "J" Sandstone.

Paleostructural Elements

Weimer (1978) noted a broad positive feature, a segment of the Transcontinental Arch, trending northeast across Colorado. This ancient basement structure influenced regional Cretaceous sedimentation patterns and erosional unconformities in the Turner–Codell and basal Niobrara, stratigraphically below the Pierre Shale. On the western flank of the Denver Basin, this regional arch is crossed on its southern flank by a second–order, west–trending basement paleostructure (Wattenberg structure of Weimer, 1980 and 1983). Recurrent movement of this second–order structure controlled local erosional thinning and unconformities in the "J" Sandstone, Codell Sandstone, lower Niobrara, and upper Niobrara intervals.

SUMMARY DEPOSITIONAL MODEL

Lithofacies, depositional environments, time stratigraphy, and structural setting of the Hygiene and Terry sandstones indicate that paleostructure influenced both the type and distribution of these deposits. Sediments presumably were eroded from the age–equivalent embayed shoreline in western Colorado,

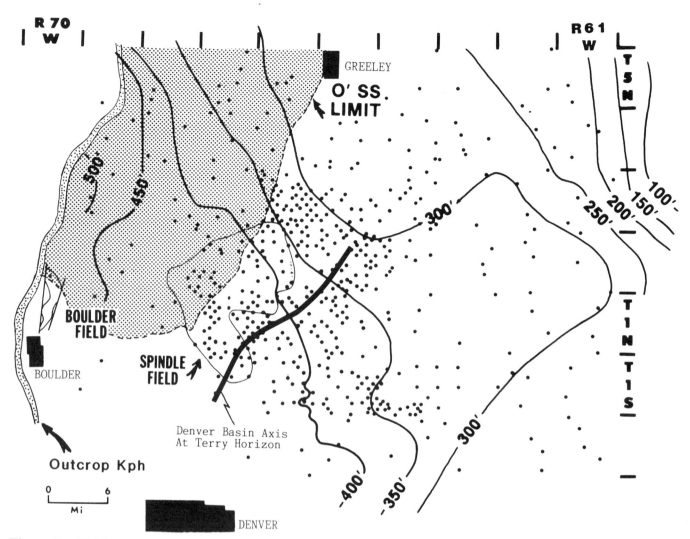

Figure 7. Thickness of Hygiene time−stratigraphic interval (unpublished data, R.J. Weimer and S.A. Sonnenberg). Distribution of cross−stratified sandstone shown stippled. Zero edge of sandstone crosses northwestern area of Spindle Field. Outcrop of Hygiene Sandstone (Kph) shown. Hygiene sandstones lie west of present structural axis of Denver Basin, updip from Spindle Field. (Data through field area from Moredock and Williams, 1976; extended to outcrop by Porter and Weimer, 1982) (6 mi = 9.7 km)

itself supplied by longshore currents from the Parkman delta in southern Wyoming (Fig. 5). These shoreline sediments were moved seaward over the shallow sea floor overlying the Transcontinental Arch during relative low stands of sea level. The sediments were transported offshore by storm−related currents and deposited in marine−shelf environments. With sea level rise, sands may have been periodically reworked by storm−dominated offshore shelf processes until transport energies diminished over the shelf, permitting deposition of mudstones (Fig. 6). Alternatively, little or no reworking may have occurred during rapid deepening of the waters.

SANDSTONE DIAGENESIS

Analyses of Hygiene and Terry central−bar sandstones from cores and outcrops indicate that diagenesis (Fig. 9) both reduced and increased porosity and permeability at different times (Porter and Weimer, 1982; Pittman, 1988 and this volume).

"Squashing" of sedimentary argillaceous lithics and glauconite was an early diagenetic event that generated extensive pseudomatrix. Calcite formed pervasively in amounts up to 25%, both as intergranular cement and intragranular grain replacement material. These processes, combined with growth of authigenic clays and quartz overgrowths, reduced the primary porosity and permeability of central−bar sandstones, initially rendering them nonreservoir rock.

Diagenesis During Oil and Gas Generation

The event most significant to reservoir development was the creation of solution porosity. The present macro− and microporosity in Spindle Field was created largely by leaching of calcite (Phase III of Fig. 9), although some primary intergranular porosity is preserved. Porter and Weimer (1982) point out that this event reflects a marked change in pore−fluid chemistry; they postulate that acidic, CO_2−rich solutions expelled from source rocks during early hydrocarbon maturation dissolved the calcium carbonate.

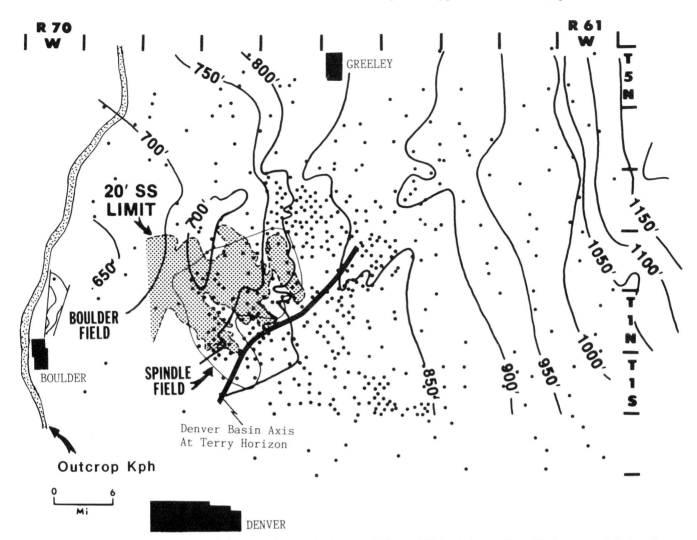

Figure 8. Thickness of Terry time-stratigraphic interval (unpublished data, R.J. Weimer and S.A. Sonnenberg). Distribution of cross-stratified sandstones thicker than 20 ft (6 m) shown stippled in field area (data from Moredock and Williams, 1976). The 20-ft limit was chosen because the zero edge of Terry sandstones is not well defined in the field area. (6 mi = 9.7 km)

Consistent with this, Pittman (1988) reports brackish formation water in the Terry. However, in light of recent work (cf. Surdam, et al., this volume), it seems more likely that the acidic solutions were caused by high concentrations of organic acids, rather than of CO_2.

Petroleum source beds for the Hygiene and Terry sandstones, as for most Cretaceous reservoirs in the Denver Basin, are the marine shales of the Benton Group (Mowry, Graneros, Greenhorn, and Carlile formations) lying 2,000 to 3,000 ft (620 to 930 m) stratigraphically below the middle Pierre sandstones (Clayton and Swetland, 1980). Fluid pressures would have been sufficient, according to Momper (1978), both to reopen earlier fractures and to generate new ones.

Emplacement of oil and gas was critically timed between development of secondary porosity and occlusion of that porosity by pore-filling kaolinite. As with the dissolution of calcite, the precipitation of authigenic kaolinite implies acidic pore fluids.

Effect of Paleostructure

The Terry and Hygiene sandstones have significantly different areal distribution, but a common area of oil and gas production that is only partly controlled by the distribution of central-bar sandstone. Hygiene central-bar sandstones are both widely distributed and of increasing thickness northwest of Spindle Field; however, production is limited to the southeastern area of sandstone development, where it overlies the Wattenberg paleostructure. Thick Hygiene sandstones structurally updip are tight and nonproductive. Production from Terry sandstones, which are best developed east and south of the Hygiene, extends the field across the paleostructure. In both intervals, production is coincident with secondary porosity and paleostructure. Conduits for the vertical migration of fluids may have been numerous tensional fractures and small faults associated with recurrent movement of the Wattenberg paleostructure.

DIAGENETIC EVENT		EFFECT ON Ø AND K
DEPOSITION UNDER HIGH-ENERGY CONDITIONS		Ø AND K INITIALLY GOOD
PHYSICAL COMPACTION	CLOSER GRAIN CONTACTS PSEUDOMATRIX	PORE SPACE REDUCTION
AUTHIGENIC CHLORITE RIMS		PERMEABILITY REDUCTION
QUARTZ OVERGROWTHS		PORE SPACE REDUCTION AND OCCLUSION
? CONTINUOUS SOLN. OF SHELL MATERIAL		
II CALCITE INVASION	CORROSION, REPLACEMENT CEMENTING	NEARLY COMPLETE PORE SPACE OCCLUSION
III SOLUTION OF CALCITE		SECONDARY POROSITY
IV AUTHIGENIC KAOLINITE (+ MINOR ILLITE)		PORE SPACE REDUCTION

Figure 9. Sequential relationship of diagenetic events observed in Hygiene and Terry central–bar sandstones. Ø = porosity; K = permeability. Stage–III calcite dissolution was crucial to development of reservoir–quality sandstones.

At Wattenberg Field, production of gas from the "J" Sandstone marine facies as well as gas and oil from the Codell Sandstone occur where these units overlie the Wattenberg structure. Production from fractured shales of the Hygiene interval at Boulder Field also is positioned on this paleostructure (Fig. 7).

Effect of Temperature

Hygiene and Terry sandstones at Spindle Field probably never were buried more deeply than 1,000 ft (305 m) below their present depth. This depth is not sufficient to place these rocks at the depths of 8,000 to 11,000 ft (2,500 to 3,400 m) generally considered necessary for subsurface leaching under normal fluid pressures and temperatures. Possibly the abnormally high thermal gradient in this part of the Denver Basin reported by several researchers (e.g., Weimer and Sonnenberg, this volume) was sufficient to initiate leaching. Whether or not high heat flow was a factor, the leaching that enhances porosity in these sandstones apparently was limited to where these sandstones overlie the Wattenberg paleostructure.

PETROPHYSICAL ASPECTS

Moredock and Williams (1976) first discussed the petrophysics and reservoir evaluation of the Hygiene and Terry sandstones. Conventional log analyses of Hygiene and Terry sandstones generally show high water saturations, thought to be caused by bound water associated with authigenic clays and glauconite. Such log analysis problems, caused by the lithologic character of the reservoir rock, have been a continuing challenge to field development and further exploration.

Core studies have proven helpful in the calibration of log response to lithology. In one good producing well, log responses (Fig. 10) can be compared to core lithologies in two central–bar intervals. The lower interval (4,672.5 to 4,686 ft, or 1,424 to 1,427.8 m, core depths) contains high–energy cross-stratified

sandstone with abundant transported glauconite in the upper three feet (one m) (Fig. 11). The SP and resistivity readings (4,674–4,685 ft log depths) suggest that most of the interval is shaly. However, the gamma ray log indicates "clean" sandstone, except in the upper three feet (one m). An interpretation of these data is that: 1) principally authigenic clays cause the shaly SP and resistivity signature of the lower part of the interval; 2) the low gamma–ray readings in the lower part of the interval are due to the lack of potassium in the dominantly kaolinitic clays; and 3) the shaly signature on all logs of the upper three–foot (one m) zone is due to the abundant glauconite with its characteristic high potassium content.

The upper central–bar sandstone (core interval 4,659–4,667.5 ft) contains much less glauconite. The SP log reads shaly in the lower part, while the gamma ray log indicates clean sandstone throughout. Density porosity readings are low in both authigenic clay– and glauconite–rich intervals.

The current completion practice in the field is to perforate and fracture stimulate all wells that show some thickness of clean sandstone on the gamma ray log. Drill–stem testing is seldom conducted because permeabilities are low (averaging 2 md), with the result that little fluid enters the borehole during the test.

CONCLUSIONS

The Hygiene and Terry sandstones represent shelf deposition associated with fluctuating sea levels in an overall regressive sea. Water depths, energy levels, and sediment transport and distribution were influenced both by first–order (Transcontinental Arch) and by second–order (Wattenberg paleostructure) basement structure. Early diagenesis, recorded in the development of pseudomatrix, quartz overgrowths, and authigenic clays, followed by a pervasive invasion of calcite, largely occluded primary porosity in the sandstones. Development of secondary porosity in the area of the field relates to calcite dissolution by acidic fluids generated during early hydrocarbon maturation at depth. Conduits for these fluids and for the subsequent migration of oil and gas were tensional fractures associated with the Wattenberg paleostructure. Late-stage development of authigenic kaolinite reduced secondary porosity and permeability, and affected the performance of individual wells in the field.

ACKNOWLEDGMENTS

The assistance of Amoco Production Company personnel with field and reservoir data is gladly acknowledged. Great appreciation is expressed to R.J. Weimer and S.A. Sonnenberg for permission to use their previously unpublished time–stratigraphic interval isopach maps (Figs. 7 and 8). Acknowledgment is also made to AAPG and SEPM for release of several figures republished in this paper.

REFERENCES

Clayton, J.L., and P.J. Swetland, 1980, Petroleum generation and migration in Denver Basin: AAPG Bull., v. 64, p. 1613–1633.

Davis, T.L., and R.J. Weimer, 1976, Late Cretaceous growth faulting, Denver Basin, Colorado, in R.C. Epis and R.J. Weimer, eds., Studies in Colorado Field Geology: CSM Prof. Contrib. No. 8, p. 280–300.

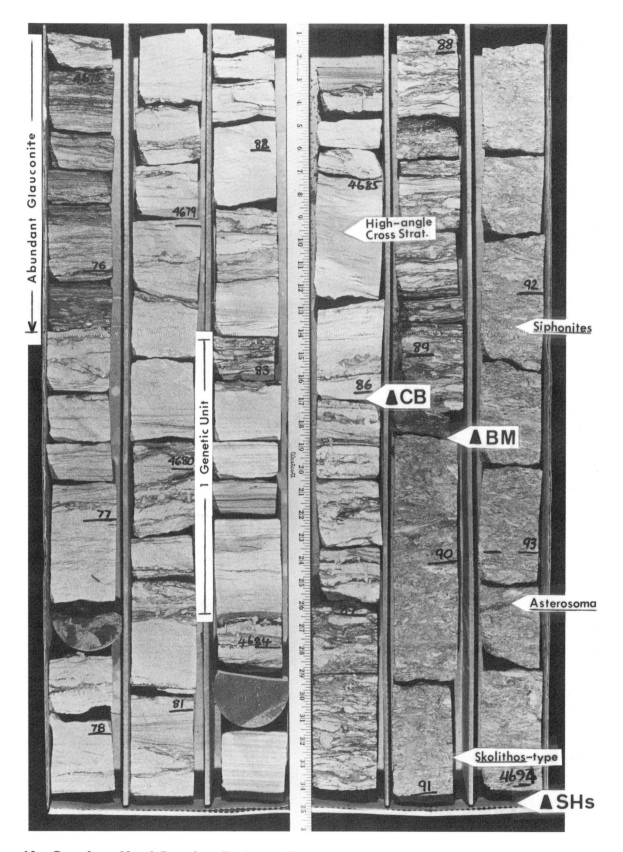

Figure 10. Core from No. 1 Premium Turkey well. Interval 4,675–4,694 ft (1,441–1,448 m). Letter symbols are same as Figure 10. Zone at top of interval contains abundant glauconite. One genetic unit of storm deposition (central–bar sandstone overlain by thin, burrowed mudstone) is indicated. (Adapted from Weimer, et al., 1985; reprinted by permission of SEPM).

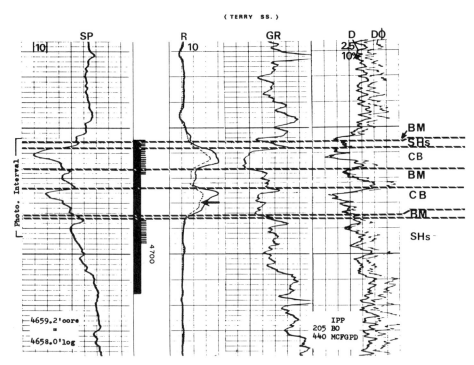

Figure 11. Well logs from Amoco Production Co. No. 1 Premium Turkey well (Sec 22 T2N R67W, Weld Co., Colorado). SP = spontaneous potential; R = resistivity; GR = gamma ray; D = density; Dφ = density porosity. Solid black bar indicates cored interval; core-to-log depth correction given at lower left. Perforated zones indicated by short horizontal lines. Long-dashed horizontal lines separate lithofacies: CB = central bar; BM = bar margin; SHs = sandy shelf. Photo interval of Figures 11 and 12 shown at far left. (Adapted from Weimer, Porter, and Land, 1985; reprinted by permission of SEPM) (Major divisions on log are 10 ft, or 3 m.)

Fouch, T.D., T.F. Lawton, D.J. Nichols, W.B. Cashion, and W.A. Cobban, 1983, Patterns and timing of synorogenic sedimentation in Upper Cretaceous rocks of central and northeast Utah, *in* M.W. Reynolds and E.D. Dolly, eds., Mesozoic Paleogeography of the West-central United States – Rocky Mountain Paleogeography Symposium 2: RMS-SEPM, p. 305-336.

Gill, J.R., and W.A. Cobban, 1961, Stratigraphy of lower and middle parts of the Pierre Shale, northern Great Plains, *in* USGS Prof. Paper 424-D, Short Papers in the Geologic and Hydrologic Sciences, Articles 293-435: Article 352, p. 185-191.

Gill, J.R., and W.A. Cobban, 1973, Stratigraphy and geologic history of the Montana Group and equivalent rocks, Montana, Wyoming, and North and South Dakota: USGS Prof. Paper 776, 37 p.

Hunter, Z.M., 1955, Geology of the foothills of the Front Range in northern Colorado: RMAG, unnumbered map.

Kiteley, L.W., 1978, Stratigraphic sections of Cretaceous rocks of the northern Denver Basin, northeastern Colorado and southeastern Wyoming: USGS Chart OC-78, 3 sheets.

Momper, J.A., 1978, Oil migration limitations suggested by geological and geochemical considerations, *in* Physical and chemical constraints on petroleum migration: AAPG Short Course No. 8, p. B-1 to B-60.

Moredock, D.E., and S.J. Williams, 1976, Upper Cretaceous Terry and Hygiene Sandstones, Singletree, Spindle and Surrey Fields, Weld County, Colorado, *in* R.C. Epis and R.J. Weimer, eds., Studies in Colorado field geology: CSM Prof. Contrib. No. 8, p. 264-274.

Pittman, E.D., 1988, Diagenesis of Terry Sandstone (Upper Cretaceous), Spindle Field, Colorado: JSP., v. 58, p. 785-800.

Porter, K.W., 1976, Marine shelf model, Hygiene Member of Pierre Shale, Upper Cretaceous, Denver Basin, Colorado, *in* R.C. Epis and R.J. Weimer, eds., Studies in Colorado field geology: CSM Prof. Contrib. No. 8, p. 251-263.

Porter, K.W., and R.J. Weimer, 1982, Diagenetic sequence related to structural history and petroleum accumulation: Spindle Field, Colorado: AAPG Bull., v. 66, p. 2543-2560.

Scott, G.R., and W.A. Cobban, 1959, So-called Hygiene Group of northeastern Colorado, *in* J.D. Haun and R.J. Weimer, eds., Symposium on Cretaceous Rocks of Colorado and Adjacent Areas: RMAG, 11th Ann. Field Conf. Guidebook, p. 124-131.

Scott, G.R., and W.A. Cobban, 1965, Geologic and biostratigraphic map of the Pierre Shale between Jarre Creek and Loveland, Colorado: USGS Map I-439.

Surdam, R.C., L.J. Crossey, E.S. Hagen, and H.P. Heasler, 1989, Organic-inorganic interactions and sandstone diagenesis: AAPG Bull., v. 73, p. 1-23.

Weimer, R.J., 1978, Influence of Transcontinental arch on Cretaceous marine sedimentation – A preliminary report, *in* J.D. Pruit and P.E. Coffin, eds., Energy Resources of the Denver Basin: RMAG Symp., p. 211-222.

Weimer, R.J., 1980, Recurrent movement on basement faults – a tectonic style for Colorado and adjacent areas, *in* H.C. Kent and K.W. Porter, eds., Colorado Geology: RMAG, p. 23-53.

Weimer, R.J., 1983, Relation of unconformities, tectonics, and sea level changes, Cretaceous of the Denver Basin and adjacent areas, *in* M.W. Reynolds and E.D. Dolly, eds., Mesozoic Paleogeography of the West-central United States – Rocky Mountain Paleogeography Symposium 2: RMS-SEPM, p. 359-376.

Weimer, R.J., K.W. Porter, and C.B. Land, 1985, Depositional modeling of detrital rocks, with emphasis on cored sequences of petroleum reservoirs: SEPM, Core Workshop No. 8, p. 164-166.

Depositional Environment and Mineralogy of the Upper Cretaceous Teapot Sandstone, Well Draw Field, Powder River Basin, Wyoming[1]

STEVEN P. CONNER[2]
JOHN J. SULLIVAN[3]
THOMAS T. TIEH[4]

[1]Received August 8, 1988; Revised January 1, 1989
[2]Department of Earth Sciences, University of North Carolina, Wilmington, North Carolina
[3]Midland, Texas
[4]Department of Geology, Texas A&M University, College Station, Texas

The Teapot Sandstone is the uppermost member of the Upper Cretaceous Mesaverde Formation in the Powder River Basin. At Well Draw Field, it consists of a sequence of turbidite deposits bounded by marine shales. Hydrocarbon production is obtained from massive sandstones that average 14.2% porosity and 4.3 md permeability. These sandstones are fine to very fine-grained feldspathic litharenites. Major authigenic minerals are carbonate cement, quartz overgrowths, and clay minerals. These constitute an average of 27% of the bulk rock.

Porosity and permeability of the massive sandstones depend on the extent of grain and cement dissolution as well as the distribution, abundance, and nature of occurrence of authigenic minerals, particularly clays. There are four types of authigenic clay: 1) alteration rims on silicate grains; 2) thin, non-oriented pore-lining chlorite and lesser kaolinite; 3) oriented pore-lining mixed layer illite/smectite; and 4) massive, poorly crystalline, pore-bridging, high-iron chlorite. Pore-lining and pore-bridging clays greatly decrease sandstone porosity and permeability.

The diagenetic sequence before hydrocarbon accumulation was: 1) compaction with limited quartz overgrowth and precipitation of grain-coating clays; 2) complete calcite cementation; 3) dissolution of carbonate cement and labile grains; and 4) precipitation of pore-lining and later pore-bridging clays. Alteration-rim development is a continuing process in sandstones outside the gas and oil column.

Hydrodynamic flow and leaching of labile detrital grains are the major controls on clay authigenesis. Downdip flow of pore fluids leached labile grains from sandstones on the eastern side of the field. As pore fluids moved downdip, they became saturated and precipitated clays in the western part of the field. The result was a decrease in reservoir-quality porosity and permeability in the downdip portion of the field.

INTRODUCTION

Well Draw Field is a stratigraphically trapped oil and gas accumulation located in the southern Powder River Basin (Fig. 1). The field produces from the Teapot Sandstone, the uppermost member of the Upper Cretaceous Mesaverde Formation in this area (Table 1). The shale underlying the Teapot is an unnamed member of the Mesaverde Formation. The overlying shale is the Lewis Formation (Gill and Cobban, 1973).

Studies by Curry (1976a,b), Isbell, et al. (1976), Almon (1980), and Coughlan and Steidtmann (1984), based on outcrop and subsurface data, contribute to understanding the complex stratigraphic, depositional, and diagenetic histories of the Teapot in the southern Powder River Basin. We studied the shallow-marine shelf deposits of the distal portion of the Teapot, where it subcrops in Well Draw Field. The objectives of this study were to document the depositional history and mineral diagenesis of the Teapot Sandstone,

FIELD DATA:	Well Draw Field
Producing Interval:	Teapot Sandstone Member, Mesaverde Formation
Geographic Location:	Converse County, Wyoming
Present Tectonic Setting:	Eastern flank of intracratonic Powder River Basin
Depositional Setting:	Shallow marine shelf
Age of Reservoir:	Upper Cretaceous
Lithology of Reservoir:	Feldspathic litharenite
Depositional Environment:	Shelf turbidite system
Diagenesis:	Carbonate cementation, carbonate dissolution, clay mineral precipitation
Porosity Types:	Intergranular and secondary, intercrystalline microporosity
Porosity:	Maximum 19.9%, average 14.2%
Permeability:	Maximum 17.0 md, average 4.3 md
Nature of Trap:	Stratigraphic pinchout of reservoir sandstones
Entrapping Facies:	Deep–marine shales of the Lewis Formation
Source Rocks:	Underlying middle Mesaverde shales, and overlying lower Lewis shale (Curry, 1976a)
Discovered:	1973
Reservoir Depth:	6,367–7,198 ft (1,941–2,194 m)
Reservoir Thickness:	Average 17.2 ft (5.2 m) (Isbell, et al., 1976)
Areal Extent:	175 sq mi (67.6 sq km)
IP (discovery well):	480 BOPD
Original Reservoir Pressure:	2,540 psi (Isbell, et al., 1976)
Cumulative Production (1/89):	27,000,000 BO, 72.8 BCFG
Approximate Ultimate Recovery:	30,500,000 BO, 91 BCFG
Oil Gravity:	42° API (Isbell, et al., 1976)
Water Saturation:	59% average (Isbell, et al., 1976)

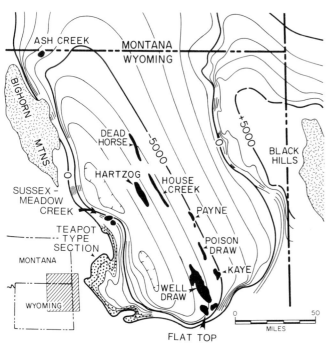

Figure 1. Structure map of the Powder River Basin using the top of the Lower Cretaceous Dakota Sandstone as a datum. Location of major Upper Cretaceous fields (shaded) and outcrop of Teapot Sandstone (stippled) are shown. Contour interval is 1,000 ft (305 m). After Berg (1975). (50 mi = 80.5 km)

and to show how they affect reservoir properties in the field.

Regional Setting

Well Draw Field lies about 18 mi (29 km) northeast of Douglas, Wyoming, in the southern Powder River Basin. The basin is bounded on the east by the Black Hills Uplift, on the west by the Casper Arch, and on the south by the Laramie Range and Hartville Uplift. The Teapot Sandstone crops out along the southwest part of the basin (Curry, 1976b; Johnson and Bryant, 1979) (Fig. 1). The type section for Teapot Sandstone is approximately 60 mi (96 km) west of Well Draw Field (Curry, 1976b). The Teapot is unconformably overlain by Tertiary sediments beginning about 32 mi (51.5 km) southwest of Well Draw Field. Depositional dip was to the southeast.

Source areas of the Teapot clastics lay to the west in the Cordilleran highlands of western Wyoming and Montana, eastern Idaho, Utah, and Arizona (McGookey et al., 1972). East of this area, an epeiric basin existed as a depocenter throughout the Cretaceous. Pulses of Sevier and Laramide orogenic activity are preserved as regressive clastic wedges. Periods of uplift, thrusting, and tectonism characterize the orogenic activity. Streams moved clastics eastward, creating progradational units. The Teapot delta of Curry (1976a) is a product of such processes. Thin, finer–grained sands and clays were deposited during periods of tectonic stability.

Table 1. Stratigraphic section for Upper Cretaceous, post–Niobrara marine rock units of the Powder River Basin. After Berg (1975).

Period	Formation	Member	Thickness Feet	Thickness Meters
Upper Cretaceous	Lewis Shale	Unnamed Shale	400	122
		Teckla Shale	100	30
		Unnamed Shale	300	92
	Mesaverde	Tepot Sandstone	100	30
		Unnamed Shale	100	30
		Parkman Sandstone	300	92
	Cody Shale (upper section)	Mitten Shale	300	92
		Sharon Springs Shale	300	92
		Sussex Sandstone	50	15

In the area around Well Draw Field, the Teapot changes eastward from porous, shallow–marine sandstones into tight, offshore siltstones and shales. Hydrocarbon migration was controlled by post–depositional dip rotation (down to the west) during basin development. The traps are sealed laterally by updip (eastward) changes into finer–grained, marine sediments with increased capillary pressures associated with grain–size changes into finer–grained marine sediments.

Production History

The Teapot sandstones in Well Draw Field lie at depths between 6,360 and 7,962 ft (1,938–2,427 m). Formation temperatures between 150° and 165°F (67 to 74°C) indicate a geothermal gradient of 1.1°F/100 ft (22.1°C/km) (Isbell et al., 1976). Approximately 3,000 ft (910 m) of Tertiary section has been removed by erosion from the study area; at maximum burial the sandstones ranged in depth from 9,300 to 10,950 ft (2,830–3,340 m). These depths and the modern geothermal gradient indicate that maximum formation temperatures were 185° to 205°F (85–96°C).

Oil and gas are produced from massive sandstones. The best wells are situated in the central portion of Well Draw Field, updip from thicker and more numerous sandstones to the west (Isbell et al., 1976). The source rocks likely are the marine shales that enclose the Teapot (Curry, 1976a).

The discovery well, the Inexco No. 1 PRE II–25, was completed in 1973 in the Teapot Sandstone from perforations between 6,936 and 6,956 ft (2,114–2,120 m), for an initial potential of 480 BOPD. Original reservoir pressure was 2,540 psi at 6,950 ft (2,118 m), indicating underpressuring (Isbell et al., 1976). Through 1989, cumulative production was 27,000,000 BO and 72.8 BCFG.

MATERIALS AND METHODS

Seven Teapot Sandstone cores with a total length of 478 ft (146 m) were used in this study (Table 2). Other data included well logs and initial production data. The seven cored wells are distributed both along structural strike and downdip in Well Draw and an adjoining unnamed field (Fig. 2). They represent a depth range of 6,766 to 7,964 ft (2,062–2,427 m) (Table 2). Each core was slabbed, described in detail, and sampled for laboratory analysis. Cored sections were correlated to electric logs, and a log character defined for each lithofacies. These data were then used in non–cored, logged wells to define lithofacies distribution, sandstone body morphology, and depositional environment. Detailed core descriptions and facies analysis are given in Sullivan (1982).

Seventy–four sandstone samples were selected for laboratory study. All represented massive, non-bioturbated sandstone. Bedsets thicker than 5 ft (1.5 m) were sampled at upper, intermediate, and lower horizons to determine if there was stratigraphic control on diagenesis within the bedset. Where pronounced variations in porosity and permeability in a core occurred, samples were taken to represent each variation. Samples were taken no more than 10 ft (2.5 m) apart. The diagenetic study is restricted to the massive sandstones. Four samples of shales found immediately above the Lewis Shale–Teapot Sandstone contact also were selected for mineralogical characterization.

Following petrographic examination of the sandstones in thin section, samples were selected for XRD, SEM, electron microprobe, and cathodoluminescence analyses. XRD analysis was used to characterize the mineralogy of the clay–size fraction separated from 18 selected sandstone samples and the Lewis Shale samples. The abundance of each mineral was estimated by Schultz's (1964) method.

STRATIGRAPHY AND SEDIMENTATION

The Teapot Sandstone represents one of many sandstone wedges deposited on the western margin of the Upper Cretaceous epeiric seaway. Depositional environment interpretations have varied from fluvial or deltaic to a mixture of marine and delta deposits, depending in part on the location of the sections studied (Curry, 1976a,b; Isbell et al., 1976; Coughlan and Steidtmann, 1984). In easterly sections, the Teapot sandstones are generally considered marine. Correlation of logs from near the outcrops to Well Draw demonstrates that reworked delta–front sandstones

Table 2. Summary of cored wells used in this study. Wells are arranged in a generally downdip trend.

Location in Field	Well (Map designation)	Depth Range Cored Ft (m)
Updip	Inexco Jack 1–28[b] (IJ 1–28)	6760 – 6830 ft (2060 – 2082 m)
	North Central Oil Federal 1[b] (NCO-1)	6769 – 6817 (2063 – 2078)
	Davis Tressie (DT-1)	6888 – 6923 (2099 – 2115)
	Inexco Robinson 1[b] (IR-1)	7021 – 7179 (2140 – 2188)
	Anadarko Lowry Estate 1[b] (ALE-1)	7150 – 7176 (2179 – 2187)
	Diamond Shamrock Lebar 1–34[a] (DSL 1–34)	7557 – 7619 (2303 – 2322)
Downdip	Anadarko Sunquist Federal 1–A[a] (ASF 1–A)	7920 – 7961 (2414 – 2426)

[a]Well is located in unnamed field west of Well Draw.
[b]Producing well.

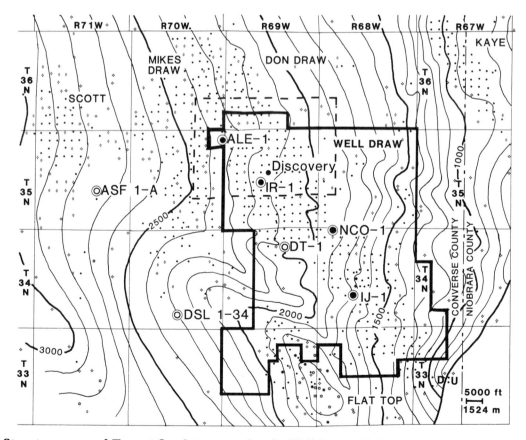

Figure 2. Structure map of Teapot Sandstone marker in Well Draw Field area. Wells used in this study are circled; dots indicate producing wells. Open circles indicate non-producing wells. Location of discovery well also shown. Area outlined by dashed line (northwest Well Draw Field) was used for detailed isopach mapping (Fig. 8). Dark outline is field boundary. Contour interval is 100 ft (30.5 m).

WEST   **EAST**

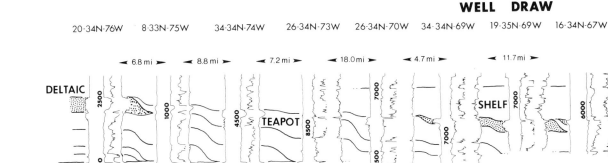

Figure 3. Electric–log stratigraphic section showing the change in Teapot lithofacies from reworked deltaic sandstones near the outcrop to shelf sandstones at Well Draw Field. No horizontal scale. Modified from Curry (1976a).

grade eastward into marine shales and siltstones (Fig. 3). Coughlan and Steidtmann (1984) concluded that at its maximum eastward progradation, the Teapot strandline was located near the present Natrona–Converse county border, 31 to 51 mi (50–82 km) west of Well Draw Field.

Depositional dip was reversed in the area of Well Draw Field by basin development. When deposited, the deltaic sandstones were updip from their marine equivalents in Well Draw Field, and both sections dipped towards the southeast. As the basin filled, its structural axis migrated westward and now lies between the paleostrandline and Well Draw Field. Modern dip is to the northwest at approximately 50 to 150 ft/mi (9.5 to 28.5 m/km).

Lithofacies Characteristics and Depositional Environments

The Teapot and adjacent sections in Well Draw Field can be divided into five distinct units, each of which can be correlated to a characteristic log response (Fig. 4). The first unit, in ascending order, is intensely bioturbated marine siltstone and shale that underlies the Teapot Sandstone. The second and third units consist of intercalated thin- and medium-bedded sandstone and shale of the Teapot. The fourth unit is composed of thick–bedded Teapot sandstone. A fifth, finer–grained unit of the Lewis Shale overlies the Teapot.

A core from the Inexco No. 1 Robinson well is typical of sections within the producing area (Fig. 5). Unit 1 is 5 ft (1.5 m) thick in this core and grades upward into unit 2, which is 7 ft (2.1 m) thick. Unit 2 consists of thin–bedded, dark gray to black shale and intensely bioturbated, silty sandstone (Fig. 5F). Much of the internal stratification and dominance of shale beds has been obscured by bioturbation. Where preserved in the lower part of unit 2, sequences of sedimentary structures are repetitive and consist of Bouma turbidite bedsets of the ABE, ACE, and BCE

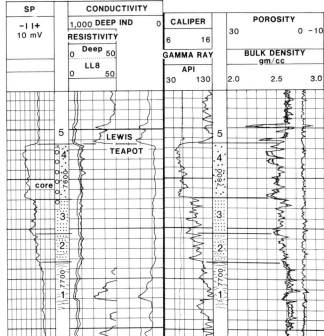

Figure 4. Electric– and density–log character of Teapot sandstones, Diamond Shamrock No. 1–34 Lebar, Well Draw Field vicinity, showing response of depositional units. The Teapot Sandstone marker occurs at 7,547 ft (2,300 m). Depth divisions are 10 ft (30.5 m) apart.

types that alternate with thin, rippled CE intervals (Bouma, 1962). Basal contacts of these graded sandstones are sharp, with local evidence of scour. Shale clasts occur at bases of sandstone beds. These thin sandstones were deposited by storm–generated turbidity currents in a deep water setting. The alterna-

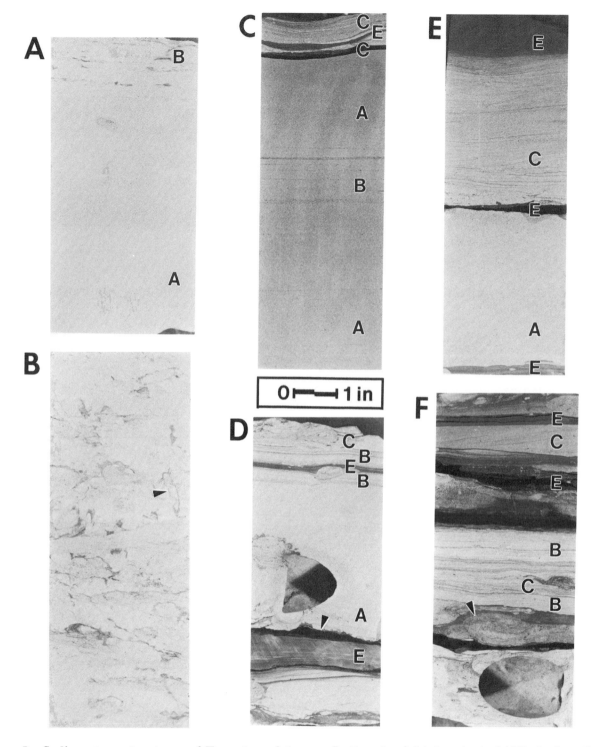

Figure 5. Sedimentary structures of Teapot sandstones. Letters to right denote turbidite bedset divisions. All samples are from Inexco No. 1 Robinson well. (1 in. = 2.54 cm)

A. Massive sandstone unit overlain by faint horizontal laminae separating stacked massive sandstones (depositional unit 4). This interval is typical of the producing horizons in Well Draw Field.

B. Intensely bioturbated sandstone masking primary sedimentary structures (unit 4). Note abundant *Ophiomorpha* and vertical burrow (arrow).

C. Stacked A and AB sandstones without shale marker, followed by thin CE intervals (unit 3).

D. Graded sandstone and shale with sharp basal contacts (arrow) (unit 3)

E. Interbedded sandstone and shale (unit 3). Sandstones are thicker than in unit 2.

F. Thin-bedded, clay-rich sandstone with abundant shale layers and bioturbation (arrow) (unit 2).

tion of intensely bioturbated sandstone with bedded sandstone indicates quiet bottom conditions between storm events. During storm events when sandstones were deposited in rapid succession, graded bedsets were preserved with little bioturbation. Quiet–water deposition occurred between storms, allowing repopulation of the substrate by infaunal and epifaunal organisms. The result is intensely bioturbated muds and finely rippled traction deposits.

Unit 2 is characterized by 4–ft thick (1.2 m) "stacks" of graded sandstones separated by lenticular-bedded intervals of rippled sandstone and shale. The dark gray to black color of the shales indicates partially anoxic substrate conditions. Trace fossils present in core slabs suggest depths no greater than inner neritic (Fig. 6) (Chamberlain, 1978; Sullivan, 1982).

The contact between units 2 and 3 is marked by an upward gradation in bedforms from rippled to "microhummocky". Bedsets are both thicker and more uniform in unit 3, consisting of AE, ACE, and CE sequences (Figs. 5D, 5E). Sandstones are separated by thin shale beds. Massive sandstone divisions appear stacked, often lacking shale interbeds (Fig. 5C). These sandstones may have been deposited as channel–margin sands. An upward increase in bedset thickness, loss of shale, and a decrease in bioturbation indicate deposition in an area that became progressively closer to main avenues of sediment delivery. Unit 3 is 11 ft (3.4 m) thick in this core.

The boundary between units 3 and 4 is placed at the uppermost beds of shale and the beginning of thick–bedded, massive sandstones. The most obvious feature of unit–4 sandstones is a lack of primary bedding. Bedsets consist of massive to indistinctly laminated Bouma A divisions ranging in thickness from 1.5 to 6.0 ft (0.4–3.4 m) (Fig. 5A). Bedsets are marked by thin, dark shale laminae, by presence of shale clasts, and by contrasting degrees of bioturbation. Where present, shale interbeds are paper thin, very micaceous, and undulose. Massive sandstones are in sharp contact with beds below. Intense burrowing occurs within intervals of slower deposition (Fig. 5B). This unit is 37 ft (11.3 m) thick in this core. Stacked massive sandstones of unit 4 are interpreted as deposits of channelized turbidity currents.

Sedimentary structures within the overlying Lewis Shale (unit 5) consist of lenticular–bedded, very fine-grained sandstone and siltstone. Some faint, undulose bedding occurs where it was preserved from bioturbation. The lenses of sandstone were deposited by low flow–regime bottom currents in deeper water.

While most cores show a sequence of sedimentary structures similar to that described above, in the Inexco No. 1–28 Jack the sequence is different. The core consists mainly of a repeated sequence of units 2 and 3; unit 4 does not appear. There is no upward decrease in bioturbation. Mean grain size is smaller and the shale content higher. Average bedset thickness is less. These characteristics denote a more distal position in the sediment system.

The main productive lithofacies is unit–4 massive sandstones. Units 2 and 3 also include some massive sandstone intervals; these intervals produce in some areas.

Morphology of Sandstone Bodies

Open–hole well logs were used in mapping the morphology of the Teapot Sandstone. Thick–bedded sandstone sections were subdivided into lithofacies (Fig. 7). These lithofacies can be correlated widely and are termed, in ascending order, the "A", "B", and "C" sandstones; other sandstones are of limited extent. Net sandstone isopach maps of these lithofacies were constructed across a portion of the study area to show the local thickness and morphology of each lithofacies (Fig. 8).

The "A" lithofacies contains dip–trending, massive sandstone bodies (Fig. 8A), with maximum thicknesses of 25 ft (7.6 m). Well control does not allow precise definition of channel morphology, yet the channels are seen to bifurcate down depositional dip and grade into the shaley marine lithofacies. These channel bodies are bounded laterally by thinner (less than 20 ft, or 6.1 m) channel–margin or overbank sandstones. The "B" and "C" lithofacies are similar to the "A" facies in trend and thickness (Figs. 8B, C).

The morphology and local distribution of lithofacies further support the interpretation of Teapot sandstones as deposits of constructional channel, channel-margin, and overbank environments (Fig. 9). The sandstone channels clearly show northeast trends in the direction of depositional dip, further supporting the turbidite interpretation. Development of turbidites on a shallow shelf most likely was related to return flow of storm surge. Therefore, the Teapot Sandstone

BIOGENIC SEDIMENTARY STRUCTURE	DEPOSITIONAL UNIT				
	5	4	3	2	1
Terebellina (single)	▬				
Helminthoida / Scalarituba	▬				
Ophiomorpha (vertical)		▬			
Ophiomorpha (horizontal)		▬▬▬			
Asterosoma (unzoned)		▬▬▬			
Terebellina (plural)		▬▬▬▬			
Rosselia / Cylindrichnus			▬▬		
Skolithos			▬▬▬▬		
Teichichnus			▬▬▬▬		
Terebellina (single)				▬▬▬▬	
Chondrites				▬▬▬▬	
Asterosoma (zoned)				▬▬▬▬	
Rhizocorallium					X
Helminthoida / Scalarituba					▬▬
Intense bioturbation					▬▬

Figure 6. Trace fossils in relation to depositional units. Traces suggest that the Teapot was deposited at depths of no greater than inner neritic. Bars denote range, x = single occurrence.

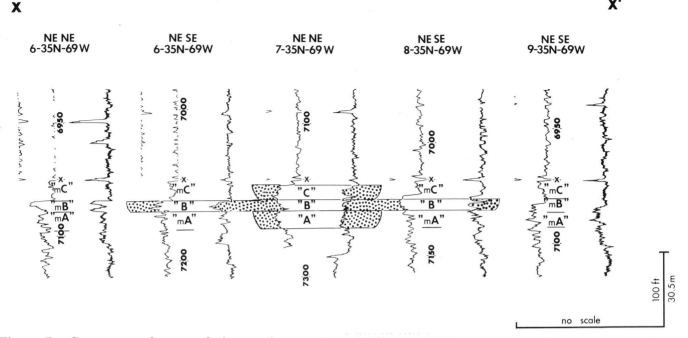

Figure 7. Gamma-ray log correlation section, northern Well Draw field area (X to X' on Figs. 8 A–C), showing the Teapot "A", "B", and "C" channel sandstones (stippled), and Teapot sandstone marker (x) as datum. Channel lithofacies thin and are replaced laterally by channel–margin (m) and overbank facies. No horizontal scale.

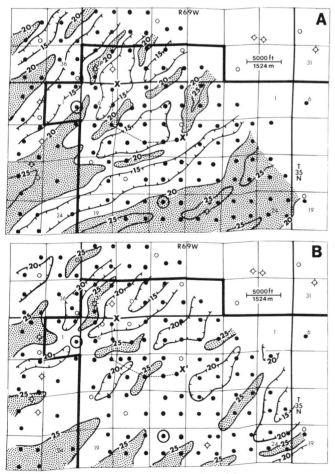

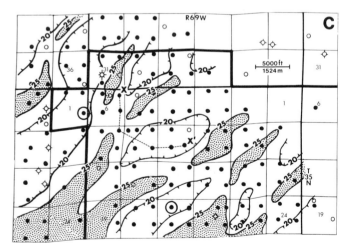

Figure 8A. Net-sandstone isopach map for Teapot "A" sandstones. Stippled areas are channel sandstones with total sandstone thickness greater than 20 ft (6 m). Other areas are either channel–margin or overbank sandstones. Map area is shown in Figure 2. Cross section X-X' is shown in Figure 7. Contour interval is 5.0 ft (1.5 m).

Figure 8B. Net-sandstone map for Teapot "B" sandstones. Symbols same as Figure 8A.

Figure 8C. Net-sandstone map for Teapot "C" sandstones. Symbols same as Figure 8A.

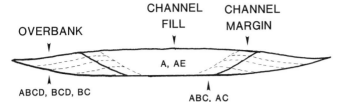

Figure 9. Diagrammatic cross section of facies and associated bedsets across a turbidite channel (after Jones, 1980).

is interpreted as a series of storm–generated shelf turbidite deposits.

PETROGRAPHY AND DIAGENESIS

The thick, massive sandstone comprising unit 4 is the primary reservoir in the area around Well Draw Field. Samples selected for diagenetic study were taken mostly from this unit. Samples also were taken from massive sandstones in units 2 and 3 because these horizons produce in some areas. More detailed discussions of diagenesis were presented by Conner (1983), who concentrated on the Teapot in Well Draw Field and by Coughlan (1983), who discussed the Teapot in both the subsurface and in outcrop in Converse and Natrona counties.

Petrography

The massive Teapot sandstones are well sorted, very fine–grained feldspathic litharenites (Fig. 10, Table 3) (Folk, 1974). The composition shows variation due in part to diagenetic alteration of labile detrital grains such as feldspars and rock fragments.

Authigenic constituents of the sandstones include silica and carbonate cements and clay minerals. Porosity in these sandstones is mostly secondary and due to dissolution of labile grains and cements, and to the development of authigenic phases. Silica cement ac-

counts for approximately 3.2 vol% of all samples. Carbonate cement, clay minerals, and secondary porosity are highly variable, with two–thirds of the samples showing clay:carbonate ratios greater than 2:1 (Fig. 11).

Diagenesis

Major diagenetic processes observed include (in approximate temporal order): 1) compaction, 2) alteration of detrital grains to form clay rims, 3) calcite cementation, 4) calcite dissolution, and 5) clay precipitation (Fig. 12). Modification of grain mineralogy and/or morphology through dissolution, recrystallization, and precipitation has been active since deposition, forming kaolinite rims on feldspar grains; combined smectite, illite, mixed–layer clay, and chlorite rims on rock fragments; intragranular porosity due to partial dissolution of rock fragments or feldspars; and carbonate replacements of silicate grains (Plate 1B, C, and D). Rock fragments and feldspar grains are more affected than are quartz grains (Plate 1C), reducing their relative abundance in more heavily altered sections. Post–oil emplacement alteration has been negligible in the oil column due to the inhibiting effect of hydrocarbons (Porter and Weimer, 1982).

Compaction during early and intermediate burial produced long or tangential quartz grain boundaries and deformation of ductile grains (Plate 1A). Compaction was halted permanently by carbonate cementation.

Carbonate cementation may have occurred over a wide depth range, encompassing several cementation events. The last stage of carbonate cementation halted compaction, impeded fluid flow and development of alteration rims, and replaced silicate grains. Replacement of silicates by carbonate cement formed etched grain boundaries in every sample examined (Plate 2), with feldspar replacement often occurring preferentially along cleavage planes. In rocks that have retained cement, authigenic carbonate constitutes up to 47% of the sandstone. However, subsequent carbonate dissolution created most of the present porosity (Plate 1B).

Clay minerals formed in the sandstones both prior to carbonate cementation and after carbonate dissolution. Clay precipitates are here distinguished from clay rims (discussed above) because they are direct precipitates from circulating pore fluids and restrict pore space. These pore–restricting clay precipitates occur in three forms: non–oriented pore–lining clays, oriented pore–lining clays, and pore–bridging clays. They are discussed below in their order of formation.

Non–oriented pore–lining clays are thin (less than 10 microns) coatings of very fine clay crystals on grains, with random crystal orientations with respect to grain surfaces (Fig. 13A). They appear as "dust rims" in thin section (Plate 1B) and consist of mixtures of kaolinite and chlorite. Their distribution in pore throats and high crystallinity indicate that they were developed in situ. Non–oriented pore–lining clays are present in all of the samples, and are the earliest clay precipitates in most samples. These clays began to form prior to or during carbonate cementation (cf. Tillman and Almon, 1979, and Coughlan and Steidtmann, 1984); and coeval with silica cement-

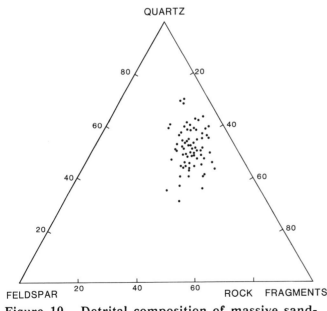

Figure 10. Detrital composition of massive sandstones.

Table 3. Average petrographic data, by well. All samples are from massive sandstones. Wells are arranged in a generally downdip trend.

Well	Quartz Size[a]		Detrital Composition[b]				Cements[c]		
	Mean (mm)	Max (mm)	Qtz	Feld	Rx	Other	Clay	Silica	Carb
			(Normalized to 100%)					(% of Total)	
IJ 1–28	0.13	0.36	56.0	10.5	25.5	8.0	12.8	3.8	11.7
NCO–1	0.13	0.34	56.5	8.6	31.9	3.0	12.3	3.1	6.1
DT–1	0.14	0.35	44.8	14.7	32.3	8.2	14.1	4.3	10.6
IR–1	0.14	0.34	48.6	15.0	32.1	4.3	14.2	3.9	4.4
ALE–1	0.13	0.25	41.0	14.0	32.6	12.4	7.8	3.4	12.5
DSL 1–34	0.15	0.38	41.0	17.8	34.4	6.8	15.2	3.8	13.2
ASF 1–A	0.15	0.28	41.0	16.3	33.3	9.4	20.5	1.7	9.4
Average	0.14	0.33	47.0	13.8	31.7	7.0	13.8	3.4	9.7

[a]From long axis measurements on 50 monocrystalline quartz grains.
[b]Qtz = monocrystalline quartz, Feld = feldspar, Rx = rock fragments, including polycrystalline quartz, Other = other fragments, as described in text.
[c]Clay = authigenic clay as alteration rims and precipitates, Silica = quartz overgrowths and chert, Carb = carbonate.

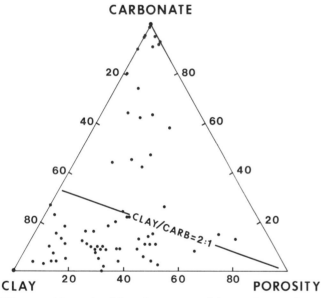

Figure 11. Authigenic composition of massive sandstones. Note that two-thirds of the samples have a clay:carbonate ratio of greater than 2:1. Porosity values include microporosity in clay matrices.

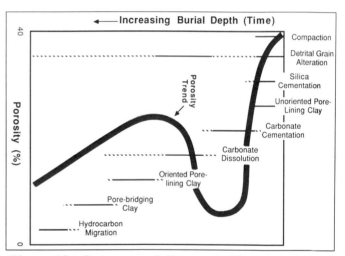

Figure 12. Summary of diagenetic history and porosity evolution of Teapot sandstones. Dashed lines indicate intervals during which process acted either slowly or was intermittent.

ation. The clay rims inhibited quartz overgrowths on some surfaces (Heald, 1965), but not on others (Plate 1B, Fig. 14).

Fluids capable of dissolving calcite entered the sandstones at or near the time of maximum burial. The abundance and ordering of the mixed–layer clays in shales adjacent to the Teapot Sandstone, the age of the shales, and the maximum formation temperatures suggest that the conversion of smectite to illite has begun, but not yet gone to completion. The fluids released during this clay transformation may become undersaturated with respect to calcite through such

processes as charging by CO_2 generated during hydrocarbon maturation (Jonas and McBride, 1977); addition of organic acids from kerogen diagenesis (Surdam et al., 1984 and this volume; Crossey, et al., 1986); or release of ferric iron from the smectite structure, subsequent reduction of the iron by methane oxidation, and consequent production of excess H^+ (McMahon, 1986). Expulsion of these fluids into the Teapot Sandstone would then cause carbonate dissolution.

The second type of clay precipitate formed mainly after dissolution of carbonate cement. Oriented pore-lining clays occur as thin to very thick (greater than 0.3 mm) rims of coarse–crystalline clay oriented with the platelets perpendicular to pore walls (Plate 2C and D, Fig. 13B). They typically retain some centrally

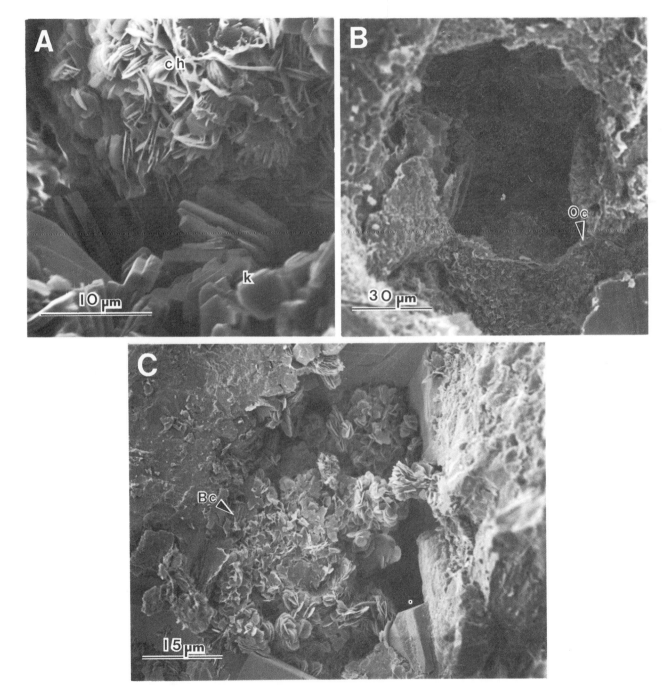

Figure 13. SEM photomicrographs of clay precipitates.

A. Non-oriented pore-lining clay assemblage. Kaolinite (k) and chlorite (ch) coat grain surfaces but do not appreciably decrease pore-throat size. Sample from NCO-1 6,805.5 ft (2,074 m).

B. Oriented pore-lining clay (Oc) assemblage. Note reduction of pore space without complete occlusion. Sample from IR-1, 7,047.5 ft (2,148 m).

C. Pore-bridging clay (Bc) assemblage. This clay type consists of poorly crystalline, iron-rich chlorite. Sample from IR-1, 7,036.5 ft (2,145 m).

Figure 14. SEM photomicrograph of quartz precipitates coeval with and succeeding unoriented pore–lining clay. Arrows indicate quartz succeeding clay. Sample from IR–1, 7036.5 ft (2,145 m).

located porosity (Plate 1C, D, and Plate 2B). The clays are mixed–layer illite/smectite clays with lesser amounts of chlorite. Oriented pore–lining clays are present in 33% of the samples.

Pore–bridging clays are aggregates of smaller, poorly crystalline particles of iron–rich chlorite found in 31% of the samples (Fig. 13C). These clays were the last precipitate in the sandstones (Fig. 12) and essentially fill intergranular pores, leaving only very restricted porosity and microporosity (diameter less than 2 microns, Neasham, 1977).

Tillman and Almon (1979), Almon and Davies (1979), and Coughlan and Steidtmann (1984) recognized diagenetic sequences in sandstones of the Powder River Basin that parallel the sequence described above. However, the Teapot in Well Draw Field is more complex; it saw clay precipitation subsequent to carbonate dissolution.

ORIGIN AND DISTRIBUTION OF POROSITY

Model for Porosity Evolution

Diagenesis created and destroyed porosity and permeability at different times. Initially, compaction reduced primary porosity by closer packing of detrital grains, and by deformation of more–ductile grains. Early–formed alteration rims generally created abundant microporosity. Non–oriented pore–lining clays do not appear to reduce porosity appreciably. Coeval quartz overgrowths reduced the effects of compaction, but occluded porosity only slightly. Removal of this type of cement was accomplished only to a limited degree by carbonate replacement and subsequent dissolution. Carbonate cementation essentially eliminated primary porosity. This ended the first stage of porosity evolution.

The second stage began with removal of carbonate cement, and formed most of the present porosity in Teapot sandstones. Dissolution of calcite removed

both cement, to restore intergranular porosity, and calcite replacements of silicate grains, creating new intragranular porosity.

This pore network was altered significantly by formation of authigenic clays. Oriented pore–lining clays appreciably reduced porosity. Loss of permeability due to clays of this type is more significant than is porosity loss. However, the greatest porosity loss was due to precipitation of late pore–bridging clays. Sandstones that contain pore–bridging clays average 0.28 md permeability and are nonproductive.

Variations in Diagenesis and Porosity Distribution

Diagenesis and destruction of secondary porosity did not occur uniformly in all sections. Framework–grain composition shows an increasing abundance of rock fragments and feldspars downdip in a westerly direction (Fig. 15). Clay minerals also increase westward (or down present dip) through the study area (Fig. 16).

These trends are interpreted as resulting from diagenesis, not from deposition. The precipitation of clays is controlled in part by the movement of pore fluids. Teapot sandstones were deposited dipping eastward and likely retained that dip direction through at least shallow burial. However, post–depositional rotation reversed dip to the northwest. This dip reversal is reflected in sandstone compositions. Less stable rock fragments and feldspars were leached out of updip (eastern) sandstones by downdip flow of fluids. These waters became progressively more saturated with dissolved ions, and thus less effective solvents and more effective sources of diagenetic miner-

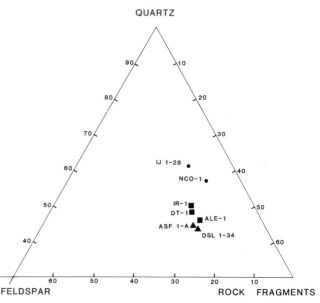

Figure 15. Average framework grain composition, by well. Note the trend toward more rock fragments and feldspars from updip wells (circles) through intermediate (squares) to downdip (triangles). Note that scales are different from Figure 10, causing data to appear to plot in a different area.

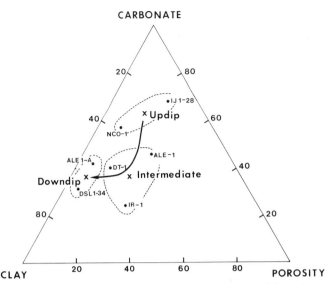

Figure 16. Average authigenic composition by well. Note downdip trend towards more abundant clay precipitates. X indicates average group values.

als, as they moved through the sandstones. This process rendered the downdip sandstones nonproductive.

Similar trends in mineralogy have been documented in other studies and attributed to depositional processes such as decrease of labile grains with distance from source area; change in mineralogy due to a change in source rock, bioturbation, or grain size (Tillman and Almon, 1979); or variation in mineral-

ogy reflecting different depositional environments. These mechanisms do not apply to the Teapot at Well Draw Field for several reasons. First, the source area was hundreds of miles to the west; it is unlikely that the large change in content of labile grains observed in the cores is due solely to depositional processes. Second, the source for the Teapot remained essentially constant throughout deposition, especially with respect to the broad classifications on a QFL diagram. Third, the samples were selected from non–bioturbated, massive sandstones in which variation in mean grain size is insignificant (Table 3). Finally, the samples were selected to avoid variations in depositional environment.

Reservoir Properties and Performance

Production curves (Fig. 17) show a normal decline in oil production from Well Draw Field, but a sudden increase in gas starting in 1981–1982. This may be due to pressure decline in the reservoir. Analysis of the decline curve for oil (Fig. 17B) suggests recoverable reserves of approximately 30,500,000 BO. Recoverable gas is approximately 91 BCF.

Teapot sandstones at Well Draw Field average 12.1% porosity and 0.69 md permeability for all cored intervals. Producing intervals average 14.2% porosity and 4.3 md permeability. Nonproducing sandstones have 11.4% porosity and 0.12 md permeability. Depositional control of porosity and permeability is illustrated by comparing non–cemented (less than 15% authigenic material) unit–4 massive sandstones with sandstones from units 2 and 3 (Fig. 18A); sandstones in units 2 and 3 are less porous and permeable because they are finer-grained, thinner-bedded, and

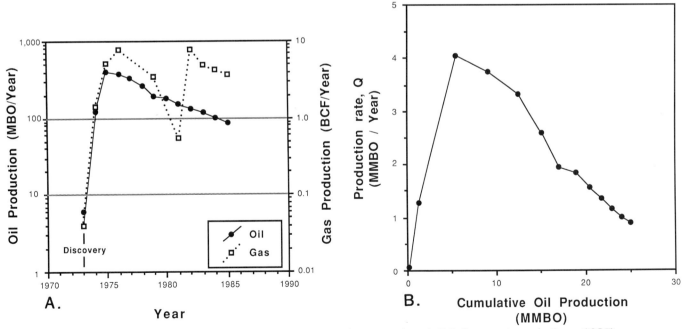

Figure 17. Production curves for Well Draw Field. (International Oil Scouts Association, 1987).

A. Oil and gas production rates versus time. Oil production followed a normal trend, but gas production increased sharply in 1981.

B. Oil production rate versus cumulative oil production. Decline curve suggests recoverable reserves of 30,500,000 BO.

shalier. Unit–4 sandstones have reservoir-quality porosities and permeabilities because they are coarser-grained and include very little depositional clay matrix. Overlap between the two sandstone types is due to the presence of massive sandstone intervals with reservoir-quality porosity and permeability in units 2 and 3, and to the presence of porosity-occluding authigenic material in some unit–4 sandstones.

In sandstone reservoirs, porosity and permeability generally decrease with increasing abundance of authigenic materials. This is the case for Teapot sandstones. Unit–4 sandstones with greater than 15% authigenic minerals display significant loss of porosity and nearly complete loss of permeability when compared to unit–4 sandstones with greater than 15% authigenic material (Fig. 18B).

Examples of the Effect of Clays

Oriented pore-lining clays decrease porosity and permeability less than carbonate cement or pore-bridging clay. Clay rims do not fill pores or clog pore throats to any significant extent.

One example is the Inexco No. 1 Robinson well (Fig. 19). Initial completion was in unit–4 sandstones for 623 BOPD, 893 MCFGPD, and 94 BWPD from a perforated interval of 26 ft (7.9 m). Average porosity is 14.1%. Average permeability is 0.97 md. The authigenic clay content averages 8.9%. Most of these clays are alteration rims on labile grains, an occurrence that does not occlude pores. As a result, the sandstone is relatively porous, permeable, and productive.

By contrast, the Diamond Shamrock No. 1–34 Lebar well (Fig. 20) contains abundant authigenic clay (average 15.2%); most of the clay is of the pore-bridging type. Unit–4 sandstones are thicker in this well, but the abundance of authigenic clay has reduced permeability to nonproductive levels (average 0.2 md). Note that there is 11.7% porosity, but this is microporosity in the clay aggregates.

CONCLUSIONS

Teapot sandstones produce oil and gas from stratigraphic traps throughout the southern Powder River Basin, including Well Draw Field. These shallow-marine shelf turbidites are characterized by thick AE bedsets in productive intervals and by thinner, more-complete bedsets interbedded with shales in nonproductive intervals. Diagenesis has pervasively altered the reservoir texture, mineralogy, and porosity distribution through grain alteration, cementation, dissolution, and clay mineral precipitation. Porosity developed in four stages: 1) loss of primary porosity due to compaction, 2) further loss due to carbonate cementation, 3) formation of secondary porosity by carbonate dissolution, and 4) modification of this porosity by clay precipitation. Microporosity in clay rims was at best a minor source of porosity for hydrocarbon migration and storage.

Downdip hydrodynamic flow of pore fluids caused greater dissolution of detrital grains and cement in the eastern part of the field, where the most productive wells are located. This same flow caused greater precipitation of authigenic clay minerals in downdip areas, rendering the sandstones generally nonproductive.

Extension of this study to additional wells likely would allow mapping the diagenetic facies that control distribution of productive and nonproductive zones. This would be useful in development and enhanced

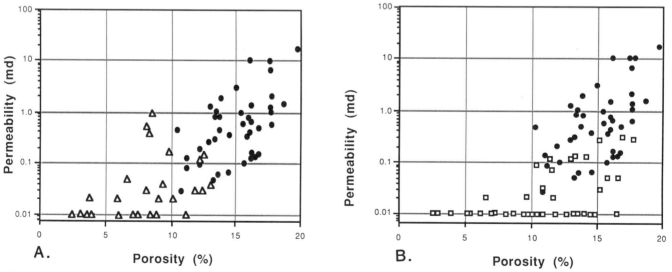

Figure 18. Controls on Teapot porosity and permeability.
A. Depositional control. Dots = non-cemented unit–4 sandstones (less than 15% authigenic material). Open triangles = samples from units 2 and 3. Unit–4 sandstones have higher porosity and greater permeability than do unit–2 and –3 sandstones because of finer grain size and higher clay content in latter units.
B. Diagenetic control. Dots = non-cemented unit–4 sandstones (less than 15% authigenic material). Open squares = cemented unit–4 sandstones (greater than 15% authigenic material). "Clean" unit–4 sandstones are more porous and permeable than cemented unit–4 sandstones due to occlusion of pores by cements. Scatter in cemented-sandstone values is due to differences in cement abundance and mineralogy.

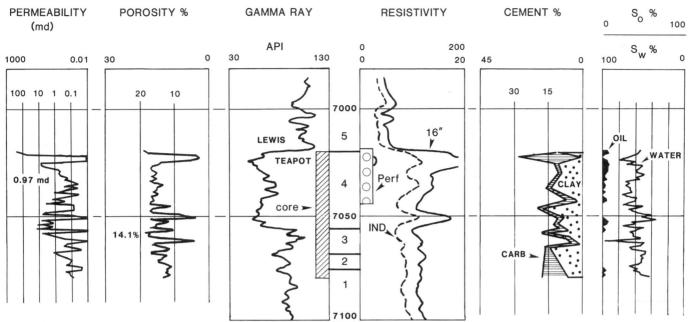

Figure 19. Log and reservoir characteristics for Inexco No. 1 Robinson well. Numbers 1–5 in depth tracks correspond to lithologic units described in text and in Figure 4. Unit 4 (massive sandstones) contains the potential reservoir sandstones. Note that net sandstone is greater in Diamond Shamrock well (Fig. 20). Average permeability and porosity are given on the figure. S_{oi} = oil saturation, S_{wi} = water saturation, CARB = carbonate cement, CLAY = authigenic clay. Saturation data are from Core Labs analyses of core samples. Relatively low authigenic content is reflected in high permeability and low water saturations. Initial production from the indicated perforations (Perf) was: 643 BOPD, 893 MCFGPD, 94 BWPD. (50–ft depth divisions = 15.2 m)

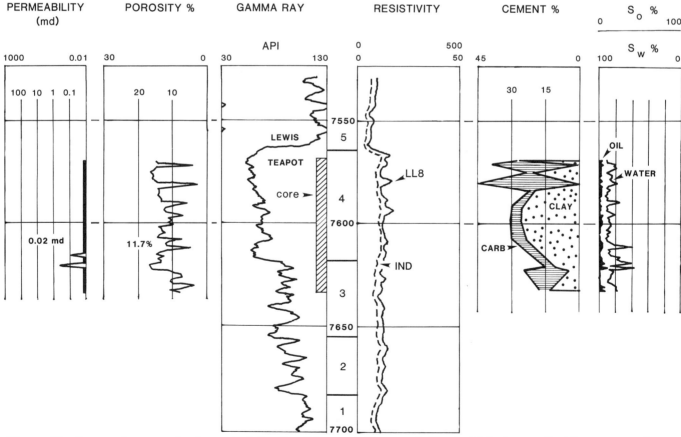

Figure 20. Log and reservoir characteristics for Diamond Shamrock No. 1–34 Lebar well. The greater abundance of clay precipitates is reflected in higher water saturations and greatly decreased permeability. The clays have rendered sandstones in this part of the field nonproductive. Symbols same as for Figure 19.

oil projects within the field, and might assist in interpreting production patterns in similar reservoirs.

ACKNOWLEDGEMENTS

We would like to thank Dr. R.R. Berg for his assistance in this study. We are grateful for the comments and critical reviews of E.B. Coalson and Drs. E.D. Pittman and C.W. Keighin. The cores were obtained from the USGS core library in Denver, Colorado. This study was funded in part by a grant from the Center for Energy and Mineral Resources, Texas A&M University, College Station, Texas, 77843.

REFERENCES

Almon, W.R., and D.K. Davies, 1979, Regional diagenetic trends in the lower Cretaceous Muddy Sandstone, Powder River Basin, *in* P.A. Scholle and P.R. Schluger, eds., Aspects of Diagenesis: SEPM Spec. Pub. 26, p. 379-400.

Berg, R.R., 1975, Depositional environment of Upper Cretaceous Sussex Sandstone: AAPG Bull., v. 59, p. 2099-2109.

Berg, R.R., 1986, Reservoir Sandstones: Prentice-Hall, Inc., Englewood Cliffs, NJ, 481 p.

Bouma, A.H., 1962, Sedimentology of some flysch deposits: a graphic approach to facies interpretation: Elsevier Pub. Co., Amsterdam, 168 p.

Chamberlain, C.K., 1978, Recognition of trace fossils in cores: *in* P.R. Basan, ed., Trace Fossil Concepts: SEPM Short Course No. 5, p. 133-184.

Conner, S.P., 1983, Diagenesis of the Upper Cretaceous Teapot Sandstone, Well Draw Field, Converse County, Wyoming: unpub. MS thesis, Texas A&M University, College Station, TX, 154 p.

Coughlan, J.P., 1983, Depositional environment and diagenesis of the Teapot Sandstone (Upper Cretaceous), Converse and Natrona counties, Wyoming: unpub. MS thesis, U. of WY, Laramie.

Coughlan, J.P., and J.R. Steidtmann, 1984, Depositional environment and diagenesis of the Teapot Sandstone, southern Powder River Basin, Wyoming: Mtn. Geol., v. 21, p. 91-103.

Crossey, L.J., R.C. Surdam, and R. Lahann, 1986, Application of organic/inorganic diagenesis to porosity prediction: *in* D.L. Gautier, ed., Roles of Organic Matter in Sediment Diagenesis: SEPM Spec. Pub. 38, p. 147-156.

Curry, W.H., III, 1976a, Late Cretaceous Teapot delta of southern Powder River Basin, Wyoming: WGA, 28th Ann. Field Conf. Guidebook, p. 21-28.

Curry, W.H., III, 1976b, Type section of the Teapot Sandstone: WGA, 28th Ann. Field Conf. Guidebook, p. 29-32.

Folk, R.L., 1974, Petrology of Sedimentary Rocks: Austin, Texas, Hemphill Pub. Co., 182 p.

Gill, J.R., and W.A. Cobban, 1973, Stratigraphy and geologic history of the Montana Group and equivalent rocks, Montana, Wyoming, and North and South Dakota: USGS Prof. Paper 393-A, 73 p.

Heald, M.T., 1965, Lithification of sandstones in West Virginia: WV Geological Survey Bull., no. 30, 28 p.

International Oil Scouts Association, 1987, International oil and gas development yearbook, (review of 1984-1985) part II, production: IOSA Yearbook v. 55/56, p. 869-870.

Isbell, E.B., C.W. Spencer, and T. Seitz, 1976, Petroleum geology of the Well Draw Field, Converse County, Wyoming: WGA, 28th Ann. Field Conf. Guidebook, p. 165-174.

Johnson, B.B., and P.F. Bryant, 1979, Field trip road log - Upper Cretaceous sandstones - Casper - Salt Creek - Tisdale Mountain: WGA, Earth Science Bull., v. 12, no. 12, p. 6-16.

Jonas, E.C., and E.F. McBride, 1977, Diagenesis of sandstone and shale: applications for petroleum exploration: Continuing Education Program Publications No. 1, Austin, TX, p. 1-165.

Jones, J.W., 1980, Depositional environment and morphology of Canyon sandstone reservoirs, central Midland Basin, Texas: MS thesis, Texas A&M University, College Station, TX, 147 p.

McGookey, D.P., J.D. Haun, L.A. Hale, H.G. Goodell, D.G. McCubbin, R.J. Weimer, and G.R. Wulf, 1972, Cretaceous System: RMAG, Geologic Atlas of the Rocky Mountain Region, p. 190-228.

McMahon, D.A., Jr., 1986, The reduction of ferric iron by methane and the development of secondary porosity in Tertiary sandstones of the Gulf Coast [abs.]: GSA Abstracts with Programs, v. 18, no. 6, p. 691.

Neasham, J.W., 1977, Applications of scanning electron microscopy to the characterization of hydrocarbon-bearing rocks: Scanning Electron Microscopy, v. 1, p. 101-108.

Porter, K.W., and R.J. Weimer, 1982, Diagenetic sequence related to structural history and petroleum accumulation, Spindle Field, Colorado: AAPG Bull., v. 66, p. 2543-2560.

Schultz, L.G., 1964, Quantitative interpretation of mineralogical composition from x-ray and chemical data for the Pierre Shale: USGS Prof. Paper 391-C, 31 p.

Sullivan, J.J., 1982, Environment of deposition and reservoir properties of Teapot sandstones (Upper Cretaceous), Well Draw Field, Converse County, Wyoming: unpub. MS thesis, Texas A&M University, College Station, TX, 172 p.

Surdam, R.C., S.W. Boese, and L.J. Crossey, 1984, The chemistry of secondary porosity, *in* D.A. McDonald and R.C. Surdam, eds., Clastic Diagenesis: AAPG Mem. 37, p. 127-149.

Tillman, R.W., and W.R. Almon, 1979, Diagenesis of Frontier Formation offshore bar sandstones, Spearhead Ranch Field, Wyoming: *in* P.A. Scholle and P.R. Schluger, eds., Aspects of Diagenesis: SEPM Spec. Pub. 26, p. 337-378.

Petrology and Reservoir Characteristics of the Almond Formation, Greater Green River Basin, Wyoming[1]

C. Wm. KEIGHIN[2]
B.E. LAW[2]
R.M. POLLASTRO[2]

[1]Received September 1, 1988; Revised January 15, 1989
[2]U.S. Geological Survey, Box 25046, MS 971, Denver CO

The Upper Cretaceous Almond Formation of the Mesaverde Group is one of the most important hydrocarbon–bearing units in the Rocky Mountain region. Through 1986, it had produced about 100,000,000 BO and 0.7 TCFG. Production is found in both conventional and unconventional low–permeability ("tight") reservoirs.

The Almond consists of a sequence of interbedded sandstones, siltstones, mudstones, carbonaceous shales, and coals. Environments of deposition range from nonmarine in the lower part to marginal marine in the upper part.

Petrophysical and petrographic (thin section and SEM) analyses indicate that pores in fine to very fine–grained Almond sandstones are small (less than 20 microns) and formed in part by dissolution of framework grains and authigenic cements. Intergranular micropores occur between crystals of authigenic clay. The sandstones contain 15 to 30% clay, which is predominantly illitic. Local concentrations of kaolinite occur, but chlorite is rare. Smectite clay minerals were not detected. Distribution of cements, as well as of detrital feldspars, is variable.

Along the eastern flank of the Rock Springs Uplift, Almond sandstones lie at depths of 4,000 to 5,000 ft (1,200 to 1,500 m), and have relatively high porosities (16 to 22%) and permeabilities (20 to 80 md), measured under ambient conditions. In the Great Divide and Washakie basins where the Almond lies at depths of 10,000 to 13,000 ft (3,050 to 3,970 m), porosities and permeabilities are much lower (3 to 10% and 0.02 to 55 md). As is typical with low–permeability sandstone, permeability is significantly reduced by confining stress, in some cases to the nannodarcy range.

Not only porosity, permeability, and depth, but also vitrinite reflectance seem to be related in both conventional and unconventional Almond reservoirs. It may be possible to define an approximate depth at which overpressuring may occur based on these data.

INTRODUCTION

Marine and nonmarine strata of the Upper Cretaceous Almond Formation of the Mesaverde Group produce oil and gas throughout the eastern portion of the Greater Green River Basin in Wyoming (Figs. 1 and 2). Production is obtained from both conventional and unconventional ("tight") reservoirs. Although the Almond Formation has been the subject of numerous investigations, most of these have focused on stratigraphy, sedimentology, and producing fields. Stratigraphic and sedimentologic studies include: Schultz (1909), Sears (1924), Hale (1950), Weimer (1960, 1961, 1965, 1966), Barlow (1961), Lewis (1961), Jacka (1965), McCubbin and Brady (1969), Meyers (1977), Van Horn (1979), and Harbridge (1980). Oil and gas field studies include those on the Desert Springs Field by Earl and Dahm (1961) and May (1961). Table Rock Field is discussed by White (1955) and by Mees and others (1961). Patrick Draw was studied by Burton (1961), Lawson and Crowson (1961), Cox (1962), and Weimer (1966). Investigations dealing primarily with petrography and diagenesis of the Almond Formation are limited to Jacka (1970), Thomas (1978), and Lanham (1980). Some samples described by Lanham, however, were

REGIONAL DATA:

Producing Interval:	Almond Formation of the Mesaverde Group
Geographic Location:	Sweetwater County, Wyoming
Present Tectonic Setting:	Wamsutter Arch, eastern flank of Rock Springs Uplift, and northeastern flank of Washakie Basin
Depositional Setting:	Western flank of Cretaceous seaway
Age of Reservoir:	Upper Cretaceous
Lithology of Reservoir:	Very fine to fine grained, lithic, illitic, kaolinitic, and quartzose sandstones
Depositional Environments:	Upper Almond is estuarine, littoral, and shallow–water neritic; lower Almond is fluvial dominated
Diagenesis:	Carbonate and/or silica cements; authigenic kaolinite; dissolution of carbonate cement and some framework grains
Porosity Types:	Intergranular, secondary, and microporosity
Porosity:	15–18% at 4,500 ft (1,400 m); 6–12% at 9,500 ft (2,900 m)
Permeability:	0.1–10 md
Fractures:	Rarely observed
Nature of Traps:	Stratigraphic and anticlinal closures
Entrapping Facies:	Shales of Almond and Lewis formations
Source Rock:	Gas from interbedded coals and from Lewis Formation. Oil probably from Cretaceous source
Timing of Hydrocarbon Migration:	Middle to Late Tertiary

FIELD DATA: Patrick Draw area–Arch Unit (Street, 1979; Wyoming Oil and Gas Commission, 1989)

Discovered:	1960
Reservoir Depth:	4,500–5,700 ft (1,370–1,740 m)
Reservoir Thickness:	Average 20 ft (6 m)
Areal Extent:	8,010 acres (3,242 ha): 5,770 acres (2,335 ha) oil, 2,240 acres (906.5 ha) gas
IP (discovery well):	F 484 BOPD, 333 MCFGPD
Original Reservoir Pressure:	1,790 psi at +2,000 ft (620 m) datum
Cumulative Production (1/88):	78,500,000 BO, 258 BCFG (total Patrick Draw fields)
Approximate Ultimate Recovery:	23,400,000 BO (Arch Unit only)
Oil Gravity:	42° API

FIELD DATA: Patrick Draw area–Monel Unit (Street, 1979; Wyoming Oil and Gas Commission, 1989)

Discovered:	1959
Reservoir Depth:	4,400–5,300 ft (1,340–1,620 m)
Reservoir Thickness:	Average 20 ft (6 m)
Areal Extent:	8,530 acres (3,452 ha): 6,650 areas (2,691 ha) oil, 1,880 acres (760.8 ha) gas
IP (Discovery Well):	F 792 BOPD, 533 MCFGPD
Original Reservoir Pressure:	1,790 psig at +2,000 ft (620 m) datum
Cumulative Production:	See Arch Unit above
Approximate Ultimate Recovery:	39,400,000 BO
Oil Gravity:	42° API

FIELD DATA: Wild Rose Field (Coalson, 1979; Wyoming Oil and Gas Commission, 1989)

Discovered:	197.
Reservoir Depth:	9,600–9,800 ft (2,930–2,990 m)
Reservoir Thickness:	Average 20 ft (6 m)
Areal Extent:	10,140 acres (4,104 ha)
IP (Discovery Well):	F 1,184 MCFGPD and 73.5 BCPD
Original Reservoir Pressure:	Variable
Cumulative Production (1/89):	2,100,000 BO, 80.5 BCFG
Character of Gas:	1,150 BTU, 0.75 sp gr
Condensate Gravity:	44° API

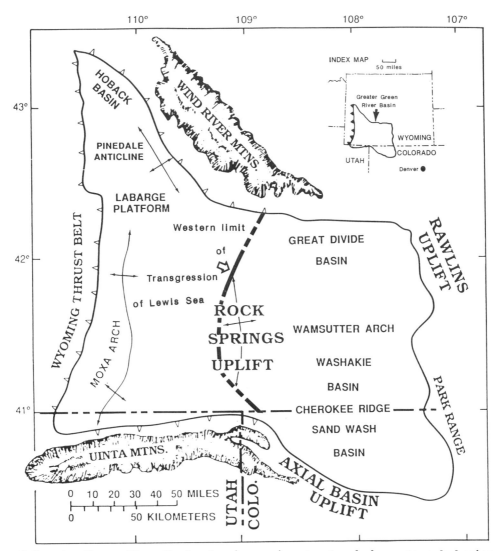

Figure 1. Map of Greater Green River Basin showing major structural elements, sub–basins, and maximum westward transgression of Lewis sea (heavy broken line).

later interpreted by Law to be from stratigraphically below the Almond Formation.

The purpose of this investigation was to compliment previous studies through description of certain aspects of petrography and diagenesis, and their influence on reservoir properties. Also important were examination of variations in porosity and permeability, and of possible relationships between porosity, permeability, burial depth, and thermal maturity.

STRUCTURAL SETTING

The area of investigation is in the Rocky Mountain foreland structural province, and includes the Great Divide and Washakie basins, the Rock Springs Uplift, and the Wamsutter Arch (Fig. 1). The Great Divide and Washakie basins are structurally deep; Precambrian rocks lie at depths of about 24,000 ft (7,300 m) in the Great Divide Basin, and more than 30,000 ft (9,100 m) in the Washakie Basin. The Great Divide Basin is bounded by thrust faults along the northern and eastern margins (Figs. 3 and 4), producing marked asymmetry. By comparison, the Washakie

Basin is more symmetrical. The two basins are separated by an east–plunging, structurally high ridge called the Wamsutter Arch. Barlow (1961) and Weimer (1966) presented stratigraphic evidence indicating that the Wamsutter Arch was present during deposition of the Upper Cretaceous Lewis Shale, which overlies the Almond Formation.

Most of the structural features in the area probably resulted from compressional deformation during the Laramide Orogeny. However, there is evidence that some features may have a pre–Laramide origin, for example along the northeastern margin of the Great Divide Basin in the northern part of the Rawlins Uplift (Reynolds, 1976).

STRATIGRAPHIC SETTING

The Almond Formation was deposited in nonmarine and marine environments during the final transgression of the Cretaceous seaway into southwestern Wyoming. Almond sediments most likely were shed eastward from highlands in western Wyoming and eastern Idaho. Throughout the region, the

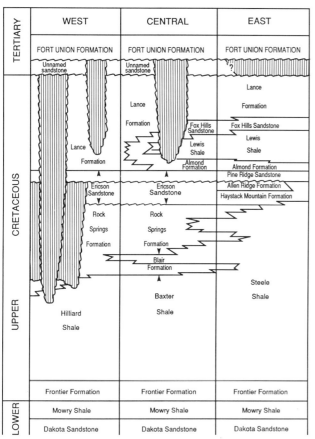

Figure 2. Stratigraphic column of Cretaceous and lower Tertiary units found in the Greater Green River Basin. Vertical hatching indicates unconformities.

Almond conformably overlies the Upper Cretaceous Ericson Sandstone and equivalent units, and conformably underlies the Upper Cretaceous Lewis Shale (Fig. 2). In the Green River Basin west of the maximum westward transgression of the Lewis sea (Fig. 1), the Almond is not formally recognized; approximately equivalent beds are found in the lower few hundred feet (100 m) of the Lance Formation.

The Almond ranges in thickness from 250 to 750 ft (76 to 230 m) and in most of the area is informally subdivided into two parts. The lower part is composed of sandstone, siltstone, mudstone, carbonaceous shale, and coal deposited in dominantly fluvial environments (Weimer, 1965, 1966; Jacka, 1965; McCubbin and Brady, 1969). The upper part is lithologically similar to the lower part, but contains less coal and was deposited in estuarine, littoral, and shallow-water neritic environments (Weimer, 1965; McCubbin and Brady, 1969). These divisions cannot always be recognized reliably on well logs (Fig. 5).

Although diagnostic fossils have not been found in the Almond, the ammonite *Baculites eliasi*, an early Maestrichtian index fossil in the western interior, has been found in the lower 100 ft (30 m) of the Lewis Shale near Rawlins, Wyoming (Bader and others, 1983). Thus, the age of the Almond is inferred to be early Maestrichtian.

OIL AND GAS PRODUCTION

The Almond Formation is one of the most important producing units in southwestern Wyoming. Within the area studied, approximately 65 fields produce from the Almond (Fig. 6). Cumulative oil and gas production through 1986 (Wyoming Oil and Gas Conservation Commission, 1987) was 100,000,000 BO and 0.5 to 0.8 TCFG. Because many of the fields produce from more than one stratigraphic interval, it is not simple to accurately determine cumulative production for individual reservoirs. However, over 95% of the produced oil is from two fields: Patrick Draw (78,500,000 BO) and Arch (18,200,000 BO).

Gas reservoirs can be subdivided into conventional and unconventional ("tight") categories. The generally used dividing point between conventional and unconventional gas reservoirs is 0.1 md permeability and 8% porosity. Also, tight reservoirs commonly are overpressured and produce little or no water. By these criteria, conventional reservoirs account for approximately 80% of the total Almond gas production. The largest conventional gas fields have produced 872 BCFG. These include Patrick Draw (255 BCFG), Desert Springs (240 BCFG), Canyon Creek (230 BCFG), Arch (82 BCFG), Playa (35 BCFG), and Desert Springs West (30 BCFG). The largest unconventional fields include Echo Springs (113 BCFG), Standard Draw (73 BCFG), and Wild Rose (61 BCFG).

MINERALOGIC COMPOSITION OF THE ALMOND FORMATION

Bulk mineralogic composition was determined by X-ray powder diffraction (XRD) for sandstones and shales of the uppermost Almond Formation (Table 1). Carbonate minerals include calcite, dolomite, ankerite, and minor amounts of siderite. Sandstones from conventional reservoirs at depths from 4,500–7,500 ft (1,400–2,300 m) in Patrick Draw and other nearby fields on the Wamsutter Arch tend to contain more carbonate minerals (as much as 55 wt%) and less quartz than do deeper reservoir sandstones found to the east. The percentage of carbonate varies dramatically on the scale of a few inches. The most carbonate-rich sandstones are tightly cemented by ankerite and retain virtually no intergranular porosity. The ratio of calcite to dolomite-plus-ankerite decreases in the deeper sandstones; diagenetic evolution from calcite cement to the more stable ferroan dolomite and ankerite cements with increasing depth has been reported for many other sandstone sequences (Land and Dutton, 1978; Pitman and others, 1982; Dickinson, 1985).

Total feldspar content of Almond sandstones averages approximately 5% and rarely exceeds 10%. Much of the detrital feldspar has been removed by dissolution (Plate 1E, Fig. 7E); some has been replaced by carbonate. Potassium feldspar commonly is more abundant than is plagioclase in samples from depths less than 6,000 ft (2,000 m). Plagioclase is more common in deeper sandstones, in which potassium feldspar is rare or absent.

Almond sandstones contain between 15 and 30 wt% clay minerals (Table 1). Kaolinite is the most

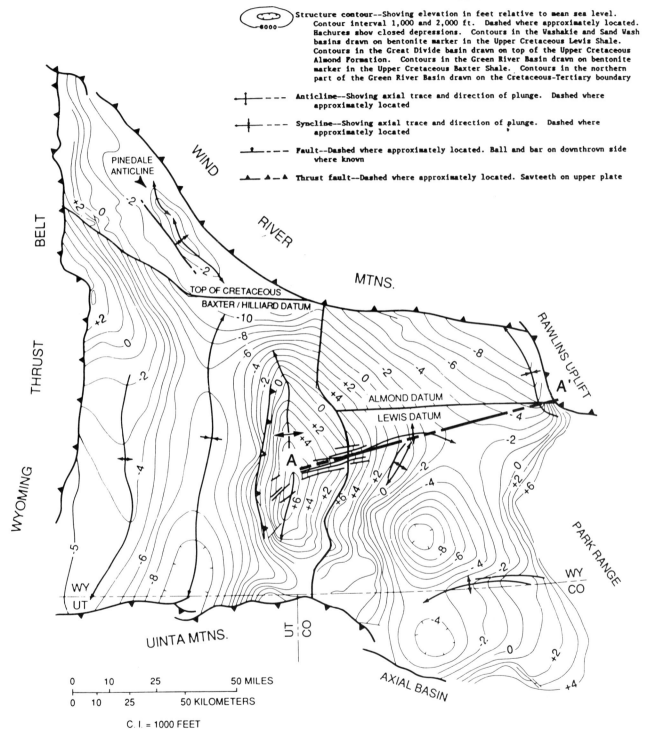

Figure 3. Structure contour map of the Greater Green River Basin (modified from Lickus and Law, 1988). Location of cross section A – A' (Fig. 4) is shown.

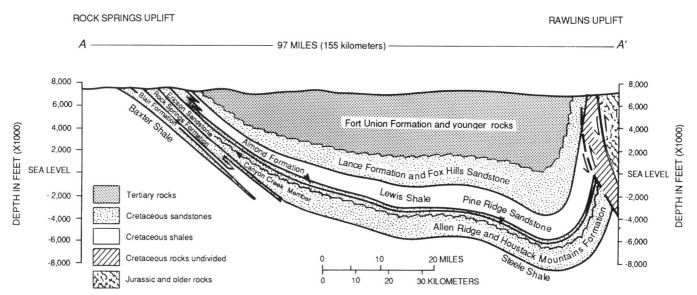

Figure 4. Structural cross–section A – A' showing relationships from the Rock Springs Uplift to the Rawlins Uplift. Location of cross–section is shown in Figure 3. Great Divide Basin is strongly asymmetric and overridden by thrusts on the flank of the Rawlins Uplift.

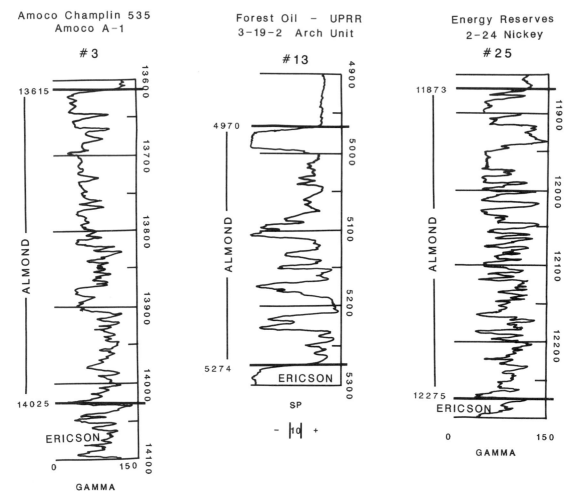

Figure 5. Representative SP and gamma ray logs showing the Almond Formation in selected drill holes (see Table 3 for locations). The Almond is informally divided into upper (marine) and lower (nonmarine) members. (100 ft = 30.5 m)

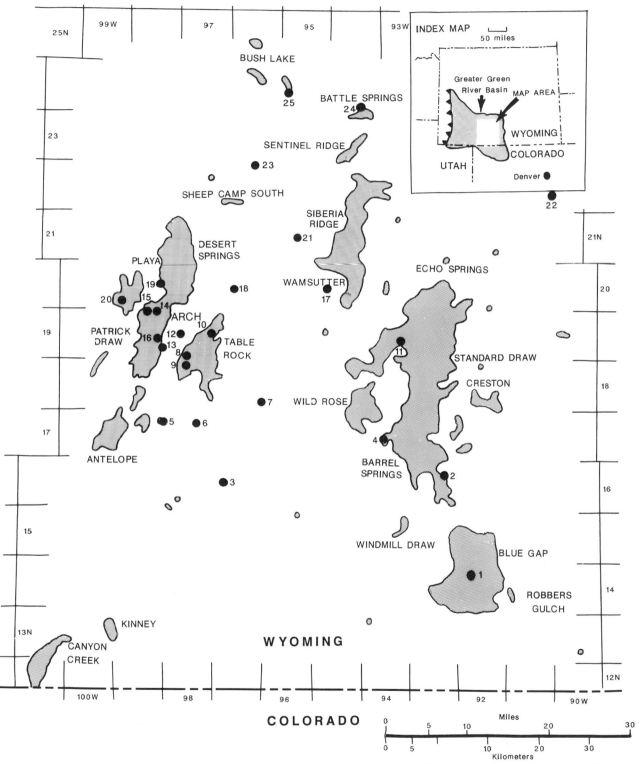

Figure 6. Oil and gas fields that produce primarily from the Almond Formation (modified from Stephenson and others, 1987). Numbers refer to wells cited in Table 3.

abundant clay in the shallower reservoir sandstones, which commonly are extensively cemented by authigenic kaolinite (Table 2; Figs. 7 and 8; Plate 1F). Kaolinite abundance decreases with increasing

Table 1. Range and mean whole-rock mineralogic composition of 46 sandstone and 30 shale samples of uppermost Almond Formation. Analysis from X-ray powder diffraction in weight percent. Wells sampled are listed in Table 3; location of wells shown in Figure 6.

	Shallow core samples (4,500 – 7,500 ft) (1,372 – 2,287 m)		Deep core samples (9,600 – 13,700 ft) (2,928 –4,178 m)	
	Sandstone	Shale	Sandstone	Shale
Quartz:				
range	25 – 81	22 – 52	38 – 91	22 – 43
mean	57	37	67	33
Clay:				
range	13 25	44 – 67	3 – 26	47 – 72
mean	18	51	18	59
Carbonate:				
range	0 – 55	0 – 19	0 – 42	0 – 31
mean	20	10	12	5
calcite	8	2	3	<1
dolomite	4	5	3	3
ankerite	8	<1	6	<1
siderite	–	<1	<1	1
Feldspar:				
range	0 – 15	2 – 5	0 – 12	1 – 6
mean	5	3	3	3
Pyrite:				
mean	–	2	–	2

Table 2. Mean clay-mineral compositions of sandstone and shale of the Almond Formation. Analyses determined from X-ray powder diffraction of less-than-two micron fraction in relative weight percent. Wells sampled and depths are listed in Table 3; location of wells shown in Figure 6.

	Shallow core samples (4,500 – 7,500 ft) (1,372 – 2,287 m)		Deep core samples (9,600 – 13,700 ft) (2,928 –4,178 m)	
	Sandstone	Shale	Sandstone	Shale
illite	23	36	44	41
illite/smectite	30	48	51	47
kaolinite	47	14	5	9
chlorite	0	2	0	3

depth; it normally is rare or absent in sandstone below 9,000 ft (2,800 m). Chlorite was not detected in any sandstone samples. Illitic clays dominate the smaller-than two micron assemblage below 9,000 ft (2,800 m), and include discrete illite and inter-stratified illite/smectite. Little smectitic clay is found in either sandstones or shales. The illite/smectite is of the ordered variety and contains less than 25% expandable layers, as estimated by the method of Reynolds and Hower (1970). These characteristics suggest that even the shallowest rocks, now at depths of approximately 4,500 ft (1,400 m), may once have been buried to depths where the temperature exceeded 212 °F (100 °C) (Hoffman and Hower, 1979), or may have experienced a heating event as suggested by Law and others (1986).

Illite and illite/smectite are the dominant clay minerals in interbedded shales (Table 2). The shales commonly also contain about 10% kaolinite and 5% chlorite.

DIAGENESIS OF ALMOND RESERVOIR SANDSTONES

Most of the porosity in the more-porous sandstones of the upper Almond Formation, occurring at depths between 4,500 and 5,800 ft (1,400 m and 1,800 m) in Patrick Draw Field, is due to dissolution of mineral grains and cement (Fig. 7; Plate 1). Dissolution of ferroan calcite cement accounts for much of the intergranular porosity in all shallower reservoir sandstones. Extensive intragranular and moldic porosity was formed by dissolution of feldspars, chert, and shale fragments.

By contrast, some shallow sandstones remain tightly cemented by ankerite. Ankerite cement was observed in all sandstones examined as replacements of calcite and quartz cements and, more commonly, as overgrowths on detrital dolomite grains.

Silica overgrowths on detrital quartz grains were observed in all samples studied (Plate 1A and 1E). Although most silica cement precipitated during early burial, some formed later as small pyramidal crystals in secondary pores (Fig. 8A and 8C). Approximately 5 to 15% of the primary porosity in the sandstones has been occluded by silica cementation.

Cementation and replacement by kaolinite also is extensive in the shallower sandstone reservoirs in the Patrick Draw area (Plate 1F, Figs. 7 B, C and 8B). Kaolinite replaces detrital chert and quartz grains, as well as shale rock fragments (Plate 2); it also replaces clay matrix where present. Much microporosity occurs within masses of kaolinite which occupy pores formed by dissolution of calcite cement, or where it has replaced detrital grains.

Formation of illite cement represents a major diagenetic stage in the history of the Almond, particularly in units at depths greater than 8,000 ft (2,400 m). This middle- to late-stage diagenetic event included the development of "flame-structured" and acicular illite and illite/smectite cements in secondary pores (Fig. 8C), or as overgrowths on detrital clay-rich grains or clay substrates (Fig. 8D). However, because the samples studied were not subjected to critical-point drying, the true *in situ* texture of the

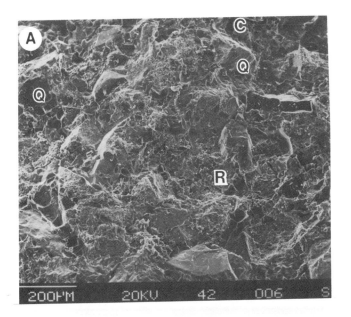

Figure 7. SEM images of sandstones from the Almond Formation.

A. Detrital quartz (Q) surrounded by microporous rock fragments (R) and carbonate cement (C). No large pores are visible. Sample from 4,480 ft (1,366 m), Forest Oil Corp., No. 63-2-2 Government.

B. Medium-grained sandstone in which many of the intergranular pores between detrital quartz grains (Q) are filled with masses of kaolinite (K). Sample from 4,494 ft (1,371 m), No. 63-2-2 Government. Area outlined in white appears in 7C.

C. Detail of area outlined in 7B. Note the abundant microporosity associated with kaolinite booklets.

D. Intergranular and intragranular porosity in a fine-grained sandstone. Sample from Forest Oil Corp. No. 3-19-2 Arch Unit. Area outlined in white appears in 7E.

E. Detail of area outlined in 7D. Intragranular pores formed by leaching of plagioclase feldspar. Some microporosity was created by this process. Such intragranular pores may not contribute much to permeability.

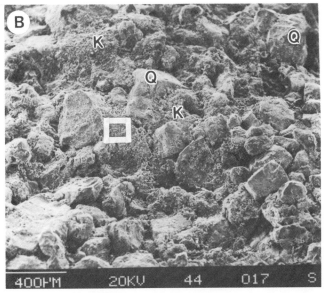

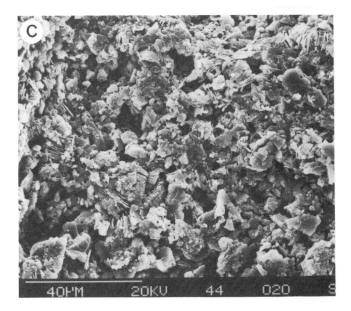

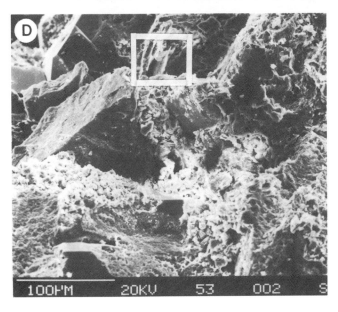

Figure 8. SEM images of authigenic clay and quartz in sandstones of the Almond Formation. Scale bars represent 10 microns.

A. Pyramidal quartz (Q) and flame-structured authigenic illitic (I) clay. Sample from 7,487 ft (2,284 m), Forest Oil Corp. No. 63-2-2 Arch Unit.

B. Extensive cementation and replacement by kaolinite. Sample from 4,491 ft (1,370 m), No. 63-2-2 Arch Unit.

C. Acicular illitic (I) clay in secondary pore. Clay is closely associated with authigenic quartz (Q); both authigenic phases may have coprecipitated, although illite may be later and replaces quartz. Clays appear to be easily damageable by fluid flow or acid reactions. Sample from 9,616 ft (2,933 m), Amoco Production Co. No. 1 Amoco Champlin 446 A.

D. Overgrowths of authigenic illite on detrital shale fragment. Again, sandstone may be easily damageable by workover fluids. Sample from 13,670 ft (4,169 m), Amoco Production Co. No. 1 Amoco Champlin 535 A.

illitic clays under reservoir conditions may be quite different than that observed in this investigation (Pallatt and others, 1984). Illitic clays partially replacing rock fragments were observed in thin sections over the depth range of 4,500 to 12,000 ft (1,400 to 3,700 m). The development of authigenic illite cements and overgrowths is thought to be due in part to the conversion of smectite to illite (Pollastro, 1985), and to the earlier dissolution of potassium feldspars within the sandstones and, perhaps, within interbedded shales.

RESERVOIR QUALITY

The diagenetic history of the Almond marine reservoirs is quite complex (Fig. 9). Due to the varied nature of the rocks and their diagenesis, their reservoir quality also is highly variable. Reservoir sandstones typically are fine to very fine–grained and commonly contain a significant volume of labile rock fragments such as chert and shale. These rock fragments make the reservoirs sensitive to compression, with consequent reduction of porosity and permeability (Plate 2). They also display variable degrees of alteration, including formation of microporosity through partial dissolution or replacement by clays.

Swelling clays were not common in the samples examined. However, the distribution and habits of kaolinite and illite in the sandstone suggest that the reservoirs may be sensitive to migration of fines during completion and production (Priisholm and others, 1987).

Porosity

Figures 10 and 11 are graphs of depth versus porosity and porosity versus vitrinite reflectance. The data are from conventional core analysis for 23 wells, the locations of which are given in Table 3 and shown in Figure 6.

Porosity commonly is presented by plotting porosity versus depth (Fig. 10). However, the apparent relationships between porosity and depth have come under critical review in recent years (Siever, 1983; Scherer, 1987; Schmoker and Gautier, 1988). Schmoker and Gautier suggest that thermal maturity,

a measure of integrated time–temperature history, is a better variable for porosity development, and permits inter–basinal comparison of rock sequences.

Figure 10 indicates a trend of decreasing porosity with depth of burial. The data plot in two populations, with slight overlap at a depth of approximately 9,000 ft (2,743 m) and porosity of 8%. In the shallower sandstones, porosity ranges up to 22% and corresponds to reservoirs generally considered conventional. In the deeper samples, porosity ranges from 3.5 to 8%, and relates primarily to unconventional reservoirs.

In Figure 11, a plot of porosity versus vitrinite reflectance, line "A" indicates a generic trend of decreasing porosity with increasing thermal maturity. Curve "B", composed of segments "B1", "B2", and "B3" indicates data from this study. The interpretation of the segments is highly speculative, but thought to be associated with the origin of abnormal pressures in low–permeability gas–bearing sequences (Law and Dickinson, 1985). These authors concluded that during the thermal generation of gas and the development of overpressuring, gas–saturated pore water was forcefully expelled from the overpressured rocks into overlying water–bearing, normally pressured rocks. We hypothesize that prior to dewatering and the development of overpressuring, the porosity curve for these sandstones was linear, and similar to curve "C"

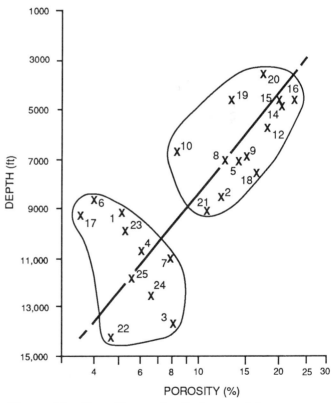

Figure 10. Porosity vs. depth for sandstone core samples from the Almond Formation. See Table 3 and Figure 6 for locations of wells. Note greater scatter in trend for low–permeability rocks as compared to higher–permeability rocks.

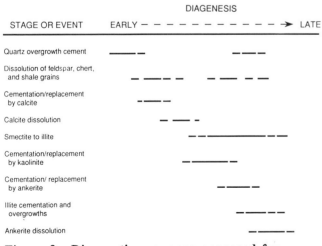

Figure 9. Diagenetic sequence proposed for sandstones in uppermost (marine) Almond Formation.

Table 3. Porosity, permeability, and vitrinite reflectance data from cores in the Almond Formation, southwestern Wyoming. Location of wells shown in Figure 6.

Well No.	Well Name	Location	Core Interval (ft)	Porosity (range and average %)	Permeability (range and average md)	R_o %
1	Colorado Interstate Gas 2-8-14-92 Blue Gap 11	SW1/4 SW1/4 Sec. 8 T. 14 N., R. 92 W.	9,059 – 9,091	1.7 – 10.0 (5.0)	0.01 – 5.9 (0.75)	0.80
2	Pan American Barrel Springs 3	NE1/4 NE1/4 Sec. 11 T. 16 N., R. 93 W.	8,407 – 8,441	7.4 – 16.1 (12.0)	0.01 – 0.30 (0.07)	0.70
3+	Amoco 1 Champlin 535 Amoco A	C SW1/4 Sec. 17 T. 16 N., R. 97 W.	13,645 – 13,674	2.4 – 11.5 (8.0)	0.02 – 1.7 (0.34)	1.64
4*+	Amoco Champlin 336 Amoco A-1	NE1/4 SW1/4 Sec. 21 T. 17 N., R. 94 W.	10,626 – 10,649	2.6 – 12.0 (5.9)	0.01 – 0.65 (0.08)	1.12 P
5	Champlin Higgins 13A	NW1/4 NE1/4 Sec. 7 T. 17 N. R. 98 W.	6,992 – 7,013	8.2 – 17.1 (13.8)	0.02 – 1.9 (0.48)	0.59
6	Amoco 1 Champlin 440 Amoco A	NW1/4 NW1/4 Sec. 11 T. 17 N., R. 98 W.	8,590 – 8,638	1.5 – 6.2 (3.9)	<0.01 – 4.9 (0.35)	0.84
7	Amoco 1 Champlin 534	C SW1/4 Sec. 31 T. 18 N., R. 96 W.	10,969 – 10, 990	3.9 – 11.0 (7.8)	0.02 – 0.1 (0.07)	0.76
8	Champlin Federal 44-4	SE1/4 SE1/4 Sec. 4 T. 18 N., R. 98 W.	6,841 – 6,897	2.3 – 19.2 12.4	0.03 – 24.0 (2.40)	0.75
9	Champlin UPRR 44-9-2	SE1/4 SE1/4 Sec. 9 T. 18 N., R. 98 W.	6,780 – 6,836	10.5 – 17.5 (14.6)	0.24 – 6.06 (1.83)	0.71
10	Texaco Table Rock 68	NE1/4 SW1/4 Sec. 19 T. 19 N., R. 97 W.	6,577 – 6,731	0.8 – 17.7 (8.1)	<0.01 – 2.39 (0.33)	0.73
11*	Marathon 1-23 Tierney II	C SW1/4 Sec. 23 T. 19 N., R. 94 W.	*	N.A.	N.A.	N.A.
12	Forest 9-G-1	SW1/4 NE1/4 Sec. 9 T. 19 N., R. 98 W.	5,754 – 5,770	14.0 – 21.4 (17.7)	0.23 – 41.0 (12.02)	0.62
13	Forest 3-19-2 Arch	SW1/4 SW1/4 Sec. 19 T. 19 N., R. 98 W.	*	N.A.	N.A.	N.A.
14	Forest 1-8 Arch 70	SE1/4 NE1/4 Sec. 1 T. 19 N., R. 99 W.	4,794 – 4,812	11.5 – 23.9 (19.8)	3.1 – 102 (23.57)	0.68 P
15*+	Forest 63-2-2 Arch	SE1/4 SE1/4 Sec. 2 T. 19 N., R. 99 W.	4,485 – 4,527	14.9 – 23.2 (19.5)	1.5 – 88.0 (31.0)	0.67
16	Fores 20-23-4 Arch	SW1/4 NE1/4 Sec. 21 T. 19 N., R. 99 W.	4,497 – 4,528	18.8 – 25.6 (22.1)	0.21 – 135 (43.96)	0.57 P
17	Amoco Champlin 441 Amoco A	C SE1/4 Sec. 21 T. 20 N., R. 95 W.	9,142 – 9,178	0.9 – 5.7 (3.5)	0.01 – 0.09 (0.03)	0.80
18+	Forest Mustang 1-22-1	NE1/4 SE1/4 Sec. 22 T. 20 N., R. 97 W.	7,452 – 7,513	12.3 – 18.9 (16.1)	<0.01 – 0.9 (0.4)	0.60
19	Luff 1-23 Champlin-Playa	SE1/4 SE1/4 Sec. 23 T. 20 N., R. 99 W.	4,577 – 4,600	7.6 – 16.7 (13.0)	0.08 – 13.0 (2.94)	0.60
20	Luff 4-29 Champlin	NW1/4 SE1/4 Sec. 29 T. 20 N., R. 99 W.	3,474 – 3,481	14.7 – 19.6 (17.3)	0.43 – 18.0 (7.9)	0.47 P
21	Amoco Champlin 527 Amoco A-1	C SW1/4 Sec. 19 T. 21 N., R. 95 W.	8,971 – 9,061	2.3 – 15.2 (10.7)	0.01 – 0.93 (0.20)	0.65
22	Amoco 1 Champlin 446 Amoco A	NE1/4 SW1/4 Sec. 15 T. 22 N., R. 90 W.	14,256 – 14,271	1.0 – 8.1 (4.5)	0.01 – 0.14 (0.07)	1.34
23*+	Amoco 438 Amoco A	C SE1/4 Sec. 5 T. 22 N., R. 96 W.	9,910 – 9,931	3.6 – 7.9 (5.1)	0.08 – 0.22 (0.11)	0.82
24	Michigan-Wisconsin Red Desert 1-33	NW1/4 SE1/4 Sec. 33 T. 24 N., R. 94 W.	12,515 – 12,586	3.4 – 9.1 (6.5)	<0.01 (<0.01)	1.64 P
25+	Energy Reserves 2-24 Nickey	NW1/4 SE1/4 Sec. 24 T. 24 N., R. 96 W.	11,884 – 11,916	1.8 – 7.6 (5.3)	<0.01 – 1.8 (0.18)	1.60

+samples studied by x-ray diffraction and (or) in thin section; data are summarized in Tables 1 and 2.
*samples for special core analyses data are summarized in Table 4; R_o = vitrinite reflectance. P = projected vitrinite reflectance values from interval above or below cored interval shown; N.A. = not available.

in Figure 11. Subsequent to the initiation of over-pressuring, curve "C" was modified into the non-linear trend represented by curve "B".

Thus, the "B2" segment represents a transitional state between normally pressured, water-bearing rocks and overpressured, gas-bearing rocks. Segment "B1" represents samples from normally pressured conventional reservoirs. We suggest that the more steeply sloping "B2" segment represents reduction of porosity due to precipitation of minerals from gas-saturated fluids which originated in overpressured rocks. The intersection of the "B2" and "B3" segments at a vitrinite reflectance value of 0.8% is interpreted to mark the top of overpressuring. In southwestern Wyoming, the top of overpressuring commonly occurs at vitrinite reflectance values of approximately 0.8% (Law, 1984).

Porosity along curve segment "B3" increases from 4.0 to 6.5%, possibly due to dissolution porosity created by the migration of gas-saturated fluids from overpressured rocks. This apparent increase in porosity may, however, be a function of incomplete data. Law and Dickinson (1985) suggest that, in overpressured rocks, porosity may not change significantly, because the pore system in these rocks is relatively closed.

Another potentially important aspect of the development of porosity is the observation by Law, et al. (1986) of evidence that sandstone reservoirs in the Almond Formation in the Patrick Draw fields had ex-perienced a heating event. They concluded that the unusually high levels of thermal maturity in these fields were due to hot fluids migrating upward along faults and fractures. Under these conditions, porosity could have been enhanced or decreased, depending on composition of the fluids.

Permeability and Pore-Throat Sizes

Porosity–permeability data from the same wells as discussed above display two distinct permeability domains (Fig. 12). The more porous sandstones show a well-defined trend of increasing permeability with greater porosity. However, data from the low-porosity/low-permeability rocks display greater scatter and a poorly defined trend. The reasons for this poor correlation are not completely understood, but may be related to the lesser accuracy of conventionally determined permeabilities in low-permeability rocks. In addition, low-permeability rocks are very sensitive to stress, and may react unpredictably to stress reduction during core retrieval. Our investigations as well as those of numerous other investigators (Vairogs, 1971;

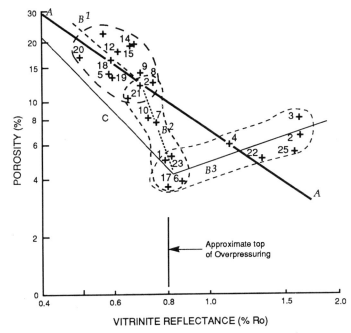

Figure 11. Porosity vs. vitrinite reflectance for core samples from the Almond Formation. See Table 3 and Figure 6 for locations of wells. Curve A is a generic relationship. Curves B1 – B3 are visual best-fit lines through each of the domains outlined. Curve C is a hypothetical porosity-vitrinite reflectance trend during early burial. Development of secondary porosity by fluids associated with gas generation is inferred from data.

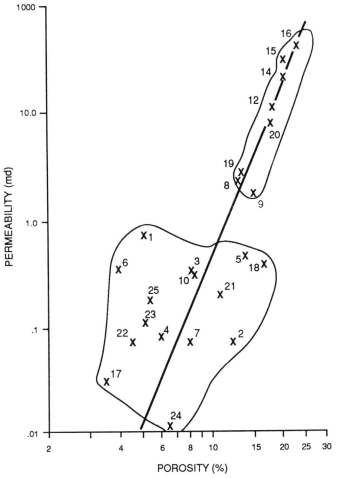

Figure 12. Permeability vs. porosity for sandstone core samples from the Almond Formation, showing visual best-fit correlation of the data. Numbers refer to wells listed in Table 3 and shown in Figure 6. Note greater scatter for low-permeability rocks as compared to higher-permeability rocks.

Thomas and Ward, 1972; Jones and Owens, 1980; Keighin and Sampath, 1982; Sampath and Keighin, 1982; Brower and Morrow, 1983; Ostensen, 1983) indicate that low–permeability rocks are much more sensitive to confining stress than are high–permeability rocks (Table 4). Pore throats in Almond sandstones commonly are smaller than one micron, based on thin sections and on mercury injection–capillary pressure data from five wells (Fig. 13).

CONCLUSIONS

Through 1986, the conventional reservoirs in the Almond Formation accounted for almost all of the oil and 80% of the gas produced in the study area. Graphs of porosity vs. depth and porosity vs. vitrinite reflectance seem to provide a method of distinguishing between conventional and unconventional reservoirs. Boundary conditions between these types of reservoirs occur at a depth of approximately 9,000 ft (2,750 m), vitrinite reflectance of about 0.8%, and porosity of approximately 8%.

Most of the effective porosity in Almond reservoirs is secondary, produced by the dissolution of detrital mineral grains or earlier diagenetic cements. The nature and distribution of pores and associated narrow pore throats, in conjunction with widely distributed authigenic illite and kaolinite, indicate that the reservoirs should be sensitive to formation damage (Krueger, 1986). Many of the sandstones are very sensitive to the changes in confining stress that occur during production. Mineralogy and pore geometry should be taken into consideration in order to minimize potential formation damage during drilling, completion, stimulation, or production of wells.

The evolution of porosity was dramatically affected by generation of overpressures and migration of gas into the reservoirs. The normal reduction of porosity attendant with increases in depth was altered or even halted in some cases.

ACKNOWLEDGMENTS

This work was funded by the U.S. Department of Energy under Interagency Agreement DE–A121–83MC20422. We appreciate the help of Doug Battin, Home Petroleum Corp.; Van Leighton, Amoco Production Co.; Dave Reffert, Celsius Energy Co.; and Lee Robinson, Union Pacific Resources for providing porosity and permeability data in selected areas.

REFERENCES

Bader, J.W., J.R. Gill, W.A. Cobbin, and B.E. Law, 1983, Biostratigraphic correlation chart of some Upper Cretaceous rocks from the Lost Soldier area, Wyoming, to west of Craig, Colorado: USGS Misc. Field Studies MF–1548.

Barlow, J.A., Jr., 1961, Almond Formation and Lower Lewis Shale, east flank of Rock Springs uplift, Sweetwater County, Wyoming: WGA Guidebook, 16th Ann. Field Conf., p. 113–115.

Brower, K.R., and N.R. Morrow, 1983, Fluid flow in cracks as related to low-permeability gas sands: SPE/DOE preprint 11623, SPE/DOE Symposium on Low Permeability Reservoirs, Denver, CO, March 14–16, p. 201–212.

Burton, G., 1961, Patrick Draw area, Sweetwater County, Wyoming: WGA, 16th Ann. Field Conf., p. 276–279.

Coalson, E.B., 1979, Wildrose field: WGA, Wyoming Oil and Gas Fields Symposium, Greater Green River Basin, p. 423.

Cox, J.E., 1962, Patrick Draw area, Sweetwater County, Wyoming: BGS Paper no. 1, p. 1–17.

Dickinson, W.W., 1985, Isotope geochemistry of carbonate minerals in nonmarine rocks; northern Green River Basin, Wyoming: unpub. PhD diss., U. of CO, Boulder, 150 p.

Earl, J.H., and J.N. Dahm, 1961, Case history – Desert Springs gas field, Sweetwater County, Wyoming: Geophysics, v. 16, p. 673–682.

Hale, L.A., 1950, Stratigraphy of the upper Cretaceous Montana Group in the Rock Springs uplift, Sweetwater County, Wyoming: WGA Guidebook, 5th Ann. Field Conf., p. 49–58.

Harbridge, C.B., 1980, Wamsutter Arch tight gas play, southern Wyoming – new look at an old area [abs.]: AAPG Bull., v. 64, p. 718.

Hoffman, J., and J. Hower, 1979, Clay mineral assemblages as low-grade metamorphic geothermometers – application to the thrust faulted disturbed belt of Montana, U.S.A., *in* P.A. Scholle and P.K. Schluger, eds., Aspects of Diagenesis: SEPM Spec. Pub. 26, p. 55–79.

Jacka, A.D., 1965, Depositional dynamics of the Almond Formation, Rock Springs uplift, Wyoming: WGA Guidebook, 19th Ann. Field Conf., p. 81–100.

Jacka, A.D., 1970, Principles of cementation and porosity-occlusion in upper Cretaceous sandstones, Rocky Mountain region: WGA Guidebook, 22nd Ann. Field Conf., p. 265–285.

Jones, F.O., and W.W. Owens, 1980, A laboratory study of low-permeability gas sands: JPT, v. 32, p. 1631–1640.

Keighin, C.W., and K. Sampath, 1982, Evaluation of pore geometry of some low-permeability sandstones, Uinta Basin, Utah: JPT, v. 34, p. 65–70.

Krueger, R.F., 1986, An overview of formation damage and well productivity in oilfield operations: JPT, v. 38, p. 131–152.

Land, L.S., and S.p. Dutton, 1978, Cementation of a Pennsylvanian deltaic sandstone – isotopic data: JSP, v. 48, p. 1167–1176.

Lanham, R.E., 1980, Petrography and diagenesis of low-permeability sandstones of the lower Almond Formation, southwestern Wyoming: U. of CO, unpub. MS thesis, Dept. of Geological Sciences, 113 p.

Law, B.E., 1984, Relationships of source-rocks, thermal maturity, and over-pressuring to gas generation and occurrence in low-permeability Upper Cretaceous and Lower Tertiary rocks, Greater Green River Basin, Wyoming, Colorado, and Utah, *in* J. Woodward, F.F. Meissner, and J.L. Clayton, eds., Hydrocarbon Source Rocks of the Greater Rocky Mountain Region: RMAG, p. 469–490.

Law, B.E., and W.W. Dickinson, 1985, Conceptual model for origin of abnormally pressured gas accumulations in low-permeability reservoirs: AAPG Stud. in Geol. 24, p. 253–269.

Law, B.E., M.R. Lickus, and M.J. Pawlewicz, 1986, Fluid migration pathways: Evidence from thermal maturity mapping in southwestern Wyoming [abs.], *in* L.M.H. Carter, ed., USGS Research on Energy Resources–1985, Program and Abstracts: USGS Circ. 974, p. 35.

Lawson, D.C., and C.W. Crowson, 1961, Geology of the Arch Unit and adjacent areas, Sweetwater County, Wyoming: WGA Guidebook, 16th Ann. Field Conf., p. 280–299.

Lewis, J.L., 1961, The stratigraphy and depositional history of the Almond Formation in the Great Divide Basin, Sweetwater County, Wyoming: WGA Guidebook, 16th Ann. Field Conf., p. 87–95.

Lickus, M.R., and B.E. Law, 1988, Structure contour map of the Greater Green River Basin, Wyoming, Colorado, and Utah: USGS Misc. Field Studies MF–2031.

May, B.E., 1961, The Desert Springs Field: WGA Guidebook, 16th Ann. Field Conf., p. 290–293.

McCubbin, D.C., and M.C. Brady, 1969, Depositional environment of the Almond reservoirs, Patrick Draw Field, Wyoming: Mtn. Geol., v. 6, p. 3–26.

Mees, E.C., J.D. Capen, and J.C. McGee, 1961, Table Rock Field, Sweetwater County, Wyoming: WGA Guidebook, 16th Ann. Field Conf., p. 294–300.

Meyers, W.W., 1977, Environmental analysis of Almond Formation (Upper Cretaceous) from the Rock Springs uplift, Wyoming: unpub. PhD diss., Tulsa U., 366 p.

Ostensen, R.W., 1983, Microcrack permeability in tight gas sandstone: SPEJ, December, p. 919–927.

Table 4. Summary of data relating conditions under which porosity, Klinkenberg permeability, and pore volume compressibility were measured, and response of samples from different depths in various fields. See Table 3 for location of wells.

Depth (ft)	Confining Pressure (psia)#	Porosity (%)	Percent Ambient Porosity	Klinkenberg Permeability (md)	Percent Ambient Perm.	Pore Volume Compressibility (cc/cc/psi)
FOREST OIL CORPORATION NO. 63-2-2 UNIT						
(see Table 3, no. 15)						
4480	ambient*	1.1	100.0	0.026	100.0	
	1750	1.0	98.4	–	–	
	2250	1.0	88.3	0.0013	5.0	
	2750	1.0	87.8	0.0068	2.6	2×10^{-6}
4487	ambient	18.2	100.0	1.88	100.0	
	1750	17.5	96.3	–	–	
	2250	17.2	94.5	1.64	87.2	
	2750	17.0	93.2	1.54	81.9	8×10^{-6}
4494	ambient	21.2	100.0	42.4	100.0	
	1750	18.1	85.2	–	–	
	2250	18.0	84.9	31.5	74.3	
	2750	17.9	84.4	27.5	64.9	3×10^{-6}
4519	ambient	21.0	100.0	36.6	100.0	
	1750	19.4	92.1	–	–	
	2250	19.3	91.8	26.9	73.5	
	2750	19.3	91.3	26.2	71.6	4×10^{-6}
4527	ambient	14.7	100.0	0.485	100.0	
	1750	14.5	98.3	–	–	
	2250	14.4	98.1	0.275	56.7	
	2750	14.4	97.7	0.248	51.1	3×10^{-6}
FOREST OIL CORPORATION NO. 3-19-2 UNIT						
(see Table 3, no. 13)						
4969	ambient	22.3	100.0	55.3	100.0	
	2000	20.1	90.1	–	–	
	2500	19.9	89.2	38.6	69.8	
	3000	19.9	89.0	37.1	67.1	4×10^{-6}
4969[1]	ambient	20.1	100.0	11.1	100.0	
	2000	17.3	86.1	–	–	
	2500	17.2	85.5	8.67	74.1	
	3000	17.1	85.1	7.44	63.6	5×10^{-6}
4971a[1]	ambient	18.7	100.0	8.68	100.0	
	2000	16.8	89.9	–	–	
	2500	16.7	89.8	5.25	60.5	
	3000	16.7	89.2	4.39	50.6	3×10^{-6}
4971b	ambient	21.2	100.0	5.05	100.0	
	2000	16.5	78.1	–	–	
	2500	16.4	77.5	3.38	66.9	
	3000	16.4	77.4	3.28	65.0	4×10^{-6}
4983.5	ambient	17.2	100.0	18.1	100.0	
	2000	16.0	93.3	–	–	
	2500	15.9	92.6	14.1	77.9	
	3000	15.8	92.2	13.4	74.0	5×10^{-6}
4983.5[1]	ambient	20.8	100.0	20.7	100.0	
	2000	16.9	81.4	–	–	
	2500	16.4	80.9	16.3	78.7	
	3000	16.4	80.6	15.9	76.8	3×10^{-6}

(Table 4. Contiued)

Depth (ft)	Confining Pressure (psia)	Porosity (%)	Percent Ambient Porosity	Klinkenberg Permeability (md)	Percent Ambient Perm.	Pore Volume Compressibility (cc/cc/psi)
AMOCO PRODUCTION COMPANY NO. 1 AMOCO-CHAMPLIN 336 A						
(see Table 3, no. 4)						
10,626.5	ambient	6.2	100.0	0.054	100.0	
	4800	6.0	97.2	–	–	
	5300	6.0	96.6	0.0001	0.2	
	5800	6.0	96.7	<0.0001	0.0	9×10^{-7}
AMOCO PRODUCTION COMPANY NO. 1 AMOCO-CHAMPLIN 438 A						
(see Table 3, no. 23)						
9658.7	ambient	9.6	100.0	0.118	100.0	
	4250	9.2	95.1	–	–	
	4750	9.1	94.2	0.0059	5.0	
	5200	9.0	93.1	0.0021	1.8	4×10^{-6}
9660.2	ambient	11.1	100.0	0.073	100.0	
	4350	10.8	96.9	–	–	
	4850	10.8	96.7	0.0049	6.7	
	5350	10.7	96.5	0.0048	6.6	7×10^{-7}
9691	ambient	12.4	100.0	0.354	100.0	
	4350	12.1	97.0	–	–	
	4850	12.0	96.0	0.01202	2.9	
	5350	12.0	96.4	0.0093	2.6	1×10^{-6}
MARATHON OIL COMPANY NO. 1-24 TIERNEY II						
(see Table 3, no. 11)						
9495[2]	ambient	2.3	100.0	0.0617	100.0	
	4250	2.2	95.6	–	–	
	4750	2.2	95.4	0.0068	11.0	
	5250	2.2	95.0	0.0064	10.4	2×10^{-6}
9885	ambient	10.1	100.0	0.0742	100.0	
	4450	10.1	99.9	–	–	
	4950	10.1	99.7	0.0194	26.1	
	5450	10.1	99.6	0.0145	19.5	7×10^{-7}

\# Confining pressures at which Klinkenberg permeability and helium porosity were determined are 500 psi less than half the sample depth; half the sample depth; and 500 psi greater than the sample depth.
* Ambient conditions are 0 psi for porosity measurements and 250 psi for permeability measurements.
[1] Plug cut perpendicular to bedding.
[2] Fractured.

Pallatt, N., J. Wilson, and B. McHardy, 1984, The relationship between permeability and the morphology of diagenetic illite in reservoir rocks: JPT, v, 36, p. 2225-2227.

Pittman, J.K., T.D. Fouch, and M.B. Goldhaber, 1982, Depositional setting and diagenetic evolution of some Tertiary unconventional reservoir rocks, Uinta basin, Utah: AAPG Bull., v. 66, p. 1581-1596.

Pollastro, R.M., 1985, Mineralogical and morphological evidence for the formation of illite at the expense of illite/smectite: Clays and Clay Minerals, v. 33, p. 265-274.

Priisholm, A., B.L. Nielson, and O. Haslund, 1987, Fines migration, blocking, and clay swelling of potential geothermal sandstone reservoirs, Denmark: SPE Formation Evaluation, v. 2, p. 168-178.

Reynolds, M.W., 1976, Influence of recurrent Laramide structural growth on sedimentation and petroleum accumulation, Lost Soldier area, Wyoming: AAPG Bull., v. 60, p. 12-32.

Reynolds, R.C., Jr. and J. Hower, 1970, The nature of interlayering in mixed-layer illite-montmorillonites: Clays and Clay Minerals, v. 18, p. 25-36.

Sampath, K., and C.W. Keighin, 1982, Factors affecting gas slippage in tight sandstones of Cretaceous age in the Uinta Basin: JPT, v. 34, p. 2715-2720.

Scherer, M., 1987, Parameters influencing porosity in sandstones: a model for sandstone porosity prediction: AAPG Bull., v. 71, p. 485-491.

Schmoker, J.W., and D.L. Gautier, 1988, Sandstone porosity as a function of thermal maturity: Geology, v. 16, p. 1007-1010.

Schultz, A.R., 1909, The northern part of the Rock Springs coal field, Sweetwater County, Wyoming: USGS Bull. 341-B, p. 256-282.

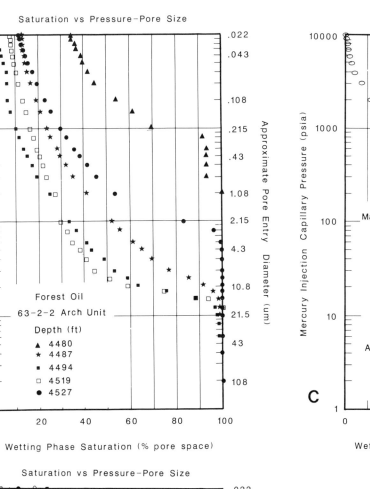

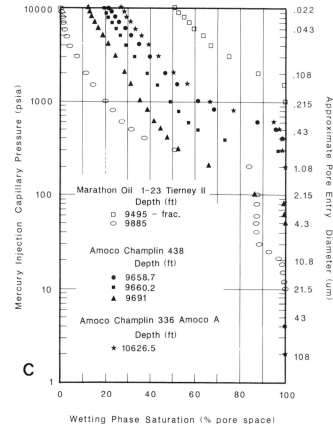

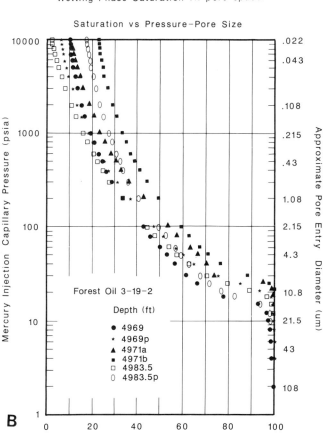

Figure 13. Mercury injection-capillary pressure and calculated pore-throat sizes. Porosities and permeabilities for each sample are summarized in Table 4. Well locations are found in Table 3 and on Figure 6. Size and size-sorting of pore throats is moderate to poor in all cases.

A. Samples from Patrick Draw Field. Small pore throats in sample from depth of 4,480 ft (1,366 m) are due to the presence of abundant carbonate cement (Plate 1B). Pore throats for other samples show some variability, but breakthrough of mercury indicates effective size of pore throats is approximately 15 microns.

B. Patrick Draw Field, Forest Oil Corp. No. 3-19-2. These samples are more homogeneous than those illustrated in Figure 13A. Entry of injected mercury indicates nearly uniform distribution of pore-throat sizes between samples; mercury entry begins with pore throats of approximately 10 microns.

C. Samples from deeper sandstone reservoirs. Note wide variation in pore-throat sizes. This variation is due in part to differences in grain size, amount of carbonate cement present, and presence or absence of microfractures. This scatter is reflected in the porosity-permeability relationships (Fig. 12).

Sears, J.D., 1924, Geology and oil and gas prospects of part of Moffat County, Colorado and Sweetwater County, Wyoming: USGS Bull. 751, p. 269–319.

Siever, R., 1983, Burial history and diagenetic reaction kinetics: AAPG Bull., v. 67, p. 684–691.

Stephenson, T.R., A.J. VerPloeg, and L.S. Chamberlain, 1984, Oil and Gas Map of Wyoming: Geological Survey of WY, Map Series MS-12.

Thomas, J.B., 1978, Diagenetic sequences in low–permeability argillaceous sandstones: Journal of the Geological Society, v. 135, pt. 1, p. 93–99.

Thomas, R.D., and D.C. Ward, 1972, Effect of overburden pressure and water saturations on gas permeability of tight sandstone cores: JPT, v. 24, p. 120–124.

Vairogs, J., C.L. Hearn, D.W. Dareing, and V.W. Rhodes, 1971, Effect of rock stress on gas production from low- permeability reservoirs: JPT, v. 23, p. 1161–1167.

Van Horn, M.D., 1979, Stratigraphy of the Almond Formation, east-central flank of the Rock Springs uplift, Sweetwater County, Wyoming: a mesotidal shoreline model for the late Cretaceous: unpub. MS thesis, CSM, 150 p.

Wardlaw, N.C., and J.p. Cassan, 1979, Oil recovery efficiency and the rock-pore properties of some sandstone reservoirs: Bulletin Canadian Petroleum Geology, v. 27, no. 2, p. 117–138.

Weimer, R.J., 1960, Upper Cretaceous stratigraphy, Rocky Mountain area: AAPG Bull., v. 44, p. 1–20.

Weimer, R.J., 1961, Uppermost Cretaceous rocks in central and southern Colorado: WGA Guidebook, 16th Ann. Field Conf., p. 17–28.

Weimer, R.J., 1965, Stratigraphy and petroleum occurrences, Almond and Lewis Formations (Upper Cretaceous), Wamsutter arch, Wyoming: WGA Guidebook, 19th Ann. Field Conf., p. 65–81.

Weimer, R.J., 1966, Time-stratigraphic analysis and petroleum accumulation, Patrick Draw Field, Sweetwater County, Wyoming: AAPG Bull., v. 50, p. 2150–2175.

White, V.L., 1955, Table Rock and Southwest Table Rock gas fields: WGA Guidebook, 10th Ann. Field Conf., p. 170–171.

Wyoming Geological Association, 1979, Wyoming Oil and Gas Fields Symposium, Greater Green River Basin, 2 volumes, 428 p.

Wyoming Oil and Gas Conservation Commission, 1987, Wyoming oil and gas fields and units of production, 1986, part I, in Wyoming Oil and Gas Statistics, 87 p.

Fine grained sandstone in which feldspar (F) grains are commonly leached, and pores are partially to completely filled with authigenic kaolinite (K). Point Lookout sandstone, Sec 5 T32N R13Q, La Plata Co., Colorado. Depth 925 ft (282 m). Photo donated by Bill Keighin.

Appendix I—Color Plates

Conceptual Models for the Prediction of Porosity Evolution with an Example from the Frontier Sandstone, Bighorn Basin, Wyoming

Ronald C. Surdam, Thomas L. Dunn, Donald B. MacGowan, Henry P. Heasler

PLATE 1. Thin-section photomicrographs of Frontier and Wagon Bed sandstones, Bighorn Basin, Wyoming.

A. Partially dissolved hornblende grain rimmed with smectite, Fe-Mn oxides, and heulandite. Upper Eocene Wagon Bed Formation, Wyoming. Field of view is 1.5 mm.

B. Fine-grained feldspathic lithic arenite of the Frontier Formation, illustrating feldspar and quartz overgrowths. A partially dissolved and albitized feldspar also is visible. From Bighorn Basin axis, depth of 8,270 ft (2,533 m). Partially crossed polars.

C. Moldic porosity after feldspar, with relict authigenic feldspar overgrowths. Upper Frontier Formation, upper fine-grained feldspathic lithic arenite. Minute dark nodules of siderite (s) also are visible; note the many grain-to-grain contacts.

D. Carbonate cement formed prior to quartz overgrowth development, but after significant grain-packing changes and ductile grain deformation. Upper Frontier Formation, very fine-grained laminated lithic quartz arenite, Bighorn Basin axis. Sample from depth of 14,670 ft (4,495 m).

E. Vermicular kaolinite and dissolved feldspar grain in upper fine-grained feldspathic litharenite. Upper Frontier Formation, west flank of the Bighorn Basin, 2,401 ft (730 m).

F. Dolomite cement in a medium-grained Frontier sandstone. West flank of the Bighorn Basin, 2,387 ft (731 m).

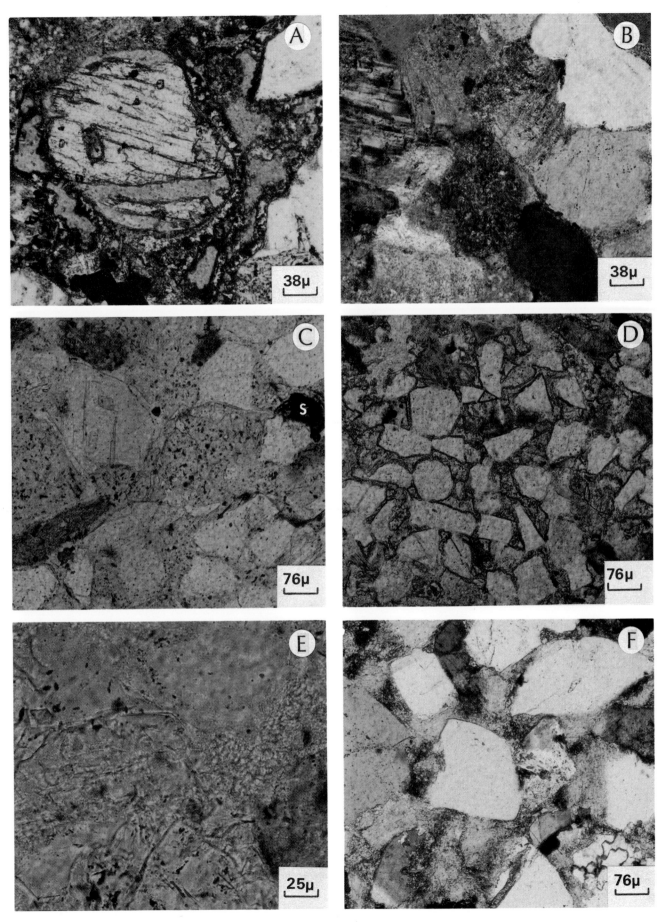

Conceptual Models for the Prediction of Porosity Evolution with an Example from the Frontier Sandstone, Bighorn Basin, Wyoming (continued)

PLATE 2. Thin-section photomicrographs of Frontier sandstones, Bighorn Basin, Wyoming.

A. Late pore-filling and replacive carbonate cement (post-quartz and feldspar overgrowths) in an upper fine-grained, feldspathic, lithic arenite from the Frontier Formation, Bighorn Basin axis, 14,719.5 ft (4,510.1 m). Crossed polars.

B. Microporous molds of microcrystalline rock fragments (upper left) in a quartz cemented upper fine-grained, feldspathic, lithic arenite. The quartz overgrowths have included sparse chlorite rosettes (the dark spots). Chlorite also occurs in the microporous fragment molds. Bighorn Basin axis, 14,719.5 ft (4,510.1 m).

C. Chlorite rosettes occur as late pore-filling cement associated with the partial dissolution of rock fragments. Chlorite and quartz overgrowths show ambiguous textural relations, usually indicative of contemporaneous growth. Much of the chlorite appears to have formed after quartz overgrowth formation. Small amounts of chlorite are visible as inclusions in incomplete quartz overgrowths. Bighorn Basin axis, 14,719.5 ft (4,501.1 m).

D. Late (formed after quartz overgrowth development) dissolution of carbonate cement in a fine-grained, lithic arenite. Bighorn Basin axis, 8,270 ft (2,533.9 m).

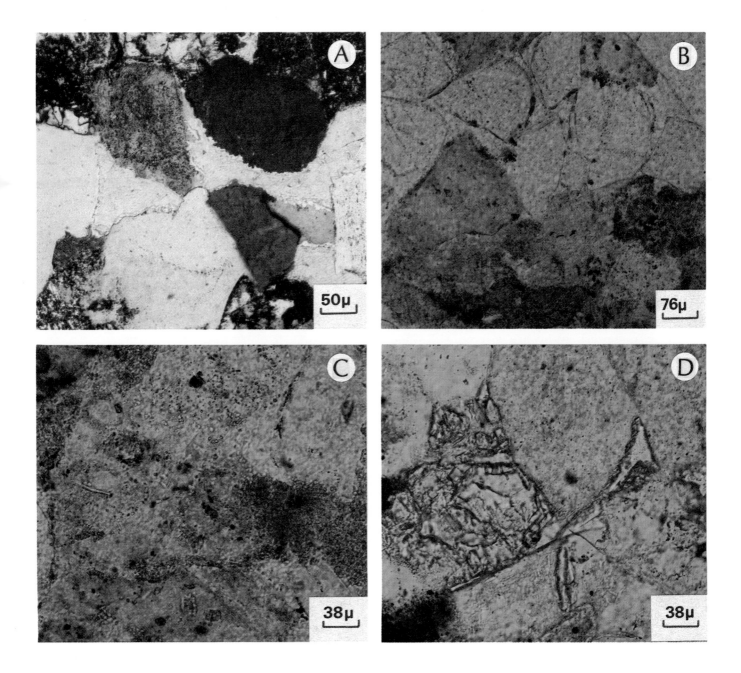

Sedimentology, Diagenesis, and Reservoir Potential of the Pennsylvanian Tyler Formation, Central Montana

Peter T. Stanton, Matthew R. Silverman

PLATE 1. Petrographic information, Tyler sandstones

A. Low magnification view of a typical well sorted, medium–grained quartzarenite. Porosity (stained blue) is comprised of intergranular and grain–dissolution pores. Sample from Polumbus No. 1–6 Kincheloe, 4,779.8 ft (1,455.9 m), plane light.

B. Sequential cementation by ferroan dolomite (stained dark blue, D) followed by calcite (stained pink). Dissolution of calcite has generated secondary porosity (P). Dead oil (arrows) forms brown meniscus rims on the calcite surface, indicating that oil infiltration followed calcite dissolution. Sample from Petro–Lewis No. 15–5 Mang, plane light.

C. Cementation by poikilotopic crystals of ferroan dolomite (stained dark blue) and anhydrite (pale yellow). Ferroan dolomite exhibits a euhedral crystal face against anhydrite (arrow) suggesting that dolomite postdates and locally replaces anhydrite. Sample from Polumbus No. 1–6 Kincheloe, 4,779.8 ft (1,455.9 m), crossed polars.

D. Crystal aggregates of rhombohedral siderite (arrow) in a pore throat. Surrounding framework grains are covered with smooth syntaxial quartz overgrowths (Q) which locally engulf siderite rhombs. The scale bar (long bar, upper left) is ten microns. Sample from GPE No. 71 Ranch, 4,818.0 ft (1,467.6 m).

E. Brown, spheroidal siderite which has partially filled intergranular pores. Reflected light microscopy indicates that opaque bands in some spheroids (arrow) are pyrite. Sample from GPE No. 71 Ranch, 4,835.1 ft (1,472.8 m), plane light.

F. Sequential cementation by chlorite (C) followed by syntaxial quartz overgrowths (Q) and ferroan dolomite (D). The dolomite crystal is replacing a brown mudstone fragment. Sample from GPE No. 3 BNI, plane light.

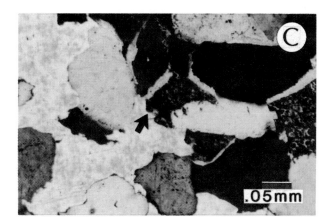

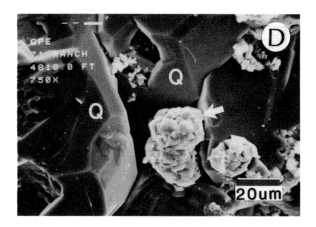

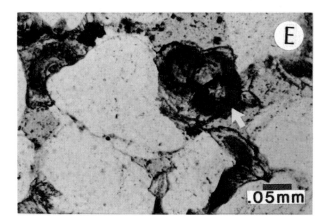

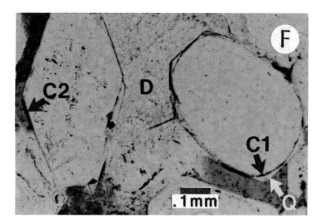

Sedimentology, Diagenesis, and Reservoir Potential of the Pennsylvanian Tyler Formation, Central Montana (continued)

PLATE 2. Petrographic information, Tyler Sandstone

A. Brown and white, banded, authigenic silica (right of center) which probably was precipitated as opaline cement. A thin band of siderite (S) occurs in the silica layers. A large dissolution void is filled with anhydrite (A) and ferroan dolomite (D). Opaque grains are hematitic rock fragments. Sample from GPE No. 3 BNI, 4,859.3 ft (1,480.1 m)), plane light.

B. Spheroidal siderite (S) rimmed by radial quartz crystals (Q) forms an authigenic siderite–quartz concretion. Authigenic chlorite (arrow) has precipitated on the quartz surface. Sample from GPE No. 3 BNI, 4,847.1 ft (1,476.4 m), plane light.

C. Dissolution of the core of a ferroan dolomite rhomb (center) suggests compositional zoning in the crystal. Dolomite abuts euhedral quartz overgrowths and pore-filling kaolinite (K). The scale bar (long bar at upper left) is ten microns. Sample from Marnell No. 1 Hydra Federal, 1,182.5 ft (360.2 m).

D. Replacement of anhydrite (blue–green) by kaolinite (K) is evidenced by the caried margin of the anhydrite crystal (arrow). Sample from Polumbus No. 1–6 Kincheloe, 4,775.9 ft (1,454.7 m), crossed polars.

E. Sequential cementation by chlorite (platy, grain–rimming crystals), quartz overgrowths (Q), and pore–filling anhydrite (A). Grooves in the surface of anhydrite indicate partial dissolution. Curved indentations in anhydrite formed where the crystal was in contact with other framework grains. The scale bar (long bar at upper left) is ten microns. Sample from GPE No. 3 BNI, 4,836.0 ft (1,473.0 m).

F. Dissolution of a ferroan dolomite rhomb (arrow, stained dark blue) has left a thin crystal rim. The leached interior of the rhomb is partially filled with pyrite (black, opaque mineral) and calcite (stained pink). Sample from Marnell No. 1 Hydra Federal, 1,182.5 ft (360.2 m), plane light.

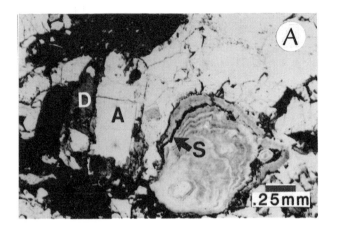

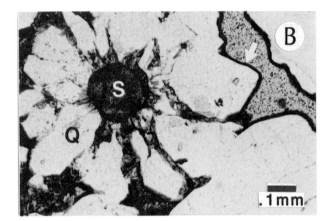

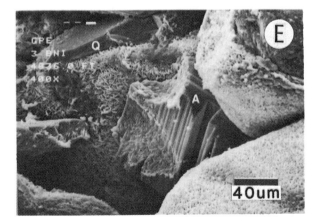

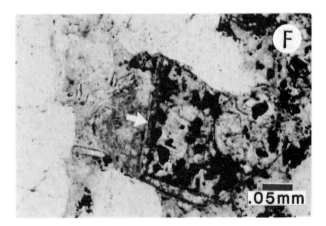

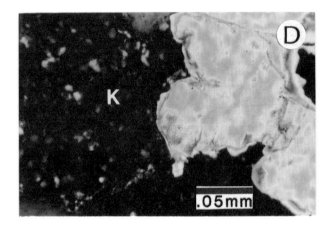

Petrologic Character of a Morrowan Sandstone Reservoir, Lexington Field, Clark County, Kansas

Martin Emery, Peter G. Sutterlin

PLATE 1. Photomicrographs of Morrowan "A" sandstones.

A. Glauconitic (G), cherty (Ch) quartz arenite. Porosity is filled with blue–dyed epoxy. Scale bar is 0.1 mm. Plane light.

B. Silica cementation (S), underlying dust rims (DR), carbonate cement (C), and porosity (P). Scale bar is 0.1 mm. Crossed nicols.

C. Calcite (C) and ankerite (A) cementation. Porosity (P) is effectively occluded by carbonate cementation and pyrite (Py). Scale bar is 0.1 mm. Plane light.

D. Intertidal subfacies porosity, including oversize pores (OP), intercrystalline porosity (IC), reduced interparticulate porosity (RI), and inhomogeneity of packing. Q = detrital quartz grain, C = carbonate cement. Scale bar is 0.1 mm. Plane light.

E. Porosity in channel–bank subfacies, including oversize pores with floating grains (OP), intercrystalline porosity in authigenic clay minerals (IC), reduced interparticulate porosity (RI), and inhomogeneity of packing. Q = detrital quartz grain, C = carbonate cement. Scale bar is 0.1 mm. Plane light).

F. Porosity in tidal–channel sandstone, including partial dissolution porosity (PD) of carbonate cement (C) and shrinkage porosity (SP) adjacent a shale clast (SC). Scale bar is 0.1 mm. Plane light.

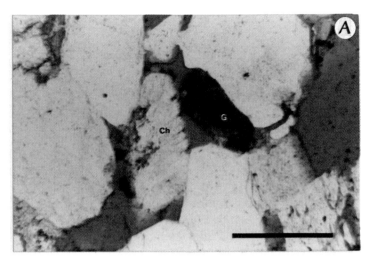

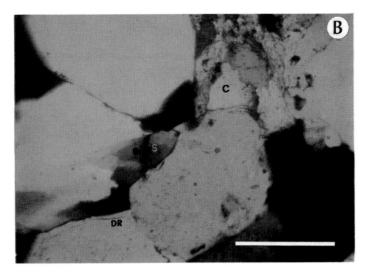

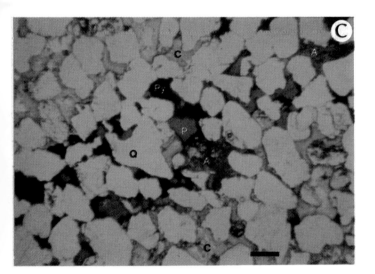

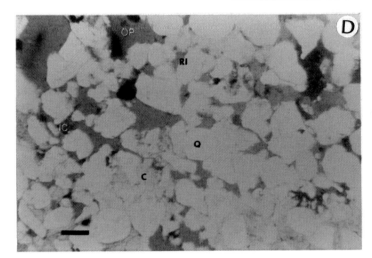

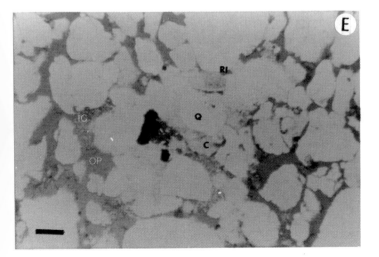

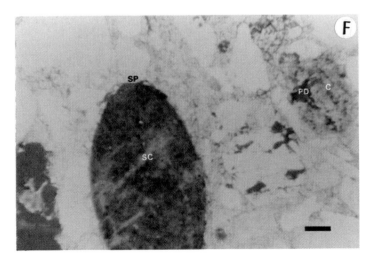

The Weber Sandstone at Rangely Field, Colorado

Kent A. Bowker, William D. Jackson

PLATE 1. Thin–section photomicrographs of the major Weber facies. Samples are from the No. 139Y UPRR. Thin sections came from the same respective depths as samples in Figure 4. All photomicrographs taken with plane light. Bars at lower right corner of each photomicrograph represent 200 microns. Each sample was impregnated with blue epoxy, and stained with Alizarin Red–S and potassium ferricyanide.

A. Wind–ripple lamina. Grain size coarsens upward within the lamina. The very fine-grained (lower porosity) portion of the overlying lamina can be seen at the top of the photomicrograph. 5,657.7 ft (1,724.5 m).

B. Massive bioturbated sandstone. Calcite crystals in the center of the photomicrograph have iron–rich outer rims. Dolomite and ferroan dolomite also are present. 5,963.1 ft (1,817.6 m).

C. Wind–ripple lamina. Dolomite cements the lower, very fine-grained portion of the lamina. Asphaltene (opaque material) lines some of the pores. 5,657.7 ft (1,724.4 m).

D. Massive bioturbated sandstone. Note low porosity (approximately 5%), abundant carbonate cement, and clay coatings. 5,963.1 ft (1,817.6 m).

E. Upper portion of a wind–ripple lamina. Ferroan dolomite (stained dark blue) fills three pores in the center of the photomicrograph. Asphaltene lines a few of the pores. 5,657.7 ft (1,724.4 m).

F. Arkosic fluvial sandstone. Note poor sorting and angular grains. Porosity is not effective (see text and Fig. 10). 6,160.7 ft (1,877.8 m).

G. Massive bioturbated sandstone. Notice decrease in porosity compared to cross-laminated sandstones. Porosity is occluded with calcite, ferroan calcite, dolomite, and ferroan dolomite; quartz overgrowths also are present. Clay lines some of the pores. 5,963.1 ft (1,817.6 m).

H. Arkosic fluvial sandstone. Note poor porosity and poor connectivity of pores. 6,160.7 ft (1,877.8 m).

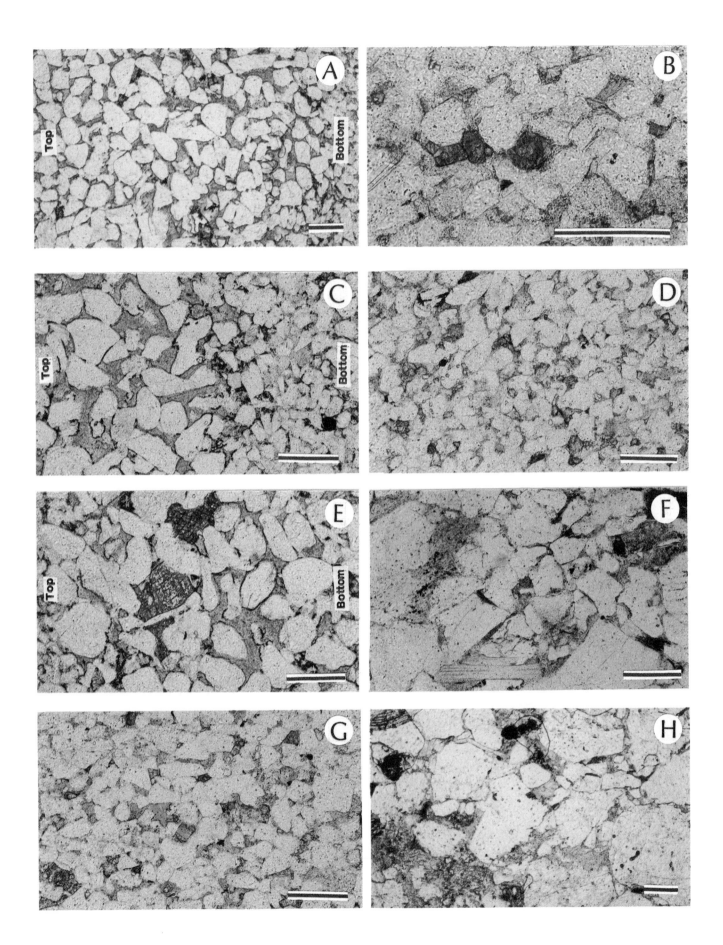

Diagenetic History and Reservoir Characteristics of a Deep Minnelusa Reservoir, Hawk Point Field Powder River Basin, Wyoming

Susan W. James

PLATE 1. Portion of slabbed core of Minnelusa "C" Sandstone reservoir in the Total Ickes No. 42–30. Photographs illustrate the upper dune complex, the best reservoir rock in the well. Black laminae are bitumen–stained. Brown sandstones are oil–stained. White laminae are anhydrite–cemented. Color contrasts accentuate eolian sedimentary structures. Avalanche deposits are characterized by fade–out laminae (11,355.5 ft, or 3,461.2 m; 11,358.8 ft, or 3,462.2 m; 11,360 ft, or 3,462.5 m; and at bottom of interval) and high angle crossbed sets. Slabbed sections show apparent dip in some cases. Ripple laminations are well preserved from 11,359 to 11,360 ft (3,462.2–3,462.5 m). Note spotty anhydrite below 11,361 ft (3,462.8 m). Capping the dune sets at 11,355.5 ft (3,461.2 m) is a band of wavy–laminated anhydrite that is overlain by a very fine–grained sandstone containing dolomite and spotty anhydrite cement; this sandstone is interpreted as a sand–sheet deposit. The bitumen in this interval is trapped in microporous dolomite cement. These differences in cementation, bitumen content, live oil staining, and depositional environments make the Hawk Point reservoir complex.

Diagenetic History and Reservoir Characteristics
of a Deep Minnelusa Reservoir,
Hawk Point Field Powder River Basin, Wyoming (continued)

PLATE 2. Thin–section photomicrographs from cores of the Minnelusa "C" Sandstone in the Total No. 42–30 and No. 31–30 Ickes wells.

A. Faintly laminated, fine to very fine-grained sandstone. Laminations extend diagonally from lower left to upper right. In this sample, dolomite is the dominant cement; an isolated patch of remnant poikilotopic anhydrite is present between large grains (upper left). Large, oversized pores are preserved between coarser grains with planar and point contacts (lower right); concavo-convex grain contacts predominate in the fine-grained laminae. Note the black bitumen preserved in the smaller pores. Porosity and permeabilty are 13.4% and 36 md. No. 42–30 Ickes, 11,367 ft (3,464.7 m). Plane light.

B. Abundant intergranular porosity in fine-grained sandstone. Large, oversized pores (center photo) are lined with euhedral dolomite crystals and black bitumen. Aggregate clusters of dolomite (left-center photo), replacement products of carbonate and feldspar grains, are accentuated by bitumen staining. No. 42–30 Ickes, 11,357 ft (3,461.6 m). Porosity and permeability are 18% and 104 md. Plane light.

C. Poikilotopic anhydrite in plane– (left photo) and cross-polarized (right photo) light. Anhydrite dissolution progressed from the crystal/grain contact, outward along the crystal cleavage, creating irregular birefringence zonation. Black oil stain helps to delineate the contact. No. 31–30 Ickes, 11,419 ft (3,480.5 m). Porosity and permeability are 13% and 21 md.

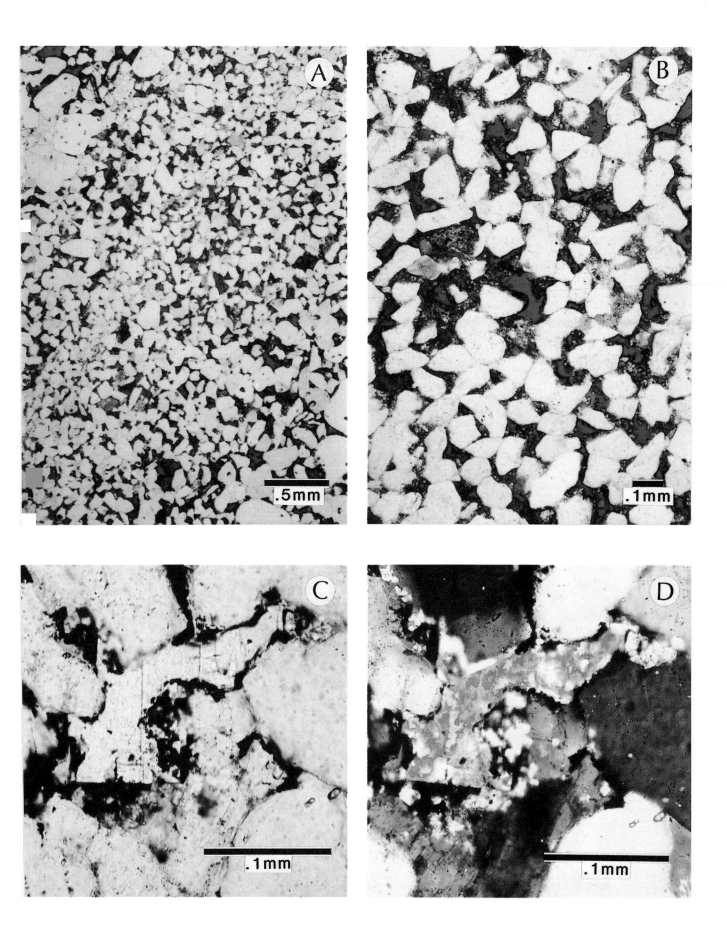

Sedimentary Facies and Reservoir Characteristics of the Nugget Sandstone (Jurassic), Painter Reservoir Field, Uinta County, Wyoming

Laura E. Tillman

PLATE 1. Thin section photomicrographs of major Nugget reservoir facies. Core from No. 44–1D PRU well.

A. The dune facies, characterized by well–sorted, well–rounded grains and well–connected intergranular porosity. Core porosity 16.3%, horizontal plug permeability 196 md, vertical plug permeability 13 md. 10,000 ft (3,048 m). Plane light.

B. Dry interdune/sand sheet subfacies, characterized by alternating finer– and coarser–grained laminae. Grains in the finer–grained laminae are poorer sorted, more angular, and more tightly packed than are grains in the coarser–grained laminae. Core porosity 10.2%, horizontal plug permeability 4.5 md, vertical plug permeability 0.67 md. 9,971.6 ft (3,039.3 m).

C. Dune facies, composed of well–sorted, well–rounded, medium and coarse grains, with poikilotopic carbonate cement. Core porosity 14.3%, horizontal plug permeability 113 md, vertical plug permeability 36 md. 9,975.1 ft (3,040.4 m).

D. A high–angle fracture (microfault) filled with quartz gouge resulting from the crushing of grains with movement, and with quartz cement. Core porosity 13.1%, horizontal plug permeability 2.2 md, vertical plug permeability 0.42 md. 10,121 ft (3,084 m).

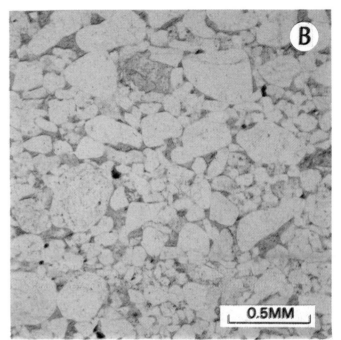

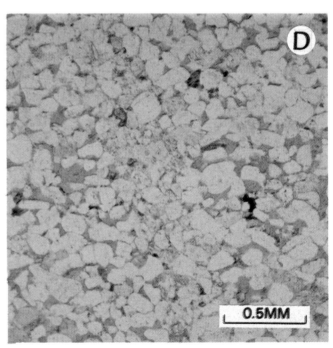

Petrography, Diagenesis, and Reservoir Properties of the Dakota Sandstone of West Lindrith Field, Rio Arriba County, New Mexico

Stanley P. Franklin, Thomas T. Tieh

PLATE 1. Photomicrographs illustrating the petrography and textural relations of various authigenic cements within the Dakota Sandstone.

A. Example of prohibitive effect of clay on silica cementation. The right portion contains extensive silica cement (s) whereas the left portion contains abundant clay (mx) and intergranular porosity (p). Scale bar represents 300 microns. Plane light.

B. Calcite (c) replacing a feldspar grain (f) with associated authigenic kaolinite (k). Scale bar represents 100 microns. Crossed nicols.

C. Sequence of cementation. Silica cement (s) formed first, followed by calcite (c) and later by non-ferroan dolomite (d). Scale bar represents 250 microns. Plane light.

D. Fine-grained dolomite rhombs (d) nucleated within pore-filling detrital matrix (mx). Scale bar represents 50 microns. Plane light.

E. Well-developed intergranular porosity network (blue) with fracture porosity (arrows) increasing the pore space interconnection. Scale bar represents 250 microns. Plane light.

F. Secondary porosity produced by dissolution of feldspar (f), biotite (b), and glauconite (g). Scale bar represents 50 microns. Plane light.

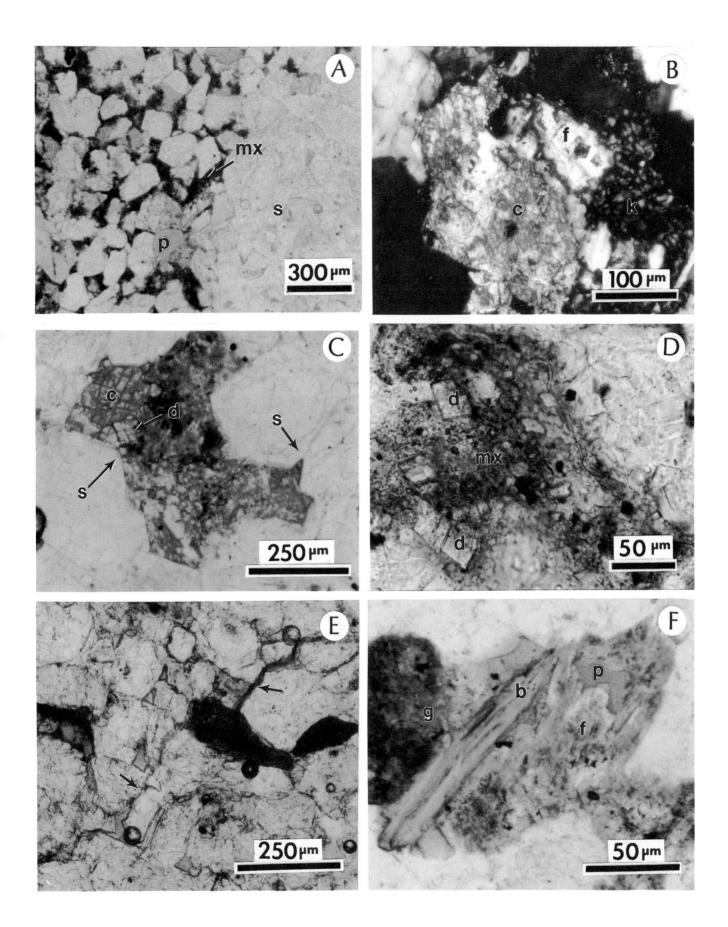

Petrography, Diagenesis, and Reservoir Properties of the Dakota Sandstone of West Lindrith Field, Rio Arriba County, New Mexico (continued)

PLATE 2. Photomicrographs of three samples most representative of the three end members calculated by factor analysis, with corresponding frequency histograms illustrating the compositional characteristics unique to each end member. The histograms reveal the relative amounts of selected petrographic variables; monocrystalline quartz (MQ), polycrystalline quartz (PQ), feldspar (F), rock fragments (RF), detrital matrix (Mx), authigenic clays (Clay), silica cement (Sil), carbonate cement (Carb), and petrographic porosity (Por).

A. End Member 1: quartzose sandstones have very low clay content and relatively high porosity. Note the well-developed intergranular porosity.

B. End Member 2: carbonate-cemented sandstones contain abundant calcite and dolomite cements with very low porosity. Note the floating grains and the lack of silica cement, indicating very early cementation.

C. End Member 3: clay-rich sandstones contain abundant detrital matrix and rock fragments with low porosity. Note the fine-grained nature of these sandstones.

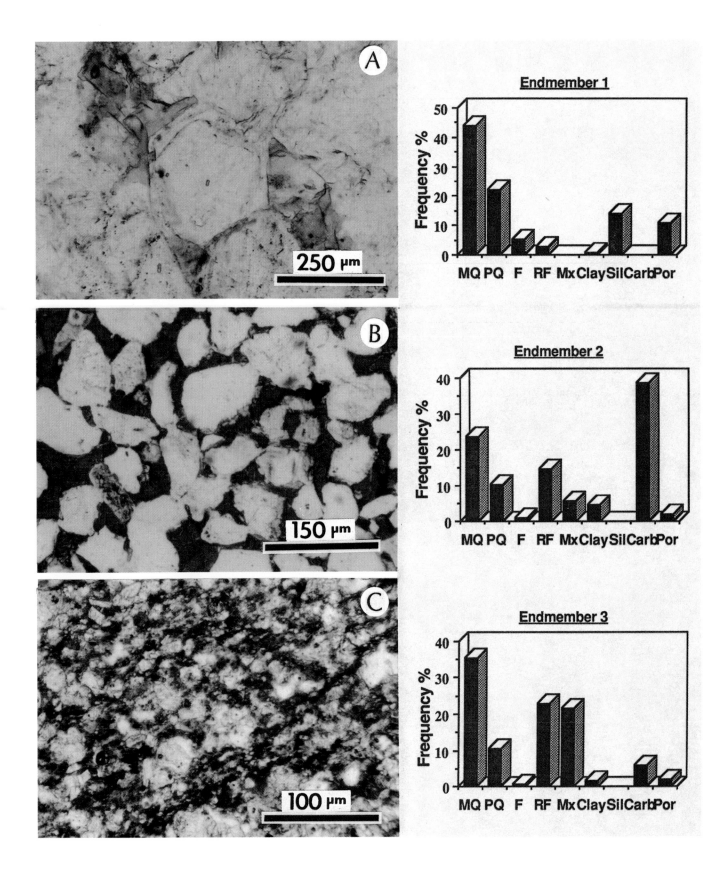

Paleostructural Control of Dakota Hydrocarbon Accumulations on the Southern Moxa Arch, Southwest Wyoming and Northeast Utah

K.D. Reisser, Steve J. Blanke

PLATE 1. Cores illustrating sedimentary structures and textures of Lower Dakota sandstone. (1 in. = 2.54 cm)

A. Chert-pebble conglomerate showing erosional cut-and-fill characterist̲ ̲ ̲ ̲-energy, episodic deposition. Sample from Sun No. I-11 Luckey Ditch Fe̲ ̲ ̲ ̲ (15,589 ft; 4,807.6 m).

B. Erosional truncation of high-angle cross-bed sets by a younger trough cross-stratified point-bar sequence. Sun No. D-6 Luckey Ditch Federal (14,864 ft; 4,584.1 m).

C. Mottling of reservoir-quality point-bar sandstone by diagenetic kaolinite. Sun No. I-11 Luckey Ditch Federal (15,633 ft; 4,821.3 m).

D. Moderate-angle trough cross-stratification emphasized by laminae containing abundant carbonaceous debris. Sample from Sun No. G-9 Luckey Ditch Federal (15,563 ft; 4,799.6 m).

E. Soft sediment deformation near the base of a point-bar sequence. Note mottling by diagenetic kaolinite. Sun No. E-7 Luckey Ditch Federal (14,607 ft; 4,504.7 m)

F. Diagenetic mottling and dead oil stain in reservoir-quality point-bar sandstone. Sun No. G-9 Luckey Ditch Federal (15,525 ft; 4,787.9 m).

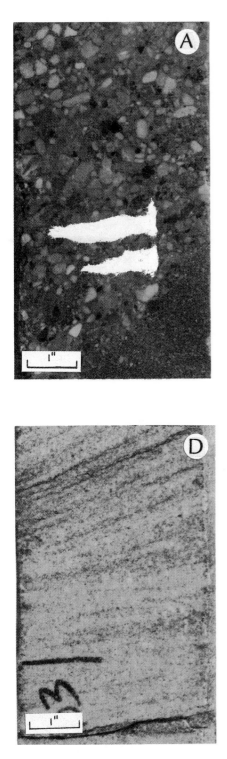

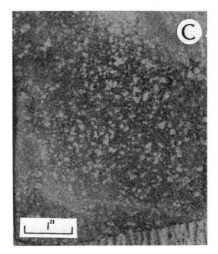

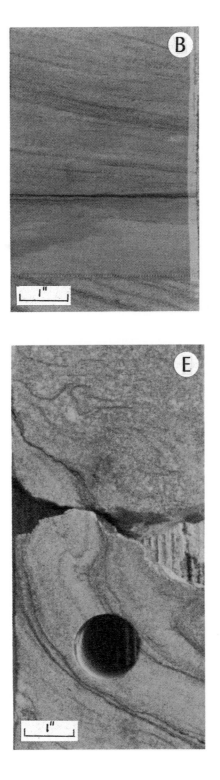

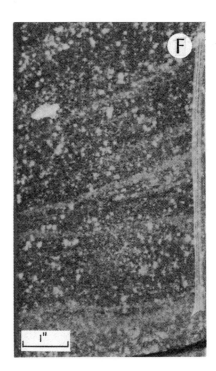

Paleostructural Control of Dakota Hydrocarbon Accumulations on the Southern Moxa Arch, Southwest Wyoming and Northeast Utah (continued)

PLATE 2. Thin section photomicrographs illustrating lower Dakota cement types, textures, and porosity types.

A. Reservoir-quality point-bar sandstone lacking appreciable diagenetic clays. Sun No. G-9 Luckey Ditch Federal (15,559 ft; 4,798.6 m).

B. Local concentration of kaolinite cement completely occluding intergranular pore space. Sun No. G-9 Luckey Ditch Federal (15,559.5 ft; 4,798.55 m).

C. Tarry, dead oil coating grains in point-bar reservoir sandstone. Sun No. I-11 Luckey Ditch Federal (15,648 ft; 4,825.8 m).

D. Tightly cemented coastal-plain sandstone. Cement consists of silica, carbonate, and authigenic clays. Sun No. E-7 Luckey Ditch Federal (14,594.5 ft; 4,500.9 m).

E. Reservoir-quality point-bar sandstone from above the oil/water contact. Sun No. 1 Flash Federal (15,240 ft; 4,700.0 m).

F. Tightly cemented point-bar sandstone from below the oil/water contact. Sun No. 1 Flash Federal (15,245 ft; 4,701.6 m).

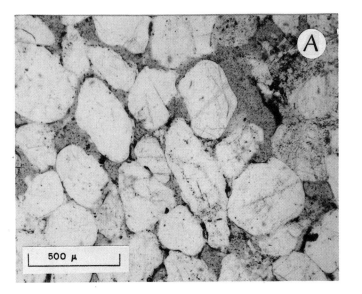

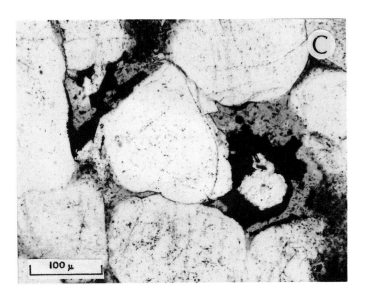

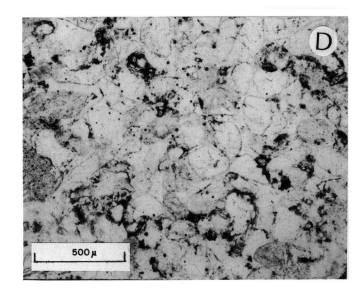

Diagenetic and Petrophysical Variations of the Dakota Sandstone, Henry Field, Green River Basin, Wyoming

Margaret M. Muller, Edward B. Coalson

PLATE 1. Photographs of Dakota sandstones, Henry Field area.

A. Photomicrograph of clay matrix completely filling the intergranular areas in fluvial channel lithofacies. XRD indicates that this matrix clay is predominantly composed of finely crystalline kaolinite (Table 1). Sample from the Forest Oil No. 2 Reed, NW SE Sec 9 T13N R114W. Log depth 13,915.5 ft (4,241.4 m).

B. Crossbedded fluvial channel sandstone. Laminae are defined by concentrations of organic material, or "coffee grounds". Forest Oil No. 8 Henry, NE SE Sec 33 T14N R113W. Log depth 13,844 ft (4,219.7 m).

C. Intergranular/intercrystalline mesoporosity (blue areas) in a fluvial channel sandstone. Forest Oil Henry 1, NE SW Sec 5–T13N–R113W. Log depth 13,283.5 ft.

D. Vuggy macroporosity and well–rounded framework grains showing relatively little compaction in fluvial channel lithofacies. An earlier carbonate cement (which has been removed) was probably responsible for inhibiting compaction. Sample from the Forest Oil No. 14 Henry (NE SW Sec 28 T14N R114W). Log depth 13,423.5 ft (4,091.5 m).

E. Partially dissolved poikilotopic calcite cement in fluvial channel lithofacies. Dissolution of calcite resulted in the formation of secondary porosity. Sample from Marathon No. 16–1 Federal (NW NW Sec 16 T13N R113W). Core depth 13,597.8 ft (4,144.6 m).

F. Partially dissolved saddle dolomite cement in fluvial channel lithofacies. Dissolution of dolomite resulted in the formation of secondary porosity. Sample from the American Quasar No. 35–14 Taylor Federal (Sec 35 T13N R114W). Log depth 14,242 ft (4,341.0 m).

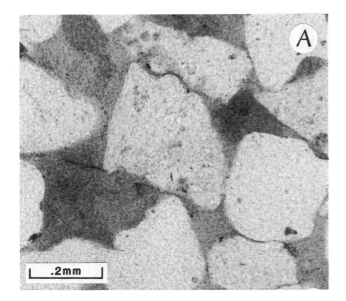

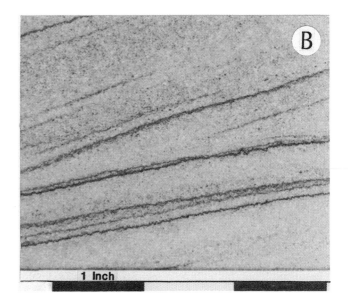

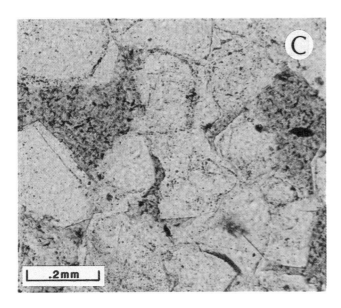

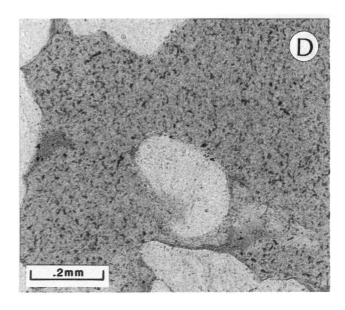

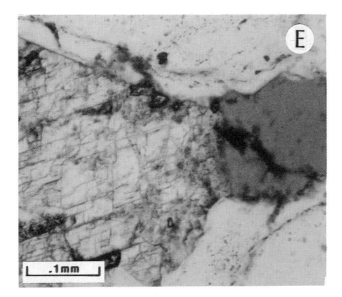

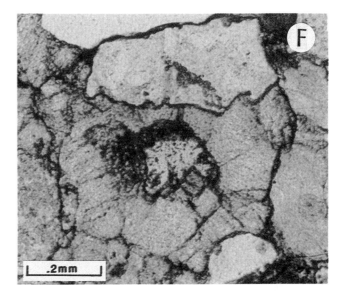

Diagenetic and Petrophysical Variations of the Dakota Sandstone, Henry Field, Green River Basin, Wyoming (continued)

PLATE 2. Photographs of Dakota sandstones, Henry Field area.

A. Poikilotopic calcite cement completely filling intergranular areas has peripherally replaced the margins of detrital quartz grains, producing deep embayments. Sample from Forest Oil No. 12 Henry (Sec 17 T13N R113W). Log depth 13,609 ft (4,148.0 m).

B. Quartz grain with highly embayed margins. The rhombic shape of the embayment indicates that carbonate at one time replaced quartz. Sample from Forest Oil No. 11 Henry (NW SE Sec 8 T13N R113W). Log depth 13,543 ft (4,127.9 m).

C. Rooted siltstone which is common in overbank deposits. Forest Oil No. 1 Henry (NE SW Sec 5 T13N R113W). Log depth 13,304 ft (4,055.1 m).

D. Intercrystalline microporosity is the predominant type of pore geometry present in the overbank lithofacies. These sandstones typically have abundant microporosity and low permeabilities (Fig. 9). Sample from Forest Oil No. 1 Henry (NE SW Sec 5 T13N R113W). Log depth 13,270 ft (4,044.7 m).

E. Interbedded very fine-grained sandstone and silty shale, common in the restricted-marine lithofacies. No. 35-14 Taylor Federal (W/2 SW Sec 35 T13N R114W). Log depth 14,147 ft (4,312.0 m).

F. Intercrystalline microporosity in a poorly sorted quartz wacke. Sample from the Forest Oil No. 2 Henry (NW SW Sec 6 T13N R113W). Log depth 13,461 ft (4,102.9 m).

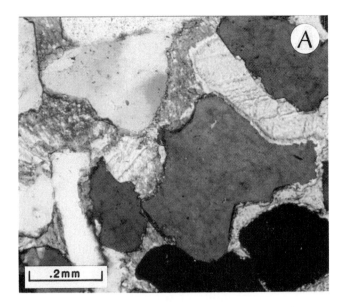

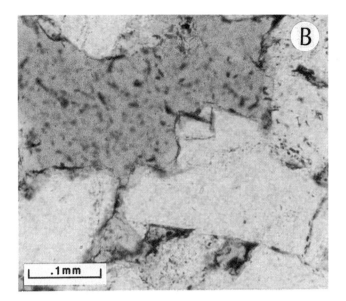

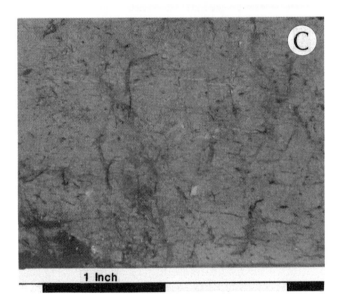

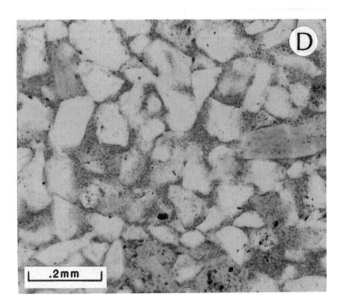

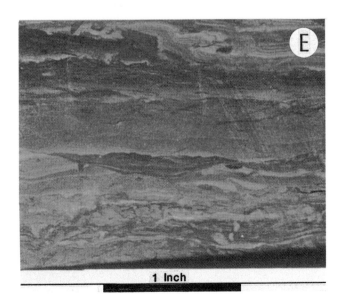

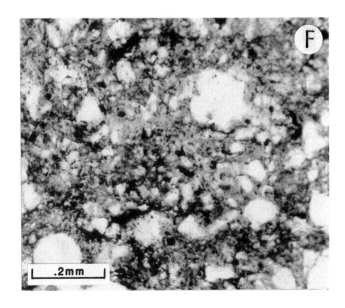

Geological and Engineering Evaluation of Barrier Island and Valley-Fill Lithotypes in Muddy Formation, Bell Creek Field, Montana

Michael Szpakiewicz, Richard Schatzinger, Matt Honarpour, Min Tham, Roderick Tillman

PLATE 1. Slabbed cores of Muddy Formation, Bell Creek Field, Unit "A"

A. Depositional disconformity between barrier island and lagoonal rocks at 4,420.2 ft (1,346.4 m) in well P-1. (For location, see Fig. 1.) Permeability of silty, shaly, ripple-laminated lagoonal sandstones above disconformity (at 4,441.8 ft, or 1,353.9 m) is only 0.78 md. Permeability of back-beach sandstones just below the disconformity (4,440.6 ft, or 1,353.5 m) is 275 md; one ft (0.3 m) deeper, permeability is nearly 1,000 md. Prominent black horizontal line in this photo is depth marking of core at 4,400 ft (1,341.1 m). Note that alluvial channel fill is absent; lagoonal rocks directly overlie barrier island sandstones.

B-D. Core from well 7, located about 1,000 ft (305 m) southwest of well P-1. Cored interval is 4,405.0 ft to 4,433.1 ft (1,342.6-1,345.2 m).

Interval from 4,405.0 to 4,413.0 ft (1,342.6-1,345.1 m) consists of lagoon or estuary deposits. Interval from 4,413.0 to 4,414.0 ft (1,345.1-1,345.4 m) is channel fill deposits with an unconformity at the base. From 4,414.0 to 4,415.0 ft (1,345.1-1,345.7 m), the Muddy consists of swamp deposits. Alluvial channel-fill rocks with an unconformity at the base are found from 4,415.0 to 4,419.3 ft (1,345.7-1,347.0 m). In the interval 4,419.3 to 4,425.9 ft (1,347.0-1,349.0 m) is found back-shore sandstone. From 4,415.9 to 4,432.8 ft (1,349.0-1,351.1 m), middle shoreface sandstone dominates. The bottom of the interval, from 4,432.8 to 4,433.1 ft (1,351.1-1,351.2 m), contains lower shoreface sandstone.

In this well, permeability of alluvial channel-fill sandstone found immediately above the disconformity at 4,419.3 ft (1,347.0 m) is 1.7 md. Permeability of back-beach sandstone below the disconformity, at 4,419.5 ft (1,347.1 m) is 1,730 md, but decreases drastically below 4,425 ft (1,348.7 m) in middle shoreface sandstones because of clay cementation (lighter-colored part of core).

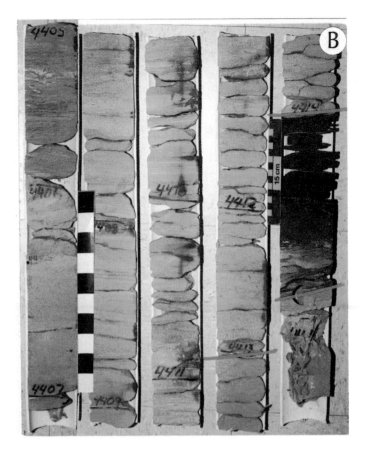

Geological and Engineering Evaluation of Barrier Island and Valley–Fill Lithotypes in Muddy Formation, Bell Creek Field, Montana (continued)

PLATE 2. Thin section photomicrographs of Muddy Formation, Bell Creek Field. All scale bars are 100 microns.

A. Inclusion–poor quartz overgrowth predating clay cement (reddish color). Sample from well C–6, 4,409.8 ft (1,344.1 m).

B. Siderite cement (S) and quartz grains have interpenetrating margins (arrow). This is evidence that siderite precipitated prior to compaction.

C. This sample displays compacted microporous sedimentary rock fragment (RF), oversize pores with preserved leached remnant (in D), and "clean" oversize pores that are all the same size. This provides strong evidence that oversized pores resulted from leaching of sedimentary rock fragments. Postcompaction creation of oversized pores (as in D) is evidence for late–stage leaching. Sample from well P–2, 4,437.1 ft (1,352.4 m).

D. Bimodal size distribution is the result of diagenesis. Silt particles in normal and oversize pores are leached remnants of original framework grains. Sample from well C–8, 4,365.4 ft (1,330.6 m).

E. Pseudomatrix (PS) was created by compaction of sedimentary rock fragments between more rigid framework grains. Sample from well C–6, 4,422.6 ft (1,348.0 m).

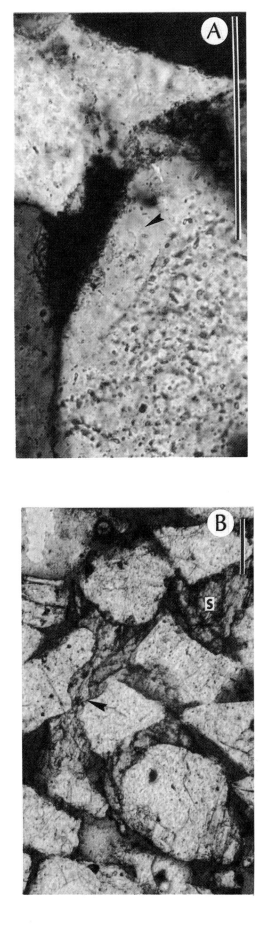

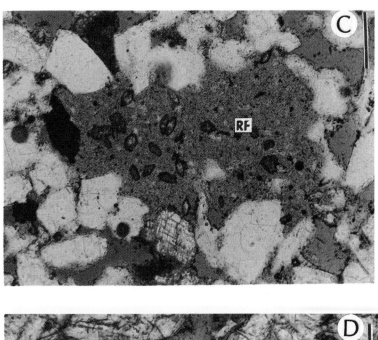

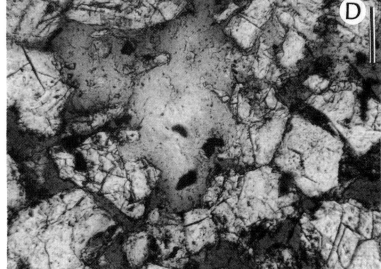

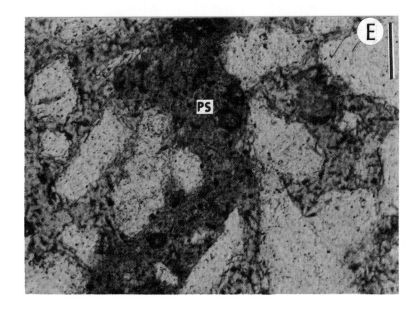

Influence of Depositional Environment and Diagenesis on Regional Porosity Trends in the Lower Cretaceous "J" Sandstone, Denver Basin, Colorado

Debra K. Higley, James W. Schmoker

PLATE 1. Thin-section photomicrographs illustrating textures and cements of the "J" sandstone, Wattenberg and Kachina fields. Blue epoxy fills pore spaces. Red bars represent 0.1 mm.

A. The solution seam (S) cutting across the photomicrograph contains hydrocarbons. Bioturbated, very fine-grained sandstone in the No. 1 G.W. Steiber Unit well. Cross polarized light.

B. Excellent intergranular porosity is enhanced by extensive dissolution of quartz, chert, and mudstone grains. Quartz (Q) overgrowths (O) are minor and indistinct. Trough cross-bedded, fine to medium-grained quartzose sandstone, No. 6 Sheetz well. Cross polarized light.

C. Calcite (C) is minor, occurring as localized poikilotopic cement. Extensive dissolution (D) of quartz and chert by calcite, and later dissolution of calcite borders is present in the lower half of the figure. Matrix clay and mudstone fill pore spaces in the upper half. Some original quartz overgrowth boundaries and quartz dust rims are preserved (R). Bioturbated, very fine-grained sandstone in the No. 1 G.W. Steiber Unit well. Cross polarized light.

D. Where present, poikilotopic calcite forms as cement and replaces lithic grains. Chert and polycrystalline quartz cement (CT) is minor and follows dissolution of calcite. Excellent intergranular porosity is enhanced by extensive dissolution (D) of quartz, chert, and mudstone grains. Dead oil (arrow) is present in some pores. Trough cross-bedded, fine to medium-grained quartzose sandstone. No. B-1 Sheetz drillhole. Plane light.

E. Feldspar (F) and quartz (Q) grains are corroded; dissolution pits (D) are filled with chlorite (CH) and other clays. Chlorite blades form rims perpendicular to lithic fragments. Bioturbated very fine-grained sandstone in the No. 1 G.W. Steiber Unit well. Cross polarized light.

F. Microporosity in pore-filling clays is very minor; kaolinite (K) and hydrocarbons fill some pore spaces. Trough cross-bedded, fine to medium-grained quartzose sandstone, No. 6 Sheetz well. Cross polarized light.

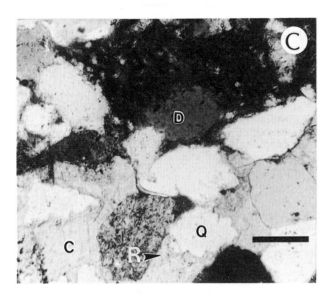

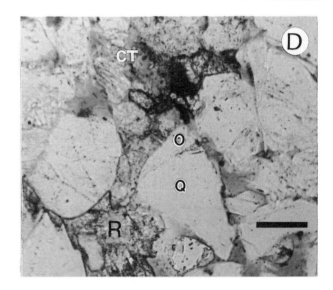

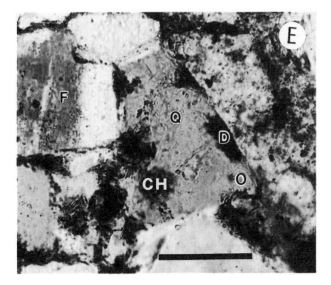

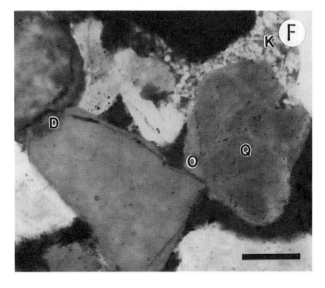

Petrography and Petrophysics of the Upper Cretaceous Turner Sandy Member of the Carlile Shale at Todd Field, Powder River Basin, Wyoming

Dawaduen Charoen–Pakdi, James E. Fox

PLATE 1: Photographs of the Turner Sandy Member of the Carlile Shale at Todd Field, Weston County, Wyoming; photomicrographs with crossed nicols.

A. Well–cemented, coarse–grained, sublitharenite from a depth of 7,045 ft (2,147.3 m), No. 1–8 Cities Service Federal well. Note the variety of detrital grains, calcite cement, and oil stain on carbonate fragments. Qm = monocrystalline quartz, Cn = carbonate rock fragments, Cc = authigenic calcite, Os = oil stain.

B. Medium–grained litharenite from a depth of 7,046 ft (2,147.6 m), No. 1–8 Cities Service Federal well. Note authigenic calcite penetrated by kaolinite (arrows), and poor porosity and permeability. Qm = monocrystalline quartz, Sh = shale, Cn = carbonate rock fragments, Cc = authigenic calcite, Kc = kaolinite.

C. Coarse–grained sublitharenite from a depth of 7,048 ft (2,148.2 m), No. 1–8 Cities Service Federal well. Note the elongate phosphatic fossil fragment which was partially dissolved and subsequently filled with oil. Qm = monocrystalline quartz, Cc = authigenic calcite, Fs = phosphatic fossil fragment, P1 = partial dissolution pore (secondary).

D. Medium–grained litharenite from a depth of 7,050 ft (2,148.8 m), No. 3–5 Todd Federal well. Note quartz overgrowths at the center of the photo and partial dissolution of feldspar grain. Also note the good porosity (poor permeability). Qm = monocrystalline quartz, Qc = quartz overgrowths, F = feldspar, P1 = partial dissolution pore, P6 = pore developed around corroded grain.

E. Medium–grained litharenite from a depth of 7,054 ft (2,150.1 m), No. 3–5 Todd well. Note all pores filled with kaolinite, and poor porosity (poor permeability). Qm = monocrystalline quartz, Kc = kaolinite.

F. Photomicrograph of litharenite from a depth of 7,029 ft (2,142.4 m), No. 1–4 Bruce Federal well. Note medium–grained litharenite with variety of detrital grains, authigenic cements, and poor porosity and permeability. Qm = monocrystalline quartz, Qc = quartz overgrowths, F = feldspar, ch = chert, P = primary pore, P1 = partial dissolution pore (secondary).

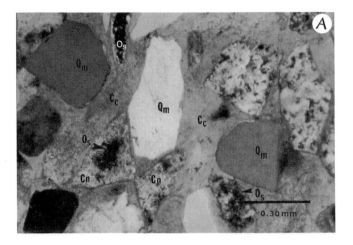

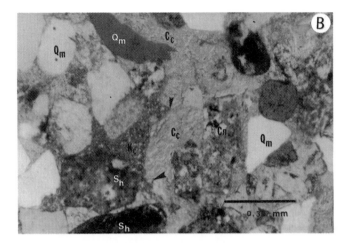

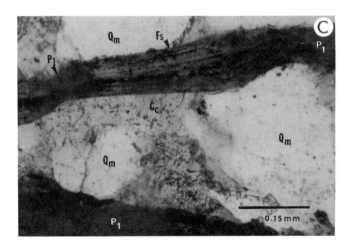

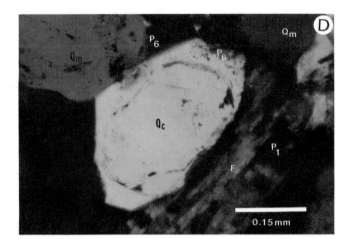

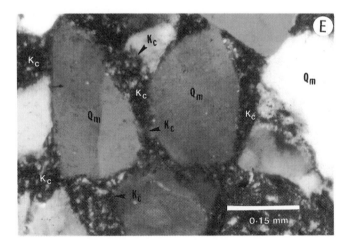

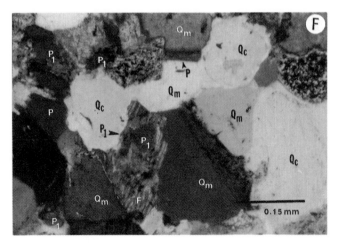

Nature of the Terry Sandstone Reservoir,
Spindle Field, Colorado

Edward D. Pittman

PLATE 1. Petrographic data for Terry sandstones. Data on locations of samples were not approved for publication, as it was considered proprietary.

A. Greenish and brownish glauconite pellets have undergone extensive ductile deformation, leading to loss of primary intergranular porosity.

B. Reservoir facies with intergranular and intragranular porosity (blue). Note brownish chlorite coats; calcite (C) cement, stained red; and dolomite (D) cement, which is unstained.

C. Reservoir facies with a significant amount of patchy pore–filling chlorite (CH). Blue–dyed epoxy fills intergranular porosity.

D. A sandstone with extensive calcite cement (stained red) that formed relatively early, judging from the open grain packing. Note that the calcite also partially replaces silicate grains.

E. View of heterogeneous texture resulting from bioturbation of Facies No. 2. Note the patchy intergranular porosity (blue).

F. Argillaceous sandstone formed by bioturbation of Facies No. 2. This type of sandstone is highly microporous due to the abundance of clay matrix and clay in lithic fragments.

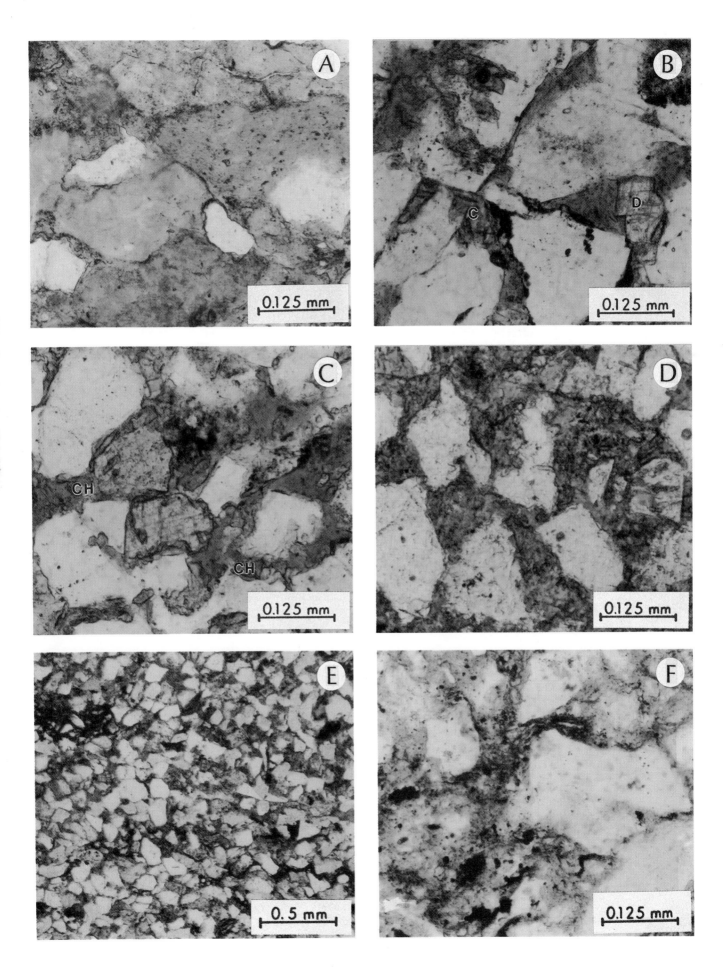

Depositional Environment and Mineralogy of the Upper Cretaceous Teapot Sandstone, Well Draw Field, Powder River Basin, Wyoming

Steven P. Conner, John J. Sullivan, Thomas T. Tieh

PLATE 1. Thin section photomicrographs of Teapot sandstone samples. Porosity filled with blue–dyed epoxy. Scale bars = 80 microns.

A. Compaction effects include deformation of biotite (B) and long grain boundaries between quartz grains (L). Plane light. Sample from ASF 1–A, 7,929.5 ft (2,147 m).

B. Non–oriented pore–lining clay (Uc) overgrown by quartz cement. Note also intergranular (A) and intragranular (B) porosity types. Plane light. Sample from IR–1, 7,030.5 ft (2,143 m).

C. Differential silicate alteration and clay–rim formation. A nearly unaltered rock fragment (R1) is adjacent to a degraded rock fragment (R2) with a well–developed clay rim (arrow). Rim consists of clay minerals, likely a combination of mixed layer illite/smectite, illite, smectite, and lesser chlorite. Plane light. Sample from IJ 1–28, 6,763.5 ft (2,062 m).

D. Carbonate–cemented (C) sandstone. Note replacement of feldspar and etched grain boundaries on feldspar (arrow) and most other grains. Crossed nicols. Sample from DT–1, 6,903.5 ft (2,105 m).

Depositional Environment and Mineralogy of the Upper Cretaceous Teapot Sandstone, Well Draw Field, Powder River Basin, Wyoming (continued)

PLATE 2. Thin–section photomicrographs of Teapot sandstones. Scale bars on A, C, and E = 80 microns. Scale bars on B, D, and F = 20 microns. All photos are in plane light.

A. Carbonate cement (C) dissolution and resultant formation of secondary porosity (P). Arrow indicates carbonate detailed in Plate 2B. Sample from DT–1, 6,901.5 ft (2,103.6 m).

B. Detail of area marked by arrow in Plate 2A. Carbonate grain shows dissolution texture and adjacent secondary porosity. Note also alteration rim on rock fragment and microporosity in rim. Sample from DT–1, 6,901.5 ft (2,103.6 m).

C. Oriented pore–lining clay (Oc) and remnant secondary porosity (RP). Other pores in vicinity are also lined with clay; some have been completely occluded. Sample from ASF 1–A, 7,929.5 ft (2,416.9 m).

D. Detail of pore labeled in Plate 2C. Oriented pore–lining clay partially occludes porosity, reducing reservoir quality in some sections. Note that clay platelets are oriented perpendicular to pore wall. Sample from ASF 1–A, 7,929.5 ft (2,416.9 m).

E. Pore–bridging clay (Bc) completely occluding most pores. Carbonate cement (C), which predated clay precipitation, continued to dissolve after clay formation and has resulted in recovered pore space. Sample from DSL 1–34, 7,511.0 ft (2,289.4 m).

F. Detail of pore–bridging clay from area marked in Plate 2E. Note that clay fills the pore, and that clay platelets have no systematic orientation. This type of clay has rendered some sections of the Teapot nonproductive. Sample from DSL 1–34, 7,511.0 ft (2,289.4 m).

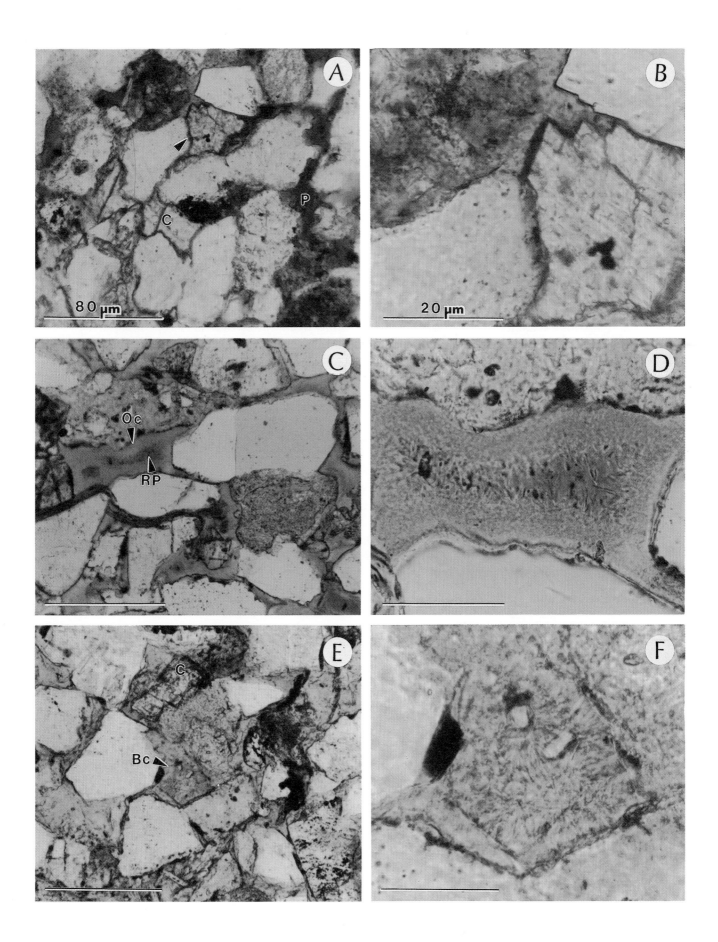

Petrology and Reservoir Characteristics of the Almond Formation, Greater Green River Basin, Wyoming

C. Wm. Keighin, B.E. Law, R.M. Pollastro

PLATE 1. Thin-section photomicrographs of Almond sandstone samples. All photos taken with plane-polarized light; scale bars represent 0.5 mm.

A. Very fine-grained sandstone composed primarily of detrital subangular quartz grains (Q) and compacted chert grains (arrow). Some organic matter (dark brown) and siltstone fragments are present. Lack of blue-dyed epoxy indicates very low porosity and/or very small pores. Sample from 9,495 ft (2,896 m), Marathon Oil Co. No. 1-23 Tierney II.

B. Pore network developed largely through the dissolution of unstable rock fragments; most pores are clay free. Sample from 4,969 ft (1,516 m), Forest Oil Corp. No. 3-19-2 Arch Unit.

C. Sandstone tightly cemented by iron-free (C) and iron-bearing (arrow) carbonate; authigenic potassium feldspar (K) is common. Sample from 4,480 ft (1,370 m), Forest Oil Corp. No. 63-2-2 Government.

D. Partially leached grains of plagioclase feldspar (F) contribute to porosity produced by dissolution. Most pores are clay free. Sample from 4,971 ft (1,516 m), No. 3-19-2 Arch Unit.

E. Potassium feldspar (K) is common in this sample; grains of iron-bearing carbonate are scattered. Both clean (P) and kaolinite-filled (arrows) pores contribute to the pore network. Sample from 4,495 ft (1,371 m), No. 63-2-2 Government.

F. Same sample as above, but from a different area on the thin section. Abundance of kaolinite-filled pores (arrow) illustrates heterogeneity of pore network which may be found within one sample.

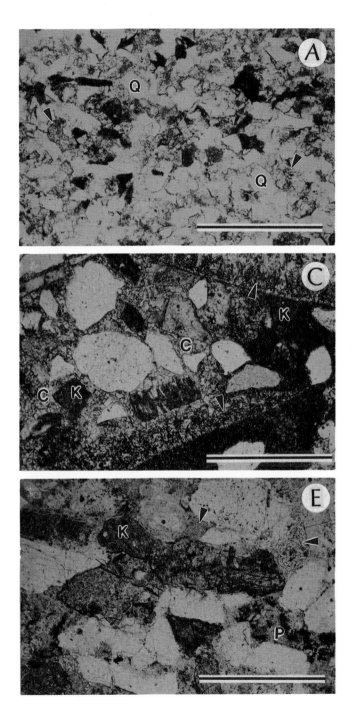

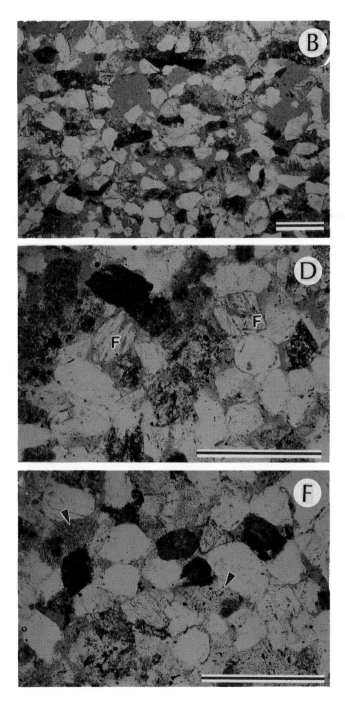

Petrology and Reservoir Characteristics of the Almond Formation, Greater Green River Basin, Wyoming (continued)

PLATE 2. Core photographs and thin-section photomicrographs of Almond sandstone samples.

A. Core of interbedded sandstones and shales. Samples from 11,884–12,026 ft (3,625–3,668 m), Energy Reserves Group No. 2–24 Nickey. Locations of following thin sections marked with red diamonds.

B. Crossed-polar thin-section photomicrograph illustrating abundance of clay-rich rock fragments (R), primarily chert, which have been compacted between detrital grains of quartz (Q) and plagioclase feldspar (P). Porosity is low, mainly because of compaction. Small pores are found in altered rock fragments. Bar scale represents 0.5 mm. Sample from 11,884.5 ft (3,625 m) in No. 2–24 Nickey.

C. Plane light thin-section photomicrograph showing quartz grains (Q) surrounded by low-porosity pseudomatrix formed by compaction of labile rock fragments. Sample from 11,905.2 ft (3,631 m) in No. 2–24 Nickey. Bar scale represents 0.5 mm.

D. Crossed-polar thin-section photomicrograph of fine-grained, low-porosity sandstone composed primarily of detrital quartz grains and clay-rich rock fragments. Sample is similar in properties to those illustrated above. Sample from 10,627.3 ft (3,241 m), No. 1 Amoco-Champlin 336 A. Bar scale represents 0.5 mm.

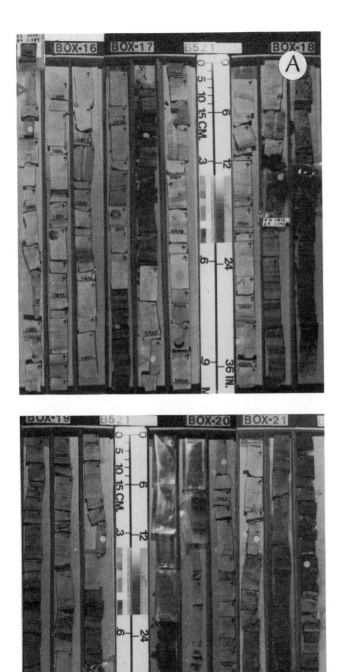

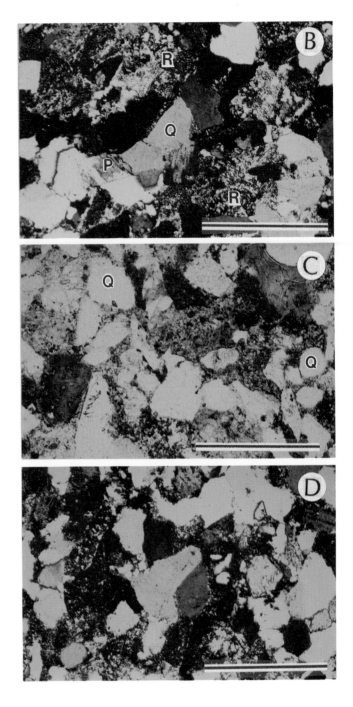

INDEX

Remnant of partially leached framework grain of feldspar (F); sandstone also commonly contains authigenic kaolinite (K) which may fill pores. Point Lookout sandstone, sec 5 T32N R13W, La Plata Co., CO. Depth 925 ft (282 m). Photo donated by Bill Keighin.

Overleaf: Cumulative production from the 50 largest fields in the Rocky Mountain area that produce primarily from sandstone reservoirs, as of August, 1988. Listing is part of a larger study of 155 sandstone-reservoir fields in the Rocky Mountains that have produced more than 10,000,000 BOE (1 BOE = 6 MCFG). Limitations on accuracy are created by data from older fields in which production was comingled (e.g., Tensleep–Phosphoria fields). Dataset does not include New Mexico or Arizona fields, some of which (e.g., Basin Dakota) are quite large. Accompanying graphs (see pages 6 and 80) were generated from the same dataset. Production data compliments of Petroleum Information. Compiled by John W. Robinson, 1989.

	NAME	LOCATION	DISCYR	TRAPTYPE	RESERVOIR	AVPOR	AVPRM	RSRVR2	RSRVR3
1	RANGELY	RIO BLANCO CO., CO	1902	STRUCTURE	WEBER	12.50	10.00	MANCOS	MORRISON
2	SALT CREEK	NATRONA CO., WY	1889	STRUC-STRAT	FRONTIER	19.10	52.00	TENSLEEP	SUNDANCE
3	ELK BASIN, GREATER	PRK CO, WY, CRBON CO,MT	1915	STRUCTURE	TENSLEEP	17.00	150.00	MADISON	FRONTIER
4	OREGON BASIN	PARK CO,. WY	1912	STRUCTURE	TENSLEEP-PHOS	15.00		MADISON	CLOVERLY
5	HAMILTON DOME	HOT SPRINGS CO., WY	1918	STRUCTURE	TENSLEEP-PHOS	14.00	99.00	MADISON	CURTIS
6	BEAVER CREEK	FREMONT CO., WY	1938	STRUCTURE	TENSLEEP			MUDDY-LAKOTA	FRONTIER
7	CUT BANK	GLAC-TOOLE-PONDERA, MT	1932	STRAT	CUT BANK	15.00	110.00	SUNBURST	MOULTON
8	BIG PINEY	LINC-SUBLETTE COS.,WY	1938	STRUC-STRAT	FORT UNION	27.00	200.00	MESAVERDE	P SAND
9	LOST SOLDIER	SWEETWATER CO., WY	1916	STRUCTURE	TENSLEEP	12.00	60.00	MADISON	FLATHEAD
10	GRASS CREEK	HOT SPRINGS CO., WY	1914	STRUCTURE	FRONTIER	21.00	81.00	TENSLEEP-PHOS	CURTIS
11	ANSCHUTZ RANCH EAST	SUMMIT CO., UT	1980	STRUCTURE	NUGGET			ANKAREH	
12	GARLAND	BIG HORN-PARK CO., WY	1906	STRUCTURE	TENSLEEP-PHOS			MADISON	FRONTIER
13	IGNACIO-BLANCO	LA PLATA-ARCHLTA CO.,CO	1950	STRUC-STRAT	MESAVERDE	9.00	0.05	DAKOTA	FRUTLN-PIC CLF
14	LITTLE BUFFALO BASIN	HOT SNGS-PARK CO., WY	1914	STRUCTURE	TENSLEEP			PHOSPHORIA	FRONTIER
15	BELL CREEK	CARTER-PWDR RIV CO., MT	1967	STRAT	MUDDY	24.00	999.00		
16	PATRICK DRAW	SWEETWATER CO., WY	1959	STRAT	ALMOMD	19.60	36.00		
17	LANCE CREEK	NIOBRARA CO., WY	1918	STRUCTURE	LEO	13.00	100.00	SUNDANCE	DAKOTA
18	BYRON, GREATER	BIG HORN CO., WY	1918	STRUCTURE	TENSLEEP	14.00		PHOSPHORIA	FRONTIER
19	FRANNIE	PARK CO., WY	1928	STRUCTURE	TENSLEEP			MADISON	
20	WERTZ	CARBON-SWTWTR CO., WY	1920	STRUCTURE	TENSLEEP	11.90	70.00	CLOVERLY	MUDDY
21	WATTENBURG	ADMS-BLDR-LRMR-WELD, CO	1970	STRAT	MUDDY J				
22	HILITE	CAMPBELL CO., WY	1969	STRAT	MUDDY	15.00	110.00	MINNELUSA	
23	BRADY, GREATER	SWEETWATER CO., WY	1973	STRUCTURE	WEBER	9.00	14.00	NUGGET	DAKOTA
24	WILSON CREEK	RIO BLANCO CO., CO	1938	STRUCTURE	MORRISON	19.40	11.00	SUNDANCE	MINTURN
25	STEAMBOAT BUTTE	FREMONT CO., WY	1943	STRUCTURE	TEMSLEEP	13.60	60.00	NUGGET	PHOSPHORIA
26	TABLE ROCK, GREATER	SWEETWATER CO., WY	1946	STRUCTURE	ALMOND	16.50	2.30	NUGGET	LEWIS
27	SPINDLE	ADAMS-BLDR-WELD CO., CO	1971	STRAT	SUSSEX			SHANNON	NIOBRARA
28	WINKLEMAN	FREMONT CO., WY	1917	STRUCTURE	TENSLEEP	15.00		PHOSPHORIA	LAKOTA
29	WORLAND	WASHAKIE CO., WY	1946	STRUCTURE	FRONTIER	14.00	13.00	PHOSPHORIA	
30	BIG SAND DRAW	FREMONT CO., WY	1918	STRUCTURE	TENSLEEP	32.00		LAKOTA	FRONTIER
31	GLENROCK, SOUTH	CONVERSE CO., WY	1950	STRUC-STRAT	DAKOTA	14.70	33.00	MUDDY	
32	ADENA	MORGAN CO., CO	1953	STRAT	MUDDY J	19.70	356.00	MUDDY D	
33	PAINTER RESERVOIR	UINTA CO., WY	1977	STRUCTURE	NUGGET	14.10	22.80		
34	HARTZOG DRAW	CMPBELL-JOHNSON CO., WY	1975	STRAT	SHANNON	12.00	12.00		
35	CLARETON, GREATER	NIOBRARA-WESTON CO., WY	1944	STRAT	MUDDY	12.00			
36	MEADOW CREEK, GREATER	JOHNSON CO,. WY	1949	STRUCTURE	TENSLEEP	11.00	31.00	SHANNON	SUSSEX
37	TIP TOP	SUBLETTE CO., WY	1928	STRUC-STRAT	FRONTIER	16.00	0.40	NUGGET	FORT UNION
38	FIDDLER CREEK, GREATER	WESTON CO., WY	1948	STRAT	MUDDY				
39	HOGSBACK	LINC-SUBLETTE CO., WY	1955	STRUC-STRAT	FRONTIER	16.00	1.10	NUGGET	MUDDY
40	BIG MUDDY and EAST	CONVERSE CO.,WY	1916	STRUC/STRAT	FRONTIER	17.00	60.00	DAKOTA	SHANNON
41	CHURCH BUTTES	SWTWTR-UINTA CO., WY	1949	STRUCTURE	DAKOTA	15.00	200.00	FRONTIER	MORGAN
42	SLEEPY HOLLOW	RED WILLOW CO., NB	1960	STRUC-STRAT	REAGAN	22.00	999.00	LANSG-KAN CTY	
43	POWDER WASH	MOFFAT CO., CO	1931	STRUCTURE	FORT UNION			WASATCH	
44	ROCK RIVER	CARBON CO., WY	1918	STRUCTURE	DAKOTA	14.50		LAKOTA	MUDDY
45	SUMATRA	ROSEBUD CO., MT	1949	STRUC-STRAT	TYLER	15.00	200.00	AMSDEN	
46	GRIEVE	NATRONA CO., WY	1954	STRAT	MUDDY	16.00			
47	MADDEN	FREMONT CO., WY	1969	STRUCTURE	FORT UNION	16.20	10.00	LANCE	CODY
48	RAVEN CREEK	CAMPBELL CO., WY	1956	STRAT	MINNELUSA	15.00	100.00		
49	CANYON CREEK	SWEETWATER CO., WY	1941	STRUCTURE	ERICSON	10.00	0.10	ALMOND	LANCE
50	BONANZA	BIG HORN CO., WY	1950	STRUCTURE	TENSLEEP	24.00	800.00		

CUMLBOE	CUMLOIL	CUMLGAS	AVDPTH	BASIN	REFERENCE	NAME	
852975000	735229000	706476000	5700	DOUGLAS CRK ARCH	RMAG 1961	RANGELY	1
636346000	627890000	50741000	2000	POWDER RIVER	WGA 1957, 1981	SALT CREEK	2
601719000	540522000	367187000	4000	BIG HORN	WGA 1957, MGS 1985	ELK BASIN, GREATER	3
415653000	385303000	182101000	3400	BIG HORN	WGA 1957	OREGON BASIN	4
267176000	267156000	121000	3000	BIG HORN	WGA 1957	HAMILTON DOME	5
217810000	81104000	820204000	11000	WIND RIVER	WGA 1957	BEAVER CREEK	6
211263000	162034000	295376000	2950	SWEETGRASS ARCH	MGS 1985, BGS 1958	CUT BANK	7
200704000	34365000	998667000	3050	GREEN RIVER	WGA 1979	BIG PINEY	8
196516000	191046000	32821000	5000	GREAT DIVIDE	WGA 1957, 1981	LOST SOLDIER	9
185771000	184327000	7426000	750	BIG HORN	WGA 1957	GRASS CREEK	10
179861000	74896000	629791000	11000	THRUST BELT		ANSCHUTZ RANCH EAST	11
176194000	154005000	133134000	3250	BIG HORN	WGA 1957	GARLAND	12
144990000	48000	869941000	5000	SAN JUAN	FCGS 1978, RMAG 1961	IGNACIO-BLANCO	13
137601000	117785000	118899000	4600	BIG HORN	WGA 1957	LITTLE BUFFALO BASIN	14
135651000	129146000	39031000	4500	POWDER RIVER	MGS 1969, 1985	BELL CREEK	15
135419000	58600000	460917000	4900	GREEN RIVER	WGA 1979	PATRICK DRAW	16
131038000	107741000	139782000	5300	POWDER RIVER	WGA 1957	LANCE CREEK	17
122632000	120479000	12891000	5500	BIG HORN	WGA 1957	BYRON,GREATER	18
115665000	115613000	312000	2600	BIG HORN	WGA 1957	FRANNIE	19
105001000	98627000	38247000	5800	GREAT DIVIDE	WGA 1957, 1979	WERTZ	20
104269000	14430000	539036000	7200	DENVER		WATTENBURG	21
104202000	75240000	233773000	10000	POWDER RIVER	WGA 1981	HILITE	22
99327000	53743000	273505000	16500	GREEN RIVER	WGA 1979	BRADY, GREATER	23
93760000	83291000	62819000	6700	WHITE RIV UPLIFT	RMAG 1961	WILSON CREEK	24
91462000	89612000	11104000	6980	WIND RIVER	WGA 1957	STEAMBOAT BUTTE	25
89535000	4213000	511933000	6300	GREEN RIVER	WGA 1957, 1981	TABLE ROCK, GREATER	26
87645000	48785000	233165000	6400	DENVER		SPINDLE	27
86159000	85844000	1892000	2980	WIND RIVER	WGA 1957	WINKLEMAN	28
84599000	18192000	398442000	7600	BIG HORN	WGA 1957	WORLAND	29
79833000	56735000	138590000	7100	WIND RIVER	WGA 1957	BIG SAND DRAW	30
78914000	73837000	30463000	5900	POWDER RIVER	WGA 1957,1981	GLENROCK, SOUTH	31
78634000	63521000	90683000	5600	D-J	RMAG 1961	ADENA	32
74292000	31098000	259167000	10200	THRUST BELT	WGA 1979,	PAINTER RESERVOIR	33
68706000	64378000	25970000	12000	POWDER RIVER	WGA 1981	HARTZOG DRAW	34
61845000	58306000	21237000	6500	POWDER RIVER	WGA 1957,1981	CLARETON, GREATER	35
61554000	43209000	110074000	9000	POWDER RIVER	WGA 1957, 1981	MEADOW CREEK, GREATER	36
56660000	3667000	317957000	5370	LA BARGE PLAT.	WGA 1957, 1971, 1979	TIP TOP	37
56580000	55278000	7814000	5200	POWDER RIVER	WGA 1957,1981	FIDDLER CREEK, GREATER	38
56512000	8501000	288067000	7000	LA BARGE PLAT.	WGA 1981	HOGSBACK	39
55970000	53647000	13397000	4300	POWDER RIVER	WGA 1957, 1981	BIG MUDDY and EAST	40
55445000	2658000	316723000	12500	GREEN RIVER	WGA 1957,1979	CHURCH BUTTES	41
49165000	49109000	339000	3500	DENVER	RMAG 1961	SLEEPY HOLLOW	42
44108000	7198000	221465000	3800	NO. SAND WASH	RMAG 1961	POWDER WASH	43
44067000	42525000	9256000	3400	LARAMIE	WGA 1957	ROCK RIVER	44
43765000	42653000	6673000	4400	CENT. MT. TROUGH	MGS 1985	SUMATRA	45
42535000	29462000	78438000	6650	WIND RIVER	WGA 1957	GRIEVE	46
41554000	405000	246904000	7000	WIND RIVER	WGA 1971, 1978	MADDEN	47
41476000	41472000	29000	8270	POWDER RIVER	WGA 1961, 1971, 1981	RAVEN CREEK	48
41372000	1253000	240715000	5500	GREEN RIVER	WGA 1957,1979	CANYON CREEK	49
41309000	41309000	0	2900	BIG HORN	WGA 1957	BONANZA	50